JUDICIAL REVIEW, SOCIO-EC(
AND THE HUMAN RI(

In the United Kingdom during the past decade, i......viuuais and groups have increasingly tested the extent to which principles of English administrative law can be used to gain entitlements to health and welfare services and priority for the needs of vulnerable and disadvantaged groups. One of the primary purposes of this book is to demonstrate the extent to which established boundaries of judicial intervention in socio-economic disputes have been altered by the extension of judicial powers in sections 3 and 6 of the Human Rights Act 1998, and through the development of a jurisprudence of positive obligations in the European Convention on Human Rights 1950. Thus, the substantive focus of the book is on developments in the constitutional law of the United Kingdom. However, the book also addresses key issues of theoretical human rights, international law and comparative constitutional law. Issues of justiciability in English administrative law are therefore explored against a background of two factors: a growing acceptance of the need for balance in the protection in modern constitutional arrangements afforded to civil and political rights on the one hand and socio-economic rights on the other hand; and controversy as to whether courts could make a more effective contribution to the protection of socio-economic rights with the assistance of appropriately tailored constitutional provisions.

Volume 10: Human Rights Law in Perspective

Human Rights Law in Perspective
General Editor: Colin Harvey

The language of human rights figures prominently in legal and political debates at the national, regional and international levels. In the United Kingdom the Human Rights Act 1998 has generated considerable interest in the law of human rights. It will continue to provoke much debate in the legal community, and the search for original insights and new materials will intensify.

The aim of this series is to provide a forum for scholarly reflection on all aspects of the law of human rights. The series will encourage work that engages with the theoretical, comparative and international dimensions of human rights law. The primary aim is to publish over time books that offer insights into human rights law in its contextual setting. The objective is to promote an understanding of the nature and impact of human rights law. The series is inclusive, in the sense that all perspectives in legal scholarship are welcome. It will incorporate the work of new and established scholars.

Human Rights Law in Perspective is not confined to consideration of the United Kingdom. It will strive to reflect comparative, regional and international perspectives. Work that focuses on human rights law in other states will therefore be included in this series. The intention is to offer an inclusive intellectual home for significant scholarly contributions to human rights law.

Volume 1 Importing the Law in Post-communist Transitions
by Catherine Dupré

Volume 2 The Development of the Positive Obligations under the European Convention on Human Rights by the European Court of Human Rights
by Alastair Mowbray

Volume 3 Human Rights Brought Home: Socio-legal Studies of Human Rights in the National Context
edited by Simon Halliday and Patrick Schmidt

Volume 4 Corporations and Transnational Human Rights Litigation
by Sarah Joseph

Volume 5 Human Rights in the Community: Rights as Agents for Change
edited by Colin Harvey

Volume 6 Human Rights, Culture and the Rule of Law
by Jessica Almqvist

Volume 7 Property and the Human Rights Act 1998
by Tom Allen

Volume 8 Gender, Culture and Human Rights
by Siobhán Mullally

Volume 9 Monetary Remedies for Breach of Human Rights: A Comparative Study
by Lisa Tortell

Judicial Review, Socio-Economic Rights and the Human Rights Act

Ellie Palmer

·HART·
PUBLISHING

OXFORD AND PORTLAND, OREGON
2009

Published in North America (US and Canada) by
Hart Publishing
c/o International Specialized Book Services
920 NE 58th Avenue, Suite 300
Portland, OR 97213-3786
USA
Tel: +1-503-287-3093 or toll-free: (1)-800-944-6190
Fax: +1-503-280-8832
E-mail: orders@isbs.com
Website: www.isbs.com

© Ellie Palmer 2007
First published in 2007. Reprinted in paperback in 2009.

Ellie Palmer has asserted her right under the Copyright, Designs and Patents Act 1988,
to be identified as the author of this work.

Hart Publishing, 16C Worcester Place, Oxford, OX1 2JW
Telephone: +44 (0)1865 517530 Fax: +44 (0)1865 510710
E-mail: mail@hartpub.co.uk
Website: www.hartpub.co.uk

British Library Cataloguing in Publication Data
Data Available

ISBN: 978-1-84113-372-0 (hardback)
ISBN: 978-1-84113-976-0 (paperback)

Typeset by Hope Services Ltd, Abingdon
Printed and bound in Great Britain by
CPI Antony Rowe, Chippenham, Wiltshire

In memory of Mike and to our wonderful children

Preface to the Paperback Edition

Since this book was first published in August 2007, world events have forced the subject of socio-economic rights onto global and domestic policy agendas. As the impact of the credit crunch continues to bite beyond the lives of the traditionally less vocal beneficiaries of minimalist social policies, centrist governments have been obliged to confront, if not to recast, the growing imbalance between the excesses of private power on one hand, and state responsibilities to provide homes and a decent standard of living for individuals in their jurisdictions on the other.

Moreover, although at the time of writing, the attention of political actors in the United Kingdom has focused primarily on economic solutions that might re-establish the flow of capital in markets, strident demands are being made for the domestic protection of labour rights, or for public construction programs or rental schemes that will address the long term deterioration and impact of privatisation on public services, particularly in the field of social housing. Thus, in the United Kingdom, for the first time in many decades, political and economic commentators have been forced to recognise the extent to which regulatory failures and the collapse of the housing market, will result in changing roles and responsibilities of local authorities, particularly through increased demand for social housing. Moreover, concerns have been raised, (even by commentators most ardently committed to the market in public services) about the extent to which the shoring up of financial markets will impact on the investments necessary for the delivery of the Government's public services agenda[1] and its 'long-term commmitment to alleviating poverty and social exclusion'.[2] Nevertheless, notably, despite the regulatory failures and shameful disparities in wealth and opportunity highlighted by the excesses of the banking sector, questions of accountability for government, or indeed private sector failures, to protect the fundamental socio-economic rights of every citizen to receive adequate health care, welfare, the right to work and a decent standard of living, remain firmly off the political agenda.

However, following a consultation process begun during the first glimmers of the impending crisis, in August 2008 the Joint Committee on Human Rights

[1] In May 2008 the Prime Minister unveiled the Government's draft legislative programme for the coming year in Parliament. Eighteen bills including, *The Community Empowerment, Housing and Economic Regeneration Bill* were underpinned by the key theme of Economic Stability Fairness and Improving Public Services.

[2] See *Housing Social Exclusion and Welfare Reform: Safeguarding Public Services from the Impact of the Credit Crunch*: conference organised by the Centre for Parliamentary Studies. December 2008 http://publicpolicyexchange.co.uk/events/8L10-PPE.php

published a comprehensive report on *A Bill of Rights for the United Kingdom?*[3] which, addressed the question about the place of socio-economic rights in a future bill of rights, and asked what those rights should be. The Committee accepted that, rights conferred over the past sixty years by the wwelfare state, such as 'the right to health, housing or education' have come to be regarded in the public perception as core fundamental rights of the United Kingdom constitution. Nevertheless, although sympathetic to the idea of including some form of protection for popular socio-economic rights such as health, welfare and education in a bill of rights, the Committee was satisfied to rehearse the well-worn constitutional objections, that 'including fully justiciable and legally enforceable economic and social rights in any bill of rights, carries too great a risk that the courts will interfere with legislative judgments about priority setting'.[4] Thus, the Committee concluded that the rights in question should only be justiciable as an aid to the construction of legislation, and only in so far as they are 'relevant to the assessment of the 'reasonableness of measures taken to achieve their progressive realisation'.[5]

The Committee focused on a limited selection of socio-economic rights, as a possible blue print for the imposition of human rights values in the delivery of public services. However, the Committee failed to address with any rigour, more challenging questions about the extent to which private power and economic wealth have become a surrogate for political power in the modern world. Nor did they consider the need for constitutionally protected socio-economic rights, rather than as a constraint on the *legislature,* to serve as a brake on the decision-making powers of common law judges who continue to champion the outmoded imbalance between private property and individual rights; that historically underpins the unwritten constitution of the United Kingdom. Thus, although clearly attracted to the idea of a more balanced constitution, the Committee was not persuaded that human rights should have direct horizontal effect, regarding such a step as 'revolutionary'; and one which would cut across 'the well-established categories of private law liability, 'giving rise in practice to difficult questions of practice and procedure'.[6]

It is true that the wholly unexpected decision of the House of Lords in *YL v Birmingham City Council (Secretary of State for Constitutional Affairs intervening)*[7] attracted the Committee's censure, largely as a case of misguided legislative interpretation. However, there was little attempt to address its more serious constitutional implications, in particular the scope for untutored assumptions by common law judges as to the unassailable ascendancy of private property interests over constitutionally entrenched human rights. Moreover, perhaps even greater cause for alarm should have been the extent to

---

[3] HL 165-I/HC 150-I Vol 1, 10 August 2008
[4] Para 36, p 98
[5] Ibid para 38
[6] Para 286- p 75
[7] [2007] 3 WLR 112

which, in its determination to uphold this outmoded constitutional imbalance, the majority in the House of Lords had demonstrated such profound indifference to the clearly expressed views of the legislature, our senior human rights judges[8] and the Joint Committee on Human Rights on these issues. Nevertheless, against this background, developments in Strasbourg continue to emphasise that the proper functioning of a twenty-first century liberal democracy, requires an appropriate balancing between the security of private property interests and the protection of fundamental human rights.

In the first of three challenges against the United Kingdom, *Stec v UK*[9] the ECtHR has firmly rejected a distinction which, since the HRA, has consistently been relied on by UK courts, to limit the scope of judicial intervention in disputes over access to welfare entitlements. Therefore, contrary to the reasoning of the House of Lords in *Carson and Reynolds'* cases (fully discussed in Chapter 7) the ECtHR has concluded that:

> 'If . . . a Contracting State has in force legislation providing for the payment as of right of a welfare benefit—whether conditional or not on the prior payment of contributions—that legislation must be regarded as generating a proprietary interest falling within the ambit of Article 1 of Protocol No. 1 for persons satisfying its requirements.'[10]

The second decision, *Tsfayo v the United Kingdom*[11] concerned the application of Article 6 ECHR to a decision by a Housing Benefit Review Tribunal, to refuse payment of housing benefit to a non-English speaking asylum seeker because she had failed to show 'good cause' why she had not submitted her renewal claim on time. On her complaint to Strasbourg, the ECtHR decided that the tribunal had been in breach of Article 6; irrespective of whether the claimant had had access to a traditional judicial review hearing on appeal. Moreover, although purporting to distinguish the House of Lords decision in *Runa Begum v Tower Hamlets London BC*[12] (discussed in Chapter 8) the ECtHR decision showed nothing of the emphasis by the House of Lords in *Runa Begum's* case on the distinction between public and private property rights, as a measure of the claimant's right to a full and impartial hearing by an independent and impartial tribunal.

Finally, brief mention should be made of the more recent decision of the ECtHR in *McCann v UK*[13], a case which in 2008 fell to be scrutinised by the House of Lords in *Docherty and others v Birmingham City Council*.[14] This is not the place to discuss the ECtHR decision in detail; it will certainly continue

---

[8] The widely held expectation that the House of Lords would adopt a compassionate 'human rights' response to the resolution of this dispute is discussed in Chapter 3 II-I p 142

[9] Application Nos. 67531/01 and 65900/01 12 April 2006

[10] *Stec v UK*, ECtHR admissability decision, para 54, July 6th 2005.

[11] Application No. 60860/00, November 2006

[12] [2003] UKHL 5;

[13] Application No. 19009/04, 13 May 2008

[14] [2008] UKHL 57

to be extensively scrutinised elsewhere. Suffice it to say, that contrary to the House of Lords opinions in *Kay* (discussed fully in Chapter 4) the ECtHR has once again signalled in *McCann*, that for compliance with Article 8, domestic law must always allow the proportionality of a person's removal from her home to be determined by an independent tribunal.

Thus, as the effects of the credit crunch continue to bite, and administrative courts are overwhelmed by the applications of an ever widening constituency of 'intentionally homeless' families, there must be growing uncertainty in lower courts, as to whether, in refusing to take account of Strasbourg jurisprudence concerning the proportionality of housing repossessions, they are giving real and effective protection to fundamental human rights in the ECHR. Therefore, in light of growing dissonance between the ECtHR and the House of Lords, and the imminence of the newly established Supreme Court, questions about a 'new bill of rights' that might act as a brake on the untutored allegiance of senior judges to the ascendancy of private economic power over fundamental human rights values have gained heightened significance.

Ellie Palmer
Colchester
March 2009

Preface

This book is concerned with issues of state responsibility for the meeting of health and welfare needs in a post-welfare landscape. Historically, legal mechanisms for protecting socio-economic rights have been subordinated to those for the protection of civil and political rights. However, against a background of the growing recognition of the moral and existential overlap between civil and political rights on the one hand and socio-economic rights on the other hand, there has been a flowering of research on the constitutional propriety and efficacy of various methods of protecting socio-economic rights at international, European regional and domestic levels. One of the primary aims of the book is to contribute to that growing body of international scholarship.

In relation to the law of the United Kingdom, one of the main objectives here is to explore the extent to which, following the Human Rights Act (HRA) 1998, international fundamental human rights standards might be used by the judiciary to protect the social and economic welfare of vulnerable citizens. Thus, the context-sensitive doctrine of deference by which senior members of the UK judiciary have defined the boundaries of their legitimate intervention under the HRA in sensitive policy disputes, has been examined against the background of a more holistic international public law discourse that seeks to reconcile the tension between legal and political spheres of decision-making through the prism of fundamental human rights law.

The project has been long, complex and very absorbing. I thank my friends and family who have been patient and supportive throughout. I also thank my colleagues Maurice Sunkin, for his encouragement and shared fascination with the subject, and Brigid Hadfield, for her meticulous assistance with chapter 3. Thanks are also due to Darren Calley, who willingly helped me with the referencing in chapter 2 and with final preparation of the manuscript. Finally, I would like to thank Lisa Gourd of Hart Publishing for her very insightful and thorough editorial assistance.

23 May 2007

Contents

Preface to the Paperback Edition   vii

Preface   xi

Table of Cases   xix

Table of Legislation   xxxiii

INTRODUCTION   1

1 THE ROLE OF COURTS IN THE PROTECTION OF SOCIO-ECONOMIC RIGHTS: INTERNATIONAL AND DOMESTIC PERSPECTIVES   11

I.   The Indivisibility of Human Rights   11

A.   Understanding Socio-economic Rights as Human Rights   11

B.   Two Faces of Liberty: Conflicting Ideologies of Socio-economic and Civil and Political Rights   15

C.   Socio-economic Rights, Resources and the Negative–Positive Dichotomy   19

D.   A Unified Approach to Human Rights: To 'Respect, Protect and Promote' the Rights   22

E.   The Normative Content of Socio-economic Rights: Programmatic Aspirations and the 'Minimum Core'   24

II.   The Protection of Socio-economic Rights in Domestic Courts   26

A.   Issues of Justiciability: Achieving Social Justice in the Round?   26

i.   Institutional Competencies   26

ii.   Welfare Politics, Courts and Conflicting Theories of Constitutional Review   29

B.   The Protection of Socio-economic Rights through the Traditional Canon of Civil and Political Rights   34

C.   The Dedicated Pursuit of Social Justice: The South African Model   39

D.   The Enforcement of Socio-economic Rights: Cooperative Dialogue in the South African Constitutional Court?   42

III.   Conclusion   47

2 THE REGIONAL PROTECTION OF SOCIO-ECONOMIC RIGHTS: EUROPE   49

I.   Introduction   49

II.   The European Convention on Human Rights (ECHR) 1950   49

A.   Background and Context: The Negative–Positive Dichotomy Revisited   49

B. Incremental Development of Positive Obligations in ECHR
Rights   53
C. Methodological Issues: Grafting a Jurisprudence of Positive
Obligations onto the ECHR Rights   59
D. Reconciling the Development of Positive Obligations with the
Negative Thrust of the ECHR   62
E. Theoretical Justifications for Positive Obligations and the
Problem of Resources   64
III. The Protection of Socio-economic Rights in the ECHR   65
A. Developing Core Values in the ECHR Rights   65
B. Article 2: A Right to Health Treatment?   67
C. Article 3: Respect for Human Dignity   69
D. Article 8: Protecting Physical and Psychological Integrity   74
E. Article 14: The Equal Distribution of Public Goods?   79
F. Article 6: Due Process in Public Law Challenges   82
IV. The Protection of Socio-economic Rights in EC/EU Law   86
A. The Development of a Doctrine of Fundamental Rights in
EC/EU Law   86
B. The Charter of Fundamental Rights of the European Union   90
C. The European Court of Justice (ECJ): Social Solidarity and
Access to Public Services in Member States   94
i. Undue Delay   96
ii. Article 49 EC Treaty   100
V. Conclusion   102

3 COURTS, THE UK CONSTITUTION AND THE HUMAN RIGHTS ACT 1998   105

I. Introduction   105
II. Reading and Giving Effect to ECHR Rights in UK Courts   105
A. The Background and Political Context of the Human Rights
Act (HRA) 1998   105
B. The Purpose and Structure of the HRA   109
C. General Principles of Constitutional Interpretation in the
United Kingdom   115
D. The Interpretation of Section 3 HRA   117
E. Deference: The Boundaries of Interpretative Possibility under
Section 3 HRA   120
F. Section 2 HRA and the Scope of ECHR Rights: Taking Account
of Strasbourg Jurisprudence   130
i. *Stare Decisis*   136
G. Section 6 HRA: The Duty of Public Authorities to Act Compatibly
with the ECHR Rights   138
I. Human Rights or Economic Liberalism: Contested Interpretations
of Section 6(3)(b) HRA   142

III. Conclusion   150

4 JUDICIAL REVIEW: DEFERENCE, RESOURCES AND THE HUMAN RIGHTS ACT   151

   I.   Introduction   151
   II. The Constitutional Foundations of Judicial Review   152
      A. Ultra Vires or Rights?   152
      B. The Reception of Human Rights in English Law prior to
          the HRA   156
      C. Resistance to Human Rights in English Administrative Law   157
      D. Judicial Deference, Resources and the Ultra Vires Paradigm of
          Review   162
   III. Public Law, Deference and the Human Rights Act   165
      A. The Limits of Judicial Intervention under Section 6 HRA   165
        i.   Context and Proportionality: A Bright-line Division in
            Public Law?   168
      B. Justification, Transparency and Reasons to Defer   172
      C. Deference Embedded: The Artificial Division between Policy
          and Law   175
      D. Deference in Context: Landlord and Tenant Repossession Cases 178
      E. Deference, the Subject Matter of Disputes and the Nature of
          the Rights   187
      F. Democracy, Human Rights Values and the 'Unity of Public Law'   189
   IV. Conclusion   195

5 FROM NEED TO 'CHOICE' IN PUBLIC SERVICES: THE BOUNDARIES OF JUDICIAL
  INTERVENTION IN PRIORITISATION DISPUTES   197

   I.   Introduction   197
      A. From Need to Choice in NHS and Public Authority Services:
          The Post-welfare Landscape of the United Kingdom   200
   II. NHS Rationing: The Role of Courts in Disputes over Access to
      Medical Services   208
      A. The Limits of Judicial Intervention in Health Care Rationing:
          R v Cambridge Health Authority, ex parte B (Re B)   208
      B. NHS Policies under Scrutiny: Legitimate Interventions in
          Public Administrative Law   210
        i.   Legitimate Expectation: The Meeting of Individual Needs   211
        ii. Irrational Allocation Policies: Distinguishing *Re B*   214
      C. Choice, Socio-economic Entitlements and EU Law:
          Challenging the Status Quo   217
   III. Local Authority Resource Allocation Disputes   220
   IV. Interpreting Local Authority Statutory Duties Post-HRA   225
      A. Section 17 Children Act 1989: Accommodating Children and
          their Families   225

B. Orthodoxy Reasserted: The Retreat from *Kujtim*?   230
C. Positive Obligations to Protect the Vulnerable: The Approach
     in *Bernard*   233
D. A Human Rights Approach to Statutory Interpretation:
     Comparing *Bernard* and *G*   237
V. Conclusion   239

6 ARTICLES 3 AND 8 ECHR: FAILURE TO PROVIDE AND POSITIVE OBLIGATIONS
    IN THE SOCIO-ECONOMIC SPHERE   241

I. Introduction   241
II. *Anufrijeva*, Article 8 ECHR and Maladministration in the
      Provision of Welfare   243
A. The Acceptance of the Inadequacy of the Positive–Negative
     Dichotomy   244
B. When Does Breach of Public Authority Statutory Duties
     Constitute Breach of Section 6 HRA?   246
C. Maintaining the Family Unit: Levels of Culpability and the
     Failure to Provide   251
III. Article 3 ECHR: Respect for Dignity   254
A. No Welfare for the Destitute: The Asylum Seekers' Story   254
B. Withdrawing Asylum Support: The Policy Background   255
C. A Crisis in the Administrative Courts   257
D. *Limbuela*: The Court of Appeal   262
E. *Limbuela*: The House of Lords Abhors the Subtraction of
     ECHR Rights   265
F. Revisiting *D v UK*: *N v Secretary of State for the Home
     Department* and the Limits of State Responsibility to Provide
     Life-saving Treatment under Article 3 ECHR   270
IV. Conclusion   274

7 ARTICLE 14 ECHR AND THE UNEQUAL DISTRIBUTION OF PUBLIC GOODS AND
    SERVICES IN THE UNITED KINGDOM   277

I. Introduction   277
II. Socio-economic Entitlements and the Limits of Substantive
      Fairness in Article 14 ECHR   279
III. Carson's Case: Refusal of Up-rated Payments to Pensioners Abroad 283
A. 'Suspect Categories', Respect for Persons and 'Weighty
     Reasons' for Review   284
B. Consistency of Treatment or Substantive Outcome:
     The Malleable Concept of Equality   287
IV. Reynolds' Case: The Intensity of Scrutiny in Other 'Status Disputes' 291
V. Equality and Human Rights   294

A. Beyond the *Michalak* Formula: The Search for a 'Material and
Relevant Difference' in Article 14 ECHR Disputes 294
B. Competing Rights and Social Values: A Human Rights
Approach 297
VI. Conclusion 301

8 ARTICLE 6 ECHR: JUDICIAL REVIEW, DUE PROCESS AND THE PROTECTION OF
SOCIO-ECONOMIC RIGHTS 303

I. Introduction 303
II. What is a Civil Right for the Purposes of Article 6 ECHR? 304
A. The Autonomous Concept of Civil Right in Article 6 ECHR:
The Substantive Procedural Dichotomy Revisited 304
B. *R (on the Application of Kehoe) v Secretary of State for Work
and Pensions* 307
III. The Quality of Administrative Justice: The Scope of Article 6
ECHR 311
A. 'A fair hearing by an independent and impartial tribunal
established by law' 311
B. Housing Reviews: Independence and the Right to a Full Hearing 316
C. Civil Rights and Welfare Needs: The House of Lords in *Begum* 320
D. Law, Fact and Homelessness Disputes 322
E. The Standard of Judicial Review in Welfare Needs Disputes 325
F. The Compatibility of Section 55(10) of the Nationality
Immigration and Asylum Act 2002 with Article 6 ECHR 330
IV. Conclusion 331

AFTERWORD 335

Index

Table of Cases

Canada

Baker v Canada (Minister of Citizenship and Immigration) [1999]
2 SCR 817 ....166, 190–2, 194
Chaoulli v Quebec [2002] 4 SCR 429 21
Chaoulli v Quebec [2005] SCC 35; [2005] 1 SCR 791 ....3, 38
Eldridge v British Columbia (Attorney General) [1997] 3 SCR 624............36G
Gosselin v Quebec (Attorney General) [2002] 4 SCR 429 ....21, 38
JG v New Brunswick (Minister of Health and Community Services)
(1990) 177 DLR (4th) 124 20
Law v Canada (Minister of Employment and Immigration) [1999]
1 SCR 497...36, 194
R v Ascov (1990) 2 SCR 1199 20
Schachter v Canada (1991) 43 Dominion Law Report 4th 1; [1992]
2 SCR 679 36
Tetrault Gadoury v Canada (Employment and Immigration Commission)
[1991] 2 SCR 22...36

European Court and Commission of Human Rights

A v UK (1999) 27 EHRR 611 ....57, 58, 69
Abdulaziz v UK (1985) 7 EHRR 471...54, 280, 286
Aerts v Belgium (2000) 29 EHRR 50..72, 84
Ahmed v UK (2000) 29 EHRR 1 85
Airey v Ireland (1979) 2 EHRR 305..53, 65, 76, 82–3
Aksoy v Turkey (1997) 23 EHRR 553 84
Amegnigan v Netherlands App no 25629/04, unreported 74, 272
Andersson and Kullman v Sweden (1986) 46 DR 251............................246
Anguelova v Bulgaria (2004) 38 EHRR 31..68
Artico v Italy (1981) 3 EHRR 1..53
Ashingdane v UK (1985) 7 EHRR 528 ....305–6, 309
Askar v UK App No 26373/95, 16 October 1995..................................252
Asmundsson v Iceland (2005) 41 EHRR 42 294
Assenov v Bulgaria (1998) 28 EHRR 652 ....57, 71
Association X v UK App No 7154/75 (1978) 14 DR 31 67
BB v France [1998] H.R.C.D. 853 272
Beale v UK (2005) 40 EHRR SE6..285
Benkessiouer v France (2001) 33 EHRR 55......................................85

Belgian Linguistic Case (1979-80) 1 EHRR 252 297
Bensaid v UK (2001) 33 EHRR 10 ....245, 272–3
Blecic v Croatia (2005) 41 EHRR 13 ....137, 178, 182
Botta v Italy (1998) 26 EHRR 241...................51, 75–8, 233, 235, 245, 247, 299
Bryan v UK (1996) 21 EHRR 342 ....84, 86, 312–4, 321, 323–4, 330, 332
Bucholz v Germany (1981) 3 EHRR 597 83
Buckley v UK (1997) 23 EHRR 101...79
Budak v Turkey App No 57345/00, 7 September2004 285
Calvelli and Ciglio v Italy, Judgment of 17 January 2002,
    CEDH 2001-I..66, 68
Chahal v UK (1997) 23 EHRR 413 ....55, 57, 73, 258, 269
Chapman v UK (2001) 33 EHRR 399 ....77–8, 178, 246, 250, 275
Connors v UK (2000) 29 EHRR 293...78-9, 81, 137, 178,
                                                            182–5, 187, 189, 246, 250
Cruz Varas v Sweden (1992) 14 EHRR 73
Cyprus v Turkey (2002) 35 EHRR 731...51, 66, 68
D v UK (1997) 24 EHRR 423 ....57, 73–4, 264, 270–4
De Wilde, Ooms and Versyp v Belgium (1979-80) 1 EHRR 388...................53
Deumeland v Germany (1996) 21 EHRR 342 321
Dougoz v Greece (2002) 34 EHRR 330..51, 57, 70
Dyer v UK (1984) 39 DR 246 306
Editions Periscope v France (1992) 13 EHRR 597...84
Edwards v UK (2002) 35 EHRR 487 56
Erikson v Italy (2000) 29 EHRR CD152..68
Fayed v UK (1994) 18 EHRR 393..82, 306
Feldbrugge v Netherlands (1986) 8 EHRR 425 ....83–4, 321
Ferrazzini v Italy (2002) 34 EHRR 1068 84
Fogarty v UK (2001) 34 EHRR 302 306
Frydlander v France (2001) 31 EHRR 52...85
G v UK (2000) 3 FCR 193...54, 245
Gaskin v UK (1990) 12 EHRR 77
Gaygusuz v Austria (1998) 23 EHRR 365...............................80–1, 280, 286
Gillow v UK (1986) 11 EHRR 35...78, 134, 182
Golder v UK (1979) 1 EHRR 524 ....53, 304, 306, 309
Goodwin v UK (2002) 35 EHRR 18... 51, 79, 189
Guerra v Italy (1998) 26 EHRR 359..51, 66
Gul v Switzerland (1996) 22 EHRR 92...54, 245
H v UK (1987) 10 EHRR 95...252
Handyside v UK (1979-80) 1 EHRR 737 ....59, 65
Hatton v UK (2002) 34 EHRR 1 79
Henao v Netherlands App No 13669/03, judgment of 24 June 2003........74, 272
Hepple v UK App Nos 65731/01 and 65900/01 ....80, 281
Herczegfalvy v Austria (1993) 15 EHRR 437 71–2
Hoffman v Austria (1993) 17 ECHRR 293 286

Hold Monasteries v Greece (1994) 20 EHRR 1 84
Humber v France (1998) 26 EHRR 457 85
Hurtado v Switzerland A.280A (1994) 70, 71
Ilhan v Turkey (2002) 34 EHRR 36 ....57, 71
Ireland v Untied Kingdom (1979-80) 2 EHRR 25 69–70
Iskcon v UK (1994) 18 EHRR CD 133..312
James v UK (1986) 8 EHRR 142..293, 306, 309–10
Jankovic v Croatia (2000) 30 EHRR CD 183 ....80, 280
Johansen v Norway (1997) 23 EHRR 33..60
Johnston v Ireland (1986) 9 EHRR 203 296
JW and EW v UK App No 9776/82 283
Kaplan v UK (1980) 4 EHRR 64 ....85, 313
Karakurt v Austria CCPR/C/74/D/965/2000..52
Karara v Finland App No 40900/98 ....74, 272
Keenan v UK (2001) 33 EHRR 913 ....57, 66, 68, 71–2
Kingsley v UK (2001) 33 EHRR 288..312, 324
Kjeldsen v Denmark (1976) 1 EHRR 711 ....282, 285
Konig v Germany (1978) 2 EHRR 170 83
Koua Poirrez v France (2005) 40 EHRR 34 ....80, 277–8, 280, 302
Langborger v Sweden (1989) 12 EHRR 416..83
LCB v UK (1998) 27 EHRR 212..51, 67–8
Le Compte v Belgium (1985) EHRR 533 82
Lombardo v Italy (1992) 21 EHRR 18..84
Lopez Ostra v Spain (1995) 20 EHRR 277..51, 60, 74, 180
M v UK (2006) 42 EHRR 45 ....77, 244–5
MM v Switzerland App No 43348/98, unreported, 14 Sept 1998..............................74, 272
Mahmut Kaya v Turkey, Judgment of 28 March 2000, CEDH 2000-III 28.....56
Marckx v Belgium (1979) 2 EHRR 330..54, 62, 64, 235, 282
Marzari v Italy (1999) 28 EHRR CD 175 ....51, 76–8, 180, 185, 233, 247, 250
McCann v UK (1995), (1996) 21 EHRR 97)..51
McGinley and Egan v UK (1999) 27 EHRR 1 84
Mellacher v Austria (1989) 12 EHRR 391 ....79, 189
Muller v Austria (1975) 3 DR 25 ....80, 280
National & Provincial Building Society v UK (1998) 25 EHRR 127 84
Ndangoya v Sweden App No 17868/03 22 June 2004..272
Niemietz v Germany (1992) 16 EHRR 97 ....75, 135
Nitecki v Poland App No 65653/01, 21 March 2002 216
Oneryildiz v Turkey (2004) 39 ECHR 12..56, 66
O'Rourke v UK App No 39022/97, Judgment of
  26 June 2001 ....69, 74, 185, 247, 267
Osman v UK (1999) 29 EHRR 245..................20, 51, 55–6, 58, 68, 83, 162, 251
Ostra Lopez v Spain (1999) 28 EHRR CD 175...180
Peers v Greece (2001) 33 EHRR 1192..51, 69–70
Pellegrin v France (1999) 31 EHRR 651 85

Petrovic v Austria (1998) 4 BCHR 232..81, 188
Philis v Greece (No 1) (1999) 13 EHRR 741...390
Pinder v UK (1984) 7 EHRR 462 305–6
Plattform 'Artze fur das Leben' v Austria (1990) 12 EHRR 1 ....51, 62
Powell & Rayner v UK (1990) 12 EHRR 355 ....54, 60–1
Pretty v UK (2002) 35 EHRR 1..................61–2, 70, 189, 245, 258–61, 263, 279
Price v UK (2002) 34 EHRR 1285.............................57, 69, 71–2, 103, 178
Procola v Luxembourg (1995) 22 EHRR 193...84
Pudas v Sweden (1988) 10 EHRR 380 83
Rees v UK (1987) 9 EHRR 56 61
Ringeisen v Austria (No 1) (1971) 1 EHRR 455...................................82, 83, 85
Salesi v Italy (1993) 26 EHRR 187..84–5, 315
Salgueiro da Silva Mouta v Portugal (1999) 31 EHRR 1055, 1071 286
SCC v Sweden App No 46553/99, unreported......................................74, 272
Schouten and Meldrum v Netherlands (1994) 19 EHRR 432....................84, 85
Scialacqua v Italy (1998) 26 EHRR CD 164...68
Selmouni v France (2000) 29 EHRR 403 70
Sen v Netherlands (2003) 36 EHRR 81..54, 245–6
Sentges v Netherlands App No 27677/02 ....64, 76
Sinnott v Ireland and Minister of Education 33
Smith and Grady v UK (1999) 29 EHRR 493 ....54, 78, 165, 168–9, 182
Soerig v UK (1989) 11 EHRR 439 ....55, 59, 73, 270
Sprl ANCA v Belgium, 40 DR 170 84
Steel and Morris v UK [2005] EMLR 15..83
Stefan v UK (1998) 25 EHRR CD 130, 135 312
Stjerna v Finland (1994) 23 EHRR 194..60
Stran Greek Refineries v Greece (1995) 19 EHRR 293 84
Stubbings v UK (1996) 23 EHRR 213 306
Süßmann v Germany (1998) 25 EHRR 64 82
Tatete v Switzerland App No 41874/98, Judgment of 18 Nov 1998,
    E Com HR...74, 272
Tavares v France App No 16593, (1991) EComm HR 68
Thlimmenos v Greece (2001) 31 EHRR 411 52
Tinnelly & Sons Ltd v UK (1998) 27 EHRR 249..306
Tyrer v UK (1979-80) 2 EHRR 1 ....64, 133
Van der Mussele v Belgium (1983) 6 EHRR 183.............................284, 289, 296
Van Raalte v Netherlands (1997) 24 EHRR 518-19...286
Velikova v Bulgaria, Judgment of 18 May 2000, CEDH 2000-VI 68
Vogt v Germany (1995) 21 EHRR 32...85
Waite and Kennedy v Germany (1999) 30 EHRR 261 306
X v Austria App No 7830/77, 14 DR 200..84
X v France (1991) 14 EHRR 483..84
X v Ireland (1976) 7 DR 78 66–7
X v UK (1998) 25 EHRR CD 88...312

X and Y v Netherlands (1986) 8 EHRR 235..54, 63

Z v UK (2002) 34 EHRR 97 ....57, 58, 58, 73, 83, 162

Zehnalova and Zehnal v Czech Republic App No 38624/97,
14 May 2002 ....76, 247

Zumtobel v Austria (1993) 17 EHRR 116, 132-3.....................................312

European Court of Justice and Court of First Instance

Booker Aquaculture Ltd v Secretary of State for Scotland (Case C-20/00)
[2000] Eu LR 449...90

Bosphorus v Minister for Transport (Case C-84/95) [1996] ECR I-3953.........89

Commission of the European Communities v France (Case C-381/93)
[1994] ECR I-5145 101

Commission of the European Communities v Germany (Case C-441/02)
[2006] ECR I-3449..89

Commission of the European Communities v Jego-Quere et Cie SA (Case
C-263/02) [2004] ECR I-3425 91

Decker v Caisse de Maladie des Employes Prives (Case C-120/95) [1998]
ECR I-1831 95

*Elliniki Radiophonia Tileorassi AE (ERT) v Dimotiki Etairia Pliroforissis
(DEP)* (Case C-260/89) [1991] ECR I-2925...89

Geraets-Smits v Stichting Ziekenfonds VGZ (Case C-157/99) [2001]
ECR I-5473...96–8, 100–1

Inizan v Caisse Primaire d'Assurance Maladie des Hauts de Seine (Case
C-56/01) [2006] 1 CMLR 20 ....97–8, 100–1

Keller's Heirs v Instituto Nacional de la Seguridad Social (INSS) (Case
C-145/03) [2005] ECR I-2529 98

Kohll v Union des Caisses de Maladie (Case C-158/96) [1998]
ECR I-1931...95, 97, 100–1

Luisi v Ministero del Tesoro (Case 286/82) [1984] ECR 377.......................100

Marleasing SA v La Comercial Internacional de Alimentacion SA
(Case C-106/89) [1990] ECR I-1435 126

*Muller-Faure v Onderlinge Waarborgmaatschappij OZ Zorgverzekeringen
UA* (Case C-385/99) [2003] ECR I-4509 ....96–8, 100–1

P v S and Cornwall County Council (Case C-13/94) [1996] ECR I-2143.........89

*R (on the application of Broadcasting, Entertainment, Cinematographic
and Theatre Union) v Secretary of State for Trade and Industry*
(Case C-173/99) [2001] ECR I-4881 ....90, 92

R (on the application of Watts) v Bedford Primary Care Trust C-372/04
[2006] ECR I-04235 94

Rutili v Ministre de l'linterieur (Case 36/75) [1975] ECR I-219 89

Schafer v Commission of the European Communities (Case T-52/01)
[2001] ECR IA-0015 91

*Society for the Protection of Unborn Children (Ireland) Ltd (SPUC) v
Grogan* (Case C-159/90) [1991] ECR I-4685 100

Sodemare SA v Lombardia (Case C-70/95) [1997] ECR I-3395......................95
Van der Duin v Onderlinge Waarborgmaatschappij ANOZ
    Zorgverzekeringen UA (Case C-156/01) [2003] ECR I-7045 98
Vanbraekel v Alliance Nationale des Mutualites Chretiennes (ANMC)
    (Case C-368/98) [2001] ECR I-5363...97, 100
Z v European Parliament (Case C-270/99) [2001] ECR I-9197 92

Germany

BVerfGE 83, 22...20

India

Dwivedi v Union of India AIR (1983) SC 624.....................................20
Mullin (Francis Corallie) v Administrator, Union Territory of Delhi
    (1981) 2 SCR 516, 529..39

New Zealand

Ministry of Transport v Noort [1992] 3 NZLR 271.....................................116

South Africa

Chairman of the Constitutional Assembly, ex parte; In re the Certification
    of the Constitution of the Republic of South Africa 1996 (10) BCLR
    1253 (CC) [78]...42
Government of the Republic of South Africa v Grootboom 2000 (11)
    BCLR 1169 (CC) 43–6
Grootboom v Oosteneberg Municipality 2000 (3) BCLR 277 (C) 289,
    2001 (1) SA 46 (CC)...21-2, 194
Khosa v Minister for Social Development 2004 (6) SA 505.....................43–6
Minister of Health v Treatment Action Campaign 2005 (5) SA 721 (CC) ...43–7
S v Makwanyame 1995 (6) BCLR 655 (CC) 42
Soobramooney v Minster if Health Kwa Zulu Natal 1998 (1) SA 765
    (CC) 43, 45–6

United Kingdom

A v Lambeth LBC (2001) 4 CCLR 486 ....110, 225–33, 237, 239
A v Secretary of State for the Home Department [2004] UKHL 56;
    [2005] 2 AC 68...155, 165–6, 192–4, 270
A v Secretary of State for the Home Department (No 2) [2005]
    UKHL 71 ....165, 190
A, B, X and Y [2004] EWCA Civ 662...117
Adan v Newham London BC [2001] EWCA Civ 1961............314–8, 324, 326–7

AG of Hong Kong v Lee Kong Kwut [1993] AC 951.....................................116

Al-Ameri v Kensington and Chelsea Royal LBC [2004] UKHL 4;
    [2004] 1 All ER 1049...199, 202, 206

*Alconbury Developments Ltd v Secretary of State for the Environment
    Transport and the Regions* [2001] UKHL 23; [2001] 2 All ER
    929................................... 131, 171, 187, 304, 307, 312–4, 322–3, 325–6, 330

Anderson v Secretary of State for the Home Department [2002] UKHL 46;
    [2002] 4 All ER 89; [2003] 1 AC 837; [2003] HRLR 7......118, 120, 126–8, 132

Anisminic Ltd v Foreign Compensation LBC [2004]
    1 ALL ER 833 ....111, 233, 242–9, 250–4, 274, 279, 301

Archibald v Fife Council [2004] UKHL 32; [2004] 4 All ER 303 299

Associated Provincial Picture Houses Ltd v Wednesbury Corp [1948]
    1 KB 223; [1947] 2 All E.R. 680 ....151, 153–4, 158–65, 169, 173,
                                                    194, 198, 208, 212, 214, 332

*Aston Cantlow and Wilmcote with Billesley Parochial Church Council v
    Wallbank* [2003] UKHL 37 ....114, 134, 146–8

Barrett v Enfield LBC [2001] 2 AC 550...83

Begum (FC) v Tower Hamlets LBC [2003] UKHL 5.............................86, 315

Bellinger v Bellinger [2003] UKHL 21; [2003] 2 All ER 593; [2003]
    2 AC 467 ....120, 127–9, 168, 245

Bernard and Another v Enfield LBC [2002] EWHC 2282, [2003]
    HRLR 4 ....233, 235–9, 244, 246, 249–50, 253

Brind v Secretary of State for the Home Department [1991] 1 All
    ER 720; [1991] 1 AC 696 ....158–60, 208

Carson v Secretary of State for Work and Pensions [2003] EWCA
    Civ 797; [2003] 3 All ER 577 247

Collier, The Independent, 14 March 1995 205

Council of Civil Service Unions v Minister for the Civil Service (CCSU)
    [1985] AC 374 154

Doody v Secretary of State for Home Development [1993] 3 All ER 92........329

Douglas v Hello (No 2) [2005] EWCA Civ 595...................................117, 140

E v East Sussex County Council, ex parte Tandy [1998] AC 714;
    [1998] 2 All ER 770 ....164–5, 222–4, 229, 231–2, 239

Edwards v National Coal Board [1949] 1 KB 704 135

Findlay, Re [1985] AC 318...210

Fitzpatrick v Sterling Housing Association Ltd [1999] 4 All ER 705......125, 127

Friends Provident v Secretary of State for Transport [2001] EWCH
    Admin 820 314

Gaima v Secretary of State for the Home Department [1989] Imm
    AR 205..329

Ghaidan v Mendoza [2004] UKHL 30; [2004] 2 AC 557; [2004]
    3 All ER 411 ....117–21, 124–30, 133, 140, 150, 165,
                                        179, 188, 194–5, 286-7, 295, 301–2

Hampshire County Council v Graham Beer [2003] EWCA Civ 1056 ....143, 147

Harrow LBC v Qazi [2003] UKHL 43; [2003] All ER 461......133, 136-7, 178–84
Higgs v Minister of National Security [2000] 2 AC 228 21
Howarth v Secretary of State for the Home Department [2000]
   Imm AR 205...157
Huntley v Attorney General for Jamaica [1995] 2 AC 1...............................116
International Transport Roth GMBH v Secretary of State for the Home
   Department [2002] HRLR 31..115, 117, 119, 171–3
Johnson v Havering LBC [2007] EWCA Civ 26.................................147, 300
K (H) an Infant, Re [1967] 1 All ER 226..329
Kay v Lambeth LBC [2006] UKHL 10...... 132, 136–8, 178, 182–7, 189, 241, 335
Lambeth v Howard [2001] EWCA Civ 468 178
Leeds v Price [2005] 1 WLR 1825...............................136–7, 178, 183, 235, 299
Lewis v Attorney General of Jamaica [2000] 3 WLR 1785 21
Lister v Forth Dry Dock and Engineering Co Ltd [1989] 1 All ER 1134........126
Malster v Ipswich Borough Council [2001] EWHC Admin 711....................314
Manchester City Council v Romano and Samaro (DRC as Third-party
   Intervener) [2004] EWCA Civ 834..300
Marcic v Thames Water Utilities Ltd [2002] EWCA Civ 64 246
Matadeen v Pointu and Minister of Education and Science [1999]
   1 AC 98 115–6
Matthews v Ministry of Defense [2003] UKHL 4.............52, 85, 304, 306–7, 309
McLellan v Bracknell Forest BC [2001] EWCA Civ 1510 ....314–5, 320
Ministry of Home Affairs v Fisher [1980] AC 319 116
Morris v Newham LBC [2002] EWHC 1262 ....236, 249
N v B, unreported (2004) 300
N v Secretary of State for the Home Department [2005] UKHL 31;
   [2005] AC 296................................. 133, 149, 242, 244, 251, 264, 270–2, 274
Nipa Begum v Tower Hamlets LBC [2000] 1 WLR 306 316
North West Lancashire Health Authority v A, D & G [2000]
   1 WLR 977 ....210–11, 215-7
O'Rourke v Camden LBC [1997] 3 All ER 23 ....206, 315, 320
Pepper v Hart (1993) AC 593 114
Popular Housing and Regeneration Community Association ltd v
   Donoghue [2001] EWCA Civ 595; [2001] 3 WLR 183...................118–9, 124,
                        141–4, 147–50, 171, 178–81, 185–7, 241, 253
Pickstone's v Freemans Plc [1998] 2 All ER 803 126
Pulhofer v Hillingdom [1986] 1 ALL ER 467 474 ....326–7, 331
R v A [2001] UKHL 25; [2001] 3 All ER 1; [2002] 1 AC 45 ....119, 121–6
R v Birmingham City Council, ex parte Mohammed [1998] 4 All ER 101 223
R v Cambridge Heal Authority, ex parte B (Re B) [1995] 1 FLR 1055,
   2 All ER 129................................164–5, 207, 208–10, 214, 216, 220, 223, 239
R v Chief Constable of Sussex, ex parte International Traders Ferry
   Ltd [1999] 2 AC 418 ....159, 206
R v Criminal Injuries Board, ex parte A [1999] 2 AC 330..............................326

R v DDP, ex parte Kebilene [2000] 2 AC 326; [1999]
3 WLR 972..............................115, 122, 132, 139, 170, 173, 187, 293
R v East Sussex County Council, ex parte Reprotech (Pebsham)
[2002] UKHL 8..189
R v Eastbourne (Inhabitants) (1803) 4 East 103 256
R v Gloucester, ex parte Barry [1997] AC 584, [1998]
2 All ER 770 ....164–5, 221–3, 238
R v Hasan [2005] 2 WLR 709, 62 119
R v Home Secretary, ex parte Fire Brigades Union [1995] AC 513.............206
R v Home Secretary, ex parte P and G [1995] 1 All ER 870..................206
R v Immigration Appeal Tribunal, ex parte Shah [1999] 2 AC 629.............269
*R v IRC, ex parte National Federation of Self-employment and Small
Businesses Ltd* [1981] 2 WLR 272...28
R v IRC, ex parte Preston [1985] 2 All ER 327...........................212
R v Inner London Education Authority, ex parte Ali and Murshid
[1990] 2 All ER 822...220–1, 228–30, 232
R v Inspector of Pollution, ex parte Greenpeace [1994]
1 WLR 570...28
R v Islington LBC , ex parte Rixon [1997] ELR 66...........................221
R v Kensington and Chelsea LBC, ex parte Kujtim (1999)
WL 478029...223–4, 230, 232, 234
R v Lambert [2002] 2 AC 545 118
R v Leonard Cheshire Homes, ex parte Heather [2002] EWCA
Civ 366 ....142–4, 146–50, 300
R v Lord Chancellor, ex parte Witham (1998) QBD 779............................161
R v Lyons [2003] 1 AC 976 132
R v Manchester City Council, ex parte Stennett [2002] UKHL 34................199
R v Ministry of Defence, ex parte Smith [1996] QB 517, 541;
[1995] 4 All ER 427, 445.....................................158–60, 165, 216
R v North Derbyshire Health Authority, ex parte Fisher (1998)
38 BMLR 76...207
*R v North East Devon Health Authority, ex parte Coughlan, Secretary
of State for Health and Another, Interveners* (2000) 51 BMLR 1,
[2000] 3 All ER 850...199, 202, 211–4
*R v Secretary of State for the Environment, ex parte Hammersmith and
Fulham LBC* [1991] 1 AC 521 163–4
*R v Secretary of State for the Environment, ex parte Nottingham County
Council* [1986] AC 240...163–4
*R v Secretary of State for the Environment Transport and the Regions,
ex parte Spath Homes Ltd* [2001] 2 AC 349 ....171, 187
R v Secretary of State for the Home Department, ex parte Anderson
[1984] QB 778 157
R v Secretary of State for the Home Department, ex parte Bugdaycay
[1987] AC 514 ....206, 209

R v Secretary of State for the Home Department, ex parte Daly
[2001] UKHL 26; [2001] 2 WLR 1622...................168–70, 173, 177, 209, 326
R v Secretary of State for the Home Department, ex parte Hargreaves
[1997] 1 All ER 397...212
R v Secretary of State for the Home Department, ex parte Leech (No 2)
[1994] QB 198 157
R v Secretary of State for the Home Office, ex parte Simms [1999]
3 WLR 328...160
R v Secretary of State for Social Security, ex parte Joint Council for the
Welfare of Immigrants (JCWI) [1997] 1 WLR 275 ......160–1, 195, 206, 255–6
R v Secretary of State for Social Services, ex parte Child Poverty
Action Group [1990] 2 QB 540 ....28, 198
R v Sefton, ex parte Help the Aged and Blanchard [1997]
4 All ER 449 ....198–9, 222
R v Speer [2002] 1 AC 734...132
R v Warwickshire County Council, ex parte Collymore [1995] ELR 217......210
R v Westminster City Council, ex Parte M (1997) 1 CCLR 85 256
R v Wicks [1997] 2 All ER 801...323
R v Wigan MBC, ex parte Tammadge [1998] 1 CCLR 581 ......224, 229–30, 234
R v Wolverhampton, ex parte Wattters (1997) 29 HLR 391........................204
R (on the Application of A) v Lambeth LBC [2002] HLR 57 998.............203–5
R (on the Application of A) v Partnerships in Care [2002]
EWHC 529..142–3, 146
R (on the Application of A,B,X and Y) v East Sussex County Council
(No 2) [2003] EWHC 167..90, 134, 177, 299
R (on the Application of Adam) v Secretary of State for the Home
Department [2004] EWHC 354 Admin..260
R (on the Application of Adlard) v Secretary of State for the Environment
[2002] EWCA Civ 735 314
R (on the Application of Hussain) v Secretary of State for the Home
Department [2001] EWHC Admin 852...84
R (on the Application of Khatun) v Newham [2004] EWCA Civ 55;
[2005] QB 37 149
R (on the Application of Buckland and Boswell) v Secretary of State
for the Environment, Transport and the Regions [2001] EWHC
Admin 524 178
R (on the Application of Beeson) v Dorset County Council [2002]
EWCA Civ 1812 ....314, 319–20
R (on the Application of Bernard) v Enfield LBC [2003] UKHRR 148..........111
R (on the Application of Burke) v The General Medical Council
and Disability Rights Commission [2003] EWCH 1879
Admin 134, 177, 197, 300
R (on the Application of C) v Royal Devon and Exeter NHS Foundation
Trust (DRC Interested Party), unreported (2004) 300

R (on the Application of Carson) v Secretary of State for Work and Pensions [2005] UKHL 37; [2005] 2 WLR 1369; [2005] 4 ALL ER 545..................80, 171, 188, 200, 277–8, 280–97, 301–2, 335

R (on the Application of Farrakhan) v Secretary of State for Home Department [2002] EWCA Civ 606; [2002] QB 1391.................171, 178, 188

R (on the Application of G) v Barnet LBC [2003] UKHL 57; [2004] 1 All ER 97-214...................198, 225–6, 229–33, 237–9

R (on the Application of Gezer) v Secretary of State for the Home Department [2004] EWCA Civ 1730.....................................264–5

R (on the Application of Greenfield) v Secretary of State for the Home Department [2005] UKHL 14.......................................111

R (on the Application of Hooper) v Secretary of State for Work and Pensions [2005] UKHL 29; [2006] 1 ALL ER 487.....................139–40

R (on the Application of Hussain) v Asylum Support Adjudicator [2001] EWHC 852 Admin.......................................315, 320

R (on the Application of J (Ghanaian Citizen)) v Enfield LBC [2002] EWHC 432; [2002] All ER (D) 209 Mar 225, 227–8, 238, 251

R (on the Application of Kathro) v Rhonda Cybnon Taff CBC [2001] EWCH 527..314

R (on the Application of Kehoe) v Secretary of State for Work and Pensions [2003] EWCH 1021; [2005] 4 ALL ER 905 ....110, 195, 304–5, 307-8, 310–1

R (on the Application of Limbuela) v Secretary of State for the Home Department [2005] UKHL 66...................195, 242, 248, 254, 259–70, 274–6, 279, 301–2, 335

R (on the Application of Mahmood) v Secretary of State for the Home Department [2001] 1 WLR 840..................... 169–70, 178

R (on the Application of Mukoko Batantu) v Islington LBC 224, 229–30, 234

R (on the Application of N) v Sec State for the Home Department [2003] EWCH Admin 111

R (on the Application of Pfizer Ltd) v Secretary of State for Health [2003] 1 CMLR 19 ....162, 206, 210

R (on the Application of ProLife Alliance) v British Broadcasting Corporation [2003] UKHL; [2003] 2 ALL ER977 ....115, 160, 175, 188

R (on the Application of Q) v Secretary of State for the Home Department [2003] EWCA Civ 364, [2003] 2 All ER 905 ....248, 254, 256, 258–60, 262, 265, 327–31

R (on the Application of Q, D, B, M, J and F) v Secretary of State for the Home Department [2003] EWHC 195 Admin 327

R (on the Application of Reynolds) v Secretary of State for Work and Pensions [2002] EWHC Admin 291–3

R (on the Application of Rodgers) v Swindon Primary Care Trust [2006] EWHC Admin 357.................................6, 214, 216–7

*R (on the Application of S) v Chief Constable of Yorkshire Police; R
(on the Application of Marper) v Chief Constable of Yorkshire
Police* [2004] UKHL 39 282

R (on the Application of Spink v Wandsworth LBC [2005] EWCA
Civ 320 ....199, 238

R (on the Application of T) v Secretary of State for the Home Department
[2003] EWHC 1941 Admin...258–62, 265

*R (on the Application of Tesema) v Secretary of State for the Home
Department* [2004] EWHC 295 Admin......................................261

R (on the Application of Watts) v Bedford Primary Care Trust [2004]
EWCA Civ 166..................6, 94–5, 97–8, 100–3, 160, 199, 206–7, 217–20, 239

R (on the Application of Wilkinson) v Inland Revenue Commissioners
[2005] UKHL 30; [2006] 1 ALL ER 529 139–40

*R (on the Application of Williamson) v Secretary of State for Education
and Employment* [2002] EWCA Civ 1820...................................136

Raymond v Honey [1983] 1 AC 1 157

Reyes v R [2006] 11 UKPC, [2002] 2 AC 235 189

Runa Begum v Tower Hamlets LBC [2003] UKHL 5,
1 All ER 731 ....132, 134, 303, 304, 307, 311,
314–5, 318–9, 321–7, 330–3, 335

S (Children: care plan) , Re; Re W (Children: care plan) [2002]
2 All ER 192, [2002] UKHL 10 ....118, 121, 123–5, 127–8

Salomon v Commissioners of Customs and Excise [1967] 2 QB 116.............118

Secretary of State for Education and Science v Tameside MBC
[1976] 3 All ER 665,675 325

Secretary of State for the Home Department, ex parte Rheman
[2001] UKHL 47; [2003] 1 AC 153.............................171, 175–6, 192

Shamoon v Chief Constable of the Royal Ulster Constabulary
[2003] UKHL 11; [2003] All ER 26...295–6

State v Makwantance [1995] 1 LCR 269, 311 190

Stefan v General Medical Council (No.1) [1999] 1 WLR 1293 157

*T (on the Application of Zardasht) v Secretary of State for the Home
Department* [2004] EWCH 91 ....259–60, 266

Thake v Maurice [1986] 2 WLR 337 177

Thomas v Baptiste [2000] 2 AC 1; [1999] 3 WLR 249 21

Vetterlein v Hampshire County Council [2001] EWHC Admin 560..............314

W v Lambeth LBC [2002] 2 All ER 901...225-6, 228-30, 232

W and B (Care Plan) [2001] 2 FCR 450......................................123–4

Waddington v Miah [1974] 1 WLR 683.......................................118

Walker, ex parte, The Times, November 26, 1987.......................205

Wandsworth LBC v Michalak [2002] EWCA Civ 271 ....187, 278, 294–7, 301

Wilson v First County Trust Ltd (No 2) [2001] EWCA Civ 633 ....114, 133

X (Minors) v Bedfordshire CC [1995] 3 All ER 353 205

United States of America

Brown v Board of Education 347 US 483 (1954) 5, 30, 37

Deshaney v Winnebago County Department of Social Services 489 US 189, 109
   Ct 998 (1989)..18, 30, 63

Fortiero v Richardson 411 US 677 (1973) 38

Goldberg v Kelly 397 US 245 (1970) 37, 52, 332

Los Angeles v Manhart 435 US 702 (1978) 38

Massachusetts Board of Retirement v Murgia 427 US 307 (1976)................285

Matthews v Eldridge 424 US 319 (1976) 52, 322, 332

Pyler v Doe 457 US 202 (1982) 37

San Antonio School District v Rodriguez 411 US 1 (1973) 286, 339

Table of Legislation

Canada

Charter of Fundamental Rights and Freedoms 1982 ....20, 42, 280
   s 1...37
   s 7...21, 38
   s 11 20
   s 11(b) 20
   s 15...35, 39, 279
Constitution
   Art 15(1) 194

European Union

Charter of Fundamental Rights of the European
   Union 2000 ....3, 5–6, 89–91, 94, 102
   Ch III 93
   Ch IV 91–3
   Art 5(1) 90
   Art 21 93
   Art 27 92
   Arts 27–38...92
   Art 28 92
   Art 30 92
   Art 31 92
   Art 33 93
   Art 34 93
   Art 35..93–4
   Art 36 91
   Art 37 93
Charter of Fundamental Social Rights of Workers 1989...........................88, 91
EC Treaty 1957 ....87, 91, 126
   Art 23 95
   Art 25 95
   Art 28 95
   Art 29 95
   Art 39 95
   Art 39(1) 88
   Art 43 95
   Art 46 ....101, 102

Art 49 ....95–8, 100–3, 218–20
Art 50 95
Art 81 95
Art 82 95
Art 86 95
Art 189...126
Art 234..95
European Code of Social Security 1964 289
European Constitution...90
European Social Charter 1961 ....7, 9, 15, 19, 50, 89, 157
  Pt 1 19
  Art 11 66
European Social Charter 1996 Revision................................50, 76, 88, 107, 109
  Arts 21–29..50
Maastricht Treaty 1991 9
Single European Act 1986...89
Treaty of European Union 1992 89
  Art 6 88
  Art 6(1) 88
  Art 6(2) 88–9
  Art 7 88

Regulations
Regulation 1408/71 on Social Security for Migrant Workers.......................283
  Art 22..95–8, 100, 102–3
  Art 22(2) 96
Regulation No 574/72 on the implementation of Reg.1408/71.....................283

Directives
Equal Treatment Directive..89

France

Declaration of the Rights of Man and the Citizen 1789..........................12, 116

India

Constitution...5, 39
  Pt 3...35, 38
  Pt 4...35, 38
  Art 21 38

International

Convention on the Elimination of all Forms of Discrimination against
  Women 1979 9
Convention on the Elimination of all Forms of Racial Discrimination 1965.....9
European Convention on Human Rights 1950.................2–4, 6-8, 15, 20–2, 34,
            38–9, 48–54, 59, 63–5, 67, 87–9, 91–2, 102–3, 106–10, 113,
            115, 117–8, 120, 125–9, 131, 135–6 138–41, 148–9, 151, 154–9,
            165, 167–70, 173–4, 185–6, 188–9, 195–6, 211, 213, 224,
            227–8, 231, 240, 242, 244, 256–7, 267, 276, 279, 287, 303, 336–7
  Art 1..19, 50, 57, 62–3, 114, 146, 148
  Art 2 ....20, 51, 55–8, 66-9, 114, 145, 167, 215–6, 239, 251, 300
  Art 2(1) 55-6, 66–8
  Arts 2–12...110
  Art 3 ....3, 6, 20–1, 51, 56–8, 61, 66–7, 69–4, 84, 95, 103, 111,
            145, 157, 167, 187, 195, 234–5, 241–4, 247–8, 250,
            254, 257–74, 300, 317, 326, 328, 330
  Art 5..53, 155, 167, 188
  Art 5(1) 193
  Art 5(2) 53
  Art 6..3, 7, 53, 82, 84–6, 111, 121–3, 126–7,
            134, 147, 172, 188, 300, 302–28, 330–3, 335
  Art 6(1)..82–4, 171, 305, 307–9, 311, 314, 319
  Art 6(3)(c)..20, 53
  Art 6(3)(e) 53
  Art 8................................3, 6, 51–5, 58–61, 66, 67, 74–9, 95, 103, 111, 125,
            127–30, 133, 135, 137, 139, 142, 145, 158, 166–7, 178–9,
            182–6, 188–9, 198–9, 212–3, 225, 227–8, 232–9, 241–3, 245–54,
            257, 267, 274, 278, 280–1, 291, 300, 326, 328, 330, 335
  Art 8(1)................................53–4, 59–61, 77, 129, 133, 178–80, 228, 245, 251
  Art 8(2)................................59–61, 77, 132–3, 178, 180–1, 184, 228, 250, 253
  Arts 8–10 59
  Arts 8–11 ....59, 166–7, 170
  Arts 9–11 59
  Art 10..158, 160, 166, 188
  Art 11 ....21, 166
  Art 12..127–8
  Art 13 ....111, 146, 148
  Art 14................................3, 6–7, 39, 52, 79–81, 110, 125, 129–30, 139, 158,
            179, 188, 194, 233, 269, 277–85, 288–9, 291–6, 300–1, 335
  Art 15..193
  Arts 16–8...110
  Art 24 50
  Art 25 50
  Art 52(3) 92
Protocol 1..65, 282

Protocol 1 Art 1...3, 7, 50, 52, 65, 79–80, 129–30,
139, 171, 186, 189, 280–3, 288, 291–2, 294
Protocol 1 Art 2...20, 65
Protocol 1 Art 3 20
Protocol 1 Arts 1-3 110
Protocol 6 Arts 1-2 110
Protocol 11 50
Protocol 12 Art 1 80–81
International Bill of Rights 11, 50
International Convention Relating to the Status of Refugees 1951.................9
International Covenant on Civil and Political
    Rights 1966 ....11, 14–5, 17, 35, 113, 157
    Art 1 19
    Art 26...52, 79, 116
International Covenant on Economic, Social and Cultural
    Rights 1966.................7–9, 11, 14, 17, 19–20, 24–6, 35, 41, 108–9, 113, 157
    Art 2 19
    Art 2(1) 41
    Art 4 42
    Art 6 157
    Arts 6–8 8
    Arts 6–9 25
    Arts 6–13 2
    Art 8 21
    Art 9..2, 7–8
    Art 11(1) 257
    Arts 11–14..2, 25
    Art 12 22
    Art 15 2
International Labour Organisation Social Security (Minimum Standards)
    Convention 1952..289
    Art 69...289
Treaty of Versailles 1919..12
United Nations Convention on the Rights of a Child 1989.....................9, 113
    Art 3 192
    Art 11 2
    Arts 12–14 2
    Art 27 2
United Nations Convention on the Rights of Persons with Disabilities
    2006...298
Universal Declaration of Human Rights 1948.............................3, 8, 11, 13–4,
16, 50, 63, 65, 69, 155–7

Art 23 12
Art 25 16
Art 25(1) 12
Art 26 12
Vienna Convention on the Law of Treaties 1969
  Art 31(1) 62
  Arts 31–33...62

Iraq

Constitution 35
  Art 25 35
  Art 30 35

Mauritius

Constitution 116
  s 1 116
  s 3 116

Netherlands

Sick Fund Law (ZWF) 96–7

New Zealand

Bill of Rights Act 1990...116

South Africa

Constitution 1996...5, 9, 21, 23, 35, 39–43, 187, 194, 338
  s 2..40
  s 7(2)..40
  s 9..45
  ss 24–7 40
  s 26 ....40-2, 44, 47, 187
  s 26(1) 44
  s 26(2)...40–1, 43, 45
  s 26(3)..23, 41
  s 27 ....40–2, 44–5, 47
  s 27(1)...40, 43
  s 27(2) 41, 43, 45
  s 27(3) 42–3
  s 28...42, 47

s 28(1)(c) 41
s 29(1)(c) 41
s 35(2)(e) 41
s 36 42
s 38 43
s 167 43
Social Assistance Act 1992..43

United Kingdom

Adoption and Children Act 2003 229
Anti-terrorism, Crime and Security Act 2001
s 23 193
Asylum and Immigration Act 1996
s 8 268
s 11 256
Asylum and Immigration Appeals Act 1993 255
Caravan Sites Act 1968..182, 184
Carers and Disabled Persons Act 2000 228
Child Support Act 1991 ....110, 307–11
Pt 3 109
Children's Act 1989................................123, 186, 225–6, 231–2, 238
Pt II..123
Pt III 109, 123, 198, 225–6, 229
s 17 ....198–9, 225–32, 238
s 17(1) 198, 226, 230–1
s 17(6) 198
s 17A..228, 239
s 20 ....227, 229
s 20(1) 227
s 21 224
Chronically Sick and Disabled Persons Act 1970 238
s 2(1) 9, 221–3, 231, 238
s 28A..238
Crown Proceedings Act 1947
s 10 306
s 10(1)(b) 306
Disability Discrimination Act 1995 298–9
s 19 300
Disability Rights Commission Act 1999................................298
Education Act 1944
s 68 221
s 69 221
Education Act 1980 202

Education Act 1993
  s 298...222–3, 232
Equality and Human Rights Act 2006...278
  s 9..279
  s 10(1)-(2)...278
European Communities Act 1972.......................................106, 156
Family Law Act 1996
  61(1)(a)..129
Fatal Accidents Act 1976
  s 1(3)...129
Freedom of Information Act 2000..145
Homelessness Act 2002...203–4, 225
  s 16...203
  s 161(1)..225
  s 167(1)..225
Housing Act 1988
  s 17(4)..129
  s 21...179
  s 21(4)..179
  s 22...228
  s 167(2)..203
Housing Act 1996...225
  Pt VI...225
  Pt VII...236, 316–7, 320
  s 127..314
  s 129..320
  s 161(1)..225
  s 188(1)..320
  s 193(2)..320
  s 202...315–20, 324–5
  s 203..316
  s 204...315–9, 325–6
  s 204(3)..325
Housing Grants and Construction Regeneration Act 1996
  s 23...223
Human Rights Act 1998...............2–6, 28, 33–4, 48–9, 52, 86, 105–21, 124–6,
                129, 131, 134, 149–52, 154, 156–7, 160–2, 165–8, 170, 172,
                174–5, 177–81, 189, 192–3, 195–8, 206, 211, 224, 225, 229,
                233, 239, 241, 246, 248, 253–4, 257–8, 275, 278–9, 281,
                299–300, 302–3, 311–3, 316, 325, 330, 333, 335–8
  s 1(1)..110
  s 2...110, 130, 133–4, 136–8, 150, 216
  s 2(1)...131, 271
  s 2(2)..130

s 2(3) 130
s 3 ....3, 105, 114–5, 117–29, 136, 138–40, 150,
              168, 171, 179, 198–9, 224–5, 228, 238–40, 251, 335, 337
s 3(1) 110–2, 117-8, 121–2, 126, 139, 148
s 3(2) 112
s 3(2)(a) 112
s 3(2)(b) 112, 121
s 3(2)(c) 112
s 4 ....112, 120–1, 123, 126–8, 138–9, 150, 228
s 4(5) 112, 124
s 4(6) 112
s 5(1) 112
s 5(2) 112
s 5(3) 112
s 5(4) 112
s 5(5) 112
s 6 ....3, 105, 114, 135, 138, 141–3, 145–6, 148,
              165–7, 178, 198, 241–2, 254, 257, 300, 316, 335
s 6(1) 138, 141
s 6(1)(a) 110, 147
s 6(2) 137, 139–40
s 6(2)(a) 138–40
s 6(2)(b) 138–40
s 6(3) 138, 141
s 6(3)(a) 110
s 6(3)(b) 114, 141–50, 178
s 7 ....111, 124, 148
s 7(1) 28, 110
s 7(1)(a) 110
s 7(3) 28, 110
s 8 ....111, 124, 148, 216, 242–4, 254, 308
s 8(1) 111, 234
s 9 148
s 10 123
s 12 114
s 13 114
s 14 216
s 19 ....112–3, 121, 139
Immigration and Asylum Act 1993 255
Immigration and Asylum Act 1999 ....119, 227–8, 256
Pt II..171
Pt VI 84
s 3 119
s 95 ....256, 262

s 95(3) 256–8, 267
s 103...327
s 116...256
Inheritance (Provision for Family and Dependants) Act 1975
s 1A..129
Jobseekers Act 1995 291
Local Government Act 2000
s 2...228
s 2(1) 228
Matrimonial Causes Act 1973..127
s 11(c) 127–8
Mental Health Act 1983 ....142, 149
s 117..199
Mobile Homes Act 1983...184
National Assistance Act 1948 ....148–9, 237, 249
s 21 ....199, 211, 222–4, 230–1, 236, 243–4, 249, 256
s 21(1)(a)...230, 234, 256
s 29 238
s 55 256
National Health Act 1977
s 2..207, 214
s 16A..214
s 17(a) 207
s 17(b) 207
National Health Service and Community Care Act 1990......................202, 231
National Insurance Act 1946 283
Nationality, Immigration and Asylum Act 2002................................113, 327
s 55 ....248, 254–7, 259, 261, 265, 275, 328, 331
s 55(1) 254, 256, 258–60, 262, 305, 328
s 55(5) 254, 257, 259–60, 267, 275
s 55(5)(a)..257, 266, 267
s 55(5)(b)...327
s 55(10) 256, 327, 330, 331
Race Relations Act 1976...296
Race Relations (Amendment) Act 2000...145
Rent Act 1977 125
Sch 1 para 2 125
Sch 1 para 3 125
Sex Discrimination Act 1975 296
Social Security Act 1986 255
Taxes Management Act 1970
s 1 139
Youth and Criminal Evidence Act 1999
s 3 121

s 41..121–2
s 41(3)(c)..121–2

Statutory Instruments
Allocation of Housing and Homelessness Review Procedures Regulations
    1999, SI 1999/71
    r 2...316
Civil Procedure Rules 1998, SI 1998/3132
    r 24(2) 185
    Pt 54..110
Employment Equality (Age) Regulations 2006, SI 2006/1031......................287
Human Rights Act 1998 (Designated Derogation) Order 2001,
    SI 2001/3644...193
Immigration (Restrictions on Employment) Order 1996, SI 1996/3225
    Sch Pt 1 para 3...268
Income Support (General) Regulations 1987, SI 1987/1967
    r 17(1) 297
    Sch 2 ....282, 297
Jobseeker's Allowance Regulations 1996, SI 1996/207
    r 79 291
Local Authorities (Contracting Out of Allocation of Housing and
Homelessness Functions) Order 1996, SI 1996/3205....................................317
Manual Handling Operations Regulations 1992, SI 1992/2793....................134
National health Service (Functions of Strategic Health Authorities and
Primary Care Trust and Administration Arrangements) (England)
    Regulations 2002, SI 2002/2375
    r 3(2)
Sex Discrimination (North Ireland Order) 1976, SI 1976/1042 295
Social Security Benefits Uprating Regulations 2001, SI 2001/910 282
    r 17(1) 282
Social Security (Persons from Abroad) Miscellaneous Amendments
    Regulations 1996, SI 1996/30 255
Supreme Court Fees Amendment Order 1996, SI 1996/3191
    art 3 161

United States of America

Bill of Rights...31
Constitution 17–8, 29, 31–3, 37, 63
Fifth Amendment...33
Fourteenth Amendment..33, 37, 79, 116, 279, 285
Declaration of Independence 1776...12

Introduction

D
URING THE PAST three decades individuals and groups have
increasingly tested the extent to which governments and public authorities can be held to account through the judicial system for delay or failure to provide access to welfare services such as health treatment, education and
housing.[1] However, in the absence of maladministration or flagrant breaches of
public law duties,[2] there is deep-rooted scepticism about the potential for courts
to make effective and constitutionally appropriate contributions to the resolution of such disputes.[3]

These doubts are not only based on widespread perceptions that courts are
constitutionally and institutionally ill-suited to adjudicating in politically sensitive disputes involving issues of resource allocation, but also closely related to a
prevailing understanding in Western style democracies that, by contrast with civil
and political rights, socio-economic rights—whether enshrined in international,
regional or domestic instruments—are ideological aspirations or programmatic
goals, dependent on resources for their satisfaction, and therefore inherently
unsuited to the mechanisms and techniques developed by courts for the protection of fundamental human rights.[4] Thus, whether controversy centres on fine
distinctions between the nature of civil and political rights on the one hand and
socio-economic rights on the other hand, or on the efficacy of legal measures for
their implementation and enforcement, the inextricable link between socio-
economic rights and the allocation of scarce resources remains problematic.[5]

This book is about the role of courts in disputes over access to health and welfare services, and in some cases to social security benefits, of the kind enshrined in

---

[1] For a survey of this growing phenomenon, drawing on experiences across the North–South
divide, including Canada, India, the Philippines, South Africa, Columbia and Argentina, see
F Coomans (ed), *Justiciability of Socio-economic Rights: Experiences from Domestic Systems*
(Antwerp, Intersentia, 2006). See in particular the chapter by E Palmer, 'The Role of Courts in the
Domestic Protection of Socio-economic Rights: The Unwritten Constitution of the UK'. See also
chapter 2 below for the respective roles played by the European Court of Human Rights and the
European Court of Justice in the resolution of socio-economic disputes.

[2] See C Fabre, 'Constitutionalising Social Rights' (1998) 6 *J Pol Phil* 263, 280–3; and C Sunstein,
Legal Reasoning and Political Conflict (Oxford, OUP, 1996) 179, for the argument that the case for
an assertive judicial role in 'managerial issues' can best be made out where institutions and processes
of government are defective.

[3] See generally A Eide, 'Economic Social and Cultural Rights as Human Rights' in A Eide,
C Krause and A Rosas (eds), *Economic Social and Cultural Rights*, 2nd edn (London, Kluwer, 2001)
9–28. See also D Beatty, 'The Last Generation: When Rights Lose their Meaning' in D Beatty (ed),
Human Rights and Judicial Review: A Comparative Perspective (London, Kluwer, 1994) 321–61.

[4] See Eide (*ibid*) 22ff.

[5] See generally P Alston, 'Economic and Social Rights' in H Steiner and P Alston, *International
Human Rights in Context*, 2nd edn (Oxford, OUP, 2000) 237–49.

Articles 9 and 11–14 of the International Covenant on Economic Social and Cultural Rights (ICESCR) 1966 and Article 27 of the Convention on the Rights of the Child (CRC) 1989.[6] It involves an exploration of constitutional arrangements and jurisprudential techniques by which courts can make an effective contribution to the resolution of such disputes, without transgressing the boundaries of their legitimate intervention. The book does not seek to underplay the well-known constitutional and institutional limits to the adjudication of politically sensitive resource allocation disputes by domestic courts. Nor does it seek to diminish the importance of a wide range of alternative mechanisms for the protection of socio-economic rights, which continue to be explored at international,[7] regional[8] and domestic levels.[9] However, as in many other jurisdictions across the North–South divide, courts in the United Kingdom already have a role to play in the scrutiny of decisions concerning access to social provision through the ordinary principles and procedures of public administrative law. Moreover, since the enactment of the Human Rights Act (HRA) 1998, for the first time, courts in the UK have had power to scrutinise legislation and public authority decisions—including those concerning the provision of welfare—for conformity with standards embodied in the European Convention on Human Rights (ECHR) 1950.

Thus, predicated on a firm belief in the moral and existential overlap and indivisibility of civil and political rights and socio-economic rights, this book is not only concerned to address international questions about the amenability of socio-economic rights to adjudication and enforcement but, more specifically, to examine the contribution by courts in the United Kingdom to the resolution of health and welfare needs disputes, prior to and following the HRA, which has now been in force for more than six years. Therefore, against a background of

---

[6] A group of rights, not confined to persons who are economically active, has generally been viewed as the 'social rights' referred to in the title to the ICESCR. These include the rights to an adequate standard of living (Art 11), to health (Art 12) and to education (Arts 13 and 14). Cf Art 27 CRC, which outlines the right of every child to a 'standard of living adequate for the child's physical mental physical and moral and social development'. Rights included in Arts 6–13 ICESCR have also been referred to collectively as second generation rights, by way of contrast with so-called first generation rights in the ICCPR, and with the cluster of cultural rights also known as group rights or third generation rights in Art 15 ICESCR.

[7] For an overview of the system of international human rights supervision, focusing in particular on the work of the Committee on Economic Social and Cultural Rights (CESCR), see M Craven, *The International Covenant on Economic Social and Cultural Rights: A Perspective on its Development* (Oxford, Clarendon, 1998) 6–22. The Commission on Human Rights, the largest inter-governmental human rights forum, which traditionally focused on civil and political rights by evaluating crises and appointing working groups or special rapporteurs to investigate human rights issues, has recently paid attention to socio-economic rights. Special rapporteurs have been appointed on the rights to education (1998), food (2000), adequate housing (2000) and health (2002); and specific areas of interest have been developed, including extreme poverty (1998), the right to development (1998) and structural adjustment policies and foreign debt (2000).

[8] Judicial mechanisms for the protection of socio-economic rights in the European region will be discussed in chapter 2 below.

[9] In the UK, alternative mechanisms include tribunals, ombudsmen and public watchdog bodies (the Commission for Racial Equality, the Disability Rights Commission, the Equal Opportunities Commission and four newly established Children's Commissioners. See for example, S Weir (ed), *Unequal Britain: Human Rights as a Route to Social Justice* (London, Politico, 2006) ch 4.

global privatisation of erstwhile public services and a retreat from twentieth-century welfarist ideology, it considers the extent to which public law courts can provide a democratically defensible point of reflex against legislators and administrators who, within the ostensible limits of their available resources, ignore international, regional or domestic commitments to meet basic socio-economic rights of citizens in their jurisdictions.[10]

During the past two decades in the United Kingdom, with varying success, attempts have been made to gain access to statutory health and welfare services for vulnerable and disadvantaged individuals and groups (children, the disabled and the elderly) through ordinary principles, procedures and remedies of English public law.[11] Furthermore, following the enactment of the HRA, strategic human rights lawyers were poised to test the extent to which the HRA could be used for the protection of socio-economic rights to health, social care and housing—particularly through Articles 3, 8 and 6 ECHR and Article 14 primarily taken together with Article 1 of the First Protocol. Thus, one of the central purposes of the book has been to evaluate the extent to which established boundaries of judicial intervention in disputes over access to public services have been altered by the extension of judicial powers, particularly through Sections 3 and 6 HRA; and, by calling into play core values of dignity, freedom and equality, which lie at the heart of the Universal Declaration of Human Rights (UDHR) 1948, to consider how far domestic courts have been prepared to interpret the Convention rights in accordance with positive state duties to meet the elementary human needs of vulnerable individuals.

Although much of the substantive focus of the book is on developments in English public law and on the interpretation by domestic courts of the ECHR rights, there are nevertheless international human rights and comparative constitutional issues to be addressed. Thus, questions of justiciability in English law have been explored against a background of, on one hand, growing acceptance in Europe and beyond of the need for balance in the protection of civil and political and socio-economic rights in modern constitutional arrangements;[12] and, on the other hand, continuing controversy as to whether courts can be assisted in their task of differential rights adjudication by including socio-economic rights in a country's constitution, whether as aspirations or as legally enforceable rights

[10] Compare the controversial intervention of the Supreme Court of Canada in *Chaouilli v Quebec* [2005] 1 SCR 791, where the Court used socio-metric indicators from foreign health care systems rather than international human rights principles to justify its finding that a provincial ban on private health care insurance unjustifiably violated the right to security of the person.

[11] See generally E Palmer, 'Resource Allocation, Welfare Rights: Mapping the Boundaries of Judicial Restraint in Public Administrative Law' (2000) 20 *OJLS* 63.

[12] This has been a core premise of the EU Charter of Fundamental Rights 2000. See M Craven, 'A View from Elsewhere: Social Rights, International Covenant and the EU Charter of Fundamental Rights' in C Costello (ed), *Fundamental Social Rights: Current European Legal Protection and the Challenge of the EU Charter on Fundamental Rights and Freedoms* (Dublin, Irish Centre for European Law, 2001). For the seeds of such a constitutional debate in the UK, see KD Ewing, 'Constitutional Reform and Human Rights: Unfinished Business' (2001) *Edinburgh LR* 297; KD Ewing, 'The Unbalanced Constitution' in T Campbell, KD Ewing and A Tomkins (eds), *Sceptical Essays on Human Rights* (Oxford, OUP, 2001).

to the meeting of elementary human needs such as food, basic health treatment, housing or the wherewithal to acquire them.[13]

Notwithstanding, detailed comparative analysis of the extent to which socio-economic rights can be enhanced either by general statements of principle or precise formulations of specific socio-economic rights in domestic constitutions—an issue that has been vigorously debated elsewhere in relation to the drafting of new constitutions and the restructuring of old ones since the end of the Cold War—is beyond the scope of this book.[14] Since the primary focus here is on the United Kingdom, our concern is the extent to which, in the absence of express constitutional protection of socio-economic rights, a set of liberal, so-called negative rights, of the kind enshrined in the ECHR, said to be securely grounded in the Enlightenment's values of possessive individualism,[15] can be used to impose positive obligations on governments to meet the socio-economic needs of individuals in their jurisdictions.

In chapter 1 therefore, without overlooking the fundamental importance of their constitutional distinctiveness, we have touched on decisions by constitutional courts in jurisdictions other than the United Kingdom, including the United States, Canada and India, where protection has been afforded to socio-economic rights through the interpretation of the traditional canon of civil and political rights.[16] However, since our primary concern has been to highlight the potential to protect socio-economic rights even in the absence of their express constitutional protection, comparative discussion of different historical or cul-

---

[13] See generally, D Beatty, 'The Last Generation: When Rights Lose their Meaning' in DM Beatty (ed), *Human Rights and Judicial Review: A Comparative Perspective* (Dordrecht, Martinus Nijhoff, 1994) 321–61. One of the main protagonists in this debate has been the American academic Cass Sunstein. See C Sunstein, 'Against Positive Rights: Why Social and Economic Rights Don't Belong in the New Constitutions of Post-communist Europe' (1993) 2(1) *East European Constitutional Review* 35–38, where the author argued vehemently at the time of the break-up of the Soviet Union that the inclusion of such rights in former Soviet Bloc constitutions would be wholly inappropriate for the economic and political climate. But compare C Sunstein, 'Social and Economic Rights? Lessons from South Africa' (2001) 11 *Constitutional Forum* 123; and C Sunstein, *Designing Democracy* (Oxford, OUP, 2001) ch 10, where the author suggests that even the poorest countries cannot overlook socio-economic rights completely. See also DM Davis, 'The Case against Inclusion of Socio-economic Rights in a Bill of Rights except as Directive Principles' (1992) 8(4) *South African Journal on Human Rights* 475–90. But compare D Davis, 'Adjudicating the Socio-economic Rights in the South African Constitution: Towards "Deference Lite"?' (2006) 2(2) *South African Journal on Human Rights* 282–300. Also compare F Michelman, 'The Constitution, Social Rights and Liberal Political Justification' (2003) 1(1) *Int'l J of Constitutional Law* 13–14.

[14] Since the fall of the Soviet Union, rights to basic levels of health, education, welfare and a clean environment find their place with increasing frequency alongside the traditional first generation of rights. See, for example, new constitutions in Hungary, the Czech and Slovak republics and Portugal, as well as in Namibia and South Africa.

[15] The phrase 'possessory individualism' is generally attributed to the political theorist CB McPherson, whose influential book, *The Critical Theory of Possessive Individualism* (Oxford, Clarendon, 1962) assigned primacy to liberty as non-interference and questioned the potential for liberal theories of justice to protect a wider range of basic human interests than those traditionally afforded the status of legal protection in Western democracies.

[16] See DM Davis, 'Constitutional Borrowing: The Influence of Legal Culture and Local History in the Reconstitution of Comparative Influence: The South African Experience' (2003) 1(2) *Int'l J of Constitutional Law* 181–95.

tural factors, or aspects of constitutional drafting that may have contributed to these rulings[17]—or indeed the consistency of judicial decisions or lack thereof—are beyond the scope of the present enquiry.[18]

By contrast, more detailed attention has been paid to the 'transformative' South African Constitution of 1996.[19] There is growing academic support for the idea that questions of constitutional legitimacy should be based on evaluation of how courts have approached the resolution of disputes in practice, rather than on more abstract theorising about the nature and limits of constitutional review.[20] Thus, we have focused on developments in South Africa not only because it provides an example of a constitution in which protection had been afforded to legally enforceable civil political and socio-economic rights but also because, in light of its shared common law traditions, the UK House of Lords has paid considerable attention to the reasoning of the South African Constitutional Court when addressing some of the most challenging constitutional issues to have arisen since the HRA came into force. Therefore, our purpose has been not only to highlight efforts in the drafting of the South African Constitution to address constitutional difficulties associated with the adjudication of such resource intensive rights, but also to draw attention to the reasoning in a small number of practically feasible and morally persuasive decisions concerning access to health and welfare benefits, where in reaching its conclusions on the reasonableness of government decisions, the Constitutional Court appears to have remained strategically outside the political arena of budgetary allocation.[21]

[17] For a defence of comparative constitutionalism in the socio-economic rights context, despite the negative impact of *Lochner,* see S Choudhry, 'The *Lochner* Era and Comparative Constitutionalism' (2004) 2(1) *Int'l J of Constitutional Law* 1–55.

[18] For discussion of the chequered history of socio-economic labour rights before the US Supreme Court in the so-called *Lochner* era (which established contractual freedom as the cornerstone of the Constitution) as evidence of the subjectivity of constitutional judicial review, see generally LH Tribe, *American Constitutional Law,* 2nd edn (New York, Foundation Press, 1988). Compare the progressive decision of the US Supreme Court in relation to socio-economic rights in *Brown v Board of Education* (1954) 347 US 483. For a criticism of the impact of decisions by authoritarian US Supreme Court judges on the ability of the federal institutions to deliver on their promises of rights, see M Tushnet, 'Scepticism about Judicial Review: A Perspective from the United States' in Campbell, et al (eds) (note 12 above).

[19] The idea of transformative consitutionalism in the South African context has been attributed to K Klare, 'Legal Culture and Transformative Constitutionalism' (1998) 14 *South African Journal on Human Rights* 146, 151–6. Elsewhere there has been extensive discussion of the use of Directive Principles enshrined in the Indian Constitution and in the EU Charter of Fundamental Rights to impose positive welfare obligations on states. For example, see S Muralidhar, 'Judicial Enforcement of Economic and Social Rights: The Indian Scenario' in Coomans (ed) (note 1 above) at 237. For the suggestion that embryonic principles for the development of positive obligations have begun to be articulated by UK courts, see S Fredman, 'Human Rights Transformed: Positive Duties and Positive Rights' (2006) *Public Law* 498.

[20] See D Beatty, *The Ultimate Rule of Law* (Oxford, OUP, 2004) 34, for the argument that rather than focusing on competing abstract political theories about the nature and constitutional limits of judicial review, judicial reasoning should inform our understanding of what 'the entrenchment of constitutional and international human rights actually does for people'. See also M Ignatieff, *Human Rights as Politics and Idolatry* (Princeton, Princeton University Press, 2001).

[21] For discussion of the reasoning of the South African Court, see the second section of chapter 1 below.

In light of these brief preliminary remarks, the scheme of the book is as follows. The first two chapters provide a theoretical and contextual framework for our subsequent review of the justiciability of disputes over socio-economic entitlements in English public law. Chapter 1 provides an overview of the artificial division between civil and political rights on the one hand and socio-economic rights on the other, and examines the place of socio-economic rights in the international human rights regime, against a background of political, philosophical and juristic debate about the status of socio-economic rights as fundamental human rights, and their amenability to adjudication by courts. Chapter 2 is concerned with the protection of socio-economic rights in the European region. It highlights the respective roles of the Council of Europe and EU institutions, including the ECtHR and the European Court of Justice (ECJ) in the protection of socio-economic rights; and, in light of contemporary constitutional debate, it considers the significance of attempts to marry economic, social and civil and political rights in the Charter of Fundamental Rights 2000.

Thereafter, the focus of the book is on the law of the United Kingdom and the role of courts in the protection of socio-economic rights in English public law. Chapter 3 presents an account of the operation and structure of the HRA. Chapter 4 provides the constitutional and jurisprudential foundations for our subsequent examination of politically sensitive public law challenges in which questions of socio-economic policy or resource allocation are at issue. Chapter 5 provides an extensive case study of key administrative law disputes over the rationing of health and welfare services before and after the HRA. Thus, it includes an examination of recent Court of Appeal decisions in *Rodgers*[22] and in *Watts*,[23] which have signalled respectively: (a) that refusal by National Health Service (NHS) providers to afford access to potentially life-saving medical treatment must be based on rationally formulated policies that are consistently applied in light of the clinical needs of individual claimants; (b) that in considering applications to receive health treatment abroad in accordance with legally enforceable rights in EU law, NHS Trust decisions must be attuned to the clinical needs and circumstances of individual claimants at the time of decisions, rather than on blanket justifications for delay or refusal, such as the impact on existing waiting lists or on the countervailing rights of others in the queue.

Chapters 6 and 7 concern the use of specific ECHR rights (in Articles 3, 8 and 14) to impose positive obligations on central government and local authorities in the socio-economic sphere. These chapters therefore provide a critique of leading cases in which UK courts have struggled to accommodate developments in Strasbourg jurisprudence, primarily in light of three factors: (a) traditional perceptions about the limited potential of a negative instrument directed at reconciliation in post-war Europe to impose positive obligations in the social sphere; (b) the extent to which resources are to be taken into account in

[22]   R *(on the application of Roger) v Swindon PCT* [2006] EWCA Civ 392.
[23]   R *(on the application of Watts) v Bedford Primary Care Trust* [2004] EWCA Civ 166.

determining the limits of judicial intervention in domestic courts; and (c) the extent to which, in the absence of clear direction in Strasbourg jurisprudence, core values such as equality or respect for the dignity of human persons, which lie at the very heart of the ECHR rights, can be used to define the limits of state obligations to provide a minimum level of basic socio-economic entitlements for vulnerable individuals in need. Finally, in chapter 8, in light of Strasbourg developments in the interpretation of due process rights in Article 6 ECHR, the spotlight is turned on the quality of administrative justice itself.

Before proceeding, a number of preliminary points should be made. First, as indicated above, the primary focus is on socio-economic rights to health and welfare benefits in kind, rather than on purely economic benefits. However, some of the cases have been concerned with fairness in the distribution of social security benefits or pension entitlements. Thus, for example, challenges in chapter 7 that are founded on Article 14 take together with Article 1 of the First Protocol have included claims to equal provision of up-rated pension benefits for retired persons living abroad, equal distribution of job seekers allowance and pension entitlements from the Ministry of Defence. Challenges founded on Article 6 have concerned attempts to bypass the established system for receipt of child support from absent parents. Moreover, it is notable that these are socio-economic disputes in which the vulnerability or financial circumstances of claimants have not always been in point.[24]

Secondly, it is important to emphasise that cultural rights, often described as third generation rights in relation to the ICESCR trio, have not been directly addressed in this book.[25] Moreover, labour rights, although prominent in the ICESCR and in the European Social Charter (ESC) 1961 and traditionally the focus of the socio-economic rights movement in the UK, are beyond the scope of our substantive examination of UK cases.[26] It is also noteworthy that although we have used the nomenclature of socio-economic rights in the title and throughout the book, discretionary entitlements to health and welfare benefits of the kind with which we are primarily concerned are traditionally referred to as social rights, as was arguably intended by the drafters of the ICESCR 1966.[27]

---

[24] Article 9 ICESCR provides that 'State Parties to the present Covenant recognise the right of everyone to social security including social assistance'. For the scope of the right, see M Scheinin, 'The Right to Social Security' in Eide, Krause and Rosas (eds) (note 3 above) 211–21.

[25] The concept of the generations of rights—the first being civil and political rights, the second comprising economic, social and cultural and the third consisting of collective rights such as minority rights or indigenous peoples rights—has been widely used. It has, however, been criticised as concealing different patterns of national evolution and the overlap between the different generations. See generally P Alston, 'Peoples' Rights: The State of the Art at the Beginning of the 21st Century' in P Alston (ed), *Peoples' Rights: Collected Courses of the Academy of European Law* (Oxford, OUP, 2001); and A Eide and A Rosas, 'Economic Social and Cultural Rights: A Universal Challenge' in Eide, Krause and Rosas (eds) (note 3 above).

[26] See generally, eg, S Fredman, 'Scepticism under Scrutiny: Labour Law and Human Rights' and KD Ewing, 'The Unbalanced Constitution' both in Campbell, et al (eds) (note 12 above).

[27] See P Hunt, *Reclaiming Social Rights: International and Comparative Perspectives* (Aldershot, Dartmouth, 1996). The author rejects the fruitless search for a definition of social rights but includes 'an adequate standard of living food shelter health and education' as examples. But compare Fabre's

Nevertheless, despite the distinction that has generally been drawn between rights with an economic component, such as labour rights or social security benefits,[28] and what have traditionally been conceived of as social rights, we have preferred the use of the composite phrase. This is not only because of its familiar deployment in human rights discourse by way of contrast with the traditional canon of civil and political rights, but also because its use reflects the inextricable link between the economic and social policy spheres intended by the drafters of the ICESCR. Moreover, this is an approach that can be contrasted with efforts in the post-welfare era to dissociate them,[29] often with the purpose of asserting the ascendancy of unregulated market freedom over state obligations to protect public welfare.[30]

It is well known that much of the ambiguous drafting of the ICESCR seeks to achieve a compromise between various states over important economic and political differences. It is also true, as Daintith has suggested, that the drafters of the ICESCR were at the time more preoccupied with ideological questions as to whether first generation civil and political rights should be accorded equal status with second generation socio-economic rights, or whether the latter were indeed justiciable.[31] However, the rationale for the fusion of social and economic rights in the ICESCR remains clear. There was an overriding commitment to the philosophy of the international labour movement—that education, shelter and health treatment are necessary precursors to the facilitation of economic independence through work, and that social and economic protection is necessary whether or not individuals are economically active.

It cannot be denied, however, that such a fluid approach to the classification of rights in international treaties and in European regional treaties has exacerbated the practical problems of domestic constitutional drafting in the post-welfare era. It has also afforded opportunity for distortion of the aims of the ICESCR by neo-Conservative political theorists who are bent on according

---

elaborate definition of socio-economic rights as 'needs standardly' rights to '(i) a minimum income calculated by taking into account the cost of what is minimally required for us to live in our society; (ii) a right that the state does not deprive us of that minimum income once it has been in place; and (iii) a right that the state pass laws laying down a minimum wage if it has decided to entrust employers with securing us with a minimum income': C Fabre, *Social Rights under the Constitution: Government and the Decent Life* (Oxford, OUP, 2000) 107–8. The positive and negative elements of 'a right to housing' have similarly been spelt out by Fabre.

[28]   A group of rights, the majority relating to employment, which precede those relating to health and welfare, have generally been regarded as the economic rights. These include the right freely to give and be remunerated for the fruits of one's labour (Arts 6–8) and the right to social security (Art 9). It is notable that no mention has been made of the right to property in this cluster of rights, although it does however make its appearance elsewhere in the International Bill of Rights, for example in the ECHR and in the UDHR.

[29]   See T Daintith, 'The Constitutional Protection of Economic Rights' (2004) 2(1) *Int'l J of Constitutional Law* 56–9.

[30]   See S Fredman, 'Social Economic and Cultural Rights' in D Feldman (ed), *English Public Law* (Oxford, OUP, 2004) 534–6. For further discussion of this tension see chapter 2 below.

[31]   Daintith (note 29 above) 57.

priority to market freedom over welfare protection.[32] Thus, for example, it has been claimed by Ernst-Ulrich Petersmann, who has classified labour rights as social rights, that strictly speaking economic rights consist of 'rights to use, possess, exchange and otherwise dispose of property'.[33] On the basis of this subjective classification, Petersmann argues that by focusing on social rights and in failing to protect what he describes as the 'welfare-increasing effects of economic and political competition', the ICESCR organs have undermined the indivisibility of social and economic rights.

Finally and perhaps most importantly, it should be emphasised that depending on context, the term socio-economic rights has different usages. Thus, in human rights discourse it is a normative construct that conveys the idea that within a framework of fundamental human rights values, the repositories of collective power have corresponding moral obligations to protect the social and economic welfare of individuals in their jurisdictions. Secondly, it connotes a set of legal rights, for example rights enshrined in treaties such as the ICESCR and CRC and in the ESC and the South African Constitution, which impose corresponding legal obligations on states for their realisation. Thirdly, the term socio-economic rights may be used to connote legally enforceable individual entitlements, for example in EU law, or occasionally in some Nordic jurisdictions, legislative subjective individual rights to public welfare provision.[34] Finally, it is also notable that mandatory legislative socio-economic entitlements of the aforementioned kind should be distinguished from discretionary entitlements to welfare provision in the UK, which are more usually referred to as welfare 'benefits' in order to connote their essentially discretionary nature.[35]

---

[32] E Petersmann, 'Time for a United Nations Global Compact' (2002) 13 *European J of International Law* 621. Compare P Alston, 'Resisting the Merger and Acquisition of Human Rights by Trade Law' (2002) 13 *European J of International Law* 815; and R Howse, 'Human Rights in the WTO' (2002) 13 *J of International Law* 651.

[33] E Petersman, 'Taking Human Dignity, Poverty and Empowerment of Individuals More Seriously' (2002) 13 *European J of International Law* 845, 851.

[34] See M Schienin, 'Economic and Social Rights as Legal Rights' in Eide, Krause and Rosas (eds) (note 3 above) 51. The author notes a general trend in Nordic countries towards securing various benefits, as 'individual subjective social rights'. In Finland the right to municipal child care for small children and the right to housing and services for the severely handicapped have been defined as subjective individual rights in Acts of Parliament. Compare Section 2(1) of the Chronically Sick and Disabled Persons Act 1970, which at the height of the welfare era in the United Kingdom purported to afford legally enforceable subjective welfare rights to chronically sick and disabled persons. See chapter 5 below.

[35] Apart from the ICESCR, the United Kingdom has ratified five other major UN treaties that reinforce protections of socio-economic rights for particular groups—namely, the Convention Relating to the Status of Refugees 1951; the International Convention on the Elimination of All Forms of Racial Discrimination (CERD) 1965; the Convention on the Elimination of All Forms of Discrimination against Women (CEDAW) 1979; and the Convention on the Rights of the Child (CRC) 1989. Britain also subscribes to the wide-ranging protections of labour rights enshrined in the treaties of the International Labour Organisation. At a regional level, the Council of Europe's European Social Charter and the revised European Union's Social Chapter (part of the Maastricht Treaty 1991), which parallel those at the international level, have been ratified. See further Weir (ed) (note 9 above) 41–50.

1

The Role of Courts in the Protection of Socio-economic Rights: International and Domestic Perspectives

All Human Rights are universal, interdependent and interrelated. The international community must treat human rights globally in a fair and equal manner, on the same footing and with the same emphasis.

UN Vienna Declaration and Programme of Action, 25 June 1993

The shocking reality [is] . . . that states and the international community as a whole, continue to tolerate all too often breaches of economic social and cultural rights, which if they occurred in relation to civil and political rights, would provoke expressions of horror and outrage and lead to immediate calls for action.

UN Vienna World Conference 1993[1]

I. THE INDIVISIBILITY OF HUMAN RIGHTS

A. Understanding Socio-economic Rights as Human Rights

THE CONCEPT OF human rights straddles the boundaries of moral, political and legal discourses. It is the central element in a normative system that recognises that every human person has an equal right to claim conditions of human existence, such as liberty and personal autonomy or integrity of the person, without which it is impossible to maintain the fundamental dignity of human kind.[2] This position was summarised in the Preamble to the Universal Declaration of Human Rights (UDHR),[3] which was adopted by the UN General Assembly in 1948:

---

[1] Statement by UN Committee on Economic Social and Cultural Rights (CESCR) UN Doc E/1993/22, Annex III, para 5.

[2] See generally, C Palley, *The United Kingdom and Human Rights* (London, Sweet & Maxwell, 1991) for a historical account of the evolution of human rights and the place of economic, social and cultural rights in the normative regime for the protection of human rights.

[3] The International Bill of Rights, which lies at the core of the international human rights regime, comprises the UDHR, ICESCR and the ICCPR. The UDHR seeks to give broad expression to civil, political, social, economic and cultural rights on an equal footing by recognising a core range of

[T]he peoples of the United Nations have in the Charter reaffirmed their faith in fundamental human rights, in the dignity and worth of the human person, and in the equal rights of men and women, and have determined to promote social progress and better standards of life in larger freedom.

Although traces of human rights thinking can be found in much earlier religious and political systems,[4] the international regime in operation at the beginning of the twenty-first century has its origins in Eurocentric traditions of religious, moral, philosophical and political thought.[5] It is also recognised that although the evolution of human rights in Western democracies has been complex, diffuse and shaped by their unique political and religious pasts, the origins of the contemporary system are to be found in British, French and American thinking of the seventeenth century.[6] It is therefore accepted that, within the Eurocentric tradition, a set of specific concerns about the overweening power of kings and princes, followed by more abstract concerns about any form of oppressive state power, was gradually absorbed into a moral and political philosophy that is based on ideas of respect for human dignity, equality and autonomy in relation to the conduct of states towards individuals in their jurisdiction.[7]

Thus, historically, human rights claims first covered such 'natural rights' as rights to life, liberty, property and religion. Later, however, they came not only to cover traditional civil liberties and rights to public participation, but in the early part of the twentieth century, influenced by the growing international labour movement,[8] also to include 'social, economic and cultural rights,[9]

economic, social and cultural rights within one consolidated text. It is today accepted as declaratory of international customary law of human rights. Art 25(1) UDHR states: 'Everyone has the right to a standard of living adequate for the health and well-being of himself and of his family, including food, clothing, housing and medical care and necessary social services, and the right to security in the event of unemployment, sickness, disability, widowhood, old age or other lack of livelihood in circumstances beyond his control'. Art 26 recognises the right to education; Art 23 establishes rights to and in work.

[4] For a general history, see A Eide, 'Economic Social and Cultural Rights as Human Rights' in A Eide, C Krause and A Rosas (eds), *Economic Social and Cultural Rights*, 2nd edn (London, Kluwer, 2001) 12ff.

[5] See Palley (note 2 above) 1–49.

[6] As proclaimed in the American Declaration of Independence 1776 and the French Declaration of the Rights of Man and the Citizen 1789.

[7] See Palley (note 2 above) 3–50. The idea of respect for persons as a basis for public morality is prominent in Christian thought. For development in moral philosophical thought of 'respect for persons' as a fundamental principle of social morality, which is antecedent to the three principles of utility, equality and liberty, see TS Downie and E Telfer (eds), *Respect for Persons* (London, George Allan and Unwin, 1969). See also more recently, J Waldron, *God, Locke and Equality: Christian Foundations of Locke's Political Thought* (Cambridge, Cambridge University Press, 2002) for an exploration of the theme of equality and the proposition that human beings are all one another's equals.

[8] The International Labour Organisation (ILO) was founded following the signing of the Treaty of Versailles 1919 'to establish fair and humane conditions of labour'. For a history of the role of the ILO in the origins of socio-economic rights in an international context, see 'Economic and Social Rights' in H Steiner and P Alston (eds), *International Human Rights in Context*, 2nd edn (Oxford, OUP, 2000) 242–6.

[9] Much earlier traces of socio-economic rights can also be found in the Eurocentric tradition of political thought from the middle of the eighteenth century onwards. See Palley (note 2 above)

which reflect the duty of states to provide for material conditions of human existence, such as education, welfare benefits and a minimally decent standard of living. Therefore, on the common understanding that social provision is no less essential to human dignity and integrity of the person than rights to physical security or to public participation in elections, the Preamble to the UDHR looks forward to

> the advent of a world in which human beings shall enjoy freedom of speech and belief *and* freedom from fear and want . . . [as] . . . the highest aspiration of the common people.[10]

The point that we therefore wish to emphasise is that during the twentieth century, it gradually became a respected tenet of socio-political,[11] political[12] and moral philosophical[13] thought, that individual interests in such basic social and economic necessities as food, shelter and the wherewithal to pay for them, carry sufficient moral force to justify the imposition of corresponding obligations on states for their protection, and that they should be accorded the status of human rights.[14]

62–75, where the author notes in particular that in the second part of the *Rights of Man*, Thomas Paine, the most influential advocate of human rights around the world, 'argued for benefits similar to those found in the modern welfare state'. See T Paine, *The Rights of Man* (1791–92) Part II, Chapter 5 in M Foot and I Kramnick (eds), *The Thomas Paine Reader* (London, Penguin, 1987). Compare the notion of charity in Locke's chapter 'Of Property' in JW Gough (ed), *The Second Treatise of Civil Government* (Oxford, Blackwell, 1946).

[10] For a brief but illuminating account of the drafting of the UDHR and the personal histories and political and philosophical backgrounds of the men who shaped it, see MA Glendon, 'Reflections on the UDHR' (1998) *First Things* 23–7. See also MA Glendon, 'The Rule of Law in the Universal Declaration of Human Rights' (2004) 2 *Northwestern U Journal of International Human Rights* 5.

[11] See TH Marshall, *Citizenship and Social Class* (London, Routledge, 1959). The chronological paradigm of rights promoted by Marshall was influential from the late 1950s onwards. Optimistically rooted in an evolving concept of citizenship, Marshall believed: civil rights were the principal achievement of the eighteenth century (allowing all members of society to share equality before the law); political rights (allowing for broader participation in sovereign power) were the triumph of the nineteenth century; and social rights, the achievement of the twentieth century, afforded citizens equal opportunities to enjoy economic and social well-being. In some quarters, this historical account has been criticised because it fails to explain the emergence of socio-economic rights at the beginning of the twentieth century in the Weimar Republic and other European democracies. See Eide (2001) (note 4 above) 13 It has also been argued by proponents of socio-economic rights that compartmentalisation of civil, political and socio-economic rights into first and second generation categories affords opportunity to critics on both sides of the ideological divide to claim the superiority of one class of rights over others, thereby obscuring their unitary moral heritage.

[12] In his famous address on the State of the Union in 1941, President Roosevelt asserted: 'True individual freedom cannot exist without economic security and independence. . . . We have accepted, so to speak, a second bill of rights, under which a new basis of security and prosperity can be established for all.'

[13] See generally, MR Ishay, *The Human Rights Reader* (New York, Routledge, 1997) 403–6. See J Raz, *The Morality of Freedom* (Oxford, Clarendon, 1988).

[14] See R Plant, *Community and Ideology: An Essay in Applied Social Philosophy* (London, Routledge and Keegan Paul, 1974); R Plant, *Modern Political Thought: An Introduction* (London, Routledge and Keegan Paul, 1984); R Plant, H Lesser and P Taylor Gooby (eds), *Political Philosophy and Social Welfare: Essays on the Normative Basis of Welfare Provision* (London, RKP, 1980); J Waldron, *Theories of Rights* (Oxford, OUP, 1985); and J Waldron, *Liberal Rights: Collected Papers* 1981–91 (Cambridge, Cambridge University Press, 1993). This last work argues that our moral response to poverty and homelessness should be based on values that underlie traditional liberal philosophy.

Nevertheless, against this background, during the Cold War, when the international normative framework for the protection of human rights was in the process of negotiation by the United Nations, it is well known that ideological tensions between civil and political and socio-economic rights were played out in the context of conflicting political philosophies of the West and the former Soviet Bloc countries. Thus, while socio-economic rights were being crudely characterised, particularly in the US, as derivatives of the philosophies of totalitarian regimes and committed to state dependency and the uniform provision of basic welfare services, civil and political rights were being championed as the bedrock of economic freedoms on which Western-style democracies had traditionally flourished.

In this ideological battleground, much play was made of the positive–negative distinction between the two sets of rights. It was claimed that while the traditional canon of civil and political rights were negative in orientation (seeking to protect individuals against unwarranted state intrusion) and free of resource implications, socio-economic rights were positive rights—involving claims to public goods, which would invariably and inappropriately impose financial obligations on states for their protection.

Accordingly, in 1952, anticipating widespread rejection by powerful Western democracies if the two sets of rights were included in a single instrument, the UN General Assembly passed a resolution to divide the rights and aspirations proclaimed in the UDHR into two separate Covenants—one containing civil and political rights, the other addressing economic, social and cultural rights.[15] Different treaties were therefore drafted for the protection of civil and political rights on the one hand, and social, economic and cultural rights on the other: the International Covenant on Civil and Political Rights (ICCPR) 1966[16] and the International Covenant on Economic Social and Cultural Rights (ICESCR) 1966.[17] Socio-economic rights were thus excluded from the enforcement machinery available for the protection of civil and political rights.[18]

A similar division was followed in the regional framework for the protection of human rights among the countries of the newly established Council of

---

[15] G A Res 543 (VI) 5 Feb1952 (overturning Res 421 (V) 4 Dec 1950).

[16] The ICCPR adopted by G A Res 2200 A (XXI) 16 Dec 1966 entered into legal force on 23 March 1976. From the outset, the UN Human Rights Committee, composed of independent experts, was set up to monitor compliance with the ICCPR and to monitor states' reports on their progress. The UN General Assembly adopted an Optional Protocol to the ICCPR, enabling the Committee to receive complaints alleging violations of rights set forth in the covenant.

[17] ICESCR adopted 2200 A (XXI) entered into legal force on 3 Jan 1976.

[18] The Economic and Social Council was given the task of monitoring progress on the ICESCR. However, the current expert monitoring agency, the Committee on Economic Social and Cultural Rights (CESCR), was appointed only in 1984 and did not meet until 1987. Although there is increasing support internationally for an Optional Protocol that would enable the CESCR, like the Human Rights Committee, to receive and respond to individual complaints, as yet no firm moves have been taken in that direction. See further, M Craven, *The International Covenant on Economic Social and Cultural Rights* (Oxford, OUP, 1995) for a study of the origins and development of the ICESCR, drawing on the work of the Committee.

Europe. Again two separate treaties were drafted—the European Convention on Human Rights (ECHR) 1950 and the European Social Charter (ESC) 1961, with priority accorded to the ECHR and correspondingly different mechanisms established for enforcement and monitoring.[19] In summary therefore, in the major regimes established for the international and regional protection of human rights in the twentieth century, ideological perceptions about differences between the two sets of rights were allowed to undermine the persuasive logic of their unitary moral foundations.[20]

B. Two Faces of Liberty: Conflicting Ideologies of Socio-economic and Civil and Political Rights

It can be seen that the constructs of civil and political rights and socio-economic rights are products of different political philosophies with correspondingly different ideas of the relationship between individual and state, and the role of the individual as citizen in society. Whereas civil and political rights are the creatures of political philosophies that conceive of the state as a potential threat to individual liberty,[21] socio-economic rights are associated with moral and political theories of citizenship in which positive state action is essential to the attainment of liberty.[22]

At the time of President Roosevelt's State of the Union Address in 1941, notions that freedom from want *and* freedom from fear should be among the four freedoms to shape the future world order[23] were in step with the emerging international consensus. Since then, however, for many American political theorists these different types of freedom have come to be regarded as mutually unsustainable.[24] Furthermore, this position has increasingly been taken up since the end of the Cold War by political theorists on the right, who have argued that socio-economic rights are inevitably inimical to economic freedom and conducive of state dependency and economic stagnation.[25]

---

[19] See further chapter 2 below.

[20] The preamble of the ICCPR states: 'The ideal of free human beings enjoying civil and political freedom and freedom from fear and want can only be achieved if conditions are created whereby everyone may enjoy [her] civil and political rights as well as her economic, social and cultural rights.'

[21] See generally F Hayek, *The Constitution of Liberty* (Chicago, University of Chicago Press, 1960); R Nozick, *Anarchy State and Utopia* (New York, Basic Books, 1974); and C Fried, *Right and Wrong* (Cambridge, MA, Harvard University Press, 1994).

[22] See generally Marshall (note 11 above)

[23] President Roosevelt's 'Four Freedoms' were: freedoms of speech, religion, from fear and from want—summarised in the aphorism that 'necessitous men are not free men'.

[24] See D Kelly, *A Life of One's Own: Individual Rights and the Welfare State* (Washington, DC, Cato Institute, 1998). Kelly has argued that notions of democratic freedom, on one hand from want and the other from fear and oppression, although skilfully juxtaposed by President Roosevelt, are in fact mutually exclusive. See also L Lomasky, 'Liberty and Welfare Goods: Reflections on Clashing Liberalisms' (2000) 4(1) *Journal of Ethics* 99–113.

[25] See note 21 above.

However, such views are plainly inconsistent with the conception of social democracy that has prevailed in Europe and in many new democracies since the end of the World War II, governments having accepted international and domestic obligations to safeguard traditional democratic freedoms, while at the same time protecting the well-being of citizens by ensuring varying levels of economic and social provision. Thus, throughout the latter half the twentieth century, social democratic theorists have continued to argue that affirmative state duties to protect citizens, for example against poverty and homelessness, are implicit in the traditional liberal values that are founded on equal respect for the dignity of persons and enshrined in the Declaration of Human Rights.[26]

At the beginning of the twenty-first century, as vast, manmade catastrophes (often perpetrated in the name of democratic freedom) continue to unfold, it is not difficult to see that denying individuals access to health treatment, water, sanitation and other basic necessities of life makes a mockery of the elevation of civil and political freedoms (such as to participate equally in free and fair elections) or economic rights (such as to engage freely in contractual bargaining) above other responsibilities of the state. Thus, in human rights discourse it has continued to be argued that socio-economic rights must be seen as equal in status to civil and political rights (or in some cases superior), on grounds that without access to food, shelter, education and health, rights such as the freedom of speech or the right to trade freely become meaningless.[27]

However, the argument has been used in both directions. Economic philosopher Amartya Sen, no less critical of claims by totalitarian states that political rights are likely to have adverse effects on economic growth,[28] has argued that the articulation of what constitutes a 'need' as opposed to a 'want' is necessarily a product of the political process.[29] Therefore, without seeking to overstate the effectiveness of democratic processes to reverse all our perceptions of human

[26] The work of Jeremy Waldron has been influential in this regard. In particular, see J Waldron, 'Liberal Rights: Two Sides of the Coin' in Waldron (1993) (note 14 above) 31: 'As an abstract matter we can say, with the drafters of Article 25 of the UDHR, that everyone has "the right to a standard of living adequate for the health and well-being of himself and his family". But that may not necessarily emerge as a specific legal or constitutional guarantee: a just society may not have a rule to that effect, or even any particular agency charged with administering this standard. There may be a variety of provisions and arrangements . . . all of which taken together may represent the best . . . that can be done in an institutional framework to honour the underlying claim for the individuals in whose behalf it can be made.'

[27] See generally the works by Plant (note 14 above) for this enduring theme. See recently, R Plant, 'Social Justice, Rights and Social Democracy' in N Pearce and W Paxton (eds), *Social Justice: Building a Fairer Britain* (London, Politico's, 2005).

[28] Arguments of the kind are associated with modern left-wing dictatorships, for example in Singapore or North Korea.

[29] See A Sen, 'Freedom and Needs', *The New Republic*, 10/17 January 1994, 31, 32, cited in Steiner and Alston (note 8 above) 269–71. For a recent empirical investigation of state reconstruction in Africa, see G Hesselbein, F Goloomba-Mutebi and J Putzel (eds), *Economic and Political Foundations of State-making in Africa: Understanding State Reconstruction* (London, LSE Crisis State Research Centre, 2006), where it is argued that in countries where state reconstruction is being attempted, the international community needs to pay more attention to planned internal economic growth rather than focusing most energy on the launching of electoral processes.

deprivation, Sen has continued to argue that democracy is a primary weapon—for example in ensuring that governments respond appropriately to mass catastrophes—and that freedoms of speech or association can also be crucial tools in exposing the failure of governments to take action for less obvious human deprivations than famines or earthquakes. Thus, observing that our conception of human needs are necessarily fashioned by society's evolving interpretation of human deprivations and what can be done about them, Sen has claimed that 'political rights including freedom of expression and discussion are not only pivotal in inducing political responses to economic needs, they are also central to the conceptualisation of economic needs themselves.'[30]

Thus, against a background in which democracy has increasingly become a central pawn in the international war of words, the human rights community has continued to endorse its belief in the central tent of the UDHR, that rights contained in the separate covenants are 'universal, indivisible interdependent and interrelated'—a position that was reaffirmed at the second World Conference on Human Rights in Vienna in 1993.[31] Nevertheless, during the past decade, against a political backdrop of widespread retreat from twentieth-century welfarist ideology and the corrosive influence of neo-Conservative economic liberalism,[32] many governments have ratified both the and the ICCPR and the ICESCR, but few have attempted to adopt legislative or administrative provisions to give legal force to the rights in the ICESCR.[33] Moreover, since the end of World War II, many US administrations have been notable for their ambivalence, while others have been downright hostile to the recognition of socio-economic rights, both in the international arena and at home[34]—often relying on the 200-year-old Constitution to counter suggestions that protection should be afforded to socio-economic rights.[35]

Interpreting the libertarian US Constitution (the very foundations of which rest on the prohibition of state interference with democratically enshrined freedoms) in accordance with a conception of positive state responsibilities for

---

[30] Sen, cited in Steiner and Alston (note 8 above), 271.

[31] See the epigraphs at the beginning of this chapter.

[32] See W Hutton, *The World We're In* (London, Abacus, 2002) for a critique of the influence in Europe of the American Conservative 'neo-liberal' political philosophy, which asserts the ascendancy of free market economics and rampant individualism over ideas of social justice and the good society.

[33] See Steiner and Alston (note 8 above) 238.

[34] Not only have successive US administrations since the time of the Cold War been opposed to ratifying either treaty, as noted by Steiner and Alston (note 8 above), US delegations at UN conferences in Rome and Istanbul also obstructed any proposals for enhancing the protection of socio-economic rights, refusing to endorse proposals for the formulation of a right to adequate food and shelter respectively (250).

[35] See L Henkin, 'International Human Rights and Rights in the United States' in T Meron (ed), *Human Rights in International Law* (New York, Oxford University Press, 1984) 43: 'The United States is not a welfare state by compulsion. . . . Indeed it became a welfare state in the face of powerful constitutional resistance. . . . Jurisprudentially the United States is a welfare state by grace of Congress and of the states' (cited by Steiner and Alston (note 8 above) 251).

public welfare is clearly a difficult task.[36] Thus, much has been made of the famous *De Shaney* case,[37] where the majority in the US Supreme Court refused to accept that there could be any room for a twentieth-century interpretation of the Bill of Rights, in accordance with even the most minimal notions of the benevolent state or an idea of the constitution as a repository of affirmative welfare duties:

> Like its counterpart in the Fifth Amendment the Due Process Clause of the Fourteenth Amendment was intended to prevent government . . . from abusing its power or employing it as an instrument of oppression. . . . Consistent with these principles our cases have recognised that the Due Process Clauses generally confer no affirmative right to governmental aid even where such aid may be necessary to secure life, liberty, or property interests of which the government itself may not deprive the individual.

While priding itself on a legacy of compassionate welfarism—albeit a dwindling one[38]—the US has seemed dominated by the originalist view that welfare protection should continue to develop as a 'matter of grace'[39] rather than by constitutional prompting, let alone by an entrenched constitutional mandate. This is in contrast to other jurisdictions that have defined their constitutional settlements in the last three decades or so. Nevertheless, without seeking to deny the limitations of the 200-year-old liberal constitution, there has also been a body of communitarian scholarship in which the Bill of Rights has been viewed as part of a larger constitutional structure of social rights and responsibilities, which 'includes more than a set of negatively formulated civil and political liberties'.[40] Arguing that the Constitution permits, although it does not *require*, 'a responsive affirmatively active state', Glendon, a leading constitutional comparatist, has criticised the Supreme Court decision in *Deshaney* for placing undue emphasis on the 'no duty to rescue rule' and interpreting the Constitution in a way that 'put statutory welfare rights in tension with our basic constitutional values'.[41]

---

[36] For the problems of an originalist interpretation of the US Constitution, see C Sunstein, *The Partial Constitution* (Cambridge, MA, Harvard University Press, 1995), in particular ch 4. For a useful summary of enduring controversy in the US as to how 'an eighteenth-century design for government could be seen to fit with the modern regulatory state' or whether the Fourteenth Amendment harbours vestiges of the 'protective state', see MA Glendon, 'Rights in Twentieth-century Constitutions' in GR Stone, RA Epstein and CR Sunstein (eds), *The Bill of Rights and the Modern State* (Chicago, University of Chicago Press, 1992) 519–38.

[37] *Deshaney v Winnebago County Department of Social Services* 489 US 189, 109 Ct 998 (1989).

[38] Following World War II, the United States, in contrast with many other constitutional democracies, was conspicuous for the unusual structure of its welfare state in leaving pensions, health insurance and other benefits to be organised privately, mainly through the work place rather than the public sector.

[39] See Henkin (note 35 above) 83, cited in Steiner and Alston (note 8 above) 251.

[40] M Glendon has energetically continued to pursue this theme. See also a more recent contribution: C Sunstein, *The Second Bill of Rights: FDR's Unfinished Revolution and Why We Need It More than Ever* (New York, Basic Books, 2004), which argues that 'economic rights' of the kind proposed by Roosevelt are vital to the security of the nation.

[41] See MA Glendon, *Rights Talk: Impoverishment of Political Discourse* (New York, Free Press, 1998) 96.

Sadly, in that decision, the Supreme Court unnecessarily contributed to a dynamic that was to shape 'the future course of those commitments'.[42]

C. Socio-economic Rights, Resources and the Negative–Positive Dichotomy

It would be misleading to suggest that obstacles to the adjudication of socio-economic rights can be attributed entirely to their ideological foundations.[43] Since it is axiomatic that socio-economic rights are generally dependent on resources, which in poor and developing countries are often unlikely to be available for their realisation, the orthodoxy has prevailed in the international arena, not only that socio-economic rights are positive in orientation, but that they are in fact mere aspirations or programmatic goals that lack the characteristic of enforceability, which is regarded as one of the essential pillars of human rights.[44]

Moreover, this view has arguably been reinforced in the drafting of the international Covenants. Whereas Article 1 of the ICCPR proclaims that 'parties to the ICCPR undertake *to give effect* to the rights recognised in the Charter', Article 2 of the ICESCR stipulates that 'state parties undertake steps . . . to the maximum of their available resources, with a view to achieving progressively the full realisation of the rights in the present Covenant'.[45] Similarly, while Article 1 of the ECHR provides that parties 'shall secure to everyone within their jurisdiction, the rights and freedoms' defined in the Convention, the ESC specifies that 'the Parties accept as the aim of their policy, to be pursued by all appropriate means both national and international in character, the attainment of conditions in which the following rights and principles may be effectively realised.'[46] Moreover, the related idea that the cultural historical and

---

[42] *Ibid.*

[43] In the international arena it has been argued that economic and social rights are by their very nature non-justiciable (incapable of being invoked in courts of law and applied by judges) because of the quintessentially political character of the ICECSR treaty obligations. M Cranston is most frequently associated with the view, given wide currency in the 1970s, that socio-economic rights are not rights at all. See M Cranston, *What are Human Rights* (London, Bodley Head, 1993). See also EG Vierdag, 'The Legal Nature of the Rights Granted by the International Covenant on Economic Social and Cultural Rights' (1978) 9 *Netherlands Yearbook of International Law*. A distinction has also been drawn between obligations of *result* (legally enforceable) and obligations of *conduct*; the majority of ESCR rights are generally relegated to the latter category. See A Eide, 'Future Protection of Economic and Social Rights in Europe' in A Bloed, LL Leicht, M Nowak and A Rosas (eds), *Monitoring Human Rights in Europe: Comparing International Procedures and Mechanisms* (Dordrecht, Martinus Nijhoff, 1993).

[44] See generally Eide (2001) (note 4 above) 9–28.

[45] It has generally been recognised that one of the greatest challenges for the architects of the ICESCR was to accommodate the reality that many participating states would be unlikely to have the necessary resources to implement the rights—either immediately or in the foreseeable future. Thus, it was considered necessary to qualify the rights by reference to the availability of resources and their programmatic realisation.

[46] Part 1 ESC 1961.

geographical relativity of socio-economic rights sets them apart from the universality and inalienability of civil and political rights has become deeply engrained in twentieth-century human rights thinking.[47]

Nevertheless, it has long been recognised that the different resource implications of socio-economic rights and civil and political rights have been overplayed and, furthermore, that the majority of socio-economic rights have some aspect that is justiciable.[48] For example, the enforcement of rights within the traditional canon of civil and political rights, such as the right to a fair trial, may also require substantial government expenditure.[49] A case in point involves the Canadian Charter of Fundamental Rights and Freedoms 1982, many provisions of which echo the rights in the ECHR, including a provision that 'any person charged with an offence has the right . . . to be tried within a reasonable time'.[50] Accordingly, in *R v Ascov*[51] the Supreme Court of Canada held that a delay of thirty-four months from the defendant's first appearance to the dismissal of the case, violated the right in section 11 of the Canadian Charter. As a result, 50,000 criminal charges in Ontario were set aside, and the provincial government had to spend over 28 million dollars on improving court resources and recruiting more personnel to reduce delays in the criminal process.[52]

Indeed, as we shall see further in chapter 2 below, the ECHR, which predominantly protects civil and political rights, contains several provisions expressly demanding expenditure by the state regarding the right to free legal assistance when charged with criminal offences (Article 6(3)(c)); the right to education (Article 2, Protocol 1); and the state duty to hold free and periodic elections (Article 3, Protocol 1). Moreover, even where rights have been cast in terms of negative state duties to refrain from inflicting harm on individuals in their jurisdictions, they have been interpreted by Strasbourg in accordance with positive state duties requiring financial expenditure, for example to ensure that state agents or non-state parties refrain from torturing or taking life (Articles 2 and 3 ECHR).[53] Furthermore, similar examples can be found on the domestic

---

[47] See generally P Alston, 'US Ratification of the Covenant on Economic Social and Cultural Rights: The Need for an Entirely New Strategy' (1990) 84 *American J of International Law* 365–93.

[48] See the 'Limburg Principles' (1986), produced by a group of international experts examining the potential for implementation of the ICESCR rights: UN doc.E/CN.4/1987/17.

[49] See S Sunstein and C Holmes, *The Cost of Rights: Why Liberty Depends on Taxes* (New York, Norton, 1999) 48; and Sunstein (1995) (note 36 above) 69–75.

[50] Section 11(b) of the Canadian Charter.

[51] (1990) 2 SCR 1199.

[52] See also the decisions of: Germany's Constitutional Court, [1967] 22 Bverf GE 83; the Supreme Court of India, *Dwivedi v Union of India* AIR (1983) SC 624; Canada, *JG v New Brunswick (Min of Health and Community Services)* (1999) 177 DLR (4th 124), where traditional guarantees of equality and due process have been read in accordance with a positive obligation to provide legal counsel for people who need but cannot afford it. See generally M Cappaletti and W Cohen, *Comparative Constitutional Law* (New York, Bobbs Merril, 1999).

[53] For example, the state's duty to protect the right to life in Article 2 ECHR includes the 'obligation to install effective criminal law provisions to deter the commission of offences against the person, backed up by law enforcement machinery for the prevention and suppression of breaches of such provisions'. See *Osman v the UK* (1999) 29 EHRR 245, para 115. See further chapter 2 below.

plane. For example, the potential of section 7 of the Canadian Charter of Rights and Freedoms[54] to impose positive obligations involving financial expenditure in the context of health and welfare provision has long been the subject of debate in Canada.[55]

Conversely, it is also possible for certain rights usually categorised as socio-economic rights to contain negative elements, which require no more than the state should not interfere with their exercise. The right to join a trade union and not be penalised for doing so[56] is most frequently cited as an example, although the force of this illustration is somewhat weakened when we recall that a similarly drafted right to freedom of association is frequently entrenched as a civil or political right.[57] A more potent modern example can be found in the South African Constitution, where the right not to be evicted unlawfully from one's dwelling has been held to be an actionable part of the right to housing.[58]

Despite the fact that the allocation of resources may be a factor in determining whether there has been a violation of civil and political rights, it has been argued that these anomalies arise in the narrowest of circumstances, for example where individuals are pursued through the criminal justice system, in which case the imbalance of resources is extreme; or where the state itself has created or exacerbated the situation in which rights violations have occurred, for example in the case of prisoners who have been reduced to a condition of state dependency.[59] However, while there is force in the argument that positive financial obligations are more likely to be found in such contexts, state dependency or prison confinement is no longer a prerequisite for the imposition of positive financial or welfare obligations on states under the ECHR.[60] Thus,

---

[54] Section 7 provides: 'Everyone has the right to life liberty and security of the person and the right not to be deprived thereof except in accordance with the principles of fundamental justice.'

[55] See I Morrison, 'Security of the Person and the Person in Need: Section 7 of the Charter and the Right to Welfare' (1998) 4 *J of Law and Soc Policy* 1; and I Johnstone, 'Section 7 of the Charter and Constitutionally Protected Welfare' (1988) 46 *UT Fac Law Rev* 1. For the potential of s 7 to engender a positive right to social security before the Supreme Court, see *Gosselin v Quebec (Attorney General)* [2002] 4 SCR 429. See also the later case of *Chaoulli v Quebec(Attorney General)* [2005] SCC 35, in which the Supreme Court expressed reluctance to interpret s 7 in accordance with a positive obligation to provide adequate health care for those who could not afford private insurance, conversely concluding that a provincial ban on private health care insurance unjustifiably violated the right to security of the person. For a critique, see J King, 'Constitutional Rights and Social Welfare: A Comment on the Canadian *Chaouilli* Health Care Decision' (2006) *MLR* 631.

[56] See Art 8 ICESCR.

[57] Compare Art 11 ECHR (freedom of assembly and association), which provides that 'no restriction shall be placed on the exercise of these rights other than prescribed by law . . .'.

[58] See *Grootboom v Oosteneberg Municipality and Others* (2000) (3) BCLR 277 (C) 289, (2001) 1 SA 46 CC. For further discussion of the South African position, see the final section of this chapter.

[59] See the rejection of the resources defence to the denial of constitutional rights in cases concerning the treatment of death row prisoners: *Lewis and Others v Attorney General of Jamaica* [2000] 3 WLR 1785. But compare *Thomas v Baptiste* [2000] 2 AC 1; and *Higgs v Minister of National Security* [2000] 2 AC 228.

[60] The question as to whether positive obligations, for example to provide medical services to prison detainees for violations of Art 3 ECHR, may be applicable outside the prison walls is explored further in chapter 2 below.

although there may be stronger moral argument for imposing positive obligations, where the state itself has given rise to or exacerbated the circumstances
giving rise to an alleged violation of rights,[61] developments in ECHR jurisprudence have demonstrated that they are no longer a prerequisite for the imposition of positive protective measures requiring financial expenditure in welfare
needs contexts.

D. A Unified Approach to Human Rights: To 'Respect, Protect and Promote' the Rights

So long as battle lines were firmly drawn around differences in the nature of civil
and political rights on the one hand and socio-economic rights on the other,
there was a failure in the international arena to develop an explanatory or prescriptive theory of human rights that accommodated the difficulties of enforcement in disputes arising from issues of resources allocation, whatever the nature
of the rights involved. It has only been during the past two decades or so that a
functional approach has been developed, which on one hand addresses the conceptual weakness of the positive–negative classification of rights, and on the
other, accepts that particular problems of adjudication and enforcement arise in
cases where human rights compliance necessitates the imposition of long-term
financial obligations on governments, whatever the category of the right.[62]

Thus, after many years of unproductive juristic controversy, inspired by the
seminal work of Henry Shue,[63] a paradigm has emerged that identifies a cluster
of correlative obligations inherent to all human rights, whether civil and political or socio-economic. This model not only recognises that threats to civil and
political *and* socio-economic rights may in some cases give rise to immediate

---

[61] This approach has been adopted by the South African Constitutional Court. For example, in
Grootboom (note 58 above), where conditions complained of had been exacerbated by the state policy of apartheid, this was taken into account when interpreting the scope of the right not to be
refused emergency medical treatment and when considering the scope of the right to housing. See
also section II, C and D below.

[62] See for example the important work of Toebes in structuring the programmatic right to health
in accordance with different types of state obligations. Art 12 ICESCR provides: 'State Parties to the
present Covenant recognise the right of everyone to the enjoyment of the *highest attainable standard*
of physical and mental health.' See B Toebes, *The Right to Health as a Human Right in International
Law* (Antwerp, Intersentia/Hart, 1999).

[63] See H Shue, *Subsistence, Affluence and US Foreign Policy*, 2nd edn (Princeton, Princeton
University Press, 1996). In an earlier edition of his book, Professor Shue identified duties to (i) 'avoid
depriving', (ii) 'protect from deprivation', and (iii) 'aid the deprived'. By using the example of the
most familiar basic right—to physical security (the right not to be tortured executed or assaulted)
etc—he identified a cluster of three correlative duties for every person's basic right to physical
security: (i) 'a duty not to eliminate a person which is the primary negative duty to avoid depriving';
(ii) 'a positive duty to protect people against deprivation of their security, requiring positive measures to be taken by security forces and other people to protect from deprivation'; and (iii) 'duties
to provide for the security of those unable to provide for their own security, ie to aid the deprived'.
Subsequently Professor Shue went on to reclassify the duty 'to avoid depriving persons of their basic
rights' as the duty 'to respect' those rights.

perfunctory obligations to spend resources for the avoidance of future violations; it also recognises that in both cases, compliance with human rights obligations may give rise to long-term commitments, often of a procedural kind, which facilitate progress towards the attainment of the rights.

In his seminal work, Professor Shue argued that breaches, or threatened breaches, of all human rights give rise to a cluster of concomitant obligations: a primary obligation 'to respect', a secondary obligation 'to protect', and a tertiary obligation 'to promote'. He therefore postulated that, whereas primary obligations require the state itself to refrain from violating rights, secondary obligations require it to protect the right against interference by others. Moreover, tertiary obligations, which were further divided by Shue into the 'duty to facilitate' and the 'duty to promote', require the state to aid people's access to resources and facilitate their effective use in achieving independent satisfaction of the right. The threat would thus be less likely to be of the kind against which an individual or group would be unable to defend themselves (circumstances in which by contrast the state would have a primary obligation to fulfil the right directly). In determining the scope of government duties, Shue's model forgoes the earlier preoccupation with the negative or positive orientation of rights, instead directing the normative enquiry towards the consideration of the seriousness of threats against rights.

Nevertheless, Shue accepted that civil and political rights, which are generally framed in terms of negative duties, most frequently give rise to primary obligations which are immediate and perfunctory. However, he also recognised that although this occurs less frequently, socio-economic rights may be cast in terms of negative duties, which also give rise to primary obligations. An example is provided by the South African Constitution, where the right to a home has been expressed *inter alia* in terms of a primary obligation on the state not to carry out forced evictions.[64] Moreover, as we shall see further, whether in the interpretation of negatively or positively formulated rights, the Strasbourg organs have required states to take positive measures of protection (secondary obligations) of a kind usually identified with positive socio-economic rights, for example to provide police forces; effective child protection systems; procedures for the better protection of mental health patients; effective legal aid systems; and so on.

Shue's tripartite theory of obligations not only provides an explanation for what have been dismissed as narrow anomalies in the adjudication of civil and political rights, but also offers constitution drafters, human rights theorists and judges a working model with which to identify different levels of state responsibility in accordance with the seriousness of threats to rights.[65] However, perhaps most importantly for our purposes, in human rights disputes where

[64] S 26(3) of the constitution of the Republic of South Africa 1966 provides: 'No one may be evicted from their home, or have their home demolished without an order of court made after considering all the relevant circumstances. No legislation may permit arbitrary evictions.' For further discussion, see section II, C and D below.

[65] See Toebes (note 62 above) n 76.

issues of resource allocation are raised, it provides a basis for moderating the standard of judicial scrutiny, not in accordance with the classification of rights as either socio-economic or civil and political, but in accordance with the tripartite duties inherent in all human rights and the extent to which resources are implicated in their satisfaction.[66]

It should be stressed at this juncture, however, that although secondary duties of protection may also have difficult resource implications, tertiary duties (duties to facilitate or to promote), which need only be realised progressively *and* in accordance with available resources, give rise to the greatest difficulties when it comes to determining breaches and the appropriate standard of judicial scrutiny to be applied. Thus, as we shall see further, in our substantive discussion of UK cases, where programmatic duties and resources collide, the greatest challenge for courts and adjudicators is to carve out a constitutionally defensible role, without simply throwing up their hands and denying that there is any duty at all.

E. The Normative Content of Socio-economic Rights: Programmatic Aspirations and the 'Minimum Core'

In light of the resource dependency, programmatic nature *and* cultural and geographical relativity of the enforcement of socio-economic rights in the international system, which also have bearing on the role of courts in domestic litigation, a related objection is that it is impossible for adjudicators and courts to determine the standard to which the conduct of government must fall in order to constitute a violation of the right.[67] In the absence of a 'universal and non-arbitrary standard for distinguishing need from luxury', how are courts to determine questions of violation?

Of course, as has been accepted above, there are heightened difficulties of adjudication whenever legal rights, whether embodied in domestic legislation or international instruments, are expressly formulated (or interpreted by courts) in terms of progressive realisation or 'targets',[68] which are subject to the availability of resources. However, the UN Committee on Economic Social and Cultural Rights (CESCR) has argued that the impossibility of determining the standard to which the conduct of government must fall in order to constitute a violation of the rights in the ICESCR has been overstated. Thus, in its General Comment No 3 on the nature of state party obligations under the ICESCR, the Committee has required:

---

[66] Questions about the moderation of judicial scrutiny in accordance with different obligations engendered by rights will be explored more fully in the context of Strasbourg and UK jurisprudence.

[67] This issue lies at the heart of the series of asylum benefit disputes in the United Kingdom, examined in chapter 6 below.

[68] The idea of a 'target duty' has been used to define many of the discretionary legislative public law duties relating to social provision in the United Kingdom.

a minimum core obligation to ensure the satisfaction of at very least, minimum essential levels of which each of the rights is incumbent on every state party. Thus for example a state party in which any significant number of individuals is deprived of essential foodstuffs, of primary health care, of basic shelter and housing, or of the most basic forms of education is *prima facie* failing to discharge its obligations under the Covenant.[69]

Moreover, highlighting the gradual way in which the normative content of civil and political rights has been developed by their on-going interpretation by courts in concrete cases, it has been claimed that problems associated with ICESCR rights have been compounded by their historical exclusion from the adjudicative processes available in the case of civil and political rights.[70]

Furthermore, in this context jurists have also relied on a distinction between different types of obligations—obligations of *result* and obligations of *conduct*—which reflect different levels of state involvement and urgency in satisfying different kinds of rights.[71] Thus, while a *result* obligation, an example of which is found in the facilitative self-help aspects of labour rights, is directed towards the achievement of long-term progress and change,[72] while obligations

---

[69]   The Nature of State Parties Obligations (Art 2, para 1) General Comment No 3 (1990) para 10, UN Doc E/1991/23.

[70]   See S Liebenberg, 'The Protection of Economic Social and Cultural Rights in Domestic Legal Systems' in Eide, Krause and Rosas (eds) (2001) (note 4 above) 61. While admitting that it is easier for national bodies such as courts and tribunals to determine more precise standards, in their own cultural settings, the CESCR has proceeded on the commonsense understanding that it should not be difficult, as suggested by Beetham, 'to establish benchmarks for determining when girls are discriminated against in access to education, when children have died through lack of food or clean water or when people sleep rough because they have no access to housing . . .' See UN General Comment 3 (*ibid*) para 10. See also D Beetham, 'What Future for Economic Social and Cultural Rights?' (1995) 43 *Political Studies* 41. The author argues that despite the relativity of needs, 'both the defenders of a "basic needs" approach within development economics and human rights theorists would converge on a minimum core of rights such as the following: the right to food of an adequate nutritional value to clothing to primary basic health care . . .'. The CESCR has embarked on the protracted task of identifying minimum standards for socio-economic rights in the international context and identifying relevant factors to be taken into account in determining the scope of the rights. For example, forced evictions, harassment and other threats have been identified as key components of a universal right to housing, along with positive aspects, such as access to safe drinking water, energy for heating and lighting, sanitation and washing facilities.

[71]   See Eide (2001) (note 4 above) 23, where the author argues that fundamental to a realistic understanding of state obligations under the ICESCR is that the individual 'who is the active subject of all economic and social development is expected wherever possible through his or her own efforts and by use of his own resources to find ways to ensure the satisfaction of his or her own needs'.

[72]   This distinction is generally attributed to O Khan Freund. See O Khan Freund, 'The European Social Charter' in FG Jacobs (ed), *European Law and the Individual* (Amsterdam, North Holland Publishing Co, 1976). Examination of the rights in the ICESCR reveals that different kinds of state responses are envisaged for the protection of both the social and economic clusters in the ICESCR. Thus, many of the so-called economic or labour related rights in arts 6–9 cast the state in the role of facilitator rather than that of direct provider. For example, rights to fair wages and a healthy working environment, seek to promote values of equality, autonomy and economic independence through fostering appropriate conditions of employment. By contrast, many of the rights in arts 11–14 presuppose direct provision or access by the state to economic and social goods. Moreover, although the protection of the majority of the rights unequivocally presupposes some form of

of *conduct* require state parties to take steps towards goals that should be 'deliberate, concrete and targeted' and directed 'as clearly as possible towards meeting the obligations recognised in the Covenant'.[73] Thus, not only should it be possible to determine whether appropriate steps towards anticipated goals are in place in the case of long-term facilitative duties, in the case of obligations of conduct, it should also be possible without direct scrutiny of competing resource commitments to decide whether reasonable steps towards compliance have been taken in light of the urgency of human needs.[74]

Finally, it should be noted in relation to the enforceability of ICESCR rights that, although the CESCR has accepted that judicial processes are not the only or even most appropriate means of protecting socio-economic rights,[75] the majority of rights in the ICESCR have some element that is justiciable.[76] By thus rejecting the rigid dichotomy that has put socio-economic rights beyond the reach of courts, the CESCR has argued that to accept such a position 'would drastically curtail the capacity of courts to protect the rights of the most vulnerable and disadvantaged groups in society'.[77] The challenge for domestic courts is therefore to develop appropriate standards to adjudicate the different sorts of obligation engendered by resource-dependent rights, particularly those requiring long-term strategic planning by states.

II. THE PROTECTION OF SOCIO-ECONOMIC RIGHTS IN DOMESTIC COURTS

A. Issues of Justiciability: Achieving Social Justice in the Round?

i. Institutional Competencies

Many objections to the adjudication of socio-economic rights in the international arena have their counterparts in domestic law. It has been argued in Western-style democracies that since socio-economic rights are political, legislative matters involving primary issues of resource distribution, the judicial review of legislative or executive decisions concerning their implementation and enforcement constitutes an illegitimate intrusion into the policy affairs of the elected branches of government and a breach of the traditional doctrine of the

positive state action, in other cases, particularly in relation to the labour rights, there is a presupposition of negative restraint.

[73] See generally Eide (2001) (note 4 above) 23–5; and CESCR General Comment No 3 (note 69 above) 83, para 2.

[74] See CESCR General Comment No 3 (note 69 above) 83–7.

[75] The CESCR has argued that many of the other available mechanisms such as ombudsmen, tribunals or parliamentary scrutiny Committees (such as the recently established Joint Committee of Human Rights (JCHR) in the UK) may provide more appropriate mechanisms. See CESCR General Comment No 10 (1998) UN Doc E/1999/22, 122–3.

[76] *Ibid*, paras 1–6.

[77] CESCR General Comment No 9 (1998) on the domestic application of the ICESCR, UN DocE/1999/22, 117–21, para 4.

separation of powers. Moreover, hand in hand with the first objection, there is a related argument that inured in a system of bipolar adversarial dispute resolution, courts are institutionally ill-suited to adjudicate in complex polycentric socio-economic disputes raising sensitive issues of resource allocation.[78] Thus, it is claimed that, although adept at interpreting and applying determinate rules of law and fact that arise in private law disputes, judges in public law lack the necessary training and analytical skills of economic forecasting; furthermore, courts as institutions lack the necessary infrastructure to make an effective contribution to the resolution such polycentric disputes that give rise to far-reaching and often unforeseeable economic repercussions.[79]

However, not only does the first objection reflect a rigid formalistic conception of the balance of powers, which sits uneasily with the powers of legislative scrutiny afforded to courts in modern constitutional democracies, the second objection is inconsistent with developments in public law adjudication, where domestic and regional courts have increasingly become fora for the resolution of complex polycentric public interest disputes, for which new rules of standing and evidentiary and remedial procedures have evolved.[80] Regarding the justiciability of disputes that involve issues of resource allocation in English administrative law, Lord Steyn has recently argued:

> Most legislation is passed to advance a policy. And frequently it involves in one way or another the allocation of resources. . . . What I am saying is that there cannot be a legal principle requiring the court to desist from making a judgement on the issues in such cases. . . . There is in my view no justification for a court to adopt an a priori view in favour of economic conservatism. . . . In common law adjudication, it is an everyday occurrence for courts to consider, together with principled arguments, the balance sheet of policy advantages and disadvantages. It would be a matter of public disquiet if the courts did not do so. Of course in striking the balance courts may arrive at a result unacceptable to Parliament. In such cases Parliament can act with great speed to reverse the effect of a decision. . . . But there is no need to create a legal principle requiring the courts to abstain from ruling on policy matters or resource allocation issues.[81]

---

[78] See generally L Fuller, *The Forms and Limits of Adjudication* (1978) 92 *Harvard Law Rev* 353.

[79] See for example, A Chayes, 'The Role of the Judge in Public Law Litigation' (1976) 89 *Harvard Law Rev* 1281. For these arguments in relation to the role of courts under the HRA, see M Loughlin, 'Rights, Democracy and Law' in T Campbell, KD Ewing and A Tomkins (eds), *Sceptical Essays on Human Rights* (Oxford, OUP, 2001) 42.

[80] See RA Dahl, 'Decision-making in a Democracy: The Supreme Court as National Policy Maker' (1957) *J of Public Law* 297. One of the strongest justifications for public interest litigation in the US (associated with Dahl) was located in theories of pluralist and participatory democracy, where it was argued that priority should be accorded to direct participation in civil society by citizens, operating not only through the constricted medium of political parties but also through a plurality of interest groups. See also M Perry, *The Constitution, the Courts, and Human Rights: An Enquiry into the Legitimacy of Constitutional Policy-making by the Judiciary* (New Haven, Yale University Press, 1982). See for example the controversial development of public interest litigation by the Indian Supreme Court in A Desai and S Murahildar, 'Public Interest Litigation Potential and Problems' in B Kirpal (ed), *Supreme But Not Infallible: Essays in Honour of the Supreme Court of India* (New Delhi, OUP, 2000).

[81] Lord Steyn, 'Deference: A Tangled Story' (2005) *Public Law* 351, 356–7. These issues are discussed in relation to the UK in chapter 4 below.

Thus, despite the potential disruption of the collective democratic balance, during the past four decades, public interest 'group' litigation, of a kind whose origins can be traced to the 'collective rights' US movement of the 1970's (which was founded on the idea that lack of legal access for disadvantaged members of society constitutes a serious gap in welfare protection) has burgeoned in Western-style democracies.[82] Whether in constitutional democracies or in countries such as the UK where the constitution is unwritten, remedial devices, managerial rules of procedure and developments in the rules of standing—often developed by the courts themselves—have allowed complex political polycentric disputes, relating to the environment, economic labour relations or to public health issues, to be adjudicated under the rubric of public law or constitutional law.[83]

This is not to suggest that there has been uniformity in the evolution of public interest litigation in Western jurisdictions.[84] In the UK, developments have been more diffuse, gradual and surreptitious than in the US, and to a large extent facilitated by courts themselves, through the development of the rules of standing in public administrative law.[85] Moreover, it is notable that in the UK, in addition to what are readily identifiable public interest 'group' cases (where, for example, the protagonists are Friends of the Earth or the Association of Small Businesses),[86] the institutional trappings of group litigation have also been afforded in individual test cases backed by political NGOs such as Shelter or Liberty in public administrative law.[87] Indeed, despite the confinement of actions based on the Human Rights Act (HRA) to victims,[88] campaigning groups such as Shelter and the Child Poverty Action Group have increasingly been invited by courts to appear as third-party interveners in politically sensitive individual test cases concerning access to public services.[89]

---

[82] The 'access to justice' movement, spearheaded by M Cappelletti in the US, had a bias towards collective group action.

[83] For the development of public interest litigation in the United Kingdom, see C Harlow and R Rawlings, *Pressure Through Law* (London, Routledge, 1992); C Harlow, 'Public Law and Popular Justice' (2002) *MLR* 1–18; and M Cappaletti, *The Judicial Process in Comparative Perspective* (Oxford, Clarendon, 1989) 268–308.

[84] For a comparative analysis of the complex relationship between prevailing ideas of democracy and development of the 'forms, procedures and substance of public law' to advance public political aims, see D Feldman, 'Public Interest Litigation and Comparative Theory in Perspective' (1992) *MLR* 44. For the potential use of public interest litigation to override the welfare interests of disadvantaged minorities, see Desai and Murahildar (note 80 above) 172–3.

[85] The phenomenon of group product liability litigation that took hold in the US has not followed the same path in the UK.

[86] See P Cane, 'Standing up for the Public' (1995) *Public Law* 276. See for example, *R v Inspector of Pollution, ex parte Greenpeace* [1994] 1 WLR 570; *R v Inland Revenue Commissioners, ex p National Federation of Self-employed and Small Businesses Ltd* [1981] 2 WLR 272.

[87] See *R v Secretary of State for the Social Services, ex parte Child Poverty Action Group* [1990] 2 QB 540.

[88] Under ss 7(1) and 7(3) HRA only a person who is or would be a victim of a violation can bring an action.

[89] See further chapters 5–8 below.

ii. Welfare Politics, Courts and Conflicting Theories of Constitutional Review

It is something of a truism that one of the defining characteristics of our age has been a prevailing belief in the power of the judiciary to control the possible excesses of the democratically elected majority through the exercise of constitutional review. [90] It is also the case that until the growth of this phenomenon during the past fifty years or more, the idea of looking to the courts as the final arbiters in urgent matters of political or social conflict had for long been an exclusively American phenomenon.[91] Thus, it was possible for Ronald Dworkin to pronounce with satisfaction at the end of the twentieth century (by which time diverse models of constitutional democracy had been established on every continent) that the concept of judicial review and enforcement of basic human rights had been the most important and enduring contribution made by the United States to political theory.[92]

Clearly, however, such developments have not been universally welcomed.[93] In the first instance, they are thought to threaten the constitutional principle of the separation of powers, potentially bolstering or replacing the tyranny of the majority with an unrepresentative judicial hegemony. Moreover, it is axiomatic that broadly formulated and malleable concepts such as equality, liberty and the inviolability of life, of the kind enshrined in the 200-year-old US constitution, offer little practical assistance to courts when giving answers to the factual contemporary questions that confront them: whether same sex couples have a right to marry, whether religious communities have a right to establish and seek support for separate so-called faith schools; whether fair decisions about access to health treatment or social security entitlements should include considerations of age or immigration status; and so on.[94]

Thus, whether constitutional texts are replete with negative duties, for example regarding non-violation of life and interference with the use and enjoyment of property, or whether (more unusually) they contain positive guarantees such as the right to emergency medical treatment or housing, it is clear that concepts such as freedom, equality and respect for human dignity cannot of themselves provide answers to questions of public morality or the limits of state responsibility for

---

[90] See D Beatty, *The Ultimate Rule of Law* (Oxford, OUP, 2004).

[91] See M Cappalletto, *Judicial Review in the Contemporary World* (Indianapolis, Bobbs-Merrill, 1971).

[92] R Dworkin, *Freedom's Law* (Cambridge, MA, Harvard University Press, 1996) 71. Compare R Posner, 'Against Constitutional Theory' (1998) 73 *NYU Law Review* 1; and R Posner, *The Problematics of Moral and Legal Theory* (Cambridge, MA, Harvard University Press, 1999).

[93] There is a vast critical and sceptical literature on the role of courts in judicial review. For example, see J Waldron, *Law and Disagreement* (Oxford, Clarendon, 1999) Part III; M Tushnet, *Red, White, and Blue: A Critical Analysis of Constitutional Law* (Cambridge, MA, Harvard University Press, 1988). In Canada, see for example M Mandel, *The Charter of Rights and the Legalisation of Politics* (Toronto, Wall and Thompson, 1989). In the UK, see for example R Bellamy, 'Constitutive Citizenship versus Constitutional Rights: Republican Reflections on the EU Charter and the Human Rights Act' in Campbell, Ewing and Tomkins (eds) (note 79 above) 15; and Loughlin (note 79 above) 42.

[94] For a critique of originalism in the US, see Beatty (note 90 above) 5–11.

social provision: the substantive content of these concepts must be fleshed out by courts in accordance with their readings of constitutions in contemporary democracies.

Early constitutional theory in the US took refuge in the notion that constitutional review, like the exercise of contractual interpretation, requires no more than the construction of concepts in accordance with the 'sense of the terms and intentions of the parties'.[95] However, as we have seen in *Deshaney,* the resolution of contemporary social, political and moral conflicts in accordance with perceived understandings of the original drafters of a constitution remains problematic.[96] Originalist theorists have struggled to show not only how simple factual questions of contemporary significance might have been addressed by the ancient fathers, but also how the level of judicial neutrality to which they aspire can be achieve in light of the open-textured nature of the Constitution's broadly drafted commitments.[97]

Thus, in the US two further political theories of judicial review, each in their own ways seeking to address criticisms of judicial activism associated with the so-called Warren era, have been added to the originalist stance. Whereas moral theorists such as Dworkin have appealed to the judiciary to develop a political philosophy of constitutional law that is informed by principled judicial understandings of the competing moral claims that lie at the heart of every constitutional case,[98] for 'process theorists', the aim of the judiciary should be little more than to ensure that the processes and institutions of politics work fairly and effectively rather than to focus on outcomes.[99]

John Ely's process theory sought to address claims of partisanship in the Supreme Court in the Warren era, by arguing that the first concern of a constitutional court should be to protect the interests of the 'politically disadvantaged,' ensuring equal participation in and equal benefit from the democratic process. Ely therefore argued that the process of judicial review should act as a corrective to the malfunctioning of the political process, by providing a channel of democratic participation that would prevent the 'inns' from 'choking off the channels of political change' and from 'systematically disadvantaging some

---

[95] See for example R Posner, 'Against Constitutional Theory' (1998) 73 *NYU Law Review* 1.

[96] For example, see R Bork, 'The Impossibility of Finding Welfare Rights in the Constitution' (1979) *Washington U Law Quarterly* 695; and R Bork, 'The Constitution, Original Intent, and Economic Rights' (1986) *San Diego Law Review* 823.

[97] The weakness of the originalist position became all too apparent during the so-called Warren period in the US Supreme Court, which was associated with a number of active interventionist judgements. See for example *Brown v Board of Education* (1954) 347 US 483, which concluded that segregated schools denied black Americans equal protection of the law. See R Dworkin, *Life's Dominion* (New York, Vintage Books, 1994) 138–43; M Klarman, '*Brown*, Originalism, and Constitutional Theory: A Response to Professor McConnell' (1995) 81 *Virginia Law Review* 1881–936.

[98] See Dworkin (1996) (note 92 above); and R Dworkin, *Law's Empire* (Cambridge, MA, Harvard University Press, 1986).

[99] See JH Ely, *Democracy and Distrust: A Theory of Judicial Review* (Cambridge, MA, Harvard University Press, 1980).

minority out of simple hostility or . . . prejudice'.[100] Thus, rather than making value judgements and defining the moral character of communities (a matter for the body politic as reflected in decisions of the legislature), Ely argued for a more minimalist judicial role: to supervise and ensure that conditions—such as formal access, fair procedures and adequate representation—are in place for the proper functioning of democracy. In short, consistent with the most significant parts of the American Constitution and the Bill of Rights, judges should lend their weight to the processes of democracy by guaranteeing that electoral rights, rights of poorly represented groups, racial minorities and individuals caught up in the criminal justice system are not disadvantaged by the political process.

Ely's process theory appeals to many theorists on grounds that it is in step with the central thrust of the US constitution; that its focus is on the interests of minorities; and that it assigns to judges a (secondary) 'role they are conspicuously well situated to fill'.[101] Nonetheless, this view has continued to be the subject of controversy and criticism, largely on grounds that in attempting to separate process from substance, it remains 'radically indeterminate and functionally incomplete'.[102] Thus, it has been claimed, and conceded to some extent by Ely himself, that the theory fails to construct a model of judicial review in which judges can avoid making value judgements of a kind that Ely considers to be inappropriate—for example, in deciding whether a law denying a benefit to a particular minority group is indicative of prejudice or not.[103] Problematically, whether a judge concludes that laws such as those against same-sex marriage or so-called faith schools or laws that hinder social mobility are examples of minority prejudice or appropriate expressions of the will of the majority, must depend on substantive moral evaluations of the kind that Ely was most anxious to avoid.

However, certain aspects of Ely's theory have continued to appeal to commentators such as Cass Sunstein, who has engaged with the idea of constitutions in which governance combines 'political accountability with a high degree of reflexiveness, and a general commitment to reason-giving'.[104] Thus, in common with many contemporary theorists, Sunstein has argued that it is appropriate that courts should be part of a community's quest for 'the ideal of deliberative democracy', albeit in a minor supportive role, and that responsible courts should interpret the constitution in this light. Moreover, like Ely, Sunstein has subscribed to the minimalist idea that the case for an assertive judiciary is most clearly made out when it is alleged that the institutions of governance are

---

[100] *Ibid*, 103.

[101] *Ibid*, 102.

[102] See L Tribe, 'The Puzzling Persistence of Process-based Constitutional Theories' (1980) 89 *Yale L J* 1063.

[103] See P Monahan, *Politics and the Constitution* (Toronto, Carswell, 1987); J Habermas, *Between Facts and Norms* (Cambridge, MA, MIT Press, 1996).

[104] C Sunstein, *Designing Democracy: What Constitutions Do* (New York, OUP, 2001a) 7. Compare W Eskridge, 'Pluralism and Distrust: How Courts can Support Democracy by Lowering the Stakes of Politics' (2005) 114 *Yale Law Journal* 1279.

malfunctioning.[105] As a consequence, he has been not only cautious about courts becoming entangled in 'managerial issues' such as poverty or health care, where considerations of public policy are at issue, but also no less wary of judicial involvement in cases of discrimination, for example on grounds of sexual orientation, where considerations of public morality are at stake.[106] As a case in point, although Sunstein accepts that the principle of equality is embedded in the US constitution, he has argued that women are more effectively protected against discrimination by the legislature than by courts.[107]

In contrast, although Dworkin, who remains pre-eminent among US moral constitutional theorists, believes like proceduralists that judicial review is a reflection of the principle of democratic accountability and the sovereignty of people in the US constitution, he rejects the idea that democracy can be reduced to a single formulaic principle of majoritarianism, or that courts can be shielded from the highly charged and often agonising moral dilemmas in the hard cases that come before them. Instead, for Dworkin, democratic decision-making *and* the judicial enforcement of human rights are expressions of a fundamental principle in liberal political thought, which recognises that each individual is entitled to equal concern and respect by the state.[108] Thus, rather than appeals to what he regards as impossible judicial neutrality, Dworkin embraces a political theory that will not only assist courts in finding the 'fit' for the words of the constitution itself, but also furnish a set of principled criteria against which the moral value of judicial decision-making can effectively be judged.[109] In other words, the prevailing judicial ambition should be to develop 'the best conception of constitutional moral principles . . . that fits the broad story of a country's constitutional record.'[110]

For Dworkin, principled readings of texts, history and precedent cases dictate answers in the majority of constitutional cases, leaving little room for the infiltration of personal moral convictions. Thus, it is claimed that the majority of cases are not hard cases, so that the requirement that there should be a 'fit' with the constitution 'sharply limits the latitude the moral reading gives to individual

---

[105] C Sunstein, *Legal Reasoning and Political Conflict* (New York, OUP, 1996) 179.

[106] In such cases, Sunstein argues, the judicial role should be 'catalytic' as opposed to 'preclusive'. See Sunstein (2001a) (note 104 above) 9–11 and 205–6. But compare more recently C Sunstein, 'Social and Economic Rights? Lessons from South Africa' (2001b) 11 *Constitutional Forum* 123. For an even less compromising view, see Monahan (note 103 above), where the author argues that the court's role is no more than to protect the basic infrastructure of liberal democracy. The author is therefore opposed to the judicial enforcement of socio-economic rights because to take such a step would significantly undermine 'the scope for democratic dialogue and deliberation rather than expand it' (126). Compare F Michaelman, 'Welfare Rights in a Consitutionalist Democracy' (1979) *Washington U Law Quarterly* 659.

[107] Sunstein (2001a) (note 104 above) 156, 157.

[108] See Dworkin (1996) (note 92 above).

[109] For Dworkin, this is not to deny the importance of the Constitutional text when interpreting distinctive general statements of the kind found in the US Constitution, the importance of history as an interpretative aid, the structural design of the Constitution as a whole or the dominant lines of past communication by other judges. See *ibid*.

[110] *Ibid*, 11.

judges'.[111] Problematically however, in his extensive application of the theory of fit and value in hard cases, Dworkin sometimes accepts that in themselves the demands of constitutional fit are sufficient and controlling. Thus, while on one hand agreeing that people living in poverty cannot be said to command the equal concern and respect to which they are entitled, on the other, Dworkin considers that American judges must accept that positive rights against the state are not part of the 'settled understandings . . . of the broad story of America's historical record'.[112] Therefore, he argues that in contrast to the interpretation of cases concerning different kinds of life-and-death issues such as euthanasia and abortion, where answers are to be found in the realm of high moral and philosophical principle, interpreting the far-reaching guarantees of liberty and equality in the Fifth and Fourteenth Amendments to include positive socio-economic rights would be wholly inconsistent with the US Constitution. Indeed, it has long been recognised as a fundamental flaw in Dworkin's theory that there is nothing to explain how, in cases where the constitution is factually silent, courts are to decide whether moral and philosophical principle should play a more significant role than history, precedent and arguments of constitutional fit.[113]

Since the enactment of the HRA 1998 in the United Kingdom, longstanding opponents of a British Bill of Rights have continued to be caught up in a mood of general scepticism about the democratic deficit implicit in the process of constitutional review.[114] However, in acceptance that the HRA has legitimated a shift in the balance between judicial and collective power, there has been some revival of interest in theories associated with American writers such as Ely and Robert Dhal.[115] In other words, some British commentators now believe that the process of human rights adjudication, rather than being destructive of democracy, might be used to forge a channel of participation for the vulnerable and marginalised, who are most likely to be excluded from the normal channels of democratic participation—provided that judges are appropriately in tune with the fundamental

---

[111] *Ibid*, 10.

[112] *Ibid*, 11.

[113] For criticism generally of Dworkin's overarching view that judges in hard constitutional cases should reason like philosophers, see M McConnell, 'The Importance of Humility in Judicial Review: A Comment on Ronald Dworkin's "Moral Reading" of the Constitution' (1995) 65 *Fordham Law Review* 1269. For a critique of the extent to which history and precedent can be manipulated in Dworkin's theory, see C Sunstein, 'Earl Warren is Dead', *The New Republic*, 13 May 1996, 35–9.

[114] In particular, for concern about the impropriety of judicial involvement in resource allocation issues, see C Gearty, 'Tort Law and the Human Rights Act' in Campbell, Ewing and Tompkins (eds) (note 79 above) 256–7, where in appealing for restraint and 'what is required in a representative democracy', the author highlights the case of *Sinnott v Ireland and the Minister of Education*, *The Irish Times*, 13 Nov 2000 (where the constitution had been read in light of an obligation to provide life-long education for disabled adults).

[115] Dahl (note 80 above). In the UK, the thesis that the judiciary cannot act neutrally and in fact must act politically has been most closely identified with the writing of John Griffith. See generally J Griffith, *The Politics of the Judiciary*, 5th edn (London, Fontana, 1997).

values inherent in the ECHR rights.[116] Thus, focusing in particular on the difficulties confronting courts in socio-economic disputes where issues of resource allocation coincide with tertiary obligations to protect Convention rights, Sandra Fredman has suggested that courts may need 'to insert a third dimension, in the form of democratic constraints', which 'could take the form of judicially enforced requirements of participation by affected parties as well as accountability via transparency and the articulation of intelligible reasons'.[117]

Focusing on the collaborative safeguards implicit in the HRA itself, and without denying the need for judicial deference in appropriate cases, others have looked to constitutional democracies such as Canada and South Africa, where non-confrontational 'cooperative' models of adjudication have been posited, both in respect of judicial powers of legislative review[118] and scrutiny of executive decisions involving hard choices about sensitive policy issues.[119] According to such a model, the process of judicial review involves a 'constitutional dialogue' that allows courts where necessary and *feasible* to 'prod the legislature into action to realise the rights, while accepting the legislature's choice of means as to the most appropriate mechanisms to advance the rights'.[120]

B. The Protection of Socio-economic Rights through the Traditional Canon of Civil and Political Rights

It is axiomatic that the role of domestic courts in the protection of socio-economic rights is dictated by the nature of a country's constitution, the interpretation of that constitution by courts, and the extent to which international instruments for the protection of human rights are directly applicable in domestic law.[121] However, it is well known that even in monist systems where

---

[116] See generally the work of S Fredman, especially 'Social, Economic and Cultural Rights' in D Feldman (ed), *English Public Law* (Oxford, OUP, 2003); and S Fredman, 'From Deference to Democracy' (2006) *LQR* 53, 68, where the author considers the limitations of the procedural approach to constitutional adjudication, arguing that its emphasis on minority rights can be better understood as an aspect of the fundamental substantive value of equality in the ECHR rights.

[117] See Fredman (2003) (note 116 above) 531. See chapter 5 below for resonance with the views of Public Choice Constitutionalists in the UK.

[118] See for example E Palmer, 'Courts Resources and the HRA: Reading Section 17 of the Children Act 1989 Compatibly with Article 8 ECHR' (2003) *European Human Rights Law Review* 308–24. See further chapter 3 below.

[119] For example, see RE Edwards, 'Judicial Deference under the HRA' (2002) *MLR* 859. For further discussion of these issues, see chapters 3, 4 and 5 below.

[120] Liebenberg (2001) (note 70 above) 59. See generally C Scott and J Nedelsky, 'Constitutional Dialogue' in J Bakan and D Schneiderman (eds), *Social Justice and the Constitution: Perspectives on Social Union in Canada* (Ottowa, Carleton University Press, 1992) 59. For a critique of the Canadian inspired theory of 'institutional dialogue', see LB Tremblay, 'The Legitimacy of Judicial Review: The Limits of Dialogue between Courts and Legislatures' (2005) 3(4) *Int'l J of Constitutional Law* 617–48.

[121] For a useful account of the relationship between these three components in diverse jurisdictions, including Canada, the UK, Hungary, the Phillipines and India, see F Coomans (ed), *Justiciability of Socio-economic Rights: Experiences from Domestic Systems* (Antwerp, Intersentia, 2006). For an overview of the role of domestic courts in the protection of socio-economic rights, see also Liebenberg (2001) (note 70 above) 55.

international treaties are directly applicable and in Western jurisdictions that have ratified both the ICCPR and the ICESCR, little use has been made of the latter treaty in domestic courts.[122]

Nevertheless, in many democracies that have framed or reframed their constitutions following the end of the World War II, some level of commitment to the provision of public welfare has been acknowledged, although often, as in the international arena, mandatory remedies of enforcement have been reserved for members of the traditional canon of civil and political rights.[123] Furthermore, in the wave of constitutionalism that followed the break-up the Soviet Union, although many states have been preoccupied with securing the rolling back of state powers/government,[124] broadly formulated expressions of state responsibility for public welfare can nonetheless often be found sitting, one might argue incongruously, side by side with so-called 'economic rights'.[125]

Moreover, in those jurisdictions where legal protection has been afforded to socio-economic rights, it is notable that different methods have been used to enlist the assistance of courts. Thus, for example, whereas the Hungarian constitution contains a number of specific social welfare rights that are legally enforceable,[126] the South African Constitution contains a list of socio-economic provisions that have been formulated in terms of instructions to government to 'respect, protect and fulfil' the rights. In other jurisdictions, of which India provides the oldest example, rather than as legally enforceable individual or collective rights, socio-economic rights have been protected in terms of directive principles of state policy.[127]

It is much more usual for socio-economic rights to be protected in domestic law through legislative provisions, which simultaneously afford an institutional

---

[122] See generally Liebenberg (2001) (note 70 above) 75–9. For comparison of the use made of the ICESCR in diverse jurisdictions across the North–South divide, see generally Coomans (ed) (*ibid*).

[123] See generally Beatty (note 90 above) 324. For examples of modern jurisdictions that have included legally enforceable socio-economic rights, see Hungary, Colombia and South Africa—each of which have been discussed in Coomans (ed) (note 121 above).

[124] For attempts to secure the rolling back of the state in domestic constitutions, see T Daintith, 'The Constitutional Protection of Economic Rights' (2004) 2(1) *Int'l J of Constitutional Law* 56–9.

[125] For a recent example of this juxtaposition of untrammelled private power and state responsibility for public welfare, see the full text of the Iraqi Constitution at <http://www.export.gov/?iraq/?pdf/?iraqi_constitution.pdf>. Under the heading 'Social and Economic Liberties', Art 25 provides: 'The State guarantees the reform of the Iraqi economy in accordance with modern economic principles to ensure the full investment of its (extensive public) resources and the encouragement and the development of the private sector.' However, Art 30 also provides: 'the state shall guarantee to the individual and the family—especially children and women—social and health security and the basic requirements for leading a free and dignified life. The state also ensures the above a suitable income and appropriate housing.'

[126] See R Uitiz and A Sajo, 'Welfare Rights in Hungarian Constitutional Jurisprudence' in Coomans (ed) (note 121 above) 97–127.

[127] See generally S Muralidhar, 'Judicial Enforcement of Economic and Social Rights: The Indian Scenario' in Coomans (ed) (note 121 above) 237–67. For a more extensive critique, see also Desai and Murahildar (note 80 above). Civil and political rights (for example the right to life, the right to equality and freedom of speech and expression) are found in Part III of the Indian Constitution. Economic social and cultural rights, which include the right to free legal aid, education, health and a minimum wage for workers, are expressed as Directive Principles of State Policy in Part IV.

framework for the delivery of public services and prescribe the respective responsibilities of government and services providers. They are usually widely formulated as discretionary duties. However, in addition to South Africa, recently Columbia and Argentina have included legally enforceable socio-economic rights. Nevertheless, although protection of socio-economic rights as justiciable rights in domestic constitutions is still relatively rare,[128] even in democracies such as the United States, where the Constitution is silent on such matters, or in Canada, where only a few references to socio-economic rights have been included in the Charter,[129] during the latter part of the twentieth century, fair process norms and equality provisions, which provide the bedrock of traditional libertarian constitutions, have sometimes been invoked to secure the protection of socio-economic rights.[130]

Our first example is a much cited decision by the Canadian Supreme Court, *Eldridge v British Columbia (Attorney General)*,[131] in which section 15 of the Canadian Charter of Fundamental Rights and Freedoms 1982 was successfully relied on to require the provision of sign language for deaf patients, as part of a publicly funded scheme for medical care.[132] Section 15 provides:

> Every individual is equal before and under the law and has the right to equal protection and benefit of the law without discrimination and in particular without discrimination based on race, national or ethnic origin, colour, religion, sex, age or mental or physical disability.

The Court famously rejected the defendant's claim that governments should be entitled 'to provide benefits to the general population without ensuring that disadvantaged members are accorded the resources' on grounds that the argument 'bespoke a thin and impoverished version of section 15(1)'.[133]

---

[128] The CESCR has recognised that a sound legislative foundation is critical for the effective implementation and enforcement of socio-economic rights within national jurisdictions.

[129] There are limited references to labour and education rights in the Canadian Charter of Rights and Freedoms 1982. For a very informative account of the role of the Supreme Court, see D Wiseman, 'Methods of Protection of Social and Economic Rights in Canada', in Coomans (ed) (note 121 above) 173–205.

[130] This approach has also been taken in the UN system, where the UN Human Rights Committee has occasionally heard socio-economic complaints under the non-discrimination provision in Art 26 CCPR. See M Scheinin, 'Economic and Social Rights as Legal Rights' in Eide, Krause and Rosas (eds) (note 4 above) 32.

[131] *Eldridge* [1997] 3 SCR 624. For a full account of the use of Art 15 and the development of a 'right to equality' by the Supreme Court in *Law v Canada (Minister of Employment and Immigration)* [1999] 1 SCR 497, see Wiseman (note 129 above) 199–203. For the successful use of Art 15 in the field of employment, see *Tetrault Gadoury v Canada (Employment and Immigration Commission)* [1991] 2 SCR 22 (protecting the economic well-being of older workers); and *Schachter v Canada* (1991) 43 Dominion Law Report 4th 1, [1992] 2 SCR 679.

[132] Each of the applicants had been born deaf, and their preferred means of communication was sign language. They contended that the absence of interpreters impaired their ability to communicate with their doctors and other health care providers and thus increased the risk of misdiagnosis and ineffective treatment.

[133] *Eldridge* (note 131 above) 635, para 72 (La Forest J). As noted by Wiseman, although at first sight the case is suggestive of a substantive conception of equality, subsequent cases have treated it more narrowly as authority for the proposition that where a government opts to provide a public program, it must ensure that it does so without discrimination. See Wiseman (note 129 above) 202.

Furthermore, in reaching the conclusion that 'discrimination can accrue from a failure to take positive steps to ensure that disadvantaged groups benefit equally from services offered to the general public', the Court refused to accept that failure by the Medical Services Commission to provide the service could be construed as a 'reasonable limitation' of the equality right, in accordance with the general limitation provision afforded in section 1 of the Charter.

Even in the United States, where there has been overwhelming opposition to reading the Constitution in accordance with positive guarantees of social protection, following the success of *Brown v Board of Education of Topeka*,[134] courts have held legislative provisions that deny basic assistance and welfare services to women[135] and members of various religious communities[136] to be unconstitutional.[137] Furthermore, the widely formulated Fourteenth Amendment was successfully relied on before the Supreme Court in *Plyler v Doe*[138] to challenge the constitutionality of a Texas statute that withheld state funds and permitted local district authorities to refuse school enrolment to the children of illegal aliens, thereby harming their educational opportunities. However, although *Plyler v Doe* has been celebrated for the Court's view that discrimination of that kind would lead to the creation of a 'sub-class of illiterates'; that the statute was irrational; and that it did not further a substantial goal of the state, the case has also been seen to reflect the partisanship of the US Supreme Court at that particular time. A more deferential stance has more usually been taken by the Court when reviewing welfare policy choices by legislatures, where generally only a minimum standard of rationality is required.[139]

Nevertheless, much earlier, in *Goldberg v Kelly*,[140] at the highwater mark of the due process movement in the United States, the Supreme Court held that the Fourteenth Amendment right to due process of law required that welfare recipients be afforded evidentiary hearings to determine their eligibility before their benefits were terminated by welfare authorities. Since then, many examples can be found in which the Supreme Court has been prepared to shape the broadly conceived right to due process enshrined in the Fourteenth Amendment to

---

[134] 347 US 483 (1954). In *Brown* (discussed at note 97 above) and a series of cases that followed during the Warren era, by holding that educational programmes which were blatantly racist were in breach of the Fourteenth Amendment, the Supreme Court is said to have given birth to substantive concept of 'equal opportunity'.

[135] See for example *Turner v Dept of Employment Security* (1975) 423 US 508; and *New Jersey Welfare Rights v Cahill* (1973) 411 US 619.

[136] See *Thomas v Review Board of Indiana Employment Security Div*, 450 US 707 (1981).

[137] This can be contrasted in subsequent cases. However, much of the early activity in the area of economic relations involved striking down laws deemed to violate the principle of equal opportunity in the context of pension rights for men and women.

[138] 457 US 202 (1982), 242 and 230.

[139] See LH Tribe, *American Constitutional Law*, 2nd edn (Mineola, NY, Foundation Press, 1988) 1439–51.

[140] 397 US 245 (1970).

ensure that, for example, administrative laws governing salaries and pension scales respect basic norms of non-discrimination and proportionality.[141]

We have already noted the extent of controversy in Canada about the potential to derive a positive right to medical care, welfare or social assistance from the right to life guarantee in section 7 of the Canadian Charter of Fundamental Rights. On one central point, however, there has been agreement, which mirrors developments in ECHR jurisprudence: in addition to the negative duty not to detract from a person's enjoyment of life, there is potential to fashion a social right from the amorphous positive right to the protection of a person's psychological and integrity in section 7.[142] Moreover, although in relation to section 7, such an approach, which is to combine social rights with other foundational rights such as the right to dignity or the maintenance of psychological and physical integrity, has met with limited success before the lower Canadian courts, the Supreme Court appears to have left the question open in *Gosselin*, where very diverse views were expressed on the issue.[143] However, more recently in *Chaoulli*,[144] although accepting that a provincial prohibition on private health insurance for medically necessary services threatened the claimant's life and security (in light of the potentially deleterious impact of waiting lists), every member of the Court expressed its reluctance to interpret section 7 in accordance with a positive obligation to provide adequate health care for those who can not afford private insurance.

To date, however, what has been dubbed the 'social rights plus' approach to human rights has been most creatively developed by the Indian Supreme Court, which has responsibility to ensure that the state in its legislative capacity applies a set of social and economic objectives contained in Directive Principles of State Policy, which are aimed at securing social justice and the meeting of needs, including education, public health and decent working conditions.[145] Thus, although it has been provided in the Constitution that the Directive Principles do not to confer individual rights and that they are unenforceable by courts, the Indian Supreme Court has accorded them primary importance in interpreting the scope and content of such legally enforceable fundamental rights as the right to life contained in Part III of the Indian Constitution. Accordingly, what appears at first sight to be a form of negative protection, not to be deprived of the right to life in Article 21, has been interpreted to include the right to live in human dignity—and all that it implies, namely 'the bare necessities of life such as adequate nutrition, clothing and shelter and facilities for reading, writing and

---

[141] For example, see *Los Angeles v Manhart* (1978) 435 US 702; and *Frontiero v Richardson* (1973) 411 US 677.

[142] See generally chapter 2 below.

[143] *Gosselin v Quebec (Attorney General)* (note 55 above). *Gosselin* involved a challenge to the inadequacy of a lower rate of social assistance for younger recipients, classed as 'employable'. See also *Chaoulli v Quebec (Attorney General)* [2005] SCC 35. For a robust critique of the decision, see King (note 55 above) 631.

[144] [2005] SCC 35.

[145] See Part IV of the Indian Constitution.

expressing oneself and in diverse forms, freely mixing and commingling with fellow human beings'.[146] Moreover, although the majority of such cases have stopped short of the imposition of mandatory orders to provide basic necessities to the most vulnerable individuals in need, important protection has been afforded against the threatened withdrawal or deprivation of socio-economic benefits, by requiring the establishment of just and fair procedures in law.

No attempt has been made in this preliminary account to address the extent to which constitutional drafting, cultural factors or indeed the political complexion of courts may have contributed to what in some cases may have been uncharacteristically protective rulings. However, it is important before proceeding to emphasise that although there may be greater scope for the protection of socio-economic rights in liberal constitutions drawn up since the end of World War II than in the 200-year-old US constitution, diversity in the drafting of substantive rights which have typically been enshrined in constitutional democracies since the end of World War II, cannot be overlooked when determining the potential for protecting socio-economic rights through the traditional canon of civil and political rights. Thus, for example, by contrast with Article 14 ECHR, the equality provision under section 15 of the Canadian Charter spells out that every individual has a right to equal benefit and protection of the law without discrimination and, in particular, without discrimination based on race, national or ethnic origin, colour, religion, sex, age, mental or physical disability.[147]

C. The Dedicated Pursuit of Social Justice: The South African Model

South Africa in part shares with the United Kingdom a common law legal system. Thus, courts in the United Kingdom have looked to the experiences of the South African Constitutional Court as a model of good practice in constitutional interpretation. However, little attention has been paid by UK courts to the judgements of the South African Constitutional Court in welfare needs disputes, on the assumption that, unlike the ECHR, the South African Constitution has carefully spelt out its uniquely dedicated commitments to social justice. Notwithstanding, elsewhere there has been growing interest (even among erstwhile US critics of positive legally enforceable socio-economic rights such as Sunstein) in the extent to which the careful structuring of rights and obligations in the South African Constitution have assisted the Constitutional Court in

---

[146] See *Francis Corallie Mullin v the Administrator, Union Territory of Delhi* (1981) 2 SCR 516, 529. For an account of the creative interpretation of the Right to Life under the Indian Constitution and the political activism of he Court through its development of public interest litigation, see Muralidhar (note 127 above) 239–45. For criticism of the cavalier role played by the Indian Court in a number of recent decisions, see generally Desai and Muralidhar (note 80 above) 172–3.

[147] Compare the narrower range of specified grounds (the absence of age, mental or physical disability) under Art 14 ECHR.

maintaining an appropriate constitutional distance when considering the 'reasonableness' of decisions concerning the allocation of scarce resources.[148]

It is well-known that the South African Constitution not only enumerates a range of protected socio-economic rights, but is said to differ from traditional liberal models in that it is 'transformative': it does not simply place limits on the exercise of collective power but requires collective power to *advance* ideals of freedom, equality, dignity and social justice.[149] Thus, in terms of content, the most significant aspect of the Constitution to set it apart from traditional liberal models is a *positive requirement*, expressed at various points, that collective state power must be exercised in accordance with the ideals of the Constitution, rather than predominantly in accordance with a set of negative restraints. Accordingly, whereas section 2 requires the state to implement or 'fulfil' its constitutional duties, section 7(2) requires it to 'respect, protect, promote and fulfil rights'.[150] Furthermore, the enumerated socio-economic entitlements have been expressed in terms of positive state obligations to take 'reasonable legislative and other measures to realise rights within their available resources'.[151] For example, under sections 26 and 27 respectively, the state is required to take 'reasonable legislative measures' to realise the right 'to have access to adequate housing' and the right to have access to health care services', including 'reproductive services', 'sufficient food' and 'social security'.[152]

The enumerated socio-economic rights in the South African Constitution not only provide a framework for evaluating the decision-making functions of the legislature, executive and other administrators, but also allow for the reasonable enactment of procedural and substantive rights to socio-economic entitlements such as social assistance for individuals who fall within a defined and deserving class.[153] Therefore, as Danie Brand has commented, the formulation

---

[148] See generally Sunstein (2001b) (note 106 above).

[149] See generally D Brand, 'Introduction to Socio-economic Rights in the South African Constitution' in D Brand and C Heyns (eds), *Socio-economic Rights in South Africa* (Pretoria, Pretoria University Law Press, 2005) 1–56. See also K Klare, 'Legal Culture and Transformative Constitutionalism' (1998) 14 *South African Journal of Human Rights* 146, 151–6.

[150] S 7(2): 'The state must respect, protect, promote and fulfil the rights in the Bill of Rights.' At a general level these different types of obligation correspond to Shue's typology. For closer analysis of the distinction between the duty to promote and to fulfil, see S Liebenberg, 'The Interpretation of Socio-economic Rights' in S Woolman, et al (eds), *Constitutional Law of South Africa*, 2nd edn (Landsdowne, Juta, 2002) ch 33, 25; G Budlender, 'Justiciability of Socio-economic Rights: Some South African Experiences' in YP Ghai and J Cottrell (eds), *Economic and Social Rights in Practice: The Role of Judges in Implementing Economic, Social and Cultural Rights* (London, Interights, 2004) 33, 37.

[151] Liebenberg has viewed the 'within available resources' qualification as a double-edged provision. On one hand, it allows the state to attribute its failure to realise a socio-economic right to budgetary constraints; on the other, it imposes an obligation on the state to make resources available for the realisation of a right. See Liebenberg (2002) (*ibid*) 44.

[152] Among the enumerated socio-economic rights in ss 24–7 (environment, property, housing, health care, food, water and social security), s 26(2) (housing) provides that the state must take reasonable and other legislative measures within its available resources to achieve the progressive realisation of the rights.

[153] S 27(1) provides: 'Everyone has the right to have access to (a) health care services including reproductive health care; (b) sufficient food and water; and (c) social security including, if they are unable to support themselves and their dependents, appropriate social assistance.'

of socio-entitlements in the Constitution, which are more concrete and clearly defined than the general commitments of other modern constitutions, together with corresponding legislative socio-economic entitlements, offer a promising route to the attainment of public resources.[154] Thus, the author suggests that when placed under scrutiny, legislative individual entitlements that correspond to specified categories are more likely to be robustly interpreted by courts who are 'not to the same extent confronted with the concerns of separation of powers, institutional legitimacy and technical competency that have so directly shaped and limited their constitutional socio-economic rights jurisprudence'.[155] Moreover, since individual socio-economic entitlements in South Africa have the advantage of constitutional protection, by contrast with similar legally enforceable statutory entitlements, for example in Nordic jurisdictions,[156] they are unlikely to fall prey to interference by the legislature if there is a change in political climate following their enactment.[157]

Rights in the South African Constitution have been formulated in three different ways, each of which requires different responses from the courts. The first type has been formulated as a set of entrenched 'basic' rights, which, by contrast with rights in the ICESCR,[158] are not constrained by reference to programmatic realisation or the availability of resources.[159] By contrast, however, in respect of the second type of rights, which includes the majority of specific socio-economic rights (access to adequate housing, health care, food, water and social security), the state is 'required to take *reasonable* legislative and other measures, within its available resources to achieve the progressive realisation of the rights'.[160] However, there is also a third category in which rights have been negatively formulated, prohibiting the state from interfering with the enjoyment of the other rights. Thus, for example, in section 26 (the right to housing) the state is directly prohibited from evicting people from their homes 'without an order of the court made after considering all the relevant circumstances',[161] and in section 27 there

---

[154] See Brand (2005) (note 149 above) 12–16.

[155] *Ibid*, 14–16.

[156] *Ibid*, 15.

[157] *Ibid*, 15. See also LA Williams, 'Welfare and Legal Entitlements: The Social Roots of Poverty' in D Kairys (ed), *The Politics of Law: A Progressive Critique* (New York, Basic Books, 1998) 569; and WH Simon, 'Rights and Redistribution in the Welfare System' (1986) 38 *Stanford Law Review* 1431, 1467–77, where the authors describe cutbacks in statutory welfare rights as a result of altered public perceptions about the sustained viability of comprehensive welfare and the erosion of the idea that the state should provide for basic needs. Notably, these arguments could be applied with equal force to legislative changes that are gradually and surreptitiously eroding the principle of equal access to health care on the basis of need in the United Kingdom.

[158] Art (2)(1) ICESCR sets out the nature of state party obligations.

[159] This category consists of children's socio-economic rights to basic nutrition, shelter, health services and social services (s 28(1)(c)); the right of everyone to basic education, including adult basic education (s 29(1)(c)); and the socio-economic rights of detained persons, which require states to provide 'conditions of detention that are consistent with human dignity, including at least exercise and the provision of state expense, of adequate accommodation, nutrition, reading material, land and medical treatment' (s 35 (2)(e)).

[160] Emphasis added. See ss 26(2) and 27(2).

[161] See s 26(3).

is a negatively framed right 'prohibiting the refusal of emergency medical treatment'.[162] Finally, all of the rights (civil and political, socio-economic and cultural) are subject to a general limitations clause. Thus, the Constitution provides that any limitation to a right must be in terms of law of general application and is only 'permissible to the extent that the limitation is *reasonable and justifiable in an open and democratic society based on human dignity equality and freedom*'.[163]

D. The Enforcement of Socio-economic Rights: Cooperative Dialogue in the South African Constitutional Court?

The Constitution of the Republic of South Africa 1996 has been described as 'different' from other constitutions in that it represents 'a decisive break from, and ringing rejection of that part of the past which is disgracefully racist, authoritarian and insular . . . and a vigorous identification of a commitment to a democratic universalistic caring and aspirationally egalitarian ethos'.[164] It is also unique for the inclusive consultative process that preceded its adoption, and has aroused curiosity and scepticism in equal measures for its entrenchment of a wide range of legally enforceable socio-economic rights, together with civil and political rights, in a single instrument, thereby breaking down traditional barriers and affording the potential for an unusual degree of judicial intervention in the resource allocation affairs of the executive.[165]

Nevertheless, in the certification case the Constitutional Court had already sounded a note of caution:

> These rights are at least to some extent justiciable . . . [M]any of the civil and political rights entrenched . . . will give rise to similar budgetary implications without compromising their justciability. The fact that socio-economic rights will almost inevitably give rise to such implications does not seem to us to be a bar to their justiciability. At the very minimum the socio-economic rights can be negatively protected from improper invasion.[166]

---

[162] S 27(3).

[163] S 36, emphasis added. This clause is similar to the general limitations clause in the Canadian Charter of Rights and Freedoms, which is discussed above. Similarly, under Art 4 ICESCR, state parties may subject the rights in the Convention 'only to such limitations as are determined by law only insofar as they may be compatible with the nature of these rights and solely for the purpose of promoting the general welfare in a democratic society'.

[164] *S v Makwanyame* (1995) 6 BCLR 665 (CC) [262] (Mohammed J).

[165] See generally D Brand, 'Socio-economic Rights and Courts in South Africa: Justiciability on a Sliding Scale' in Coomans (ed) (2006) (note 121 above) 207–36. See Davis for recent criticism of the Court's 'failure to impose additional policy burdens on government or exercise supervision over the executive by sticking to a small legal repertoire' (ss 26, 27 and 28); failing adequately to 'break down the division between negative and positive rights' or to 'adopt different remedies': DM Davis, 'Adjudicating the Scoio-economic Rights in the South African Constitution: Towards "Deference Lite"?' (2006) 22(2) *South African Journal of Human Rights* 301–27.

[166] *Ex parte Chairman of the Constitutional Assembly: In re the Certification of the Constitution of the Republic of South Africa* (1996) (10) BCLR 1253 (CC) [78].

Since then, in four key decisions, the Constitutional Court has demonstrated not only its reliance on the tripartite structuring of state obligations in seeking to maintain an appropriate constitutional balance[167] but also creative use of strategically tailored remedial orders, in its efforts to stay outside the vexed arena of budgetary allocation, while reinforcing the Constitution's commitment to the promotion of social justice.[168]

The now familiar case of *Soobramooney v Minster of Health Kwa Zulu Natal*,[169] the first of these decisions, concerned a challenge by a patient against a hospital authority decision to refuse life-prolonging dialysis treatment, on grounds that his case fell outside established prioritisation criteria. The second case, *Government of the Republic of South Africa v Grootboom and Others*,[170] challenged the scope of the state's obligation under section 26(2) to make provision for emergency housing for homeless applicants and others in similar positions. The third case, *Minster of Health v Treatment Action Campaign*,[171] challenged inter alia the constitutionality of the state policy to limit the provision of Nevirapine (a drug to stop mother-to-child transmission of AIDS) to a restricted number of public health facilities. Finally, *Khosa v Minister of Social Development*[172] concerned a challenge against provisions of the Social Assistance Act 1992, which excluded people with permanent residence status from access to social assistance.

The idea of judicial restraint was certainly at the fore in *Soobramooney*, the first case in which the Constitutional Court considered the enforceability of the category of rights that are qualified by reference to resources. Relying on the distinction between rights subject to immediate fulfilment and those allowing for progressive realisation and resource constraints, the Court first decided that the patient's claim to receive dialysis lay outside the negatively framed right not to be refused 'emergency medical treatment' in section 27(3). Since the mandatory provision was directed at catastrophes, it could not be used to *require* provision of life-prolonging treatment for ongoing life-threatening conditions.[173] Instead, since it fell within the ambit of the positive right of 'access to health care services' in section 27(1), the scope of the state's duty was circumscribed by the 'progressive realisation within available resources' qualification afforded by section 27(2).

---

[167] Brand (2005) (note 149 above) has suggested that as a general point of strategy it is preferable in lower courts to characterise breaches of any of the socio-economic rights as negative rather than positive on grounds that courts will generally scrutinise breaches of negative duties imposed by socio-economic rights more strictly than they would failures to meet positive duties (26).

[168] S 38 determines that courts must provide 'appropriate relief' including a 'declaration of rights', while s 167 empowers courts to declare law or conduct inconsistent with the Constitution to be invalid and, more expansively, to provide any order that is 'just or equitable'.

[169] (1998) 1 SA 765 CC.

[170] Note 58 above.

[171] (2005) 5 SA 721 (CC).

[172] (2004) 6 SA 505.

[173] *Ibid*, [20–2].

Accordingly, the Court was clear that a large margin of discretion should be afforded not only to the provincial government responsible for establishing budgetary priorities, but also to hospital administrators at the forefront of 'difficult decisions' concerning resource allocation: 'a court will be slow to interfere with rational decisions taken in good faith by the political organs, and by medical authorities who have the responsibility of dealing with such matters'.[174] Instead, suggesting that the absence of *any* eligibility criteria would have afforded a more appropriate type of administrative challenge, the Court deemed the authority's eligibility criteria to be reasonable and to have been 'fairly and rationally' applied; it therefore refused to issue an order for the provision of dialysis.[175]

In *Grootboom* however, the Court took a more proactive stance, albeit issuing a form of declaration rather than mandatory order of enforcement, stating that the national housing programme was inconsistent with the right in section 26 of the Constitution, which affords access to adequate housing.[176] Although it was decided that there was no provision in national, provincial or local policy 'to rescue people in desperate need', the Constitution required measures to 'provide relief for people who have no access to land, no roof over their heads, and who are living in intolerable conditions or crisis situations'.[177] However, here again the court made it clear that it was not for the judiciary to second-guess the government on its housing policies, but rather to assess whether its measures represented 'reasonable' progress towards satisfying the housing rights of South Africans. Thus, in the structuring of its remedial orders, the court avoided direct intervention in the resource allocation functions of government: the first order enforced a settlement between the local authority and the squatters, giving the latter basic shelter and services such as sanitation and running water, while stressing that the judgment must not be seen as an approval of 'land invasion' in order to gain advantage in the allocation of resources. The second order declared that the state was obliged to 'devise and implement within its existing resources a comprehensive and coordinated programme progressively to realise the right of access to adequate housing'.[178]

By contrast, in *Treatment Action Campaign,* the Court's decision was, at least at first sight, more interventionist, since it issued a declaration that the inadequacy of the measures taken by the state to prevent the mother-to-child spread of AIDS constituted a breach of section 27 and accordingly directed the state to remedy its programme. Similarly, in *Khosa,* the Court took a robust stance, holding that the exclusion of certain permanent residents from access to statutory social assistance grants was inconsistent with the prohibition on

---

[174] (2004) 6 SA 505, [29].

[175] This approach echoes that used in administrative law disputes in the UK when courts are required to consider the reasonableness of hospital authority decisions to refuse services on grounds of scarce resources. See chapter 5 below.

[176] See s 26(1).

[177] *Grootboom* (note 58 above) [43].

[178] *Ibid,* [44].

unfair discrimination in section 9 of the Constitution (read together with the right of access to social assistance in section 27). Appropriate words were therefore read into the statute to remedy this defect.

Nevertheless, examination of all four cases reveals that the Constitutional Court achieved resolution with minimum scrutiny of the reasonableness of budgetary decisions or circumspectly avoided resource allocation issues altogether. In *Soobramooney*, for example, in accepting the authority's defence of limited resources without demur, the Court made no effort to scrutinise the central budget allocation or the manner of its use at provincial level.[179] Indeed in that case, rather than address the issue of available resources as a separate issue, the Court reasoned that issues of resources were already addressed in the Constitution by defining the reach of the specific rights.[180] Moreover, since fortuitously in *Grootboom* the wider issue before the Court was whether the state was under a duty to fulfil the right to make provision for people who have no access to land, there was no need for consideration of the availability of resources question required by section 26(2). Likewise in *Treatment Action Campaign,* insofar as the Court was asked to consider whether the provision of Nevirapine should be extended beyond pilot health centres to others with the necessary infrastructure, questions of resource allocation policy could be avoided, especially since the manufacturers had undertaken to provide the drug free of charge.[181]

By contrast, in the case of *Khosa*, budgetary issues could not altogether be avoided since the issue for the Court was the reasonableness of the state's defence that budgetary constraints justified the exclusion of the claimant group from access to a specific social security benefit under section 27(2).[182] Here again, however, although the Court was clear that the burden must be on the state generally to prove the non-availability of resources, the Court subsequently considered the reasonableness of the state defence without further examining the validity of the evidence on which it was based. Moreover, in respect of the primary argument in *Khosa* and the secondary argument in *Treatment Action Campaign* that the state was obliged to extend programmes to facilities that did not have the necessary infrastructure, the Court noticeably skirted around budgetary allocation issues by more firmly fastening on extraneous reasons to undermine the resource constraints argument and avoiding close scrutiny of the state's budgetary allocation at a macro-economic level.

Thus, in *Khosa*, relying on crude assessments of the projected costs of extending social assistance to 'permanent residents' by comparison with the overall social assistance budget, the Court concluded that far from breaking the camel's back, the additional burden on the state would be small in relative terms.[183] Further, in *Treatment Action Campaign*, inter alia lighting on the state's

---

[179] Brand (2005) (note 149 above) 52–3.
[180] *Ibid.*
[181] For discussion of these issues, see Brand and Heyns (ed) (note 149 above) 52–4.
[182] S 27(2): 'The state must take legislative and other measures within its available resources'.
[183] See Brand (2005) (note 149 above) 53.

argument that significant additional resources had already been allocated to the HIV pandemic, the Court took the view that pre-existing problems of resource constraints had now been satisfactorily removed.

Perhaps the reserved type of administrative law scrutiny that the Court has continued to emphasise, which is reminiscent of that in UK courts, was most clearly encapsulated in *Treatment Action Campaign*, where, rejecting the idea even of a minimum core content to the rights and reiterating that the courts are ill-suited to adjudicate upon issues where court orders could have multiple social and economic consequences, the Court stated:

> The Constitution contemplates rather a restrained and focused role for the courts, namely to require the state to take measures to meet its constitutional obligations and to subject the reasonableness of these measures to evaluation. Such determinations of reasonableness may in fact have budgetary implications but are not in themselves directed at rearranging budgets. In this way the judicial legislative and executive functions achieve appropriate constitutional balance.[184]

Nevertheless, as Brand has commented, the demarcation of the judicial and executive functions by a distinction between 'rearranging budgets and taking decisions that may have the consequences of rearranging budgets' may be 'something of a fiction'.[185] Brand argues that such a covert approach was amply demonstrated in *Khosa*, where in any event the *effect* of the decision was that 'the state has to allocate additional resources however relatively slight to an item which it was not minded to finance'.[186] Moreover, a similarly deferential approach to the exercise of the Court's powers has been detected by Brand in relation to what he describes as a 'shifting standard of reasonableness' when scrutinising legislative measures or administrative decisions in accordance with the qualification of 'available resources', in order to achieve the 'progressive realisation' of the rights. Thus, whereas in *Soobramooney* the Court applied a 'basic rationality and good faith' test, in *Grootboom* and *Treatment Action Campaign* a more stringent 'means–end effectiveness test' was applied, later superseded in *Khosa* by a more stringent proportionality test.[187]

Although the Court has not yet done so, it would be constitutionally appropriate in the determination of the reasonableness of legislative measures or the exercise of executive powers, for the Court to adjust the intensity of its scrutiny in accordance with it its own assessment of the core content of specified rights. However, Brand suggests that such factors as 'the position of claimants in society, the degree of deprivation complained of, the extent to which the breach of the right in question affects their dignity, or the extent to which the complaint

---

[184] *Treatment Action* (note 171 above) [38]. For a critique, see D Bilchitz, 'Right to Health and Access to HIV/AIDS Drug Treatment' (2003) 1(3) Int'l J of Constitutional Law 534–40.
[185] Brand (2005) (note 149 above) 43–4. See also Brand (2006) (note 165 above) 227–30.
[186] Brand (2005) (note 149 above) 54.
[187] *Ibid*, 43–4.

involves undetermined complex policy questions', or whether it also constitutes a breach of other protected rights, have instead been 'tacitly' significant.[188]

This is not the place for more detailed examination of the extent to which the South African Court has kept faith with its constitutional mandate in the socio-economic sphere. It is clear from this brief discussion, however, that despite the scope of that mandate, it has at times felt itself to be subject to the same kinds of tensions and constraints as in other common law jurisdictions such as the UK, where courts are called upon to scrutinise the reasonableness of resource allocation decisions in the area of socio-economic provision.

Some commentators have expressed frustration and disappointment at the Court's failure more openly to challenge or impose mandatory orders on the South African government, and to recognise the distributional implications of all constitutional rights. Thus, arguing that there is already a small but significant body of decisions of the Court that support the development of a 'more fused conception of rights', including the 'recognition that the concept of legality may impose positive obligations on the state',[189] Davis has recently criticised the Court's failure 'to impose additional policy burdens on government, or exercise supervision over the executive' by its adherence to a 'small legal repertoire' in sections 26, 27 and 28.[190] Further, he has argued that the Supreme Court has failed adequately to 'break down the division between negative and positive rights, or to 'adopt different remedies', claiming that there has been 'a judicial and academic retreat into administrative law with the occasional, mechanistic application of international law'.[191]

Other commentators have been less critical. Accepting the pragmatic concern of the Constitutional Court that it should not be criticised for pre-empting the prerogatives of a government elected under proportional representation, strategists such as Brand have suggested that through its development of a sliding scale of deference, the Constitutional Court has arrived, albeit covertly and gradually, at a number of morally defensible and practically feasible decisions that are consistent with the advancement of social justice in South Africa.[192]

III. CONCLUSION

The purpose of this chapter has been to provide a historical, theoretical and legal framework for subsequent analysis of the justiciability of socio-economic rights in UK courts. Although traditional doubts about the amenability of socio-economic rights to adjudication and enforcement persist, it is well known that

---

[188] *Ibid*, 55.
[189] See Davis (note 165 above) 301–27. See also the Comment to the *Treatment Action Campaign* case (note 184 above).
[190] Davis (note 165 above) 301.
[191] *Ibid*.
[192] See for example Brand (2006) (note 165 above).

in common law jurisdictions such as the United States and, more recently, Canada, courts have sporadically afforded protection to socio-economic rights through the interpretation of equality provisions or due process clauses in the traditional canon of civil and political rights. However, critics have frequently objected that in such cases, socio-political and cultural factors—or indeed the political complexion of courts—have resulted in inappropriately protective or, conversely, reactionary rulings that flout the intention of the constitution's drafters. Thus, in addition to the potential to develop principles of equality and respect for human dignity that are consistent with welfarist conceptions of the social democratic state, attention has increasingly focused on the potential for the principled adjudication and enforcement of socio-economic rights through the tailoring of appropriately drafted constitutional provisions, as in South Africa.

In the United Kingdom, debate about the nature and limits of constitutional review has traditionally been conducted against the backdrop of American social and political history and theories of deliberative democracy, which has informed the work of leading American political theorists writing at the end of the twentieth century. However, since the enactment of the HRA in 1998, students of English public law have also been confronted with their own more immediate questions about the boundaries of constitutional review in relation to the ECHR, which was drafted in a very different context, at a very different period of social history in Europe at the end of World War II. Thus, one of the aims of this chapter has been to provide a thematic background for discussion in the following chapters about the novel powers of UK courts in the exercise of constitutional review, and to prepare the ground for discussion about the extent to which values enshrined in an old-fashioned instrument such as the ECHR can be called into play to protect individuals from threats to fundamental human rights arising in the socio-economic sphere.

Thus, we have not only sought to demonstrate the weakness of the positive–negative dichotomy as a means of regulating the limits of judicial intervention in sensitive socio-economic disputes of the kind at issue, but also emphasised throughout the chapter the need to moderate the remedial consequences of all human rights violations in accordance with a range of considerations, including the extent to which resources are implicated in their satisfaction and the type of action necessary to protect the rights.

2

The Regional Protection of
Socio-economic Rights: Europe

I. INTRODUCTION

THIS CHAPTER IS concerned with the protection of fundamental rights in the European region. Its purpose is to highlight developments in European Convention on Human Rights (ECHR) jurisprudence that are relevant to our subsequent evaluation of the role of courts in disputes over access to health and welfare services in English administrative law. The chapter demonstrates the extent to which the development of a jurisprudence of positive obligations in the ECHR rights has increased the likelihood of socio-economic challenges in domestic law following the enactment of the Human Rights Act (HRA) 1998; and the way in which the Strasbourg organs have defined the limits of their legitimate intervention in resource allocation disputes of the kind with which we are concerned.

Our primary concern here is thus with Strasbourg jurisprudence. However, developments in the European Union, including the expansion of the internal market in the area of social provision, and the role of the European Court of Justice (ECJ) in the protection of fundamental rights have increased the impact of EU law not only on domestic policy issues, but also on the role of domestic courts in disputes over access to socio-economic entitlements. Thus, the final part of this chapter provides a brief outline of EU legal developments insofar as they have import for our discussion of substantive case law and the role of UK courts in subsequent chapters of the book.

II. THE EUROPEAN CONVENTION ON HUMAN RIGHTS 1950

A. Background and Context: The Negative–Positive Dichotomy Revisited

We have seen in chapter one above that during the establishment of a human rights framework for the European region, the divide between civil and political rights on the one hand and socio-economic rights on the other hand was strategically maintained. Thus, while a complex system of adjudication and enforcement was afforded under the ECHR,[1] no enforcement machinery was provided under its sister treaty, the European Social Charter (ESC) 1961 or the revised ESC 1996.[2] Moreover, although the opening paragraphs of the preamble to the ECHR obliquely refer to the Universal Declaration of Human Rights (UDHR) 1948, 'which is aimed at securing the universal and effective recognition of the rights therein declared', there is little ostensible protection of socioeconomic rights in the ECHR itself.[3] Nevertheless, over time, a dynamic approach to the interpretation of ECHR rights has opened avenues for the protection of vulnerable individuals in respect of claims to receive a minimum standard of living consistent with their basic human dignity and the maintenance of their psychological and physical integrity.

In the aftermath of World War II, the concern of the Council of Europe was the drafting of a legally binding Convention that would safeguard individuals against interference with their fundamental human rights, in the types of circumstances in which they had recently been so horrendously violated. State parties were enjoined to desist from unlawful killings, torture and slavery and not to interfere with free speech or fair trials.[4] Thus, the attention of the drafters was more immediately focused on protection against negative interference with fundamental human rights than on the positive actions that might be necessary to safeguard rights. However, in its dynamic interpretation of ECHR rights, the Strasbourg organs have progressively recognised that in order to 'to secure to everyone within their jurisdiction the rights and freedoms set out in the Convention,' as required by Article 1, negative 'hands-off restraint' by state par-

---

[1] The Convention has strong enforcement mechanisms, allowing for both individual and state applications. Under Art 24, any party can bring an application alleging a breach of the Convention by another party simply on the basis that each has ratified the Convention. Under Art 25 (more important in practice), a party may make a declaration accepting the right of an individual, regardless of nationality, who claims to be a victim of a breach of the Convention, to bring an application against it. Following restructuring under Protocol 11 ('Restructuring the Control Machinery Established Thereby', European Treaty Series No 155) (Strasbourg, 1994)), the Commission and the original Court have been replaced by a new full-time body, which began to operate fully in 1998. See further L Betton and N Grief, *EU Law and Human Rights* (London, Longman, 1998) 35–8.

[2] By comparison with the preamble to the ECHR, the preamble to the ESC 1961 is vague, stating: 'the Contracting Parties are resolved to make every effort to improve the standard of living and to promote the social well being of their populations by means of appropriate institutions and actions'. For the contents of the ESC 1961 and the Revised ESC 1996, see Betton and Grief (*ibid*) 42–52. The provisions of the ESC, by contrast with rights in the ECHR, cannot be invoked by individuals or NGOs in national courts or before international treaty bodies. The supervisory mechanism consists of a reporting procedure, a 'mixture of quasi-judicial and political supervision' (Arts 21–9 ESC). There have been sustained criticisms of the Charter's composition and reporting systems despite some improvements since 1991. See Betton and Grief (*ibid*). See further D Harris, *The European Social Charter*, 8th edn (Charlottesville, University of Virginia Press, 1984).

[3] See Art 1, Protocol 1 ('Protection of Property'); Art 2, Protocol 1 ('Right to Education').

[4] See generally L Lester and D Pannick, *Human Rights Law and Practice*, 2nd edn (Butterworths, London, 2004). For a recent account of the negotiating process and the extent to which individual drafters, from the time of the conception of the International Bill of Rights, anticipated the looming problems of universality and sought to accommodate them, see also MA Glendon, 'Reflections on the UDHR' (1998) *First Things* 23–7, available at http://www.leaderu.com/?ftissues/?ft9804/?articles/?udhr.html.

ties is not enough: the protection of ECHR rights increasingly requires positive action as well.[5]

Thus, during the past three decades, whether complaints have been founded on allegations of interference (so-called negative breach) or of failure to take protective or preventive measures to safeguard rights (positive breach), a growing range of procedural and substantive affirmative duties have been recognised as necessary to ensure the protection of the ECHR rights against interference by state agents and third parties. Moreover, affirmative action has not only been deemed necessary in high-profile sensitive contexts where civil and political freedoms are often most visibly at risk, such as national security,[6] prison detention[7] and the administration of justice;[8] the Strasbourg organs have indicated a readiness, albeit fluctuating, to accept that the protection of ECHR rights demands positive action by state parties in further areas of governmental responsibility, including environmental protection, child protection, public health and, very tentatively, the securing of welfare benefits.

As a case in point, the European Court of Human Rights (ECtHR) has recognised that positive procedural measures may be necessary to protect individuals against the hazards of environmental pollution under Article 8.[9] Moreover, drawing on the core values of respect for human dignity and psychological and physical integrity, which are recognised as immanent in all ECHR rights,[10] the Court has identified an embryonic duty to make public health provision under Article 2 (the right to life);[11] to provide appropriate medical welfare provision for vulnerable individuals in the care of the state under Article 3 (freedom from torture); and in a small number of cases, to ensure access to welfare provision, even in the form of shelter, for vulnerable disabled applicants under Article 8 (the right to respect for private and family life).[12]

In chapter one above it was demonstrated that protection of socio-economic rights has often been achieved in domestic jurisdictions through the application of due process or non-discrimination provisions or through principles of

---

[5] For a review of positive obligations under the Convention, see A Mowbray, *The Development of Positive Obligations under the European Convention on Human Rights by the European Court of Human Rights* (Oxford, Hart, 2004).

[6] For example, to undertake investigations into killings by the security forces in Turkey (*McCann v United Kingdom* A.324 (1995), (1996) 21 EHRR 97); or to provide police protection for the exercise of rights of association or lawful assembly (*Plattform 'Artze fur das Leben' v Austria* A.139 (1988), (1990) 12 EHRR 1).

[7] To provide suitable conditions of detention to prisoners (*Dougoz v Greece* CEDH 2000-II 6.03.2002, (2002) 34 EHRR 330; *Peers v Greece*, CEDH 2001-III 16.04.2002, Judgment of 19 April 2001, (2001) 33 EHRR 1192).

[8] The administration of justice (*Osman v United Kingdom* 1998-VIII no 95, (2000) 29 EHRR 245).

[9] *Guerra v Italy* (1998) 26 EHRR 359; and *Lopez Ostra v Spain* (1995) 20 EHRR 277.

[10] See for example *Christina Goodwin v United Kingdom* (2002) 35 EHRR 399, in which the Court noted at para 90 that 'the very essence of the Convention is human dignity . . .'.

[11] *LCB v United Kingdom* (1998) 27 EHRR 212; and *Cyprus v Turkey* (2002) 35 EHRR 731.

[12] *Botta v Italy* (1998) 26 EHRR 241; and *Marzari v Italy* ECHR Ct Admissibility Decision 04/05/1999, (1999) 28 EHRR CD 175.

reasonableness and proportionality in public administrative law.[13] This has similarly occurred under the ECHR. Thus, despite well-established limits to the non-discrimination provision in Article 14, it has been relied on in conjunction with Article 1, Protocol 1 ECHR and with Article 8 ECHR to afford protection in socio-economic disputes.[14] Moreover, as has occasionally happened under Article 26 of the International Covenant on Civil and Political Rights (ICCPR) 1966, the so-called fair trial clause in Article 6 ECHR has been used to provide protection in socio-economic disputes.[15]

Since the incorporation of ECHR rights in the United Kingdom through the HRA, there has been intense controversy over a number of related issues: the extent to which, in light of developments in Strasbourg jurisprudence, the ECHR rights give rise to positive financial obligations in socio-economic or welfare needs contexts; the appropriate standard of scrutiny in ECHR disputes that require the review of executive or administrative decisions involving issues of resource allocation; the related question as to whether the margin of discretion afforded by the Strasbourg organs should be replicated in UK courts; and the extent to which the growing recognition of positive obligations in Strasbourg jurisprudence can be reconciled with a rigorous method of human rights adjudication, which has evolved in accordance with the primarily negative thrust of the Convention rights.

It is recognised that in addressing these questions, incremental developments in the Convention jurisprudence, together with the reluctance of the ECtHR to provide a coherent rationale for the imposition of positive obligations on member states in accordance with values enshrined in the sixty-year-old Convention, have made it difficult for UK courts to quantify, as Lord Hoffman put it in *Matthews v Ministry of Defence*,[16] *how much* protection is afforded to positive socio-economic rights. Nevertheless, since the HRA, UK courts are required, when relevant, to take account of the Strasbourg jurisprudence when determining the scope of ECHR rights. It is therefore with the Strasbourg side of the story that we first begin.

---

[13] For example, in *Goldberg v Kelly* 397 US 254 (1970) the Supreme Court held that the Fourteenth Amendment right to due process of law required that welfare participants should be afforded an evidentiary hearing to determine their eligibility, before benefits were peremptorily terminated by welfare authorities. But compare *Matthews v Eldridge* 424 US (1976).

[14] In *Thlimmenos v Greece* (2001) 31 EHRR 411 the Court reaffirmed that 'the right under Article 14 not to be discriminated against in the enjoyment of the rights guaranteed under the Convention is violated when States treat differently persons in analogous situations without providing an objective and reasonable justification . . .' (para 44). Likewise, the failure to take into account the 'significantly different' situations of individual persons without an objective and reasonable justification also amounts to a violation of Art 14.

[15] See generally M Scheinin, 'Economic and Social Rights as Legal Rights' in A Eide, C Krause and A Rosas (eds), *Economic, Social and Cultural Rights*, 2nd edn (London, Kluwer, 2001) 32–4. See also for example *Karakurt v Austria* CCPR/C/74/D/965/2000, 29 April 2002.

[16] [2003] UKHL 4. For further discussion of *Matthews*, see chapter 8 below.

B. Incremental Development of Positive Obligations in ECHR Rights

In the case of some ECHR rights, notably Article 5 (the right to freedom and security) and Article 6 (the right to a fair trial), the need for affirmative action is expressed in the text of the ECHR itself.[17] Thus, for example, Article 5(2) states that 'everyone who is arrested shall be informed promptly in a language which he understands of the reasons for the arrest and the nature of the charge'— thereby requiring interpreters to be available for non-native speakers.[18] Moreover, while Article 6(3)(c) requires that everyone charged with a criminal offence who has insufficient means to pay for legal assistance should be given it free, 'when the interests of justice so require', Article 6(3)(e) provides that a defendant 'who cannot understand or speak the language used in court' should also have 'the free assistance of an interpreter'.[19]

However, there are few instances when positive duties have been expressed directly in the text of the ECHR. Rather, they have been inferred, in accordance with an interpretative process whereby the Strasbourg organs have concluded that, even in the absence of an express obligation, it may be necessary, to read a positive element into the rights in order to afford their *effective* protection. Thus, despite the absence of any such affirmative duty, so long ago as 1979 the court decided, in *Golder v United Kingdom*,[20] that Article 6 ECHR should be read in accordance with a positive substantive obligation to provide legal assistance for the pursuit of civil claims.[21] Moreover, shortly after that decision, it was concluded in *Airey v Ireland*[22] that in specific circumstances, Article 6 should be read in accordance with a positive requirement for state parties to provide legal aid in civil hearings, despite the absence of such an express requirement in the text.

In the case of some rights, however—most notably Article 8—the words of the text have lent themselves to the inference of positive obligations. Thus, the flexible notion of 'respect' in Article 8(1)[23] has increasingly provided a springboard for the development of a wide range of procedural and substantive duties

[17] For an early discussion of the scope of positive obligations expressly mandated by the right to liberty and security in Art 5, see *De Wilde, Ooms and Versyp v Belgium* A.12 (1971), (1979–80) 1 EHRR 388. For positive obligations deemed to arise from the text of Art 6 (the right to a fair trial), see *Artico v Italy* A. 37 (1980), (1981) 7 EHRR 528.

[18] Art 5 provides: 'everyone has the right to liberty and security of person. No one shall be deprived of his liberty, save in the following cases and in accordance with a procedure prescribed by law'.

[19] Art 6(3)(c) provides that everyone charged with a criminal offence has the minimum right to 'defend himself in person or through legal assistance of his own choosing or, *if he has not sufficient means to pay for legal assistance, to be given it free when the interests of justice so require*' (emphasis added).

[20] (1979) 1 EHRR 524.

[21] (1979) 2 EHRR 305.

[22] A-32 (1979), (1979–80) 2 EHRR 305.

[23] Art 8(1) states: 'everyone has the right to respect for his private and family life, his home and his correspondence'.

in the ECHR. Indeed, over two decades ago it was recognised by the ECtHR in the case of *X and Y v the Netherlands* that 'although the positive notion of respect, in Article 8(1), is essentially that of protecting an individual against arbitrary interference by the public authorities, it does not merely compel the state to abstain from interference . . . but also imposes positive duties to protect and safeguard aspects of private and family life.'[24]

Since then, in conjunction with expansive interpretations of the substantive elements of Article 8 (private family life and home and correspondence), the Strasbourg organs have allowed the Janus-headed notion of 'respect' in Article 8(1) to act as a catalyst for the development of a wide range of positive obligations of a procedural[25] and substantive kind.[26] Thus, in complaints founded on allegations of interference with aspects of 'private life' (for example, investigation by the Ministry of Defence into the sexual orientation of services personnel) is challenged, the duty of 'respect' has supported the inference that compliance with Article 8 requires negative, 'hands-off' restraint by state parties.[27] By contrast, however, in cases involving state interference with family life (for example, when family members have been deported, or children have been taken into care), the duty of 'respect' has been no less apt to justify the conclusion that Article 8 gives rise to positive mandatory obligations to reunite family members.[28]

From the outset, however, the ECtHR has acknowledged that, so far as positive obligations are concerned, the notion of respect is not clear-cut. Thus, in *Abdulaziz v UK*,[29] a case concerning the reunion of an immigrant with his family, the ECtHR acknowledged:

> Having regard to the diversity of the practices followed and the situations obtaining in the Contracting States, the notion's requirements will vary considerably from case to case . . . in particular . . . in an area in which the Contracting Parties enjoy a wide

[24] (1986) 8 EHRR 235, in which the ECtHR unanimously found that the absence of appropriate provisions in Dutch criminal law to safeguard a mentally handicapped young person from serious sexual abuse by an adult constituted a breach of Art 8.

[25] See *Glazer v UK* [2000] 3 FCR 193, 208–9. The Court stated that 'positive obligations inherent in effective "respect" for family life may include . . . both the provision of a regulatory framework of adjudicatory and enforcement machinery protecting individuals' rights and the implementation, where appropriate, of specific steps' ((2001) 33 EHRR 1, para 63).

[26] For examples see *Marckx v Belgium* (1979) 2 EHRR 330, A. 31 (1979) (a duty to provide legal recognition of the family relationships between parents and their illegitimate children); and *Powell & Rayner v UK* A/172 (1990) 12 EHRR 355 (a duty to protect a person's home and family life from the negative interference of environmental pollution).

[27] *Smith and Grady v United Kingdom* (1999) 29 EHRR 493.

[28] The ECtHR has recognised a wide variety of situations in which states are under a positive obligation to introduce systems to preserve respect for family life. See the list identified by R Clayton and H Tomlinson, *The Law of Human Rights*, vol 1 (Oxford, Oxford University Press, 2000) 927 (para 13.118). For example, a state might be under an obligation to admit relatives of settled immigrants in order to develop family life. See *Gul v Switzerland* (1996) 22 EHRR 92. Such an obligation was also recently recognised by the ECtHR in *Sen v Netherlands* (2003) 36 EHRR 81.

[29] (1985) 7 EHRR 471. The applicants, who were permanently settled in the UK, alleged that their right to respect for private and family life was infringed because their husbands were not permitted to come and live with them.

margin of appreciation in determining the steps to be taken to ensure compliance with the Convention with due regard to the needs and resources of the community and individuals. . . . [The] extent of a state's obligation to admit to its territory relatives of settled immigrants will vary according to the particular circumstances of the persons involved.[30]

Although Article 8 has generated the widest range of affirmative procedural and substantive duties, it has been part of a much wider phenomenon in which positive duties have been recognised in the majority of rights. For example, the words of Article 2[31] also disclose both a positive 'protective' aspect and a negative injunction to refrain from intentional killing except in lawful circumstances.[32]

Osman v UK[33] provided the Court with its first opportunity to consider the scope of the positive protective element in Article 2(1). It involved a complaint concerning the failure of the UK police to prevent the applicant's death at the hands of a dangerous third party, a stalker whose life-threatening tendencies had on numerous occasions been reported to them.[34] In that case the primary question for the Court was the extent to which *failure* by the police to take appropriate operational measures to prevent criminal deaths at the hands of third parties could constitute a breach of Article 2, in cases where the authorities had some prior knowledge of the risk.

The ECtHR was clear that 'not every claimed risk to life could entail a Convention requirement to take operational measures to prevent the risk from materialising'.[35] It was also aware that the positive obligation under Article 2(1) must be 'interpreted in a way, which does not impose an impossible or disproportionate burden on authorities'.[36] Nevertheless, the Court reached the conclusion that, although there had been no infringement in the instant case, there could in principle be a violation of the positive injunction in Article 2(1) in circumstances where an applicant could show that 'the authorities did not do all that could reasonably be expected of them, to avoid a real and immediate risk to life of which they have or ought to have knowledge.'[37]

The case of *Osman v UK* has therefore not only been regarded as authority for the narrow proposition that in certain circumstances the state will be obliged to protect an individual whose life is at risk from the criminal acts of others. It

---

[30] Para 67.

[31] Art 2(1) provides: 'Everyone's right to life shall be protected by law. No one shall be deprived of life intentionally, save in the exception of a sentence of a court, following his conviction of a crime for which this penalty is provided by law.'

[32] *Soerig v the UK* (1989) 11 EHRR 439, para 88. See *Chahal v the UK* (1996) 23 EHRR 413.

[33] Note 8 above.

[34] It was accepted by the UK government that the positive aspect of Art 2(1) extends beyond a primary duty to put in place effective measures of deterrence in the criminal law, 'backed up by law enforcement machinery for the prevention suppression and sanctioning of breaches of such provisions' (para 115).

[35] *Osman v UK* (note 8 above) para 116.

[36] *Ibid.*

[37] *Ibid.*

is also widely regarded as laying down a more general principle that *failure* by public authorities (not just the police) to do all that could reasonably be expected of them in the protection of the lives of individuals of whose life-threatening circumstances they have real or constructive knowledge, may constitute a violation of the positive protective duty in Article 2.[38]

However, the Court has been slow to extend the *Osman* principle beyond the context of prison and police operations. Moreover, it is also notable that even in those contexts, infringements of the positive obligation in Article 2(1) have most frequently been found when there are unanswered questions about positive violations that may have contributed to deaths in custody. Indeed, in *Osman,* despite much evidence to the contrary, the Court was surprisingly satisfied that 'in light of all the circumstances' at the time of the killing, the authorities neither 'knew or ought to have known' of the existence of 'a real and immediate risk to life of which they had or ought to have knowledge'.[39]

Nevertheless, the Court has not entirely turned its back on the general principle in *Osman* that *preventive* measures may be necessary in cases where vulnerable individuals are in the care of the state. In the later case of *Paul and Audrey Edwards v the United Kingdom*[40] (a complaint involving failure by the UK prison authorities to prevent the death of the applicant's son at the hands of a violent prisoner diagnosed with schizophrenic symptoms), the Court considered that operational failures by the prison authorities, in conjunction with those of a range of other agencies, had cumulatively amounted to a violation of Article 2. Moreover, the recent willingness of the Court to accept that negligent failure to take appropriate safety measures at a rubbish tip in Turkey constituted a breach of the positive obligation in Article 2, continues to demonstrate the possibility of liability under Article 2 in further areas of governmental responsibility to include negligent omissions 'liable to give rise to a serious risk for life or various aspects of the right to life'.[41]

Turning to Article 3, there is little to associate its archetypically negative formulation with the imposition of positive obligations. Article 3 tersely provides that 'no one shall be subjected to torture or inhuman or degrading treatment or punishment'. However, during the past decade, the Court has concluded that state parties may be required to undertake a growing range of affirmative duties

---

[38] See for example *Oneryildiz v Turkey*, Judgment of 18 June 2002, [2002] ECHR 48939/99, (2004) 39 ECHR 12.

[39] *Osman v UK* (note 8 above) paras 116, 119–122. Nevertheless, in other jurisdictions, the principle of state liability for the criminal acts of third parties has since been successfully pursued in even more extreme circumstances than *Osman*. See for example *Mahmut Kaya v Turkey*, Judgment of 28 March 2000, CEDH 2000-III 28. Against a backdrop of an extremely volatile security situation and politically motivated killings, the Court determined, citing *Osman*, that Art 2 had been violated by the failure of the Turkish authorities to take effective measures to protect a doctor who, to the knowledge of the authorities, was at particular risk of falling victim to unlawful attacks by contra guerrillas.

[40] Judgment of 14 March 2002, (2002) 35 EHRR 487.

[41] *Oneryildiz v Turkey* (note 38 above) para 64. The opinion of the Divisional Court was endorsed by the Grand Chamber in November 2004.

in order to be Article 3 compliant. These have included duties to undertake investigations into the causes of maltreatment in detention;[42] to provide sufficient[43] and appropriate[44] conditions of detention; to provide adequate medical services to detainees;[45] and to take positive steps to protect children from degrading and inhuman treatment, suffered as a result of the acts or omissions of state agents or third parties.[46]

Moreover, the Court has not only concluded that preventive measures may be necessary to ensure that individuals *within their jurisdictions* are thus protected; it has also recognised that the positive duty in Article 3 extends to cases in which there is a real risk that a course of conduct might expose individuals to torture or inhuman treatment in other jurisdictions.[47] Uncertainty has remained, however, about the extent to which positive welfare obligations identified in the context of prison detention are applicable in other areas of governmental responsibility where individuals are deprived of liberty through mental illness, old-age or other infirmity.[48]

In *A v UK*[49] the Court first considered the extent of the positive obligation under Article 3 to protect individuals from abuse suffered at the hands of private parties, in a complaint involving the persistent beating of a six-year-old boy by his stepfather in a manner that by any standards appeared to go far beyond reasonable parental chastisement. Following his stepfather's acquittal of a charge of assault occasioning actual bodily harm, the applicant complained to Strasbourg, alleging inter alia that the failure of the UK government to protect him against such abuse constituted a breach of Article 3. The Court unanimously agreed with the European Commission of Human Rights finding that the persistent and serious maltreatment of the child amounted to conduct prohibited by Article 3.[50] Further, it was recognised by the Court and conceded by the UK government that there was a lacuna in the criminal law that failed adequately to protect children against treatment of the kind prohibited by Article 3. Thus, the Court concluded that 'in the circumstances of the case', there had been a violation of Article 3.

It may be concluded that the decision in *A* is authority for no more than the proposition that domestic criminal law must provide adequate deterrent

---

[42] As in the case of Art 2, the Court has held that the combined effects of Arts 1 and 3 is to require effective official investigation into credible allegations of serious ill treatment by state agents (*Assenov v Bulgaria* (1998) 28 EHRR).

[43] *Dougoz v Greece* (note 7 above); and *Peers v Greece* (note 7 above).

[44] *Price v United Kingdom*, Judgment of 10 July 2001, (2002) 34 EHRR 1285.

[45] *Ilhan v Turkey* (2002) 34 EHRR 36; and *Keenan v United Kingdom* (2001) 33 EHRR 913.

[46] *Z and Others v United Kingdom* (2002) 34 EHRR 97.

[47] *Chahal v United Kingdom* (1997) 23 EHRR 413; and *D v United Kingdom* (1997) 24 EHRR 423.

[48] For consideration of these questions in the United Kingdom, see in particular the comments of Sullivan J in the important case of *R (Bernard) v London Borough of Enfield* [2003] UKHRR] 148, paras 29–30, referred to in chapters 3 and 6 and discussed fully in chapter 5 below.

[49] (1999) 27 EHRR 61.

[50] Without determining whether the beatings amounted to 'torture', 'degrading or inhuman treatment' or 'punishment', all prohibited by Art 3.

measures to prevent abuse of children by third parties—in the instant case, by a clearer definition of what constitutes reasonable chastisement. Nevertheless, it was not only recalled that children and other vulnerable persons are entitled to effective protection in the law against breaches of their personal integrity by third parties; in finding a violation of Article 3, the ECtHR observed:

> [T]he obligation on the High Contracting Parties . . . to secure to everyone within their jurisdiction the rights and freedoms defined in the Convention, taken together with Article 3, requires states to take positive steps, to ensure that individuals within their jurisdictions are not subjected to conditions amounting to torture or inhuman and degrading treatment and punishment, including such ill treatment by private individuals.[51]

The broader principle in *A*—that failure to take preventive steps to protect vulnerable individuals from maltreatment at the hands of state agents or third parties—was subsequently endorsed by the Court in the case of *Z and Others v United Kingdom* (hereafter *Z*),[52] a complaint involving failure by a network of relevant authorities, including social services, to protect four children against prolonged abuse and neglect by their parents. Citing *Osman*,[53] the Court reasoned in *Z* that Article 3 obliges state parties 'to take reasonable steps' to prevent vulnerable persons from being subject to ill treatment that the relevant authorities 'had or ought to have had knowledge'.[54] In the instant case, reasonable steps should have been taken to effect the physical removal of the children from such protracted suffering. Thus, it follows that despite its negative formulation, compliance with Article 3, no less than in the case of Article 2, may require the undertaking of operational measures with far-reaching financial repercussions, to ensure the protection of vulnerable individuals for whom there is a real risk of maltreatment (of which the authorities ought to have had knowledge) at the hands of state agents or third parties.

This section is not the place to provide an examination of positive obligations required of state parties in relation to all the ECHR rights. However, by focusing on Articles 2, 3 and 8, we have sought to demonstrate two key aspects of the phenomenon of positive obligations in the ECHR: first, that positive steps may need to be taken by state parties themselves (whether to provide legal or institutional structures or resources) *to protect* an individual's ECHR rights; secondly, that it is no longer only the state that is capable of infringing the rights of others. Positive protective measures may be necessary to guarantee protection of core elements of the ECHR rights, whether violation is threatened by state agents or private third parties.

---

[51] *A v UK* (note 49 above) para 22.
[52] Note 46 above.
[53] Note 8 above.
[54] *Z v UK* (note 46 above) para 73.

C. Methodological Issues: Grafting a Jurisprudence of Positive Obligations onto the ECHR Rights

The framework of the ECHR discloses a dual purpose. In upholding the principle of democracy, it seeks to balance the rights of the individual in society against other public interests. At the same time, in accordance with the rule of law (see the Preamble), it seeks to ensure that the 'tyranny of the majority' is not allowed disproportionately to interfere with the rights of minorities in member states.

Thus, consistent with this duality of purpose, the Strasbourg organs have not only recognised that 'inherent in the framework of the Convention is a search for a fair balance between the demands of the whole community and the protection of fundamental rights',[55] but also sought to ensure that limitations on individual rights are imposed only if they are prescribed by law, intended to achieve a legitimate objective and necessary in a democratic society. In other words, infusing the Convention in its entirety is the concept of proportionality, which requires a judicial evaluation of whether state interference is 'necessary in a democratic society'. In practice, this requires that restrictions on rights must be justified by 'a legitimate aim' that is 'proportionate to the need at hand'—further interpreted in the case law as meaning a 'pressing social need'.[56]

In addition to general principles for determining the legitimacy of interference in the case of some rights, specific limits have been implied or, in the case of Articles 8–10, expressly provided in the Articles themselves. Thus, for example Article 8(2) provides:

> There shall be no interference by a public authority with the exercise of this right except such as is in accordance with the law and necessary in a democratic society, in the interests of national security, public safety or the economic well-being of the country, for the prevention of disorder or crime, for the protection of health or morals, for the protection of the rights and freedoms of others.

Therefore, in complaints founded on allegations of negative intrusion, a jurisprudential method has evolved, whereby once it has been demonstrated to the satisfaction of the court that a complaint falls within the ambit of a particular Convention right (the right is said then to be engaged), limitations and restrictions of the kind included in Articles 8–11 ECHR are applied in order to determine whether there has been a substantive violation.[57]

Thus, typically, in Article 8-based claims of state interference, the Court decides first whether the right in Article 8(1) encompasses a specific duty (for

---

[55] *Soering v United Kingdom* (1989) 11 EHRR 439, para 89.

[56] *Handyside v United Kingdom* (1979–80) 1 EHRR 737, para 48. For an overview of the limitations and restrictions on ECHR rights, see generally J Wadham, H Mountfield, and A Edmundson, *Blackstone's Guide to the Human Rights Act 1998*, 3rd edn (Oxford, OUP, 2003) 29–41.

[57] This format and wording is closely followed in Arts 9–11, although the restrictions, some of which are tailored to the rights, are different. For example, only Art 8(2) refers to the economic well-being of the country.

example, to involve natural parents in the decision-making process when children have been removed into care[58]), then whether there has been an interference with that right, before finally seeking a fair balance between the competing interests of the individual and the community, as required by the defensive precepts in Article 8(2). Once a duty has been recognised as falling within the scope of the right in Article 8(1), the state, as duty bearer, is required by Article 8(2) to show that interference with the complainant's right is 'in accordance with the law', 'necessary in a democratic society' and 'in the interests of . . . the economic well-being of the country . . . or for the protection of rights and freedom of others'.[59]

By this methodology, complainants have benefit of the rigorous enquiry afforded by Article 8(2), which finally seeks to determine whether the measure impugned is necessary in a democratic society. For example, where positive duties encompassed by Article 8 give rise to state expenditure, Article 8(2) affords an internal mechanism of appreciation, by which the Court must seek to balance the economic interests of the whole community and the rights and interests of others, with those of the individual complainant. Moreover, despite the wide margin that the Strasbourg organs have notionally allowed to state parties in matters of resource allocation (see below), in the case of *Lopez Ostra*,[60] which concerned the state's failure to protect the applicant against harm caused by toxic omissions from a privately owned chemical plant, it was firmly concluded that in this exercise of appreciation under Article 8(2), a mere incantation of scarce resources will not be enough.[61]

However, commentators have noted a difference in the treatment of Article 8 claims, depending on whether they have been framed as allegations of negative or positive breaches of state duties.[62] This is because, it is argued, in complaints framed as positive breaches of duty (failure to take action to protect the right), it is all too easy for the question of breach to be conflated with the logically prior question of the scope of the duty encompassed by Article 8(1).[63] It has therefore been observed that in complaints framed as positive breaches of duty, both parties may lose the benefit of the complex balancing exercise that has traditionally followed the preliminary enquiry, and which has marked the evolution of the ECHR as a sophisticated mechanism of differential rights adjudication.

Nevertheless, in *Powell and Rayner v UK*,[64] the Court was anxious to dispel such concerns. The applicants, who lived near Heathrow Airport, complained

---

[58] See for example *Johansen v Norway* (1997) 23 EHRR 33.

[59] *Ibid*, paras 78–95.

[60] Note 9 above.

[61] Since the applicant complained of the state's failure to protect her against a direct violation of her rights, the case of *Lopez Ostra* (note 9 above) was cast in terms of a negative interference.

[62] See C Warbrick, 'The Structure of Article 8' (1998) 1 EHRLR 32–44.

[63] See the remarks of Judge Wildhaber in *Stjerna v Finland* (1994) 24 EHRR 194, where it was recognised that it was difficult to address complaints founded on positive breaches of duty by means of the traditional methodological approach to determining whether there has been an intrusive violation of Art 8.

[64] Note 26 above.

that excessive noise from the Airport breached their right under Article 8 to respect for their private life and home. As a preliminary issue, the government questioned whether the complaint disclosed the necessary 'interference by a public authority', because Heathrow Airport and the traffic using it were not owned or controlled by the government or its agents. However, the Court was clear that, whether the case was analysed in terms of a positive state duty to take reasonable and appropriate measures to secure the applicant's rights under Article 8(1), or was framed in terms of 'an interference' by a public authority, the same approach should be applied. Thus, it was observed:

> [I]n both contexts, regard must be had to the fair balance that has to be struck, between the competing interests of the individual and the community as a whole; and in both contexts the State enjoys a certain margin of appreciation in determining the steps to be taken to ensure compliance with the Convention.[65]

Further, it was suggested that in complaints of positive breaches of duty involving state omissions, in striking a fair balance, the specific aims listed in Article 8(2) afford relevant and important guides to determining whether there has been infringement of Article 8.[66]

Similar concerns have been raised about the methodology in complaints of positive breaches of Article 3. It has been accepted that the absence of an express requirement for proportionate interference in Article 3 means that the right contained therein is an absolute or unqualified right, in the sense that once the prohibited interference has taken place, there is no room for executive judgement as to whether the interference was legitimate. However, it is also recognised that issues of proportionality may arise when, for example, it is argued, as in the case of *Pretty v UK*,[67] that a public authority such as the Director of Public Prosecutions is under an implied obligation to do something to avoid an incompatibility for which he is not directly responsible. In such instances and in the absence of balancing factors of the kind found in Article 8(2), how are courts to determine the limits of state liability?

In answer to that question, the Court in *Pretty v UK* endorsed the reasoning in the case of *Rees v UK*,[68] where it had been concluded, as in *Powell*,[69] that the defensive precepts in Article 8(2) are no less appropriate as yardsticks for determining the limits of state liability for positive breaches of duty under Article 3 ECHR. The Court furthermore held that:

> . . . while states may be absolutely forbidden to inflict the proscribed treatment on individuals within their jurisdictions, the steps appropriate to discharge a positive

---

[65] Para 41.

[66] *Ibid*.

[67] No 2346/02ECHR 2002-III, (2002) 35 EHRR 1.

[68] A.106 (1986), (1987) 9 EHRR 56. The applicant claimed that refusal by the UK government to allow her legally to alter her birth certificate so as to reflect her gender reassignment constituted a positive breach of her Art 8 right to respect for private life.

[69] Note 26 above.

obligation may be more judgemental, more prone to variation from state to state, more dependent on the opinion and beliefs of the people and less susceptible to any universal injunction.[70]

D. Reconciling the Development of Positive Obligations with the Negative Thrust of the ECHR

Recognition that positive action may be necessary to ensure that state parties and individuals conform to human rights standards embodied in the ECHR may be viewed as progress, from an individualised system of compensatory justice to an international regime that participates more widely in the monitoring and development of international human rights standards.[71] Nevertheless, for state parties, not only may the dynamic developments in ECHR jurisprudence that dictate the imposition of positive obligations in diverse areas of government responsibility be difficult to square with their understanding of the negative obligations that they had undertaken at the time of ratification; positive obligations in sensitive areas of policy such as immigration, national security or social provision, may also be in tension with dominant values and customs in individual member states.

Nevertheless, the ECtHR has declined to offer a unified theory to explain the expansion of affirmative duties in the ECHR rights.[72] In some cases, the identification of positive duties has been tersely explained by reference to an overriding obligation 'to ensure to everyone the rights and freedoms set out in the Convention'[73] or to ensure that rights guaranteed by the Convention are not merely 'theoretical and illusory' but 'practical and effective'.[74] In other cases, judicial creativity has been justified by reference to the general interpretative obligation to ensure that the 'the object and purpose' of the Convention are fulfilled.[75] Moreover, by reference to the Preamble, the Court has specified the 'maintenance and further realisation of human rights'; 'the protection of individual human rights; and the promotion of the ideals and values of a democratic society' as being among the Convention's objects.

Commentators have accepted the increased inference of affirmative duties as a necessary part of the effective protection of ECHR rights[76] or as a facet of the

---

[70] *Pretty v UK* (note 67 above) para 15.

[71] See A Clapham, *Human Rights in the Private Sphere*, (Clarendon, Oxford, 1993).

[72] *Plattform 'Arze fur das Leben' v Austria*, note 6 above.

[73] Art 1 ECHR.

[74] *Marckx v Belgium* (note 26 above).

[75] The Convention is an international treaty and as such should be interpreted in accordance with Arts 31–3 of the Vienna Convention on the Law of Treaties 1969, which provides in Art 31(1) that 'A treaty shall be interpreted in good faith, in accordance with the ordinary meaning to be given to the terms of the treaty, in their context and in light of its object and purpose.'

[76] See JG Merrils, *The Development of International Law by the European Court of Human Rights*, (Manchester, Manchester University Press, 1993) 102. See also R Singh, *The Future of Human Rights in the United Kingdom: Essays on Law and Practice* (Oxford, Hart, 1997) 54.

'dynamic interpretation of the Convention, in light of changing social and moral assumptions'.[77] However, there has been criticism of the ECtHR's reluctance to provide a theory by which to set clearer limits to the scope of positive obligations required of state parties.[78] Thus, while recognising that the principle of effectiveness justifies the inference of a limited range of affirmative duties in the ECHR rights, JG Merrills, in one of the earliest critiques, questioned the unpredictable development of positive obligations in what he described as a 'Convention concerned, not with what a state must do, but with what a state must not do'.[79] In a passage that echoes traditional objections to the inference of positive duties in the US Constitution,[80] Professor Merrills furthermore argued that the negative orientation of ECHR rights should, except in a small number of cases, inhibit the expansion of positive obligations by the ECtHR.

There is no doubt that the ECHR provides primarily a set of negative restraints on government action, which at the time of drafting were aimed at the protection of traditional civil and political freedoms. However, it is also clear that there is a profound difference between the nature of the ECHR and the US Constitution. Unlike the latter, the text of which is hostile to any form of positive state intrusion in the original constitutional settlement, the ECHR is an international Convention *dedicated to the protection* of human rights. Thus, not only is it recalled in the Preamble that the UDHR (the basis of the Convention) is aimed at 'securing the universal and effective recognition and observance of the rights declared therein' (thereby encompassing civil, political *and* socio-economic rights); under Article 1 ECHR, the general obligation on state parties is 'to secure to everyone in their jurisdiction the rights and freedoms defined in . . . the Convention'.

Therefore, despite its primarily negative orientation and its embodiment of traditional civil and political liberties, and by contrast with the US Constitution, the ECHR is primarily meant 'to safeguard human dignity, even in the sphere of individuals among themselves', rather than 'to safeguard individual freedom from over-mighty government'.[81] Once this proposition is accepted, however, it is for the Strasbourg institutions to identify the limits of such positive duties and to determine the extent to which they should be context-bound. Problematically, however, there has been a lack of coherent guidance.

---

[77] D Feldman, *Civil Liberties and Human Rights in England and Wales*, 2nd edn (Oxford, OUP, 2002).

[78] See for example Wadham, Mountfield and Edmundson (note 56 above) 25–6.

[79] Merrills (note 76 above) 103.

[80] See *DeShaney v Winebago Social Services Department* (1989) 489 US 189.

[81] See *X and Y v Netherlands*, A. 91 (1985), (1986) 8 EHRR 235. See also K Starmer, 'Positive Obligations under the Convention' in J Jowell and J Cooper (eds), *Understanding Human Rights Principles* (Oxford, Hart, 2001) 203.

E. Theoretical Justifications for Positive Obligations and the Problem of Resources

As we have seen in chapter one, the idea that the types of action necessary for the protection of human rights can be determined by their positive or negative orientation has long been discredited. Thus, recalling Shue's tripartite theory of obligations, we are reminded that in every right, there is a set or cluster of both positive and negative obligations and that 'what one cannot find in practice is a right that is fully honoured, or merely even adequately protected, only by nega-tive duties or positive duties'.[82] According to Shue:

> If one looks concretely at specific rights and the particular arrangements that it takes to defend or fulfil them, it always turns out in concrete cases to involve a mixed bag of actions or omissions . . .[83]

Of course, we have also seen in the international arena that reluctance to accept that affirmative duties may be necessary for the effective protection of human rights is related to the likelihood that financial consequences may fol-low. Thus, in questioning the unguarded expansion of positive obligations in ECHR rights, Merrills has pointed in particular to the dangers of their expan-sion in areas of social and economic policy. While conceding that governments that have signed the treaty may have understood that policies would have to be modified in some areas, he has argued that 'what a government may not bargain for, is to find itself put to considerable trouble and expense . . . as a result of an obligation to advance particular social or economic policies which it may not wholly support'.[84]

Only on rare occasions have the ECHR organs adopted an originalist stance to the interpretation of the treaty rights.[85] Instead, the ECtHR has continually affirmed its determination to treat the Convention as a living instrument that must adapt to the changing political and social mores of member states.[86] At the same time however, the Strasbourg organs have embraced a principle of general application in international law, that in sensitive areas of social policy, particu-larly those involving complex resource allocation issues, supervision by inter-national adjudicators should give way to state discretion in the enforcement of domestic laws.[87] Thus, the concept of the 'margin of appreciation' has been

---

[82] See H Shue, *Basic Rights: Subsistence, Affluence and US Foreign Policy*, 2nd edn (Princeton, Princeton University Press, 1996) 155.

[83] *Ibid.*

[84] Merrills (note 76 above) 106.

[85] *Marckx v Belgium*, note 26 above.

[86] *Tyrer v UK* A/26 (1979–80) 2 EHRR 1.

[87] See recently *Sentges v Netherlands*, Application No 27677/02, Judgment of 18 July 2003, ECtHR (Second Section), where the ECtHR starkly reaffirmed this principle. Finding the Applicant's claim to be 'manifestly unfounded', the ECtHR stated that 'regard must be had to the fair balance that has to be struck between the competing interests of the individual and of the com-munity as a whole and to the wide margin of appreciation enjoyed by States in this respect in deter-mining the steps to be taken to ensure compliance with the Convention. . . . This margin of

used to connote a principle of review that allows the standard of scrutiny to be determined in accordance with the complexity or sensitivity of the subject matter and the greater potential for appropriate decision-making by the national authorities themselves.[88] It has furthermore been used more broadly to refer to a general interpretative obligation by the Strasbourg organs to respect domestic cultural traditions and values when determining the meaning and scope of ECHR rights. In this context, it has been criticised as being vague and indeterminate.

There are two ways of viewing the margin of appreciation deployed in international law. For commentators and members of the ECtHR who emphasise the need to respect the diversity of values and different democratic traditions in member states, the margin of appreciation is a welcome concept. However, for those who applaud the development of the Court's role in promoting common values and standards of respect for human dignity in member states, the use of the doctrine to restrict the standard of review reflects an abnegation of the Court's primary duty to determine the proportionality of domestic governments' conduct.[89] Moreover, it is not always clear whether restraint by the Strasbourg organs has been exercised on grounds of international constitutional propriety, or whether a particular dispute has been regarded as inherently unsuitable for adjudication due to its subject matter or policy domain. Therefore, as we shall see, for UK courts and tribunals that are required to scrutinise public authority decisions for compatibility with ECHR rights, there is uncertainty about the application of the margin of appreciation in sensitive resource allocation disputes.

III. THE PROTECTION OF SOCIO-ECONOMIC RIGHTS IN THE ECHR

A. Developing Core Values in the ECHR Rights

With the exception of the First Protocol, the ECHR focuses almost entirely on the traditional canon of civil and political rights.[90] At first sight, it has little to say about the protection of freedoms from want and squalor or the promotion of 'social progress and better standards of life in larger freedom', which are aspired to in the Preamble to the UDHR. Nevertheless, so long ago as *Airey v Ireland*[91] the ECtHR recognised that there is some overlap between civil, political and socio-economic rights in the treaty. Human rights commentators

appreciation is even wider when, as in the present case, the issues involve an assessment of the priorities in the context of the allocation of limited State resources . . .'.

[88] See for example *Handyside*, note 52 above, paras 48–51.

[89] For a general critique of the doctrine, see P Mahoney, 'Marvellous Richness of Diversity or Invidious Cultural Relativism' (1998) 19 *Human Rights Law Journal* 1.

[90] Arts 1 and 2 of the First Protocol concern the 'Right to Property' and the 'Right to Education' respectively.

[91] Note 22 above.

therefore once optimistically considered the possibility that Article 2 might be developed by the Strasbourg organs to furnish a positive 'social right' (encompassing health treatment, shelter or a healthy environment) of the kind developed by the Indian Constitutional court.[92] Alternatively, it was suggested that the positive aspect of Article 2 might be fashioned into a general right to health treatment, of the kind enshrined in Article 11 of the European Social Charter.[93]

Nevertheless, an examination of the case law shows that during the past decade, in its interpretation of Article 2(1), the ECtHR has not moved far from an orthodox conception of 'life protection' that is aimed at protecting individuals against unlawful killings in the traditional contexts of national security and policing. Moreover, with the exception of the 'progressive' opinions of Judges Jambreck and Ward in *Guerra v Italy*,[94] there is little in the jurisprudence to suggest the willingness of the Court either to explore different aspects of the fundamental right to life, such as the psychological and physical integrity of claimants or the protection of human dignity, or to apply them in diverse areas of governmental responsibility. Thus, although the Court has confirmed the potential of Article 2 to protect against environmental hazards[95] and has found an infringement of Article 2 in the prison context, in circumstances where failure to protect did *not* result in death,[96] only in a small number of cases has the protection of Article 2(1) been extended to the public health or welfare arena.[97]

Significantly, however, creative developments of the kind proposed by the minority in *Guerra* have taken root in different quarters. Not only has the Court recognised that a stark injunction to protect human dignity, implicit in Article 3

[92] See generally D Harris, M O'Boyle and C Warbrick, *Law of the European Convention on Human Rights* (London, Butterworths, 1995) 41. See *X v Ireland* (1976) 7 DR 78, where the Commission's statement that Art 2(1) 'enjoins the state not only to refrain from taking life intentionally but also to safeguard life' encouraged expectations that Art 2 might provide the foundations of a positive social right.

[93] See Clayton and Tomlinson, note 28 above, 356, para 7.40.

[94] Note 9 above. Judge Jambrek expressed the view that 'protection of health and physical integrity was closely associated with the right to life' (387).

[95] In *Guerra* (note 9 above) the Court found it unnecessary to consider the alleged violation of the applicant's Art 2 rights due to the prior finding of a breach of the State's positive obligations under Art 8. The judgment in *Guerra* has since been applied in *Oneryildiz v Turkey* (note 38 above), in which the court explicitly acknowledged that 'that a violation of the right to life can be envisaged in relation to environmental issues . . .' (para 64).

[96] Although to the author's knowledge there have been no cases up to the time of writing that explicitly deal with this issue, it is clear from *Keenan v United Kingdom* (note 45 above) that the obligation under Art 2 upon prison authorities encompasses both the duty to take proportionate and reasonable steps to guard against the risk of death and injury suffered in custody, and that this 'obligation is particularly stringent where that individual dies' (para 90).

[97] See for example *Cyprus v Turkey* (note 11 above), considered by Mowbray as authority for the proposition that Art 2 may be invoked when a State 'fails to meet its own declared standard [of health care provisions] . . . in a life threatening case' and 'tantalisingly' to suggest that 'Article 2 may also require the provision of a minimum level of health by a member State.' Whilst this minimum level will vary from State to State due to the reluctance of judges to secondguess the allocation of scarce resources and the divergent economies of many Member States, Mowbray does suggest that the role of states will also extend to the regulation of private sector medical treatment providers. See *Calvelli and Ciglio v Italy*, Judgment of 17 January 2002, CEDH 2001-I; and Mowbray, note 5 above.

and immanent in all the ECHR rights, may require state parties to take positive steps to meet the health and welfare needs of vulnerable claimants; it has also recognised that the right of respect for physical and psychological integrity, which lies at the heart of the complex right in Article 8 ECHR, may give rise to positive obligations to meet the health and welfare needs of vulnerable claimants suffering from disabilities. Thus, notably, in complaints of failure to protect individual health and welfare interests, even though recognising that Article 2 is engaged, the Court has preferred to decide cases on the basis of Articles 3 or 8.

B. Article 2: A Right to Health Treatment?

The possibility that the Strasbourg organs might be prepared to fashion a general social right or an individual right to health treatment from Article 2(1) was first suggested by two well-known public health cases heard by the European Commission of Human Rights. In the first case, *X v Ireland*,[98] the parents of a severely disabled child claimed that their daughter had not been allowed free medical treatment by the state. The Commission accepted that the right to life was engaged by the case, although this question was in the event not pursued, on grounds that she had in fact received *some* medical care, and her life had not been endangered. Further, in *Association X v United Kingdom*,[99] which involved the administration of a voluntary vaccination scheme in which many children died, the Commission, although holding the complaint to be inadmissible on the facts, famously stated that Article 2 requires state parties not only 'to refrain from taking life *intentionally* but also to safeguard life'.[100]

Optimism was further fuelled by the later case of *LCB v UK*,[101] which involved a failure to warn the applicant or her father of environmental hazards to her health caused by activities of the state, or subsequently to monitor her health in light of those hazards.[102] The Court unanimously agreed that Article 2 was engaged in the case but, in the event, concluded that there had been no breach of the positive obligation in Article 2(1), particularly in light of the limited knowledge of the risks to her health available at the relevant time. Nevertheless, in principle the Court accepted in *LCB* that the positive obligation of state parties 'to take appropriate steps to safeguard the lives of those within its jurisdiction' would in some circumstances require the undertaking of procedural and

---

[98] Note 92 above.

[99] Application 7154/75 (1978) 14DR 31, E Comm HR.

[100] *Ibid*, para 32. It was decided that appropriate steps had been taken with a view to safe administration of the scheme.

[101] (1998) 27 EHRR 212.

[102] The applicant, whose father had been involved in atmospheric nuclear tests before her birth, was diagnosed with leukaemia at the age of four. Following a report that provided evidence of a high degree of cancer among children of parents involved in the nuclear test programme, she complained to Strasbourg, *inter alia*, on grounds that the failure to warn her parents of the risks of exposure or to monitor her health before the development of her illness constituted a breach of Art 2.

substantive measures, of precisely the kind that had been denied in the applicant's case.

Moreover, following *LCB*, the ECtHR seemed to establish the far-reaching principle in *Osman*[103] that 'it would be sufficient for an applicant to show that, "the authorities did not do all that could reasonably be expected of them, to avoid a real and immediate risk to life, of which they have or ought to have knowledge"'.[104] This raised further expectations that the positive aspect of Article 2 might be used to hold public authorities to account for failure to provide *appropriate* health services. Despite the promise of *Osman*, however, an examination of subsequent case law demonstrates that the Court has been slow to develop a positive right to health services under Article 2(1).[105]

Thus, although positive breaches of Article 2 have increasingly been found in cases where police or prison authorities failed to provide appropriate medical services to detainees who subsequently died in custody,[106] there have been very few complaints that have led to the conclusion that a failure by public authorities or private health agencies to take appropriate preventive health measures constituted an infringement of Article 2.[107]

Nevertheless, despite the reluctance of the ECtHR to intrude in national health care operations, it has not ruled out the possibility that the positive aspect of Article 2 might in future be relied on to facilitate access to public health services for individuals and groups that have been denied treatment that is made generally available to the rest of the population. Thus, in the recent interstate case of *Cyprus v Turkey*,[108] it was held that Article 2 was engaged by a series of complaints that the Turkish authorities in Northern Cyprus had failed to facilitate the receipt of adequate medical services by several hundred Greek Cypriots and Maronites remaining in the Northern region of Cyprus, though the services were made available to the population generally.

---

[103] Note 8 above. See also further discussion of the case above.

[104] *Osman* (note 8 above) para 116.

[105] In *Scialacqua v Italy*, Application 34151/96, (1998) 26 EHRR CD 164, the applicant's complaint of failure by the state to provide for the cost of unlisted medical treatment was judged by the Commission to be 'manifestly unfounded'. However, the Commission appeared to accept that Art 2 could be interpreted as imposing a positive obligation on state parties to cover the costs of medical treatment necessary to save life. Compare *Tavares v France*, Application 16593/90, (1991) EComm HR, where the wife of the applicant had died during childbirth. Her application was judged to be inadmissible on grounds that the hospital had followed all its established procedures. Also see *Erikson v Italy*, unreported, Application 37900/97, 26 Oct 1999, where it was suggested that the positive obligation to protect life 'includes the requirement for hospitals to have regulations for the protection of their patients' lives'.

[106] See *Keenan* (note 45 above). See also a series of detention cases in which states have breached their obligations under Art 2: *Velikova v Bulgaria,* Judgment of 18 May 2000, CEDH 2000-VI, in which the failure of the Bulgarian authorities to provide adequate medical treatment to a seriously injured detainee who subsequently died as a result of his injuries, contributed to the Court's conclusion that there had been a breach of Art 2; likewise, in *Anguelova v Bulgaria*, Judgment of 13 June 2002, CEDH 2002-IV, the Court unanimously found a breach of Art 2 on grounds that the authorities had failed to provide timely medical care to a seriously injured detainee.

[107] *Calvelli and Ciglio v Italy* (note 97 above).

[108] Note 11 above, para 36.

C. Article 3: Respect for Human Dignity

Violations of Article 3 have increasingly been recognised by the ECtHR in complaints of state failure to provide conditions of human existence that satisfy the fundamental right to respect for human dignity, which lies at the heart of the UDHR. Moreover, although a positive duty to meet the health and welfare needs of vulnerable individuals has most frequently been found in the context of prison or police custody, beyond those areas of governmental responsibility, it has also been recognised that failure to make social provision for vulnerable claimants suffering from disabilities may, in cases of sufficiently acute individual need, constitute infringement of Article 3.[109]

Like Article 2, Article 3 is one of the most fundamental provisions of the ECHR, a fact that is said to be reflected in its absolute formulation and non-derogable status: once there has been a direct interference with the right—that is, once the prohibited conduct has been directly inflicted—there can be no excuse of lawful interference. Early in the case law, a distinction was drawn by the Strasbourg organs between the types of conduct prohibited by Article 3. Thus, while torture stands apart as '*deliberate* inhuman treatment causing very serious and cruel suffering', 'inhuman treatment' has been characterised as that which causes 'intense physical and mental suffering' and 'degrading treatment' as that which 'arouses in the victim a feeling of fear anguish and inferiority capable of humiliating and debasing the victim and possibly breaking his or her physical or moral resistance'.[110] However, the Court has not always found it necessary to identify which type of maltreatment has been suffered, ether inhuman or degrading treatment/punishment, before reaching the conclusion that there has been a violation of Article 3.[111] Moreover, while it is notable that torture necessarily involves the deliberate infliction of suffering, inhuman and degrading treatment/punishment can be suffered without any intention to humiliate or debase.[112]

Clearly, however, not every type of indignity amounts to degrading or inhuman treatment within the meaning of Article 3. The yardstick is said to be 'a minimum level of severity', which is relative to the duration of the treatment, its physical and mental effects and, in some circumstances, the sex, age and state of health of the victim—a standard applied both in determining whether the treatment falls into the categories of inhuman or degrading, and in distinguishing

---

[109] *O'Rourke v United Kingdom*, Application No 39022/97 (unreported), Judgment of 26 June 2001, where the Court recognised that failure to provide shelter does not by itself amount to degrading or inhuman treatment but did not rule out the possibility that such a positive obligation might arise.

[110] *Ireland v United Kingdom* (1979–80) 2 EHRR 25.

[111] *A v United Kingdom* (note 49 above).

[112] See for example *Peers v Greece* (note 7 above). However, it should be noted that in *Price v United Kingdom* (note 44 above), the Court stated, 'In determining the amount of the award it has regard, inter alia, to the fact . . . that there was no intention to humiliate or debase the applicant' (para 34).

between those types of treatment and torture.[113] Moreover, it has recently been recognised by the Court that since the Convention is a living instrument, acts that have previously been regarded as inhuman treatment might in future be regarded as torture.[114]

In the recent case of *Pretty v UK*,[115] the Court had opportunity to consider the scope of the positive obligation to refrain from the types of maltreatment prohibited by Article 3. The question at issue was whether failure by the UK government to provide a lawful opportunity for assisted suicide, in circumstances of significant physical and mental suffering (experienced by a woman in the advanced stage of motor neurone disease), amounted to inhuman or degrading treatment within the meaning of Article 3. In the first instance, the Court was clear that it is impossible to cover every human condition that will engage Article 3 by a single definition. Nevertheless, highlighting the subjective experiential approach of previous case law, it concluded in summary that

> ill treatment prohibited by Article 3 is that which 'attains a minimum level of severity and involves actual bodily injury or intense physical or mental suffering' or which 'humiliates or debases an individual showing lack of respect for, or diminishing his or her human dignity' or 'arouses feelings of fear, anguish or inferiority capable of breaking an individual's moral and physical resistance'.[116]

The Court also recognised:

> The suffering which flows from naturally occurring illness, physical or mental, may be covered by Article 3 where it risks being exacerbated by treatment, *whether flowing from conditions of detention, expulsion or other measures*, for which the authorities can be held to be responsible.[117]

Thus, in the context of prison detention (where subjective indignities are likely to be exacerbated by the deprivation of liberty), the Court has found positive breaches of Article 3, in cases of failure to provide adequate food or recreation,[118] suitable physical conditions or appropriate medical care, even when the suffering has been endured for a relatively short period of time.[119] For example, *Peers v Greece*[120] involved the complainant being obliged to share a one-person cell with another inmate, to use the cell toilet in the other's presence and to suffer the deprivation of natural light and ventilation. Observing that the

---

[113] *Ireland v UK* (note 110 above) para 162.
[114] *Selmouni v France* (2000) 29 EHRR 403, para 101.
[115] Note 67 above.
[116] *Pretty* (note 67 above) para 52.
[117] *Ibid* (emphasis added).
[118] In *Dougoz v Greece* (note 7 above), the detention centre in which the applicant, a Syrian national, had been held for 18 months was severely overcrowded (100 detainees were held in 20 cells); there were inadequate facilities for heating, sanitation food, recreation and contact with the outside world. The Court concluded that serious overcrowding and absence of sleeping facilities, combined with the inordinate length of the period during which he was detained in such conditions, amounted to degrading treatment under Art 3.
[119] *Hurtado v Switzerland* A.280A (1994).
[120] *Peers v Greece* (note 7 above).

'the prison conditions complained of diminished the applicant's human dignity and aroused in him feelings of anguish and inferiority capable of debasing him and possibly breaking his physical and moral resistance', the Court unanimously concluded that the treatment which he suffered constituted a breach of Article 3. In reaching this conclusion, the Court furthermore commented that, although the applicant had been subjected to these conditions for a relatively short period of two months, during that time, the authorities had taken no positive steps to improve them.

It has been made clear by the Court that although an intention to debase will be a factor in determining whether treatment is 'degrading', the absence of such a purpose cannot conclusively rule out a finding that there has been a violation of Article 3. Thus, recently in *Price v the UK*,[121] where the applicant, a Thalidomide victim with severely impaired mobility, was committed to prison for seven days for contempt of court, the ECtHR stated that 'to detain a severely disabled person in conditions where she is dangerously cold, risks developing sores because her bed is too hard and unreachable, and is unable to go to the toilet and keep clean, without the greatest of difficulty, constitutes degrading treatment contrary to Article 3'.[122] While recognising that the applicant's degradation was not due to any *intention* to debase her, the majority concluded that the failure of the prison to meet her individual physical and medical needs constituted an experiential infringement of Article 3.

Almost a decade before the decision in *Price,* the Commission had expressed the opinion that under Article 3 the states have a 'specific positive obligation to protect the physical well being of persons deprived of liberty' and that 'the lack of medical treatment in such a situation must be classified as inhuman treatment.'[123] Moreover, when the omission of such medical treatment is calculated to inflict harm, it may, depending upon circumstances, amount to torture.[124] Thus, focusing in particular on *Herczegfalvy v Austria*,[125] the Court in *Keenan v UK*[126] recognised that 'the assessment of whether the treatment or punishment

---

[121] Note 44 above.

[122] The duty under Art 3 can also extend to a duty to investigate allegations of serious ill-treatment by state agents. See for example *Assenov and Others v Bulgaria* 1998-VIII (1999) 28 EHRR 652, in which the Court stated that 'where there were reasonable grounds to believe that an act of torture or inhuman or degrading treatment or punishment had been committed, the failure of the competent domestic to carry out a prompt and impartial investigation in itself can constitute a violation of Article 3' (para 104).

[123] *Hurtado v Switzerland* A.280A (1994), para 79.

[124] See for example *Ilhan v Turkey* (2002) 24 EHRR 36, in which the applicant claimed that his brother Abdüllatif had been the victim of an assault by members of the Turkish security forces during his arrest. Finding a violation of Art 3, the Court held that '[n]otwithstanding visible injuries to his head and the evident difficulties which Abdüllatif Ilhan had in walking and talking, there was a delay of some thirty-six hours in bringing him to a hospital. . . . Having regard to the severity of the ill-treatment suffered by Abdüllatif Ilhan and the surrounding circumstances, including the significant lapse in time before he received proper medical attention, the Court finds that he was a victim of very serious and cruel suffering that may be characterised as torture' (paras 86–7).

[125] (1993) 15 EHRR 437.

[126] Note 45 above.

concerned is incompatible with the standards of Article 3 has to, in the case of mentally ill persons, take into consideration their vulnerability and their inability, in some cases, to complain coherently or at all about how they are being affected by any particular treatment'.[127] Nevertheless, although continuing to endorse these opinions, the Court has been slow to find that failures by the authorities to provide appropriate medical treatment for detainees, even when they are suffering from acute diagnosed psychiatric conditions, constitute infringements of Article 3.

The case of *Keenan*[128] may indicate a change of position. In that case it was concluded by the ECtHR that failure to provide appropriate medical care to a detainee diagnosed with an acute schizophrenic condition and known as a suicide risk constituted an infringement of Article 3. The Court stressed that the 'lack of informed psychiatric input into the prisoner's assessment and treatment' amounted to inhuman and degrading treatment and punishment within the meaning of Article 3, but it also considered the imposition of a severe disciplinary punishment to have been a contributing factor, 'which might well have threatened his physical and moral resistance'.[129]

As Alastair Mowbray has suggested, the Court's reluctance to find violations of the positive duty to provide appropriate psychiatric services to extremely vulnerable detainees is likely to have been coloured by the deplorable lack of appropriate treatment for offenders suffering from acute mental illness in many member states. In his comment on the unduly lenient judgment in *Aerts v Belgium*,[130] Mowbray no doubts gets close to the truth when he suggests that we can only speculate that

> the Court was being tolerant of a poor level of psychiatric care by prison authorities, because of the endemic nature of this deficiency in many member states, and the consequent large financial costs of raising the standards of mental health provision in such institutions.[131]

The reasoning in cases such as *Price* is therefore important, since it demonstrates that the Court, disengaged from the political minefield of psychiatric care, has

---

[127] *Ibid*, paras 110–11. See for example *Herczegfalvy* (note 125 above) 25–6, para 82; and *Aerts v Belgium*, (2000) 29 EHRR 50, judgment of 30 July 1998, Reports 1998-V, 1966, para 66.

[128] *Keenan* (note 45 above).

[129] *Ibid*, para 115.

[130] Note 127 above. In this case, the Applicant had been held for many months in the psychiatric wing of Lantin Prison. Despite a psychiatrist's recommendation that the Applicant be moved as a matter of urgency to a more appropriate institution, Aerts remained in the prison wing for seven more months. Notwithstanding an independent report describing the facilities of the prison wing as carrying 'an undeniable risk of causing [patients'] mental state to deteriorate' and the uncontested assertion that the conditions of the wing as being 'unsatisfactory' and falling 'below the minimum acceptable from an ethical and humanitarian point of view', the majority in the ECtHR found no breach of Art 3 due to the lack of proof that Mr Aerts himself had suffered a deterioration in his mental health. Although it was recognised that Mr Aerts' severe mental disturbance may have had a detrimental effect upon his abilities to communicate the extent to which the conditions in the prison wing had further affected him, the Court found that Mr Aerts had not conclusively established that he had been subject to inhuman or degrading treatment.

[131] Mowbray (note 5 above) 54.

less difficulty in drawing a direct correlation between the extent of individuals' disabilities and the positive obligations of state parties to provide services tailored to their health and welfare needs.

Let us turn then to the issue raised at the beginning of our discussion, namely the extent to which, outside prison walls and beyond the context of prison or police detention, state parties are obliged under Article 3 to meet the health and welfare needs of vulnerable individuals in their jurisdictions. How far does the positive obligation in Article 3 require the taking of measures to protect vulnerable individuals from degradation and suffering caused by the deprivation of elementary needs such as food, shelter, health care and a subsistence income?

Outside the context of compulsory detention, few complaints have come before the Strasbourg organs, alleging that failure to provide for the health or welfare needs of vulnerable claimants has constituted breaches of Article 3. This is not surprising, given the wide margin of appreciation afforded to member states in matters of social and economic policy. Nevertheless, as we have seen, the Court has made it clear in *Z v UK*[132] that preventive measures may be necessary to protect individuals from degrading and inhuman circumstances of the kind prohibited by Article 3, in cases where authorities know that there is a real risk of such an occurrence. Moreover, two frequently cited cases heard by the Court during the past decade have been accepted as authority for the proposition that state parties may be liable for violations of Article 3 in extreme circumstances where there is a real risk that degradation and suffering are likely to be exacerbated by the failure of state parties to provide for the elementary health and welfare needs of individuals presently in their jurisdictions.

In the first case, *D v United Kingdom*,[133] the applicant, a drug dealer from St Kitts with an extensive criminal record, was suffering from AIDS. Following a proposal by the UK government to return him to his country of origin, where there was generally a very low standard of health care and where treatment and ancillary support for AIDS sufferers was virtually non-existent, he complained to Strasbourg that the decision to deport him constituted a violation of Article 3.

In a series of cases (starting with *Soerig v UK*[134] in 1989) the ECtHR has interpreted Article 3 to include an absolute prohibition on extradition or expulsion when there is a sufficient risk that the complainant will face serious ill-treatment if returned to another state—thereby demonstrating the willingness of the Court to extend the concept of state responsibility beyond its immediate territory.[135] Moreover, the protection afforded by Article 3 in such cases has included contexts in which an individual has been at risk of being subjected to any of the treatment prohibited by Article 3, *either* as a result of intentionally inflicted acts of public authorities in the receiving state, *or* in circumstances where state

---

[132] Note 54 above.
[133] Note 47 above.
[134] Note 32 above.
[135] See for example *Cruz Varas v Sweden* (1992) 14 EHRR; and *Chahal v United Kingdom* (1996) 23 EHRR 413.

authorities are unable to provide adequate protection. Furthermore in such cases Article 3 has retained the absolute character of its protection. Thus, in *D v UK*, in a hearing that took place when the applicant was in the final stages of his illness, the Court was influenced by such factors as the imminence of the applicant's death, the lack of sanitation in the hospital in St Kitts and the fact that there may not even be a bed for him there; the Court therefore concluded that the proposed deportation would indeed amount to a violation of Article 3.

In the second case, *O'Rourke*,[136] the applicant was a vulnerable individual who on coming out of prison was provided with temporary accommodation, pending a decision by the local authority as to whether he was eligible for housing as a homeless person. Following his eviction by the authority from temporary accommodation, he lived rough on the streets for fourteen months, eventually complaining to Strasbourg that his eviction and the subsequent failure to provide him with accommodation constituted violations of Articles 3 and 8 ECHR. Although the ECtHR considered the suffering that followed his eviction to have reached the requisite level of severity to engage Article 3, he was considered to be largely the author of his own misfortune (since he had failed to visit a night shelter and had indicated his unwillingness to accept temporary accommodation), and the state was deemed not liable for breach of Article 3. Thus, it was recognised that, as in the case of *D v the United Kingdom*, compliance with the negatively framed duty in Article 3 can give rise to such positive undertakings, where a course of conduct pursued by the state (in these cases, deportation or eviction) is likely to result in inhuman or degrading consequences of the requisite severity for the individual concerned.[137]

D. Article 8: Protecting Physical and Psychological Integrity

Perhaps the most unexpected development in the jurisprudence of positive obligations has been the ECtHR's willingness to recognise that compliance with Article 8 requires state parties to protect the health of individuals in their jurisdictions by undertaking substantive and procedural measures to avoid environmental hazards.[138] However, it is not only in the field of so-called third generation rights that such positive obligations have been recognised as necessary. Recent case law has shown that under Article 8 state parties may be required to

---

[136] Note 109 above.

[137] However, see further *Karara v Finland*, App No 40900/98, unreported, 29 May 1998; *MM v Switzerland*, App No 43348/98, unreported, 14 Sept 1998; *SCC v Sweden*, App No 46553/99, unreported, 15 Feb 2000; *Henao v Netherlands*, App No 13669/03, unreported, 24 June 2003; *Ndangoya v Sweden*, App No 17868/03, unreported, 22 June 2004; *Amegnigan v Netherlands*, App No 25629/04, unreported, 25 Nov 2004; and *Tatete v Switzerland*, App No 41874/98, judgement of 18 Nov 1998, E Com HR.

[138] In *Lopez Ostra* (note 9 above), the European Commission had found admissible a violation of Art 3 on torture or inhuman or degrading treatment. While the Commission did not find the violation to be serious enough, the case nevertheless points to the possibility of using the prohibition on inhuman or degrading treatment or situations not traditionally associated with torture.

take positive measures to protect the health of individuals in their jurisdictions even in respect of social provision. Thus, it has been recognised that, in addition to a continuing negative obligation not to interfere with enjoyment of private family life and home, in cases of individuals suffering from disabilities or of minorities such as gypsies for whom a nomadic way of life is an integral part of their cultural heritage, state parties may be required to take positive steps to provide for their socio-economic needs.

The Court first considered the extent to which Article 8 gives rise to positive obligations to make social provision for vulnerable individuals in their jurisdictions in *Botta v Italy*,[139] which involved a physically disabled man who took his holiday at a seaside resort, where he was then unable to gain access to a private beach and the sea because they were not equipped with disabled lavatories or access ramps. Testing the scope of Article 8, he complained of 'impairment of his private life and the development of his personality', resulting from the Italian government's failure to take appropriate measures to remedy the omissions of the private bathing establishments. The essence of his complaint was that his Article 8 rights had been infringed because if his inability to enjoy a normal social life, 'which would enable him to participate in the life of the community, by the exercise of his essential non-pecuniary personal rights'.[140]

It was first recognised by the ECtHR that a person's physical and psychological integrity is part of his or her private life, which under Article 8, states are under an obligation to protect. Therefore, recalling *Niemietz v Germany*,[141] the Court stated that '[p]rivate life . . . includes a person's physical and psychological integrity' and that 'the guarantee afforded by Article 8 is primarily intended to ensure the development, without outside interference, of the personality of each individual in his relations with other human beings.'[142] Further, it was recognised that the duty to protect physical and emotional integrity could arise even when there is no direct interference on the part of the state.[143]

However, the Court refused to find that there had been a violation of Article 8 in this case, where the right asserted by the applicant (to gain access to a beach and sea at a place distant from his normal place of residence during the holidays) 'concerned interpersonal relations of such broad and indeterminate scope that there could be no conceivable direct link between the measures the State was urged to take and the applicant's private life'.[144] At the same time, however, it was recognised that in principle Article 8 could give rise to precisely the type of

---

[139] Note 12 above.

[140] *Ibid*, para 27.

[141] (1992) 16 EHRR 97, in which the Court indicated that 'private life' includes at least two elements. First, there is the notion of an 'inner circle' in which the 'individual may live his own personal life as he chooses'. Secondly, the Court considered that 'respect for private life must also comprise to a certain degree the right to establish and develop relations with other human beings' (para 29).

[142] *Botta* (note 12 above) para 32. The Court in essence concluded that the crucial question is the extent to which the life of a particular individual is so circumscribed and so isolated as to be deprived of the possibility of developing his personality.

[143] *Ibid*, paras 32–3.

[144] *Ibid*, para 35.

affirmative duties for which the applicant had contended, in cases where it was possible to establish 'a direct and immediate link between the measures sought by an applicant and the latter's private and/or family life'.[145]

In their concurring opinion, the minority of the Commission in *Botta* agreed that the precise aim and nature of the measures to be undertaken for the protection of handicapped people would vary from place to place and that this is an area where a wide discretion would be left to national governments. However, the ECtHR also recalled the more restrictive opinion of the majority, namely that, in light of the resource implications for the state in satisfying the claim, the 'social nature' of the rights at issue rendered them more suitable for protection under the 'flexible' machinery of the ESC.[146] However, despite the emphasis that has since been placed by commentators on this aspect of the Commission's opinion, the judgment of the ECtHR in *Botta* continues to provide important authority for the proposition in *Airey v Ireland*[147] that there is no watertight division separating the sphere of social and economic rights from the field covered by the Convention.

Thereafter, the extent of the obligation outlined by the Court in *Botta* was tested in the case of *Marzari v Italy*,[148] which provides one of the clearest statements by the ECtHR that the positive duty in Article 8 to respect private family life, although not creating a right to a home per se, does not absolve the government of all responsibilities in respect of housing needs. In that case, the applicant, who suffered from a rare metabolic disease, had a prolonged history of grievances against Trento public authorities, including eviction for non-payment of rent; he claimed a failure to provide him with accommodation suitable for his severe disability following that eviction. The Court concluded:

> Although Article 8 does not guarantee the right to have one's housing problems solved by the authorities, a refusal of the authorities to provide assistance in this respect to an individual suffering from a severe disease might in certain circumstances raise an issue under Article 8.[149]

---

[145] *Botta* (note 12 above), para 34.

[146] *Botta* (note 12 above) 'Proceedings before the Commission', 246–55. For concurring minority opinion on the application of the margin of appreciation (Judges Liddy, Tune, Pellonpää, Bratza, Sváby, Perenic and Schermers), see 251–2. Compare the majority Commission opinion on the subject of the more 'flexible monitoring system' of the ESC (para 28), referred to in the ECtHR judgment (249, para 36). Since *Botta v UK*, there have been further restrictive judgments in which the Strasbourg Court has found that many inaccessible public buildings are not sufficiently closely linked to a person's private and family life to attract the protection of Art 8 (eg, *Zehnalova and Zehnal v the Czech Republic*, Application 38621/97, 14 May 2002, unreported). Further, in *Sentges v the Netherlands* (note 87 above) the Court found that state provision of a robotic arm for an individual with progressive muscular degeneration cannot be considered an obligation under Art 8 once regard has been had to the wide margin of appreciation afforded to states in determining how to ensure compliance with the European Convention.

[147] Note 22 above.

[148] Note 12 above.

[149] *Ibid*, 179.

Further, in determining whether the interference complained of was necessary in a democratic society, the Court stressed that the applicant's medical condition was particularly relevant to his need for accommodation: the applicant had to be hospitalised as a consequence of his living in a camper van after his eviction. As in *Botta*, the Court concluded that there had been no violation of Article 8 in the applicant's case, but in performing the exercise of appreciation in *Marzari*, the Court took the important step of recognising that in cases of people suffering from disabilities, the burden of justifying the refusal of accommodation under Article 8(2) may be greater than in other cases.

The extent to which Article 8 may require positive measures to respect a person's enjoyment of their home in the concrete physical sense has also been tested in a number of cases concerning the rights of gypsies to remain on land. The important case of *Chapman v United Kingdom*[150] concerned the refusal of planning permission to a gypsy woman to station caravans on her own land and the eviction measures that were taken in respect of her continued occupation of the land. The ECHR Court accepted that the refusal to allow the applicant to remain on her land and the enforcement measures taken by the authorities had constituted an interference with her right to respect for her private and family life and her home within the meaning of Article 8(2).

However, when considering whether the interference with the applicant's Article 8 right was justified as being 'necessary in a democratic society', the Court stated:

> [W]hile it is clearly desirable that every human being has a place where he or she can live in dignity and which he or she can call home, there are unfortunately in the Contracting States many persons who have no home. Whether the State provides funds to enable everyone to have a home is a matter for political not judicial decision.[151]

Thus, despite the recognition that the right to respect in Article 8(1) encompasses positive duties state duties, the court emphasised in *Chapman* that Article 8(1) does not encompass the right to a home.[152]

The aphoristic statement that Article 8 affords no right to a home in *Chapman* was not novel. It has long been clear from ECHR jurisprudence that the right to respect for private and family life does not afford a right to a home per se. However, as we have seen, it had been recognised in *Marzari*[153] that there are positive obligations in Article 8 relating to an applicant's enjoyment of private and family life *and* home. This was highlighted in *Chapman* in a strong

---

[150] (2001) 33 EHRR 399.

[151] *Chapman (ibid)* para 99.

[152] Even in cases of state inaction as opposed to arbitrary interference, the right to respect for private and family life has been extended to encompass positive duties, for example to allow access to foster care or social care records of childhood. See *Gaskin v United Kingdom*, Series A No 160 (989) 12, (1990) 12 EHRR 36; and *M v United Kingdom* (unreported 2002) (regarding a positive obligation to provide access to social care records of childhood).

[153] Note 12 above.

dissenting judgment, in which eight members of the ECtHR recalled that although the essential object of Article 8 is to protect individuals against arbitrary action by public authorities, there may in addition be positive obligations inherent in an effective 'respect for private and family life and home'. Further, it was recognised in the dissenting opinion that positive duties to respect may arise even in cases where there has been no state interference of the kind that had been identified in *Chapman*. Thus, in considering whether the applicant's eviction served a 'pressing social need', the minority referred to the judgments of the Court in *Marzari* and *Botta*,[154] recalling that 'where there is a direct and immediate link between the measures sought by an applicant and the latter's private life, positive obligations may be imposed on states'.[155]

Moreover, importantly for our purposes, since the case of *Chapman*, it has been confirmed in *Connors v United Kingdom*[156] that in sensitive 'accommodation' cases, whether founded on allegations of interference or on state policies concerning failure to provide, the Strasbourg Court will not uniformly apply the strict margin of appreciation, which has come to be associated with disputes that raise sensitive socio-economic issues of resource allocation or issues of general housing policy. Thus, in *Connors* (which concerned the legality of a gypsy's forced eviction from a local authority caravan site, on grounds of the alleged misbehaviour of his extended family), the Court was in the first instance at pains to emphasise that 'a margin of appreciation must inevitably be left to the national authorities', who 'by reason of their direct and continuous contact with the vital forces of their countries, are in principle better placed than an international court to evaluate local needs and conditions'.[157] Notably, however, citing *Smith and Grady v United Kingdom*,[158] the Court also stressed that while in general 'it is for the national authorities to make the initial assessment of necessity, the final evaluation as to whether the reasons cited are relevant and sufficient, remains subject to review by the Court for conformity with the requirements of the Convention.'[159]

Accordingly, the Court has emphasised that the margin would vary, 'according to the nature of the Convention right in issue, its importance to the individual and nature of the activities restricted, as well as the aim pursued by the restrictions'.[160] Therefore, on one hand, 'the margin [would] tend to be *narrower* where the right at stake is crucial to the individual's effective enjoyment of intimate or key rights';[161] on the other hand, however, a wide margin of appreciation would be more likely to be applied in contexts such as planning,

---

[154] Note 12 above.
[155] *Chapman* (note 150 above) para 7 (joint dissenting opinion of Judges Pastor Ridruejo, Bonello, Tulkens, Straznica, Lorenzen, Fischbach and Casadevall).
[156] [2004] ECHR 223, Judgment of 27 May 2004.
[157] *Ibid*, para 82.
[158] (2000) 29 EHRR 493, para 88.
[159] *Ibid*, para 81.
[160] *Gillow v United Kingdom*, A.104 (1986) 11 EHRR 335, para 55.
[161] *Connors* (note 156 above) para 82.

insofar as 'the exercise of discretion involving a multitude of local factors is inherent in the choice and implementation of planning policies'.[162] Recalling *Mellacher and Others v Austria*,[163] the Court has therefore stated that 'in spheres such as housing, which play a central role in the welfare and economic policies of modern societies' (particularly in cases where Article 1 Protocol 1 is in play), the legislature's judgement as to what is in the general interest, will generally be respected, 'unless the judgement is manifestly without reasonable foundation'.[164]

Significantly, however, the Court was anxious to distinguish *Mellacher*, 'a case involving an imputed breach of Article 1, Protocol 1', from disputes founded on Article 8, which, as with *Connors*, crucially 'concern rights of central importance to the individual's identity, self determination, physical and moral integrity, maintenance of relationships with others and a settled and secure place in the community'.[165] Moreover in *Connors*, citing *Hatton v United Kingdom*,[166] the Court was clear that where general social and economic policy considerations arise under Article 8, 'the scope of the margin of appreciation depends on the context of the case, with particular significance attaching to the extent of the intrusion into the personal sphere of the Applicant'.[167] Applying this reasoning to the facts, it was concluded in *Connors* that the eviction of the applicant and his family from the site had not been attended by the requisite procedural safeguards, 'namely the requirement to establish proper justification for the serious interference with his rights'. The eviction could not therefore be regarded as either justified by a 'pressing social need' or 'proportionate to the legitimate aim being pursued'. Accordingly, the Court found a violation of Article 8 of the Convention.

E. Article 14: The Equal Distribution of Public Goods?

By contrast with more wide-ranging provisions in many written constitutions and human rights instruments, most notably the very broad formulation of the 14th amendment of the US Constitution,[168] Article 14 ECHR has been restricted in two ways. Firstly, the substantive arena in which discrimination is forbidden has been restricted to the 'enjoyment of the rights and freedoms set forth in [the] Convention'. Secondly, the *grounds* upon which discrimination is forbidden have been restricted to 'any ground such as [the specified grounds] or other

---

[162] *Buckley v United Kingdom*, Judgment of September 1996, (1997) 23 EHRR 101, para 75.
[163] Judgment of 19 Dec 1989, A.169 (1989) 12 EHRR 391.
[164] *Connors* (note 156 above), para 82.
[165] *Pretty v UK* (note 67 above); and *Christine Goodwin v the UK*, No 28957/95, ECHR 2002–VI, para 90.
[166] (2002) 34 EHRR 1, paras 102 and 123.
[167] *Connors* (note 156 above) para 82.
[168] Compare also Art 26 ICCPR.

status'.[169] However, the Strasbourg organs have adopted an expansive approach to the interpretation of both types of restriction, for example, by gradually bringing allegations of discriminatory treatment in the allocation of social security benefits within the ambit of Article 14. Indeed, early in the case law, in *Muller v Austria*,[170] the Commission decided that by analogy with the proprietary right of a contributor to a private pension fund, a claim to contributory benefits in the Austrian municipal system was a 'possession', thereby grounding the complaint within Article 14 together with the Convention right protected by Article 1 of the First Protocol.[171]

Although the reasoning in *Muller v Austria* has since been followed by the ECtHR,[172] the analogy between private economic interests and social security entitlements has continued to be problematic in countries such as the United Kingdom, where, as noted by Lord Hoffman in *R (on the Application of Carson) v Secretary of State for Work and Pensions*,[173] 'contributions to the social security fund are hardly distinguishable from general taxation'.[174] This difficulty has been surmounted in Strasbourg by the general argument that although a claim to a social security benefit is a possessory right that falls within the ambit of Article 1 of Protocol 1, it does not entitle the claimant to 'anything in particular'.[175] Moreover, the argument has controversially taken a new twist in the recent case of *Koua Poirrez v France*,[176] in which the difference between contributory and non-contributory systems was relied on by the ECtHR as *justification* for further expanding the ambit of Article 14 in the socio-economic sphere.[177]

---

[169] Art 14 states: 'The enjoyment of the rights and freedoms set forth in this Convention shall be secured without discrimination on any ground, such as sex race colour language, religion, political or other opinion, national or social origin, association with a national minority birth or other status'. Cf the Twelfth Protocol, Art 1(as yet unsigned by the United Kingdom), which covers much greater territory: (1) 'The enjoyment of any right set forth by law shall be secured without discrimination on any ground such as sex, race, colour language, religion political or other opinion, national or social origin, association with a national minority, property birth or other status'; (2) 'No one shall be discriminated against by any public authority on any grounds such as those mentioned in Paragraph 1.'

[170] (1975) 3 DR 25.

[171] Art 1, Protocol 1 provides that 'Every natural or legal person is entitled to the peaceful enjoyment of his possessions. No one shall be deprived of his possessions except in the public interest and subject to the conditions provided for by law and by the general principles of international law.'

[172] See *Gaygusuz v Austria* (1997) 23 EHRR 365.

[173] [2005] UKHL 37, [2005] 2 WLR 1369, [2005] 4 All ER 545.

[174] *Ibid*, [12].

[175] *Jankovic v Croatia* (2000) 30 EHRR CD 183.

[176] (2005) 40 EHRR 34, 45, para 37.

[177] In the applicant's submission, the allowance for disabled adults amounted to a 'possession' within the meaning of Art 1 of Protocol 1, and the refusal to award it to him had breached his right to peaceful enjoyment of that possession. He argued that the refusal had been based on a discriminatory criterion, namely the fact of his being a foreign national from a non-European Union country that had not signed a reciprocity agreement in respect of the allowance for disabled adults. He submitted that the concept of 'possession' had been widely extended by the Court's case law. This issue is shortly to be considered by the Grand Chamber in the case of *Hepple v UK*, App Nos 65731/01 and 65900/01. However, now see also the key case of *Stec v UK (Stec)* App Nos 67531/01 and 65900/01 12 April 2006 referred to in the preface of the paperback edition, at page vii.

As noted above, Article 14 does not guarantee a free-standing right not to be discriminated against. It merely prohibits discrimination in 'the enjoyment of the rights and freedoms set forth in [the] Convention'. Efforts to remedy this defect were therefore made in the enactment of Protocol 12 ECHR.[178] However, questions have been raised as to whether state parties that fail to ratify the Protocol may rely on the very fact of its existence to question developments in the Strasbourg jurisprudence that move towards a more independent self-standing right to non-discrimination in Article 14. From the outset, the Strasbourg organs have insisted that for Article 14 to be applicable, the facts at issue must 'fall within the ambit' of one or more of the Convention rights. Thus, the Court has explained that Article 14 comes into play whenever the subject matter of the alleged disadvantage 'constitutes one of the modalities' of the exercise of a right guaranteed, or wherever the measures complained of are 'linked' to the exercise of a guaranteed right.[179]

However, during the past decade there has been evidence of greater willingness on the part of the Court to create a nexus between the alleged disadvantage and the substance of protected rights. For example, in *Gaygusuz v Austria*[180] the denial of social assistance to a Turkish migrant worker on grounds of nationality created a sufficient link with the Property Clause in the First Protocol to call Article 14 into play. Therefore, commentators have suggested that there is now sufficient evidence in the case law to indicate that even the most tenuous link with another provision of the Convention will be enough to call Article 14 into play.

It can be seen from *Gaygusuz* that when a sufficient link has been established, Article 14 can provide the means for minority groups to gain access to social provision. If it can be shown that there is a sufficient link between a discriminatory practice (for example, the refusal of housing to asylum seekers or gypsies on grounds of nationality) and the enjoyment of private and family life and home, then in theory Article 14 should provide an important avenue for securing positive rights to social provision for minority groups. However, even when the Court has recognised that there is a sufficient link, it has been slow to find breaches of Article 14 in cases where violations of the subsidiary right have not been established. Moreover, in cases where there has been violation of the subsidiary right (for example, in the recent case of *Connors*[181]), the court has subsequently found it unnecessary to consider whether there has been violation of Article 14.

---

[178] Which states in Art 1 that (1) 'The enjoyment of any right set forth by law shall be secured without discrimination on any ground such as sex, race, colour, language, religion, political or other opinion, national or social origin, association with a national minority, property, birth or other status' and (2) 'No one shall be discriminated against by any public authority on any ground such as those mentioned in paragraph 1.'

[179] *Petrovic v Austria* (1998) 4 BCHR232, paras 22 and 28.

[180] (1996) 23 EHRR 365.

[181] Note 156 above; discussed in section III.D above.

F. Article 6: Due Process in Public Law Challenges

The fair trial clause in Article 6 ECHR has provided an important avenue for the indirect protection of socio-economic rights in ECHR jurisprudence.[182] As we have seen, the right to free legal assistance as a 'social' dimension of the right to a fair trial was emphasised by the ECtHR in *Airey*.[183] More recently, the fundamental right in Article 6 has been extended to encompass a right of access to courts in disputes over discretionary socio-economic entitlements in public administrative law.

Article 6 covers all proceedings, whether between two private individuals or between an individual and a state, the result of which is 'decisive' for civil rights and obligations.[184] However, a remote connection between the subject matter of the dispute and the concept of civil rights will not be sufficient to bring Article 6 into play. It has been said that civil rights and obligations must be the object, or at least one of the objects, of the 'contestation'.[185] Moreover, the result of the proceedings must be determinative of the right.[186] Thus, in the seminal case of *Le Compte v Belgium*[187] it was decided by the ECtHR that Article 6 applied to proceedings before a medical disciplinary tribunal hearing that had suspended a group of doctors, because the proceedings were decisive of their private law right to practice medicine.[188]

In the drafting of the ECHR, the term 'civil rights' in Article 6, the roots of which lie in the Continental notion of legally enforceable private law claims, was not intended to cover administrative decisions, which are conventionally subject to review, if at all, by administrative law courts.[189] Since it was recognised by the Council of Europe that administrative decision-making raises special problems of independence and impartiality, it was considered necessary

---

[182] Art 6(1) of the Convention provides that in the determination of their 'civil rights and obligations', everyone is entitled to a fair hearing by an independent and impartial tribunal established by law.

[183] Note 22 above.

[184] *Ringeisen v Austria (No 1)* (1971) 1 EHRR 455, para 94, which concluded that proceedings before administrative tribunal for the statutory approval of a contract between private individuals for the sale of land fell within Art 6(1). It also includes constitutional court proceedings. See *Süßmann v Germany* (1998) 25 EHRR 64.

[185] *Le Compte v Belgium Application* Nos 7299/75; 7496/76, (1985) EHRR 533, para 27.

[186] *Ibid*, paras 27–8.

[187] Note 185 above.

[188] By contrast, in *Fayed v United Kingdom* (1994) 18 EHRR 393, the mere fact that an official investigation had made findings detrimental to the applicants did not bring the investigation within the scope of Art 6, since the report was not determinative of any civil right.

[189] For an account of the intention of the Covenants drafters in this regard, see F Newman, 'Natural Justice, Due Process and the New International Covenants on Human Rights: Prospectus' (1967) *Public Law* 274. See further P Van Dijk, 'The Interpretation of Civil Rights and Obligations by the European Court of Human Rights: One More Step to Take' in F Matscher and H Petzhold (eds), *Protecting Human Rights: The European Dimension (Studies in Honour of Gerard J Wiarda)* (Koln, Carl Heymanns Verlag, 1988) 131.

to leave issues of fair process in public law disputes for future consideration.[190] However, when no further action was taken, the ECtHR, mindful that state parties might try to avoid the control of Article 6 by the removal of private law claims into the territory of domestic public law, extended the notion of 'civil right' in Article 6 to cover disputes in public law as well.[191]

It is also well established in the jurisprudence of the ECtHR that the concept of 'civil right' in Article 6 is autonomous, which means that it takes into account 'any uniform European notion in the law of the contracting parties' as to the nature of the right at issue, so that the classification of the right in domestic law cannot be decisive.[192] For example, even though the right to health insurance benefits under social security schemes is treated as a public law right in the Netherlands, in *Feldbrugge v Netherlands*[193] it was held by the ECtHR to constitute a civil right within the autonomous meaning of Article 6(1).[194]

It is axiomatic that the rights and obligations of private persons in their relations between themselves are always civil rights and obligations. Thus, civil rights and obligations have readily been found in tort law,[195] family law,[196] employment law[197] and the law of real property.[198] However, the application of Article 6 in disputes that contain both public and private law aspects, and where there is room for interference by public authorities with the enjoyment of private law rights (for example, the right to claim maintenance costs for children of estranged fathers), is clearly problematic. The court has therefore devised a general rule whereby rights and obligations have been identified as civil rights in any case in which state action is said to be determinative of the right in question. Accordingly, civil rights have been identified in decisions

---

[190] *Pudas v Sweden* (1988) 10 EHRR 380: an autonomous right in the Convention jurisprudence is one that has a particular meaning devised by the ECtHR and that may go beyond the usual or domestic meaning.

[191] See for example *Ringeisen v Austria* (note 184 above) para 94. For a critique of this judicial expansion, see J Herberg, A le Sueur and J Mulcahy, 'Determining Civil Rights and Obligations' in Jowell and Cooper (eds) (note 81 above). The authors argue that the framers of the Convention intended the adjective 'civil' to be by way of contrast to 'criminal' in the same sentence.

[192] See *Feldbrugge v Netherlands* (1986) 8 EHRR 425.

[193] *Ibid.*

[194] See also *Konig v Germany* (1978) 2 EHRR 170. The ECtHR concluded that the right to practice medicine in West Germany was a civil one. The fact that the medical profession did not provide a 'public service' in Germany was taken into account in reaching this conclusion.

[195] *Osman* (note 8 above). See also *Steel and Morris v United Kingdom* [2005] EMLR 15, where the denial of legal aid to the applicants in the 'McLibel' case deprived the applicants of their chance to present their case effectively and thus constituted a violation of Art 6(1). Since the enactment of the HRA, the majority of negligence claims raising Art 6(1) issues have, like *Osman*, been claims by private individuals against public bodies. Prior to *Osman*, negligence claims against public bodies were generally disposed of under 'striking out' procedures in the Civil Pocedure Rules. Post-*Osman*, and despite the subsequent backtracking of the ECtHR in *Z and Others v UK* (note 46 above), domestic courts have generally erred on the side of caution, concluding that to give full effect to an individual's rights under Art 6(1), a full investigation of the facts is required. See for example *Barrett v Enfield London Borough Council* [2001] 2 AC 550.

[196] *Airey v Ireland* (note 22 above).

[197] *Bucholz v Germany*, Series A No 42 (1981) 3 EHRR 597 ECtHR.

[198] *Langborger v Sweden*, Series A No 155 (1989) 12 EHRR 416 ECtHR.

concerning the expropriation of property,[199] the application of planning laws,[200] bankruptcy[201] and patent rights.[202] Furthermore, rights to engage in commercial activity or to receive compensation for financial loss resulting from illegal state acts, including claims in respect of personal injury or ill-treatment by the state,[203] have been identified as civil rights for purposes of Article 6.[204] However, a more general approach has recently emerged in cases concerning access to socio-economic entitlements. Thus, it has been suggested that all rights of a pecuniary nature (except perhaps in relation to taxation) are civil rights within the meaning of Article 6.[205]

In the specific area of social security, social assistance and welfare disputes, the ECtHR initially approached the question of whether there was a 'civil' right by examining the nature of the benefit, for example by weighing the private law features of a domestic insurance scheme against its public law features.[206] More recently however, the Court has held that the principle of equality of treatment dictates that Article 6 should apply to social insurance claims in domestic jurisdictions, even when a benefit is a discretionary, non-contributory form of public assistance granted unilaterally by the state.[207] Moreover, it has been held that this is the correct approach even when the cost is fully borne by the public purse without any link to a private contract of employment.[208] Thus,

---

[199] *Holy Monasteries v Greece* (1994) 20 EHRR 1, ECtHR, para 85.

[200] *Bryan v United Kingdom* (1995) 21 EHRR 342.

[201] *Sprl ANCA v Belgium*, App No 10259/83, 40 DR 170 (1984).

[202] *X v Austria*, App No 7830/77, Commission Decision of 13 July 1978, DR 14, 200.

[203] *X v France* (1991) 14 EHRR 483 involved a claim for damages for negligence for contracting AIDS from blood transfusion. See *Aerts v Belgium* (note 127 above) para 60: the right to liberty of an arrested person detained in the psychiatric wing of a prison was a 'civil right' because the person was 'seeking a declaration that the domestic court had jurisdiction to award compensation for unlawful imprisonment'. See also *Aksoy v Turkey* (1996) 23 EHRR 533 ECtHR, especially para 29, where the claim for compensation in respect of ill-treatment by the state constituted a violation of Art 3.

[204] This category may be wide enough to include claims for compensation for damage caused by an illegal decision by a public authority on a tax matter. See *National & Provincial Building Society, the Leeds Permanent Building Society and the Yorkshire Building Society v The United Kingdom* [1997] ECHR 87, judgment of 23 Oct 1997. In that case it was held that judicial review proceedings relating to claims for restitution of moneys paid as tax fell within Art 6(1). However, compare *Ferrazzini v Italy* (2002) 34 EHRR 1068, where the Grand Chamber held that tax disputes between an individual and the state, although of direct financial interest to the individuals, do not involve civil rights and obligations.

[205] See *Editions Periscope v France* (1992) 14 EHRR 597, which was followed in *Stran Greek Refineries and Stratis Andreadis v Greece*[1994] ECHR 48; and *Procola v Luxembourg* (1995) 22 EHRR 193, paras 38–9. However, compare *Schouten and Meldrum v Netherlands* (1994) 19 EHRR 432, paras 50–7, where the court held that the fact that a dispute is pecuniary in nature is not always sufficient to bring it within the scope of Art 6.

[206] *Feldbrugge* (note 192 above). In the UK, this approach has been followed, for example, in *R (Hussain) v Secretary of State for the Home Department* [2001] EWHC Admin 852, where it was held by the Divisional Court that a destitute asylum seeker receiving benefits under Part VI of the Immigration and Asylum Act 1999 has a civil right under Art 6(1) to the continuation of support, subject to the conditions in and under the Act. See generally chapter 8 below.

[207] *Salesi v Italy* (1993) 26 EHRR 187.

[208] A fortiori, where a pension is linked to employment, even to employment in the civil service, the ECtHR has held that Art 6 will be engaged. See *Lombardo v Italy* (1992) 21 EHRR 18, paras 14–17; and *McGinley and Egan v United Kingdom* (1999) 27 EHRR 1, para 84.

in *Salesi*[209] the definition of a civil right was said to cover social security and welfare benefits regarded as 'sufficiently well defined to be analogous to rights in private law' and of 'economic significance to the claimant'.[210] Therefore, the majority in *Salesi* decided that, since the features of private law claims predominated, the right to social security benefits was a civil right within the meaning of Article 6.[211] Notably, however, such a broad approach to the determination of civil rights has not been applied in other cases of state involvement in the economic life of individuals.[212]

Nevertheless, the erosion of the public–private divide in Article 6 remains problematic. In many jurisdictions including the United Kingdom, it has been deemed constitutionally appropriate to afford different types of judicial hearing in public and private law disputes and to adopt a more intrusive form of scrutiny in cases where the legality as opposed to the fairness of an administrative decision has been impugned. In many jurisdictions it has also been deemed appropriate to deny appeals to a judicial tribunal on the facts or the merits of decisions by primary decision-makers. The ECtHR has therefore long recognised that the requirement of a 'full hearing' under Article 6 might disturb existing models of administrative dispute resolution and the public–private jurisdictional division in member states. To avoid this result, it was argued in a powerful dissent by the Commission in *Kaplan v UK*[213] that it would be more appropriate to confine the protection of Article 6 to administrative disputes in which the lawfulness rather than the fairness of decisions had been impugned.

Nevertheless, the Strasbourg Court has declined to follow that approach, instead deciding that the full judicial model afforded in private law disputes can be substantially modified in public law disputes that engage civil rights. Thus, the Court has decided that prima facie an administrative decision that is 'a determination of civil rights and obligations' must be made by an independent

---

[209] Note 207 above.

[210] *Ringeisen v Austria (No 1)* (note 184 above).

[211] This was despite a powerful dissent from seven members of the court, who said that the distinctions between public and private law were being eroded in ways that would cause great uncertainty.

[212] The ECtHR has rejected claims by public employees concerning appointment or dismissal conditions of service and discipline as being outside the scope of the Convention. See *Huber v France* (1998) 26 EHRR 457. But compare *Vogt v Germany* (1995) 21 EHRR 205; and *Ahmed v UK* (1998) 29 EHRR 1, where the ECtHR held that there is no principle that civil servants fall outside the Convention. See also *Schouten and Meldrum v Netherlands* (1994) 19 EHRR 32, para 50, where the ECtHR concluded that a more restrictive approach than benefit entitlements should be used in disputes over benefit contributions. In *Pellegrin v France* (1999) 31 EHRR 651, para 66, the ECtHR recognised that its case law on civil servants contained 'a margin of uncertainty' and sought to fashion a test that would exclude only public employees whose functions involved the exercise of public powers falling outside the scope of Art 6. However, notably in *Matthews v Ministry of Defence* [2003] UKHL 4, the House of Lords decided that the 'public service exclusion' is confined to disputes over conditions of service. (See chapter 8 below.) In disputes involving public servants other than those relating purely to conditions of employment, the ECtHR has held that Art 6 applies. See *Frydlander v France* (2001) 31 EHRR 52; and *Becessiouer v France* (2001) 33 EHRR 1317.

[213] (1980) 4 EHRR 64, 90, para 161.

and impartial tribunal. However, it has conceded that when the necessary degree of independence is manifestly lacking in the initial procedure, it will be permissible to consider whether the composite procedure of administrative decision-making, together with a right of appeal, is sufficient to satisfy the guarantees afforded by Article 6.

Adopting this flexible approach to the idea of a full hearing, the ECtHR in the case of *Bryan v UK*[214] concluded that 'full jurisdiction' in public administrative law means jurisdiction to deal with the case as the nature of the decision requires, in accordance with the dictates of 'democratic accountability, efficient administration and the sovereignty of Parliament'.[215] Problematically however, there is no clear guidance as to how the criteria enunciated in *Bryan* are to be applied in national jurisdictions, as a result of which, in the UK there has been intense due process litigation since the HRA has been in force.[216]

IV. THE PROTECTION OF SOCIO-ECONOMIC RIGHTS IN EC/EU LAW

A. The Development of a Doctrine of Fundamental Rights in EC/EU Law

Following World War II, initiatives were taken in the European region to promote human rights and establish institutional cooperation in the economic sphere. While the Council of Europe had the task of ensuring the protection of fundamental human rights, a comprehensive framework devoted to economic recovery and integration was established under the auspices of the European Communities.

The question of dealing with human rights protection within the European Economic Community (EEC) framework was considered but rejected. It was decided that since economic integration provided the *raison d'etre* of the Community institutions, the issue of fundamental rights was a more appropriate concern for the Council of Europe.[217] Not only was there an assumption that the creation of better economic conditions in the EEC would contribute to the avoidance of future violations of human rights; it was also assumed that the primary goal of market integration could be pursued without impinging on national systems of social protection, including legislative labour rights and industrial relations policies and programmes.[218]

---

[214] (1996) 21 EHRR 342.

[215] *Begum (FC) v London Borough of Tower Hamlets* [2003] UKHL 5, paras 35 and 43 (Lord Hoffman).

[216] For a full discussion of these issues in welfare needs contexts, see chapter 8 below. Also now see the important case of *Tsfayo v the United Kingdom (Tysafo). Tysafo v UK* referred to in the preface to the paperback edition.

[217] See generally Betton and Grief (note 1 above) ch 3, 55–77 for a discussion of the policy decision to keep human rights out of the EEC framework.

[218] For an excellent critique of the EU's 'ambivalent constitutionalism', see J Kenner, 'Economic and Social Rights in the EU Legal Order: The Mirage of Indivisibility' in T Hervey and J Kenner (eds), *Economic and Social Rights under the EU Charter of Fundamental Rights* (Oxford, Hart Publishing, 2003) 5.

Accordingly, when the EEC treaty was signed in 1957, references to fundamental human rights were omitted. Furthermore, the so called 'social provisions', such as the right to equal pay for men and women,[219] regarded as the 'fundamental rights' of the EU legal order, were intended as no more than a network of policies and programmes rather than an enforceable set of legal principles.[220] In other words, the primary objective having been to establish a common market and the functional apparatus to uphold it, 'other considerations, moral and social remained secondary'.[221]

However, by the early 1970's, the underlying tension between the economic goals of the EEC and the constitutional protection of fundamental rights in member states had become increasingly apparent.[222] This tension was progressively highlighted by the expanding competencies of the EU in areas of social policy such as free movement of persons, discrimination and asylum.[223] Moreover, concerns in the region about the difficulties of reconciling the advance of the internal market with prevailing traditions and values of a growing European family of nations, dedicated to different levels of employment and social protection, continued to grow. In particular, concerns were raised about the detrimental impact in the social sphere, of the so-called 'race to the bottom', which implies an invidious lowering of social standards by member states in order to compete effectively. Thus, from the 1970s onwards, alternative visions of a political and social union that was capable of embracing a concept of citizenship based on the recognition and protection of common values inherent in fundamental human rights, had began to capture the imagination of European political actors.[224] Notwithstanding these developments, the Community political institutions remained ambivalent, and no steps were taken towards the protection of human rights until the Single European Act (SEA) 1986.[225]

The third recital of the Preamble to the SEA for the first time referred to all those human rights 'recognised in the constitutions and laws of the Member States; in the Convention for the Protection of Human Rights and Fundamental

---

[219] Arts 117–12 EEC.

[220] See G de Burca, 'The Language of Rights and European Integration' in J Shaw and G More (eds), *New Legal Dynamics of European Union* (Oxford, Clarendon, 1995) 29–54.

[221] Kenner (note 218 above) 5.

[222] This applied to fundamental human rights entrenched in domestic constitutions and in the ECHR. For example, the German *Bundesverfassungsigerciht* rejected the ECJ's assertion of the supremacy of EC law unless there was a guarantee that there was a concomitant respect for fundamental rights in EC law and that the acts of the Community institutions could be reviewed for compatibility with fundamental human rights. See Betton and Grief (note 1 above) 54–66 for the origins of the conflict and the development of the ECJ role in the recognising the rights in the ECHR as part of the fundamental principles of EC law.

[223] See generally J Shaw (ed), *Social Law and Policy in an Evolving European Union* (Oxford, Hart, 2000). In particular, see the chapter by T Hervey entitled 'Social Solidarity: A Buttress Against Internal Market Law?'.

[224] See the 'Report by Mr Leo Tindemans, Prime Minister of Belgium, to the European Council' ('The Tindemans Report'), *Bulletin of the European Communities*, Supplement 1/76, 1975, 26–7.

[225] OJL 169 of 29 June 1987, in force as of 1 July 1987.

Freedoms *and* in the European Social Charter'.[226] Subsequently building on what could be dismissed as no more than a symbolic aspiration in the SEA, a more specific obligation was included in Article 6(2) of the Treaty of European Union (TEU) 1992, requiring EU institutions to respect both the fundamental rights in the ECHR and those derived from 'the constitutional traditions of member states'. A power was furthermore added in Articles 6(1) and 7 TEU to impose sanctions on member states for persistent failures to protect the fundamental rights encompassed by Article 6, albeit with emphasis clearly placed on ECHR rights.[227]

Although these developments were welcomed by some commentators, by failing to make reference to the ESC, the European Union was open to criticism that in the TEU it had taken the retrograde step of perpetuating the traditional subordination of socio-economic to civil and political rights.[228] Moreover, against this political backdrop, the ECJ continued to be involved in its own institutional struggle to resolve the constitutional clash between the goals of market integration and the protection of fundamental rights—a task made all the more difficult in the context of free movement provisions, wherein the vocabulary of fundamental rights has traditionally been used to justify the limits of public power in face of uninhibited free market competition.[229] Thus, according to fundamental rights as conceived in the European market model, any rule having a detrimental impact on trade can be struck down, even if its origins lie in domestic social policy concerns, unless the rule is necessary to attain an objective that is justified in regard to Community law.[230]

Although the route has been tortuous, since the 1970s the ECJ has nevertheless gradually come not only to accept the relevance of human rights standards

---

[226] 'Determined to work together to promote democracy on the basis of fundamental rights recognised in the constitutions and laws of the Member States, in the Convention for the Protection of Rights and Fundamental Freedoms and the European Social Charter, notably freedom, equality and social justice'.

[227] See Kenner (note 218 above) 10.

[228] Against this background, the European Commission had long been preoccupied with its own proposal for a 'social charter', which culminated in 1989 (during the French Presidency) in an instrument concerned with the rights of 'workers' exclusively rather than those of 'citizens'. See the Community Charter of the Fundamental Social Rights of Workers (COM (89) 471, 1), otherwise known as the Community Social Charter. For a critique, see generally Kenner (note 218 above) 8–13. Kenner has suggested that, although remarkably effective as a 'soft law tool' and as 'an impulse for change', the effectiveness of the Community Social Charter has been constrained by 'its limited vision of social citizenship and its place at the periphery of the integration process' (13).

[229] Art 39(1) EC.

[230] See generally Betton and Grief (note 1 above) 53–73. An early effect of this approach to social rights was witnessed in the decisions on Sunday trading. In these cases the Court held that limitations of Sunday trading, although based on social concerns, could be subjected to strict scrutiny because they reduce the sale of imported goods from other Member States. National court were left with the difficult task of deciding whether the social concerns behind Sunday trading restrictions could be justified as compatible with the exceptions set out in Community law.

in EC/EU law[231] but, in cases such as *Rutili v Ministre d l'Interieure*[232] and *ERT*[233], also to accept the 'special significance' of the ECHR as a source of principles of EC/EU law.[234] Moreover, the development by the ECJ of its fundamental rights jurisprudence has not been confined to the acts of the EC/EU institutions, but has also been directed at the acts of member states. Thus, the ECJ has concluded that when implementing Community rules or applying national rules that fall within the ambit of Community law, member states must do so in a manner that is compatible with fundamental rights, derived in particular from the ECHR. Thus, in *Bosphorus v Minister for Transport*[235] the Advocate General noted that for practical purposes the Convention can be regarded as Community law and can be invoked as such both in the ECJ and in national courts where Community laws are at issue.[236]

Nevertheless, so far the ECJ has been slow to review the acts of member states by reference to ECHR jurisprudence. Moreover, it is not clear how far, when applying ECHR standards for the resolution of disputes, the ECJ is prepared to follow principles and standards of review applied by the ECtHR, or indeed whether the ECJ's conceptions of ECHR standards are entirely consistent with those of the Strasbourg organs. Moreover, it is notable that, with few exceptions and despite the relevance of socio-economic rights standards in the ESC (and the revised ESC), the ECJ has continued to view ECHR standards—and ECHR standards alone—as the most important source of 'common traditions'.[237]

Given the difficulties of reconciling a free market ethos with the protection of social values in many member states, the omission of legally enforceable socio-economic rights from the TEU is not surprising. Indeed, against the background that was outlined in chapter one above, the historic inclusion of socio-economic rights along with a range of civil and political rights in the Charter of Fundamental

---

[231] In Advisory Opinion 2/94 [1996] ECR 1759, the ECJ held that, although the EC did not have competence to sign the Convention, 'it is well settled that fundamental rights form an integral part of the general principles of law whose observance the court ensures. For that purpose the Court draws inspiration from the constitutional traditions common to the Member states and from the guidelines supplied by international treaties for the protection of human rights on which Member States have collaborated and or of which they are signatories' (para 33).

[232] Case 36/75 [1975] ECR 1219.

[233] *Elliniki Radiofonia-Tileorasi AE v Dimotiki*, Case 260/89 [1991] ECR I-2925.

[234] Human rights principles have been used both to interpret the scope of rights guaranteed by the ECHR and to decide the extent of derogations that are permitted from it. See for example the opinion of Advocate General Tesauro in *P v S and Cornwall County Council*, Case C-13/94 [1996] ECR 1-2143, where the ECJ used Convention principles to decide that the EC Equal Treatment Directive prohibited discrimination against the Applicant following gender re-assignment.

[235] Case C-84/95, [1996] ECR I-3953.

[236] *Ibid*, para 53.

[237] For instance, in a number of recent cases the ECJ has referred to the ECHR as containing the 'fundamental rights which, according to the court's settled case-law, restated by the preamble to the Single European Act and by Article 6(2)EU, are protected in Community law.' As an example involving free movement of persons, see *Commission v Germany*, Case C-441/02, Judgment of 27 April 2006.

Rights of the European Union 2000 has been much more remarkable.[238] In the Charter, fundamental rights have been arranged in chapters, not in accordance with their civil and political or social welfare content, but in accordance with several major concepts: human dignity, fundamental freedoms, equality, solidarity, citizenship and justice.[239]

Directed at a 'Europe of peoples as distinct from markets', the Charter's primary objective is to make the process of European integration more democratic and participative by furnishing it with a layer of rights 'embodying values with which intrinsically most people can readily identify'.[240] Therefore, as Kenner puts it, promulgation of the Charter as a unified composite text can be understood 'as part of a much broader fundamental rights dialogue that seeks to transcend the artificial . . . debate about the labelling of "rights" and places emphasis on the institutional duties of states and international bodies to respect core rights and values as a matter of obligation'.[241]

B. The Charter of Fundamental Rights of the European Union 2000

The Charter of Fundamental Rights of the EU,[242] which is addressed to the institutions and bodies of the EU and to its Member States 'when implementing Community law',[243] requires states to promote the rights contained therein. However, its legal status was notoriously left to a future date, after which time it would be binding and apply to all EU institutions. Its future has now become very tenuous following rejection in French and Dutch referenda.[244] Even with-

---

[238] For a brief history of the origins and iconographic significance of the Charter, which has been said to encapsulate the values of a 'Europe of peoples as distinct from markets', see Kenner (note 218 above) 1–5. In 1996, the Report of an ad hoc *Comite des Sages* ('For a Europe of Civic and Social Rights' (Luxembourg, European Communities, 1996)) called for a 'Bill of Rights' encompassing both civil and political rights. For the full text of the Charter with explanatory notes produced on behalf of its promulgators (a body known as 'the Convention'), see CHARTE4473/00 CONVENT 49; European Council, 'Explanations Relating to the Complete Text of the Charter' (Luxembourg, Office for Official Publications of the European Communities, 2001).

[239] The first recital to the Preamble to the Charter of Fundamental Rights and Freedoms 2000 proclaims on behalf of the 'peoples of Europe' that 'in creating an ever closer union among them they are resolved to share a peaceful union based on common values'.

[240] Kenner (note 218 above) 4.

[241] *Ibid*.

[242] For wide-ranging commentary on (inter alia) the implications for future law and the policy of including socio-economic rights in the Charter, see the collection of essays in Hervey and Kenner (eds) (note 218 above).

[243] Art 5(1) EUCFR. The Charter has now been discussed in a number of Advocate Generals opinions, including *R v Secretary of State for Trade and Industry, ex parte Broadcasting, Cinematographic and Theatre Union [BECTU]*, Case C-173/99, 8 Feb 2001, [2001] ECR I-4881 and *Booker Aquaculture Ltd v Secretary of State for Scotland*, Case C-20/00, 10 July 2003; and as a source of law in UK courts. For example, see the reference to the Charter by Munby J in *R (on the Application of A, B, X and Y) v East Sussex County Council No 2* [2003] EWHC 167, discussed in chapter 3 below.

[244] The Charter was to have formed part of the Treaty Establishing a Constitution for Europe ('The European Constitution'), signed in Rome on 29 October 2004 by representatives of the

out ratification, however, the Charter—although not a source of law in the strict sense—can be consulted insofar as it proclaims, reaffirms or elucidates the content of those human rights that are generally recognised throughout the European family of nations, in particular those fundamental rights that have been guaranteed in the ECHR.[245] Moreover, the Commission has stated before the Court of First Instance that it considers itself to be bound by the EU Charter.[246] Nevertheless, the ECJ has demonstrated reluctance to make reference to the Charter in its judgments, despite a number of invitations by the Advocates General to so.[247]

In purporting to promote the 'common values' of EU citizens, the Charter brings together a wide range of modern economic and social rights with more established civil and political rights in a single text, thereby underlining their 'relevance and importance' and rendering them more visible to EU citizens.[248] Thus, the fundamental rights in the Charter have been drawn from the EC Treaty, Community legislation and the jurisprudence of the ECJ and the ECtHR, as well as a variety of international and national sources, including UN human rights instruments, the Council of Europe and the European Community's Charter of the Fundamental Social Rights of Workers 1989. Moreover, a guarantee now replicated in many contemporary constitutions can be found among the Solidarity Rights in Chapter IV of the Charter. Thus, somewhat incongruously, next to the 'right to health' there is a right of access to 'services of general economic interest'—demonstrating a general commitment in the countries of the EU to the transference of erstwhile public services to the private sector.[249]

---

25 Member States. However, during the ratification process, as demonstrated first by the voters of France and then by those in the Netherlands who rejected the Constitution in referenda (*The Times,* 2 June 2005), it failed to capture the public imagination. Following these 'setbacks', the Heads of State issued a Declaration on the status of the Constitution ('Declaration by the Heads of State or Government of Member States of the European Union on the Ratification of the Treaty Establishing a Constitution for Europe', Brussels, 18 June 2005, SN 117/05) that affirmed the Council's commitment to the Constitution but declaring a 'period of reflection' until mid-2006. By August 2006, the Commission was still involved in dialogue with citizens.

[245] See generally the Preamble: 'This Charter reaffirms, with due regard for the powers and tasks of the Community and the Union and the principle of subsidiarity, the rights as they result, in particular, from the constitutional traditions and international obligations common to the Member States, the Treaty on European Union, the Community Treaties, the European Convention for the Protection of Human Rights and Fundamental Freedoms, the Social Charters adopted by the Community and by the Council of Europe and the case law of the Court of Justice of the European Communities and of the European Court of Human Rights'.

[246] The Commission has stated before the Court of First Instance that it considers itself to be bound by the EU Charter: *R Jurgen Schafer v Commission,* Case T-52/01, Order [2001] ECR IA-0015.

[247] See *Commission of the European Communities v Jego Quere et Cie SA,* Case C-263/02, 30 April 2004.

[248] European Union Institute, *Leading by Example: A Human Rights Agenda for the European Union for the Year 2000* (Florence, EUI, 2000).

[249] Art 36 provides: 'The Union recognises and respects access to services of general economic interest as provided for in national laws and practices, in accordance with the Treaty establishing the European Community, in order to promote the social and territorial cohesion of the Union.'

The contents of the Charter are divided into six chapters: I) Dignity; II) Freedoms; III) Equality; IV) Solidarity; V) Citizens' Rights; and VI) Justice. A final chapter contains general clauses, which relate to the Charter's scope and applicability, bodies to which it is addressed, and its relationship to other legal instruments, including the ECHR. With regard to the relationship between the Charter and other international human rights instruments, Article 52(3) provides:

> In so far as this Charter contains rights which correspond to rights guaranteed by the [ECHR], the meaning and scope of these rights shall be the same as those laid down by the said Convention. This provision shall not prevent Union law providing more extensive protection.[250]

Notably, however, it has been generally decided that, like the Indian Constitution, the Charter is premised on a fundamental difference between specific rights and freedoms, which are legally enforceable, and general principles, which are unenforceable. Thus, although arguably the reference to a collection of 'rights, freedoms and principles' in the seventh recital of the Preamble may be regarded as neutral, many commentators have insisted that this is not the case. For example, in an independent comment in 2000 on the scope of the Charter, Lord Goldsmith, at that time UK Attorney General, emphasised that 'unenforceable principles do not equate with rights and are not truly fundamental'.[251] Arguing moreover that the economic and social rights in the Charter are merely principles, he concluded that they would be realised as exercisable rights only 'to the extent that they are implemented by national law or in those areas where there is competence by Community law'.[252] In line with general view of the UK political establishment, Lord Goldsmith claimed that economic and social rights are different because they are 'usually non-justiciable' and further, by implication, that they are less important than civil and political rights.[253]

Chapter IV of the Charter ('Solidarity', Articles 27–38) contains the majority of the social rights. It includes core labour rights, such as workers' rights to information and consultation;[254] the right of collective bargaining and the right to strike,[255] protection against unjustified dismissal;[256] and the right to fair and just working conditions.[257] Moreover, Chapter IV also 'recognises' the right of

---

[250] This has been explored in two cases: first by Advocate General Jacobs in his opinion in *Z v European Parliament*, Case C-270/99P, para 40; and by Advocate General Tizzano in his opinion in *ex parte BECTU* (note 243 above).

[251] Lord Goldsmith, 'A Charter of Rights Freedoms and Principles' (2000) 38 *Common Market Law Review*, 1201, 1212.

[252] *Ibid*, 1213.

[253] *Ibid*, 1212. For an alternative analysis of the significance of the general principles in the Charter, see J Toose, 'Social Security and Social Assistance' in Hervey and Kenner (eds) (note 218 above) 161.

[254] Art 27.

[255] Art 28.

[256] Art 30.

[257] Art 31.

the family to enjoy legal economic and social protection[258] and 'recognises and respects' the right to social security and the right to housing assistance.[259] Additional rights in Chapter IV include access to health care[260] and a 'high level' of environmental and consumer protection (Article 37). Rights that might be expected in the above grouping can be found elsewhere, including the right to education, freedom to choose an occupation and engage in work, equality between men and women, rights of children and rights of the elderly. For example, a far-reaching non-discrimination provision that prohibits discrimination on many grounds, including birth, disability and sexual orientation, is located in Chapter III (Article 21),[261] the previous Article tersely proclaiming that everyone is equal before the law.

There are notable omissions from this eclectic range of socio-economic provisions, including the right 'to work', to 'fair remuneration' and to 'housing'; and for sceptics, these omissions have cast further doubt on the Charter's integrity[262] and reaffirmed old doubts, particularly among labour lawyers, about the seriousness of claims by the Charter's progenitors that it affords equal protection to citizens in respect of their civil, political and socio-economic rights. While it might be understandable that rights with such overwhelming resource implications are excluded as mandatory provisions, this does not explain why such fundamental socio-economic rights could not at least have been included as aspirations subject to resource qualifications.[263]

Indeed, there is much room for scepticism about the potential for the Charter to enhance the multi-layered goals of political and socio-economic integration envisaged by its drafters. Nevertheless, and despite the lack of opportunity for citizen participation in a process that purported to give expression to the common democratic values of EU citizenry, there is no doubt that the Charter project has ignited crucial debate, not only about the substance of the rights, but also more generally about the relevance of a human rights approach to shaping the development of EU law and policy and about the possibility of reconciling

---

[258] Art 33.

[259] Art 34.

[260] Art 35 provides for the right of access to preventive health care and the right to benefit from medical treatment under the conditions established by national laws and practices, to which has been added a statement of intent 'that a high level of human health protection shall be ensured in the definition and implementation of all Union policies and activities'.

[261] Article 21. Prohibited grounds include sex, race, colour, ethnic or social origin, genetic features, language, religion or belief, political or any other opinion, membership in national minorities, property, birth, disability, age or sexual orientation.

[262] These omissions have been justified by Lord Goldsmith (note 251 above) on grounds that economic and social rights are not justiciable in the same way as other rights. As noted in chapter 1 above, labour lawyers have traditionally been sceptical about a fundamental rights approach to the protection of socio-economic rights. See B Fitzpartick, 'European Union Law and the Council of Europe Conventions' in C Costello (ed), *Fundamental Social Rights: Current Legal Protection and the Challenge of the EU Charter of Fundamental Rights* (Dublin, Irish Centre for European Law, 2001) 101; and KD Ewing, *The EU Charter of Fundamental Rights: Waste of Time or Wasted Opportunity'* (London, Institute of Employment Rights, 2002).

[263] See generally Kenner (note 218 above).

such an approach to socio-economic provision on the one hand, with a market-inspired response to social cohesion on the other hand.[264] This is not the place for an elaborate rehearsal of debates that raise complex questions about the relationship between EU law, social policy and issues of fundamental rights, which have been extensively and expertly conducted elsewhere. Instead, as indicated in the introductory remarks, the purpose here is to provide a brief outline of EU legal developments insofar as they have import for our discussion of the role of UK courts in politically sensitive disputes over the prioritisation of public services. For this purpose, therefore, the recent reference to the ECJ[265] in the case of *Yvonne Watts v Bedford Primary Health Trust* (hereafter *Watts*),[266] which will be discussed below, graphically demonstrates an approach to protecting social rights in EU law that is very different from that envisaged in the Charter.[267] The case furthermore provides a timely snapshot of the impact of EU law on UK policy concerning the management of supply and demand through waiting lists; and underscores a very clear tension with the traditional English administrative law approach to the scrutiny of policy decisions to delay or refuse public services on grounds of lack of resources.

C. The European Court of Justice (ECJ): Social Solidarity and Access to Public Services in Member States

As indicated above, European social policy has become an important aspect of European integration and has effects on domestic policy to the extent that member states are required to fit their regulatory regimes within the provisions of Community law.[268] Moreover, although for some time it was assumed that national health and welfare policies were to remain largely immune from Community law and policy,[269] recent developments, including attempts by indi-

---

[264] See generally Shaw (ed) (note 223 above). The 'European Social Model' has been described as a diffuse amalgam of ideas and principles constructed principally by the Commission to justify social policy interventions on the part of the EU, particularly in relation to labour interventions. See J Shaw, 'Introduction' in Shaw (ed) (note 223 above) 3. Shaw questions whether the concentration of policy agendas on a labour market orientation (those potentially or actually employed) can convincingly be 'reconciled with the parallel increase in commitment claimed by the EU institutions to excluded groups such as those in poverty, children, third-country nationals, racial and ethnic minorities and other groups such as the disabled, gays and lesbians' (4).

[265] [2003] EWHC 2228.

[266] *R (on the application of Watts) v Bedford Primary Care Trust* C-372/04 [2006] ECR I-04235.

[267] In particular, see T Hervey, 'The Right to Health in European Union Law' in Hervey and Kenner (eds) (note 218 above), where the author questions whether a 'right to health' (included in Art 35 of the Charter) within EU law and policy makes a difference to the resolution of conflicts, for example in cases concerning 'relationships between minorities and majorities, "insiders and outsiders", resource allocation, spheres of competence or others' (193).

[268] See also Hervey (2000) (note 223 above) 31. This requirement applies to labour law standards, consumer policy, education environmental policy and even sport.

[269] See generally M Dougan and E Spaventa, 'Introduction' in M Dougan and E Spaventa (eds), *Social Welfare and EU Law* (Oxford, Hart, 2005) for the argument that traditional assumptions that Member States enjoy exclusive competence over social provision have given way to the realisation

viduals in member states to rely on free movement provisions in order to receive public goods and services across national boundaries, have demonstrated that this is no longer the case.[270] It is also clear from a number of decisions by the ECJ[271] that when welfare goods and services are provided through market mechanisms,[272] as increasingly occurs in member states, the norms of the internal market and competition law apply.[273] Concerns have therefore been raised not only about the impact of the market on the rights of member states to develop and maintain their own prioritisation systems, but also about the potential for what may be regarded as opportunistic welfare tourism of the kind that has now become a reality across the EU.

The much publicised test case of *Watts*[274] concerned delays in the treatment of a 72-year-old woman who, having been diagnosed as having osteo-arthritis in both hips, was told that the waiting time for medical treatment was about one year. In light of UK government policy of sending people to mainland Europe in order to reduce waiting lists, and on the basis of legally enforceable rights in EU law, she asked her Primary Care Trust (PCT) to support her application for treatment overseas. However, without waiting for a final response, she had the surgery in France, after which she was informed that her request had been rejected and that the waiting list had in fact fallen to four months.

Before the UK High Court, it was agreed that established principles of English law denied her an effective remedy and significantly that her case fell outside the protection of more vulnerable claimants in Articles 3 and 8 ECHR. She therefore relied instead on Article 49 EC Treaty and on Article 22 of the Council Regulation (EEC) 1408/71 as amended (hereafter 'Article 22 Council

---

that 'they are now "semi-sovereign welfare states", whose policy choices are subject to increasing scrutiny under Community law, and therefore reshaping the legal environment of welfare provision across Europe' (1).

[270] See for example A Pieter Van der Mei, *Free Movement of Persons within the European Community: Cross-border Access to Public Benefits* (Oxford, Hart, 2003), where the author explores the extent to which European Community law confers upon individuals the right to gain access to public services in other Member States and questions whether Community law has regard for Member States' concerns about 'welfare tourism'.

[271] EU internal market and competition law is enforceable at the suit of individuals in national courts. Challenges can then be heard by the ECJ under Art 234 of the EC preliminary rulings procedure.

[272] For examples of different pressures that EU internal market and EU competition law can place on national welfare systems, see *Sodermare SA v and Others v Region Lombardie*, Case C-70/95 [1997] ECR 1 3395, which concerned the provision of social welfare services of a health care character to residential homes for the elderly in Lombardy and questioned whether national subsidies to non-profit-making homes that are almost exclusively Italian indirectly discriminated against commercially operated homes on grounds of nationality. See also *Decker v Caisse de Maladie des Employes Prives*, Case C-120/95 [1998] ECR 1-1831; and *Kohll v Union des Caisses de Maladies*, Case C-158/96, [1998] ECR 1-1931. However see Hervey (2000) (note 223 above) for a discussion of the concept of 'social solidarity as a way of defusing the potentially deregulatory thrust of EU law'.

[273] See Arts 23, 25, 28 29, 39, 43 49 50 81, 82 and 86 EC.

[274] Note 266 above.

Regulation'),[275] the effect of which was to confer a legally enforceable right to be treated in another member state at public expense.

i. Undue Delay

On the question of the reasonableness of the waiting period, the trial judge in the UK decided that 'any national authority properly directing itself' in accordance with the principles laid down by the ECJ in *Geraets-Smits* and *Peerbooms*[276] and *Muller-Faure* and *Van Reit*[277] should have concluded that the anticipated delay of approximately one year was 'undue' delay,' sufficient to trigger the claimant's right under Article 49 EC Treaty to reimbursement of the costs of receiving more timely treatment in another member state. However, on the facts, it was concluded that the applicant had failed to establish 'undue delay', since by the time she went to France she had been reassessed and the anticipated waiting time for her treatment reduced to four months. It was further concluded that the test of what constituted undue delay was significantly higher under Article 22 Council Regulation than under Article 49 EC Treaty. Both the applicant and the Secretary of State for Health therefore appealed to the Court of Appeal.

The claimant's appeal was based primarily on the dismissal of her application for reimbursement and on the conclusion at first instance that national waiting times are relevant to a determination of what constitutes undue delay in Article 49 EC and also central to the proper application of Article 22 Council Regulation. By contrast, the Secretary of State's appeal was based on the more challenging contention that National Health Service (NHS) patients are not entitled to rely on the free movement of services provision in Article 49 EC Treaty because, in contrast with citizens in systems funded by insurance such as the Netherlands Sick Fund Law (ZWF) scheme, patients in the publicly funded NHS have no entitlement to receive services under Article 49; Mrs Watts' case should therefore be governed exclusively by Article 22 Council Regulation.

In view of these institutional differences, the Court of Appeal applied to the ECJ for a preliminary ruling,[278] asking for clarification of the extent to which principles in the case law relating to the free movement of services provision in

---

[275] Art 22(2), subpara 2 of the regulation provides that authorisation for treatment in another Member State is mandatory to the extent that 'it shall not be refused by the member state of insurance' in circumstances where 'the treatment cannot be provided within the time normally necessary for obtaining the treatment necessary in the member state of residence, taking account of his current state of health and the probable course of his disease'.

[276] *BSM Geraets-Smits v Stichting Ziekenfonds; HTM Peerbooms v Stichting CZ Groep Zorgverzekeringen*, Case C-157/99 (2001).

[277] *VG Muller-Fauré v Onderlinge Waarborgmaatschappij OZ Zorgverzekeringen UA; Van Riet v Onderlinge Waarborgmaatschappij OZ Zorgverzekeringen UA*, Case C-385/99 (2003).

[278] Following the Advocate General's Opinion in December 2005, the Grand Chamber gave its ruling in May 2006.

Article 49 EC were applicable to the NHS system,[279] which, in contrast with other systems previously considered, is wholly public in character.[280] Moreover, a further question relating specifically to Article 22 Council Regulation raised the key issue of what constitutes a legitimate delay when refusing to authorise treatment abroad, an issue that was also relevant to the decision regarding whether the refusal to authorise treatment under Article 49 EC had been objectively justified.

Advocate General Geelhoed,[281] and later the Grand Chamber,[282] went over familiar ground about the difficulties of harmonisation raised by compartmentalised national systems of health care and health insurance in an internal market common to twenty-five member states. It was also conceded that tensions are even more acute in cases in which the financing of health care has traditionally been addressed by the balancing of demand and supply within the confines of the national system, as with the NHS. Nevertheless, with the proviso that answers previously given might require further refinement in the context of the NHS, it was considered that basic principles for resolving the problems of funding cross-border provision of medical services, laid down over the past 10 years, are sufficiently well-established for the guidance of national courts.[283]

In its preliminary remarks, the Grand Chamber agreed with the opinion of Advocate General Geelhoed[284] that the applicability of Article 22 Council Regulation, which confers a legally enforceable entitlement under domestic law to receive services in kind in another member state, did not preclude the case from falling also within the scope of Article 49 EC.[285] Simply put, the court

---

[279] *Geraets-Smits and Peerbooms* (note 276 above); *Muller-Fauré and Van Riet* (note 277 above); and *Inizan v Caisse Primaire d'Assurance Maladie des Hauts de Seine*, Case C-56/01, 23 Oct 2003, [2006] 1 CMLR 20.

[280] For example, under Art 49, was there any distinction between a state-funded national health service such as the NHS and insurance funds such as the Netherlands ZFW scheme, particularly when considered that under the NHS, there is no fund out of which to make such reimbursements? Is the NHS obliged to authorise such payment, given that it is not obliged to authorise and pay for such treatment if it were to be carried out privately by a UK services provider? Is it material in answering these questions to establish whether hospital treatment provided by the NHS is itself a provision of services under Art 49?

[281] In *Watts* Case C-372/04, [2005], para 101. See also note 265 above.

[282] Note 265 above.

[283] Important issues concerning the relationship between Art 49 EC and Art 22 Council Regulation, which were relevant to the instant case, have also recently been addressed in the cases of *Vanbraekel v Alliance Nationale des Mutualities Chretiennes*, Case C-368/98, [2001] ECR I-5363; and *Inizan* (note 279 above).

[284] According to the Advocate General's opinion (para 101), there is no reason that seriously justifies different interpretations depending on whether the context is Art 22 EC or Art 49 Council Regulation.

[285] *Kohll v Union des Caisses de Maladies* (note 272 above) para 25. The fact that a national measure such as Article 49 (directed at states rather than at individuals) may be consistent with a provision of secondary legislation does not have the effect of removing that measure from the scope of the provisions of the Treaty. Specifically, the applicability of Art 22 Council Regulation to the situation in question did not mean that the person concerned may not simultaneously have the right under Art 49 EC to have access to health care in accordance with rules about costs in Art 49 that are different from those laid down by Art 22 Council Regulation. See also *Vanbraekel* (note 283 above) paras 37–53.

considered that in the case of both provisions, the crux of the matter is whether the hospital treatment required by the patient's medical condition can be provided in the territory of the member state of residence within an acceptable time, so as to ensure its usefulness and efficacy.

However, before considering issues of funding and reimbursement under Article 49 EC, the ECJ recalled that in the context of the general objectives of the treaty, Article 22 Council Regulation is one of a number of measures designed to allow a patient who is covered by the legislation of one member state to enjoy under the conditions specified in the regulation, benefits in kind in other member states, whatever the national institution with which he or she is registered and whatever the place of his or her residence.[286] Accordingly, Article 22 bestows a legally enforceable entitlement on a patient who is covered by the legislation of one member state and has received prior authorisation to be treated in the other Member state, to reimbursement conditions that are as favourable as those enjoyed by persons covered by the legislation of the host state.[287]

Thus, the Court regarded it as a crucial factor that Article 22 Council Regulation affords opportunity to an insuring state, such as the UK in Mrs Watts' case, to consider in advance whether to grant authorisation. Indeed, it is settled law that a patient failing to receive prior authorisation will not be entitled to reimbursement, unless authorisation has been wrongfully refused.[288] However, on the question of whether refusal was justified, the ECJ recalled its earlier rulings[289] in which it had decided that in determining whether treatment that is 'equally effective for the patient' can be obtained without 'undue delay' in a member state of residence, account must be taken not only of the patient's general medical condition but also of such factors, if appropriate, as the degree of pain or the nature of the patient's disability[290] and of his medical history at the time when authorisation is sought.[291]

---

[286] *Van der Duin and ANOZ Zorgverzekeringen* [2003] ECR 1-7045, para 50; *Juzgado de lo Social n° 20 de Madrid Heirs of Annette Keller v Instituto Nacional de la Seguridad Social (INSS) and Others*, Case C-145/03 [2005] ECR I-2529, para 45.

[287] *Watts* (Grand Chamber) (note 267 above) para 53. See *Inizan* (note 279 above) para 45: Art 22 Council Regulation helps to facilitate the free movement of patients and, to the same extent, the provision of cross-border medical services between Member States. See also *Vanbraekel* (note 283 above) para 32; and *Inizan* (note 279 above) para 21.

[288] *Inizan* (note 279 above) para 45; *Muller-Fauré and Van Riet* (note 277 above) para 89; and *Geraets-Smits and Peerbooms* (note 276 above) para 103.

[289] *Geraets-Smits and Peerboom* (note 276 above) para 104; *Muller-Fauré and Van Riet* (note 277 above) para 90.

[290] As a notable example, the condition might make it extremely difficult to carry out a professional activity.

[291] *Watts* (Grand Chamber) (note 265 above) para 62, citing *Inizan* (note 279 above). Moreover, the ECJ recalled that in *Muller-Fauré* it had similarly been concluded in relation to Art 49 that, in determining whether a treatment that is 'equally effective' is 'available without undue delay from an establishment in the territory of the member state of residence', the competent institution cannot base its decision exclusively on the existence of waiting lists, without taking account of the specific circumstances of the patient's medical condition (para 92).

Furthermore, although recognising that there is a tension between the role of waiting lists as an instrument for managing and allocating limited resources on one hand, and the interests of patients in receiving adequate and timely treatment on the other, the ECJ was clear that in accordance with recent case law, this tension must be addressed by the imposition of 'a number of conditions . . . on the way in which waiting lists are managed'. Thus,

> in order to be entitled to refuse authorisation . . . on the ground of waiting time, the competent institution must establish that the waiting time arises from objectives relating to the planning and management of the supply of hospital care, pursued by the national authorities on the basis of generally predetermined clinical priorities, within which the hospital treatment required by the patient's state of health may be obtained in an establishment forming part of the national system.[292]

In short, therefore, the ECJ agreed with the thrust of Advocate General Geelhelds' opinion:

> The setting of waiting times should not be confined to 'registering that a given patient is eligible for a given type of treatment with a given degree of urgency'. Instead, they should be managed actively, 'as dynamic and flexible instruments, which take into account the needs of patients as their medical condition develops'.[293]

As to the Secretary of State's argument that a notion of what constitutes 'undue delay' which is patient-oriented rather than determined by reference to standardised waiting times, would undermine the rationality of the prioritisation scheme and existing budgetary arrangements, the ECJ did not agree. Rather, it was concluded that if waiting times resulting from general planning objectives do not exceed medically acceptable waiting times in accordance with criteria determined by earlier case law, then the competent institution is entitled to refuse authorisation. Thus, patient migration would only have an adverse impact of the kind envisaged if the competent authority was bound to authorise patients to go elsewhere for treatment at its own expense, even when it could be supplied within a medically acceptable period within the hospitals covered by the service.[294]

Thus, in conclusion it was considered that despite the UK government's fears, the interpretation of the words 'the time normally necessary for obtaining the treatment necessary in the member state of residence, taking account of [the patient's] current state of health and the probable course of his disease' would be unlikely to undermine the power of national competent authorities to manage available hospital capacity in their area by use of waiting lists, 'provided, the

---

[292] *Ibid*, para 68.

[293] Advocate General's opinion (note 265 above) para 86, cited by the Grand Chamber (note 265 above) para 69.

[294] The fact that authorisation would require the establishment of a financial mechanism to enable it to satisfy requests for reimbursement to meet 'benefits in kind' received in the host member state was no more a legitimate reason for refusal in the publicly funded NHS than in the case of other types of systems.

existence of such lists does not prevent their taking account in each individual case of the medical circumstances and clinical needs of the person concerned when he requests authorisation to receive medical treatment in another Member State at the expense of the system with which he is registered'.[295]

Accordingly, the answer to the question posed by the Court of Appeal was that the words in the second subparagraph of Article 22 Council Regulation must be interpreted as meaning that:

> in order to be entitled to refuse authorisation, on the ground that there is a waiting time for hospital treatment, the competent institution is required to establish that that time does not exceed the period which is acceptable on the basis of an objective medical assessment of the clinical needs of the person concerned in light of all the factors characterising his medical condition at the time when the request for authorisation is made or renewed as the case may be.[296]

ii. Article 49 EC Treaty

The Court of Appeal's reference in *Watts* had essentially asked in what circumstances an NHS patient is entitled under the general principles of EU law reflected in Article 49 EC Treaty, to receive hospital treatment in another member state at the expense of the national service. It further questioned the relevance of the facts that there is no fund available to NHS bodies out of which such treatment may be paid and that the NHS has no duty to pay for private hospital treatment received by NHS patients in England and Wales. Moreover, subsumed in these questions was a further question as to whether hospital treatment provided by the NHS constitutes 'services' within the meaning of Article 49. If it does, a range of factors could legitimately be relied on in refusing to grant prior authorisation for treatment in another member state, and these factors could be taken into account in deciding whether there has been undue delay so as to justify refusal.[297]

It has long been established that medical services that are provided for payment fall within the scope of provisions on the freedom to provide services within Article 49 EC.[298] Further, it has been held that the freedom to provide services also includes the freedom for recipients of services, including persons in need of medical attention, to go to another member state to receive those services there.[299] More recently, it has also been established that the subsequent

---

[295] *Watts* (Grand Chamber) (note 265 above) para 75.
[296] *Ibid*, para 79.
[297] See the end of this subsection several paragraphs below.
[298] See inter alia: *Society for the Protection of Unborn Children Ireland v Grogan* [1991] ECR I–4685, para 18; *Kohll v Union des Caisses de Maladies* (note 272 above) para 29 (no need to distinguish between care provided in a hospital environment and care provided outside such an environment); *Vanbraekel* (note 283 above) para 41; *Geraets-Smits and Peerbooms* (note 276 above) para 53; *Muller-Fauré and Van Riet* (note 277 above) para 38; and *Inizan* (note 279 above) para 16.
[299] See joined cases *Graziana Luisi and Giuseppe Carbone v Ministero del Tesoro* [1984] ECR 377, para 16.

seeking of reimbursement for the hospital treatment in question from a publicly funded national health service does not mean that rules on the freedom to provide services guaranteed by the treaty do not apply.[300]

Thus, the ECJ concluded in *Watts* that in accordance with the case law on free movement of services, when a person such as Mrs Watts goes to another member state and receives treatment for payment, the situation falls within the scope of the provisions on freedom to provide services under Article 49 EC. Moreover, the fact that in her case reimbursement had been sought from a nationally funded health service did not mean that the rules on freedom to provide services guaranteed by the treaty do not apply.[301] Nor, according to recent case law, did it mean that that a supply of medical services ceases to be such, within the meaning of Article 49, because after paying the foreign supplier for her treatment, the patient has subsequently sought reimbursement from a national health service.[302] Thus, regardless of the way in which a national system of residence operates, circumstances such as those of Mrs Watts, where prior payment was made to the host provider, fall within the ambit of Article 49 EC.

Despite repeating its now familiar refrain that Community law does not detract from member state powers to organise their social security systems, and that it is for each to determine their own conditions under which social security benefits are granted, the ECJ nonetheless insisted that member states are prohibited from introducing or maintaining unjustified restrictions in the health care sector. What matters is that prioritisation polices comply with Community law, and in particular with the provisions on freedom of services.[303]

It is now established in the case law that Article 49 EC precludes national rules that render the provision of services between member states more difficult than the provision of services purely within one member state (for example, when provisions deter or even prevent individuals from applying to other member states).[304] Thus, at first sight UK rules prohibiting treatment abroad without prior authorisation are less favourable than those applying to the NHS, where no prior authorisation is needed for treatment.[305] Therefore, taking into account the derogations applicable under Article 46 EC, the next step for the ECJ to consider was the extent to which the need for prior authorisation could be justified in accordance with settled case law, so as to ensure that it does not

---

[300] *Muller-Fauré and Van Riet* (note 277 above).

[301] To that effect, see *Geraets-Smits and Peerbooms* (note 276 above) para 55; and *Muller-Fauré and Van Riet* (note 277 above).

[302] *Muller-Fauré and Van Riet* (note 277 above) para 103.

[303] See, inter alia, *Muller-Fauré and Van Riet* (note 277 above) para 100; and *Inizan* (note 279 above) para 17. For discussion of the implications of these decisions generally, see Hervey (2000) (note 223 above).

[304] See *Commission of the European Communities v France*, Case C-381/93 [1994] ECR I-5145; *Kohll* (note 272 above) para 33; and *Geraets-Smits and Peerbooms* (note 276 above) para 61.

[305] Even though there is no similar obligation to authorise or undertake the cost of private treatment in UK institutions (para 98). Accordingly, it was decided that the system deters or even prevents patients from applying for health treatment in other member states, so as to constitute an obstacle to the freedom to provide services.

exceed what is objectively necessary, and whether the same result could not be achieved by less restrictive rules.

The ECJ rejected a number of traditional grounds that had been proposed by the Court of Appeal as possible justifications for refusal of authorisation: the fact that it would seriously undermine the NHS system of administering medical priorities through waiting lists; that it would permit patients with less urgent medical needs to gain priority over patients with more urgent medical needs; that it would have the effect of diverting resources to pay for less urgent treatment for those who are willing to travel abroad, thereby adversely affecting others; that costs would increase for NHS bodies; that it may require the United Kingdom to provide additional funding for the NHS budget or restrict the range of treatments; that the costs of treatment in other member states may be more expensive.

Most importantly, however, as under Article 22 Council Regulation, the Court reiterated that in the context of Article 49, refusal to grant prior authorisation cannot be based merely on the existence of waiting lists enabling the supply of hospital care to be managed on the basis of predetermined clinical priorities, 'without carrying out in the individual case an objective medical assessment of the patient's medical condition, the history of the possible course of his illness, the degree of pain he is in and or the nature of his disability at the time when the request for prior authorisation was made.'[306]

V. CONCLUSION

This chapter has laid the foundations for discussion in the following chapters about the extent to which fundamental international human rights standards enshrined in the ECHR have been used by the judiciary to protect the social and economic welfare of vulnerable citizens in the United Kingdom. As we shall see, some of the most politically sensitive public law challenges under the HRA have tested: (i) its potential to enhance access to basic socio-economic entitlements for vulnerable individuals and groups caught up in the health and welfare systems; (ii) the extent to which notions of fairness in the distribution of public goods in Strasbourg should be replicated in the domestic arena; and (iii) the extent to which the quality of administrative justice in ordinary administrative disputes over the allocation of public resources (housing, social security benefits, asylum support) can be compatible with due process rights in the ECHR.

In this chapter we have also highlighted a problematic tension between the use of human rights standards under the ECHR and the EU Charter of Fundamental Rights on one hand, and the concept of socio-economic rights in

---

[306] *Watts* (Grand Chamber) (note 265 above) para 119. The ECJ had already held that Art 46 EC permits member states to restrict the freedom to provide medical and hospital services insofar as the maintenance of treatment capacity or medical competence on national territory is essential for public health or even the survival of the population.

EU law on the other. Fundamental differences of approach are necessary in determining the proportionality of prioritisation decisions when questions of legally enforceable socio-economic entitlements in EU law are at issue. We have thus seen how in its reference to the ECJ in *Watts*, the UK High Court was clear that although the claimant fell outside the kind of protection afforded to vulnerable claimants in Articles 3 and 8 ECHR, she could successfully rely on Article 49 of the EC Treaty and on Article 22 of the Council Regulation (EEC), the effects of which were to confer legally enforceable rights to be treated in another member state at public expense. In *Watts*, the claimant exercised an a priori legally enforceable right derived from her status as a citizen of the EU.

By contrast, we have seen how in *Price v UK* a majority of the ECtHR held that the detention of a severely disabled person in conditions where, among other physical and intensely personal indignities suffered, she had risked developing sores because her bed was too hard and unreachable, constituted a failure to provide care appropriate to her needs and was therefore an infringement of Article 3 ECHR.[307] In other words, at the heart of the claimant's right in *Price* to receive appropriate and timely care consistent with her needs were issues of human dignity and the effect of treatment on the claimant's psychological well-being.

Like the case of *Watts*, many of the challenges that will be examined in subsequent chapters concern attempts to gain access to public services in the face of limited local authority or central government resources. Thus, in the NHS health sector of the UK, where the so-called postcode lottery has received greatest publicity, courts have increasingly been confronted with individual or public interest group challenges, for example to receive expensive life-prolonging treatment or to prevent the closure of hospitals that have run into debt.

As noted in the Introduction of this book, questions about the extent to which UK courts might be assisted in their task of differential rights adjudication by the inclusion of carefully tailored socio-economic rights to health care or to an adequate standard of living are beyond the scope of our enquiry. Notwithstanding, our purpose in this chapter has been not only to demonstrate the inadequacy of an absolute 'right to health care' as a means of determining the share of available resources to which citizens have a right, but also to suggest that at the very minimum, fundamental values of respect for dignity and personal integrity enshrined in the ECHR should inform UK public service prioritisation decisions—whoever has ultimate responsibility for the allocation of scarce resources to meet basic human needs.[308]

---

[307] Note 44 above. See also note 112 above.
[308] See M Brazier, 'Rights and Health Care' in R Blackburn (ed), *Rights of Citizenship* (London, Mansell, 1993) 58.

3

Courts, the UK Constitution and the Human Rights Act 1998

I. INTRODUCTION

I N PREPARATION FOR the examination in the following chapters of substantive case law concerning the impact of the Human Rights Act (HRA) 1998 on the role of UK courts in decisions about access to health and welfare services, this chapter provides an account of the structure and operation of the Act. It analyses the approach of courts to their novel powers of legislative scrutiny under section 3 HRA and considers whether the degree of judicial deference accorded to Parliament in the interpretation and exercise of their HRA obligations has been consistent with collaborative constitutional safeguards surrounding the design and structure of the Act. Where relevant, the role of courts in socio-economic disputes has been highlighted.

In chapter four below we will focus more closely on the tension between the orthodox approach to the review of public authority decision-making in English administrative law on the one hand, and the justificatory techniques of human rights adjudication presupposed by section 6 HRA on the other hand. However, in light of the inexorable retreat from welfare to market in the delivery of public services, the final section of this chapter considers one of the most controversial issues under the HRA: the extent to which its central thrust against the conduct of public authorities, as defined in section 6, is apt to control the decision-making powers of private bodies performing erstwhile public functions such as the delivery of health, education and community care services, irrespective of the legal derivation of their powers.

II. READING AND GIVING EFFECT TO ECHR RIGHTS IN UK COURTS

A. The Background and Political Context of the Human Rights Act 1998

Prior to the enactment of the Human Rights Act in 1998 there was protracted controversy as to whether a Bill of Rights should be adopted in the unwritten constitution of the United Kingdom.[1] Opponents of an entrenched Bill of Rights focused in particular on the implications for the doctrine of parliamentary sovereignty and questioned the potentially significant decision-making role of non-elected judges in political matters deemed more appropriately to belong to the elected organs of government.[2] However, following a sustained campaign by liberal rights constitutionalists,[3] a number of NGOs[4] and indeed many senior members of the judiciary themselves,[5] the New Labour government, despite having thrown its weight behind the movement for a Bill of Rights before coming to office, instead incorporated the rights contained in the ECHR into domestic law through the HRA.[6]

For a small number of key campaigners, the promise of the HRA lay in its perceived potential to generate a new culture of rights in the United Kindom, which would protect and respect the rights of the vulnerable as well those who can afford litigation.[7] It was contemplated that in a climate of heightened awareness, citizens might develop a greater sense of fundamental rights and responsi-

---

[1] See generally J Jowell and D Oliver (eds), *The Changing Constitution*, 5th edn (Oxford, OUP, 2004). The impact of the European Communities Act 1972 on the sovereignty of Parliament lent force to arguments for adopting a constitutional Bill of Rights. See for example A Lester, 'The Constitution: Decline and Renewal' in Jowell and Oliver (eds) (*op cit*); and A Lester, et al, 'A British Bill of Rights', Institute of Public Policy Research, Consultation Paper No 1, 1990.

[2] See generally JAG Griffiths, *The Politics of the Judiciary*, 5th edn (London, Fontana, 1997). Although the orthodox model of parliamentary sovereignty no longer matches the balance of power between courts and Parliament in the UK, since the HRA, questions about the protection of fundamental rights in domestic courts have continued to be debated in terms of opposing supremacies: rights versus parliamentary sovereignty. For analyses of these rival constitutional discourses, see for example N Walker, 'Setting English Judges to Rights' (1999) *Oxford Journal of Legal Studies* 133; and M Elliott, 'Reconciling Constitutional Rights and Constitutional Orthodoxy' (1997) *Cambridge Law Journal* 474, 476.

[3] For a brief history of the campaign for incorporation, see L Lester and D Pannick, *Human Rights Law and Practice*, 2nd edn (Butterworths, London, 2004) 11–14.

[4] For example, the National Council of Civil Liberties (now Liberty), JUSTICE, the Constitutional Reform Centre, the Institute for Public Policy Research and Charter 88.

[5] See Lord Scarman, *English Law: The New Dimension* (London, Hamlyn, 1976); and T Bingham, 'The European Convention on Human Rights: Time to Incorporate' (1993) 109 *Law Quarterly Review* 390–400. Sir Thomas Bingham (as he then was), now the most senior Law Lord, was most prominent in the campaign for incorporation.

[6] The incorporation of the ECHR rights through the HRA was promulgated as a balanced compromise between the increased protection of human rights and the preservation of the constitutional supremacy of the Queen in Parliament. See Lord Lester of Herne Hill, '"The Art of the Possible": Interpretation of Statutes under the Human Rights Act' (1998) 3 *European Human Rights Law Review* 665–75, 668; Lord Irving of Lairg, 'The Development of Human Rights in Britain under an Incorporated Convention of Human Rights' (1998) *Public Law* 221; Sir W Wade, 'Human Rights and the Judiciary' (1998) 3 *European Human Rights Law Review* 520; and D Feldman, 'The Human Rights Act 1998 and Constitutional Principles' (1998) 19 *Legal Studies* 165–206. But compare T Campbell, 'Incorporation through Interpretation' in T Campbell, KD Ewing and A Tomkins (eds), *Sceptical Essays in Human Rights* (Oxford, OUP, 2001) 79–101. The author considers that 'the interpretative techniques . . . licensed by the HRA, would make judges the determinate body with respect to a wide body of policy issues which have hitherto been in the sphere of parliamentary responsibility' (79).

[7] The work of F Klug, *Values of a Godless Age* (Harmondsworth, Penguin, 2000) has been influential in this regard. See also J Wadham, H Mountfield, and A Edmundson, *Blackstone's Guide to the Human Rights Act 1998*, 3rd edn (Oxford, OUP, 2003) 14.

bilities gained by virtue of their common humanity, rather than by dint of state patronage. Furthermore, there was a degree of optimism that fundamental rights principles would be 'mainstreamed' into the design and delivery of government policy, legislation and public services[8] and that 'obligations imposed by the HRA would go beyond negative interference with rights and require public bodies to take active steps to protect peoples' rights.'[9]

Nevertheless, in the prolonged controversy that preceded the HRA, little attention was paid to the content of the rights to be incorporated into UK law.[10] Indeed, it was narrowly assumed by most supporters that liberal democratic rights of the kind enshrined in the ECHR would provide an entirely apposite foundation and that there would be no need to fashion a home-grown Bill of Rights for the United Kingdom.[11] Belatedly, however, constitutional commentators have raised concerns about the lack of balance reflected in the incorporation of an 'outmoded' treaty such as the ECHR into the fabric of UK constitutional law.[12] Critical of what is perceived as the limited potential of the ECHR rights to protect, at best, a very basic minimum standard of living,[13] various appeals have been made for the International Covenant on Economic, Social and Cultural Rights (ICESCR) 1966 to be incorporated into UK law;[14] for the adoption of a novel constitutional framework that would protect both sets of rights;[15] and for courts, in their interpretation of the ECHR rights, to follow the example of the Strasbourg organs in having regard to other international treaties (to which the United Kingdom is signatory), such as International Labour Organization (ILO) Conventions and the Council of Europe's revised Social Charter (ESC) 1996.[16]

---

[8] The work of the British Institute of Human Rights (BIHR), a charity whose mission is to 'raise awareness and understanding about the importance of human rights', has promoted these twin objectives, focusing especially on the promotion of a culture of rights in the delivery of public services.

[9] Wadham, et al (note 7 above) 14.

[10] In the UK, socio-economic rights have continued to be viewed as policy matters of discretionary entitlement that are subject to democratic change, inherently non-justiciable and therefore different from civil and political rights.

[11] Normative liberal rights constitutionalists such as Lord Lester drew inspiration from the work of Ronald Dworkin, whose claims for the ascendancy of principles of individual freedom over collective goals and policies were based on notions of fair and just treatment and respect for the human dignity of others. For example, see R Dworkin, *A Matter of Principle* (Oxford, OUP, 1985) ch 8.

[12] See KD Ewing, 'Constitutional Reform and Human Rights: Unfinished Business' (2001) *Edinburgh Law Review* 297; and G Van Beuren, 'Including the Excluded: The Case for an Economic Social and Cultural Rights Act' (2002) *Public Law* 456.

[13] E Metcalfe, 'Justice Response to the *Inquiry into the Concluding Observations of the UN Committee on Economic Social and Cultural Rights*', E/C.12/1/Add.79, by the Joint Committee on Human Rights (JCHR), 2003, available at http://www.justice.org.uk, para 17.

[14] *Ibid*.

[15] Van Beuren (note 12 above).

[16] K Ewing, 'The Unbalanced Constitution' in Campbell, Ewing and Tomkins (eds) (note 6 above), where the author highlights use made by the Strasbourg organs of other international treaties. Although remaining highly sceptical, he suggests that when taking account of relevant Strasbourg jurisprudence under s 2, UK courts should engage with other international treaties that reflect social values as well as liberal constitutional values enshrined in the ECHR.

However, orthodox perceptions about differences in the nature of civil and political rights on the one hand and socio-economic rights on the other remain embedded in the thinking of the UK political establishment, as can be seen in a dismissive response by the Blair government, following the HRA, to a proposal that the ICESCR might be incorporated into UK law. When asked by the Parliamentary Joint Committee on Human Rights (JCHR) to comment on the concluding observations of the United Nations Committee on Economic, Social and Cultural Rights (UNCESCR) following the United Kingdom's fourth periodic report in 2002,[17] a junior minister at the Foreign and Commonwealth Office who gave evidence said:

> I think there would be real difficulties with full legal incorporation. To give you a flavour of what I mean by that, if you look at the rights of adequate food, clothing and housing, these are issues for which there is no absolute standard, and are rightly the business of governments and their electorates through general elections, to determine what standard we should achieve.[18]

In face of such intransigence, it has been left largely to the efforts of strategic human rights campaigners and practitioners[19] to see how far UK courts might be prepared to travel on the uncharted sea of socio-economic rights protection through their interpretation of the ECHR.[20]

There is indeed a need for an informed debate in the United Kingdom about the extent to which the protection of positive socio-economic rights (for example, rights to a reasonable standard of health care, to adequate housing or to

---

[17] The concluding observations were made on 5 June 2002, following an unfavorable periodic report (the UK's fourth under the International Covenant on Economic Social and Cultural Rights) in which the UNCESCR expressed its regret that 'the Covenant has still not been incorporated in the domestic legal order and that there is no intention by [the UK] to do so in the near future'.

[18] Evidence of Bill Rammell MP, then Parliamentary Under-Secretary of State, Foreign and Commonwealth Office, 15 September 2003, reply to Q24.

[19] Campaigning lawyers, with the support of JUSTICE and large pressure groups such as Shelter, Help the Aged and the Public Law Project (PLP), had in the decade previous to the HRA been active in the pursuit of socio-economic rights protection through ordinary principles of public administrative law. An independent legal charity, the PLP aims to 'improve access to public law remedies, for those whose access is restricted by poverty, discrimination or other similar barriers'. See http://www.publiclawproject.org.uk. Following the enactment of the HRA, the British Institute of Human Rights (BIHR) has actively supported the promotion of a culture of human rights in public services for the vulnerable. For the role of pressure groups in the UK, see C Harlow and D Rawlings, *Pressure Through Law* (London, Routledge, 1992). For a more recent critique of American style 'group litigation' in the UK where the author argues that the growth of 'campaigning' style advocacy in the UK contributes to a blurring of the traditional distinctions between the legal and political process, see C Harlow, 'Public Law and Popular Justice' (2002) 65 *Modern Law Review* 1. For further discussion, see also chapter one, section II A–C above.

[20] The metaphor is borrowed from Sedley LJ, 'The Rocks or the Open Sea: Where is the Human Rights Act Heading?' (2003) *Legal Action* 1. In an annual address to the Legal Action Group (LAG), Sedley LJ recognised the potential use of the HRA, if not to create access to litigation, at least to raise awareness that certain rights are there to be claimed: 'The indignities which the elderly and infirm sometimes suffer in institutions are only one of many examples . . . The treatment of prisoners' families is another. And when it comes to enforcement, we are starting to appreciate that there are large geographical and social gaps in the legal profession's ability to provide advice and representation' (1).

other basic services) might be enhanced by either the incorporation of the ICESCR, the revised ESC or other international treaties, or indeed through the design of a wholly novel constitutional settlement dedicated to the protection of both civil and political rights *and* socio-economic rights.[21] However, further constitutional debate of the kind which has taken place elsewhere in Europe and beyond during the latter part of the last century—about the potential for greater judicial protection to socio-economic rights through dedicated constitutional arrangements—is beyond the scope of this book. Instead, the following chapters are primarily concerned with the specific responses of UK courts to the efforts of campaigning human rights advocates, who have been testing the potential of the HRA to give rise to positive obligations in diverse areas of public service provision.[22]

B. The Purpose and Structure of the HRA

The purpose of the HRA, which came fully into force on 2 October 2000, is to 'bring home'[23] certain of the rights enshrined in the ECHR, by giving 'further effect'[24] to those rights in English law.[25] Not only was it contemplated that public power would be constrained by courts in circumstances where it impinged unjustifiably on those rights and whenever it fell short of principles of proportionality and non-discrimination; more expansively, it was claimed that the HRA would provide the foundations for a lasting culture of human rights that would be central to the lives of individuals in society. Thus, on the second reading of the Bill in the House of Lords, the Lord Chancellor stressed that 'our

[21] For the potential of the ICESCR to enhance the protection of socio-economic rights in the UK, see S Weir, *Unequal Britain: Human Rights as a Route to Social Justice* (London, Methuen, 2006). See Afterword below (335).

[22] These include public housing; community care services for adults; services for Children under Part III of the Children Act 1989; accommodation services for the disabled and other vulnerable adults; and basic support for destitute asylum seekers.

[23] Human Rights Unit (Home Office), 'Rights Brought Home: The Human Rights Bill' (White Paper) CM 3782, October 1997. In the Preface to the White Paper, it was explained by Prime Minister Tony Blair that the HRA 1998 is intended to 'give people in the UK opportunities to enforce their rights under the European Convention in UK courts, rather than having to incur the cost and delay of taking a case to the European Court of Human Rights in Strasbourg'.

[24] The Lord Chancellor, Lord Irvine of Lairg, explained during the Committee stage of the Bill in the House of Lords that the reason the long title uses the word 'further' is that our courts already apply the Convention in many different circumstances. See Hansard HL Official Report (5th series) vol 583 col 478 (18 Nov 1997) [2.03]. He then amplified this, stating that 'The HRA 1998 does not create new human rights or take away rights. It provides better and easier access to rights that already exist.' The use of human rights in UK courts before the HRA (including rights contained in the ECHR) will be discussed further in chapter 4 below.

[25] Instead of giving direct effect to the ECHR rights by their incorporation into UK law, the stated objective was to weave the Convention into the existing legal system by requiring all courts to consider Convention arguments and rights, which can obtain in Strasbourg. It was argued that by avoiding the incorporation of the Convention rights as rights, which take precedence over other common law and statutory rights, the sovereignty of Parliament will be maintained.

courts will develop human rights throughout society. A culture of awareness of human rights will develop.'[26]

The rights to be 'brought home' are contained in section 1(1) HRA.[27] Notably, however, the ECHR rights did not become rights in English law. Instead, they are given domestic effect as laid down under the HRA, which makes it unlawful for a public authority to act in a way that is incompatible with a Convention right.[28] Moreover, since 'public authority' is defined to include courts,[29] the courts—in addition to having judicial powers to read legislation 'so far as is it is possible to do so' compatibly with the ECHR rights[30] and to review the acts of public authorities that are alleged to be ECHR non-compatible—are themselves bound to act compatibly with ECHR rights, an obligation that extends to their role in developing the common law. Furthermore, under section 2 HRA, although not bound by decisions of the Strasbourg organs, all courts and tribunals must take account of the Convention jurisprudence,[31] an obligation that meets one of the primary objectives of the Act—to limit the need for future recourse to Strasbourg.

A key aspect of the process of 'bringing rights home' to the United Kingdom was to ensure the availability of effective remedies for breach. Thus, a victim[32] of an act by a public authority that infringes Convention rights is permitted to bring proceedings in 'the appropriate court or tribunal'.[33] Moreover, although

---

[26] Hansard HL Official Report (5th series) vol 582 col 1228 (3 Nov 1997). See also Lord Williams' observation that every public authority 'will know that its behaviour its structures, its conclusions and executive actions will be subject to this culture' (col 1308).

[27] They are Arts 2–12 and 14 ECHR; Arts 1–3 Protocol 1 to the ECHR; and Arts 1–2 Protocol 6 to the ECHR. Moreover, all must be read subject to Arts 16–18 ECHR and have effect subject to any designated derogation or reservations.

[28] S 6(1)(a) HRA.

[29] S 6(3)(a) HRA.

[30] S 3(1) HRA.

[31] When ruling on a question that has arisen in connection with a Convention right, a court or tribunal must take into account, inter alia, any judgment decision or advisory opinion of the ECHR court, whenever given. See subsection F below.

[32] Any legal or natural person can use the Act. Accordingly, the HRA can be relied on by companies. In accordance with ss 7(1) and 7(3) HRA, proceedings can only be brought under the Act by a person who is, or would be, a victim of the violation. At first sight this precludes the possibility of public law challenges by public interest groups of the kind possible under the rules of standing employed in public law disputes under Part 54 Civil Procedure Rules. However, in effect, the position has been mitigated by the relaxed rule on third-party interventions and *amicus* briefs, which evolved prior to the HRA. Thus, written submissions on the wider implications of cases have been produced by third-party interveners, such as Shelter or Help the Aged. See for example the role played by Shelter in *A v Lambeth LBC* (2002) 4 CCLR 487; and *W v Lambeth LBC* [2002] 2 ALL ER 901. (See further chapter 5 below.) For further discussion of the issues raised by the 'victim limitation', see Wadham, et al (note 7 above) 92; and S Hannnett, 'Third Party Intervention: In the Public Interest' [2003] *Public Law* 128.

[33] S 7(1)(a). The 'appropriate court or tribunal' in essence means that claims go to the court or tribunal most accustomed to dealing with claims of the kind disputed. Thus, for example, family courts are likely to deal with human rights issues relating to care proceedings; and human rights issues concerning enforcement of rights to payment under the Child Support Act 1991 are more appropriately dealt with in the administrative court. See for example *R on the application of Kehoe v Secretary of State for Work and Pensions* [2003] EWCH 1021, [2005] 4 All ER 905.

the HRA does not include Article 13 ECHR,[34] it contains a crucial remedial provision, which authorises a court that has found an act or proposed act of a public authority to be unlawful, to grant 'such relief or remedy or make such order, within its powers as it considers just and appropriate'.[35] In effect therefore the HRA has created a far-reaching novel cause of action,[36] which may found a claim for relief, including damages against a public authority that has acted in breach of the ECHR rights. Thus, in *R (on the Application of Bernard) v London Borough of Enfield*,[37] a case to which we shall return, compensatory damages were awarded for the first time under the HRA in public law, for breach of the positive duty of respect for private and family life in Article 8 ECHR.[38]

Significantly, a number of constitutional checks and balances have been incorporated into the HRA, which demonstrates that 'bringing rights home' was intended to be a collaborative endeavour between Parliament, the executive and judiciary.[39] Thus, while the interpretative obligation in section 3(1), which

[34] Art 13 concerns the duty to afford an effective remedy for violation of Convention rights. The rationale for its omission was that the Human Rights Act in itself constituted compliance with Art 13.

[35] S 8(1) HRA.

[36] There has been acute controversy over the relationship between the HRA and existing remedies in public and private law and the extent to which ss 7 and 8 HRA have, taken together, created a novel public law tort. See for example L Lester and D Pannick, 'The Impact of the Human Rights Act on Private Law: The Knights Move' (2000) 116 *Law Quarterly Review* 380. For damages under the HRA, see generally Law Commission, 'Damages under the Human Rights Act 1998' (Law Com No 266 Cm 4853, 2000); M Amos, 'Damages for Breach of the Human Rights Act 1998' (1999) *EHRLR* 178; D Fairgreave, 'The Human Rights Act 1998: Damages and Tort Law' (2001) *Public Law* 695; and R Clayton, 'Damage Limitation: The Courts and Human Rights Act Damages' (2005) *Public Law* 429. In the important Court of Appeal decision of *Anufrejiya v Southwark London Borough Council* [2004] 1 All ER 833 (discussed in ch 6 below), the Court of Appeal had opportunity to consider the scope of the power to award damages under the HRA in public law challenges founded on breach of statutory duty. In giving the judgement of the Court of Appeal, Lord Woolf held that damages were not recoverable as of right where Convention rights had been breached and courts were to look critically at such claims; further, since the concern in such cases was usually to bring the infringement to an end, compensation was of secondary importance. An equitable approach to the award of damages was therefore required, and the need for damages should be ascertainable from an examination of the correspondence and witness statements. See also *R on the application of Greenfield v Sec State for the Home Department* [2005] UKHL 14, where the House of Lords decided in relation to breach of Art 6 that, in determining whether to award damages or the amount of an award, the Court must take into account the principles applied by Strasbourg in affording just satisfaction to the injured party.

[37] [2003] UKHRR 148. *Bernard* was concerned with the failure by a public authority to meet the accommodation needs of a severely disabled person within a reasonable period of time, when the urgency of the person's needs had been recorded by assessment.

[38] See also *R on the Application of N v Secretary of State for the Home Department* [2003] EWCH Admin. The claimant brought a successful action for judicial review and damages against the Secretary of State, contending that the delay in granting him refugee status constituted breach of the positive duty of respect for private and family life in Art 8 (although not of Art 3), arising from maladministration in the handling of his asylum claim, which caused him psychiatric illness. His claim, one of three conjoined appeals, was upheld by the Court of Appeal in *Anufrejiya* (note 36 above).

[39] For the intended balance between judiciary legislature and the executive under the HRA generally, see TR Hickman, 'Constitutional Dialogue, Constitutional Theories and the Human Rights Act 1998' (2005) *Public Law* 306.

applies to 'primary legislation and subordinate legislation whenever enacted',[40] requires that 'so far as it is possible to do so, primary and subordinate legislation must be read and given effect to in a way which is compatible with the Convention rights',[41] section 3(2) allows that 'this does not affect the validity, continuing operation, or enforcement of any incompatible primary legislation'.[42]

Although in deference to the authority of the legislature, there is no judicial power to strike down non-conforming legislation, there is nevertheless a non-remedial power in section 4 HRA that allows courts[43] to make a formal 'declaration of incompatibility'—although notably once again this does not affect the 'validity continuing, operation or enforcement' of the offending provision.[44] The cooperative nature of the HRA endeavour is further emphasised in section 5, which requires a court when considering whether to make a declaration of incompatibility to give notice to the Crown, which is entitled to be joined as a party to the proceedings.[45] Furthermore, the crucial involvement of Parliament is contemplated by section 19, which seeks to ensure that in the preparation of Bills and in their passage through Parliament, consideration is given to any implications they may have in relation to Convention rights.[46]

Since the implementation of the HRA there has been continuing controversy about the extent to which the intended constitutional balance between courts and the executive has been achieved by judicial interpretations of the HRA.[47] Less attention has been paid, however, to the crucial role of the JCHR in ensuring that balance.[48] Composed of members of both Houses of Parliament, the

[40] See s 3(2)(a) HRA.

[41] S 3(1) HRA.

[42] S 3(2)(b). Similarly, s 3(2)(c) provides that 'the validity continuing operation or enforcement of incompatible subordinate legislation' will be unaffected 'if primary legislation . . . prevents removal of the incompatibility'.

[43] S 4(5) provides that for this purpose, 'court' includes the House of Lords, the Privy Council, the High Court and Courts of Appeal.

[44] S 4(6) HRA. It was envisaged in Parliamentary debates that if used sparingly, such a declaration of incompatibility would attract the attention of Parliament and the public to the need for legislative reform in outstanding cases of incompatibility, thereby still avoiding recourse to Strasbourg.

[45] See ss 5(1)–(5) HRA.

[46] S 19 HRA provides that a Minister of the Crown in charge of a Bill in either House of Parliament must, before the second reading of the Bill, either make a statement that in their view the provisions of the Bill are compatible with the Convention rights (a statement of compatibility), *or* that although incompatible, the government nevertheless wishes the House to proceed with the Bill. On the second reading of the Bill in the House of Lords, the Lord Chancellor recognised that s 19 would have a significant impact on the scrutiny of draft legislation within government: 'Clause 19 imposes a new requirement on Government Ministers when introducing legislation. In future they will have to make a statement either that the provisions of the legislation are compatible with the Convention or that they cannot make such a statement but nevertheless wish Parliament to proceed to consider the Bill . . . Where such a statement cannot be made, Parliamentary scrutiny of the Bill will be intense' (Hansard HL Official Report, 2nd Reading (5th series) vol 582, Col 1233 (3 Nov 1997).

[47] See the discussion in subsections D and E below.

[48] The Committee was established in 1999. For an account of the history of the JCHR, see Wadham, et al (note 7 above) 15. The authors note that the idea of such a Committee was inspired by the monograph produced by Liberty: F Klug, *A People's Charter: Liberty's Bill of Rights* (London, NCCL, 1991). For the role of the Committee generally, see Lester and Pannick (note 3 above) 603–18. For a recent discussion of the importance of its constitutional role in developing a

Committee is overseen by a fulltime legal adviser,[49] who reviews all Bills once introduced, for compatibility not just with the ECHR rights but with all UK human rights obligations,[50] thereby shifting some of the onus from the courts. Independent of the executive and uninhibited by constitutional constraints to which judges are subject by virtue of the doctrine of the separation of powers, the JCHR is competent to provide both Houses of Parliament and courts with informed legal opinions on all matters relating to human rights in the UK, including the compatibility of enacted or proposed legislation with UK international treaty obligations. Therefore, in circumstances of potential conflict between courts and the executive over sensitive public interest or socio-political issues, JCHR Reports can provide democratic support[51] for a strong judicial stance against legislation that appears to fly in the face of international treaty obligations, including those in the ECHR.[52]

Thus, as we shall see further, the monitoring work of the JCHR potentially has a crucial role to play in securing the compatibility of present and future UK legislation with all UK international human rights obligations, and especially with rights incorporated by the HRA. The Committee's work not only serves to highlight the collaborative nature of the human rights endeavour (by demonstrating that Parliament, the executive and the courts together have responsibility for human rights protection), but also affords an important opportunity to bring home to both Houses of Parliament and to courts the overlapping nature of civil, political and socio-economic rights and the ways in which positive socio-economic rights can be protected through the ECHR.

In our areas of interest, to date there have been influential Reports on the meaning of public authority under the HRA; the compatibility of the Mental Health Bill 2002 with ECHR rights; a critical Report on the compatibility of the Homelessness Bill 2001 with international treaty obligations, including those in the CRC 1989; and, as we shall see further, a crucial Report on provisions in the Immigration and Asylum Seekers Act 2001 concerning the refusal or withdrawal of basic living support from destitute asylum seekers without any other means

---

culture of human rights and for comparison with Canada and New Zealand, see JL Hiebert, 'Parliament and the Human Rights Act' (2006) 4(1) *Int'l Journal of Constitutional Law* 1–38. See further the final section of this chapter.

[49] The expert adviser notifies the Committee about aspects of Bills that raise questions of human rights compatibility and advises them on questions to be put to ministers and departments.

[50] The Joint Committee on Human Rights (JCHR) terms of reference are wide and general. Although the Committee has a specific role in relation to questioning ministers with regard to statements of incompatibility under s 19 (see notes 44 and 46 above), it can also question them on compatibility questions, for example those arising under the ICCPR, the ICESCR and the CRC.

[51] As we shall see further, in addition to crucial work in relation to crisis legislation concerning asylum, immigration and 'the threat of terror', the Committee has provided critical scrutiny of legislation concerning socio-economic rights for compatibility with international treaties, including the ICESCR and the UN Convention on the Rights of the Child (CRC) 1989. The Committee will publish its 'Tenth Report' on 30 March 2007: JCHR, 'Tenth Report: Treatment of Asylum Seekers' (2006–07) HL 81 HC 60.

[52] However, notably under the HRA, the judicial role is confined to scrutiny of legislation compatibly with ECHR rights.

of support, pending the hearing of their claims. The Committee has also been singularly active in reminding the government of the difficulties of dissociating the human rights of children from those of the adults on whom they depend, challenging the government on the reasons for its failure to establish a Commissioner for Children's Rights[53] and closely questioning the Minister for Children in relation to the concerns of the UN Committee for Children's Rights in relation to its obligations under its most recent Report. Furthermore, the JCHR has responded to concerns about the unequal treatment of mentally ill patients by their exclusion from legislation that authorises the fining of social services for failure to provide accommodation for patients ready to be discharged from hospital. Finally, as we shall see, the courts as public authorities have themselves been the subject of trenchant criticism in a JCHR Report, in relation to their interpretation of the scope of section 6(3)(b) HRA.[54]

The HRA has been fulsomely praised (not only by commentators who had a hand in its creation) for its clever and intricate structure, and in general it has been clearly drafted.[55] Moreover, although the use of Parliamentary material as a legitimate aid to judicial interpretation of the HRA has been rejected by the House of Lords,[56] the protracted Parliamentary debates that preceded the HRA contain a wealth of background commentary on its objects and purpose.[57] Its enactment was furthermore accompanied by a deluge of academic commentary, much of which came from influential practitioners who had long been active in Strasbourg.[58] Thus, by the time the HRA was in force, senior judges were in no

---

[53] Children's Commissioners have now been appointed for England, Scotland, Northern Ireland and Wales.

[54] See the final section of this chapter. The JCHR has also recently published its 'Ninth Report': JCHR, 'Ninth Report: The Meaning of Public Authority under the Human Rights Act' HL (2006–07) 77 HC 410 (28 March 2007).

[55] 'The HRA 1998 is beautifully drafted. Its structure tight and elegant, marred only by the interpolation of sections 12 and 13' (so as to include Arts 1 and 2 of the sixth protocol within the scope of the Convention rights against the wishes of the government): *Wilson v First County Trust Ltd (No 2)* [2003] 3 WLR 568, 619 (Lord Rodger). See generally Wadham, et al (note 7 above) for a concise and logical exposition of the intricate structure and operation of the HRA.

[56] In light of the decision of the House of Lords in *Pepper v Hart* (1993) AC 593, one of the most intense controversies following the HRA has concerned the legitimate use of Parliamentary material in determining the scope of the HRA—both in relation to the scope of judicial powers when interpreting legislation under s 3, and in relation to the meaning of a hybrid public authority under s 6(3)(b). For the origins of the debate generally, see F Klug, 'The Human Rights Act 1998: *Pepper v Hart* and All That' (1999) *Public Law* 246; and A Kavanagh, 'Pepper and Hart and Matters of Constitutional Principle' (2005) 121 *Law Quarterly Review* 98. In *Aston Cantlow and Wilmcote with Billesley Parochial Church Council v Wallbank* [2003] UKHL 295, the House of Lords concluded that courts should not look to Hansard for the meaning of s 6, 'since it is the words used by Parliament in the legislation that must be interpreted' (37). See also *Wilson v First County Trust Ltd (No 2)* (*ibid*). However, inevitably Hansard has provided a rich background source of information as to what ministers regard as the purpose of the statutory provisions.

[57] See J Cooper and AM Williams (eds), *Legislating for Human Rights* (Oxford, Hart, 2000) for a useful compilation of the Parliamentary debates that preceded the enactment of the HRA.

[58] Following the enactment of the HRA, courts frequently referred to the authoritative pronouncements, articles and textbooks of human rights practitioner advocates such as Lester and Pannick (note 3 above), Clayton (note 36 above) and Tomlinson. See also R Clayton and H Tomlinson, *The Law of Human Rights* (Oxford, OUP, 2000) in determining the scope of the HRA rights.

doubt that their distinctive role would be the interpretation of a novel constitutional settlement, which, although potentially subject to repeal, had redefined the boundaries of their legitimate intervention vis-à-vis the elected organs of government and other public authorities acting on their behalf. For example, even prior to the implementation of the HRA, it was robustly claimed by Lord Hope in *R v DPP, ex parte Kebilene*[59] that the UK government had subjected the 'entire legal system to a fundamental process of review, and where necessary, reform by the judiciary', in a manner that was designed to achieve a major change in the formal balance of power between courts and the executive.[60]

Nevertheless, it is a commonplace observation that in the unwritten constitution of the UK, prior to the HRA and consistent with the doctrine of Parliamentary sovereignty, courts have long been wedded to a narrow process of statutory construction, whereby meaning is attributed to legislation by searching for the presumed intention of Parliament in the language of the text. Therefore, although they now emphasise the fundamental shift in the balance of power between courts and legislature that is intended in the HRA, courts have experienced difficulty in adapting to the purposive style of constitutional adjudication implicit in their HRA powers. Thus, the notion of deference has been used to justify the boundaries that have been set by courts around their powers of legislative scrutiny under section 3, which is the provision that most directly challenges the authority of the democratic majority.[61] Furthermore, as we shall see further in chapter four, deference has provided a pivotal conceptual tool for determining the limits of judicial intervention in public law disputes in which questions about the proportionality of executive or other public authority conduct has been at issue.[62]

C. General Principles of Constitutional Interpretation in the United Kingdom

Although not entrenched, the HRA has been accepted by courts as having the force and status of a constitutional instrument—that is, an instrument that contemplates the future shaping of UK governance in accordance with moral and social values enshrined in the ECHR. For example, before the enactment of the HRA, Lord Hoffman, in comparing the nature of those democracies that have entrenched constitutional protection of fundamental rights with those that do not, observed that the HRA would introduce a modified form of constitutional review that, in practice, would not be very different from that which would apply if the Act had been entrenched.[63] From the outset, therefore, it has been

---

[59] [1999] 4 All ER 801; [2001] 2 All ER 926; [2002] 2 AC 381.

[60] *Ibid*, 838.

[61] See for example *International Transport Roth GMBH v Secretary of State for the Home Department (Roth)* [2002] HRLR 31.

[62] See for example *R (on the application of ProLife Alliance) v British Broadcasting Corporation* [2003] UKHL; [2003] 2 ALL ER 977 (discussed more fully in chapter five below).

[63] *Matadeen v Pointu and Minister of Education and Science* [1999] 1 AC 98 PC, 108, para 7.

made clear that, in interpreting the provisions of the HRA, courts should adopt the generous techniques of statutory interpretation applied in other jurisdictions that, during the past two decades or more, have adopted constitutional Bills of Rights.[64]

Thus, reference has frequently been made to pronouncements by senior judges in Privy Council decisions, on the nature and practice of constitutional interpretation: courts must avoid the 'austerity of tabulated legalism'; adopt a generous interpretation 'which would give individuals the full measure of the fundamental rights and freedoms referred to';[65] and 'achieve the attainment of a constitution's objectives . . . according to [its] true intent, meaning and spirit'.[66] Furthermore, courts have been reminded that the process of constitutional review should involve a purposive search for the 'substance and reality of what [is] involved' rather than emphasis on technicalities that might offer little assistance in arriving at the true meaning and spirit of what was intended by the constitution's drafters.[67]

On the other hand, courts have not been allowed to forget that instinctive virtues of 'realism, good sense and proportionate responses' are no less relevant to the exercise of constitutional interpretation.[68] To this end, Lord Hoffman's observation that constitutional interpretation does not allow courts to depart entirely from the language of the text, 'in order to give free rein to whatever they consider *should have been* the moral and political views of the framers of the constitution',[69] has frequently been cited. Lord Hoffman's conclusion that in the final analysis, whether interpreting commercial documents or constitutions, courts must examine the precise language used by the drafters, has served as a caution that purposive constitutional interpretation has its limits.[70]

Nevertheless, in advising courts about their novel interpretative obligations, it has also clearly been necessary to distinguish their role from that of courts in other common law jurisdictions that have framed their constitutions only during the past two decades or so. UK courts do not begin with a tabula rasa. In

---

[64] See generally Lester and Pannick (note 3 above) 84–100. Since the implementation of the HRA, UK courts have frequently looked to the jurisprudence of the Constitutional Court of South Africa, the Supreme Court of Canada and the New Zealand Court of Appeal.

[65] *Ministry of Home Affairs v Fisher* [1980] AC 319 PC, 328 G–H (Lord Wilberforce).

[66] *Ministry of Transport v Noort* [1992] 3 NZLR NZCA 271 (Lord Cooke), commenting on the New Zealand Bill of Rights Act 1990.

[67] *Huntley v Attorney General for Jamaica* [1995] 2 AC 1 PC, 12 G–H (Lord Woolf).

[68] *AG of Hong Kong v Lee Kong Kwut* [1993] AC 951 PC, 975 B–C (Lord Woolf).

[69] *Matadeen v Pointu* (note 63 above) 108 E–F (emphasis added). *Matadeen* concerned an interesting appeal to the Privy Council concerning the conclusion of the Supreme Court of Mauritius that it was permissible when construing the Constitution of Mauritius to have regard inter alia to the Declaration of the Rights of Man (adopted in 1793 when the island was a French colony) and to Art 26 of the International Covenant on Civil and Political Rights, to which Mauritius was a party. Both contained a right to substantive equality. It was therefore argued that so construed, and when taken together with ss 1 and 3, the Constitution conferred a general right to equality of laws and executive action enforceable by the Courts. In a single speech given by Lord Hoffman, the Privy Council unanimously disagreed. Compare expansive interpretations of the Fourteenth Amendment.

[70] *Ibid.*

interpreting and giving effect to ECHR rights, they are required not only to take relevant Strasbourg jurisprudence into account, but also to grapple with the principles and adjudicative techniques developed over time by the Strasbourg organs, in giving practical effect to the objects and purpose of a supranational treaty.[71] Thus, UK courts have been required both to adapt to the rigorous justificatory techniques of human rights adjudication subsumed in the concept of Strasbourg proportionality and to adhere to the dynamic approach that has been used by the Strasbourg organs, to ensure that in domestic law, ECHR rights are given as wide an interpretation as in ECHR jurisprudence.[72] Furthermore, early in the domestic jurisprudence it was accepted that there could be no place for the application of the margin of appreciation deployed by Strasbourg—insofar as it reflects the deference of a supranational treaty body to the expertise of national institutions safeguarding human rights—although as we shall see, UK courts have developed their own 'margin of appreciation' when exercising their novel powers of scrutiny under the HRA.[73]

D. The Interpretation of Section 3 HRA

From the time of its inception, section 3 has been recognised as a key provision in the scheme of the HRA, affording a 'democratic underpinning to the common law's acceptance of constitutional rights'.[74] Its importance has also been said to lie in its 'legal pervasiveness':[75] it affects legislation whenever enacted *on any subject matter* and applies to contested statutory provisions in litigation between private parties, just as it does in disputes between the executive or other public authorities and private individuals.[76] Section 3(1) provides:

> So far as it is possible to do so, primary legislation and subordinate legislation must be read and given effect in a way which is compatible with Convention rights.

Thus, although a side-note refers to the 'interpretation of legislation', section 3 clearly may be read as containing two separate complementary obligations: to read *and* to give effect to Convention rights—thereby connoting not only a strong interpretative obligation by use of the word 'must' but also a remedial power to ensure that rights are effectively brought home to the United Kingdom.[77] However, notably, section 3(1) is not a measure directed exclusively

---

[71] See generally chapter 2 above.
[72] See Lester and Pannick (note 3 above) 83–90.
[73] For detailed discussion of this issue see further chapter four below.
[74] *Roth* (note 61 above) para 71 (Laws LJ).
[75] See generally A Kavanagh, 'The Elusive Divide between Interpretation and Legislation under the Human Rights Act 1998' (2004a) 24(2) *Oxford Journal of Legal Studies* 259.
[76] See for examples *A, B, X and Y* [2004] EWCA Civ 662; *Ghaidan v Mendosa* [2004] UKHL 30, [2004] 2 AC 557, [2004] 3 All ER, 411, 425; and *Douglas and Others v Hello (No 2)* [2005] EWCA Civ 595.
[77] See Lord Steyn in *Ghaidan v Mendosa* (*ibid*) 425, para 42.

at courts. It obliges everyone who may have to interpret and give practical effect to legislation, which clearly includes public authorities in the performance of their duties, to do so in a Convention-compatible manner.[78] It is true, however, that insofar as section 3(1) has been the subject of academic controversy, focus has generally been on the role of the judiciary in interpreting legislation compatibly with the Convention.

It was made clear in the Home Office White Paper 'Rights Brought Home'[79] that when ECHR rights are in play, courts are required to interpret statutory provisions in a manner and to an extent that goes far beyond what was legitimate before the incorporation of the HRA, so as to accord with the purpose of the Convention, unless the legislation itself is so clearly incompatible with the Convention that it is impossible to do so.[80] Furthermore, following the implementation of the HRA, it soon became clear that this 'far-reaching approach to the construction of statutes'[81] does not require any ambiguity or uncertainty in the statutory provision in order to call section 3 into play.[82]

Thus, it has often been repeated that section 3(1) is 'a powerful tool whose use is obligatory. It is not an optional canon of construction. Nor is its use dependent on the existence of ambiguity'.[83] In light of this strongly purposive mandate, it was assumed by some commentators when the HRA came into force that section 3 would not be treated as a separate canon of construction, to be called into play only when a Convention-compatible meaning cannot be discovered through traditional rules of statutory construction.[84] However,

---

[78] See Lord Steyn in *Ghaidan v Mendosa* (*ibid*) 448, para 106.

[79] Note 23 above.

[80] Home Office White Paper (note 23 above) para 2.7. On the second reading of the Bill, during the Committee stage in the House of Lords, the Lord Chancellor (note 24 above) stated that s 3 'will ensure that if it is possible to interpret a statute in two ways, one Convention compatible and one not, the courts will always choose the interpretation which is compatible'.

[81] *R v Lambert* [2002] 2 AC 545, para 7 (Lord Hope). In *Poplar Housing and Regeneration Community Association Ltd v Donoghue* (hereafter *Donoghue*) [2001] EWCA Civ 595, [2001] 3 WLR 183, 204, [2001] 4 All ER 605, shortly after the implementation of the HRA, Lord Woolf famously stated that whenever s 3 applies, 'The courts have to adjust their traditional role in relation to interpretation so as to give effect to the direction in section 3. It is as though legislation, which predates the HRA and conflicts with the Convention has to be treated as subsequently amended to incorporate the language of section 3' (para 75).

[82] Prior to the HRA, courts were permitted to, but did not have to, use the Convention as an interpretative tool in cases of ambiguity. See *Salomon v Commissioners of Customs and Excise* [1967] 2 QB 116; and *Waddington v Miah* [1974] 1 WLR 683. This has been affirmed on many occasions. See for example *Donoghue* (*ibid*) para 59 (Lord Woolf); *Re S* (*children: care plan*) *Re W children: care plan* (hereafter *Re S*) [2002] 2 All ER 192, [2002] UKHL 10, para 37 (Lord Nicholls); and *Anderson v Secretary of State for the Home Department* [2002] UKHL 46, [2002] 4 All ER 89, [2003] 1 AC 837, [2003] HRLR 7, para 30 (Lord Bingham).

[83] *Re S* (*ibid*) para 37 (Lord Nicholls).

[84] See RA Edwards, 'Generosity and the HRA: The Right Interpretation?' (1999) *Public Law* 400. See also for example D Rose and C Weir, 'Interpretation and Incompatibility: Striking the Balance' in J Jowell and J Cooper (eds), *Delivering Rights* (Oxford, Hart, 2003). The authors argue that 's 3 and the generous purposive approach that it requires should be seen as integral to the process of construction in any case where it is alleged that a statutory provision or the exercise of powers pursuant to a provision is incompatible with the Convention' (40).

despite a lack of methodological consistency in the early case law,[85] it was soon confirmed by senior courts that the first step to be taken in a case of alleged incompatibility is to determine, using ordinary principles of statutory construction (literal or purposive), whether primary legislation is incompatible with the Convention right. Only when such an incompatibility is found should the application of section 3 be considered.[86]

We can therefore conclude from the above that there has been general agreement about many aspects of section 3—its democratic credentials, its novelty and its central role in the operation and structure of the HRA—and an overall refusal to accept that 'Parliament intended that the operation of section 3 should depend critically on the particular form of words by the parliamentary draftsman in the statutory provision under consideration'.[87] Thus, as Lord Nicholls accepted in *Ghaidan v Godin-Mendoza*:[88]

> Section 3 is a key section of the 1998 Act. It is one of the primary means by which Convention rights are brought into this country. Parliament has agreed that all legislation existing and future should be interpreted in a particular way.[89]

This is not to suggest, however, that there has been concurrence about the limits to be set by courts in the exercise of their novel interpretative role. Although it has consistently been acknowledged that section 3 affords a very powerful interpretative mandate, it has also been recognised that a line must be drawn between acts of legitimate judicial interpretation and those that stray beyond their interpretative mandate into a zone of illegitimate judicial lawmaking, which is more appropriately the preserve of the democratically elected branches of government—an elusive Rubicon first identified by Lord Woolf in *Poplar Housing and Regeneration Community Association v Donoghue* (hereafter *Donoghue*)[90] shortly after the implementation of the HRA.[91]

Undoubtedly, since *Donoghue* the familiar slogan of interpretation versus legislation has usefully served to remind courts that in exercising their judicial functions they must not intrude on the territory of the legislature and must maintain the separate functions of courts and executive prescribed by Parliament in the HRA. However, the designation does little to inform them about the point at which, in the purposive interpretation of impugned statutory provisions, they may stray from the zone of legitimate interpretation into one

---

[85] Compare the different approaches in the House of Lords in *R v A* [2001] UKHL 25, [2001] 3 All ER 1, [2002] 1 AC 45. But see also *International Transport Roth GmbH v Secretary of State for the Home Department* [2002] EWCA Civ 158, in which the compatibility of carriers liability provisions of the Immigration and Asylum Act 1999 was at issue, and Jonathan Parker LJ first embarked on analysis of the nature and effect of the statutory scheme without reference to s 3.

[86] See *R v A (ibid)* 21, para 58 (Lord Hope); and *R v Hasan* [2005] 2 WLR 709, 62 (Lord Steyn).

[87] *Ghaidan* (note 76 above) para 31 (Lord Nicholls).

[88] *Ibid*, 502.

[89] *Ibid*, para 26 (Lord Nicholls).

[90] Note 81 above.

[91] For an excellent analysis of judicial understandings of what is contemplated by the distinction as revealed in early case law, see Kavanagh (2005) (note 56 above).

that should be inhabited only by the legislature. For example, in giving effect to the ECHR rights, should courts be prepared to remedy a perceived gap in existing legislation by reading into it a procedural requirement where no such provision existed before?[92] Would it be constitutionally appropriate for courts to arrive at a meaning that, although compatible with the Convention, is in direct contradiction with the unambiguous meaning of a statutory provision at issue?[93] Or indeed should the legislative history of an impugned statutory provision or its specific policy domain suggest that its compatibility with the ECHR rights should more appropriately be addressed by Parliament than by courts?

From the outset, such uncertainties have jostled with confident judicial assertions about the robust approach to interpretation required when reading legislation compatibly with the ECHR. Thus, on one hand it has been acknowledged that it may be necessary to read in additional words or to 'read down', in order to arrive at a narrow interpretation of legislation that renders it compatible with the ECHR rights. On the other hand, there has been a constant reminder that through the use of the words 'so far as possible to do so' in section 3 HRA, Parliament intended that there must be some barriers to the purposive reading of domestic legislation compatibly with the ECHR.[94]

E. Deference: The Boundaries of Interpretative Possibility under Section 3 HRA

Despite the strong judicial obligation to find ECHR-compatible meanings 'so far as possible to do so', the drafters of the HRA clearly contemplated that cases would arise in which no ECHR-compatible interpretation would be possible, thereby requiring courts to make a declaration to that effect.[95] The phrase has therefore been the focus of controversy, not only as to where the boundaries of interpretative possibility under section 3 should lie, but also as to the relative weight to be placed on sections 3 and 4 in ensuring the proper distribution of power between courts and Parliament and in ensuring that rights are effectively brought home to the United Kingdom.

Commentators in favour of a high threshold of interpretative possibility under section 3 have advocated that the declaratory provision in section 4 should be used as a saving provision of last resort, only to be called into play in those few cases in which Convention-compatible readings are plainly impossible under the remedial provision in section 3. By contrast, opponents, in particular those who were opposed to an increased role for courts in policy matters, have appealed for an approach that recognises that one of the overriding aims

---

[92] See for example *Re S* (note 82 above).

[93] See for example *R v A* (note 85 above).

[94] See for example Lord Nicholls in *Ghaidan* (note 76 above): 'What is not clear is the test to be applied in separating the sheep from the goats. What is the standard or criterion by which "possibility" is to be judged? A comprehensive answer to the question is proving elusive' (para 27). See also *Bellinger v Bellinger* [2003] UKHL 21, [2003] 2 All ER 593, [2003] 2 AC 467, para 67 (Lord Hope).

[95] For discussion of the effect of a 'declaration of incompatibility', see notes 44 and 46 above.

of the HRA is to ensure the preservation of parliamentary sovereignty in its structure and operation. Thus, for example, it was argued by one commentator that, consistent with the overriding concession to Parliamentary sovereignty in section 3(2)(b), the non-remedial provision in section 4 should be allowed to play a more significant role in determining the limits of interpretative possibility under section 3(1).[96] By this means, it was argued, government could be afforded a final decision as to whether to amend the offending provision with Parliament's approval, in accordance with section 19.

Divided opinions on the interpretative limits of section 3(1) have not been confined to the academic arena. Following the enactment of the HRA, there has been considerable disunity among senior members of the judiciary as to where the limits of interpretative possibility under section 3 HRA should be set. Contrasting views were propounded in a number of House of Lords decisions, particularly in cases in which a flexible purposive approach to the interpretation of domestic legislation might lead to a Convention-compatible meaning in conflict with the express or presumed intention of Parliament when it originally enacted the impugned provision. Thus, while the contrasting speeches of Lord Steyn and Lord Hope in *R v A*[97] came to be regarded as advocating very different approaches to the exercise of section 3 powers, the unanimous House of Lords decision in *Re S (children: care plan) Re W children: care plan* (hereafter *Re S*)[98] was regarded as antithetical to the expansive approach to statutory interpretation condoned by the majority in *R v A*. Subsequently, the House of Lords decision in *Ghaidan*[99] was viewed as a crucial opportunity to provide a more detailed exploration of the problematic issues surrounding the interpretation of section 3.

The case of *R v A*[100] concerned the so-called rape shield in section 41 of the Youth and Criminal Evidence Act 1999, a measure that in brief prevented a defendant from calling evidence about the complainant's prior sexual history, in respect of the issue of whether or not she had consented to his conduct.[101] When asked to determine the question of whether the discretion afforded by Parliament to the trial judge was compatible with article 6 ECHR, the House of Lords held that, subject to the application of section 3, section 41 should be read in favour of the defendant.[102] Thus, even though the interpretation proposed

---

[96] See for example C Gearty, 'Reconciling Parliamentary Democracy and Human Rights' (2002) 118 *Law Quarterly Review* 243.

[97] Note 85 above.

[98] Note 82 above.

[99] Note 76 above. See also note 88 above and accompanying text.

[100] Note 85 above.

[101] It is so called because it restricts cross-examination of a rape victim about her own sexual conduct.

[102] Moreover, a majority of the House agreed with Lord Steyn that under s 41(3)(c), 'construed where necessary by applying the interpretative obligation under section 3 . . . and due regard always being paid to the importance of seeking to protect the complainant from dignity from humiliating questions, the test of admissibility is whether the evidence (and questioning in relation to it) is nevertheless so relevant to the issue of consent, that to exclude it would endanger the fairness of the trial under art 6 of the Convention': *R v A* (note 85 above) para 46 (Lord Steyn).

flew in the face of the legislature's original intention, as gleaned from evidence of the lengthy process of consultation and debate that had preceded the enactment of section 41, it was unanimously concluded that the question of the admissibility of the applicant's previous sexual history should be remitted to the trial judge.

Despite the unanimity of the conclusion in *R v A*, Lords Steyn and Hope expressed two very different views about the limits of their interpretative role under section 3(1) HRA. Recalling Lord Cooke's description of section 3 as an 'emphatic adjuration',[103] Lord Steyn was adamant that when choosing from a range of possible interpretations, courts should, if necessary to give effect to the Convention rights, adopt an interpretation that might appear 'linguistically strained' and involve the 'reading down of express language in a statute' or the 'implication of provisions'. Most significantly, he claimed that a declaration of incompatibility, as 'a measure of last resort', should always be avoided, unless a Convention-compatible interpretation is 'plainly impossible' in the sense that a 'clear limitation on Convention rights is stated in terms'.[104]

However, Lord Hope, who was in fact the only member of the House to consider the scope of Article 6 ECHR in any detail, was more cautious. Not only did he observe that the right to lead evidence and put questions are not among the unqualified rights contemplated by Article 6. He also focused on both the mischief that section 41 of the 1999 Act had been designed to address and its impact on questions about a victim's alleged consent, finding it difficult, in contrast with Lord Steyn, to accept that it was permissible under section 3 HRA, to read into section 41 'a provision, that evidence or questioning which was required to ensure a fair trial under Article 6 of the Convention, should not be treated as in-admissible'.[105] Nevertheless, on the facts of the case and in the absence of further information about the nature of the defendant's relationship with the complainant, Lord Hope agreed with the unanimous conclusion that in this case questions about the admissibility of the complainant's past sexual history should be remitted to the trial judge.

Following the decision in *R v A*, criminal and civil liberties lawyers were incensed by the fact that the interpretation adopted by the House of Lords so clearly ran counter to the legislative purpose of section 41 of the 1999 Act, which after all had been aimed to strike, as far as possible, a fair balance between the interests of the defendant and wider community interests, with the purpose of mitigating a potential barrier to the successful prosecution of rapes. It was therefore argued by one commentator that Lord Steyn's approach afforded 'too much leeway' to the judiciary, allowing 'their own values free rein, under the cloak of using interpretative techniques', and that such an expansive reading of

---

[103] *Ibid*, para 44 (Lord Steyn), citing Lord Cooke of Thorndon in *Kebilene* (note 59 above) 373F.
[104] *Ibid*, para 44 (Lord Steyn).
[105] *Ibid*, para 108 (Lord Hope).

the limits of possibility under section 3 HRA meant that it could almost always be used to outflank sections 4 and 10 HRA.[106]

Shortly after the judgment in *R v A*, however, commentators were pleased to note that the unanimous House of Lords decision in *Re S*[107] reflected a more deferential approach to the interpretation of their section 3 powers.[108] The case concerned an appeal from the decision of the Court of Appeal in *W and B (Care Plan)*[109] in which applicants had complained of delays by local authorities in implementing care plans in accordance with their statutory obligations under the Children Act 1989. Section 3 HRA had therefore been relied on by the Court of Appeal to justify its reading of the Children Act 1989 in accordance with a novel prioritisation scheme, which involved the introduction of so called 'starred' factors into care plans.[110] It was clear however, that in setting up this starring system, the Court of Appeal had abrogated powers that had been expressly accorded to local authorities themselves, under Parts II and III of the Children Act.[111] However, claiming to have remedied a 'legislative gap' that had previously denied access to a fair hearing of complaints against local authorities in such cases, the Court of Appeal relied on section 3 HRA to interpret the Children Act as being compatible with Article 6 ECHR—in accordance with the overriding purpose of the legislation and for the benefit the children concerned.[112]

On appeal by the local authorities concerned, the House of Lords were sympathetic to the Court of Appeal's frustration about the detriment to children and their parents caused by unacceptable delays in instituting care plans.[113] However, Lord Nicholls, who gave the leading judgment of the House, was emphatic that the introduction of the starring system could not be justified as a legitimate exercise of judicial lawmaking. He accepted that the 'forthright, uncompromising language' of section 3 HRA connoted a powerful tool of

---

[106] H Fenwick, *Civil Liberties and Human Rights*, 3rd edn (London, Cavendish, 2002) 145.

[107] Note 82 above.

[108] See for example Wadham, et al (note 7 above) 60.

[109] [2001] 2 FCR 450.

[110] The Children Act 1989 had been designed to transfer responsibility for overseeing care plans (formerly held by the Court under its wardship jurisdiction) to local authorities. Although this arguably left children with inadequate protection for their Convention rights, it was concluded that the remedy would have to lie in legislative amendment rather than judicial reinterpretation of the 1989 Act.

[111] The origins of the starred scheme, which were not addressed in argument before the Court of Appeal, lay in a series of extraneous interdisciplinary conferences that took place in 1998.

[112] 'Where elements of the care plan are so fundamental that there is a real risk of a breach of Convention rights if they are not fulfilled, and where there is some reason to fear that they may not be fulfilled, it must be justifiable to read into the Children Act a power in the court to require a report on progress . . . the court would require a report, either to the court or to CAFCASS . . . who could then decide whether it was appropriate to return the case to court': *W and B (Care Plan)* (note 107 above) paras 79–80 (Hale LJ).

[113] Lord Nicholls stressed that the rejection of the Court of Appeal's innovation 'must not obscure the pressing need for the Government to attend to the serious practical and legal problems identified by the Court of Appeal' (*Re S* (note 82 above) para 106).

statutory interpretation, the use of which is 'obligatory', rather than an 'optional canon of construction' that is dependent on the existence of ambiguity in the statutory provision at issue.[114] Nevertheless, he was unable to agree with the Court of Appeal that its introduction of the starring system could be 'justified as a legitimate exercise in the interpretation of the 1989 Act in accordance with section 3 of the 1998 Act'.[115]

Reiterating the distinction drawn by Lord Woolf CJ in *Donoghue*[116] between acts of legitimate interpretation and judicial legislation, Lord Nicholls was in no doubt that the Rubicon of judicial interpretation had been crossed by the Court of Appeal in *W and B (Care Plan)*.[117] Moreover, Lord Nicholls also took the opportunity to reject the opinion of Lord Steyn in *R v A* that such a position is not reached unless there is a clear limitation on a proposed Convention-compatible reading in the legislation itself. Instead, Lord Nicholls insisted that 'a meaning that departs substantially from a fundamental feature of an Act of Parliament is likely to have crossed the boundaries between interpretation and amendment', even in the absence of such express limitations.[118]

Because of its procedural interference with an existing statutory scheme, the decision in *W and B (Care Plan)* can easily be dismissed as an eccentric example of judicial overreaching. However, the subsequent unanimous decision by the House of Lords in *Re S* was more widely viewed by commentators as a general retreat from the robust approach to interpretation advocated by Lord Steyn in *R v A*.[119] Opportunity was therefore taken by a differently constituted House of Lords in *Ghaidan*[120] not only to provide a more nuanced approach to the interpretation of section 3 HRA than afforded by the House of Lords in *Re S* but also to engage in a thorough examination of the proper relationship between sections 3 and 4 in the constitutional design of the HRA. Thus, while accepting that the Court of Appeal in *W and B (Care Plan)* had clearly exceeded the boundaries of possibility by its interference in the legislative scheme laid down by Parliament, the House of Lords reopened many of the questions that they had debated in earlier cases, in particular the question raised by Lord Steyn's analysis in *R v A* that the Rubicon of interpretative possibility is not crossed until an express or implied limitation on the proposed compatible reading can be found in the language used by Parliament when originally enacting the offending provision.

The dispute in *Ghaidan* concerned a claim to succeed to the statutory tenancy of a flat in which the applicant had lived with his same-sex partner in a 'very

---

[114] *Re S* (note 82 above) para 37.

[115] *Ibid.*

[116] Note 81 above, para 76.

[117] *Re S* (note 82 above) para 39.

[118] *Ibid*, para 40. Lord Nicholls also held that the remedial scheme established under ss 7 and 8 HRA could not provide a basis for the introduction of the starring scheme.

[119] See generally Wadham, et al (note 7 above) 62. Notably, following *Re S*, as seen from the tabulation of cases in *Ghaidan* (note 76 above), increasing use was made of the declaratory provision in s 4 HRA.

[120] Note 76 above.

close, loving and monogamous relationship' since 1972. It therefore turned on the correct interpretation of the word 'spouse' for purposes of succession by the claimant to a statutory tenancy under the Rent Act 1977 as amended.[121] Three years earlier, prior to the coming into force of the HRA, the House of Lords in the case of *Fitzpatrick v Sterling Housing Association Ltd*[122] had unanimously held that whilst a same-sex couple could constitute a 'family' for the purposes of the Rent Acts, the definition of 'spouse' to include a person 'living with the original tenant as his or her husband or wife' pointed to a gendered heterosexual relationship between one man and one woman and could not therefore be read into the legislation in order to make it ECHR-compatible. Accordingly, it was held in that case that the impugned provision in the Rent Acts was not intended to include same-sex couples. In *Ghaidan*, therefore, the question for the House of Lords was whether the section 3 HRA obligation to read and give effect to the ECHR rights dictated a different conclusion.

The applicant in *Ghaidan* argued that to afford a statutory tenancy to the survivor of a heterosexual relationship while restricting the survivor of an equivalent homosexual relationship to an assured tenancy constituted an infringement of Articles 8 and 14 ECHR. The House of Lords agreed. In other words, the majority[123] in *Ghaidan* was prepared to invoke what Lord Steyn recognised as the 'prime remedial remedy' of the Court's interpretative duty under s 3 HRA,[124] in order to arrive at the opposite conclusion of the earlier decision in *Fitzpatrick*.[125] Accordingly, it was concluded by a variety of routes (Lord Millet dissenting) that paragraph 2 of Schedule 1 to the Rent Act 1977 should be interpreted so as to include survivors of homosexual relationships as if they were the surviving spouses of the original tenants.

Moreover, far from endorsing the apparent retreat by the House of Lords in *Re S*, Lord Steyn was concerned to emphasise the correctness of the robust approach, which he had advocated in *R v A*. Arguing therefore that in earlier cases involving section 3 HRA, too much emphasis had been placed on the linguistic features of domestic legislation, he claimed that the primary focus of the courts' concern should be the significance of the fundamental rights at issue. He was therefore clear that courts should emulate the purposive approach, which had been used by domestic courts in giving effect to EU rights in cases such as

---

[121] The Rent Act 1977, Schedule 1, paras 2 and 3 provide: '2(1) The surviving spouse (if any) of the original tenant, if residing in the dwelling-house immediately before the death of the original tenant, shall after the death be the statutory tenant if and so long as he or she occupies the dwelling-house as his or her residence. Section 2(2) which is also relevant provides that for the purposes of this paragraph, a person who was living with the original tenant as his or her wife or husband shall be treated as the spouse of the original tenant. 3(1) Where paragraph 2 above does not apply, but a person who was a member of the original tenant's family was residing with him in the dwelling-house at the time of, and for the period of two years immediately before his death then, after his death, that person . . . shall be entitled to an assured tenancy of the dwelling-house by succession.'

[122] *Fitzpatrick v Sterling Housing Association* [1999] 4 All ER 705.

[123] Lord Millet dissented.

[124] *Ghaidan* (note 76 above) para 50 (Lord Steyn).

[125] *Ibid*, para 39 (Lord Steyn).

Pickstone[126] and *Litster*[127] and had been advocated by the ECJ itself in *Marleasing*.[128] He was furthermore clear that courts should avoid undue emphasis on the language of the legislative text impugned.[129]

For Lord Steyn, the reason for such an approach was uncomplicated. Recalling that one of the primary objectives of the HRA was to provide effective individual remedies without recourse to Strasbourg, he considered the words 'read and give effect to the ECHR rights' in section 3 to contain two separate complimentary judicial obligations.[130] Moreover, although he agreed that the case of *R v A*[131] had primarily come to be associated with divided judicial opinions about the scope of section 3 HRA, he stressed that in fact there had been unity of purpose in the outcome—which was to give effect to the complainant's Article 6 ECHR rights.

Of course, Lord Steyn also accepted the inevitability of cases in which it is impossible to read or give effect to legislation in a Convention-compatible manner and in which therefore 'the only alternative is to exercise, where appropriate, the power to make a declaration of incompatibility'.[132] However, he refused to accept that the remedial potential of section 3 HRA should be compromised by the existence of the saving provision in section 4—a pattern that appeared to be demonstrated by the table of cases produced in his judgment in which Articles 3 and 4 respectively had been relied on since implementation of the HRA.[133] Citing the House of Lords decisions in *Anderson v Secretary of State*

---

[126] *Pickstone's v Freemans Plc* [1998] 2 All ER 803.

[127] *Litster v Forth Dry Dock and Engineering Co Ltd* [1989] 1 ALL ER 1134. In light of the Equal Pay (Amendment) Regs 1983, *Pickstone's* case (*ibid*) implied into any contract without an equality clause modifications of any term in a woman's contract that is less favourable than a similar term in a man's. In *Litster's* case, having enquired into the purpose of the relevant EC Directive, the House of Lords famously interpreted the resulting Regulations by reading in additional words so as to protect workers even if they were not employed *immediately* before a 'transfer of undertakings' as required by the Regulations.

[128] In *Ghaidan* (note 76 above) paras 44–5, Lord Steyn observed that in determining the scope of s 3(1) the draftsman had rejected a requirement that the interpretation to be adopted must be 'reasonable', preferring instead the analogy of the obligation under the EEC Treaty defined in *Marleasing SA v LA Commercial International de Alimentacion SA*, Case C-106/89 [1990] 1 ECR 1435: 'the national court is required to interpret [national law] . . . so far as possible in the light of the wording and purpose of the directive in order to achieve the result pursued by the latter and thereby comply with Article 189 of the Treaty' (4159).

[129] *Ghaidan* (note 76 above) para 49 (Lord Steyn).

[130] *Ibid*, para 46: 'Rights could only be *effectively* brought home if s 3(1) was the prime remedial measure and s 4 a measure of last resort' (emphasis added). The idea of the duality of purpose in s 3 was emphasised by Lord Rodgers, who observed that in contrast to s 4, s 3(1) is not addressed exclusively to courts but indeed to all public authorities, who are instructed to 'read and give effect' to the primary legislation in a Convention-compatible manner: 'the broad sweep of section 3(1) is indeed crucial to the working of the HRA. It is the means by which Parliament intends that people should be *afforded the benefit* of the Convention rights, "so far as it is possible" without need for further intervention by Parliament' (para 106, emphasis added).

[131] Note 85 above.

[132] *Ghaidan* (note 76 above) para 49.

[133] *Ibid*. For the table showing the distribution between s 3 and s 4 decisions by senior courts, see the Appendix to the opinion of Lord Steyn at para 52.

for the Home Department (hereafter *Anderson*)[134] and *Bellinger v Bellinger*[135] as cases in which ECHR-compatible interpretations were impossible under section 3 HRA, and without expanding on that point, Lord Steyn concluded that 'such cases should not be difficult to identify'.[136]

In fact, all of the Law Lords reached the conclusion that, in choosing between a range of possible Convention-compatible meanings, courts should be less concerned with close contextual analysis of disputed legislation; although Lord Millett was more concerned than his colleagues that linguistic analysis should be consistent with the incremental legislative linguistic history of an impugned provision.[137] However, it was also accepted by the majority that emphasis on purposive judicial creativity should not mean that Convention-compatible interpretations are always legitimate. Thus, Lord Nicholls reiterated his view in *Re S* that although 'possible' insofar as they were consistent with the Convention, judicial interpretations of legislation would be 'inappropriate where they were inconsistent with a fundamental feature of legislation'. He also agreed with Lord Rodger that words implied into legislation must 'go with the grain of the legislation', since 'Parliament has retained the right to enact legislation in terms which are not Convention compliant'.[138]

For the majority, closely linked to this was the idea that a line can be drawn between permissible and impermissible readings of legislation, in cases in which possible Convention-compatible readings could give rise to indirect and unforeseeable consequences of a kind that courts are unable to predict. Thus, observing that 'Convention compatible interpretations are impossible where they require courts to make decisions for which they are not equipped',[139] Lord Nicholls cited *Bellinger*[140] as a clear example of the type of case 'where a

---

[134] Note 82 above. In *Anderson* the House held that the Home Secretary was not competent under Art 6 ECHR to decide on the tariff to be served by mandatory life sentence prisoners. A declaration to that effect was issued in accordance with s 4 HRA.

[135] Note 94 above. In *Bellinger v Bellinger* the House of Lords concluded, contrary to their decision in *Fitzpatrick* (note 122 above), that s 11(c) Matrimonial Causes Act was incompatible with Arts 8 and 12 ECHR.

[136] *Ghaidan* (note 76 above) para 49.

[137] Lord Millett argued that linguistic legislative history could render certain categorisations impossible—on this analysis, the field of applicability was narrowed (in this case to heterosexual couples) (paras 70–3).

[138] *Ghaidan* (note 76 above) para 33 (Lord Nicholls).

[139] *Ibid.*

[140] Note 94 above. *Bellinger* concerned the validity of a marriage in which the wife (W), a post-operative male-to-female transsexual, appealed against a decision by the Court of Appeal that she was not validly married to her husband (H) of twenty years, by virtue of the fact that at law she (W) was still a man. W contended that: (1) she should be recognised as female within the meaning of s 11(c) Matrimonial Causes Act 1973; and (2) the marriage was valid at its inception and was still subsisting on grounds that s 11(c) was incompatible with Arts 8 and 12 ECHR. The House of Lords dismissed the appeal on grounds that recognition of W as female for the purposes of s 11(c) would necessitate giving the expressions 'male' and 'female' in the 1973 Act a novel and extended meaning. A declaration that conferred validity upon W's marriage would represent a major change in the law relating to gender reassignment, which would have far-reaching ramifications and necessitate extensive enquiry and wide consultation.

Convention compatible interpretation would have exceedingly wide ramifications, raising issues ill-suited for determination by the court or court procedures'.[141] In similar vein, Lord Rodger accepted that Convention-compatible interpretations are not possible when amendment will have important practical repercussions that the court is not equipped to evaluate, 'even if the proposed interpretation does not run counter to any underlying principle of the legislation'.[142] In short, he thought, like Lord Millett, that questions of the kind at issue were 'essentially questions of social policy which should be left to Parliament'.[143]

Ghaidan has been welcomed by commentators for its clarification of the policy preference for section 3 HRA interpretations over section 4 declarations 'of last resort';[144] and for providing some tangible indicators for determining the limits of judicial intervention under section 3 HRA. Promising signposts have been identified: the House of Lords has interpreted existing statutory words as opposed to filling in gaps; no procedural modifications were necessary to give effect to the ECHR-compatible reading; and it has been suggested that there were 'no wide-ranging practical ramifications of the Convention compatible interpretation' and that 'the modification was an addition to previous legislative amendments.'[145] *Ghaidan* also exudes a robustness of tone that acknowledges and reinforces the importance of section 3 in the structure and remedial scheme of the HRA, while at the same time seeking to clarify its proper relationship with section 4.

As noted by Alison Young, however, there is little in the *Ghaidan* judgement to address the possibility that courts might inappropriately defer to the authority of the legislature in their initial determination of the reach of the ECHR rights, thereby at a stroke undermining the remedial purpose of section 3 HRA.[146] Moreover, it may be added that there is also a danger that advocates, discouraged by the emphasis on the unsuitability of social policy legislation for section 3 interpretation, may fail to do justice to Lord Steyn's reflection that

---

[141] *Ghaidan* (note above) para 34. The issues in *Bellinger* (discussed *ibid*) were deemed to be ill-suited for determination in the courts and pre-eminently a matter for Parliament, the more especially because the government had announced an unequivocal intention to introduce primary legislation on the subject. However, since it was not possible to construe s 11(c) of the 1973 Act so as to give effect to W's rights under Arts 8 and 12 ECHR, the court was compelled to make a declaration of incompatibility under s 4 HRA.

[142] *Ghaidan* (note 76 above) para 115 (Lord Rodger).

[143] *Ibid*, para 101 (Lord Millett).

[144] See generally AL Young, '*Ghaidan v Godin Mendosa*: Avoiding the Deference Trap' (2005) *Public Law* 23–34, 27. Compare pre-*Ghaidan* comments on the interplay of ss 3 and 4: D Nicol, 'Statutory Interpretation and Human Rights after *Anderson*' (2004) *Public Law* 274; and A Kavanagh, 'Statutory Interpretation and Human Rights after *Anderson*: A More Contextual Approach' (2004b) *Public Law* 537.

[145] Young (*ibid*) 27. Kavanagh (2004a) (note 75 above) has argued that when courts fail to follow the 'incremental rule', they fall into the trap of 'inappropriate' judicial legislating and are more likely to interfere with a fundamental feature of an Act of Parliament.

[146] Young (*ibid*) 28. Notably all the law lords concluded that it would not have been possible to find a Convention-compatible interpretation in *Bellinger* (note 94 above), *Anderson* (note 82 above) or *Re S* (note 82 above).

section 3 is a key remedial provision in the HRA that applies to all legislation whenever enacted.

Thus, despite the assurance with which the House of Lords distinguished *Ghaidan* from what was considered to be the unsuitable case of *Bellinger* for judicial interpretation under section 3 HRA,[147] the second signpost for determining the limits of possibility under section 3 is less than clear-cut. How far should the context of a particular judicial determination be weighed against the fundamental nature of the rights at issue, so as to deny the remedial protection of section 3? Is it possible to question the assurance with which the House of Lords separated the case of *Bellinger* from that of *Ghaidan*, leaving the applicant in the former case without a viable remedy, while unreservedly intervening on behalf of the tenant in the latter? In fact, it may be argued that the essential principle to emerge from *Ghaidan*—that it is contrary to Articles 8 and 14 ECHR to limit statutory protection in the family law field to unmarried heterosexual couples 'living together as husband and wife'—could in future be applied by courts to a wide range of existing statutory provisions;[148] and consequently, the House of Lords decision in *Ghaidan* is no less prone to unforeseeable economic repercussions than *Bellinger* would have been.

So far, we have considered the success of *Ghaidan* in light of the willingness of the House of Lords to adopt a proactive approach to the interpretation of impugned statutory provisions, without considering the question touched on by Young—that is, how they approached the logically prior question as to whether there was a violation of the applicant's Convention rights. It is clear, however, that the strength of the applicant's claim in *Ghaidan* lay in an emerging stream of ECHR jurisprudence in which applicants to Strasbourg have relied on Article 14 taken together with Article 8 or Article 1, Protocol 1 to assert proprietary claims. Thus, in anticipation of our subsequent discussion of judicial deference in landlord and tenant repossession cases, it is worth noting that the success of the claim in *Ghaidan* in this vexed area of housing law did not rest on an allegation that by lawfully terminating the original tenancy, the private landlord had interfered with the duty of respect for the tenant's private, family life and home under Article 8(1) ECHR; instead, it depended on the more potent argument that his relegation to a less beneficial 'assured tenancy' constituted discrimination, contrary to Article 8 in conjunction with Article 14 ECHR. For Baroness Hale, the dispute was thus concerned above all with the protection of the liberal values of non-discrimination and equality, recognised as fundamental not only to the scheme of the Convention as a whole, but to the very notion of democracy itself.[149]

---

[147] See Kavanagh (2004a) (note 75 above).

[148] On this point consider for example s 62(1)(a) Family Law Act 1996 (domestic violence and regulating occupation of the family home); s 1(3) Fatal Accidents Act 1976; s 1A Inheritance (Provision for Family and Dependants) Act 1975; and s 17(4) Housing Act 1988. See generally S Harris-Short, 'Family Law and the Human Rights Act 1998: Judicial Restraint or Revolution?' (2005) *Child and Family Law Quarterly* 329–61.

[149] *Ghaidan* (note 76 above) 131–2 (Baroness Hale). The Canadian Supreme Court, which has generally taken a similarly deferential approach on sensitive socio-economic issues relating to the

Moreover, the strength of the applicant's claim, resting as it did on Article 8 ECHR taken in conjunction with the non-discrimination provision in Article 14, was further highlighted by the ease with which it displaced the appellant's secondary contention that a discretionary area of judgement should be left to Parliament in such sensitive political contexts as national housing policy. Lord Nicholls agreed that 'national housing policy is a field' in which courts, 'in balancing the competing interests of landlords and tenants' and in 'taking into account broad issues of socio-economic policy', will be less ready to intervene.[150] However, at the same time, he was in no doubt that when an 'alleged violation comprises differential treatment based on grounds such as race, or sex or sexual orientation', courts 'will scrutinise with intensity any reasons said to constitute justification', even in such politically sensitive socio-economic contexts.[151]

As we have seen in chapter two above, there is a growing trend in Strasbourg jurisprudence (although not in the context of the equal treatment of same sex couples) that has permitted intensive scrutiny of the proportionality of government discriminatory practices towards minority groups under Article 14 ECHR taken in conjunction with Article 8 or Article 1 of the First Protocol. Although *Ghaidan* runs against the grain of Strasbourg jurisprudence concerning the idea of same-sex families, Article 14 ECHR jurisprudence was nonetheless allowed to justify judicial intervention in the sensitive area of national housing policy, where a wide margin of discretion has formerly generally been left to the executive and public authorities.

F. Section 2 HRA and the Scope of ECHR Rights: Taking Account of Strasbourg Jurisprudence

Under the side-note 'Interpretation of Convention' rights, section 2 HRA provides:

> A court or tribunal determining a question that has arisen in connection with a Convention right must take into account . . . any judgment, decision, declaration or advisory opinion of the European Court of Human Rights . . . whenever made or given, so far as in the opinion of the court or tribunal, it is relevant to the proceedings in which that question has arisen.[152]

Thus, although UK courts must take account of Strasbourg case law that is considered relevant, they are not bound to follow it. However, it was presumed in the Parliamentary debates preceding the HRA that, when interpreting domestic law in compliance with the ECHR rights, courts would turn to 'the wealth of

family, has similarly been much more robust in its use of the Canadian Charter where principles of equality and non-discrimination are at stake.

[150] *Ibid*, para 19 (Lord Nicholls).
[151] *Ibid*.
[152] S 2 also makes provision for how evidence of such judgements is to be given. See ss 2(2) and 2(3) HRA.

existing jurisprudence on the Convention' as relevant material to be taken into account.[153] Although not binding on courts, it was assumed that ECHR jurisprudence would be of strong persuasive authority.[154]

Since there is no system of *stare decisis* in the ECHR jurisprudence, however, questions necessarily arise as to how courts are to determine which cases and principles are to be regarded as relevant and, consequently, to be taken into account in their interpretation of UK legislation. For example, are courts free to ignore earlier Strasbourg decisions that raise issues similar to those raised in domestic disputes, in favour of later decisions that are only marginally on point? Is it appropriate for courts to dismiss as obsolete a Strasbourg decision that, although circumstantially relevant to a domestic dispute, dictates a conclusion that is at odds with legislative or common law developments on the domestic plane? How far is it envisaged that Strasbourg jurisprudence should be *followed* in giving effect to the ECHR rights in domestic jurisprudence?[155]

During the report stage of the Bill in the House of Lords, these questions were not considered to be problematic. It was stated by the Lord Chancellor:

> The interpretation of the Convention rights develops over the years. Circumstances may therefore arise in which a judgment, given by the ECtHR decades ago, contains pronouncements which it would not be appropriate to apply to the letter in the circumstances of today in a particular set of circumstances affecting this country.[156]

Secondly, he accepted not only that the *age* of Strasbourg determinations would affect their persuasive force, but also that judgements of the European Court of Human Rights (ECtHR) should carry greater hierarchical weight than those of the Commission (especially with regard to admissibility decisions). Thirdly, he stated that 'a judgement based on the doctrine of the margin of appreciation, might provide limited assistance to a national court.'[157]

Consistent with these comments, and following the implementation of the HRA, the House of Lords emphasised that in the absence of some special circumstances, any 'clear and constant' jurisprudence of the ECtHR should normally be followed[158] and that they would be unlikely to depart 'without good reason' from principles laid down in a carefully considered judgment of the

---

[153] See the Lord Chancellor, Lord Irvine of Laird, at the Second Reading of the Bill in the House of Lords (note 26 above). The requirement that courts should take account of the Convention jurisprudence can also be explained in terms of one of the Act's objectives: to reduce the flow of complainants to Strasbourg.

[154] It was explained by the Lord Chancellor at the committee stage of the Bill in the House of Lords (note 24 above) that s 2(1) HRA does not make Strasbourg judgements binding: '[Courts] may depart from existing Strasbourg decisions and on occasion it might well be appropriate to do so . . . However, where it is relevant we would of course expect our courts to apply Convention jurisprudence and its principles to the cases before them' (cols 514–15).

[155] See generally R Masterman, 'Section 2(1) of the Human Rights Act 1998: Binding Domestic Courts to Strasbourg' (2004) *Public Law* 725–37.

[156] Hansard HL Official Report vol 584 cols 1272 (19 Jan 1998).

[157] *Ibid*, cols 1270–1.

[158] See *Alconbury Developments Ltd v Secretary of State for the Environment Transport and Regions* [2001] UKHL 23, [2003] 2 AC 295, [2001] 2 All ER 929, 969, para 26 (Lord Slynn of Hadley).

Court sitting as a Grand Chamber.[159] Furthermore, it has been accepted that in taking account of ECHR jurisprudence and when considering the legitimacy of an interference by a public authority (for example, under Article 8(2) ECHR), terms such as 'the interests of national security' or 'the economic well being of the country' should not be given a more generous meaning than that which was applied by the Strasbourg organs.[160] It was also accepted, however, that special circumstances encouraging departure from decisions of the ECtHR might arise—for example, when 'the reasoning is unpersuasive'[161] or when a domestic court considers that the ECtHR 'has misunderstood or been misinformed about some aspect of English law'.[162]

It is also notable that legitimate judicial latitude does not merely allow for narrower readings of the Convention than afforded by the Strasbourg organs. Thus, in *Runa Begum v Tower Hamlets LBC*[163] Lord Hoffman considered that without seeking to preempt the possibility of the UK government adopting a different position in Strasbourg, 'domestic courts are perfectly entitled to accord greater rights than those guaranteed by the convention', so long as to do so, as in the present case, would not prevent what he regarded as a practicable outcome.[164]

What emerged from these early House of Lords decisions therefore was the expectation that, despite the absence of *stare decisis* in Strasbourg, domestic courts would provide *principled* justifications for the selection of relevant case law, and that evidence of a constant line of reasoning would be a primary factor in determining relevancy in domestic courts. Moreover, although it was agreed that greater attention might be paid to the reasoned judgments of the ECtHR than those of the Commission, there was no suggestion that embryonic developments in Strasbourg jurisprudence, even though found in strong dissenting judgements or in admissibility decisions, should be overlooked by domestic courts. The Strasbourg organs have regarded the ECHR as a living instrument to be interpreted in light of present-day conditions in national sys-

---

[159] See *Anderson* (note 82 above) para 18 (Lord Bingham of Cornhill).

[160] In *Kebilene* (note 59 above) Lord Hope first accepted that the margin of appreciation applied by the Strasbourg organs, which is premised on the greater ability of national authorities to make judgements about whether there is a pressing social need and the nature of a proportionate response in national contexts, should have no role to play in the interpretation of ECHR rights by UK courts. But compare the 'area of discretionary judgement' allowed to UK courts. See further chapter 4 below.

[161] *R v Spear* [2002] 1 AC 734 HL, 750–1 (Lord Bingham). See also *Kay v Lambeth* [2006] UKHL 10: 'There are isolated examples when a domestic court may challenge the application by the Strasbourg Court of the principles it has expounded' (para 28 (Lord Bingham)).

[162] *R v Lyons* [2003] 1 AC 976, 997, para 46 (Lord Hoffman). In *Anderson* (note 82 above), a controversial dispute concerning the Home Secretary's role in fixing mandatory sentences for life prisoners, it was concluded by the House of Lords that in relation to such matters, a UK court would be likely to depart from a previous authority (even though favourable to the UK) where in an alternative decision, it appeared that the ECtHR had considered the views of domestic courts on the issue in question and understood the political, legal and administrative context.

[163] [2003] UKHL 5, [2003] 1All ER 731.

[164] *Ibid*, para 69 (Lord Hoffman). See further chapter 8 below.

tems,[165] and problematic though this may be, it has generally been assumed that domestic courts will do the same.[166]

Over time, however, there has been criticism of the way in which some senior UK courts have approached their interpretative powers in section 2 HRA, particularly in socio-economic disputes of the kind with which we are concerned. For example, in the sensitive field of national housing policy, Ian Loveland has been highly critical of outstanding failures by some, although by no means all, Courts of Appeal and the House of Lords to offer reasoned justifications for their selections of relevant case law, often arriving at conclusions more consistent with domestic legislation and principles of common law than with principled developments in Strasbourg reasoning.[167]

Focusing on the important Court of Appeal decision in *Ghaidan*,[168] Loveland has highlighted the way in which the Court dismissed as 'obsolete' a strong line of Strasbourg jurisprudence that is hostile to the recognition of same-sex partnerships, in favour of a tangentially related sex discrimination case concerning property rights, of much less direct relevance to the central issue in the domestic dispute.[169] Further, on the pressing question about whether, even if the right to respect for the home in Article 8 ECHR is engaged, the HRA can bite 'horizontally' on a private landlord such as in *Ghaidan,* the Court of Appeal's argument that the issue was determinable by the positive or negative orientation of the right in question, namely Article 8 ECHR, has no apparent foundation in ECHR jurisprudence. In Loveland's analysis of the leading House of Lords decision in *Harrow London Borough v Qazi*,[170] he has been no less critical of the willingness of the House of Lords to ignore a clear and principled trend in Strasbourg jurisprudence, which has recognised that positive obligations of respect in Article 8 ECHR extend not only to a person's private and family life but also indirectly to her home in the concrete physical sense.[171]

---

[165] For a more recent discussion of these issues, see *N v Secretary of State for the Home Department* [2005] UKHL 31, [2005] AC 296 HL.

[166] *Tyrer v UK* (1978) 2 EHRR 1, para 31.

[167] I Loveland, 'Making It Up as They Go Along? The Court of Appeal on Same-sex Spouses and Succession Rights to Tenancies' (2003) *Public Law* 223–35. See also I Loveland, 'The Impact of the Human Rights Act on Security of Tenure in Public Housing' (2004) *Public Law* 594–611.

[168] In seeking to justify his argument that Art 8 ECHR would bite in respect of the conduct of a private as opposed to public authority landlord, Loveland notes that Buxton LJ and Keene LJ embarked on a wholly irrelevant discussion of the distinction between positive and negative obligations for which they erroneously claimed authority in the case of *Wilson v First County Trust (No 2)* [2001] EWCA Civ 633. See Loveland (2003) (*ibid*) 228. Notably, the House of Lords gave no consideration to these issues, since reading the offending legislation compatibly with Arts 8 and 14 ECHR achieved the desired horizontality.

[169] Loveland has highlighted the Court's lack of jurisprudential rigour, in particular when addressing the complex question of whether Art 8(1) ECHR is engaged in disputes concerning the termination of residential tenancy agreements.

[170] [2003] UKHL 43, [2003] All ER 461.

[171] See Loveland (2004) (note 167 above), where the author claims: 'The Majority judgments all seem to contain assertions that are not securely rooted in ECtHR precedent' (603). Loveland contrasts Lord Hope's narrow assertion on the 'privacy point'—that the object of Art 8 ECHR is to protect individuals against arbitrary interference by public authorities and that it is not concerned

Before proceeding, however, it is also important to stress that more positive changes in the quality and style of judicial reasoning in lower UK courts have also taken place since the enactment of the HRA. As courts have become familiar with the breadth and rigour of Strasbourg jurisprudence, legal representatives and judges have begun to structure their arguments in the systematic way that is done in Strasbourg: 'to identify the broad prima facie right that may have been infringed and then to consider the limitations to it.'[172] Therefore during the period that the HRA has been in force, a new generation of High Court judges has become adept at drawing out broad principles from Convention jurisprudence and deploying the formal Strasbourg style of differential rights adjudication, required in cases in which disputed Convention rights are at issue.[173]

In this regard, the decision of Munby J in *R (on the Application of A, B, X and Y) v East Sussex County Council (No 2)*,[174] although one among many, has been singled out by commentators as an exemplary application of the rigorous style of differential rights adjudication in a challenge where the disputed rights of disabled applicants and other interested parties were most finely balanced, and issues of resources were tangentially in play. The case concerned an application for a declaration in judicial review proceedings as to whether a local authority policy regarding the implementation of manual handling regulations in relation to care was consistent with the needs of two profoundly disabled young adults and their parental carers, for a certain amount of manual handling (rather than lifting by equipment) to be included in their local authority care package. Thus, the central issue in the case was the legality of the application in A and B's circumstances of the local authority's general policy on manual handling and lifting of disabled persons.

It was clear that the Manual Handling Operations Regulations 1999 required employers to avoid 'as far as reasonably practicable' the need for employees to

with a right to own or occupy property—with the statement of the ECtHR in *Gillow* (1986) EHRR 35, where, in the author's view, 'rights of occupancy seem to have been at the forefront of the court's analysis' (603). These issues will be much more fully discussed in chapter 4 below in the context of deference. Compare the willingness of the House of Lords to expand the interpretation of civil rights in *Runa Begum v Tower Hamlets* (note 163 above), where the House of Lords pragmatically accepted that such a generous interpretation of 'civil rights' under Art 6 ECHR should be counterbalanced by a limited degree of scrutiny in ordinary administrative disputes over the allocation of housing or other scarce resources. See also chapter 8 below.

[172] This aspect of the s 2 HRA obligation was endorsed by the Court of Appeal in the case of *Aston Cantlow* (note 56 above). The Court of Appeal held that its task is to draw out the broad principles that animate the ECHR.

[173] When there is potentially a Convention right in play, the domestic court or tribunal first has to identify the right in question; identify the alleged interference with the right; and look to see whether it is prescribed by law. It then has to decide what objectives are to be served by the interference and whether the interference is necessary in a democratic society for achieving these objectives.

[174] [2003] EWHC 167. See also the decision of Munby J in *R (on the Application of Burke) v the General Medical Council and Disability Rights Commission* [2004] EWCH 1879 Admin in which the claimant, who was suffering from cerebellar ataxia, sought clarification of circumstances in which life support on which he would be wholly reliant as his condition worsened could be lawfully withdrawn without his consent. In both cases the issue of resources was tangential.

perform manual lifting, which involves a risk of injury. However, it was also clear from previous authority that the risk of injury had to be a 'real risk' and that, even then, the particular circumstances of any given case had to be taken into account in balancing the health and safety of employees against the profundity of a disabled person's needs. Moreover, it was incumbent on employers, in light of their section 6 HRA obligations, to strike a fair balance between the human rights of A and B on the one hand and the corresponding rights of their carers on the other.[175]

Accordingly, recognising the ECHR as an 'important source of positive obligations both owed to and enforceable by A and B and indeed by their carers',[176] Munby J exhaustively analysed the relevant issues of policy and fact relating to the applicants' profound needs and the interests of the carers; the domestic legislative background; and the relevant human rights framework, before balancing the respective rights of the claimants and their carers in accordance with the relevant law. Having dispelled any crude assumptions that in every case the personal handling of a disabled person might be more appropriate to the dignity rights that are immanent in Article 8 and indeed in all of the ECHR, Munby J proceeded to draw together and articulate a framework of principles that would assist in the formulation of general policy and its application in such extreme circumstances as those of the applicants, where the profundity of their disabilities demanded a greater degree of personal handling than might be 'reasonably practicable' in other cases.

Although the judge recognised that the issue of 'reasonable practicability' was to be assessed on the basis of the 'cost benefit analysis' first relied on in the context of workers rights in *Edwards v National Coal Board*,[177] he emphasised that in the context of the current Regulations, 'reasonable practicability must also take into account the needs of the disabled person and the Convention rights'.[178] Accordingly, he concluded the statutory regime to be one that 'aims to avoid manual lifting insofar as it is reasonably practicable *and* commensurate with the best interests of the disabled person, their dignity and the promotion of their independence, and their Convention rights; but which also recognises (in relation to both risk avoidance and risk minimisation) that the needs of the disabled person may mean that it is not reasonably practicable to avoid a particular risk or to reduce it as much as might otherwise be appropriate.'[179]

---

[175] The fact that the carers were involved because they were being paid to do a professional service was irrelevant to the question of whether they too had 'dignity' interests, which would be protected by Art 8 ECHR. Munby J recalled that in *Niemietz v Germany* (1992) 16 EHRR 97, the ECtHR stated that there is no reason in principle why the 'private life' protected by Art 8 'should be taken to exclude activities of a professional or business nature' (*R (on the Application of A, B, X and Y) v East Sussex County Council (No 2)* (note 174 above) para 29).

[176] *R (on the Application of A, B, X and Y) (No 2)* (note 174 above) para 69.

[177] [1949] 1 KB 704.

[178] *R (on the Application of A, B, X and Y) (No 2)* (note 174 above) paras 127–9.

[179] *Ibid*, paras 128–53.

It is difficult in this brief space to do justice to the methodological rigour with which Mumby J approached his task, in a test case in which, although notably issues of resources were not to the fore, the socio-economic needs of two severely disabled applicants were at issue; or to reflect at length on the extent to which the Strasbourg style of reasoning has informed the decision-making role of lower courts in every case where the fundamental right to be treated with dignity is at issue. It is important to note, however, that with regard to that issue, the judge, as he recognised himself, was here cast in the more educative role of umpire or declaratory advisor, rather than what has proved to be the more controversial role of determining in judicial review proceedings *ex post facto* the question of whether the conduct of local authorities or other public authorities towards their most vulnerable clients has been compatible with positive obligations engendered by the Convention rights.[180]

i. Stare Decisis

Read together with section 3, section 2 HRA clearly has an impact on the UK doctrine of *stare decisis*, an issue that was addressed in the White Paper prior to the enactment of the Act.[181] There it was accepted that the section 3 rule of construction would apply to past as well as future legislation and that in 'interpreting legislation the courts will not be bound by previous interpretations. They will be able to build a new body of case law taking into account Convention Rights.'[182] However, it was decided early in the case law that the system of precedent would continue to operate to the extent that if the House of Lords had previously considered a Convention issue fully, the Court of Appeal would be 'bound by any decision within the normal hierarchy of domestic authority as to the meaning of an article of the Convention, in the same way that it is bound by such a decision as to the meaning of domestic law'; if, however, the House of Lords had only dealt with an issue briefly, the decision could not be relied on 'if the general trend of Convention authority pointed in a different direction.'[183]

Nevertheless, this issue had not been authoritatively examined by the House of Lords, until the case of *Kay and Others v London Borough of Lambeth*,[184] conjoined appeals that raised a crucial question as to whether the Court of Appeal in *Leeds v Price* (hereafter *Price*)[185] should have considered itself free to depart from the House of Lords decision in *Qazi*[186] in light of subsequent deci-

---

[180] *Ibid*, paras 163–6.

[181] Home Office White Paper (note 23 above).

[182] *Ibid*, para 2.8.

[183] See *R Williamson v Secretary of State for Education and Employment* [2002] EWCA Civ 1820, para 41 (Buxton LJ).

[184] [2006] UKHL 10.

[185] [2005] 1 WLR 1825.

[186] Note 170 above. For discussion of the wider substantive issues raised by the case, see I Loveland, 'Much Ado about Not Very Much After All? The Latest (Last Word) on the Relevance of ECHR Article 8 to Possession Proceedings' (2006) JPL 1457. See also his comment on the impact of the HRA on the possibility of regarding individual speeches as reflecting a particular stance on an

sions of the ECtHR in *Connors v UK*[187] and *Blecic v Croatia*.[188] In *Kay*, the House of Lords not only arrived at the same result as in *Qazi* in relation to the scope of Article 8 ECHR, but also adopted a unanimous front on the controversial issue of *stare decisis*, which had been raised by the *Leeds* challenge (one of the three conjoined appeals before the Court of Appeal in *Price*)—highlighting the jurisprudential chaos that would follow if they did not.

Although finding the House of Lords decision in *Qazi* to be incompatible with the ECtHR decision in *Connors,* the Court of Appeal in *Price* had concluded that the only permissible course was nonetheless to follow that earlier decision.[189] However, in *Kay*, regarding the issue of *stare decisis* it was strenuously argued by Liberty and JUSTICE as interveners that the Court of Appeal, 'barring some special circumstance', should follow the later Strasbourg ruling, if four conditions pointing to its principled authority vis-à-vis the earlier House of Lords decision were satisfied.[190] For his part, the Secretary of State who had been joined in the appeal, suggested a strictly circumscribed relaxation of the doctrine of precedent in the *Price* case, suggesting that a lower court should be allowed to depart from an earlier House of Lords decision when there is a clear inconsistency rather than a mere tension; the respondents, however, more circumspectly suggested that the Court of Appeal should depart only when it can clearly see that the House of Lords are bound to take the same decision. Thus, in *Kay*, concluding that such variable perceptions of what might be considered a sufficient degree of inconsistency would be an unsatisfactory basis for relaxation of the current position, the House of Lords decided that it was for the national courts to decide in the first instance how the principles expounded in Strasbourg were to be applied, and that the ordinary rules of precedent must continue to apply.

Pointing to the confusion in the present cases—the First Secretary of State and the Court of Appeal in *Price* having found a clear inconsistency between *Qazi* and *Connor*, while the respondents and the Court of Appeal in *Kay* found no inconsistency, and while 'some members of the House take one view, some the

issue: 'In a very general sense . . . the judgment raised the question of whether British lawyers are increasingly likely to find themselves . . . following the tortuous . . . path in US constitutional jurisprudence of having to identify ever more fragmented judicial majorities and pluralities which support particular parts of any given Supreme Court opinion' (1463). Loveland argues that singular support by individual members of the House of Lords for specific arguments raised by some judgments and not others, although not wholly unfamiliar, has increased considerably under the HRA. See also chapter 4 below for a discussion of s 2 HRA issues raised in the context of landlord and tenant housing repossession cases.

[187] (2005) 40 EHRR 9.

[188] (2005) 41 EHRR 13.

[189] *Price* (note 185 above) para 33.

[190] The four conditions were: (i) the Strasbourg ruling had been given since the domestic ruling on the point at issue; (ii) the Strasbourg ruling has established a clear and authoritative interpretation of Convention rights based (where applicable) on an accurate understanding of United Kingdom law; (iii) the Strasbourg ruling is necessarily inconsistent with the earlier domestic judicial decision; and (iv) the inconsistent domestic decision is, was or is not dictated by primary legislation so as to fall within s 6(2) of the HRA. See *Kay* (note 161 above) para 41.

other'[191]—Lord Bingham drew attention to the possibility of 'different county courts and high court judges and even different divisions of the Court of Appeal taking different views of the same issue' if the proposed modifications were allowed. Therefore in agreement with his colleagues he concluded that 'if [judges] consider a binding precedent to be, or possibly to be inconsistent with Strasbourg they may express their views and give leave to appeal as the Court of Appeal did here'.[192]

G. Section 6 HRA: The Duty of Public Authorities to Act Compatibly with the ECHR Rights

Thus far in our discussion of judicial powers of interpretation we have focused on the interplay between sections 2, 3 and 4 HRA. However, section 6 is also crucial to the interpretative obligations of courts under the HRA. Section 6(1) states that 'it is unlawful for a public authority to act in a way which is incompatible with a Convention right'. Since courts and tribunals are defined as public authorities in section 6(3) HRA,[193] they have their own primary duty to act compatibly with the Convention, an obligation that applies to all their adjudicative tasks, including their duties of statutory interpretation and their duty in developing the common law. Therefore, in addition to their obligation under section 3 HRA to interpret all legislation whenever enacted compatibly with the Convention, a court or tribunal, when, for example, resolving a private law dispute founded on the common law of nuisance or for breach of confidence, is required to develop the law horizontally so as to reach a result that is ECHR-compatible.[194]

Once again, however, under section 6 HRA respect for parliamentary sovereignty has been carefully preserved. Thus, public authorities have been exonerated from the duty to act compatibly with the ECHR rights under section 6(1), if 'as the result of one or more provisions of primary legislation the authority could not have acted differently',[195] or 'in the case of one or more provisions of, or made under primary legislation which cannot be read or given effect to in a way which is compatible with the Convention rights, the authority was acting so as to give effect to or enforce those provisions.'[196] However, although section 6 HRA enables a public authority charged with breaching a Convention right to use as a defence that it was acting to give effect to primary or secondary legisla-

---

[191] See *Kay* (note 161 above) para 43 (Lord Bingham).

[192] *Ibid.*

[193] S 6(3) HRA provides that '"public authority" includes (a) a court or tribunal and (b) any person certain of whose functions are functions of a public nature; but does not include either House of Parliament or a person exercising functions in connection with proceedings in Parliament'.

[194] See generally J Wright, *Tort Law and Human Rights: The Impact of the ECHR on English Law* (Oxford, Hart, 2001).

[195] S 6(2)(a) HRA.

[196] S 6(2)(b) HRA.

tion that 'cannot be read or given effect in away which is compatible with Convention rights', by contrast courts are not relieved of their overriding obligation under section 3 HRA to interpret all legislation so *far as is possible* compatibly with the ECHR rights.

Both sections 6(2)(a) and (b) provide public authorities with a fairly robust defence based on primary legislation, the essential purpose of which is to allow parliamentary sovereignty to take precedence over ECHR rights.[197] However, for some time following the implementation of the HRA, these obscurely framed defences were rarely relied on by authorities.[198] Thus, judicial review proceedings have much more often turned on questions concerning the proportionality of executive or other public authority acts in the performance of relevant statutory duties. However, latterly in a series of disputes culminating in the House of Lords decisions in *R (on the Application of Hooper and Others) v Secretary of State for Work and Pensions* (hereafter *Hooper*)[199] and *R (on the Application of Wilkinson) v Inland Revenue Commissioners* (hereafter *Wilkinson*),[200] the House of Lords has had occasion to examine the meanings and interrelationship between these two somewhat obscurely worded provisions. In those cases it was with the purpose of determining whether diverse legislative provisions affording pecuniary benefits or tax allowance to widows or to widowers on the death of their spouses were compatible with Article 14 ECHR, read in conjunction with Article 1 of the First Protocol and Article 8 ECHR. If so, it was asked, did sections 6(2) or 6(2)(b) HRA provide appropriate defences for the failure of the Secretary of State or the tax Commissioners to act compatibly with the Convention?

Leaving aside the detail of possible Article 14 ECHR discrimination issues for the present, it is noteworthy that in *Wilkinson* the House of Lords was satisfied that the Commissioners as public authorities were protected by section 6(2)(a) HRA. Thus, it was concluded that although they had wide discretionary powers to deal with minor or transitory anomalies or cases of hardship at the margins, their powers under section 1 of the Taxes Management Act 1970 could not be construed so widely as to allow the Commissioners to 'concede by extra-statutory concession, an allowance which Parliament could have but had not granted and on grounds not of pragmatism in the collection of taxes, but of

---

[197] However, s 6(2) should also be read in light of ss 3 and 4 HRA, which allow courts as public authorities to construe legislation so that it is compatible. However, see also Lord Steyn in *Kebilene* (note 59 above): 'It is crystal clear that the carefully and subtly drafted Human Rights Act 1998 preserves the principle of Parliamentary sovereignty. In a case of incompatibility, which cannot be avoided by interpretation under section 3(1), the courts may not disapply the legislation. The Court may merely issue a declaration of incompatibility which then gives rise to a power to take remedial action' (367). For discussion of constitutional checks and balances preserved in the HRA, see subsection B above. See also the discussion of s 19 HRA at note 46 above.

[198] See M Amos, *Human Rights Law: A Textbook for UK Lawyers* (Oxford, Hart, 2006) 111 for a detailed analysis of the nature and scope of the 'defence of primary legislation' under the HRA, in light of debate surrounding its 'intention' to preserve parliamentary sovereignty.

[199] [2005] UKHL 29, [2006] 1 ALL ER 487.

[200] [2005] UKHL 30, [2006] 1 All ER 529.

what was considered to be general equity between men and women.'[201] By contrast with the certainty expressed in *Wilkinson* however, in *Hooper*, where the Secretary of State himself was the respondent, the House of Lords decision has if anything exacerbated the confusion surrounding the intended relationship between sections 6(2)(a) and (b). Whereas Lords Hoffman and Hope considered the appropriate defence to lie in section 6(2)(b) HRA, Lords Scott and Brown preferred section 6(2)(a), and Lord Nicholls considered the important point to be that in general 6(2) HRA was a defence directed at the preservation of parliamentary sovereignty, and the question of which subsection applied was therefore of secondary importance.[202] Notably, however, in both *Hooper* and *Wilkinson* the House of Lords was clear that the alleged discrimination between men and women in the payment of statutory pensions had been and continued to be objectively justified.

Prior to the implementation of the HRA, there had been intense controversy about the extent of the so-called horizontal effects of section 6 HRA, in light of the potential for courts as public authorities to develop the common law compatibly with the ECHR rights.[203] The potential use of section 6 in disputes between private parties was questioned, both in light of the direction of the Convention, which is an international treaty protecting against the abuse of state power[204] and in light of the vertical thrust of the HRA itself, which is aimed predominantly at the control of public power. However, much of the uncertainty on this issue has abated following the implementation of the HRA. Although courts have demonstrated their willingness to protect the interests of private parties through their development of the common law and through the use of their interpretative powers in section 3,[205] the prevailing use of the HRA

---

[201] [2005] UKHL 30, [2006] 1 All ER 529, para 21 (Lord Hoffman).

[202] See Amos (2006) (note 198 above) 112.

[203] See HWR Wade, 'Horizons of Horizontality' (2000) *Law Quarterly Review* 217. Prior to the implementation of the HRA, Professor Wade argued that courts, as public authorities, would be bound to give direct horizontal effect to the Act in private law claims. Compare R Buxton, 'The Human Rights Act and Private Law' (2000) *Law Quarterly Review* 116. Buxton LJ strenuously contested that view. See also the debate in G Phillipson, 'The Human Rights Act, Horizontal Effect and the Common Law: A Bang or a Whimper?' (1999) 62 *Modern Law Review* 824. For the less radical view that courts would give indirect horizontal effect to the Act by developing private law incrementally to protect Convention rights, see M Hunt, 'The Horizontal Effects of the Human Rights Act' (1998) *Public Law* 423; and D Oliver, 'The Frontiers of the State: Public Authorities and Public Functions under the Human Rights Act' (2000) *Public Law* 476, 476. The prediction that courts would give indirect horizontal effect to the Act by incremental development of the common law began to materialise shortly after the HRA was in force. See the remarks of Sedley LJ in *Douglas v Hello Ltd* [2001] 2 All ER 321.

[204] However, from the time of the first proposals in the 1970s for the incorporation of the European Convention of Human Rights, it had been argued that such an instrument should not only bind the state but extend to private parties as well. See A Clapham, 'The Privatisation of Human Rights' (1995) *EHRLR* 20. The author challenges traditional assumptions of international and human rights law, 'that human rights law only binds and constricts government agencies'. See also A Clapham, *Human Rights in the Private Sphere* (Oxford, Clarendon, 1996).

[205] See for example the dispute between the private landlord and the tenant in *Ghaidan* (note 76 above).

has been in section 6 challenges against the proportionality of executive actions or those of other core public authorities acting pursuant to statutory powers and duties.

This has not however been the only controversy surrounding the scope of section 6 HRA. One of the most controversial issues to have arisen since its enactment concerns the extent to which the definition of a 'hybrid public authority' in section 6(3)(b) is apt to capture the wide range of private actors performing erstwhile public functions, following the gradual transfer of property and power to the independent sector in the UK during the past three decades.[206]

At first sight, the so-called 'anti-governmental' thrust of the ECHR has been maintained in the drafting of the HRA, since section 6(1) HRA provides direct protection only against core public authorities.[207] Nevertheless, recognising that protection against infringements of Convention rights is necessary—whether prison or hospital services are provided in the public or private sectors—section 6(3)(b) seeks to afford protection against bodies other than traditional public authorities, by reference to the nature of the functions they perform.[208] Thus, section 6(3) HRA provides that 'in this section "public authority" includes . . . any person certain of whose functions are functions of a public nature'.

The reach of the HRA has therefore been extended by section 6(3)(b) to include hybrid bodies performing functions that are in the nature of public functions.[209] However, since there is no definition of public function in the Act, divergent views about what constitutes a public function were initially supported by reference to the general aims of the HRA, insofar as they could be gleaned from the White Paper 'Rights Brought Home'[210] and from conflicting responses in the Parliamentary debates that preceded the Act.[211] It appears to have been assumed by Ministers that in the case of hybrid bodies encompassed by section 6(3)(b), activities such as education and medical services could be

---

[206] The extent to which the definition of a public authority would give rise to continuing controversy became apparent immediately after the HRA in the Court of Appeal decision of *Donoghue* (note 81 above). Moreover, it became clear that the issue would be particularly controversial in the under-resourced area of national housing, where there has been a relentless transfer of property and managerial power from the public to the private sector. See for example J Morgan, 'The Alchemists' Search for the Philosophers' Stone: The Status of Registered Social Landlord under the Human Rights Act' (2003) 66 *Modern Law Review* 700–25. See also E Palmer, 'Should Public Health be a Private Concern? Developing a Public Service Paradigm in English Law' (2002) *Oxford Journal of Legal Studies* 663.

[207] The Home Office White Paper 'Rights Brought Home' (note 23 above) lists the following traditional public authorities: 'central government, including executive agencies; local government; the police; immigration; prisons; courts and tribunals themselves . . .'.

[208] Hansard HC Debate vol 314 col 409 (17 June 1998). The Home Secretary Jack Straw stated that in drafting s 6, the Government decided that 'the best approach would be by reference to the concept of a public function'.

[209] *Ibid*, cols 406–14. Jack Straw listed examples of hybrid bodies performing public functions under s 6(3)(b): Railtrack in its monitoring capacity, water companies, private security firms that run prisons and the Press Complaints Commission.

[210] Note 23 above.

[211] See Oliver (note 203 above) for the wide variety of meanings that *could* in principle be attributed to the meaning of public function under the HRA.

treated as public functions, irrespective of the source of a provider's power.[212] In particular, a response by Jack Straw, then Home Secretary, to a question about the scope of section 6 HRA appears to be consistent with that assumption.[213] However, during the passage of the Bill, the Home Secretary also stated that the intention of the government was to encompass those public functions that had already been identified as public functions for purposes of judicial review.[214] Courts were therefore faced with a dilemma: unless, contrary to Jack Straw's suggestion, they were either to adopt different approaches to the meaning of public function in judicial review and under the HRA, or alternatively, to abandon the narrow approach to public function determined in accordance with the source of a body's power, which had prevailed in judicial review, then many charitable and commercial bodies providing fundamental public services would be immune from action under the HRA.[215]

I. Human Rights or Economic Liberalism: Contested Interpretations of Section 6(3)(b) HRA

Following the enactment of the HRA, there was widespread criticism by human rights advocates of the unjustifiably restrictive approach that was taken by the Court of Appeal in *Donoghue*[216] and in *R v Leonard Cheshire Homes, ex parte Heather and Others* (hereafter *Leonard Cheshire*)[217] in interpreting the meaning

---

[212] Hansard HL vol 583 col 800 (24 Nov 1997). The Lord Chancellor said that 'if a court was to hold that a hospice, because it provided a medical service, was exercising a public function, what on earth would be wrong with that? Is it not also perfectly true that schools although underpinned by a religious foundation or a trust deed might well be carrying out public functions?'

[213] Hansard (note 208 above) cols 409–10. Referring to the hybrid category in s 6(3)(b), Jack Straw said that 'one of the things with which we had to wrestle was the fact that many bodies, especially over the last 20 years have performed public functions which are private, partly as a result of privatisation, partly as a result of contracting out'.

[214] Hansard HC vol 314 cols 406–14 (17 June 1998).

[215] For a critique of the orthodox approach to the meaning of public function and its impact on vulnerable service users, see Palmer (2002) (note 206 above) 668–72.

[216] Adopting a somewhat traditional approach to determining whether a private body should be treated as a public authority under the HRA, Lord Woolf in *Donoghue* (note 81 above) observed that key factors included: 'a feature or combination of features which impose a public character or stamp on the Act', adding that 'statutory authority for what is done can at least mark the act as being public' and that 'the more closely the acts that would otherwise be of a private nature are enmeshed in the activities of a public body the more likely they are to be public' (para 65). Accordingly, an independent housing association that provides services in accordance with a complex legislative framework for the delivery of social housing is performing a public function within the meaning of Art 6(3)(b) HRA.

[217] At first instance unreported, 15 June 2001; Court of Appeal [2002] EWCA Civ 366, [2002] 2 All ER 936. *Leonard Cheshire* (one of a number of such challenges under Art 8 ECHR) concerned the sudden closing of a home owned by the LC foundation, in which a very frail elderly man expected to live for the rest of his life. Since LC provided the statutory residential service in accordance with a local authority contract, it was not performing a public function. Contrast *R (on the Application of A) v Partnerships in Care* [2002] EWHC 529, [2002] 1 WLR 2610, where it appears that a private hospital was held to be performing a function of a public nature (in part) because the complainant was compulsorily detained under the Mental Health Act 1983.

of the words 'functions of a public nature' in section 6(3)(b).[218] In light of the emphasis placed on the public source of power rather than more directly on the kind of function that a body performs,[219] it appeared that in key areas of provision such as housing or residential care for the elderly or mentally ill patients in the community, vulnerable individuals would be denied the protection of the HRA.[220]

Objections have continued to be raised that some of the most vulnerable members of society (for example, the elderly, the majority of whom are in privately owned care homes, and terminally ill people) are denied the protection of the HRA simply on grounds that the statutory services that they receive are provided in the private sector.[221] However, from the outset, such compassionate human rights responses to the interpretation of section 6(3)(b) HRA have competed with powerful strands of traditional common law thinking and constitutional theory, which are hostile to the regulation of private power through public law mechanisms. It has therefore been argued (contrary to the ostensible purpose of section 6 in the scheme of the HRA) that statutory duties imposed on private bodies should be mediated 'horizontally' through the common law of private obligations, rather than through the vertical mechanism of public law, which should be reserved so far as possible for the control of the state and its core derivative institutions.[222] At the same time, strong ideological concerns have been voiced, not only that the over-regulation of private power by a generous interpretation of section 6(3)(b) HRA would adversely affect the availability of services for vulnerable service users,[223] but also more obscurely that such an interpretation would inappropriately affect the countervailing 'human rights' of the private economic entities concerned. In the UK, Dawn Oliver has

[218] See also *Hampshire County Council v Graham Beer* [2003] EWCA Civ 1056.

[219] In *Donoghue* (note 81 above), Lord Woolf adopted a 'mixed approach', which was closely followed in *Leonard Cheshire* (note 217 above), and first accepted that 'functions of a public nature' in s 6(3)(b) should be determined in accordance with a number of features that impose a 'public character or stamp on the act'. However, turning to orthodox questions about the legal source of power, he argued that s 6(3)(b) did not make a body that had no responsibilities to the public a public body, merely because it performed acts on behalf of the public body that would otherwise have been public functions if performed by the public body itself.

[220] Compare *R (on the Application of A) v Partnerships in Care* (note 217 above).

[221] See for example: Palmer (2002) (note 206 above); P Craig, 'Contracting Out: The Human Rights Act and the Scope of Judicial Review' 92002) 118 *Law Quarterly Review* 551–68; Morgan (note 206 above); K Markus, 'What is Public Power: The Courts' Approach to the Public Authority Definition under the Human Rights Act' in Jowell and Cooper (eds) (note 84 above); and M Sunkin, 'Pushing Forward the Frontiers of Human Rights Protection: The Meaning of Public Authority under the Human Rights Act' (2004) *Public Law* 643.

[222] For the view that the HRA was not generally intended to have direct horizontal effect, see Hunt (note 203 above). However, compare Wade (note 203 above), who appealed for maximum horizontality, and Buxton (note 203 above), who argued that the effect of the HRA should be 'vertical' only.

[223] See Oliver (note 203 above). For Oliver's policy argument that a generous interpretation of s 6(3)(b) HRA might have the effect of forcing private entities to withdraw from some areas of provision, thereby impacting adversely on the vulnerable, see D Oliver, 'Functions of a Public Nature under the Human Rights Act' (2004) *Public Law* 328, 341–2.

most frequently been associated with the view that the public sphere should be narrowly confined to maximise the 'private space' in which individuals are free to 'pursue their own conception of the good'.[224] Arguments of this kind have clearly been influential in courts.[225]

Criticism of the Court of Appeal decisions in *Donoghue*[226] and *Leonard Cheshire*[227] has not been confined to the academic arena. Not only has it been recognised by the Audit Commission that these decisions condone palpable gaps in the protection offered by the HRA, particularly with reference to vulnerable groups who are dependent upon the private sector for their basic needs and support;[228] a highly critical inquiry by the JCHR has reinforced those concerns.[229]

Evidence to the JCHR on the implications of such a restrictive interpretation of section 6(3)(b) HRA has demonstrated the massive involvement of the private sector, especially in key areas such as housing[230] and social care.[231] Charities such as Help the Aged have given graphic accounts of potential violations of Convention rights that might be perpetrated in the public or private spheres.[232] Furthermore, although accepting that 'many private homes provide the highest quality of care', very grave concerns were expressed by the charity Dial UK about the lack of accountability of private service providers towards vulnerable

[224] Oliver (note 203 above) 477.

[225] It is suggested that Professor Oliver's concerns, which resonate with neo-liberal arguments in the international arena about the over-protection of social welfare at the expense of competing economic property rights, are out of place in the context of a discussion about the scope of the protection afforded to public service users intended by Parliament in s 6(3)(b) HRA—and as Alston has argued in the international context, would be better considered as a separate policy issue. See Palmer (2002) (note 206 above) 685.

[226] Note 81 above. See also discussion of *Donoghue* above.

[227] Note 217 above.

[228] Audit Commission, 'Human Rights: Improving Public Services Delivery', September 2003, 11–12.

[229] Joint Committee on Human Rights (JCHR), 'Seventh Report: The Meaning of Public Authority under the Human Rights Act' (2003–04) 39 HC 382 (hereafter 'the JCHR Seventh Report'). See generally Sunkin (note 221 above). In its 'Ninth Report' (note 54 above), the current Committee has agreed with the earlier analysis of the issues raised in the Seventh Report and, after reviewing recent developments, has concluded that 'there has been little evidence of progress in the last three years to close the gap in human rights protection arising from the narrow interpretation of the meaning of public authority' (1).

[230] Shelter reported that nearly 50 per cent of social housing is now out of Local Housing Authority (LHA) control (Memorandum from Shelter, the JCHR Seventh Report (*ibid*), ev 13). It was also reported by Government that 200 tenant management organisations currently manage 84,000 local authority homes in England; 337,000 English local authority owned homes are managed by Arms Length Management Organisations; and over 1.7 million properties are owned or managed by Registered Social Landlords (Memorandum from the Office of the Deputy Prime Minister, the JCHR Seventh Report (*ibid*), ev 1).

[231] Age Concern said that 'extremely serious' consequences flow from the fact that 'as current case law stands, residents of independent sector care homes do not have the protection of the Act'. This, they said, 'is most apparent in the case of care home closures, where there are numerous examples of residents being moved with only a few days' notice'. See Memorandum from Age Concern (JCHR Seventh Report (note 229 above) ev 9) para 3.1.

[232] Memorandum from Help the Aged (JCHR Seventh Report (note 229 above) ev 12) paras 11 and 12. See also the Memorandum from Age Concern (*ibid*).

individuals in their care.[233] A number of abuses giving rise to potential breaches of Articles 2, 3 and 8 ECHR were highlighted, such as the use of 'physical restraints in the form of locked doors or confining individuals in their chairs; chemical restraints through drug use to control behaviour; . . . and electronic restraint through tagging', all of which raise issues potentially falling under Articles 3 and 8.

In light of overwhelming evidence, the Seventh Report of the JCHR, entitled 'The Meaning of Public Authority under the Human Rights Act', expressed concerns that 'much of the new accountability the Human Rights Act brings to the delivery of public services may be undermined almost from its inception.'[234] Moreover, according to the JCHR, it is not 'just the damage done to the enforcement and redress mechanisms of the Human Rights Act' that is at issue, but also 'the confusion about where responsibility lies for actively securing and promoting the underlying standards of human rights'.[235] Thus, the Committee re-emphasised that key to the effective protection of human rights is the creation of 'a culture in public life in which these principles are seen as fundamental not just to the design of policy and legislation but also to the delivery [of] public services.'[236] In short, the JCHR asserted:

> The application of the functional public authority provision in section 6(3)(b) of the Human Rights Act leaves real gaps and inadequacies in human rights protection in the UK, including gaps that affect people who are particularly vulnerable to ill treatment. We consider that this deficit in protection may well leave the UK in breach of its international obligations to protect the Convention rights of all those in the jurisdiction and to provide mechanisms for redress where those rights are breached.[237]

The Committee extensively examined and rejected a range of proposed legal solutions, including amendments to section 6 HRA,[238] the designation of public authorities in secondary legislation[239] and the use of contracts to secure human

---

[233] Memorandum from Dial UK (JCHR Seventh Report (note 229 above) ev 11) para 2.3.

[234] Note 228 above, para 45.

[235] *Ibid*, para 47.

[236] *Ibid*, para 48.

[237] *Ibid*, para 148.

[238] The Law Society suggested the redrafting of the HRA so that when functions are delegated by a public to private body, the functions of both entities should be considered 'public' for the purposes of the HRA—a proposal viewed as giving rise to drafting difficulties and possibly a new set of anomalies and 'unintended consequences' when interpreted by the courts (JCHR Seventh Report (note 229 above) para 98). A proposal to add a schedule of public authorities like that in the Freedom of Information Act 2000 or the Race Relations (Amendment) Act 2000 was also rejected, on grounds that it was inconsistent with the flexible nature of the HRA scheme, which emphasises the public nature of functions, rather than the identity of particular bodies (JCHR Seventh Report (note 229 above) paras 101–2).

[239] The designation of public authorities in secondary legislation was rejected inter alia on grounds that the conferment of such a power would inappropriately substitute executive decisions for judicial decisions in human rights situations (JCHR Seventh Report (note 229 above) para 106). Similarly, a proposal to identify specific functions as public for purposes of the HRA, although viable in theory, raised the risk that certain functions might be overlooked (paras 107–9).

rights.[240] Although accepting that contracts might go some way to fostering a culture of human rights within the private sector, in light of a range of systemic problems relating to the contractual approach, the Committee concluded that such a culture is better promoted by 'awareness of obligations arising from direct responsibilities under section 6 HRA, than by contract and private litigation'.[241] The JCHR therefore preferred that the onus be placed on courts themselves to exercise their HRA obligations in the interpretation of section 6(3)(b). Accordingly, the JCHR posited certain principles for the interpretation of section 6(3)(b) 'appropriate to the intention of Parliament in enacting the Human Rights Act' and allowing for 'an application of section 6, that more fully satisfies the UK's international obligations under Articles 1 and 13', which would give 'true effect' to Parliament's intention to 'bring rights home'.[242]

The Committee has thus been clear that it is the *function* that the person is performing that is determinative[243] and that there is nothing in section 6(3)(b) HRA to suggest that a person's institutional proximity to the state or their coercive power in relation to the service user[244] should decide the issue. Instead, the question of whether the function performed is part of a government scheme has been seen as key to the interpretation of section 6(3)(b). The JCHR proposal is therefore that rather than relying on generic descriptions (for example, medical, dental or educational services), functions should be deemed to be public only when they are provided as part of a government programme established in the public interest.[245] Significantly therefore, the thrust of the JCHR Seventh Report is that although no blueprint is likely to be perfect, it should be possible for courts in their interpretation of what constitutes a public function to reflect a general societal conception of what makes a function public and to adapt to shifting attitudes on the issue.[246]

---

[240] This suggestion, favoured by Lord Woolf in *Leonard Cheshire* (note 217 above, para 34), has its own pitfalls (JCHR Seventh Report (note 229 above) para 112). Although contracts between a public body and a private service provider may be enforceable by the public body, they may not always be enforceable by users who are not parties to the contract. See E Palmer, 'Residential Care: Rights of the Elderly and the Third Party Contracts Act' (2000) 22 *JSWFL* 461–76. For a general analysis of the advantages to be gained by good contract practice, see the JCHR Seventh Report (note 229 above) paras 122–7. See also Palmer (2002) (note 206 above) 686.

[241] JCHR Seventh Report (note 229 above) para 120.

[242] *Ibid*, para 135.

[243] *Ibid*, para 136. See also *Aston Cantlow* (note 56 above) para 11 (Lord Hope).

[244] See *Partnerships in Care* (note 217 above), where the coercive power argument was used in part.

[245] Cf the concept of 'services of general interest' in EU law. For example, a distinction has been drawn by the JCHR (in the JCHR Seventh Report (note 229 above)) between the 'discharge of health care services' (not in itself a public function) and the doing of the work as part of a governmental programme (a public function). The Committee also recognises that although the provision of services for the elderly could be private when care is administered in private homes or by relatives, the same services will be public when provided 'as part of a Government program of state provision' (paras 138–41). See Palmer (note 206 above) 670.

[246] For a detailed analysis of the practical implications and viability of the proposal, see Sunkin (note 221 above) 655–7.

Problematically, however, despite the cogency of the JCHR argument that courts should abandon the restrictive approach adopted by the Court of Appeal in *Donoghue*[247] and *Leonard Cheshire*,[248] the House of Lords has not yet had opportunity to address the issue. Indeed, leave to appeal to the House of Lords was refused in *Leonard Cheshire*. Moreover, neither *Donoghue* nor *Leonard Cheshire* were addressed by the House of Lords when considering the wider implications of section 6 HRA in *Aston Cantlow*.[249] It has therefore been said that both cases remain unaffected by it.[250] However, when contemplating whether the House of Lords may be minded to adopt a more generous interpretation of section 6(3)(b) HRA in light of the JCHR Report on the meaning of public authority, the approach of the House in *Aston Cantlow* appears to offer some encouragement for a retreat from the restrictive interpretation previously afforded to section 6(3)(b) in cases such as *Donoghue* and *Leonard Cheshire*.[251]

As noted by Maurice Sunkin, even their Lordships who adopted a wholly traditional approach to identifying 'core public authorities' in *Aston Cantlow*, emphasised the different nature of the tests to be applied under section 6(3)(b) HRA. For example, contrasting the tasks involved in determining whether a body is a 'core' public authority under section 6(1) or whether it is a private body to be treated as a public authority under section 6(3)(b), Lord Hope stated—only in relation to section 6(3)(b)—'The single unqualified phrase "public authority" suggests that it is the nature of the person itself, not the functions which it may perform, that is determinative.'[252] Notably, he observed further that the phrase 'functions of a public nature' in section 6(3)(b) 'has a much wider reach, and is sensitive to the facts of each case. It is the function that the person is performing that is determinative'.[253]

Moreover, although uncritical of views such as those by Oliver,[254] the House of Lords in *Aston Cantlow* was nonetheless concerned to signal to lower courts that as a matter of substantive law, 'giving a generously wide scope to the

---

[247] Note 81 above.
[248] Note 217 above.
[249] Note 56 above.
[250] See *County Council v Graham Beer* [2003] EWCA Civ 1056, para 15 (Dyson LJ). A differently constituted Court of Appeal upheld the earlier Court of Appeal decisions in *Donoghue* and *Leonard Cheshire* in *Johnson v Havering LBC, the Secretary of State for Constitutional Affairs and the National Care Association; YL v Birmingham CC, Southern Cross Healthcare, OL, VL and the Secretary of State for Constitutional Affairs* [2007] EWCA CIV 26. At the time of going to press the House of Lords has reserved judgment on appeal from that decision.
[251] Sunkin (note 221 above).
[252] *Aston Cantlow* (note 56 above) para 41 (Lord Hope).
[253] *Ibid* (Lord Hope) (emphasis added). Lord Nicholls also stated: 'Clearly there is no single test of universal application' that can be applied to determine when a person is a functional public body within s 6(3)(b); '. . . [f]actors to be taken into account include the extent to which in carrying out the relevant function the body is publicly funded, or is exercising statutory powers, or is taking the place of central government or local authorities, *or is providing a public service*' (para 12, emphasis added).
[254] See note 203 above and the accompanying text to notes 223–5 above.

expression "public function" in section 6(3)(b) will further the statutory aim of promoting the observance of human rights values *without* depriving the bodies in question of the ability themselves to rely on convention rights when necessary.'[255]

Perhaps most significantly, however, in *Aston Cantlow* Lord Hope stressed (as he has done subsequently) that the importance of sections 6–9 HRA lies in their provision of a remedial structure that gives effect both to the Article 13 ECHR obligation to provide effective remedies and to the obligation in Article 1 ECHR for states to secure to everyone within their territories the rights and freedoms contained in the Convention; this emphasis suggests that, in accordance with section 3(1) HRA, judges must interpret section 6 'so far as it is possible to do so' in a manner that furthers the effectiveness and scope of the remedial system. This is a view with which the JCHR would wholly concur, as we have seen.

Reflecting on the significance of the JCHR Report on the meaning of public authority,[256] Sunkin has suggested that in light of developments under the HRA since *Leonard Cheshire* and *Donohgue,* it is unlikely that senior courts can sustain a position that so clearly runs against the grain of modern human rights thinking, 'especially in the domestic context, freed as it is from the international lawyers' preoccupation with the State as subject'[257] and where 'the prevailing view, expressed in normative terms, considers it paradoxical to seek to maximise individual autonomy by minimising the human rights protection available to individuals against bodies that exercise *actual* power over profoundly important aspects of their lives'.[258]

Referring critically to the formalistic reflection by the first instance judge in *Leonard Cheshire* that the charity should not be required to comply with the HRA, in part because the residents of Le Court had chosen to live there,[259] Sunkin has highlighted, as the group Justice did in evidence to the JCHR, the absence of an appropriate human rights response by courts to the plight of the residents,[260]

[255] *Aston Cantlow* (note 56 above) para 11 (Lord Nicholls) emphasis added. The concern was principally based on the wording of Art 34 ECHR, which only permits 'any person, non governmental organization or group of individuals' to claim be a victim of a violation of rights under the ECHR. The JCHR has doubted that it is correct as a matter of principle that core public authorities cannot enforce Convention Rights. (See the JCHR Seventh Report (note 229 above) para 23).

[256] Note 229 above.

[257] See Sunkin (note 221 above) 652, citing Andrew Clapham (who in his writing has continued to challenge traditional assumptions of international and human rights law) that 'human rights law only binds and constricts government agencies'. See Clapham (1995) and (1996) (note 204 above).

[258] Sunkin (note 221 above) 652.

[259] See *Leonard Cheshire* (note 217 above) para 35. Stanley Burnton J pointed out that 'Before she was accepted as a long-term resident, the claimant lived there for an 8-week trial period, the object of which was to see whether she would be accepted by existing residents . . . and presumably also for her to decide that she wanted to live there.'

[260] See the Justice submission to the JCHR Inquiry into the Meaning of Public Authority under the Human Rights Act (Memorandum from Justice (JCHR Seventh Report (note 229 above) ev 18)). Justice argued before the Joint Committee that 'the absence of compulsion is not sufficient to remove the public character from the discharge of a public duty by a private body' (para 21), and significantly, the very fact that a person's support has fallen to a local authority under s 21(1) NAA

for whom admittedly, unlike prisoners or patients detained under section 3 of the Mental Health Act 1983, there was no legal coercion to live in accommodation provided by the charitable foundation.[261] As JUSTICE and others have emphasised, many people are *compelled* by factors such as age, infirmity or poverty to accept and depend upon the services provided by the private sector, not only in the context of community care but also in other areas, including social housing. Thus, while accepting that 'it is plausible to distinguish for HRA purposes between public and private regimes where those subject are genuinely free to choose', JUSTICE has recognised that 'this is much less likely to be the case when the individual has no practical option but to accept private provision'.[262] The reality in such cases is that the existence or non-existence of formally coercive powers may throw no light on the actuality of choice[263] or on the quality of the relationship between a client and a service provider.[264] Such a reality calls for a more probing 'human rights response'.

This is not the place to speculate further on whether the House of Lords will adopt an approach more consistent with Parliament's intention in the enactment of section 6(3)(b) HRA with regard to the protection of vulnerable people who are in receipt of services that can reasonably be conceived of as part of governmental programmes. However, as we further consider what is entailed by a human rights response to the interpretation of the HRA, we shall see that in recent judgments, the House of Lords has been prepared with openness and humanity to confront the reality of the starkest of choices facing some of the most unfortunate complainants to have come before them, in deciding whether it might be possible to find violations of Article 3 ECHR in welfare needs contexts.[265]

---

tends to show that they lack the private means to make appropriate contractual arrangements' (para 24). Claimants are genuinely free to choose services that they receive or whether they have no practical option but to accept private provision should be subject to anxious scrutiny by the courts in each case (para 31).

[261] The idea of a 'human rights response' has been used recently by Dyzenhaus and others to connote a more open style of judicial reasoning in human rights disputes. See further chapter 4 below. Justice have pointed out that in *Leonard Cheshire* (note 217 above) neither the High Court nor the Court of Appeal referred to the alternatives available to the claimants and whether they '. . . had the option of living in a residential care home run by their local authority'.

[262] JUSTICE submission to JCHR (Memorandum from JUSTICE (note 260 above) para 30. JUSTICE argued that 'the very fact that a person's support has fallen to a local authority under s 21(1) NAA tends to show that they lack the private means to make appropriate contractual arrangements' (para 24) and that 'if "public authority" is to be interpreted generously, as the Court held in *Donoghue*', then 'the question of whether a given private regime was avoidable in practical terms must be considered by the courts with anxious scrutiny in each case' (para 31).

[263] See *R (Khatun and Others) v Newham* especially Laws LJ's criticism (at 43) of Newman J for acting on the unreal assumption that there was a situation of equal bargaining between a homeless person and the local authority.

[264] See D Cowan and S Halliday, *The Appeal of Internal Review* (Oxford, Hart, 2003) 141 for a discussion of the notion of 'coerced choice' in the context of internal reviews of homelessness decisions by Local Housing Authorities. For discussion of the chimera of choice in public service provision, see chapter 5 below.

[265] See for example *N v Secretary of State for the Home Department* [2005] UKHL 31, [2005] AC 296 HL (discussed in chapter 6 below).

III. CONCLUSION

The primary purpose of this chapter has been to provide an overview of the structure and operation of key provisions of the HRA and to consider how far in determining the limits of their interpretative powers under sections 2, 3 and 4 HRA courts have taken into account the collaborative safeguards surrounding the HRA. In so doing, the chapter has highlighted the difficulties of treading a secure path between the robust interpretative mandate imposed by section 3 and the traditional inhibitions on courts when addressing policy issues deemed to be more appropriately reserved for elected organs of government. Thus, despite the emphasis placed by the House of Lords in *Ghaidan*,[266] particularly by Lord Steyn and Lord Rodger, on the remedial importance of section 3, it has been accepted by the House of Lords that it may be necessary to 'step back' from the remedial aspect of their interpretative mandate in certain, although not all, polycentric disputes with unforeseeable economic or societal repercussions— Lord Steyn suggesting that 'like the proverbial elephant, case[s] ought generally to be easy to identify'.[267]

By highlighting judicial decisions in sensitive areas of socio-economic policy where senior courts have overlooked principled developments in Strasbourg jurisprudence, this chapter has also suggested that deference plays a significant role in respect of the interpretative obligation to take account of relevant jurisprudence under section 2 HRA. In other words, by interpreting rights either more narrowly or more broadly, UK courts have on occasion sought to arrive at decisions that are more compatible with UK policy and law than with principled developments in Strasbourg case law.

More positively, however, we have noted a continuing trend, whereby lower UK courts have kept faith with principled developments in Strasbourg jurisprudence, quickly becoming adept at structuring their arguments in accordance with the rigorous method of differential rights adjudication deployed by Strasbourg. Furthermore, in contemplating the restrictive response of Courts of Appeal in *Donoghue*[267] and in *Leonard Cheshire*[268] to the interpretation of section 6(3)(b) HRA, there appears room for optimism that a more compassionate 'human rights approach' to the adjudication of these issues is likely to be adopted by the House of Lords. The idea of a fundamental rights approach to judicial reasoning will therefore be fully explored in the following chapter.

---

[266] *Ghaidan* (note 76 above), para 50.
[267] Note 81 above.
[268] Note 217 above.

4

Judicial Review: Deference, Resources and the Human Rights Act

> Care must be taken to not to extend the notion of deference too far. . . . Parliament has its role: to choose the appropriate response to social problems within the limiting framework of the Constitution. But the courts also have a role: to determine impartially and objectively whether Parliament's choice falls within the limiting framework of the Constitution.
>
> McLachlin LJ in *RJR-MacDonald Inc v Attorney General of Canada*[1]

I. INTRODUCTION

T
HE PURPOSE OF this chapter is to provide the constitutional and jurisprudential foundations for the subsequent examination in the following chapters of politically sensitive public law challenges in which questions of socio-economic policy or resource allocation are at issue. It demonstrates the difficulties of accommodating a fundamental rights jurisprudence within the statute-based paradigm of English administrative law and questions whether, following enactment of the Human Rights Act (HRA) 1998, courts have fully engaged with their constitutional powers to review the decisions of public authorities, in accordance with justificatory techniques of human rights adjudication implicit in the rights of the European Convention on Human Rights (ECHR) 1950. Further, it examines the context-sensitive doctrine of deference, by which attempts have been made to define the boundaries of legitimate intervention in accordance with a bright-line division between policy and law, against the background of a more holistic international public law discourse that seeks to reconcile the tension between legal and political spheres of decision-making through the prism of fundamental human rights law.

The chapter is in two sections. The first section demonstrates the difficulties of accommodating an open-textured rights-based style of adjudication within the orthodox UK framework of *Wednesbury* review. The second section examines the approach of UK courts to issues of constitutional legitimacy following

---

[1] (1995) 3 SCR 199, para 133.

the implementation of the HRA. Thus, it focuses on controversial disputes in contexts such as national security and immigration, where questions about the manner and extent to which courts should defer to the elected branches of government have been most vigorously contested. However, our primary concern is with a particular type of politically sensitive dispute, namely polycentric socio-economic disputes that raise issues of resource allocation. Such issues in English administrative law have traditionally been regarded as the preserve of the elected branch of government and since the HRA have continued to be viewed as lying on the fault line between policy and law. Thus, in demonstrating the application of deference in socio-economic policy disputes, the second section of this chapter focuses specifically on controversial landlord and tenant repossession cases—in which, since the HRA has been in force, the reluctance of courts to apply the rigours of Strasbourg proportionality has been most consistently defended.

II. THE CONSTITUTIONAL FOUNDATIONS OF JUDICIAL REVIEW

A. Ultra Vires or Rights?

During the past three decades, the emergence of a common law doctrine of fundamental rights, the impact of international law and the enactment of the HRA have presented challenges to the doctrines of ultra vires[2] and parliamentary sovereignty as the constitutional foundations of judicial review. Almost two decades before the enactment of the Human Rights Act, a debate ignited over the extent to which the doctrinal 'fairy tales' of ultra vires and judicial interpretation of statutes 'in accordance with the intention of Parliament' could provide a credible theoretical basis for the legitimacy of the jurisdiction of courts on application for judicial review.[3] An alternative view was posited that the basis of jurisdiction in administrative review lies in the need to vindicate the rule

---

[2] See de Smith, Woolf and Jowell, *Judicial Review of Administrative Action*, 5th edn (London, Sweet & Maxwell, 1995): 'In essence, the doctrine of *ultra vires* permits the courts to strike down decisions by bodies exercising public functions which they have no power to make' (229). In determining the scope of public powers, courts must interpret statutes in accordance with the presumed intention of Parliament.

[3] The view that the doctrine of ultra vires is the basis of the courts' jurisdiction in public administrative law has for some time been associated with the opinions of Sir William Wade, particularly as they were expressed in his influential treatise, *Administrative Law*, 7th edn (Oxford, Clarendon, 1994) 41ff. See now HR Wade and CF Forsyth, *Administrative Law*, 8th edn (Oxford, OUP, 2000) 35–7. See also C Forsyth, 'Of Fig Leaves and Fairy Tales: The *Ultra Vires* Doctrine, the Sovereignty of Parliament and Judicial Review' (1996) 55 *Cambridge Law Journal* 122; and Lord Irvine of Lairg QC, 'Judges and Decision Makers: The Theory and Practice of *Wednesbury* Review' (1996) *Public Law* 59–78. The Rt Hon Lord Woolf of Barnes described the doctrine of ultra vires as 'fairy tale' in 'Droit Public—English Style' (1995) *Public Law* 57, 65–71. Sir John Laws used the term 'fig leaf' to refer to the fiction of Parliamentary intention in 'Law and Democracy' (1995) *Public Law* 72, 79.

of law by giving effect to fundamental constitutional rights embodied in the common law.[4]

Proponents of the orthodox model of judicial review no longer attempted to refute the latitude afforded to courts by the fiction of parliamentary intention. Even though their intellectual stance was inelegantly tied to an outmoded unitary principle of parliamentary sovereignty, they were not prepared to contemplate the development of a role that would allow non-elected judges to engage overtly in the evaluation of public authority discretion in accordance with principles and standards that lie beyond the reach of statute.[5] It was strenuously argued that since courts, in performing their supervisory role, have neither the competence nor the legitimate authority accorded to expert decision-makers, must exercise the 'rigorous standards of self imposed restraint' for which '*Wednesbury* principles' have become a convenient shorthand formula.[6]

Therefore, a mechanistic and generalised approach to the evaluation of elliptical open-textured concepts such as individual need—which goes hand in hand with a strict constructionist approach to the interpretation of statute—was deemed to reflect an appropriate division of power between courts on one hand and the legislature and executive on the other. Particularly in certain sensitive areas of policy that have historically been regarded as the preserve of elected organs of government, it was argued that essential dissatisfaction with the reasonableness of public authority decision-making is more appropriately to be expressed through the ballot box than by the sporadic interventions of non-elected judges in the affairs of executive government.

However, in the mid-1980s, dissatisfied with the lack of intellectual rigour and analytical integrity within the ultra vires paradigm of review, some constitutional scholars and judges began to posit an alternative 'rights-based' model for the legitimate control of administrative discretion in English public law. Basing their analyses on pluralist conceptions of parliamentary democracy, it was claimed that the role of courts is to give effect to those clearly defined and enduring values that lie beyond the purview of statutes and to which society is already committed in international and domestic common law.[7] Thus, not only was it claimed that judicial review 'is founded on a need to control abuse of power and protect individuals',[8] but more controversially, it was argued that

---

[4] This alternative view was presented both in the works of leading academic authors and in the extra-judicial pronouncements of senior members of the judiciary. See P Craig, *Administrative Law*, 3rd edn (London, Sweet & Maxwell, 1994) 12ff. For judicial support of the alternative view, see the influential opinions of the Lord Woolf (*ibid*); Sir John Laws, 'Is the High Court Guardian of Fundamental Constitutional Rights?' (1993) *Public Law* 59; and Laws (1995) (*ibid*) 93. For an early academic critique of the orthodox view, see D Oliver, 'Is the *Ultra Vires* Rule the Basis of Judicial Review?' (1987) *Public Law* 543, 545.

[5] It was argued that dissatisfaction with the exercise of executive discretion was more appropriately dealt with at the ballot box than through the involvement of unelected judges in matters of policy reserved for the executive.

[6] See Lord Irvine of Lairg (note 3 above) 62.

[7] For further discussion, see the final section of this chapter.

[8] See Oliver (note 4 above) 543.

the underlying purpose of judicial review is 'to promote individual rights'.[9] In short, it was contemplated that unencumbered by the constraints of ultra vires, courts might more openly engage in the principled evaluation of open-textured concepts such as individual need, which demand the balancing of diverse competing interests and claims.

A number of extra-judicial pronouncements were influential in the debate.[10] Perhaps most controversial was that of Sir John Laws, then a High Court judge and now a prominent member of the Court Appeal. At the annual Public Law Project lecture in 1994,[11] he appealed for a more rigorous and open appraisal of the 'true distinctions between judicial and elective power' and presented his view of the constitutional framework that underpins such an alternative model.[12] It is easy to take issue with the iconoclastic tenor of some aspects of Laws' address,[13] in particular with his assertion that 'Ultimate sovereignty rests, in every civilised constitution, not with those who wield governmental power, but in the conditions under which they are permitted to do so. The constitution not Parliament is in this sense sovereign.'[14] Nevertheless, the main plank of Laws' argument—that the substantive grounds of review[15] should be developed in accordance with obligations imposed on courts to give effect to fundamental rights embodied in the common law and in the ECHR—in essence reflects the aspirations of liberal proponents of human rights, now given expression in the Human Rights Act 1998.[16]

[9] See TRS Allan, 'Pragmatism and Theory in Public Law' (1988) 104 Law Quarterly Review 422. For a contemporary development of Allan's thesis, see TRS Allan, 'The Constitutional Foundations of Judicial Review: Conceptual Conundrum or Interpretative Inquiry?' (2002) 61 *Cambridge Law Journal* 87–125. See also TRS Allan, 'Common Law Reason and the Limits of Judicial Deference: Essay on the Unity of Public Law' in D Dyzenhaus (ed), *The Unity of Public Law* (Oxford, Hart, 2004).

[10] See generally M Hunt, *Using Human Rights Law in English Courts* (Oxford, Hart, 1997) especially chs 5 and 6.

[11] Subsequently published in *Public Law* as Laws (1995) (note 3 above).

[12] *Ibid*, 79. The author claimed that in the unwritten constitution of the UK, this normative divide is to be found in the 'judicially created principles which represent much of the bedrock of modern administrative review'.

[13] For Lord Irvine, the dividing line between judicial and elective power was to be drawn in accordance with the doctrine of parliamentary sovereignty: the doctrine of constitutional legitimacy had been unequivocally established by Lord Greene MR in *Associated Picture Houses v Wednesbury Corporation* [1948] 1 KB 223, 230. For trenchant criticism of the over-simplification of Laws' theory of democracy, see JAG Griffith, *The Politics of the Judiciary*, 5th edn (London, Fontana, 1997) 330.

[14] Laws (1995) (note 3 above) 92.

[15] These grounds of review were named by Lord Diplock in *Council of Civil Service Unions v Minister for the Civil Service (CCSU)* [1985] AC 374 as 'procedural propriety, legality and rationality', along with 'a possible fourth ground of proportionality to be applied in the future' (410–11C).

[16] Other senior judges had similarly argued for some time that ECHR principles were already part of the common law tradition and that courts should not shrink from recognising a general presumption of conformity with the ECHR when interpreting legislation, including statutes conferring administrative discretions. See Lord Woolf, *Protection of the Public: A New Challenge* (Hamlyn Lectures) (London, Stevens, 1990), where Lord Woolf argued for a general interpretative presumption of conformity with the ECHR: 'in reviewing the exercise of discretionary powers, on *Wednesbury* grounds, courts could justifiably assume that ministers and their officials do not wish to act inconsistently with this country's treaty obligations under the Convention and the reasonableness of their actions could be judged against the background of those assumptions' (121–2). See also Lord Browne-Wilkinson, 'The Infiltration of a Bill of Rights' (1992) *Public Law* 397.

Notably, however, in the course of extra-judicial debate, it was seldom doubted that traditional liberal values of the kind enshrined in the ECHR would provide a comprehensive moral and political framework for the control of public power.[17] Among his judicial colleagues, Sedley J, now also a prominent member of the Court of Appeal, was alone in questioning that assumption, although by contrast with other commentators on the traditional left,[18] he was not wholly opposed to the idea of constitutional adjudication—that is, of a role for courts in developing the common law consistently with internalised fundamental human rights values.[19] Nevertheless, pointing to outstanding historical failures of courts to defend the moral and political principles that are central to the idea of democracy, Sedley J argued that, rather than slavishly following the rhetoric of classical liberal theory or notions of a higher moral order law, which places principles of fundamental rights above political debate, courts should be alert and responsive to their constitutional role—which is to protect society's fundamental, albeit shifting and contingent, needs.[20]

The writings of Sedley J are important, both because they provide a significant counterpoint to the judicial supremacism that had characterised the writing of those such as Sir John Laws and because they challenge the idealisation of domestic common law as a robust defender of individual rights. For our purposes, however, perhaps their greater importance lies in their engagement with debate, which has long been dormant in the UK, about the extent to which the catalogue of rights of the kind enshrined in the ECHR and predominating in other instruments such as the Universal Declaration of Human Rights (UDHR) 1948, should continue to triumph over contemporary conceptions of what is entailed in the protection of human rights in a twenty-first century democratic state.[21]

---

[17] For analysis of different judicial contributions to the debate, see Hunt (1997) (note 10 above) 162.

[18] Compare the views of other writers on the traditional left at that time, for example Griffith (1997) (note 13 above); CA Gearty, 'The Cost of Human Rights: English Judges and the Northern Irish Troubles' (1994) 47(2) *Current Legal Problems* 19; and KD Ewing and C Gearty, *Freedom Under Thatcher: Civil Liberties in Modern Britain* (Oxford, OUP, 1990) 262–75. For a more recent twenty-first-century critique of claims that common law courts have been robust defenders of fundamental civil liberties against encroachment by the executive, or that the incorporation of the ECHR rights has enhanced their ability to do so, see K Ewing, 'The Futility of the Human Rights Act' (2004) *Public Law* 892–52. It is worth noting that the author's unqualified criticisms of the failure of courts to protect one of our most basic civil liberties, the right to a fair trial in Article 5 ECHR, was written before the House of Lords overturned the decision of the Court of Appeal in *A v Secretary of State for the Home Office* [2004] UKHL 56, [2005] 2 AC 68.

[19] For this approach, which is at once sceptical of metaphysical claims that rights represent 'a higher moral order' (of the kind made by Sir John Laws (1995) (note 3 above)) *and* receptive to the idea that fundamental human rights values and standards offer an articulated basis for decision-making in the unwritten constitution of the UK, see generally the important contributions of Sir Stephen Sedley, 'Human Rights: A Twenty-first Century Agenda' (1995) *Public Law* 386; and S Sedley, 'Governments, Constitutions and Judges' in G Richardson and H Genn (eds), *Administrative Law and Government Action* (Oxford, OUP, 1994).

[20] See Sedley (1995) (*ibid*).

[21] *Ibid*: 'In their received and accepted form, whether one takes the European Convention or the Universal Declaration as the example, they enshrine values which are universal neither in time nor place. They are in essence the Enlightenment's values of possessive individualism, derived from the

As already discussed in chapter 2, there can be little doubt of the bias reflected in instruments such as the ECHR and UDHR towards values of 'possessive individualism' or their historic concerns with principles and standards dedicated to the nurturing of post-war reconciliation.[22] Nevertheless, as observed by Murray Hunt in his appreciation of Sedley J's theoretical contributions, in his pessimistic rejection of the 'Enlightenment's values of possessive individualism', Sedley J had perhaps overlooked the extent to which principles and values, enshrined in international instruments such as the ECHR and the Universal Declaration of Human Rights, might 'include at least some of the values prized by those who take a more optimistic view of the possibilities of state action, to redress the inequalities which inevitably result from private ordering', and that many of the rights which it recognises would 'figure in any account of the minimum standards required by common humanity'.[23] Indeed, this prescient idea is one that we will return to throughout the book.

B. The Reception of Human Rights in English Law prior to the HRA

More than three decades prior to the HRA, a number of factors led to the growing use of human rights law in UK courts.[24] Increased monitoring of legislation by government for compliance with international human rights standards raised general awareness of their relevance. Moreover, from the time of the European Communities Act (ECA) 1972, it became necessary for UK courts in interpreting UK law to have regard to those fundamental rights that form part of the general principles of European Economic Community (EEC) law.[25] Once international human rights began to make their way into courtrooms by that route, their use in other areas of law also increased dramatically.

It is now commonplace that the longstanding difficulties associated with the reception of the ECHR and other international human rights treaties in UK courts, were rooted in the United Kingdom's dualist approach to international law,[26] which in its strict formulation, dictates that in order to be applicable in domestic courts, international treaty obligations to which the United Kingdom is signatory must be incorporated by legislation into domestic law.[27] However, more than three decades before the HRA, the stringency of this orthodoxy had

---

historic paradigm . . . of the conscious human actor whose natural enemy is the state—a necessary evil—and in whose maximum personal liberty lies the maximum benefit for society' (386).

[22] See for example D Nicol, 'Original Intent and the European Convention on Human Rights' (2005) *Public Law* 152.

[23] See Hunt (1997) (note 10 above) 172.

[24] See generally Hunt's seminal work (note 10 above) for a historical account of the reception and use of human rights law in UK courts.

[25] See chapter 2 above. See also Lord Scarman, *English Law: The New Dimension*, Hamlyn Lectures 26th Series (London, Stevens, 1974).

[26] See Hunt (1997) (note 10 above) 1–43.

[27] For a detailed account of the relationship between international law and domestic law, see I Brownlie, *Principles of Public International Law* (Oxford, Clarendon Press, 1990).

gradually been modified. Thus, unincorporated international standards had begun to be accepted in legal argument once they could be shown to form part of international customary law. Moreover, courts gradually developed a common law presumption that Parliament, by legislating, intends to fulfil rather than deny its international treaty obligations—a fiction that applied even when Parliament enacted legislation without any specific intention of implementing a particular treaty obligation.

Thus, by a gradual process of attrition, unincorporated international instruments to which the United Kingdom is signatory, including the UDHR, ECHR and International Covenant on Civil and Political Rights (ICCPR) 1966, came to be relied on in UK courts.[28] However, while these developments were taking place in other areas of common law, courts were slow to accept them in the sphere of public administrative law. Thus, until the implementation of the HRA it continued to be necessary to find an ambiguity in the statutory language, before courts were prepared to countenance the reception of human rights law in public law.[29] Notably therefore, the only consistency with other areas of law was that, as in many other jurisdictions, international treaties concerning socio-economic rights (such as the European Social Charter (ESC) 1961 and International Covenant on Economic, Social and Cultural Rights (ICESCR) 1966) were wholly ignored in UK courtrooms.[30]

C. Resistance to Human Rights in English Administrative Law

Although human rights arguments based on the strict construction of statutory powers in accordance with fundamental rights had some success, for example in specific contexts such as prisoners' rights of access to court,[31] UK courts continued strongly to resist appeals for the use of the ECHR, whether reviewing the

---

[28] For a chronological table of English cases in which judicial reference was made to unincorporated international human rights law prior to the HRA (mainly to the ECHR), see Hunt (1997) (note 10 above) 325.

[29] *Ibid*, 151 and ch 6.

[30] Notably, despite occasional references to the UDHR and the ICCPR, no references to the sister ESC or the ICESCR were made prior to the HRA. Cf the use of the ICESCR in the Canadian Supreme Court: D Wiseman, 'Methods of Protection of Social and Economic Rights in Canada' in F Coomans (ed), *Justiciability of Socio-economic Rights: Experiences from Domestic Systems* (Antwerp, Intersentia, 2006). Since the enactment of the HRA but before it was in force, the only successful use of the ICESCR known to this author was in the employment field where the 'right to work' in Art 6 ICESCR, although not conclusive, was relevant to the imposition of a duty on the part of the GMC to give reasons for its decision to suspend a doctor from the medical roll. See *Stefan v Medical Council (No 1)* [1999] 1 WLR 1293 PC. Post-HRA, compare *Howarth v Secretary of State for the Home Department* [2000] Imm AR 205. Although it was recognised that the denial of such rights might as a matter of 'fact degree and judgement amount to persecution of an asylum seeker in individual cases', it was said that 'breach of third category rights could not as a matter of law amount to persecution' (209 (Ward LJ)). Compare the use of Art 3 ECHR in chapter 6 below.

[31] See for example *Raymond v Honey* [1983] 1 AC 1; *R v Secretary of State for the Home Department, ex parte Anderson* [1984] QB 778; and *R v Secretary of State for the Home Department, ex parte Leech (No 2)* [1994] QB 198.

legality of executive action or as an aid to the interpretation of statutes from which public authorities had derived their power. However, courts began to acknowledge that their resistance could no longer convincingly be attributed to the dualist orthodoxy, which had been supplanted in other areas of law. Rather, resistance to the reception of international human rights treaties in public law could more accurately be attributed to an unremitting tension between the limited supervisory role of courts in English public law and the evaluative exercise that is necessary when reviewing administrative decisions for conformity with international treaty obligations such as those in the ECHR.

Awareness of this tension was certainly to the fore in the House of Lords decision in *Brind v Secretary of State for the Home Department*[32] and also in the paradigmatic case of *R v Ministry of Defence, ex parte Smith* (hereafter *Smith*),[33] where Simon Brown LJ, now a member of the House of Lords, recognised that Strasbourg proportionality was a regime that, if accepted, would 'wholly transform the methodology of public law adjudication, at least [in cases] where fundamental human rights are at stake'.[34] Nonetheless, even though it was argued that, in light of its emergence through EU law, proportionality had already become an additional separate ground for the review of executive action in public law, courts were reluctant to deviate from the high standard of *Wednesbury* reasonableness or from the approach to the construction of statute for which *Wednesbury* review continues to provide a convenient shorthand formula.

Prior to *Smith*, the House of Lords decision in *Brind* had demonstrated the difficulties of limiting the use of Strasbourg proportionality in public administrative law, while at the same time recognising the relevance of the ECHR in other areas of the common law. In the event, a majority of the House of Lords rejected the argument that Article 10 ECHR was relevant to a determination of whether the exercise of the Minister's discretion to impose a ban on viva voce interviews with terrorists had been lawful. However, in determining the reasonableness of the exercise of ministerial discretion, Lord Bridge (dissenting) argued that, in deciding whether the Secretary of State could 'reasonably impose the ban', the court was entitled to 'start from the premise' that 'any restriction of the right to freedom of expression requires to be justified and that nothing less than an important competing public interest will be required to justify it'.[35] Having thus endorsed the legitimacy of an approach that represented a significant departure from the orthodox *Wednesbury* standard of review, Lord Bridge claimed:

---

[32] [1991] 1 All ER 720, [1991] 1 AC 696, 761.

[33] [1996] QB 517, 541; [1995] 4 All ER 427, 445. The complainant challenged the rationality of the government's policy to prohibit gays from serving in the armed forces. The legality of the policy was also challenged on grounds that it breached Arts 8 and 14 ECHR.

[34] *Ibid*, 541.

[35] *Brind* (note 32 above) 723 (Lord Bridge).

While the primary judgment as to whether the competing public interest justifies the particular restriction imposed falls to the Secretary of State . . . [we] are entitled to exercise a secondary judgment by asking whether a reasonable Secretary of State on the material before him could make that primary judgment.[36]

However, diverse evasions by different members of the House of Lords in *Brind* led to continuing uncertainty in lower courts, not only as to the inter-pretative status of the unincorporated ECHR, but also as to the standard of review to be applied in cases where fundamental rights were at issue. Thus, for example, in the later Court of Appeal decision in *Smith*,[37] so as to avoid the methodological step taken by Lord Bridge towards a secondary balancing role for courts in cases where fundamental rights were at issue, *Brind* was down-played as no more than authority for the proposition that the greater the intru-sion proposed by a public body in an area where fundamental rights are engaged, the more rigorously should the Court scrutinise the decisions them-selves. Such an approach, known as anxious scrutiny, requires no departure from the *Wednesbury* principles of review, of the kind implicit in Lord Bridge's dissenting judgement.[38] Thus, in *Smith*, claiming to have captured the essence of the majority opinions in *Brind*, Simon Brown LJ expressed satisfaction that any other solution would have involved a departure from *Wednesbury* reason-ableness, which he considered would have inappropriately involved courts in the review of the merits of administrative decisions.

When claims were made for the use of proportionality as a separate head of review in cases in which fundamental rights were at issue, the resistance of UK courts was even more pronounced.[39] It was argued that that if such a use were accepted, courts would be engaged in reviewing the merits of policy issues, in accordance with a standard deemed to be considerably lower than that of *Wednesbury* reasonableness.[40] Thus, lower courts resorted to the reasoning of

---

[36] *Ibid.* However, compare the arguments against the use of proportionality as a differential stan-dard of review in the speeches of Lords Ackner (766) and Lowry (767).

[37] (Note 33 above) 445.

[38] See the remarks of Simon Brown LJ in *Smith* (note 33 above), where, taking into account the House of Lords decision in *Brind* (note 32 above), the judge held that 'when the most fundamental human rights are threatened', courts should be slow 'to overlook some minor flaw in the decision-making process or to adopt a particularly benevolent view of the Minister's evidence' (444).

[39] See P Craig, *Administrative Law*, 4th edn (London, Sweet & Maxwell, 1999) 561–3; and de Smith, Woolf and Jowell (note 2 above) 593ff. For an early account of the principle of proportion-ality in German law, French law, European Community law and European human rights law and its application in English law in currency at that time, see J Jowell and A Lester, 'Proportionality: Neither Novel nor Dangerous' in J Jowell and D Oliver (eds), *New Directions in Judicial Review* (London, Stevens, 1988) 51. More recently, see D Feldman, 'Proportionality and the Human Rights Act 1998' in E Ellis (ed), *The Principle of Proportionality in the Laws of Europe* (Oxford, Hart, 1999); and J Jowell, 'Beyond the Rule of Law: Towards Constitutional Review' (2000) *Public Law* 671.

[40] The potential clash between the doctrine of proportionality and *Wednesbury* unreasonable-ness was highlighted in the context of EU law in *R v Chief Constable of Sussex, ex parte International Trader's Ferry Ltd* [1996] QB 197 Div Ct, [1997] 2 All ER 65 CA, 1 All ER 129 HL, 192. The Divisional Court held that a decision by the Chief Constable not to deploy additional resources for the management of demonstrations against 'live exports' was not irrational because it

the majority in *Brind*, where all but Lord Templeman had refused to counte-nance the reception of proportionality outside the European law context. Following *Smith*, in cases in which human rights were engaged, rather than requiring the rigours of Strasbourg proportionality, public law courts generally attempted to emasculate the doctrine by absorbing it as an aspect of a more intense form of *Wednesbury* unreasonableness.

Nevertheless, it gradually became apparent that the use of illegality as an alternative ground of review could also avoid some of the technical difficulties associated with challenges founded on *Wednesbury* reasonableness. Thus, it was argued that in interpreting the scope of public authority duties, courts must take account of the common law presumption that statutes are to be interpreted in accordance with human rights standards and principles embodied in inter-national customary law and the common law, even though unincorporated[41]— a proposition that was endorsed by the House of Lords in *R v Secretary of State for the Home Office, ex parte Simms* (hereafter *Simms*).[42]

Prior to *Simms*, which arose shortly before the HRA, the success of such an approach had been variable. In some cases, courts resorted to the majority argu-ment in *Brind*, where it had been objected that to allow Article 10 as a source of rights and obligations in the common law would allow indirect incorporation of the ECHR by the back door. However, in the well-known case of *R v Secretary of State for Social Security, ex parte Joint Council for the Welfare of Immigrants (JCWI)*,[43] a challenge founded on the legality of the exercise of ministerial pow-ers, the use of the common law presumption that Parliament had not intended to authorise disproportionate interference with fundamental rights, met with some success.

The case, to which we will return, is well known for its tentative formulation by Simon Brown LJ of a right to common humanity in the sense of a funda-mental right to elementary human needs.[44] However, for current purposes, it is

---

involved difficult choices about the allocation of scarce resources. However, it was accepted that the decision of the Chief Constable was contrary to EU law, since it imposed *disproportionate* quanti-tative restrictions on exports. The House of Lords rejected this contention. But see the comments of Lord Steyn in the 'The Weakest and Least Dangerous Department of Government' (1997) *Public Law* 84, where his Lordship acknowledged the difficulties of reconciling the doctrines (94). For a recent example of the clash between the two standards, see of *Watts v Bedford Primary Health Trust* [2003] EWHC 2228, discussed fully in chapter 2 above and chapter 5 below.

[41] See *R v Broadcasting Complaints Commission, ex parte British Broadcasting Corporation, The Times*, 24 February 1995. In that case the judge held that in construing the statutory wording, he was entitled to have recourse to Art 10 ECHR as a guide to its meaning, not only if there was ambiguity, in which case the long-established treaty presumption applied, but also 'a fortiori when Article 10 mirrors the common law of England'. For a discussion of the implications of the case as an example of the courts using the ECHR as a mirror of the common law (in this case the common law of free-dom of expression), see Hunt (1997) (note 10 above) 222. See also the cases in note 31 above.

[42] [1999] 3 WLR 328.

[43] [1996] 4 All ER 385

[44] Citing Blackstone's *Commentaries*, Simon Brown in *JCWI* (*ibid*) famously commented: 'Either that, or the regulations necessarily contemplate for some a life so destitute, that to my mind no civilised nation can tolerate it. So basic are the human rights here at issue, that it cannot be

notable that the majority in the Court of Appeal reached the conclusion that however widely drawn, the enabling power to remove public benefits from asylum seekers, which had been proposed by the Secretary of Sate, could not have been intended to permit the degree of interference with statutory rights, or indeed with fundamental human rights, that would inevitably flow from the exercise of the Minister's discretion. Accordingly, it was concluded by the majority that a proposal to remove the benefits from destitute asylum seekers were ultra vires the widely drawn statutory power afforded by the Regulations.

To the extent that courts had thus been disposed to seek alternative ways of protecting rights through the statute-based paradigm of review, much of the controversy over contrasting approaches to judicial review could be said to be purely academic. Could it be that within the orthodox straightjacket of ultra vires, UK courts had begun to find ways of protecting human rights without disrupting the constitutional paradigm of judicial review? If so, were such efforts confined to the creative genius of a small number of judges who were already known to be intellectually wedded to the protection of fundamental rights?

Observing that challenges founded on *Wednesbury* 'rarely succeed' and that successful challenges are 'now typically put in terms of relevancy or improper purpose', Lord Irvine, then Lord Chancellor in waiting, was critical of the latitude afforded to courts by the creative use of relevancy and improper purpose.[45] For example, in *Witham*,[46] which essentially revolved around issues of resource allocation by central government, the level at which court fees had been set by the Lord Chancellor was successfully challenged. Protection of the right of access to court was given by Laws J, who read the relevant statutory instrument in terms of an overriding purpose to give effect to that most fundamental common law right, despite the direct relevance of resources.[47] However, what remains clear from challenges of that kind is that protection had been afforded to fundamental rights in public law, not by use of the open-textured principled style of reasoning that had begun to be contemplated by rights-based theorists prior to the HRA, but rather by the creative use of statutory interpretation, which, however far it departs from Parliament's true intention, can seem to avoid any overt intrusion by courts into the legislative domain.

---

necessary to resort to the European Convention on Human Rights to take notice of their violation . . . Parliament cannot have intended a significant number of genuine asylum seekers to be impaled on the horns of so intolerable a dilemma: the need either to abandon their claims to refugee status or alternatively, to maintain them as best they can, but in a state of utter destitution. Primary legislation alone could in my judgement, achieve that sorry state of affairs' (401).

[45] See Lord Irvine (note 3 above) 67.

[46] *R v Lord Chancellor, ex parte Witham* (1998) QBD 779 Div Ct, 788. But compare *R v Secretary of State for Social Security, ex parte JCWI* (note 43 above).

[47] In *Witham* the applicant applied for judicial review by way of a declaration that Art 3 of the Supreme Court Fees Amendment Order 1996 (SI 1996/3191), according to which fees had been set at allegedly prohibitive levels, was ultra vires and unlawful insofar as it prevented the applicant from suing in libel or in defamation and therefore infringed his constitutional right of access to court.

D. Judicial Deference, Resources and the Ultra Vires Paradigm of Review

It is axiomatic that the use of resources lies at the heart of administrative decision-making. Thus, a clash between decision-making functions of courts and administrators is most clearly manifested in cases where issues of resource allocation are raised. In the unwritten constitution of the UK, courts have dealt with this constitutional issue by declining to review the fairness of funding decisions in challenges founded on *Wednesbury* unreasonableness. Premised on the view that in such cases there is no legitimate decision-making role for courts that can be separated from that of administrators, a so-called doctrine of non-justiciability of resource allocation was in place prior to the HRA, even in cases where fundamental rights were at issue. However, in the context of EU law, where questions of resources are often likely to lie at the heart of complaints, concerns were frequently raised about the 'potent inhibitory effects' of the creation of such no-go areas on legally enforceable individual rights.[48]

It should be emphasised that in the unwritten constitution of the UK, there is no legal principle by which courts are prevented in the exercise of statutory interpretation from intervening in politically sensitive disputes involving issues of resource allocation.[49] However, lack of constitutional propriety, procedural limitations and sensitivity to the problems of administrators have variously been used as justifications or motives for the refusal of courts to intervene in resource allocation disputes. Such no-go areas in public and sometimes in private law[50]—even in cases in which matters of resource allocation are only tangentially raised—caused Carol Harlow to comment that, by contrast with European systems with a developed concept of the administrative state, there remained in the United Kingdom's parliamentary democracy a deeply embedded judicial conviction that matters of public finance are the preserve of the elected branches of government and not of courts.[51]

---

[48] See JWF Allison, 'Fuller's Analysis of Polycentric Disputes and the Limits of Adjudication' (1994) 53 *Cambridge Law Journal* 367, where he argues for a case-by-case approach to such disputes. See also AP Le Sueur, 'Justifying Judicial Caution: Jurisdiction Justiciability and Policy' in B Hadfield (ed), *Judicial Review: A Thematic Approach* (Dublin, Gill & Macmillan, 1996) 228, 256. For the argument that bilateral court procedures are inappropriate for the resolution of multifaceted socio-economic disputes, see JAG Griffith, 'Judicial Decision-making in Public Law' (1985) *Public Law* 564, 579. For criticism of the lack of coherent jurisprudential foundations for the doctrine of justiciability in English law and of the expansion of judicial review in general, see R Cranston, 'Reviewing Judicial Review' in Richardson and Genn (eds) (note 19 above). For a more general discussion of justiciability in a comparative context, see also chapter 1, section II above.

[49] See section IIIC below for the disagreement between Lord Steyn and Lord Hoffman concerning the validity of such a constitutional principle.

[50] For the complications of resources and no-go areas in private law tort prior to the HRA, see the cases culminating in *Osman v UK* (1998) 29 EHRR 245; *E v UK* [2003] 36 EHRR 519; and *Z and Others v UK* (2002) 34 EHRR 97.

[51] C Harlow, '*Droit prive*—English Style' (1997) *Oxford Journal of Legal Studies* 517, 523. See also C Harlow, 'Administrative Law: Back to Basics' (1997) *Public Law* 245, 252; and *R (on the Application of Pfizer Ltd) v Secretary of State for Health* [2003] 1 CMLR 19.

In the politically charged atmosphere of the 1980s, disaffected left-wing authorities engaged directly in litigation with central government with the purpose of challenging the legitimacy of budgetary reforms and the legality of their impact on the performance of local authority statutory duties.[52] As JAG Griffith observed, these challenges ultimately 'forced the courts to consider where to draw the line between intervening in the public interest and effectively transferring the decision making power from local authorities to judges'.[53] Two important decisions of the House of Lords in particular sought to mark a retreat by courts from their involvement in financial disputes between local authorities and central government.

In *R v Secretary of State for the Environment, ex parte Nottingham County Council* (hereafter *Nottingham*),[54] a number of authorities that had been adversely affected by expenditure targets imposed by the Secretary of State challenged his guidance for their implementation, on grounds of both illegality and *Wednesbury* unreasonableness. The authorities argued that the Secretary of State had unreasonably exercised his discretionary power, since the implementation of the guidance affected authorities disproportionately. Lord Scarman expressed a disinclination to review the details of the guidance on grounds of irrationality. He seemed to consider that he could only do so if a prima facie case of perversity or improper purpose had been made out. In his summing up, he formulated the standard as one in which a prima facie case must be made out that the Secretary of State 'had acted in bad faith or for an improper motive or that the consequences of his guidance were so absurd that he must have taken leave of his senses'.[55]

In the later case of *R v Secretary of State for the Environment, ex parte Hammersmith and Fulham LBC* (hereafter *Hammersmith and Fulham*),[56] the House of Lords reviewed a charge-capping decision by the Secretary of State that the local authority applicants claimed was in breach of the relevant statute. Handing down the only judgement of the Court, Lord Bridge held that while the court could intervene if the Secretary of State had acted illegally, it was very wary of review on irrationality grounds in the sphere of economic policy, unless there was some 'manifest absurdity or bad faith'.[57]

---

[52] For a historical account of the central local conflict, see M Loughlin, *Legality and Locality: The Role of Law in Central Local Government* (Oxford, OUP, 1996). Tensions inherent in the legal framework for the delivery of local services increasingly became the subject of litigation rather than negotiation. Twin processes of politicisation and juridification of the central local relationship took place. Loughlin's analysis that there was no appropriate juridical framework and no legal political language for the resolution of such disputes has been widely accepted.

[53] Griffith (1997) (note 13 above) 220.

[54] [1986] AC 240. This represented the final step in a conjoined challenge by ten local authorities against the fairness of the expenditure targets imposed by the Secretary of State for 1995–96. Lord Bridge examined the question of statutory interpretation and Lord Scarman the question of *Wednesbury* reasonableness. For a critical analysis of their judgements that highlights the difficulties experienced by their Lordships in dealing with the complexities of local government finance, see Loughlin (note 52 above) 282ff.

[55] *Nottingham* (*ibid*) 247.

[56] [1991] 1 AC 521.

[57] *Ibid*, 250.

Both of these cases were concerned with central government funding policy and were 'clearly coloured by the fact that the House of Commons had approved the Secretary of State's decisions prior to their implementation'.[58] Taken together, the cases have been read as authority for the unexceptionable proposition that the balancing of competing social and economic interests at governmental level should be subjected by courts to a very low standard of review.[59]

Even though at first sight in Lord Scarman's statements in *Nottingham* appeared to address precise constitutional questions about the boundaries of judicial power vis-à-vis elected branches of government,[60] his speech can also be read as authority for the proposition that courts are procedurally ill-equipped to deal with complex financial resource allocation issues and that a very low standard of review should be applied in such cases. Couched in the language of *Wednesbury*, Nottingham therefore served as the springboard for the draconian proposition that courts are procedurally incompetent 'to evaluate the kind of evidence which it would be necessary to assemble in order to test the validity of policy judgments of this kind' and such decisions are therefore inherently non-justiciable.[61]

Nevertheless, the over-simplification of a division of powers doctrine as a justification for judicial refusal to intervene in resource allocation disputes is highlighted by a series of challenges over access to health and welfare services, following *Nottingham* and *Hammersmith and Fulham* in the latter half of the 1990s. The first of these cases, *R v Cambridge Health Authority, ex parte B* (hereafter *Re B*),[62] challenged the reasonableness of a health authority decision to refuse expensive chemotherapy treatment to a child suffering from leukaemia. The Court of Appeal reaffirmed the non-justiciability of resource allocation decisions founded on *Wednesbury* reasonableness. By contrast, however, in *R v Gloucester, ex parte Barry* (hereafter *Gloucester*)[63] and *R v East Sussex County Council, ex parte Tandy* (hereafter *Tandy*),[64] the House of Lords demonstrated their readiness to intervene in resource allocation decisions that are taken at the highest executive level, albeit through the exercise of statutory interpretation of local authority duties.[65]

For present purposes, this trilogy of cases serves to highlight the potential use of two very different approaches—ultra vires and rights—for the resolution of

---

[58] See de Smith, Woolf and Jowell (note 2 above) 592.

[59] This test was dubbed the 'super *Wednesbury* test' by Simon Brown LJ in *Smith* (note 33 above).

[60] For the narrow constitutional reading of the case, see R Ward, 'Biting on the Bullet: The Constitutional Limits of Judicial Review' (1986) 49 *Modern Law Review* 645, 647; CT Reid, 'Parliament, the Executive and the Courts' (1986) *Cambridge Law Journal* 169, 170.

[61] Loughlin (note 52 above) 289.

[62] [1995] 1 FLR 1055, 2 All ER 129.

[63] [1997] AC 584, [1997] 2 All ER 1.

[64] [1998] AC 714, [1998] 2 All ER 770.

[65] Both *Gloucester* and *Tandy* concerned access to local authority public services.

resource allocation disputes. Nowhere more than in *Re B* has the clash between contrasting approaches to the review of administrative discretion been so poignantly illustrated as the different reasoning styles adopted by Laws J in the lower court and that of the unanimous Court of Appeal. Moreover, the contrasting approaches in the reasoning of their lordships in *Gloucester* and in the single judgment of a differently constituted House in *Tandy* also provide evidence of considerable disunity in the 1990s among senior members of the judiciary as to the limits of their appropriate intervention in the resolution of welfare needs disputes founded on breach of local authority statutory duties.

Chapter 5, which traces the approach of courts to resource allocation disputes in the field of health and local authority welfare services, will return to these three key decisions. However, for the remainder of this chapter, our purpose is to consider the extent to which, in developing a standard of scrutiny consonant with their obligations under section 6 HRA, courts have overcome the constraints dictated by the sovereignty-based conception of their traditional role in public law.[66]

III. PUBLIC LAW, DEFERENCE AND THE HUMAN RIGHTS ACT

A. The Limits of Judicial Intervention under Section 6 HRA

In recent texts that chart the progress of the HRA, prominence has been given to assertive statements by senior members of the House of Lords, in cases such as *Ghaidan*[67] and *A v Secretary of State for the Home Department*,[68] about the relative competencies of courts vis-à-vis the elected branches of government. Indeed, at first glance it might be assumed from those confident judicial

---

[66] Even after the decision of the ECtHR in *Smith and Grady* (1999) 29 EHRR 493 (where the ECtHR held that the intensive form of *Wednesbury* scrutiny proposed by Simon Brown LJ in *Smith* (note 33 above) fell short of the rigorous proportionality standard required by cases in which ECHR rights are at issue), controversy continued about possible circumstances in which it might be constitutionally appropriate to adopt the kind of anxious scrutiny proposed in *Smith* rather than Strasbourg proportionality.

[67] *Ghaidan v Mendosa* [2004] UKHL 30, [2004] 2 AC 557. See discussion of the case in chapter 3 above.

[68] Note 18 above (the House of Lords response to the government's derogation from its human rights commitments by instituting powers of indefinite detention without trial of non-UK citizens). *A v Secretary of State* has provided the most assertive statements by a majority of seven of nine members of the House of Lords of the relative institutional competencies of courts vis-à-vis the elected branches of government, and of the extent to which courts should defer in determining the proportionality of acts of the legislature or the executive branch of government. Lord Bingham stated: 'The function of independent judges charged to interpret and apply the law is universally recognised as a cardinal feature of the democratic state a cornerstone of the rule of law itself. The Attorney General is fully entitled to insist on the proper limits of judicial authority, but he is wrong to stigmatise judicial decision-making as in some way undemocratic. It is particularly inappropriate in a case such as the present in which Parliament has legislated in s 6 of the 1998 Act to render unlawful any act of a public authority including a court incompatible with a Convention right . . .' (para 42). See also *A and Others v Secretary of State for the Home Department (No 2)* [2005] UKHL 71, where in reaching their conclusions the House of Lords relied on 'the common law of England', the ECHR and principles of public international law.

pronouncements that UK courts had overcome much of their traditional reticence when evaluating the proportionality of decisions by the executive or other public authorities in public administrative law.[69] However, parallel to the story of increased judicial assertiveness, textbook writers have also traced a more complex and uncertain story about the manner and extent to which courts have determined the limits of their legitimate intervention under section 6 HRA in disputes raising contentious issues of policy—of precisely the kind that arose in cases such as *A v Secretary of State*. This section of the chapter therefore begins with this 'tangled story of deference', which has been unfolding since the HRA came into force.[70]

It is axiomatic that traditional doctrines such as the separation of powers, parliamentary sovereignty and indeed the rule of law can be of limited assistance in determining the boundaries of judicial intervention when courts are engaged in the legitimate exercise of constitutional judicial review.[71] It is also clear that under the HRA the adequacy of the doctrine of the separation of powers is most acutely challenged when courts are confronted with the review of sensitive, politically controversial decisions—when, for example, matters of national security and public interest are deemed to be in direct tension with the protection of an individual's fundamental human rights, as in *A v Secretary of State*.[72]

As seen in chapter 2, interference with qualified rights such as those in Articles 8–11 ECHR can only be justifiable if in accordance with the law and necessary in a democratic society.[73] Moreover, Articles 8–11 ECHR contain a number of defensive precepts, described as 'qualified escape routes from the application of the Convention rights', such as 'in the interests of national security' or other evaluative judgments such as what is necessary in the interests of public safety.[74] Furthermore, as recently observed by Lord Steyn, such crucial matters of public interest are ones on which the legislative and executive branches of government, by virtue of their office, are expected to have considered opinions; and in cases in which, for example, questions of public safety or 'the economic well being of

---

[69]   See for example M Amos, *Human Rights Law* (Oxford, Hart, 2006) ch 1.

[70]   See Lord Steyn, 'The Tangled Story of Deference' (2005) *Public Law* 346–59. For early contributions to the debate about deference in relation to the HRA, see D Pannick, 'Principles of Interpretation of Convention Rights under the Human Rights Act and the Discretionary Area of Judgement' (1998) *Public Law* 545; P Craig, 'The Courts, the Human Rights Act and Judicial Review' (2001) 117 *Law Quarterly Review* 589; M Elliott, 'The Human Rights Act 1998 and the Standard of Substantive Review' (2001) 60 *Cambridge Law Journal* 301; and D Clayton, 'Judicial Deference and Democratic Dialogue: The Legitimacy of Judicial Intervention under the Human Rights Act 1998' (2004) *Public Law* 33–47.

[71]   See generally D Dyzenhaus, 'Form and Substance in the Rule of Law: A Democratic Justification for Judicial Review' in C Forsyth (ed), *Judicial Review and the Constitution* (Oxford, Hart, 1999).

[72]   Note 18 above. (See also note 68 above.) See also the Canadian case *Baker v Canada (Minister of Citizenship and Immigration)* [1999] 2 SCR 817, discussed below.

[73]   See general principles discussed in chapter 2, section II above.

[74]   Questions relating to national security are specifically referred to under Arts 8, 10 and 11 ECHR; issues of public safety under Arts 8–11; the economic well-being of the country and the protection of health or morals under Art 8; and the prevention of disorder and crime under Arts 8, 10 and 11.

the country' must be balanced, they are expected to have, or to have access to, specialist expertise.[75]

Problematically, however, although it is a fundamental aspect of the ECHR regime that opinions of democratically appointed organs of government must be taken into account, they are not expected to be conclusive on crucial questions about whether alleged interference with an individual's fundamental freedoms by public authority is legitimate or necessary in a democratic society. Indeed, Strasbourg proportionality presupposes that these questions should be the subject of judicial evaluation. How then in sensitive 'public interest' contexts such as immigration, national security and the determination of what constitutes the 'economic well-being of the country' in accordance with Article 8, are domestic courts to exercise a *constitutionally appropriate* degree of restraint, without ceding questions about the legality of decisions under scrutiny to public authorities themselves?

In section II above we demonstrated that debate about such questions in English administrative law has traditionally revolved around opposing constitutional hegemonies: on one side of the divide have stood champions of fundamental rights, with courts enlisted in their protection; on the other side have been what have been described as democratic positivists, who are committed to the supremacy of the legislature and those acting on their behalf. It is not surprising, therefore, that since the HRA came into force, questions about the limits of judicial intervention under section 6 HRA have continued to be debated within the confines of this narrow administrative law discourse.[76]

Some commentators have argued that the Act squarely imposes on courts an obligation to evaluate whether an alleged interference with a Convention right is proportionate and lawful—leaving minimal room for judgement by the particular primary decision-maker, especially in cases in which unqualified rights such those in Articles 2, 3 and 5 ECHR are engaged.[77] On the other side of the debate, it has been claimed that the 'public interest' dimension of disputes, particularly when Articles 8–11 are engaged, calls for maximum restraint, on grounds that judicial deference to elected organs of government is always necessary when deciding issues that engage majority choice—leaving little room for assessment by courts of the proportionality of their decisions.[78]

---

[75] See Lord Steyn (2005) (note 70 above).

[76] For a critique of the perseverance of this narrow field of enquiry, see Allan (2002) (note 9 above) 87–125.

[77] See for example I Leigh, '"Taking Rights Proportionately": Judicial Review, The Human Rights Act and Strasbourg' (2002) *Public Law* 265. However, it is notable that even though Leigh favours a robust fundamental rights approach to the scrutiny of public authority decisions under s 6 HRA, he finds justification for a strong judicial mandate not in the fundamental values of the common law but in the democratic legitimacy afforded by the HRA itself. Thus the unqualified language of s 6 is central to the argument.

[78] See S Atrill, 'Keeping the Executive in the Picture: A Reply to Professor Leigh' (2003) *Public Law* 41–51, where the author argues that judicial deference should be permitted in relation to all rights, including the unqualified rights, and that to allow no margin of appreciation for unqualified rights conflicts with Strasbourg jurisprudence. However, compare the arguments of Leigh (*ibid*).

In the course of this continued debate, however, a functional doctrine of constitutional deference has emerged to capture the idea that in hard cases in which courts are confronted with difficult policy choices of the kind outlined above, differences in the relative institutional competencies of courts and the elected branches of government should be key to determining the limits of legitimate intervention.[79] Even before the HRA was in force, academic commentators and judges had proposed a 'margin of discretion'—different in import though similar in practice to the Strasbourg margin of appreciation—whereby greater consideration must be afforded to opinions of the legislature or the executive in certain types of policy disputes such as immigration or national security, where facts may be excluded for justifiable reasons of secrecy; or when courts are otherwise institutionally ill-suited to adjudicating in polycentric disputes with far-reaching socio-political or socio-economic repercussions.[80]

i. Context and Proportionality: A Bright-line Division in Public Law?

Shortly after the HRA came into force, the well-worn controversy as to whether proportionality is the appropriate standard of review in human rights cases[81] was finally put to rest in *R v Secretary of State for the Home Department, ex Parte Daly* (herafter *Daly*),[82] when the House of Lords confirmed the correctness of the European Court of Human Rights (ECtHR) decision in *Smith and Grady*.[83] In that case, the ECtHR had unanimously held that investigations conducted by the Ministry of Defence pursuant to a policy of excluding homosexuals from the armed forces constituted a breach of Article 8 ECHR.

---

[79] See J Jowell, 'Judicial Deference: Servility, Civility or Institutional Capacity?' (2003) *Public Law* 592. The author sought to narrow the reach of the doctrine to disputes in which courts lacked the requisite institutional competencies, socio-economic disputes in particular. For similar arguments in relation to s 3 HRA, see chapter 3, section IIE above, particularly the discussion regarding *Bellinger v Bellinger* [2003] UKHL 21, [2003] 2 All ER 593, [2003] 2 AC 467.

[80] Pannick (note 70 above); M Hunt, 'Judicial Review after the Human Rights Act' (1999) *Queen Mary and Westfield Law Journal* 14, 15–16, where the author argued for a doctrine of due deference 'whereby, depending on the context, a court should defer to the decision maker or the legislature'; and Craig (2001) (note 70 above) 590 for the view that judicial deference is part of a longstanding tradition in public law and that it is therefore unsurprising that it should continue after the HRA.

[81] See for example Craig (2001) (note 70 above); Elliot (note 70 above); Leigh (note 77 above); and R Clayton, 'Regaining a Sense of Proportion: The Human Rights Act and the Proportionality Principle' (2001) *European Human Rights Law Review* 504.

[82] [2001] UKHL 26, [2001] 2 WLR 1622.

[83] Note 66 above. As we have seen, in *Smith* (note 33 above) it had been recognised that in determining the standard of review, the human rights context was important, and that the more substantial the interference with human rights, the more the court would require by way of justification before it was satisfied that the decision was reasonable. However, it was also accepted that the threshold of irrationality that an applicant was required to surmount was a high one. Thus, although the main judgments in the High Court and the Court of Appeal challenged the reasons advanced by the government in justification of the policy, both courts concluded that the policy could not be said to be beyond the range of responses open to a reasonable decision-maker and, accordingly, could not be said to be 'irrational'.

Moreover, regarding the review of the policy by the domestic courts in *Smith*,[84] the ECtHR was clear:

> [T]he threshold at which the High Court and Court of Appeal could find the Ministry of Defence policy irrational was placed so high, that it effectively excluded any consideration by the domestic courts of the question whether the interference with the applicants' rights answered a pressing social need or was proportionate to the national security and public order aims pursued, principles which lie at the heart of the Court's analysis of complaints under Article 8 of the Convention.[85]

In addition to reaffirming this ECtHR decision, the House of Lords in *Daly* rejected the approach of the Court of Appeal in the earlier decision of *Mahmood*[86] as being too close to the language of *Wednesbury* review. Lord Steyn emphasised that Strasbourg proportionality may require a reviewing court to assess the actual balance that the decision-maker struck, rather than merely to make a decision as to whether it was within the range of rational or reasonable decisions; furthermore, 'the proportionality test may go further than the traditional grounds of review inasmuch as it may require attention to be directed to the relative weight accorded to interests and considerations'.[87]

Moreover, although recognising that in practice the intensive form of *Wednesbury* review (anxious scrutiny) might yield the same results, Lord Steyn emphasised that this would not always be so, and judicial scrutiny under the HRA should therefore always be conditioned by the two-fold requirements of Strasbourg: any limitation of rights must be necessary in a democratic society, in the sense of meeting a pressing social need; and any interference must be proportionate to the legitimate aim pursued. He concluded in unequivocal terms: 'It is therefore important that cases involving ECHR rights must be analysed in the correct way.'[88] However, agreeing with an article by Jeffrey Jowell,[89] Lord Steyn was also at pains to emphasise that there remains a fundamental distinction between proportionality and a full merits review—a distinction that allows for the difference between judicial and executive competencies. In performing the balancing exercise, courts have a secondary responsibility to 'ensure that the decision-maker has acted in accordance with the requirements of legality'.[90]

Having approved the general thrust of the Court of Appeal decision in *Mahmood*, insofar as it had implied a crucial distinction between proportionality

---

[84] Note 33 above.

[85] *Smith and Grady* (note 66 above) para 138.

[86] *R (on the Application of Mahmood) v Secretary of State for the Home Department* (hereafter *Mahmood*) [2001] 1WLR 840 (an immigration case).

[87] *Daly* (note 82 above) para 27. Lord Steyn rejected Lord Phillips MR's test in *Mahmood* (*ibid*), which was an 'objective test' as to whether 'the decision-maker could reasonably have concluded that the interference was necessary to achieve one or more of the legitimate aims recognised by the Convention' (*Mahmood* (note 86 above) para 40 (Lord Phillips)).

[88] *Daly* (note 82 above) para 28.

[89] See Jowell (2000) (note 39 above) 681.

[90] *Daly* (note 82 above) para 28 (Lord Steyn).

and a full merits review, Lord Steyn also agreed with the observation of Laws LJ in *Mahmood* 'that the intensity of review in public law cases involving Convention rights will depend on the subject matter in hand', adding that of course 'in law context is everything'.[91] As will be seen, this remark left room for some doubt as to how in practice the context or subject matter of a dispute should affect the standard of scrutiny to be applied.

Against this background, even before the HRA came into force, constitutional commentators had contemplated a similar though different notion of deference or 'margin of discretion' to be afforded to public authorities in appropriate circumstances. In *R v DPP, ex parte Kebilene*,[92] by reference to a recent book edited by Lord Lester of Herne Hill and David Pannick,[93] Lord Hope had famously stated:

> There will be times during Convention adjudication, when a court will need to recognise that difficult choices may have to be made by the executive or the legislature between the rights of the individual and the needs of society. In some circumstances it will be appropriate for the courts to recognise that there is an area of judgement within which the judiciary will defer on democratic grounds to the considered opinion of the elected body . . .[94]

Proceeding to explain how these 'discretionary areas of judgements' would be identified, Lord Hope considered that they would be most likely to arise where the Convention itself had recognised the need 'for a balance to be struck'; they would be much less likely to arise 'where the right is stated in terms which are unqualified'—such as those in Articles 8–11 ECHR. Furthermore, Lord Hope thought that it would be easier for courts to recognise the need for such discretion

> where the issues involve questions of social or economic policy, much less where the rights are of high constitutional importance or are of a kind where *the courts are especially well placed to assess the need for protection.*[95]

Thus, in the immediate aftermath of the HRA, by reference to Lord Hope's speech in *Kebilene* or to Lord Steyn's fleeting reference to context in *Daly*, deference was increasingly relied on as *a* reason if not the sole reason to deny Convention claims in diverse areas of executive power,[96] including national

---

[91] *Daly* (note 82 above) para 28 (Lord Steyn).

[92] [2000] 2AC 326 HL.

[93] L Lester and D Pannick (eds), *Human Rights Law and Practice*, 1st edn (London, Butterworths, 1999). 'The margin of discretion' propounded by Lord Hope in *Kebilene* was attributed to Lester and Pannick, who had contemplated the use of a 'margin of discretion' that was similar though not identical to the margin of appreciation deployed by the Strasbourg institutions.

[94] *Kebilene* (note 92 above) 381.

[95] *Ibid*, emphasis added.

[96] See generally L Lester and D Pannick (eds), *Human Rights Law and Practice*, 2nd edn (London, Butterworths, 2004) 99; and J Wadham, H Mountfield and A Edmundson, *Blackstone's Guide to the Human Rights Act 1998*, 3rd edn (Oxford, OUP, 2003) 82–6.

security,[97] immigration,[98] public order[99] and the allocation of public resources.[100] This did not, however, prevent continuing doubts about the manner in which deference should be applied in practice. Would it be enough for authorities merely to state the reasons for their decisions so that courts would then be exonerated from any further obligation to consider whether their reasons were justifiable?

Useful insights can be gleaned from contrasting approaches to deference in the dissenting speech of Laws LJ in *International Transport Roth Gmbh v Secretary of State for the Home Department* (hereafter *Roth*)[101] on the one hand and the opinion of Simon Brown LJ in the majority on the other. The case, which raised questions about the 'proportionality' of financially stringent measures enacted to deter carriers from bringing illegal immigrants into the UK, constituted a direct challenge to the lawfulness of the legislative scheme itself under section 3 HRA.[102] Therefore, in light of the political sensitivity of the dispute and the directness of the challenge to the legislature's authority, the Court of Appeal took opportunity to reflect in general, and at length, on the proper approach to deference in public law.

Although dissenting, the speech of Laws LJ in *Roth* received considerable attention because it set out to provide courts with what he regarded as a principled set of guidelines that should play a part in any judicial calculation as to whether or not to defer in public law disputes. These included: the fundamental nature of the rights at issue; the degree of democratic accountability of the decision-maker; and the expertise of the decision-maker weighed against that of the court in any given context.[103] Applying these guidelines, Laws LJ concluded that 'the principles of deference would require the balance struck by the

---

[97] For example, *Secretary of State for the Home Department, ex parte Rheman* [2001] UKHL 47, [2003] 1 AC 153.

[98] For example, *R (on the Application of Farrakhan) v Secretary of State for Home Department* (hereafter *Farrakhan*) [2002] EWCA Civ 606, [2002] QB 1391. Lord Phillips MR concluded that the discretionary area of judgement was broad in the context of immigration decisions because the 'European Court of Human Rights attaches considerable weight to the right under international law of a state to control immigration in its own territory' (1418, para 71).

[99] See *Farrakhan* (*ibid*) para 73.

[100] For example, *R v Secretary of State for the Environment Transport and the Regions, ex parte Spath Homes Ltd* [2001] 2 AC 349 HL; *R (on the Application of Alconbury Developments Ltd) v Secretary of State for the Environment Transport and the Regions* [2001] UKHL 23, paras 69–70 (Lord Hoffman); *Poplar Housing and Regeneration Community Association Ltd v Donoghue* (hereafter *Donoghue*) [2001] EWCA Civ 595, [2001] 3 WLR 183, 204, [2001] 4 All ER 605; and *R (Carson) v Secretary of State for Work and Pensions* [2003] 3 All ER 577.

[101] [2002] EWCA Civ 158. The case concerned a challenge by road hauliers against the penalty regime contained in Part II of the Immigration and Asylum Act 1999, which imposed fixed financial penalties on persons deemed responsible for illegal entrants to the UK, for example as in this case, those who had arrived hidden in a lorry. The majority in the Court of Appeal upheld the declaration of incompatibility imposed by the first instance judge.

[102] On grounds that certain of its provisions were in breach of Art 6(1) and Art 1 of Protocol 1 ECHR. The penalty was fixed, and there was no flexibility for degrees of fault; there was furthermore no provision for compensation if it was ultimately determined that a carrier was not at fault during the period when his vehicle had been detained.

[103] *Roth* (note 101 above) paras 83–7.

democratic powers to be accepted'—and in this case, crucially, the assessment of the 'social consequences which flow from the entry into the UK of clandestine illegal immigrants in significant numbers' lay 'obviously far more within the competence of government than of courts'.[104]

By contrast, although no less certain that a high degree of deference was owed to Parliament in evaluating the legality of the scheme under review, Simon Brown LJ in *Roth* considered that under the HRA, courts cannot subjugate their role 'as guardians of human rights' to the authority of the legislature and must intervene where Parliament has overstepped the limits of what is justifiable.[105] Claiming therefore that the question can properly be answered only if the court carries out 'a proper scrutiny' of the reasons for a public authority decision, and 'according as much deference as he believed proper to the executive', Simon Brown LJ was prepared to demand justifications for the measure from those responsible for immigration control and for their devising and enacting the legislation necessary to achieve it.[106] Accordingly, by contrast with Laws LJ, whose approach in *Roth* contemplated the truncation of a secondary judicial balancing role, Simon Brown LJ had no choice but to find the legislative scheme unfair, insofar as it imposed on carriers an excessive burden, albeit in pursuit of social goals, and was therefore incompatible with Article 6 ECHR.

In essence, therefore, the judgement of Simon Brown LJ postulates an approach whereby appropriate deference is to be determined in accordance with a range of factors *after* hearing the justifications for the measure. These could include the democratic accountability of decision makers; the political sensitivity of the matter in dispute; or the institutional suitability of the court to deal with the kind of evidence involved—all of which must be viewed in light of the justifications that the decision-maker has given for arriving at the decision in the applicant's case.

B. Justification, Transparency and Reasons to Defer

Despite the superficial appeal of a bright-line division between cases that merit the full rigours of proportionality and those that do not, both constitutional commentators and courts have expressed doubts about the creation of judicially defined zones of non-justiciability in public administrative law—a weakness over which English administrative law has for some time considered itself to have triumphed, particularly in contexts such as national security and immigration.[107]

---

[104] *Roth* (note 101 above) paras 83–7.

[105] *Ibid*, para 27.

[106] *Ibid*, paras 26–9.

[107] See generally J Jowell and J Cooper, 'Introduction' in J Jowell and J Cooper (eds), *Delivering Rights: How the Human Rights Act is Working* (Oxford, Hart, 2003). See also Jowell (2003) (note 79 above). For a survey of the expansion of judicial review into new territories, see M Belloff, 'Judicial Review 2001: A Prophetic Odyssey' (1995) 58 *Modern Law Review* 143. See also Laws (1995) (note 3 above) 75, where the author, noting the political territory covered by modern judicial review cases, asserts that apart from those few areas 'where courts have rightly or wrongly created

Thus, although the idea of a bright-line division has rarely been criticised in relation to disputes that raise issues of resource allocation, in contexts such as immigration and national security there have been doubts about the constitutional
propriety of a context-sensitive approach that limits the full use of Strasbourg
proportionality in precisely the manner proposed by Laws LJ and rejected by the
majority in *Roth*.[108]

In an early contribution to the debate,[109] Hunt argued not only that it is
impossible to isolate the multifaceted issues of human rights adjudication into
watertight compartments of the kind proposed by Lord Hope in *Kebilene*,[110]
but also that, as recognised by Lord Steyn in *Daly*,[111] the very notion of constitutional review dictates that 'it is very important that all cases involving
Convention rights be analysed in the right way'[112]—even though it might make
a difference in only a handful of cases. Thus, Hunt claimed, if deference is
applied on the basis of the subject matter *before* examining the reasons on which
public authority decisions are based, the doctrine can be used to undermine
what he regarded as one of the seminal insights in Lord Steyn's speech in *Daly*—
that 'proportionality is not so much a "test", or "standard" as a new type of
approach to adjudication which subjects the justification for decisions to rigorous scrutiny to determine their legality'.[113] Understood in this way, *Daly* is 'a
major landmark on the road to a true culture of justification implicit in all
human rights adjudication'.[114]

Nonetheless, in his article, Hunt noted that in the wake of *Daly*, 'lawyers rep-
resenting defendant authorities in public law proceedings merely preface their
familiar *Wednesbury* submissions with the words "in context" in order to justify continuing to apply the *Wednesbury* standard'.[115] Instead, he argued, 'deference from the courts must be earned by the primary decision-maker, by openly
demonstrating the justifications for the decisions they have reached and by
demonstrating why their decision is worthy of crucial respect'.[116] Furthermore,

---

a non-intrusive jurisdiction', we now possess one where 'every public body is subject to the supervision of the court as regards every decision it makes, save for the Queen in Parliament' (75).

[108] Note 101 above.

[109] M Hunt, 'Sovereignty's Blight: Why Contemporary Public Law Needs a Concept of Due
Deference' in N Bamforth and P Leyland (eds), *Public Law in a Multi-layered Constitution* (London,
Hart, 2003).

[110] Note 92 above. For example, resource allocation issues considered to be inappropriate are frequently raised in criminal law disputes, which have been characterised as particularly suitable,
because of the expertise of courts in that area.

[111] Note 82 above.

[112] *Ibid*, 1636, para 28.

[113] Hunt (2003) (note 109 above) 342.

[114] *Ibid*. Increasingly, commentators have focused on the evidence that courts should be demanding from decision makers as the price of judicial deference to their assessment of proportionality
issues. See *ibid*.

[115] *Ibid*, 342.

[116] *Ibid*, 341. See also R Edwards, 'Judicial Deference under the Human Rights Act' (2002)
Modern Law Review 859, where the author argues that a process of constitutional review requires
detailed reasoning from judges supported by detailed evidence, from the decision maker or public
authority, that the restrictions on rights and freedoms are both necessary and justified.

rejecting the conceptualisation of 'due deference' as spatially defined areas into which courts should not trespass, he cogently reasoned that the degree of deference accorded to the legislature or other administrators should be determined in accordance with the specific circumstances of each case.

In the second edition of their textbook,[117] Lester and Pannick have taken issue with Hunt's suggestion that they advocated a spatial approach to deference that should be avoided on grounds that it 'treats certain areas of decision-making ... as being beyond the reach of legality and within the realm of pure discretion in which remedies for wrongs are political only'.[118] Refuting any suggestion that their 'discretionary area of judgement' was ever intended to indicate that there are definitive 'areas of decision-making which are effectively excluded from challenge', Lester and Pannick have sought to put the record straight by explaining that 'in assessing whether a challenge succeeds, the courts will recognise a margin of judgment for the decision-maker *in some circumstances*'.[119]

Nevertheless, in the same passage, Lester and Pannick vigorously refute the second of Hunt's claims, that in practice, since the HRA, the use of such a territorial notion of deference has served to 'inhibit the proper articulation of what may be perfectly legitimate reasons for deferring'.[120] This is in fact the more speculative of Hunt's claims and one that clearly lacks empirical foundation. Nevertheless, the response of Lester and Pannick suggests that they may have missed the essential point of Hunt's argument, which was not to deny that there are a wide range of reasons, including public safety, as to *why* courts might decide to defer, but to point out that as part of the democratic balance between courts and the executive envisaged by the process of constitutional review, reasons for deferring should always so far as possible be transparent so that deference can be seen to have been *earned* by the primary decision-maker.[121]

Thus, consistent with what has increasingly been viewed in common law jurisdictions as the very essence of constitutional review, Hunt proposed that, in order to facilitate transparency in the adjudicative process and to ensure the scrutiny of administrative decisions in accordance with fundamental democratic values enshrined in the ECHR, authorities should be required whenever possible to give reasons for their decisions so that, in turn, those reasons can be weighed in the balance by courts, along with other considerations on which they might consider it appropriate to defer.[122]

---

[117] Note 96 above.

[118] Leseter and Pannick (2004) (note 96 above) 95.

[119] *Ibid.*

[120] *Ibid*, citing Hunt (2003) (note 109 above) 339.

[121] Hunt distinguishes the idea of 'due deference' from deference as submission to argue that 'the language of sovereignty' should be abandoned in favour of the language of justification. See Hunt (2003) (note 109 above) 340.

[122] Hunt has acknowledged the influence of the work of David Dyzenhaus, in particular his efforts to build on Etienne Mureinik's conception of legality as a 'culture of justification', as expounded for example in D Dyzenhaus, 'Law as Justification: Etienne Mureinik's Conception of Legal Culture' (1998) *South African Journal of Human Rights* 11. See further subsection F below. Hunt's unique contribution to the UK debate is found in the latter part of 'Sovereignty's Blight' (note

C. Deference Embedded: The Artificial Division between Policy and Law

Since the HRA, the general consensus regarding the need for appropriate deference has tended to obscure a deep division not only among academics but also
among senior members of the judiciary. This division has been particularly apparent in the judgments and extra-judicial pronouncements of Lords Hoffman and
Steyn. Even though Lord Steyn has conceded that he and Lord Hoffman have
arrived at the same conclusions in a number of controversial and highly sensitive
political disputes,[123] there has been clear disagreement between these senior
judges as to how deference should be exercised in difficult cases that engage
majority choice, particularly when there is acute tension between an alleged violation of fundamental rights and appeals by the executive to the public interest.[124]

Lord Hoffman's thesis centres around the idea of a bright-line division that
separates the judicial and executive spheres of decision-making, perhaps most
concisely summarised in his familiar speech in *R on the Application of ProLife
Alliance v BBC* (hereafter *ProLife Alliance*).[125] Starting from the non-
controversial proposition that a judgement concerning the appropriate division
of powers in a modern democratic constitution is a 'question of law, to be
decided by the courts',[126] Lord Hoffman nonetheless went on to state in *ProLife
Alliance* that the powers of courts under the HRA are also necessarily constrained by certain 'principles of law' according to which judicial 'decision-
making powers are allocated'. Arguing that 'independence makes the court
more suited to deciding some kinds of questions, and being elected makes the
legislature or executive more suited to deciding others', he concluded:

> [That] the independence of the courts is necessary for a proper decision of disputed
> legal rights or claims of violation of human rights is a legal principle . . . On the other
> hand, the principle that majority approval is necessary for a proper decision on policy
> or allocation of resources is also a legal principle. Likewise, when a court decides that
> a decision is within the proper competence of the legislature or the executive, it is not
> showing deference; it is deciding the law.[127]

---

109 above), where he moves beyond abstract theorising about 'why due deference matters' to consider 'recent decisions in "contexts" where courts have been traditionally submissive to primary
decision makers' (immigration control; town and country planning; and social and economic policy) (354–70). His purpose is to illustrate the operation of what he sees as two different approaches
and how they might make a difference in practice.

[123] For example, in *Rheman* (note 97 above), which was heard shortly after the HRA came into force.

[124] *Rheman* (note 97 above): 'It is not only that the executive has access to special information
and expertise in these matters. It is also that such decisions, with serious potential results for the
community, require a legitimacy which can be conferred only by entrusting them to persons responsible to the community through the democratic process. If the people are to accept the consequences
of such decisions, they must be made by persons whom the people have elected and whom they can
remove' (para 61 (Lord Hoffman)).

[125] [2003] UKHL 23, [2004] 1 AC 185.

[126] *Ibid*, para 85.

[127] *Ibid*.

Although superficially attractive, Lord Hoffman's approach is clearly prob-lematic. Premised on the artificial separation of the spheres of policy and law, it seeks to limit the intensity of judicial scrutiny in certain types of preordained disputes, on grounds that they are intrinsically more suited to resolution by the elected branches of government.[128]

In a public address to the Judicial Studies Board[129] Lord Steyn took the opportunity to posit a constitutional approach to deference that avoids what he saw as the pitfall in Lord Hoffman's reasoning, namely that 'courts would be required automatically to defer, on constitutional grounds, on any occasion when a qualified Convention right was claimed to be defeated by a particular public interest'.[130] Thus, one of Lord Hoffman's reasons for deferring in *Rheman*—that 'certain types of decisions can only be made by persons whom the public have elected and whom they can remove'—was rejected by Lord Steyn as 'self sufficient and controlling'.[131] Instead, Lord Steyn suggested that were courts to give effect to any 'self denying ordinance' in respect of particular classes of cases (such as immigration or resource allocation disputes), it would be palpably inconsistent with the role of courts as interpreters of statute, cre-ators of the common law and guardians of human rights.[132]

Significantly, however, Lord Steyn, like Hunt has not denied the need for the *legitimate* exercise of deference 'in the context of *a specific issue in a particular case*'.[133] Thus, Lord Steyn added that in a disputes concerning matters of national security, when decisions might be based on secret intelligence assess-ments,[134] or in cases concerning the 'allocation of scarce resources for what may be important but experimental surgery',[135] a court might decline as a matter of discretion to rule on a particular issue, on grounds that 'another branch of gov-ernment is institutionally better placed to decide the matter'.[136] Such restraint, however, would not be based on the dispute's prior labelling as a national security or resource allocation dispute. Instead, it would be based on an informed decision that there was limited potential for adjudication in light of

---

[128] Commenting on Lord Hoffman's statement, Jowell and Cooper (note 107 above) have argued: 'The vocabulary of legal principle . . . has its dangers insofar as it implies that the courts have no legal right to intervene in certain matters which engage majority choice. It is the judges now who define the scope of all Convention rights . . . And it is for the courts to decide whether and in what circumstances, to concede competence to other branches of government . . . but any conces-sion [deference] on the part of courts . . . is based less upon the law than upon a developing sense of when to recognise the limits of the court's own fact-finding capacity or expertise and an apprecia-tion of those matters which are most appropriately decided by Parliament or the executive' (4).

[129] Lord Steyn (note 70 above) 351.

[130] *Ibid*, 359. 'On this reasoning such decisions are beyond the competence of the court. Apart from Lord Hoffman's observation I am not aware of any authority for this view'. Paradoxically, in failing to explain his reference to context in the leading case of *Daly* (note 82 above), Lord Steyn had made his own contribution to the tangle that he was concerned to unravel in his public address.

[131] Lord Steyn (note 70 above) 358.

[132] See generally *ibid*, 350–8.

[133] *Ibid*, 350 (emphasis added).

[134] *Ibid*, 357.

[135] *Ibid*.

[136] *Ibid*.

circumstances surrounding the particular case, whether due to lack of evidence or the greater expertise of the primary decision-maker.[137]

In seeking to untangle the story of deference, Lord Steyn focused primarily on national security, public safety and related contexts in which he believed that 'the issue will perhaps most frequently and credibly arise'.[138] However, in appealing for a holistic approach to the adjudication of disputes that involve fundamental rights, he was no less critical of Lord Hoffman's claim that 'the principle that majority approval is necessary for a proper decision on policy or allocation of resources is also a legal principle.'[139] Observing that 'in common law adjudication, it is an everyday occurrence for courts to consider, together with principled arguments, the balance sheet of policy advantages and disadvantages', Lord Steyn noted that 'most legislation is to advance a policy', and 'frequently it involves in one way or other, the allocation of resources'.[140] He stated that if 'in striking the balance', courts may arrive at a result that is unacceptable to Parliament, that body 'can act with great speed to reverse the effect of a decision'.[141] In light of these considerations, Lord Steyn concluded:

> Courts ought not to take such decisions on a priori grounds without scrutiny of the challenged decision, since no one can know in advance whether it has been infected with manifest illegality. This is a balanced approach well suited to the needs of our mature democracy.[142]

Although Lord Steyn was minded to take a shot across the bow, stressing the importance of judicial vigilance in contexts where abrogation of the most fundamental democratic freedoms such as the right of access to court can be facilitated by overwhelming parliamentary majorities, the key purpose of his address was to appeal to courts to recognise their adjudicative responsibilities under the HRA, by ensuring 'that cases involving Convention rights must be analysed in the right way'.[143]

---

[137] *Ibid*, 352.

[138] *Ibid*, 356.

[139] Note 127 above and accompanying text.

[140] Lord Steyn (note 70 above) 357.

[141] *Ibid*, 357. See *R (on the Application of A) v East Sussex County Council (No 2)* [2003] EWHC 167; and *R (on the Application of Burke) v the General Medical Council and Disability Rights Commission* [2004] EWCH 1879 Admin for examples of judicial balancing of this kind (discussed in chapter 3 above). See also *Thake v Maurice* [1986] 2WLR 337 (a tortuous claim involving the measurement of damages for economic loss resulting from experimental surgery). In cases of these kind, courts are indeed required to make resource allocation decisions.

[142] Lord Steyn (note 70 above) 352. Here Lord Steyn was speaking of the dangers of 'democratic governments abusing their powers and abdicating their democratic and constitutional responsibilities' and 'of the need that they should face open and effective justice', by reference to the flagrant abuse of the rule of law in the detention of prisoners at Guantanemo Bay and in Iraq at Abu Ghraib.

[143] *Daly* (note 82 above) para 28 (Lord Steyn).

D. Deference in Context: Landlord and Tenant Repossession Cases

This is not the place for detailed examination of deference in the extensive range of policy areas in which it has been applied since the HRA came into force.[144] However, the application of deference in context can usefully be examined by reference to the proliferation of public sector housing repossession cases.[145] This line of cases began with the now familiar case of *Donoghue*,[146] appeared to reach a finale in the House of Lords decisions in *Qazi v Harrow LBC*[147]and resurfaced in *R (on the Application of Kay) v London Borough of Others v Lambeth* (hereafter *Kay*).[148]

In the controversial area of UK national housing policy, eviction has long been accepted as an integral tool in managing the inadequate supply of public housing, despite its potential to augment the deprivations and suffering of vulnerable individuals in cases of acute need.[149] Since *Donoghue*, the context-

---

[144] For example, regarding immigration control, see *Mahmood* (note 86 above) and *Farrakhan* (note 98 above); regarding gypsies and town and country planning, see *R (on the Application of Buckland and Boswell) v Secretary of State for the Environment* [2001] EWHC Admin. (Cf *Chapman v UK* (2001) EHRR 399, para 73.)

[145] For the substantive law in housing repossession case law prior to *Qazi v Harrow LBC* [2003] UK HL 43, [2003] 4 ALL ER 461, see J Luba, N Madge and D McConnell, *Defending Possession Proceedings*, 5th edn (London, Legal Action Group, 2002). See further I Loveland, 'The Impact of the Human Rights Act on Security of Tenure in Public Housing' (2004) *Public Law* 594, 594–611. The HRA litigation raised two questions for housing lawyers: (a) what type of residential tenancy occupancy situations fall within the notion of respect for the home in Art 8(1) ECHR; and (b) in what circumstances can Art 8(2) ECHR be invoked by a landlord or property owner to justify interference with Art 8(1)? After *Lambeth v Howard* [2001] EWCA Civ 468 (in which the Court of Appeal held that Art 8(1) ECHR is likely to be engaged whenever a person's continued occupancy of his or her home is under threat), it became progressively clear form Court of Appeal judgments that the limited effect of Art 8 ECHR on public sector landlord and tenant repossession challenges would vary according to the type of tenancy agreement at issue. See for example 'secure tenancies' and 'introductory tenancies'. Cf 'assured' or assured short-hold tenancies (granted by private sector landlords and not at first sight caught by s 6 HRA). But see *Donoghue* (note 100 above), in which Lord Woolf decided that Art 8 ECHR would bite on ostensibly private sector tenancies if, as in the applicant's case, the landlord was a public authority within the meaning of s 6(3)(b) HRA. For discussion of this aspect of the case, see chapter 3 above.

[146] Note 100 above.

[147] Note 145 above.

[148] [2006] UKHL 10. The case concerned appeals from Courts of Appeal in *R (on the Application of Kay) v Lambeth* [2004] EWCA Civ 289; and *R (on the Application of Price) v Leeds City Council* [2005] EWCA Civ 289, in which the House of Lords was asked to reconsider and depart from its decision in *Qazi* in light of later decisions by the ECtHR in *Connors v UK* (2004) 40 EHRR 189 and in *Blecic v Croatia* (2004) 41 EHRR 185, where in each case the ECtHR considered at some length the excepting conditions in Art 8(2) ECHR. See further the discussion of *Kay* and *Price* at notes 172 and 173 and accompanying text below.

[149] The government argued in *Donoghue* (note 100 above): 'The purpose of the homelessness legislation is to provide a safety net for people who have become homeless through no fault of their own and would be vulnerable if they were not provided with temporary accommodation until a more settled housing solution becomes available. If people accepted as unintentionally homeless and in priority need were provided with accommodation with security of tenure, this would displace applicants with greater claim to scarce social housing' (para 40). However, cf the position of the 'intentionally homeless' like Ms Donoghue, who have very low priority in the housing queue. See Joint Committee on Human Rights (JCHR), 'First Report: The Homelessness Bill' (2001–02)

sensitive approach to deference has not only survived but blossomed in the area of landlord and tenant repossessions—a state of affairs that, after the House of Lords decision in *Qazi*, provoked Ian Loveland to criticise that by 'blurring the distinction between hierarchy and function,' the courts have 'used the notion of deference, in effect to abdicate their traditional responsibilities at common law even to tell us what Parliament has done in enacting legislation'.[150] In contradiction to much academic and practitioner opinion prior to the HRA, the House of Lords decision in *Qazi* became authority for the proposition that in the absence of an Article 14 ECHR issue of the kind that arose in *Ghaidan*, domestic law on residential possession issues is invariably Article 8 ECHR-compliant.

The complex story of housing repossession disputes began with the now familiar case of *Donoghue*, which involved a tenant who had three children under six years old and was pregnant. She sought to resist an order for repossession of the temporary homelessness accommodation that had been granted by the council,[151] on grounds that such an order would contravene her rights under Article 8 ECHR. The trial judge refused to revoke the order, on grounds that there had been no violation of Article 8, since refusal to make a possession order in the applicant's case would 'contravene the rights of others' and enable persons who were intentionally homeless to disrupt the housing scheme. The applicant appealed.

Invoking section 3 HRA, Donoghue argued that section 21 of the Housing Act 1998 should be read compatibly with Article 8 ECHR, so as to mitigate the harsh effects of the notice to vacate her 'temporary homelessness accommodation'. Lord Woolf had no difficulty in accepting that there had been an interference with the applicant's Article 8 rights[152] and therefore agreed that the court was formally bound to consider the lawfulness of the measure, whether it served a legitimate aim and whether it was necessary in a democratic society.

As to whether the infringement satisfied 'a democratic aim', that is whether it was 'proportionate' and served a 'pressing social need', it was argued by the NGO Shelter as intervener, that in respect of the applicant's particular circumstances, the provision of temporary relief would not give rise to the 'undesirable consequences to which witnesses for the department refer' (in effect the annihilation of the legislative housing scheme).[153] However, upholding the decision of the trial judge, Lord Woolf tersely concluded:

> [The] court has to pay considerable attention to the fact, that when enacting section 21(4) of the 1998 Act, Parliament intended to give preference to the needs of those who

HL 30 HC 314, in which concerns were raised that possible loopholes in the network of support for certain groups of people in need of housing might lead to people suffering degrading treatment by reason of their homelessness.

[150] Loveland (2004) (note 145 above) 606.
[151] Granted by the claimant housing authority under s 21(4) Housing Act 1988.
[152] Lord Woolf concurred with the finding of the trial judge that Art 8(1) ECHR was engaged by the circumstances of the case 'because the eviction interfered with her family rights'.
[153] *Donoghue* (note 100 above) para 67.

are dependent on social housing as a whole, over those in the position of the [intentionally homeless] defendant.[154]

For constitutional commentators keen to observe how courts would approach their novel powers of review under the HRA, the absence in *Donoghue* of principled debate of the kind envisaged by the structure of Article 8(2) ECHR was generally considered striking.[155] The Court of Appeal did not further consider why the refusal to grant even temporary relief (as advocated in light of the family's predicament) was 'necessary in a democratic society'. Moreover, no attention was drawn to the case of *Marzari v Italy*,[156] in which the ECtHR had considered the applicant's medical condition to be highly relevant to that question; or to the case of *Ostra Lopez v Spain*,[157] in which the ECtHR concluded that general evidence of resource allocation issues are not enough to satisfy Article 8(2). Instead, in summary, Lord Woolf briefly concluded:

> [N]otwithstanding its mandatory terms, section 21(4) of the 1998 Act does not conflict with the defendant's right to family life. The question is whether the restricted power of the court is legitimate and proportionate. This is the area of policy where the court should defer to the decision of Parliament. We have come to the conclusion that there was no contravention of article 6 or article 8.[158]

Donoghue was soon followed by a plethora of challenges against the legality of repossession orders in the county courts in respect of different types of landlord and tenant contracts. Thus, finally in *Qazi*[159] the House of Lords was asked to consider two questions: the type of residency agreement that falls within the notion of respect for the home in Article 8(1) ECHR; and the circumstances in which Article 8(2) ECHR can be relied on by public landlords or property owners seeking repossession of property in accordance with relevant legislation or rules of common law.

The facts of *Qazi* were straightforward: Mr Qazi had shared a house with his former wife and their children; after his former wife, who was joint tenant, unilaterally served notice to quit and thereby terminated the tenancy, Mr Qazi remained in the house with his new family and children. The facts did not disclose circumstances of exceptional need or possible vulnerability of the children of the kind present in *Donoghue* or of any impropriety on the part of the authority concerned. The question was whether it was lawful for Harrow as a public authority to recover summary possession of its property from a former tenant in accordance with the rules of housing law, without any opportunity in existing procedures for the court to consider whether the making of such an order was proportionate.

---

[154] *Donoghue* (note 100 above) para 72 (Lord Woolf).
[155] See Edwards (note 116 above).
[156] ECtHR Admissibility Decision 04/05/1999, (1999) 28 EHRR CD 175.
[157] (1995) 20 EHRR 277.
[158] *Donoghue* (note 100 above) para 72. See Edwards (note 116 above).
[159] Note 145 above.

The House of Lords were divided three to two on the issue. Among the majority, Lord Hope first concluded that since a joint tenancy is automatically terminated by a tenant's notice to quit, the order for possession follows automatically, so a county court judge has no discretion in the matter. Lord Hope further concluded that the requirements of Article 8(2) ECHR are automatically met whenever the law affords an unqualified right to possession, on proof that the tenancy has been terminated by notice or some other means. Similarly, Lord Millet held that while Article 8(2) might call for a balance to be struck, no such balancing exercise needs to be conducted when the outcome is a foregone conclusion:

> In most cases the statutory scheme established by Parliament will provide the objective justification for the council's decision to seek possession, which need not be demonstrated on a case-by-case basis.[160]

In short, therefore, not only was the majority in *Qazi* prepared to defend the approach of *Donoghue*, but, by insisting that courts should always defer to legislative housing schemes enacted by Parliament and to the principles of the common law regarding property rights, the House of Lords went further. Thus, it was concluded that in relation to a statutory scheme whereby landlords were automatically entitled to possession on fulfilment of certain procedural criteria, there was no Article 8(2) ECHR issue to address.

Nevertheless, in forcefully worded dissenting speeches, Lord Steyn and Lord Bingham insisted that some form of justificatory exercise is always demanded by Article 8(2) ECHR, even though in certain circumstances (for example, when there is a challenge to the scope of primary legislation) it may require no more than a recognition that Parliament has already struck the Article 8(2) balance in the enactment of the impugned legislation (as Lord Woolf had done in *Donoghue*). Lord Steyn in particular expressed serious doubts as to whether the majority in *Qazi* had performed their obligations under section 6 HRA, since in his view they had effectively abnegated any responsibility for examining the Article 8 compatibility of the refusal by the landlord to renew the tenancy of a dwelling in which the applicant lived with his wife and children). He concluded in strong words:

> It would be surprising if the views of the majority or their interpretation and application of Article 8 of the ECHR as incorporated into our legal system by the HRA 1998 withstood European scrutiny. . . . It is contrary to the purposive interpretation of Article 8 read against the structure of the Convention. . . . [I]t is inconsistent with the general thrust of the Court of Human Rights and the Commission. It is contrary to the position adopted by the UK government on more than one occasion before the European Court of Human Rights. . . . [T]he decision of today does not fit into the new legal landscape created by the HRA.[161]

---

[160] *Qazi* (note 145 above) para 109 (Lord Millett).
[161] *Ibid*, paras 26–7 (Lord Steyn).

The matter did not rest there however, since the views of the minority in *Qazi* were subjected to further scrutiny by the House of Lords in *Kay*,[162] where the issue of deference in the context of Article 8 repossession disputes was reopened in the wake of later decisions of the ECtHR in *Connors v United Kingdom*[163] and *Blecic v Croatia*.[164] It was on the assumption that following *Connors*, *Qazi* was of doubtful authority, that the appeals in *Kay* were launched.[165]

It should be recalled that, characteristically, the ECtHR in *Connors* had emphasised that 'a margin of appreciation must inevitably be left to the national authorities', who 'by reason of their direct and continuous contact with the vital forces of their countries, are in principle better placed than an international court to evaluate local needs and conditions'.[166] However, citing *Smith and Grady v the UK*,[167] the ECtHR had also stressed that while in general 'it is for the national authorities to make the initial assessment of necessity, the final evaluation as to whether the reasons cited are relevant and sufficient, remains subject to review by the Court for conformity with the requirements of the Convention.'[168]

Thus, emphasising that the margin would always vary 'according to the nature of the Convention right in issue, its importance to the individual and nature of the activities restricted, as well as the aim pursued by the restrictions',[169] the Court concluded in *Connors* that the eviction of the applicant and his family from a gypsy site had not been attended by the requisite procedural safeguards: 'namely the requirement to establish proper justification for the serious interference with his rights',[170] which emanated from a failure to provide rules in national legislation that distinguish between what is appropriate to mobile homes on private sites and those on gypsy sites provided by the council.

Although the ECtHR in *Connors* focused particularly on the summary nature of the eviction regime under a specific piece of UK legislation (the Caravan Sites Act 1968), in finding a breach of Article 8 ECHR, it also gave due concern to the impact of that regime on the personal circumstances of the applicant's family. Thus, in determining the gravity of the interference with the applicant's home— and therefore the margin of appreciation that should be left to the national authority—the ECtHR made it clear that factors such as the difficulties of 'finding a lawful alternative location for their caravans, in coping with health problems and young children and in ensuring continuation of their children's education' were highly relevant to the exercise of proportionality.[171]

---

[162] Note 148 above.

[163] Note 148 above.

[164] Note 148 above.

[165] For comment on the House of Lords decision in *Kay*, see I Loveland, 'Much Ado about Not Very Much After All? Last Word on the Relevance of ECHR Article 8 to Possession Proceedings' (2006) *Journal of Planning Law* 1457.

[166] *Connors* (note 148 above) para 82. See also chapter 2 above.

[167] Nos 33985/96 and 33986/96 ECHR 1999-VI, para 88.

[168] *Ibid*, para 81.

[169] *Gillow v UK*, judgment of Nov 1986, Series A, No 104, para 55.

[170] *Connors* (note 148 above) para 95.

[171] *Ibid*, para 85.

Accordingly, relying on *Connors*, the appellants in *Kay*[172] and *R (on the Application of Price) v Leeds City Council* (hereafter *Price*)[173] appealed to the House of Lords against decisions by the Court of Appeal that Article 8 ECHR afforded no defence against actions for possession bought by local authority landlords. Like the claimants in *Connors*, the applicants in *Price* were gypsies; in this case they had *unlawfully* entered land owned by Lambeth. However, in response to an application by Lambeth for possession of the land, it was argued that in light of *Connors*: the local authority was in breach of its statutory duty to provide gypsy sites; that the circumstances of the claimants were exceptional; and that they were protected by Article 8 ECHR. In *Kay*, no such exceptional circumstances were pleaded. In that case, the applicants, although originally licensees, had become tenants following the granting by Barnett local authority of a lease of their dwellings to a housing trust. Barnett, however, then terminated the leases, seeking repossession of their 'homes' on grounds that the claimants were trespassers. Arguments therefore turned essentially on complex issues of repossessions in statutory landlord and tenant law and the law relating to eviction of trespassers at common law.

As Loveland has commented, it is very difficult to draw a tight ratio from the various judgments offered by the House of Lords in *Kay*.[174] However, there are points of agreement running through the judgments. There was agreement, for example, that in repossession challenges founded on Article 8, landowners are no longer required to go through the motions of pleading and proving that a grant of possession is 'necessary' in accordance with Article 8(2); and it seems to have been generally accepted that Article 8 is relevant only in 'exceptional circumstances'.[175]

Thus, conceding that the Court of Appeal in *Price* was 'right to hold that the decision of the ECtHR in *Connors* was "unquestionably incompatible" with the majority ratio in *Qazi* that Article 8 ECHR is always irrelevant to possession proceedings conducted in accordance with the law', Lord Bingham, with whom Lord Nicholls and Lord Walker agreed, accepted that Article 8 might be relevant in exceptional circumstances: when facts, as they do very rarely (for example, in the case of minorities such as gypsies), disclose a positive obligation of respect for home and family life under Article 8; when a disputed provision of domestic law is *per se* incompatible with the Convention; or when, assuming the law is Convention-compliant, its application by a public authority has arguably

---

[172] Note 148 above.

[173] Note 148 above.

[174] See Loveland (2006) (note 165 above): 'In a very general sense . . . the judgment raised the question of whether British Lawyers are increasingly likely to find themselves . . . following the tortuous . . . path in US constitutional jurisprudence of having to identify ever more fragmented judicial majorities and pluralities which support particular parts of any given Supreme Court opinion' (1463). For discussion on the issues of precedent raised by the case, see chapter 3 above.

[175] The House of Lords was divided in *Kay* as to what would constitute 'exceptional circumstances'. Lords Bingham, Nicholls and Walker appeared to adopt the most generous analysis.

violated Article 8 because of the particular personal circumstances of the defendant.[176]

Beyond that, however, Lord Bingham, like the majority in *Qasi*, accepted that:

> Our housing legislation strikes a balance between the competing claims to which scarcity gives rise, taking account no doubt imperfectly but as well as may be, of the human social and economic considerations involved. And it is of course to housing authorities such as the respondents that Parliament has entrusted the power of managing and allocating the local authority housing stock and the pitches on local authority gypsy sites.[177]

It was therefore concluded by Lord Bingham that once a court has accepted that the property in question is the occupier's home for the purposes of Article 8 ECHR, it should proceed on the understanding that domestic rules relating to possession have achieved the necessary fair balance required by the Convention, and that *generally* the applicable rules of law provide justification for the landlord's interference with Article 8 rights, without any need for recourse to the defensive precepts in Article 8(2).

Although the majority in *Kay* (Lords Hope, Brown and Scott and Baroness Hale) also distinguished *Connors* as an exceptional case in which interference with the applicant's Article 8 rights had required justification, they overlooked the significance placed by the ECtHR on family issues in *Connors*, concluding that what made *Connors* exceptional was not the applicant's personal circumstances but the fact that there was a procedural gap in the law relating to termination of occupancy rights for caravan dwellers, which would have to be amended to provide the necessary safeguards.[178] It was therefore concluded that only when a claimant has fallen victim to a glaring gap or defect in the common law (as under the Caravan Sites Act 1968) or statutory provisions relating to the overall housing scheme (using the term in its broadest sense) where no prior balance has been struck, could there be any room for examination of an Article 8(2) defence.

---

[176] *Kay* (note 148 above) paras 36–9 (Lord Bingham). See in particular Lord Bingham's cautionary remarks: 'I do not think it possible or desirable to attempt to define what facts or circumstances might rank as highly exceptional . . . [C]ounty court judges . . . provided always that the stringency of the test is borne in mind . . . will recognise a highly exceptional case when they see it' (para 38). However, he also added: 'I do not . . . consider that problems and afflictions of a personal nature should avail the occupier where there are public services available to address and alleviate those problems, and if under the relevant social legislation the occupier is specifically disentitled from eligibility for relief it will be necessary to consider the democratic judgment reflected in that provision. Nor can Article 8 avail a tenant, otherwise perhaps than for a very brief period, if he can be appropriately accommodated elsewhere (whether publicly or privately). Where, as notably in the case of gipsies, scarcity of land adversely affects many members of the class, an Article 8(2) defence could only, I think, succeed if advanced by a member of the class who had grounds for complaint substantially stronger than members of the class in general' (para 38).

[177] *Ibid*, para 33 (Lord Bingham).

[178] There was a gap in the law insofar as someone who had lived perfectly lawfully on a designated gypsy caravan site for many years could be evicted without good cause being shown under the Caravan Sites Act 1968, whereas someone who had lived on a site governed by the Mobile Homes Act 1983 could *only* be evicted for cause.

Sounding through the speeches of the House of Lords in *Kay* is a pragmatic concern that has been at the fore of repossession cases since *Donoghue* and has often been refuted by interveners—namely, that if *Connors* were to be followed in every case, 'the result would be to dislocate the conduct of housing claims in the county court, distort local authority housing policies and budgets and upset the important compromises inherent in property law and housing legisla-tion.'[179] Baroness Hale accordingly endorsed what she judged to have been the unanimous conclusion that 'the sequential approach adopted in Strasbourg to the cases which it declares admissible, should [not] be adopted in the general run of possession cases' because the court was entitled to assume 'first . . . that the domestic law has struck the correct balance between the competing interests involved . . . second, that the landowner, if a public authority, has acted com-patibly with the Convention rights of the individual occupier in deciding to enforce its proprietary rights'.[180]

Baroness Hale agreed that housing had been one of the most politically con-troversial issues of the twentieth century and that 'the law has been much tram-pled over by the legislature as it has tried to respond to shifting and conflicting social and economic pressures'.[181] However, she considered that in the absence of enough suitable and affordable housing, 'priorities have to be established either by Parliament or the public sector landlord, who has to allocate this scarce resource in accordance with the priorities set by Parliament'.[182] Notably, however, she went further by questioning what she understood to be the view of the minority, namely that 'there may be highly exceptional cases in which the occupier could argue that his individual personal circumstances made the appli-cation of the general law disproportionate in his case'.[183] If that were so, asked Baroness Hale, 'when if at all should the court to be able to say that even though there is no obligation to continue to provide housing, in these circumstances it is not "necessary in a democratic society" to permit the landowner to assert its property rights?'[184] Setting aside Strasbourg developments in cases such as *Marzari*[185] and *O'Rourke v United Kingdom*,[186] and taking an originalist view of the scope of the European Convention, Baroness Hale questioned how far a liberal treaty such as the ECHR, which began life as a code of individual civil

---

[179] *Kay* (note 148 above) para 31 (Lord Bingham). The appellants, supported by the First Secretary of State, strongly challenged this prediction, since it was agreed that the threshold for rely-ing successfully on Art 8, in response to an otherwise well-founded possession claim, should be very high and the number of successful defendants would be minimal.

[180] *Ibid*, para 182 (Baroness Hale). Baroness Hale considered that only if the occupier advances grounds for challenging either or both of these assumptions would there be any need for modifica-tion to present practice. Under rule 24(2) of the Civil Procedure Rules, a court may give summary judgement against a defendant if it considers that the defendant has no real prospect of successfully defending the claim (para 183).

[181] *Ibid*, para 185.

[182] *Ibid*.

[183] *Ibid*, para 189.

[184] *Ibid*.

[185] Note 156 above.

[186] Application No 39022/97 (unreported), Judgment of 26 June 2001.

and political rights, could be relied on to impose positive obligations in the context of social provision.

Moreover, when reflecting on the difficulty of determining standards by which to judge whether interference by a landlord is disproportionate so as to justify the imposition of positive obligations, Baroness Hale considered it relevant to look to the standard set by Parliament in social services law that 'defines the extent of its obligation to provide services', including 'assistance with housing for vulnerable people, such as children, the elderly, the sick and the disabled'.[187] Since she could find nothing in this repository of positive social commitments to the needy and vulnerable 'to provide assistance to an occupier whose personal circumstances are said to make eviction from this particular accommodation disproportionate', she argued that 'it is questionable that housing law should be made to do so'.[188]

Therefore, in the final analysis, without reflecting on whether aspects of English social services law may be incompatible with positive UK obligations to protect ECHR rights, Baroness Hale decided that the appellant's defences must fail, not because they disclosed 'no sufficient (highly exceptional) merit' but because they were dependent upon 'establishing a freestanding article 8 right to remain in possession incompatible with the respective claimant's clear entitlement to possession under domestic property law'.[189] Such a freestanding right to social housing could not be said to exist in the United Kingdom.

There can be no doubt that the repossession disputes that have dogged UK county courts since *Donoghue* demonstrate the unsuitability of protecting socio-economic rights by relying on an old-fashioned instrument such as the ECHR, which is primarily directed at preventing negative state interference with individuals' possessory rights in Article 1, Protocol 1, or interference with the less tangible right to respect for the home in Article 8. Indeed, it is clear that the heightened expectations of success that first propelled the long line of repossession cases through the county courts, rested on the bald proposition that eviction equals direct negative interference with Article 8 rights. Baroness Hale is certainly right to argue that the Convention is a very blunt instrument for determining the scope of positive obligations in the socio-economic sphere. However, in her argument that public authority repossessions should continue to be a no-go area of Article 8 litigation, whatever the impact on the individual

---

[187] *Kay* (note 148 above) para 191.

[188] *Ibid.* Cf the JCHR Report on the Homelessness Bill (note 149 above), in which the JCHR stated: 'we recognise that local authorities have duties to provide support for children in need under Part III of the Children Act 1989' (para 11). (See in particular section 17.) However, the Committee pointed to examples of cases as the ECtHR had done in *Connors*, where 'if a parent behaves in such a way as to be treated as unsuitable to be a tenant of the housing authority, the child's education and social life may be disrupted by homelessness and a need to move to a different area' (para 11). The JCHR therefore expressed concern that the effect of clause 13 of the Bill may be to interfere unacceptably with the right to respect for the private life and home (under Art 8 ECHR) of adult children and other members of the family to whom no duty is owed under the Children Act 1989, and that 'this should be borne in mind when deciding how to treat families regarded as unsuitable' (para 11).

[189] *Kay* (note 148 above) para 207.

circumstances of claimants, she appears to have parted company with the ECtHR in *Connors* and with Lord Steyn's position that all human rights cases should be read 'in the correct way'.

Nevertheless, in considering the force of the point made by Baroness Hale in *Kay* about the unsuitability of the Convention as an instrument for the protection of ill-defined positive socio-economic rights, it is useful to recall how even in the South African Constitution, positive obligations of fulfilment corresponding to the negative right against eviction have been carefully circumscribed. Thus, section 26 of the Constitution, which imposes a positive duty on state and other relevant role-players 'to desist from preventing or impairing the positive right of access to housing', deals specifically with *arbitrary evictions* (rather than with those that are carried out within the law). The section explicitly outlaws people being evicted on *procedural* grounds without an order of court that has been issued only after due consideration has been accorded to 'all relevant circumstances', irrespective of resource considerations.[190] These constitute issues of accountability that Baroness Hale considers to be accommodated adequately in English administrative law.

E. Deference, the Subject Matter of Disputes and the Nature of the Rights

Thus far we have primarily considered the role of deference in relation to the context or subject matter of disputes. However, it is clear from ECtHR jurisprudence that in determining the appropriate intensity of review, courts must also consider the fundamental nature of the rights at issue. Thus, in *Kebilene*[191] Lord Hope considered as a matter of course that courts are less likely to afford a wide margin of discretion to decisions of the legislature or the executive in cases where so-called unqualified rights, such as those in Article 3 ECHR, are at issue; or where rights are of special importance and require a 'high degree of constitutional protection'; or where the courts have a high degree of special expertise, as for example in relation to criminal justice.[192] Practitioner and academic texts therefore disclose a complicated array of negative *and* positive factors, 'which may conflict in individual cases' but must be balanced by courts in determining the margin of discretion to be afforded to the legislature, the executive or other public authorities.[193]

Closer examination of such a catalogue in the work Lester and Pannick[194] reveals that, in light of ECHR jurisprudence and dicta of other constitutional

---

[190] See P de Vos, 'The Right to Housing' in D Brand and C Heyns (eds), *Socio-economic Rights in South Africa* (Pretoria, Pretoria University Law Press, 2005) 85–106.

[191] *Kebilene* (note 92 above).

[192] *Ibid*, 380D (Lord Hope).

[193] See generally Lester and Pannick (2004) (note 96 above) 95–100.

[194] See for example *ibid*, p 97, para 3.21 (ii) citing: Lord Bingham in *R v Secretary of State, ex parte Spath Homes Ltd* (note 100 above) ('The allocation of public resources is a matter for ministers not courts'); Lord Hoffman in *R (Alconbury Developments Ltd) v Secretary of State* (note 100 above); *Donoghue* (note 100 above); and *Wandsworth Borough Council v Michalak* [2002] EWCA Civ 271.

courts, rights that are likely to be deemed of special constitutional significance so that 'a particularly strict level of scrutiny' might apply, are members of the traditional canon of civil and political rights, including rights to freedom of expression, especially in relation to political speech (Article 10 ECHR); liberty (Article 5 ECHR); access to courts (Article 6 ECHR); and intimate aspects of private life (Article 8 ECHR).

Of course nothing is fixed in the matter of deference, and upon probing further, we find that when a disputed right seems at first sight to attract a high level of scrutiny, domestic courts may conclude that the intensity of review should be moderated in accordance with the degree of interference that has been suffered by the claimant.[195] Thus, in *Farrakhan*, a claim based on Article 10 that involved the refusal of entry into the United Kingdom to a United States citizen by personal decision of the Home Secretary, it was stated that 'the more remote the interference from the central core of the protected right the easier it is to justify an interference'.[196] Moreover, in *Farrakhan* the Court took into account the primary consideration that the higher the constitutional status of the decision maker, the more extensive the area of discretionary judgement allowed. Thus, Lord Phillips took account of 'the fact that the decision in question is the personal decision of the Secretary of State', which 'has not been taken lightly' but was made after 'widespread consultation'.[197] Further, since the legislature had in any event precluded a statutory right of appeal, there was no further issue to address.[198]

Notably, however, consistent with developments in ECHR jurisprudence, *mutatis mutandae*, UK courts have been unwilling to afford a wide margin of discretion when there is a difference of treatment in respect of one of the conditions covered by Article 14 ECHR, particularly in respect of sex discrimination.[199] Thus, for example, as noted in chapter 3 above, Lord Nicholls explicitly stated in *Ghaidan*[200] that under Article 14 the appropriate degree of scrutiny was more intensive than would normally be applicable in the field of national housing policy.

Since *Ghaidan*, the idea that rights in the Convention should attract different degrees of deference in accordance with their place in a hierarchy of fundamental values in the ECHR, has often been endorsed by the House of Lords.[201] Thus, for example, in *R v East Sussex County Council, ex parte Reprotech*

---

[195] See *Prolife Alliance* (note 125 above).
[196] *Farrakhan* (note 98 above) para 77 (Lord Phillips MR).
[197] *Ibid*, paras 72 and 74.
[198] *Ibid*, paras 72–4.
[199] 'Where very weighty reasons' are required by way of justification for a difference in treatment. Even in that context, the ECtHR has accorded a measure of deference. See *Petrovic v Austria* (1998) 33 EHRR 307 ECtHR, 320, paras 37–8.
[200] Note 67 above.
[201] See for example *R (on the Application of Carson) v Secretary of State for Work and Pensions* [2005] UKHL 37, [2005] 4 All ER 545–672. In particular, see the discussion of the House of Lords decision in this case in chapter 7 below.

(Pebsham) Ltd,[202] Lord Hoffman stated that 'public law can also take into account the hierarchy of individual rights which exist under the Human Rights Act, so that for example the individual's right to a home is accorded a high degree of protection . . . while ordinary property rights are in general far more limited by considerations of public interest'.[203]

F. Democracy, Human Rights Values and the 'Unity of Public Law'

The HRA requires the judicial importation of democratic standards and values enshrined in the ECHR into UK public authority decision-making. However, by contrast to countries with modern constitutions, such as South Africa and Canada, that have designed their constitutional settlements often after lengthy consultation and debate, there is little guidance in the HRA as to the direction that democracy should take in the United Kingdom. For example, as Baroness Hale encourages us to ask in *Kay*,[204] how far can an old-fashioned treaty such as the ECHR—which on one hand says very little directly about the protection of human rights in the socio-economic sphere, but which on the other hand has enshrined equality and respect for human dignity and psychological integrity of every person—allow for the development by UK courts of a contemporary concept of democracy that provides at least a minimum level of social protection?

In chapter 3 we noted that, in interpreting the scope of ECHR rights, senior courts in the UK have turned to pronouncements of other common law constitutional courts, including the South African Constitutional Court and the Canadian Supreme Court, which have adopted similarly 'open-textured' constitutions in the last two decades or so.[205] For example, in reaching the conclusion that 'public opinion' is not a sufficient benchmark for determining the limits of judicial intervention in politically sensitive disputes in which fundamental rights are at issue, Lord Bingham in *Reyes v R*[206] explicitly recalled the speech of Chalkaston P in the Constitutional Court of South Africa:

---

[202] [2002] UKHL 8.

[203] *Ibid*, para 34. In *Connors* (note 148 above) the ECtHR recognised Art 8 ECHR as of 'central importance to the individual's identity, self determination, physical and moral integrity . . .' (para 82). By contrast, however, the ECtHR, citing *Mellacher v Austria* (1989) 12 EHRR 391, also stated in relation to Art 1 of Protocol 1: 'The legislature must have a wide margin of appreciation both with regard to the existence of a problem of public concern warranting measures of control and as to the choice of the detailed rules for their implementation. The Court will respect the legislature's judgement as to what is in the general interest, unless the judgment be manifestly without reasonable foundation' (*Connors* (note 148 above) para 82). See also *Pretty v UK*, No 2346/02, ECHR 2002-III; and *Christine Goodwin v the UK*, No 28957/95, ECHR 2002-VI, para 90.

[204] Note 148 above.

[205] See Clayton (2004) (note 70 above) 33–47. The author argues that the HRA strongly resembles the Canadian Charter in terms of both structural collaborative features and the open-textured nature of many of its provisions.

[206] [2002] 11 UKPC, [2002] 2 AC 235: 'In carrying out its task of constitutional interpretation the court is not concerned to evaluate and give effect to public opinion . . .' (246 (Lord Bingham)).

The very reason for establishing the new legal order and for vesting the power of judicial review of all legislation in the courts, was to protect the rights of minorities and others who cannot protect their rights adequately through the democratic process. Those who are entitled to claim this protection include the social outcasts and marginalized people of our society. It is only if there is a willingness to protect the worst and weakest among us that all of us can be secure that our own rights will be protected.[207]

During the past decade in common law jurisdictions, commentators and practitioners have increasingly taken up the idea of a shared public law discourse that is concerned with the identification of fundamental values in constitutional, public and international human rights law—a discourse that seeks to prevent vulnerable, marginalised and dispossessed individuals being placed beyond the protection of the rule of law.[208] Although this discourse has gained much greater momentum in other common law jurisdictions, its influence in the United Kingdom is reflected in the work of leading constitutional and public law theorists, and as we shall see, its presence can be detected, albeit in a small number of outstanding decisions, in the House of Lords.[209]

Thus, as David Dyzenhaus has described it, gradually across the whole of the common law world, a 'common public law' is emerging, which rejects the artificial divide between legal and political spheres of decision-making, with its tendency to cordon off certain types of sensitive policy decisions from a standard of judicial scrutiny appropriate to the fundamental rights at stake. This common system is 'reminiscent of the common law's traditional understanding of positive law, as serving a kind of evidentiary function for the enduring values of the common law articulated by judges from time immemorial'.[210] However, by contrast, with the earlier private common law tradition, which was notionally based on the creative expression of preordained common law values, the new public law, which traverses administrative law, constitutional law and international law, seeks prospectively to update and reshape public law values by viewing them through the lens of international human rights norms.

Furthermore, whereas judges developing the common law of private obligations are well aware that their function is the interpretation of a body of law

---

[207] *State v Makwanyane* [1995] 1 LCR 269, 311 (cited by Lord Bingham (*ibid*)). Compare the tenor of Lord Bingham's uncompromising view of the nature and force of the democratic mandate in *A v Secretary of State for the Home Department* (note 18 above): 'The function of independent judges charged to interpret and apply the law is universally recognised as a cardinal feature of the modern democratic state, a cornerstone of the rule of law itself. The Attorney General is fully entitled to insist on the proper limits of judicial authority, but he is wrong to stigmatise judicial decision-making as in some way undemocratic' (para 42).

[208] See the judgement of Madame L'Hereux-Dube for the majority before the Supreme Court in *Baker v Canada* (note 72 above), which 'fits with and takes forward an international judicial debate about the relationship between international rights documents and domestic legal regimes' and 'establishes for the first time in the common law world a general duty for administrative decision makers to give reasons for their decisions': D Dyzenhaus, '*Baker*: The Unity of Public Law?' in Dyzenhaus (ed) (2004) (note 9 above) 1.

[209] See for example Allan (1988) (note 9 above); and more recently Allan (2004) (note 9 above) 25.

[210] Dyzenhaus (2004) (note 208 above) 2.

'replete with values for whose presence they are themselves responsible',[211] judges who adhere to a rights-based conception of public law acknowledge that the purpose of their adjudicative task is to give creative expression to legal rights, which, in this case, individuals possess by virtue of their common humanity.[212] Thus, inspired by the celebrated case of *Baker v Canada (Minister of Citizenship and Immigration)*,[213] Dyzenhaus has identified four interrelated hallmarks of a human rights approach to adjudication:

> Human rights judges will think of public law as a unity, in which the same fundamental values underpin the whole enterprise of public law . . . [and will think] that constitutional law, in the sense of written law, is an explicit articulation of that set of values rather than their source. Correspondingly they will be alert to the impact of fundamental values as unwritten constitutional values even when, perhaps especially, when, the written texts of the constitution do not cover an exercise of public power. And they will think that other actors, besides legislatures and constituent assemblies, among whom they are likely to number judges themselves, have a legitimate role in articulating what these values are.[214]

Cleary, one of the central tenets of a 'unified' approach to public law is that the articulation and reshaping of democratic values should not be left to the legislative process alone, but should be integral to the adjudicative process as well. Moreover, despite myriad often contested analyses of what *Baker* tells us about the limits of deference in public law, constitutional commentators and administrative lawyers have agreed that if courts accept administrative decisions *without some knowledge of the reasons*, democratic rights of access to a fair hearing are 'little more than aspirations, without genuine legal support'.[215] Thus, the duty to give reasons, which *Baker* authoritatively established, is concerned not only with the removal of arbitrariness in administrative decision-making, but more fundamentally with protecting the dignity of claimants by affording them the right to be heard. It has therefore been suggested that since *Baker*, the general common law duty to give reasons has acquired a new dimension: justification has come to be seen as a central aspect of constitutional adjudication in mature democracies, the purpose of which is to allow for an appropriate interchange between primary decision-makers and courts within the boundaries of their relative institutional competencies.[216]

Baker arose because the delegates of the Canadian Minister of Immigration refused to accept that their statutory discretion to stay an order of deportation on 'humanitarian and compassionate' grounds should be exercised in the complainant's favour. The case therefore centred specifically on the degree of deference appropriate in deportation cases and more generally raised questions about the limits of deference in politically sensitive disputes involving non-citizens,

---

[211] *Ibid*, 3.
[212] *Ibid*.
[213] Note 72 above.
[214] Dyzenhaus (2004) (note 208 above) 4.
[215] Allan (2004) (note 9 above) 289.
[216] For this theme, see also Hunt (2003) (note 109 above).

which have the greatest propensity to be sealed off from the rule of law. Such disputes have most severely challenged the power of UK courts in judicial review since the HRA has been in force. In *Baker* there was also the significant complication of children whose 'best interests' needed to be taken into account.[217] Thus, on one hand, L'Hereux Dube J was clear that reasonableness was the appropriate standard of review, and since the Minister had a very wide discretion when it came to deciding whether to stay deportation on humanitarian and compassionate considerations, the courts should incline towards deference. On the other hand, however, not only did the importance of the interests affected by the decision call for greater scrutiny, if the dictates of compassion and humanity were to be satisfied, the decision would have to be read in light of the interests of Baker's four Canadian-born children.[218]

At the commencement of our discussion about deference in this chapter, we noted the confident departure by the House of Lords in *A v Secretary of State*,[219] from the rigid dualism associated with Lord Hoffman's statement in *Rheman* that 'if the people are to accept the consequence of decisions, they must be made by persons whom the people have elected and whom they can remove'.[220] In light of the foregoing discussion, it would be wrong to suggest that in their diverse speeches, the House of Lords in *A v Secretary of State* had fully embraced Dyzenhaus' four interrelated hallmarks of a unified human rights approach to public law adjudication. However, there can be no doubt that in *A v Secretary of State* there are the seeds of an approach that asserts not only that constitutional law, in the sense of written law, is an explicit articulation of fundamental human rights values rather than their source, but also that the articulation and reshaping of democratic values should not be left only to the legislative process, but should be integral to the process of adjudication itself.[221]

---

[217] Art 3 CRC provides that administrative decisions affecting children should make the 'best interests of the child' a 'primary consideration'. In her majority judgement, in addition to referring to the Immigration Act, which required officials to attend to the best interests of children when making their decisions, L'Heureux Dube J adverted to the CRC, which Canada (like the UK) had ratified but not incorporated.

[218] See L'Hereux Dube J in *Baker v Canada* (note 72 above): 'In my opinion, the approach taken to the children's interests shows that this decision was unreasonable.... . The officer was completely dismissive of the interests of Ms Baker's children. As I will outline in detail in the paragraphs that follow, I believe that the failure to give serious weight and consideration to the interests of the children constitutes an unreasonable exercise of the discretion conferred by the section, notwithstanding the important deference that should be given to the decision of the immigration officer. Professor Dyzenhaus has articulated the concept of "deference as respect" as follows: respect requires not submission but a respectful attention to the reasons offered or which could be offered in support of a decision' (para 65, citing D Dyzenhaus, 'The Politics of Deference: Judicial Review and Democracy' in M Taggart (ed), *The Province of Administrative Law* (Oxford, Hart, 1997) 279, 286). Canadian commentators remain deeply divided on the substantive issues addressed in *Baker*. For wide-ranging views on the substantive issues, see Dyzenhaus (2004) (note 208 above).

[219] Note 18 above.

[220] *Rheman* (note 97 above) para 62 (Lord Hoffman).

[221] For close textual analysis of *A v Secretary of State* in this light, see S Fredman, 'From Deference to Democracy: The Role of Equality under the Human Rights Act 1998' (2006) 122 *Law Quarterly Review* 53: 'the turbulence created by the cross currents of the political and the legal forced a new accommodation' (60).

The case of *A v Secretary of State* involved the power to detain non-UK nationals indefinitely without trial if they are suspected of being international terrorists,[222] and this involves derogating from the unqualified right to liberty in Article 5(1) ECHR.[223] The right to derogate arises only 'in time of war or other public emergency threatening the life of the nation' and only to the extent that is 'strictly required by the exigencies of the situation and provided that such measures are not inconsistent with its other obligations under international law'.[224] Thus, in accordance with the context-sensitive approach to deference in matters of sensitive public policy, at first sight there was little room for a judicial evaluation of any of these matters. It was assumed that this was a policy area in which decisions about what constitutes a sufficient public interest, as adjudged by the Home Secretary on behalf of the electorate, demand at least the highest degree of deference, if not total judicial abstinence.

Nevertheless, in light of the starkness of the denial of the applicants' rights, the House of Lords in *A v Secretary of State* felt compelled to look beyond this narrow utilitarian account of their orthodox role in public law (to balance individual human rights against the collective will of the majority), accepting instead an alternative public law vision in which human rights are constituents of democracy rather than weapons wielded by individual interests ranged against it. Lord Hope therefore cautioned against:

> the dangers that lie in store for democracy itself, if the courts were to allow individuals to be deprived of their right to liberty indefinitely and without charge on grounds of public interest by the executive.[225]

Thus, although largely derived from the authority of their legislative HRA mandate, shining through the majority of the speeches in *A v Secretary of State* are some of the most confident assertions of the judicial role vis-à-vis the democratically elected legislature to have been made since the HRA came into force. Accordingly, Lord Roger stressed that due deference does not mean abasement,[226] and Lord Bingham rejected the Attorney General's argument that protection of public security falls within the discretionary area of judgement belonging to the elected organs of government. Most notably, however, reaching beyond the authority of the HRA, Lord Bingham recognised the function of independent judges charged to interpret and apply the law to be a cardinal feature of the modern democratic state:

> The Attorney General is fully entitled to insist on the proper limits of judicial authority but he is wrong to stigmatise judicial decision making as in some way undemocratic.[227]

---

[222] S 23 Anti-terrorism, Crime and Security Act 2001.
[223] The Human Rights Act 1998 (Designated Derogation) Order 2001 (SI 2001/ 3644).
[224] Art 15 ECHR.
[225] *A v Secretary of State* (note 18 above) para 100.
[226] *Ibid*, para 176.
[227] *Ibid*, para 42.

Whether the power of detention without trial was 'strictly required by the exigencies of the situation' (that is, whether it was 'proportionate') was characteristically assumed to be a matter within the power of the Minister and therefore not subjected to the proportionality analysis.[228] However, a further question as to whether the measures served a legitimate aim was regarded as very different. Since the rules applied only to foreign nationals and not to UK nationals suspected of international terrorist activities, they were not 'strictly required'. Accordingly, a core human rights principle of equality, which serves to protect marginalised and vulnerable individuals excluded from the democratic process,[229] came to the fore—not, as in *Ghaidan*,[230] through its formal presence in Article 14 ECHR, but as a fundamental aspect of the principle of proportionality, which involves an evaluation of whether the means used can be seen to justify the aims pursued.[231]

Increasingly, the malleable concept of equality—in conjunction with respect for human dignity,[232] which permeates the South African Constitution and, as we have seen, was used in the Canadian case of *Baker*[233] to ensure the equal protection of the law—has emerged in different guises in constitutional adjudication. Thus, in Canada it has been used in conjunction with the equal treatment provision in Article 15(1) of the Canadian Constitution to secure access to equal treatment in relation to pension provision.[234] Moreover, in the United Kingdom—although lacking the welfarist connotations of *Grootboom v Oosteneberg Municipality and Others*,[235] in which the South African Court intervened on behalf of squatters to protect people against extreme indignities which a society should not tolerate[236]—Baroness Hale did observe in *Ghaidan*:

---

[228] In *A v Secretary of State* the first question to be addressed was whether there was a 'public emergency threatening the life of the nation'. However, by regarding this as a 'pre-eminently political judgement' and placing the burden on the applicants themselves, the House of Lords required them to give good reasons to displace the government's justifications. Furthermore, Baroness Hale considered that assessing the strength of the threat to the life of the nation fell squarely within the government's territory. She therefore regarded patent W*ednesbury* unreasonableness as the only possible grounds for judicial scrutiny of the measure.

[229] Cf the proclamation of Chalkaston P (note 207 above and accompanying text).

[230] Note 67 above.

[231] See generally Fredman (note 221 above).

[232] 'Respect for dignity' is an express value in the South African Constitution, where it has played a central role in the thinking of the Constitutional Court. For a critique of the amorphous concept of 'respect for dignity' as a lodestar in constitutional adjudication, see D Feldman, 'Hunan Dignity as a Legal Value' (1999) *Public Law* 682.

[233] Note 72 above.

[234] See *Law v Canada* [1999] 1 SCR 497, which concerned equal treatment in respect of pension provision. Justice Iaccobbi concluded that the purpose of the equality guarantee in Art 15(1) of the Constitution is to promote a society in which 'all persons enjoy equal recognition at law as human beings and as members of Canadian society, equally capable and equally deserving of concern, respect and consideration' (para 51).

[235] (2000) (3) BCLR 277 (C) 289.

[236] See *Grootboom* (*ibid*): 'The right of access to adequate housing is entrenched because we value human beings and want to ensure that they are afforded their basic human needs. A society must seek to ensure that the basic necessities of life are provided for all if it is to be a society based on human dignity, freedom and equality' (para 44).

Democracy is founded on the principle that each individual has equal value. Treating someone automatically as having less value than others not only causes pain and distress to that person but also violates his or her dignity as a human being.[237]

Moreover, although closely tied to formal substantive analysis of Article 3 ECHR, the idea that individuals are entitled to a minimum level of subsistence based on respect for their common humanity[238] can be found in many of the speeches in the House of Lords decision in *Limbuela*.[239] Thus, as we shall see in chapters 6–8 below, there are some signs that UK courts have begun to recognise themselves as active participants in upholding a contemporary rights-based democracy—a role that requires them to contribute to policy debate through the judicial development of values and principles enshrined in the ECHR, while at the same time paying due deference to opinions of the democratically elected organs of government. Although continuing doubts have been expressed by courts about the *extent* to which a traditional negative civil libertarian instrument such as the ECHR can give rise to positive obligations in socio-economic welfare needs contexts, as we shall see, a more sophisticated understanding of the nature of the Convention as a repository of democratic values that may cut across the traditional dichotomy between civil and political rights and socio-economic rights has begun to evolve.

IV. CONCLUSION

The primary purpose of this chapter has been to demonstrate the ways in which UK courts have determined the limits of their legitimate intervention in politically sensitive public law challenges following the HRA. In so doing, we have highlighted the problem characteristically faced by public lawyers in common law jurisdictions when a human rights instrument such as the HRA has been injected into a long-established legal system.[240] In the United Kingdom, it has been necessary not only to determine how a rights-based form of adjudication can be fitted into the constitutional parameters of English administrative law, but also to identify the points at which established rules and principles of administrative law should give way to what have been described by one commentator as 'the bigger guns of constitutional or international law'.[241] Moreover, we have also demonstrated how the shifting concept of deference—although more loosely used before the HRA to capture the notion of self-imposed judicial restraint—has, as in other

---

[237] *Ghaidan* (note 67 above) para 32.
[238] Compare the 'the right to common humanity' posited by Simon Brown LJ in *JCWI* (note 43 above). See also note 44 above.
[239] [2005] UKHL 66. This will be discussed further in chapter 6. See also Baroness Hale's view that the protection of children is a fundamental societal value and is anterior to positive law concerning the protection of children in *R (on the Application of Kehoe) v Secretary of State for Work and Pensions* [2005] UKHL 48, [2005] 4 All ER 905, [2006] 1 AC 42.
[240] See also New Zealand, where human rights have also been imported by statute.
[241] M Taggart, 'The Tub of Public Law' in Dyzenhaus (ed) (note 9 above) 456, 466.

jurisdictions such as Canada, become a term of art that seeks more precisely to define the limits of constitutional adjudication in politically sensitive public law disputes, when questions about the relative competencies of courts and the elected branches of government are at issue.[242]

This chapter is not the place to examine further the extent to which courts in the United Kingdom have begun to flesh out such malleable concepts as liberty, equality and dignity in order to shape our understanding of what is positively required of government in protecting fundamental human rights in a twenty-first-century democratic state.[243] Nor is there space to discuss further the extent to which some judges have embraced this creative aspect of their constitutional mandate; or to reflect on the extent to which senior members of the judiciary have adopted what has been described by Dyzenhaus as a 'human rights approach' to public law adjudication. These questions will be addressed in more detail in subsequent chapters of the book. However, in looking at how UK courts have wrestled with the many dichotomies used in contemporary public law debate to define the limits of their legitimate intervention,[244] it is worth reflecting on Michael Taggart's impressionistic distinction between positivist judges and human rights judges, noted by Dyzenhaus when commenting on the *Baker* case:

> [O]ne can tell almost everything about a judge in an immigration case by the way he or she starts the judgment: 'the executive has traditionally . . .' as opposed to 'in this case we are concerned with the fate of an individual who has lived in Canada for ten years and has three children . . .'.[245]

As we shall see, particularly in chapter 6 below in relation to cases involving asylum seekers, since the implementation of the HRA, a very clear division of this kind has emerged in administrative law courts in the United Kingdom.

---

[242] Moreover, as we have seen, 'adding regional and/or international human rights instruments into the mix can complicate matters further'. Administrative law disputes in the UK can raise points under EU law, the Human Rights Act and the ECHR. See P Craig, 'Judicial Review, Intensity and Deference in EU Law' in Dyzenhaus (ed) (note 9 above) 335.

[243] See generally S Fredman, 'Human Rights Transformed: Positive Duties and Positive Rights' (2006) *Public Law* 498.

[244] As we have seen, these include natural law versus positive law; legislation versus interpretation; process versus substance; legislature versus courts; and fundamental values versus statutes.

[245] Attributed to Taggert by Dyzenhaus (2004) (note 208 above) 3.

5

From Need to 'Choice' in Public Services: The Boundaries of Judicial Intervention in Prioritisation Disputes

I. INTRODUCTION

DURING THE PAST three decades, individuals and groups in the United Kingdom have increasingly tested the extent to which public authorities can be held to account in public administrative law for failure to meet the health and welfare needs of citizens. This chapter will evaluate the way in which, within the constraints of the ultra vires paradigm of review, UK courts have determined the limits of their legitimate intervention in key disputes over the rationing of health and welfare services before and after the Human Rights Act (HRA) 1998.[1] However, before proceeding it is important to emphasise that a distinction has been drawn between the role of courts in the scrutiny of public authority decisions concerning delay or refusal of public services on grounds of resources, and their role in disputes that address fundamental questions of medical ethics and human rights (for example, the artificial prolongation of life), in which issues of resource allocation are tangentially implicated.[2] It is only with disputes of the former kind that we are directly concerned in this chapter.

It is also important to emphasise at the outset that we have not underplayed the difficulties of carving out a democratically defensible role for courts in polycentric resource allocation disputes that concern access to public services, whether founded on allegations of unfairness or on breach of statutory duties. There is no suggestion that either the ordinary principles and procedures

---

[1] The term 'rationing' is used to connote both the refusal and the withdrawal of services from individuals previously assessed as eligible to receive them. In general discussion, the term has been used to mean the distribution of resources by public authorities.

[2] R (on the Application of Burke) v General Medical Council [2004] EWCH 1879 Admin: 'I must start by emphasising what this case is not about. . . . This case is not about the prioritisation or allocation of resources whether human, medical or financial' (para 26). 'The case (concerning withdrawal of ANH in the absence of consent) plainly raises . . . fundamentally important questions of medical law and ethics' (para 2 (Munby J)). See also Lord Steyn, 'The Tangled Story of Deference' (2005) Public Law 346–59, 357.

of public administrative law[3] or the extension of judicial powers in the HRA can provide a major corrective for the ills of a system in which escalating demand for health and welfare services so far exceeds supply, and where the democratic consensus has increasingly shifted towards notions of personal responsibility for the satisfaction of human needs, with concomitant emphasis on public tax reduction.

However, bearing in mind the scope of judicial obligations under sections 3 and 6 HRA, it is suggested first that in appropriate disputes concerning access to services by some of the most vulnerable claimants caught up in the social care system, the justificatory techniques of human rights adjudication can provide a more finely tuned vehicle than afforded by the traditional standard of *Wednesbury* review. Secondly, it is suggested that the remedial power of courts in section 3 HRA—which has rarely been called into play in welfare needs challenges that test the scope of local authority statutory duties—has legitimated a more open textured and principled approach to the adjudication of such disputes than that which has traditionally prevailed in this area of litigation.

The main body of the chapter is in three sections: the first is concerned with challenges against the reasonableness of National Health Service (NHS) decisions to delay or refuse access to publicly funded health care. The following section is concerned with challenges against the denial of local authority services that are founded on allegations of breach of public authority statutory duties. The last main section involves a case study of a series of challenges against the refusal of accommodation to vulnerable children and their families under Part III of the Children Act (CA) 1989, which has culminated in the House of Lords decision in *R (on the Application of G) v Barnet London Borough Council* (hereafter *G*).[4] The primary purpose of mounting the Children Act test cases (in which Shelter appeared as third-party intervener) was to test the scope of local authority duties to provide accommodation for vulnerable children in need and their families under section 17 CA.[5] However, Article 8 of the European Convention of Human Rights (ECHR) was also clearly implicated. The series of cases has therefore provided a fertile setting in which to consider not only the vagaries of the orthodox ultra vires approach for the resolution of such chal-

---

[3] For an overview of the expansion of judicial review into new territories prior to the HRA, see M Belloff, 'Judicial Review 2001: A Prophetic Odyssey' (1995) 58 *Modern Law Review* 143. See also *R v Sefton, ex parte Help the Aged and Blanchard* [1997] 4 All ER 449; *R v Child Poverty Action Group* [1998] 2 All ER 755. It had become apparent that any body with respectable political credentials would have standing. See chapter 3 above for the role of campaigning-style litigation under the HRA. Concerns about the limiting effects of the narrow definition of 'victim' under the HRA have not materialised.

[4] [2003] UKHL 57, [2004] 1 All ER 97–214.

[5] While s 17(1) CA sets out what is specifically described as a 'general' duty for local authorities to provide a wide range of services for children 'in need', s 17(6) permits that 'the services provided by a local authority in the exercise of [their] functions . . . may include giving assistance in kind or, in exceptional circumstances, in cash'. Children 'in need' are those who are disabled or whose development, health or opportunity to maintain or achieve these things will significantly be impaired without services.

lenges but also the legitimate use of section 3 HRA to interpret section 17 CA compatibly with positive obligations engendered by Article 8 ECHR.

At the heart of many of the disputes lie institutional funding issues. These include the protracted conflict between the NHS and local authorities on the distinction between nursing and personal care services;[6] controversy about the extent to which health authorities, local authorities or vulnerable individuals should have financial responsibility for care services;[7] institutional disputes between local authorities as to which local authority has primary responsibility to meet the housing needs of vulnerable claimants;[8] and more recently, the possibility of requiring the NHS to reimburse individuals for the cost of health care treatment abroad in accordance with free movement provisions in EU law.[9] The cases discussed in this chapter therefore highlight not only the complexities of the funding arrangements that have accompanied the gradual transition from welfare to market in the delivery of public services in the United Kingdom, but also the anomalies and uncertainties surrounding the intricate structure of discretionary duties superimposed on the foundational statutory regimes for health and welfare provision in the UK. Moreover, as we shall see, despite efforts by courts and central government to remain outside of the fray, strategists have continued to test the established parameters of judicial intervention in this intensely politicised area of public law litigation.

The review of cases in this chapter covers very disparate areas of public service provision, including NHS health care, education, community care and

---

[6] For example *R v North East Devon Health Authority, ex parte Coughlan, Secretary of State for Health and Another, Interveners* (2000) 51 BMLR 1, [2000] 3 All ER 850. At the heart of the challenge lay a protracted national dispute between the Department of Health and local authorities as to which of the parties had financial responsibility for nursing care to individuals assessed by local authorities as being in need of care and attention under s 21 of the National Assistance Act 1948.

[7] *R v Sefton* (note 3 above); *R v Manchester City Council, ex parte Stennett* [2002] UKHL 34 (considering whether contrary to the opinion of the DOH, social services and health authorities were entitled to charge for aftercare services (residential or non-residential) that they render to persons in their area discharged from compulsory detention under s 117 Mental Health Act 1983); and *R (on the Application of Spink) v Wandsworth LBC* (hereafter *Spink*) [2005] EWCA Civ 320 (considering whether local authorities are entitled to take into account the ability of parents to pay for home adaptations that are necessary for the safety of disabled children in accordance with their functions under s 17 CA).

[8] See for example *Al-Ameri v Kensington and Chelsea Royal London Borough Council* [2004] UKHL 4, [2004] 1 All ER 1049–172. The case concerned a dispute as to whether an 'unintentionally homeless' asylum seekers granted 'exceptional leave to enter' should be housed in a remote and wholly unfamiliar locality of Glasgow (where he had been temporarily housed in NASS dispersal accommodation) rather than in London, where he had extended family and other cultural ties. However, Kensington and Chelsea argued that the applicant and others in his position had a 'local connection' with Glasgow that arose from their temporary residence there. Furthermore, this connection had come about by their 'own choice' because they had not been 'coerced' into going there in the first instance. The House of Lords held that a destitute asylum seeker had no 'real choice' within the meaning of s 95 Immigration and Asylum Act 1999 as to the locality in which temporary accommodation was granted, and that the local authority's formalistic interpretation was wholly disingenuous.

[9] See *R (on the Application of Watts) v Bedford Primary Care Trust* (hereafter *Watts*) [2004] EWCA Civ 166. For further discussion of the decision, see chapter 2, section IV-C above and also section II-C below.

housing for vulnerable children and their families. However, despite the wide-ranging substantive issues raised by the challenges, they are conceptually underpinned by the same controversial jurisprudential and socio-political issues:[10] (i) the limits of state responsibility for the meeting of health and welfare needs in a post-welfare landscape; (ii) the extent to which the government can be held to account for the unequal distribution of medical and welfare services throughout the United Kingdom; and (iii) the meaning of choice and entitlement for citizens who live in a country in which 'social security benefits are part of an intricate and interlocking system of social welfare', which exists to maintain certain minimum standards of living and is 'an expression of what has been called social solidarity or *fraternité*, the duty of any community to help those of its members who are in need'.[11]

A. From Need to Choice in NHS and Public Authority Services: The Post-welfare Landscape of the United Kingdom

The foundational principle of the welfare state, that universal demand for services should be met by the allocation of public resources at central and local levels, has for some time been regarded by governments as no longer politically tenable or economically sustainable. Instead, the concept of a mixed economy of welfare is now prevalent in Western capitalist societies, placing emphasis on markets rather than state provision, with a reduced expectation of the extent to which individual public services ought to be sustained by resources made available through taxation.[12]

Thus, during the past two decades or more, public policy in the United Kingdom has been dominated by questions as to who should pay for welfare (public funds or private purses); who should be eligible for services; and who should be involved in making decisions about the allocation of scarce resources to pay for them. Moreover, in justifying stringent policies, successive governments have sought to attract public attention not only to the range of competing claims made by different welfare sectors on the public purse, but also to the

---

[10] See generally N Pearce and W Paxton (eds), *Social Justice: Building a Fairer Britain* (London, Politico, 2005). See also therein D Miller, 'What is Social Justice?' in which the author argues: 'The idea of social justice has been the driving force behind centre-left politics in Western societies for over a century and that to pursue social justice is to believe that society's major social and political institutions can be changed—so that each person gets a fair share of the benefits and carries a fair share of the responsibilities of living together in a community' (3). Miller posits four basic principles of social justice: equal citizenship; the social minimum; equality of opportunity; and 'fair distribution' of resources that do not form part of equal citizenship or the social minimum. See also S Weir (ed), *Unequal Britain: Human Rights as a Route to Social Justice* (London, Politico, 2006) 1–24.

[11] *R (on the Application of Carson) v Secretary of State v Secretary of State for Work and Pensions* [2005] 4 All ER 542–67, 556, para 18 (Lord Hoffman).

[12] The centre ground in British politics, represented by the New Labour administration, is not in theory ideologically committed to any formula of state, voluntary or private provision of welfare but rather to pragmatic balancing of suitable providers across a range of public services.

complex interplay of moral, clinical and economic judgments involved in individual cases of welfare rationing.[13]

Since 1979, inspired by the goal of financial expediency, which has been presented with the ideological trappings of market efficiency, successive UK governments have struggled to impose a market framework on the established order for the delivery of general and local public services.[14] Moreover, early in this transition it became clear that these structural reforms necessitated a reappraisal of the relationship between individuals and the state in the delivery of welfare services.[15] Thus, a new formative role was accorded to public law in which public choice constitutionalists sought to capture the democratic potential inherent in the role accorded to 'choice' in the economic theories of the New Right.[16] It was argued that greater executive accountability was to be achieved not necessarily by the conferment of individual rights to welfare services, but rather by the responsiveness of institutions in meeting the collective demands of citizens.[17] New forms of accountability were explored within institutional frameworks.[18] Thus, for example, under the banner of public choice, attempts were made to embody enduring values 'which will influence the choices made about objectives and the means available to achieve them' in the delivery of health care.[19]

[13] Much of the debate about the rationing of welfare has been premised on the inevitability of rationing rather than on the enhancement of services through increased taxation. See RJ Maxwell (Chief Executive of Kings Fund Trust), 'Why Rationing is on the Agenda' (1995) 15(4) *British Medical Bulletin* 761–8.; and B New (ed), *Rationing: Talk and Action in Health Care* (London, King's Fund and British Medical Journal Publishing Group, 1997). For a useful description of the development of explicit NHS rationing during the past decade, see K Syrett, 'Judicial Review in an Era of Explicit NHS Rationing' (2004) *Modern Law Review* 289, 292–4.

[14] For a scholarly and comprehensive review of the impact of the shift in focus from welfare to market on public administrative law, see C Harlow, 'Administrative Law: Back to Basics' (1997) *Public Law* 245.

[15] For constitutional analysis of the changing role of the state in the delivery of public services in the UK, see generally P Birkenshaw, I Harden and N Lewis, *Government by Moonlight: The Hybrid Parts of the State* (London, Unwin Hyman, 1990); I Harden and N Lewis, *The Noble Lie: The British Constitution and the Rule of Law* (London, Hutchinson, 1986); and I Harden, *The Contracting State* (Buckingham, Open University Press, 1992) ch 5.

[16] Public sector reforms that have taken place throughout the Western world in the transition from welfare to market have been characterised as New Public Management (NPM). The rhetorical values of NPM were encapsulated by the New Right in the slogan 'Voice Exit and Loyalty', which was borrowed from a theoretical perspective on public participation by AO Hirschman, *Exit, Voice and Loyalty: Responses to Decline in Firms, Organisations, and States* (Cambridge, MA, Harvard University Press, 1970).

[17] See generally ND Lewis, *Choice and the Legal Order: Rising above Politics* (London, Butterworths, 1996).

[18] New public choice theorists have argued that the redefining of structures of governance in the delivery of welfare services involves a search for power sharing structures that will lead to the fair distribution of public resources. See Lewis (*ibid*) 11. See also S McIver, 'Information for Public Choice' (1995) 51(4) *British Medical Bulletin* 900–3. For the importance of 'democratic responsiveness' from an ethics perspective, see A Weale, 'The Ethics of Rationing' (1995) 51(4) *British Medical Bulletin* 831–4, 831.

[19] D Longley, *Health Care Constitutions* (London, Cavendish, 1996) iii. Longley also offers a comparative analysis of the role of choice and public accountability in health care management in Canada, the UK and New Zealand.

However, while market rhetoric served to create heightened expectations of the quality and availability of public services, in every field of provision those responsible for their delivery were constrained by financial stringencies imposed by central government. For example, during the Thatcher era, the reform of community care, education and housing services imposed burdens on authorities that they claimed to be unable to meet. Thus, following the reform of the system of social care at the beginning of the 1990s and a change in the basis of grant allocation,[20] many local authorities claimed to run out of money by the middle of the financial year. It appeared that the government had introduced a new community care regime without providing sufficient funds to pay for it.[21]

During three consecutive periods of New Labour governance, the most highly publicised crises have been in the NHS health and local authority housing sectors. In particular, media attention has frequently focused on the strains placed on housing and health care resources by large numbers of immigrants, who often arrive in the most demographically disadvantaged areas.[22] However, problems have not been confined to the health and housing sectors. Competition has intensified across the whole field of local authority services—education, accommodation for vulnerable adults, personal and residential care services for the elderly and accommodation for young adults and children with disabilities.[23] Nonetheless, New Labour has continued to pursue the market-oriented policies of their predecessors and sought to deflect attention from minimalist welfare policies by further institutionalising the language of choice.[24] One example among many can be found in the Green Paper 'Quality and Choice: A

---

[20] The National Health Service and Community Care Act (NHSCCA) 1990, which introduced major reform of social care, placed new responsibilities and additional financial strains on local authorities. The funding of placements in residential and nursing homes, which had previously been supported on a national basis through the benefits system, was now to be funded by local authorities. Although the government provided additional funds to meet the new commitments, many local authorities claimed to be unable to do so. Changes to the system of resource allocation by central government, directed at reducing local financial autonomy, prevented the transference of resources across different welfare sectors. For judicial efforts to resolve continuing conflict as to whether local or health authorities must shoulder the burden of responsibility for long-term nursing care, see *R v North and East Devon Health Authority, ex parte Coughlan* (note 6 above).

[21] For an account of the crisis in community care services, see B Schwehr, 'The Legal Relevance of Resources—or Lack of Resources—in Community Care' (1995) 17(2) *Journal of Social Welfare and Family Law* 179–98, 180. See also E Palmer and M Sunkin, 'Needs, Resources and Abhorrent Choices' (1998) 61 *Modern Law Review* 401.

[22] See *Al-Ameri* (note 8 above) for an example of stringent criticism of the misuse of the language of choice in the context of housing provision for asylum seekers.

[23] See for example M Dixon and W Paxton, 'An Audit of Social Injustice in the UK' in Pearce and Paxton (eds) (note 10 above) 21–62. Compare P Toynbee and D Walker, *Better or Worse: Has Labour Delivered?* (London, Bloombsury, 2005) for a defence of New Labour's achievements.

[24] See for example N Harris, 'Empowerment and State Education: Rights of Choice and Participation' (2005) *Modern Law Review* 925–57. The author argues that although 'parent power' is based on liberal, consumerist notions of choice and participation and, in respect of children's education, has been a continuing feature of legislative changes to the governance of state education since the Education Act 1980, social rights such those in education which are based on citizenship have been weak.

Decent Home for All',[25] precursor to the Homelessness Act 2002,[26] which advanced the idea that 'many of the ills of social housing could be alleviated by changing the way it is allocated—from a system based upon bureaucratic assessment of *housing need* to one which respects and prioritises customer choice'.[27]

This is not the place for an extensive critique of the Green Paper. Notably, however, Dave Cowan and Alex Marsh have argued in its defence that it offered prospects of greater economic efficiency while addressing long-standing criticisms by neo-liberal critics of traditional points systems based on evidence of individual need. It is indeed true that in the past, typical criticisms centred on the ideas that prioritisation schemes based on needs assessment afforded too much discretion to administrators; that they often reflected subjective and institutional racism; and that there was confusion and a lack of transparency in the rules both for those implementing them and for those subject to them.[28]

However, for individuals with the most pressing social needs, the choice between accepting wholly unsuitable and unpopular housing or remaining for indefinite periods on waiting lists is problematic. The idea that consumers of public sector housing, like their low-income counterparts at the bottom of the private housing market, should have minimal expectations of their needs being met, appears to undermine the very basis of the relationship between need and public sector provision on which the welfare state was founded. This tension was to the fore in *R (A) v Lambeth London Borough Council (LBC); R (Lindsay) v Lambeth LBC* (conjoined appeal hereafter referred to as *Ex parte A and*

[25] Department of the Environment, Transport and the Regions (DETR), 'Quality and Choice: A Decent Home for All' (Green Paper, 4 April 2000). For a review of the Green Paper, see generally D Cowan and A Marsh, 'From Need to Choice: *R (A) v Lambeth LBC; R (Lindsay) v Lambeth LBC*' (2004) *Modern Law Review* 478. The authors point out that local authorities were no longer to regard themselves purely as 'housing allocators' but rather as 'providers of a lettings service responsive to the needs of and wishes of their individual clients' (Green Paper, para 9.5–7). The Green Paper therefore proposed a shift from housing prioritisation based on points accumulation to a system in which access would notionally be driven by customer choice. Cowan and Marsh note that in the subsequent White Paper (DETR, 'Quality and Choice: The Way Forward for Housing' (White Paper, December 2000)), the government, although less prescriptive about how local authorities might develop choice in lettings, still considered that 'choice should be explicitly incorporated into allocation polices as it would help to create sustainable communities and make better use of housing stock' (para 6.4.).

[26] The Homelessness Act 2002 received Royal Assent in February 2006, and allocation provisions were brought into force in January 2003.

[27] Cowan and Marsh (2004) (note 25 above) 478 (emphasis added), paraphrasing the DETR Green Paper (note 25 above) paras 9.5–9.7. Notably, s 16 Homelessness Act 2002 has retained the concept of 'reasonable preference' to those in urgent housing need, reducing the categories of households so entitled to five and giving power to determine priorities on several grounds, including financial resources and previous behaviour in s 167(2) Housing Act 1996.

[28] See Cowan and Marsh (2004) (note 25 above): 'Choice-based letting schemes operate at the juncture of neo-liberal and neo-conservative ideology. . . . In place of dependency they advocate self-reliance and personal responsibility on the part of home-seekers; they seek to mirror the market in terms of bargaining ability . . . [T]hey affirm the importance of individual choice . . . however limited that may be, and have regard to the interests of the individual over the collective. . . . Householders are no longer regarded as passive recipients of welfare, but active autonomous and responsible customers' (488).

Lindsay),[29] a challenge in which two severely disabled claimants argued that a pilot scheme set up before relevant provisions of the Homelessness Act 2002, which required households to assess their own household need by reference to their willingness and ability to wait, was illegal.

Having first made clear that the objective assessment of need is for local authorities rather than applicants to make,[30] the Court of Appeal was critical both of technical aspects of the Lambeth choice-based letting scheme and of its analysis of the meaning of choice as an expression of individual preference, which had been promoted in the Green Paper.[31] The Court of Appeal questioned how 'permitting an applicant to assess his needs so highly that he accepts inferior accommodation amounts to conferring a preference on him'.[32] Furthermore, in response to Lambeth's argument that choice had proved to be a bureaucratically rational policy, as shown by the considerable reduction in the average rate of refusals for any particular property after the implementation of self-assessment,[33] Collins J stated:

> What has helped is not necessarily choice but a greater knowledge of what an applicant was prepared to accept. . . . [I]n many ways the policy provides the antithesis of choice. A realisation that what would otherwise be regarded as substandard accommodation in an unwanted area can be the only way of avoiding an unacceptably long wait is hardly what most would regard as a real choice. It is not the sort of choice which the Green Paper seems to me to be advocating.[34]

One of the central precepts in the choice-based letting schemes proposed by the Green Paper is the idea that choice in the public sector should mirror the private sector by taking on board the harsh reality of what it means to have low bargaining power. However, Cowan and Marsh have argued that choice-based letting schemes also have all the hallmarks and the 'linguistic turn and program-

---

[29] [2002] HLR 57 998. In *R (A) v Lambeth LBC* at first instance, the decision of Sir Christopher Bellamy, 5 November 2001 (unreported), the applicant, who suffered from physical and mental disabilities, and her daughter were living in a single room in a hostel. In *R (Lindsay) v Lambeth* [2002] EWHC, the first instance decision of Sullivan J, 11 April 2002, the applicant, who did not have a priority need under homelessness legislation, lived with friends or slept rough.

[30] See for example *R v Wolverhampton, ex parte Wattters* (1997) 29 HLR 931. In that case, which set out 'a reasonable head start' principle, the Court of Appeal upheld a scheme that excluded a household from appearing on the list despite having 'a reasonable preference', arguing that a 'local authority is a public resource holder with duties to the public purse: the council has a duty to have regard to financial consequences of its actions and to the need to balance its housing revenue account' (936).

[31] This approach was in stark contrast to the non-interventionist approach of courts in similar prioritisation challenges under prior legislation.

[32] *Ex parte A and Lindsay* (note 29 above) para 38 (Pill LJ).

[33] In essence, Lambeth had argued that the policy was rational because the more refusals a property gets, the longer it remains unoccupied, thereby adversely affecting the housing revenue account. This claim was supported by evidence from a Report by the Social Exclusion Unit, which recognised that if a property remains unoccupied, it can tip an estate into being regarded as unpopular, with a more significant impact on rental income streams. See Cowan and Marsh (2004) (note 25 above) 486; and Social Exclusion Unit (Policy Action Team 7), 'Unpopular Housing' (1999).

[34] *Ex parte A and Lindsay* (note 29 above) para 49.

matic shift in government from welfarism to the empowerment of "advanced liberalism"',[35] which, in place of dependency, advocates self-reliance and personal responsibility on the part of home-seekers.[36] Cowan and Marsh therefore consider that Collins J's analysis in *Ex parte A and Lindsay* of the role of choice inappropriately harks back to bygone understandings of the notion of consumer choice in liberal contract theory, 'which presupposes that in a situation of market equilibrium, the individual customer has some considerable power'.[37] However, Cowan and Marsh also accept that the policy of 'choice' adopted by New Labour in the Green Paper is not a historical break in social housing allocation policy, and that since the mid-1980s, as a result of (post-)Thatcherite housing policy and practice, there has been an interplay between need and choice. However, they also concede that in the continuing march towards 'advanced liberalism' there has been a 'significant discursive shift in social housing policy in which the ideals of choice have overtaken the ideals of need.'[38]

It is certainly true that throughout the Thatcher era, assessment of individual need was a central component of legislative reform of local authority social services, including education, community care and children's services. Thus, since the middle of the 1980s, individuals and groups, who were encouraged to view themselves as consumers, began testing the extent to which local authorities could be held to account for failure to provide services appropriate to their individually assessed needs.[39] Courts in both public and private law were therefore confronted by claims in which issues of finite resources were crucial to the resolution of challenges against the failure of authorities to meet their perceived statutory obligations.[40] However, litigation that demonstrated the 'impossible choices' faced by decision-makers[41] often served to highlight further the relationship between fiscal policy and the allocation of scarce resources.

---

[35] Cowan and Marsh (2004) (note 25 above) 488.

[36] See N Rose, *Powers of Freedom* (Cambridge, CUP, 1999) 139; and N Rose, 'Government Authority and Expertise in Advanced Liberalism' (1993) 22 *Economy and Society* 283, 296.

[37] Cowan and Marsh (2004) (note 25 above) 487.

[38] *Ibid*, 489. See also D Cowan and A Marsh, 'From Need to Choice: Welfarism to Advanced Liberalism? Problematics of Social Housing Allocation' (2005) *Legal Studies* 22–48.

[39] See M Sunkin, L Bridges and G Meszaros, *Judicial Review in Perspective: An Investigation of Trends in the Use and Operation of Judicial Review Procedure in England and Wales*, 2nd edn (London, Cavendish, 1995). For an account of the use of judicial review by parents as ' consumers' in the education system, see generally N Harris, *Law and Education: Regulation, Consumerism and the Education System* (London, Sweet & Maxwell, 1993); N Harris, 'Judicial Review and Education' in T Buck (ed), *Judicial Review and Social Welfare* (London, Pinter, 1998).

[40] See *X and Others (Minors) v Bedfordshire CC* [1995] 3 All ER 353 in which children sued local authorities in negligence for breach of statutory powers. It was held by the House of Lords that a duty of care would not be imposed when local authority conduct raises non-justiciable issues. These included inter alia 'decisions about the allocation of finite resources' (749).

[41] Two public law challenges against Birmingham Health Authority received a great deal of emotive publicity. In *ex parte Walker*, *The Times*, 26 November 1987, a heart operation not yet vital to a baby's survival had been postponed because of a shortage of nurses. The Court of Appeal held that it was not for the court to substitute its judgment for that of the Health Authority, 'unless the allocation itself was wholly unreasonable'. In the later case of *Collier*, *The Independent*, 14 March 1995, a heart operation urgently needed was refused for the same reason to a baby at the top of the list. Simon Brown LJ refused to distinguish the earlier case.

Protective of local authorities, senior members of the UK judiciary generally recoiled from principled resolution of these disputes, distancing themselves by routinely pointing to the interdependence of competing strains upon the public purse.[42] Accordingly, in private as in public law, their judgements came to be associated with a pragmatic policy-oriented approach to the resolution of welfare needs disputes, even in cases where weaknesses within the administrative machinery resulted in outstanding failures to meet very basic standards of welfare.[43] Therefore, before the enactment of the HRA, although cases brought by destitute asylum seekers had from time to time been associated with authoritative bursts of judicial protectionism,[44] leading cases in the fields of housing and education were in general characterised by overt judicial pragmatism.[45] As indicated in chapter four, issues of resource allocation in the area of local authority services proved to be a crucial pressure point against which tensions inherent in the judicial role had been laid bare.[46]

From the mid-1980s onwards, in the NHS health care sector, structural reforms also revolved around the language of choice and empowerment. However, by contrast with the local authority welfare sector, it has generally been more clearly understood that 'the type, location, and timing of medical interventions are determined on the basis of clinical priority and availability of resources by relevant NHS bodies, rather than at the choice of the patient'.[47] Thus, although prioritisation decisions by NHS bodies can be challenged in judicial review, as noted by the Advocate General in *R (on the Application of*

---

[42] See for example *O'Rourke v Camden BC* [1997] 3 All ER 23, 30, where the local authority was held to be in breach of statutory duty to provide housing to a claimant who was homeless on leaving prison. Despite the apparent abnegation of responsibility and the arguably inhumane treatment that he received, the House of Lords unanimously rejected his claim for compensation in a private law action. Lord Hoffman bluntly observed that 'expenditure [on housing the homeless] interacts with expenditure on other public services such as education, the National Health Service and even the police' (26). More recently, see *Al-Ameri* (note 8 above): 'It would be wholly unrealistic to suggest that a child selected by Sophie for the gas chamber had died as a result of Sophie's own choice' (para 19 (Lord Bingham)).

[43] See JAG Griffiths, *The Politics of the Judiciary*, 5th edn (London, Fontana, 1997) 112–51.

[44] *R v Secretary of State for the Home Department, ex parte Bugdaycay* [1987] AC 514; and *R v Secretary of State for Social Security, ex parte JCWI* [1997] 1 WLR 275.

[45] For analysis of judicial reasoning in the House of Lords from a political science perspective and the view that the House of Lords has used statutory interpretation to impose a collectivist policy-oriented notion of welfare rights as 'public goods', see D Robertson, *Judicial Discretion in the House of Lords* (Oxford, Clarendon, 1998).

[46] For this juridical tension, in addition to rationing disputes analysed in this chapter, see for example *R v Home Secretary, ex parte P and G* [1995] 1 All ER 870; *R v Chief Constable of Sussex, ex parte International Trader's Ferry Ltd* [1996] QB 197 Div Ct, [1997] 2 All ER 65 CA, [1997] 1 All ER 129, 192 HL; *R v Home Secretary, ex parte Fire Brigades Union* [1995] AC 513; and *R (on the Application of Pfizer Limited) v Secretary of State for Health* [2002] EWCA Civ 1556, [2003] 1 CMLR 19—one of a series of challenges by the pharmaceutical giant Pfizer against the legality of the government's refusal to provide Viagra for routine treatment on the NHS.

[47] *R (on the Application of Watts) v Bedford Primary Care Trust* (hereafter *Watts*) Case C-372/04, [2005] ECR 0, para 7 (Advocate General). See also the opinion of the Grand Chamber, [2006] ECR 0, discussed further below. For additional discussion of *Watts* in the context of EU law, see chapter 2, section IV-C above.

Watts) v Bedford Primary Care Trust (hereafter *Watts*),[48] the wide discretion afforded in legislation for the delivery of health care has meant that 'the general perception has been that such challenges usually fail.'[49] Nevertheless, during the past decade, as a result of growing public awareness of issues of rationing and of the way in which allocation decisions are made in the NHS,[50] there have been increased attempts by 'consumers' to challenge decisions by Primary Care Trusts (PCTs), on grounds of failure to take account of their individual needs.

Notably, however, New Labour has attempted to mitigate the impact of the uneven distribution of health provision throughout the UK regions (the so-called 'postcode lottery') through the centralisation of policy decisions on the scope of NHS provision.[51] For example, the National Institute of Clinical Excellence (NICE) was established in 1999 to provide 'authoritative, robust and reliable guidance on current best practice'.[52] Problematically, however, individual Primary Care Trusts strapped for cash are not bound to follow NICE guidance. Thus, despite efforts to minimise complaints against the unequal distribution of national health care resources, there are signs that the courts will continue to be embroiled in the review of allocation polices, as awareness of discrepancies continues to grow.[53]

There has been longstanding support in the fields of both health policy[54] and public law[55] for some limited judicial contribution to decisions about the allocation of health care resources, as a means of 'promoting and ensuring accountability in public decision-making'[56] and of developing 'principles and processes which might assist in the positive creation of legitimate modes of implementation of public policy'.[57] The extent to which courts have moved beyond such a minimalist role in health care allocation decisions since the well-known decision in *R v Cambridge Health Authority, ex parte B* (hereafter *Re B*)[58] will be the subject of the following section.[59]

---

[48] *Ibid*. By ss 17A and 17B National Health Act 1977, the Secretary of State may give directions to Primary Care Trusts, which they must then follow. It is common knowledge that by reason of s 2 of the 1977 Act, the Secretary of State also has power to issue guidance and that trusts must have regard to such guidance: see *R v North Derbyshire Health Authority, ex parte Fisher* (1998) 38 BMLR 76, 80–1 and 89–90 (Dyson J).

[49] See the remarks of Advocate General Geelhoed in *Watts* (note 47 above) para 7.

[50] See L Locock, 'The Changing Nature of Rationing in the UK National Health Service' (2000) 78 *Public Administration* 91, 93.

[51] See R Klein, *The New Politics of the NHS*, 4th edn (Harlow, Prentice Hall, 2001).

[52] The work of NICE involves the appraisal of the clinical effectiveness and cost effectiveness of health technologies, particularly those that are new and costly. It then produces guidance on whether the technology is recommended for restricted or routine use on the NHS.

[53] At the time of writing, a judicial review of a decision by NICE to recommend the use of Ariceps for early-onset Alzheimer patients has been mounted.

[54] See generally C Ham and S McIver, *Contested Decisions* (London, Kings Fund, 2000).

[55] See generally D Longley, *Public Law and Health Service Accountability* (Buckingham, Open University Press, 1993).

[56] *Ibid*, 4.

[57] T Prosser, 'Towards a Critical Public Law' (1982) 9(1) *Journal of Law and Society* 1–19, 11.

[58] [1995] 1 FLR 1056, [1995] 1 WLR 898.

[59] See generally Syrett (note 13 above).

II. NHS RATIONING: THE ROLE OF COURTS IN DISPUTES OVER ACCESS TO MEDICAL SERVICES

A. The Limits of Judicial Intervention in Health Care Rationing: *R v Cambridge Health Authority, ex parte B (Re B)*

The well-known case of *Re B* concerned the refusal by a health authority to provide further treatment for a young girl with leukaemia, on grounds that the expenditure involved would not reflect an efficient use of resources, given the small prospect of success and the Health Authority's responsibility for the funding of other patients. Argument proceeded on the basis that the right to life was engaged.

At first instance, Laws J (as he then was) accepted that in a world of scarce resources, 'it is for the respondents to decide how resources are to be distributed'.[60] However, in such a case, where the fairness of a Health Authority decision was at issue, he questioned whether the appropriate touchstone for legality was 'the crude *Wednesbury* bludgeon'.[61] Thus, closely following the judgement of the House of Lords in *Brind*,[62] he considered that when the right to life of a ten-year-old child is engaged, the court has a secondary role to ensure that only those infringements are allowed that that can be justified by an objection of substance put forward in the public interest:

> [W]here a public body enjoys a discretion, the exercise of which may infringe a fundamental human right, it is not to be permitted to perpetrate any such infringement unless it can show a substantial objective justification on public interest grounds for so doing.[63]

In view of the limited evidence of a clear prioritisation policy by the Health Authority, Laws J therefore believed that the decision not to fund further treatment had interfered with child B's right to life; and that the reasons put forward did not constitute a substantial public interest ground which could justify the infringement. Although he accepted that the court itself should not make orders for the use of health care resources without *some* understanding of the likely effects for other patients, he went on to state: 'where the question is whether the life of a ten-year-old child might be saved by however slim a chance, the responsible authorities . . . must do more than toll the bell of tights resources'.[64]

Not only can the methodology proposed here by Laws J in *Re B* be said to be in tune with the hard-look scrutiny suggested in cases where Convention rights are engaged; his opinion that the exercise of the Health Authority discretion

---

[60] *Re B* (note 58 above) 1064 G–H.
[61] *Ibid*, 1058 H–G.
[62] [1991] 1 All ER 720.
[63] *Re B* (note 58 above) 1060 D–E.
[64] *Ibid*, 1065 A–B.

should be transparent and demonstrably fair is also a reflection of the principle now generally countenanced in public administrative law, that public authorities are obliged to give reasons for their decisions.[65] Nevertheless, in a decision that was clearly premised on the notion that there can be no evaluative role for courts distinct from that of administrators, Lord Bingham MR refused to accept that the Authority should be required to justify its decision in this way. Thus, although Lord Bingham MR expressed sympathy for the view that courts should apply the most rigorous standards of review in cases in which such 'tragic choices' had to be made by authorities, he famously decided:

> Difficult and agonising judgments have to be made as to how a limited budget is best allocated to the maximum advantage of the maximum number of patients. This is not a judgement that the court can make. In my judgement it is not something that a health authority such as this authority can be fairly criticised for not advancing before the court.[66]

Laws J at first instance had been careful in *Re B* to identify a distinct contribution that could be made by courts in complaints about the fairness of health authority rationing decisions. His measured and qualified approach was in tune not only with the established approach to human rights adjudication in public law, but also with current policy debates about the rationing of medical services, particularly in relation to the need for health care rationing to be made explicit. At the same time, his arguments chimed with the aspirations of public choice constitutionalists: that democratic accountability is to be achieved by the embodiment in public life of transparency and democratic responsiveness.[67] Indeed, as Laws J recognised himself, his opinion that Health Authority discretion should be transparent and demonstrably fair was no more than a reflection of the principle now recognised in public administrative law, that it should be incumbent on public authorities to give reasons for their decisions.

By contrast, the judgment of Lord Bingham MR is characteristic of the conservative opposition to any attempt to carve out an evaluative role for courts that is separate from that undertaken by administrators in the context of rationing decisions. Robert Lee contrasted the response of Lord Bingham MR in *Re B* with the willingness of Lord Templeman in *Bugdaycay*[68] to acknowledge human rights obligations in a case where the right of an asylum seeker was threatened by deportation.[69] Lee went on to posit that the refusal of the Court of Appeal in *Re B* to recognise an evaluative role for themselves may have been inspired not by the strictures of constitutional legitimacy, but rather by an intuition that if courts were to require authorities to justify the refusal of health services, they would expose a minefield of contradictory practices and uncertainties and the

---

[65] *R v Secretary of State, ex parte Daly* [2001] 2 WLR 16223.
[66] *Re B* (note 58 above) 1073 C–D.
[67] See note 18 above.
[68] Note 44 above.
[69] See B Lee, 'Judicial Review and Access to Health Care' in Buck (ed) (note 39 above).

absence of a clear prioritisation policy.[70] Perhaps this captures something of the truth. However, it is impossible to dissociate the response of Lord Bingham MR in *Re B* from an endemic cultural resistance to the development of an open-textured differential standard of review—which had up to this point been successfully maintained in disputes over the fairness of resources allocation decisions in welfare needs context.

B. NHS Policies under Scrutiny: Legitimate Interventions in Public Administrative Law

Although UK courts have continued to hold firmly to the position of the Court of Appeal in *Re B*,[71] since then, in a small number of rationing disputes, they have successfully utilised and in some cases expanded existing public law principles to ensure that in the exercise of discretionary powers, national policies and the individual needs of claimants are fully considered. In *North West Lancashire Health Authority v A, D & G* (hereafter *A, D & G*),[72] for example, the principle that administrators must not fetter their discretionary powers was central to a successful challenge by three transsexuals against the refusal of gender reassignment surgery. The refusal had been based on a Health Authority policy that accorded low priority to such procedures, on the assumption that they were ineffective in terms of health gains. In the most notable judgement of the Court of Appeal, Auld LJ decided that a uniform policy that failed adequately to assess the possible benefits of gender reassignment surgery constituted a fetter against the rights of the complainants to an appropriate assessment of their cases based on an evaluation of their clinical needs. The refusal was therefore quashed and the matter remitted to the authority.

Auld LJ accepted that questions about appropriate and effective medical treatment for transsexualism and its sequelae must be a matter for the medical judgment of the relevant health authority. Nevertheless, he was clear that it made a nonsense of the Authority's policy, which stated that it would not provide treatment *except* in cases of overriding clinical need, if, as a matter of prior medical judgment, no such treatment was considered viable.[73] He was thus in agreement with the trial judge that the 'precise allocation and weighting

---

[70] See B Lee, 'Judicial Review and Access to Health Care' in Buck (ed), 47.

[71] See for example *R (on the Application of Pfizer Limited) v Secretary of State for Health* [2002] EWCA Civ 1556, [2003] 1 CMLR 19.

[72] [2000] 1 WLR 977.

[73] *Ibid*, 991 (Auld, Buxton and May LJJ). Auld LJ reinforced this point by citing the trial judge: 'In my view, the stance of the authority, coupled with the near uniformity of its reasons for rejecting each of the applicants' requests for funding was not a genuine application of a policy subject to individually determined exceptions of the sort considered acceptable by Lord Scarman in *Re Findlay* [1985] AC 318. It is similar to the over-rigid application of the near "blanket policy" questioned by Judge J in *R v Warwickshire County Council, ex parte Collymore* [1995] ELR 217, 224–6, which while in theory admitting of exceptions, may not, in reality, result in the proper consideration of each individual case on its merits' (991).

of priorities is clearly a matter of judgment for each authority, keeping well in mind its statutory obligations to meet the reasonable requirements of all those within its area for which it is responsible'.[74] Furthermore, like the trial judge, he also considered it proper for an authority when adopting a general policy in relation to a particular treatment, to allow for exceptions in 'exceptional circumstances' and to leave those circumstances undefined. Therefore, following the lead of the trial judge, Auld LJ concluded:

> [A] policy to place transsexualism low in an order of priorities of illnesses for treatment and to deny it treatment save in exceptional circumstances such as overriding clinical need, is not in principle irrational, provided that the policy genuinely recognises the possibility of there being an overriding clinical need and requires each request for treatment to be considered on its individual merits.[75]

i. Legitimate Expectation: The Meeting of Individual Needs

The most striking example of the expansion of ordinary principles of judicial review to allow the intervention of the Court of Appeal in an NHS resource allocation decision has been the decision of the Court of Appeal in *Coughlan*,[76] which also arose prior to the implementation of the HRA. The facts of *Coughlan* are now well rehearsed: Ms Coughlan and five fellow residents, who were all severely disabled, had been persuaded to move from a hospital that the Health Authority wished to close to another purpose-built hospital. However, having assured the applicants that the new hospital would be their home for life, after consultation and taking into account the fact of the promise, the Health Authority decided to close the home, primarily on economic grounds. On appeal by the Health Authority from the decision of Hidden J in the Divisional Court, the Court of Appeal decided that the closure decision amounted to a breach of the applicants' legitimate expectation and a breach of Article 8 ECHR.

Prior to the decision, one of the most controversial issues in the law of legitimate expectation was the appropriate standard of review in cases in which 'a lawful promise or practice has induced a legitimate expectation of a benefit which is substantive, not simply procedural'.[77] In *Coughlan*, the Court of Appeal accepted that such cases may call for a stricter fairness or justificatory standard of review and that it is for the court 'to determine whether there is a sufficient overriding interest to justify a departure from what has been previously promised'.[78] In other words, the court must judge 'whether to frustrate the

---

[74] *A, D & G* (note 72 above) 991 (Auld LJ).

[75] *Ibid*, 993 (Auld LJ), emphasis added.

[76] Note 6 above. At the heart of the challenge lay a protracted national dispute between the Department of Health and local authorities as to which of the parties had financial responsibility for nursing care to individuals assessed by local authorities as being in need of care and attention under s 21 of the National Assistance Act 1948.

[77] *Coughlan* (note 6 above) 867, para 57.

[78] *Ibid*, 880, para 82.

expectation is so unfair that to take a new and different course will amount to an abuse of power'.[79]

In reaching this conclusion, Lord Woolf relied on the leading decision of the House of Lords in *R v IRC, ex parte Preston*.[80] That case, which arose in a very different context, was concerned with an allegation, not in the event made out, that the IRC had gone back impermissibly on their promise not to reinvestigate certain aspects of an individual taxpayer's affairs. In *Preston*, Lord Scarman had stressed the importance of fairness as a ground on which the court can in appropriate cases intervene to quash a decision made by a public officer or authority in purported exercise of a power conferred by law. However, Lord Scarman had emphatically concurred with the conclusion of Lord Templeman, that even beyond an ultra vires claim, 'unfairness in the purported exercise of a power can in itself amount to an abuse or excess of the power'.[81] Most significantly, Lord Scarman had concluded in *Preston* that 'it is unimportant whether the unfairness is analytically within or beyond the power conferred by law; on either view public law reaches it today'.[82] The Court of Appeal in *Coughlan* had thus refused to accept that the authority had justified its claim that the closure decision did not represent an abuse of power.

Since courts have generally applied a low standard of review in challenges founded on *Wednesbury* reasonableness in which policy choices about scarce resources are at issue, the Health Authority in *Coughlan* believed that they had satisfied their legal duty to the applicant by agreeing to finance her future care. However, despite previous reluctance to intervene in such cases, the Court did not accept that the Health Authority had demonstrated that the public interest in the closure of the home outweighed the interests of the applicants in being allowed to remain for as long as they chose.

In rejecting the allegation that they had acted in breach of Ms Coughlan's legitimate expectations, the Health Authority relied on their promise to continue paying for her care following closure. However, Lord Woolf considered that such a compromise missed the essential point of the promise given to the complainant. In his view, the specificity of the promise of a home—for which the applicant had indeed a right of protection under Article 8 ECHR—could not be compared with the substituted offer of 'financial care'. Thus, in weighing the right of the complainant to continue living in her home, against the duty of the Health Authority to take economically prudent decisions, Lord Woolf had no doubt that the Health Authority had erred in treating the promise as a factor,

---

[79] *Coughlan* (note 6 above) 867, para 57. Authority for departure from the seminal decision of the Court of Appeal in *R v Secretary of State for the Home Department, ex parte Hargreaves* [1997] 1 All ER 397 was to be found in those cases where the doctrine of legitimate expectation had emerged 'as a distinct application of the doctrine of abuse of power in relation to substantive as well as procedural benefits' (*Coughlan* (note 6 above) paras 67–71 and 78–81).

[80] [1985] 2 All ER 327, 329.

[81] *Preston* (ibid) 329.

[82] *Ibid*, 329, cited in *Coughlan* (note 6 above) 875, para 80 (Woolf LJ).

which although given considerable weight, could be outweighed by compelling financial reasons.

Accordingly, his Lordship found no overriding public interest to justify the decision to move Ms Coughlan against her will and in breach of the Authority's own promise. He therefore concluded that the decision was unfair since it frustrated the legitimate expectation of the applicant and amounted to an abuse of power by the Authority. Moreover, for Lord Woolf, the fact that the closure of the home clearly constituted a breach of Article 8 ECHR, to which the court would shortly have to give effect, lent weight to this conclusion. Finally, although he appeared to accept that the consultation process would have been lawful had it taken place prior to judicial proceedings, Lord Woolf considered that inadequate weight had been accorded to individual and multi-disciplinary assessments in that process.

Throughout his speech, Lord Woolf sought to confine these developments by emphasising the quasi-contractual basis of the remedy. He considered that cases in which the doctrine of abuse of power provides the basis of the court's intervention 'are likely to be in the nature of things, where the expectation is confined to promises made to one or a few people, giving the promise the character of a contract'.[83] Significantly, however, he also stressed that the remedy available to the applicants would be available only in a limited number of sensitive statutory contexts. Thus, he concluded:

> [T]he fact that the court will only give effect to a legitimate expectation within the statutory context in which it has arisen should avoid jeopardising the important principle that the executives' policy making powers should not be trammelled by the courts.[84]

Thus, one of the most significant aspects of the judgement in *Coughlan* is the conclusion that in order to avoid encroaching on the power of the executive, courts must be prepared to identify those sensitive statutory contexts in which the doctrine will be applied.

Elsewhere, there has been much valuable discussion as to the place of *Coughlan* in the incremental development of the law of legitimate expectation in domestic law.[85] It is clear that the decision to depart from previous authority reflects not only the flexibility of administrative review but also the readiness of the Court of Appeal to develop their jurisdiction in accordance with principles of EU administrative law and to give effect to their obligations to protect citizens against breach of Convention rights.[86] Commentators have highlighted those aspects of the decision that demonstrate the confidence of courts in developing a role in judicial review that is concerned not only with protecting citizens

---

[83] *Coughlan* (note 6 above) 868, para 59.

[84] *Ibid*, para 82 (Lord Woolf).

[85] See P Craig and S Schonberg, 'Substantive Legitimate Expectations after *Coughlan*' (2000) *Public Law* 684.

[86] See M Fordham, 'Legitimate Expectation: Domestic Principles' (2000) *Judicial Review* 188.

from unfairness in the restricted *Wednesbury* sense, but also with protecting them in circumstances in which through unfairness or arbitrariness the decision of an authority amounts to an abuse of power. The case also provides clear authority for the proposition that in the limited 'context sensitive' area of residential care, in weighing obligations to meet the assessed needs of patients against the availability of health authority resources, the ritual incantation of a lack of resources is no longer enough.

Moreover, at the level of procedure, the case provided an important clarification of the lawfulness of consultation procedures, which must take place prior to closure decisions by public authorities, and the relevance of individual and multi-disciplinary assessments to the legitimacy of that process. For local authorities contemplating closure of directly managed homes, even in the absence of specific promises, it became clear in *Coughlan* that high priority must be given to the assessed needs of vulnerable residents during the consultation process. However, it should also be stressed that, in light of the highly specific nature of the promise given to the applicant in *Coughlan*, the case has provided only a very narrow platform on which to challenge the fairness of resource allocation decisions by public authorities in health and welfare needs disputes.

Nonetheless, in the area of health care prioritisation, the more recent case of *R (on the Application of Rodgers) v Swindon Primary Care Trust* (hereafter *Rodgers*)[87] has reinforced the warning provided by *Coughlan* to health care providers that they must pay careful attention to the articulation *and* application of clear and rational policies when making decisions about the funding of health treatment. Moreover, the Court of Appeal in *Rodgers* reiterated the circumstances in which, by contrast with the non-justiciable complaint in *Re B*,[88] ordinary principles of public administrative law can be relied on to ensure that health care providers do so.

ii. Irrational Allocation Policies: Distinguishing Re B

In *Rodgers*[89] the claimant, who was in the primary stage of HER2 positive breast cancer, had found out that there was considerable optimism among members of the medical profession about the potential benefits of a drug named Herceptin for patients suffering from primary stage breast cancer of her type, although it was not yet licensed for that purpose. Notwithstanding, the Secretary of State had issued a weekly bulletin to NHS chief executives, which included an advisory to Primary Care Trusts[90] that they should not refuse to

---

[87] [2006] EWHC Admin 357.

[88] Note 58 above. See also discussion in subsection A above.

[89] Note 87 above.

[90] PCTs were established pursuant to s 16A National Health Act 1977. The primary duties of such a trust are set out in s 15: 'to administer the arrangements made in pursuance of this Act for the provision of primary medical services . . .' Under reg 3(2) of the National Health Service (Functions of Strategic Health Authorities and Primary Care Trust and Administration Arrangements) (England) Regulations 2002, the functions of the Secretary of State under inter alia s 2 of the 1977

fund Herceptin solely on grounds of cost and that they 'should not rule out treatments in principle, but that they should consider individual circumstances'.[91] Having found out that she was in the class of patients for whom Herceptin might be beneficial and after being made aware of possible negative effects of its use, the claimant sought funding from Swindon PCT.

In its general statement of policy, Swindon PCT outlined its 'clinical priorities for the commissioning of selected services', providing that 'where an individual patient . . . presents an exceptional need for treatment, Swindon PCT will consider such cases on their own merits'.[92] The statement also included a number of relevant circumstances to be taken into account, including: the fact that a particular drug may be off-licence and not approved by NICE; the special healthcare problems of particular patients; and financial considerations. Although neither licensed nor approved by NICE, a specific policy was issued regarding Herceptin, which was to be funded for early-stage breast cancer, *without* taking financial considerations into account, provided that it had been prescribed by a clinician and there were exceptional clinical or personal circumstances to justify its use.

There were no more than 20 or so patients with early-stage breast cancer who were suitable for treatment with Herceptin.[93] However, having considered her case, Swindon PTC decided that the drug would not be made available to the applicant on grounds of exceptional clinical or personal circumstances. She therefore argued in judicial review proceedings inter alia: that the application of the Trust's policy had been irrational and arbitrary, since there was no rational basis for deciding what constituted exceptionality; that the eligible group had been automatically pre-selected on grounds of medical suitability; and further that the PCT decision constituted a violation of Article 2 ECHR.

At first instance, the judge disagreed,[94] holding that refusal to fund the unlicensed use of Herceptin in the claimant's case was merely a reflection of the Trust's policy to provide funding only in exceptional cases, which although different from the policy applied by many other trusts, was not in itself unlawful.

Act are exercisable by '(a) Primary Care Trusts; and (b) Strategic Health Authorities but only to the extent necessary to support and manage the performance of Primary Care Trusts in the exercise of those functions'.

[91] Department of Health, *Chief Executive Bulletin*, Issue 294, 4–10 November 2005.

[92] The PCT's Clinical Priorities Committee (CPC) is made up of a range of health professionals and Primary Care Trust managers. It includes a Patient and Public Involvement Forum member and is chaired by a non-executive director of the PCT. It acts as a formal subcommittee of the PCT's Board and is responsible for considering requests for exceptions to the PCT's commissioning policies. In cases of urgency it acts through an Urgency Panel. There is a right of appeal from the decision of the CPC to an Appeal Panel, which may make a recommendation to the Board as to the decision that should be taken. The general policy of the PCT is thus not to fund off-licence or unlicensed drugs except that, 'where a patient has a special healthcare problem that presents an exceptional need for treatment', it will consider that case on its merits; in doing so, however, it will have regard to the funds available.

[93] In her formal application, the claimant's consultant, who believed that all patients in her position should be funded if they so wished, argued that his patient was not an exceptional case.

[94] In light of *A, D & G* (note 72 above).

Furthermore, the trial judge decided that since the Secretary of State's bulletin was not a Direction *requiring* Herceptin to be provided for all members of the eligible group, the argument based on Article 2 ECHR also failed.[95] The Court of Appeal, however, unanimously agreed that since there had been no basis for deciding what constituted 'exceptionality', the policy was irrational as it applied to her case.

In the Court of Appeal there was little, if any, dispute between the parties as to the standard of scrutiny. Thus, agreeing that a dispute that 'may be a life or death decision for the appellant' was enough to attract rigorous scrutiny of the kind proposed in *R v Ministry of Defence, ex p Smith*,[96] Sir Thomas Clarke MR, giving the unanimous judgment for the Court of Appeal, recalled the view of Sir Thomas Bingham (as he then was) in *Smith*:

> The more substantial is the interference with human rights, the more the court will require by way of justification before it is satisfied that the decision is reasonable in the sense outlined above.[97]

Nevertheless, the Court of Appeal in *Rodgers* highlighted a crucial difference from earlier prioritisation disputes such as *Re B*[98], which rested on the conviction that an authority could not be expected to advance justificatory reasons as to the fairness of a refusal, based on considerations of resource allocation. Thus, in *Rodgers* it was again emphasised that, by contrast with *Re B*, it was the *application* of the Trust's policy in the claimant's case that was irrational.

On this view, it was accepted that it would have been difficult to distinguish *Rodgers* from a 'resource allocation dispute' such as *Re B* had the PCT, as a hard-pressed authority, simply decided that taking into account the Secretary of State's guidance, it would as a matter of policy have 'regard to its financial constraints *and* to the particular circumstances of the individual patient in deciding whether or not to fund Herceptin treatment in a particular case'.[99] Sir Thomas Clarke MR stated that it 'would be very difficult, if not impossible, to say that such a policy was arbitrary or irrational'.[100] He therefore emphatically endorsed that part of the decision in *A, D & G*[101] where Auld LJ had confirmed the lawfulness of a policy of refusing to fund treatment save in *undefined* exceptional

---

[95] In the Strasbourg case of *Nitecki v Poland*, Application No 65653/01, 21 March 2002 (unreported), [2006] EWHC 171 Admin, the applicant was an elderly man suffering from a life-threatening condition known as amyotrophic lateral sclerosis (ALS). He was prescribed the drug Rilutek to treat the disease but could not afford to pay for it. His complaints to the European Court of Human Rights under Arts 2, 8 and 14 ECHR were found to be inadmissible. The Court held: 'an issue may arise under Article 2 where it is shown that the authorities of a Contracting State put an individual's life at risk through the denial of healthcare which they have undertaken to make available *to the population generally* . . .' (para 72 (Bean J) emphasis added).

[96] [1996] QB 517, 554.

[97] *Rodgers* (note 87 above) para 57 (Clarke LJ).

[98] Note 58 above.

[99] *Rodgers* (note 87 above) para 59.

[100] *Ibid.*

[101] Note 72 above.

circumstances: a policy that 'allows for exceptions in undefined exceptional circumstances' is not unlawful, so long as the 'the policy genuinely recognises the possibility of there being an overriding clinical need and requires each request for treatment to be considered on its individual merits'.[102] The crux of the matter was that the PCT, having established a policy that made funds available for all women within the eligible group whose clinicians prescribed Herceptin, had failed to adduce criteria whereby exceptionality could be judged.[103]

In *Rodgers*, the Court of Appeal once again spelt out what can legitimately be expected of the Administrative Court in NHS prioritisation disputes. In the case at hand, it was within the boundaries of their traditional supervisory jurisdiction to conclude that the policy—and therefore the decision taken pursuant to the policy—had been manifestly unlawful and should be quashed. However, even here it was not for the court to order decision-makers to fund the treatment concerned. Instead, it was for the PCT to formulate a lawful policy upon which to base decisions in particular cases, including that of Ms Rogers, in the future.

C. Choice, Socio-economic Entitlements and EU Law: Challenging the Status Quo

In its reference to the ECJ, the Court of Appeal in *Watts*[104] asked whether a person in the complainant's situation had an *entitlement* to receive services at the expense of the NHS under EU Law, given the fact that the NHS is a wholly publicly organised and funded health system. As Advocate General Geelhoed put it, the problem was that UK citizens such as Mrs Watts possess two contradictory qualities: on one hand, at the national level her status is determined by her 'affiliation to a national security system under which she did not enjoy any entitlement to be treated at a particular time or place'; on the other hand, from the point of view of EU law, she is 'a recipient of medical services' who, subject to justifiable restrictions imposed by national law, 'enjoys freedom in respect of the treatment she requires'.[105]

Since the very notion of entitlement under the free movement of services provisions in EC/EU law derives from the *absence* of unjustified restrictions on their

---

[102] *Ibid*, para 63 (Sir Thomas Clarke MR), citing Auld LJ: 'A policy of withholding assistance, save in un-stated exceptional circumstances . . . will be rational in the legal sense provided that it is possible to envisage, and the decision-maker does envisage, what such exceptional circumstances might be. If it is not possible to envisage any such circumstances, then the policy will be in practice a complete refusal of assistance: and irrational as such because it is sought to be justified not as a complete refusal but as a policy of exceptionality' (*A, D & G* (note 72 above) 991).

[103] When asked for examples of personal circumstances that might justify funding one woman rather than another within the eligible group, the single example proffered was a woman with a child suffering from a life-limiting condition as compared to one who had not. Since each fell within the eligible group, and funds were available for both, the example made little sense to the trial judge.

[104] Note 9 above.

[105] Opinion of Advocate General Geelhoed (note 47 above) para 61.

exercise, Advocate General Geelhoed considered it appropriate to enquire whether a refusal to fund cross-border health treatment that had taken place without prior authorisation constituted a restriction on the rights of UK residents to enjoy their freedoms—and if so, *whether it could be justified*.[106] Therefore, addressing the necessary question of whether, contrary to Article 49 EC, UK national rules present barriers to insured persons applying for health treatment abroad, the Advocate General stated that the rules consist not so much 'in a concrete provision limiting the possibility of obtaining treatment abroad, but in the absence of a clearly defined procedure for considering applications for such treatment'.[107] He concluded:

> Patients [under the NHS] have no entitlement to receive treatment at any time or location, but are dependent on clinical assessments made by care providers within the NHS . . . NHS bodies decide on the treatment which will be provided and when and where it will be provided. Persons requiring medical services are diagnosed, then classified according to the seriousness of their complaint and depending on that classification are given a place on a waiting list. It would appear that in this sense the NHS bodies enjoy unlimited discretion.[108]

The Advocate General therefore concluded in *Watts* that an administrative decision-making process that typically leaves individual patients both at the mercy of its discretionary operations and unsure as to whether costs might be paid to the care provider or reimbursed to them after treatment, can be viewed as a restriction on the right to choose treatment abroad. To the extent that patients might wish to obtain medical services in another member state, being left in a position of such fundamental uncertainty constitutes a restriction of their freedom to choose. Moreover, the Advocate General did not consider this finding to be antithetical to the well-established proposition that states may impose a 'reasonable and necessary' requirement of prior authorisation to maintain efficiency, stability and rationality in the allocation of resources, 'which would be jeopardised if persons were at liberty, regardless of circumstances, to go outside the system'.[109]

For the Advocate General, the crux of the matter was that any conditions attached to the granting of prior authorisation must be justified in accordance with 'overriding considerations of the general interest and proportionality'.[110] An authorisation scheme should not allow discretionary decisions to be taken that might negate the effectiveness of provisions of EU law. It therefore followed:

> In order for a prior administrative authorisation scheme to be justified even though derogating from such a fundamental freedom it must be based on non-discriminatory

---

[106] Opinion of Advocate General Geelhoed (note 47 above), para 64.
[107] *Ibid*, para 66.
[108] *Ibid*.
[109] *Ibid*, para 69.
[110] *Ibid*, para 70.

criteria which are known in advance, . . . so that it is not used arbitrarily . . . Such a prior administration scheme must likewise be based on a procedural system which is easily accessible and capable of ensuring that a request for authorisation will be dealt with objectively and impartially within a reasonable period of time, and refusals to grant authorisation must also be capable of being challenged in judicial or quasi judicial proceedings.[111]

Thus, in the interests of transparency, decisions regarding the treatment to be provided and its likely timeframe should be taken on the basis of clear criteria restricting the discretionary power of the decision-making body. In short, the Advocate General regarded it as insufficient for the decision-making body to reject an application for treatment abroad in accordance with the formal justification that it would be possible to provide treatment within the target set under the national system. Authorisation decisions should be taken with regard to whether the application of targets is acceptable in light of the individual pathological conditions of particular patients.

Subsequently, when considering Mrs Watts' case, the Grand Chamber[112] was also critical of the fact that NHS regulations regarding prior authorisation for treatment abroad did not set out specific criteria for their grant or refusal, and to that extent, did not 'circumscribe the exercise of national competent authorities discretionary power'.[113] Moreover, regarding the possibility of review of refusals as crucial, the Grand Chamber concluded that the 'lack of a legal framework in that regard makes it particularly difficult to exercise judicial review of decisions refusing to grant prior authorisation'.[114] By contrast with the traditional acceptance of blanket resource constraints as a justification for prioritisation decisions, the ECJ was clear that in the context of Article 49 EC Treaty,

a refusal to grant prior authorisation cannot be based merely on the existence of waiting lists enabling the supply of hospital care to be managed on the basis of predetermined clinical priorities, without carrying out in the individual case an objective medical assessment of the patient's medical condition, . . . the history of the possible course of his illness, the degree of pain he is in and or the nature of his disability at the time when the request for prior authorisation was made.[115]

Therefore, as seen earlier in chapter two, the ECJ rejected a number of general and specific grounds that were proposed by the Court of Appeal as possible justifications for refusal of authorisation: the disruption of waiting lists as a method for managing medical priorities; the possibility that patients with less urgent medical needs would gain priority over patients with more urgent medical needs; the diversion of resources to pay for less urgent treatment for those who are willing to travel abroad, which would adversely effect others; and that

---

[111] *Ibid.*
[112] *Watts* (Grand Chamber) (note 47 above).
[113] *Ibid*, para 118
[114] *Ibid.*
[115] *Ibid*, para 149.

the United Kingdom may be required to provide additional funding for the NHS budget or restrict the range of treatments because of the comparative costs of treatment in other member states.

Thus, although it recognised the conflict between the UK discretionary system of health care and one based on socio-economic entitlements, the ECJ in *Watts* at a stroke dismissed the traditional justifications relied on in the UK in challenges against the refusal of delivery of health and local authority services: that positive decisions would undermine the existing prioritisation scheme (which in the NHS was controlled by waiting lists); or that such decisions would have adverse effects on the claims of others and require a complete overhaul of the resource allocation budget. As to the first argument, it was claimed by the ECJ as a matter of logic that it would be inherent in any positive decision of an NHS body that the claimant was indeed someone in need of urgent treatment. As to the second argument regarding the impact on other patients and the subsequently necessary reallocation of the NHS budget, these economic concerns were external to the assessment of any patient's pathological condition on which decisions about treatment should be based.

In its reference in *Watts*, the Court of Appeal was concerned about the extent to which the overriding pressures of national targets and the deployment of waiting lists as a driver for efficiency at every level in the NHS can leave room for the kind of transparency and patient-centred concerns that are required when considering authorisation for elective treatment abroad under Article 49 EC Treaty, even in cases that are not 'life and death'. It has now been confirmed by the ECJ that in cases in which patients do seek authorisation for treatment abroad, much greater transparency and patient-centred decision-making processes are required than were previously considered possible or necessary within the NHS, and furthermore, in those cases, reviewing courts will have a much more active role in deciding whether refusal or delay is justified.[116]

III. LOCAL AUTHORITY RESOURCE ALLOCATION DISPUTES

In cases involving breach of local authority statutory duties, UK courts have been no less conscious than in *Re B*,[117] that to insist on provision of services in particular cases would affect the claims of others. Throughout the 1980s the courts were therefore extremely reluctant to interpret public authority obligations as absolute, in the sense that they could give rise to mandatory obligations to provide socio-economic entitlements. Typically, for example, in *R v Inner London Education Authority, ex parte Ali and Murshid* (hereafter *Ali and*

---

[116] See generally T Hervey, 'Mapping the Contours of European Health Law and Policy' (2002) 8 *European Public Law* 69.

[117] Note 58 above.

Murshid),[118] a renowned challenge against the failure of the Borough of Tower Hamlets to provide 'sufficient'[119] primary school places for children, Lord Woolf refused to accept that there was an overriding obligation on the authority to place children in schools irrespective of resources available for that purpose.[120]

Even when legislation had been framed in terms of apparent mandatory obligations to deliver services irrespective of resources (as was the case under section 2(1) of the Chronically Sick and Disabled Persons Act (CSDPA) 1970), there was an overriding presumption that resources were a factor to be taken into account, unless Parliament had made explicit references to the contrary. Thus, prior to the leading House of Lords decision in *R v Gloucester County Council, ex parte Barry* (hereafter *Gloucester*)[121] it was assumed that courts would be unlikely to enforce even explicit mandatory obligations in the community care field, 'if lack of resources was the sole reason for non-assessment or non provision'.[122]

The challenge in *Gloucester* concerned the needs of an elderly immobile man whose laundry and cleaning services had been withdrawn on grounds that the local authority did not have sufficient resources to meet his needs.[123] The primary issue was whether a local authority could take its own resources (or lack thereof) into account in determining whether to meet the needs of the disabled under section 2(1) CSDPA. Enacted at the high-water period in the delivery of welfare services in 1970, section 2(1) purports to create legally enforceable rights

---

[118] [1990] 2 All ER 822. The challenge concerned the failure of the Borough of Tower Hamlets to provide sufficient places for children of school age, as a result of which they remained at home. Lord Woolf refused to accept an overriding obligation on the authority to place children in schools irrespective of available resources. The duty of the Secretary of State was a 'target' duty and did not give rise to a right to sue for private law damages.

[119] See P Cane, *An Introduction to Administrative Law*, 3rd edn (Oxford, Oxford University Press, 1996) for analysis of the ambit of discretion in the 'sufficient' schools provision. Cane distinguishes between the core duty, a fundamental breach of which is justiciable, and the discretionary penumbra, where courts have left the exercise of discretion to the authority alone in such politically and morally contentious areas. This approach has since been applied in the context of special needs provision and in the area of general higher education.

[120] *Ali and Murshid* (note 118 above). The challenge arose under ss 68 and 69 Education Act 1944. It was held by Lord Woolf before the Divisional Court that (i) the duty of the Secretary of State to provide 'sufficient' schools could not give rise to legally enforceable rights in private law; and (ii) the duty that enured not for individual children, but rather for the benefit of the general public, was a 'target duty' owed to the public at large. In *R v London Borough of Islington, ex parte Rixon* [1997] ELR 66, Sedley J described the target duty as a 'metaphor' that recognises that 'the statute requires the authority to aim to make the provision but does not regard failure to achieve it without more as a breach' (69 D).

[121] [1997] 2 All ER 1.

[122] B Schwehr, 'The Legal Relevance of Resources' (1995) 17(2) *Journal of Social Welfare and Family Law* 181. For a discussion of the issues raised by cases such as *Gloucester*, see Palmer and Sunkin (note 21 above).

[123] Following substantial cuts in central government funding, disadvantaged local authorities had withdrawn services to individuals already assessed as eligible to receive them. The Gloucestershire case was one of a series of test cases supported by the Public Law Project.

for the disabled to receive a wide range of specific and general services in accordance with their individually assessed needs.[124]

However, despite the apparent mandatory force of section 2(1) CSDPA, the House of Lords in *Gloucester* concluded that the local authority could take its own resources into account, both in the primary assessment of needs and subsequently in deciding whether it was necessary to make arrangements to meet the needs of a disabled person. Any other conclusion, it was claimed, would render the authority liable to open-ended budgetary commitment. However, there was one caveat: it was held that once a local authority deems it necessary to make arrangements to meet the needs of the disabled under section 2(1) CSDPA, 'the duty is owed to the disabled person absolutely' and can give rise to legally enforceable individual rights to sue for private law damages. Services could not be withdrawn without a reassessment.[125]

However, a very different result was reached by the House of Lords in *R v East Sussex County Council, ex parte Tandy* (hereafter *Tandy*).[126] That case concerned the special educational needs of a sick child who had been unable to attend school for seven years and was living in an area where the local authority had introduced a blanket policy by which home tuition for children in the claimant's category of need had been reduced from five to three hours weekly. The issue was whether the Council could take its own resources into account in making an assessment of what constitutes a 'suitable education'.

It is clear that despite the very different policy backgrounds of section 2(1) CSDPA and section 298 Education Act 1993, the challenges in *Tandy* and *Gloucester* both revolved around parallel debates concerning textual analysis of discretionary statutory duties and the collateral issues of social justice. Under both legislative provisions, requirements for services were to be met by local authorities on the basis of assessments of claimants' needs. In both challenges, the crucial question was whether an absolute mandatory duty owed to an individual claimant could give rise to a corresponding right to have assessed needs met irrespective of resources. However, by contrast with section 2(1) CSDPA, where the purported needs of claimants were defined in terms of an impracticably wide range of specific services, under section 298 of the 1993 Act, claimants'

---

[124] It is clear from the history of the Act that those responsible for its drafting believed that they had successfully created legally enforceable rights for the disabled.

[125] In light of the conclusion in *Gloucester* that in one sense 'there could never be an unmet need', local authorities across the country began to renege on other community care duties on grounds of lack of resources. In *ex parte Help the Aged and Blanchard* (note 3 above), Help the Aged challenged the refusal by Sefton Borough Council to pay for residential accommodation for an elderly member of the Borough in accordance with nationally applicable regulations. The Court of Appeal reluctantly accepted that in light of the elasticity imported into the concept of need by the House of Lords in *Gloucester*, the local authority could take its own resources into account both in making an assessment of applicant's need for residential care under s 21 National Act 1948 and in deciding whether it would be necessary to make arrangements to meet the need. However, it was concluded that once an authority had acknowledged the necessity of such arrangements, it could not thereafter refuse to meet its obligations to fund the applicant's future care in a lawful manner.

[126] [1998] 2 All ER 770.

requirements were expressed in terms of a 'suitable education'. An evaluation of 'suitability' was to be carried out by an authority in accordance with objectively defined criteria: efficiency, suitability to a child's 'age, ability and aptitude' and to any special educational needs he or she may have.

In contrast with *Gloucester*, an entirely differently constituted House of Lords in *Tandy* refused to 'downgrade duties to discretions over which courts could have very little real control'.[127] They therefore unanimously interpreted section 298 of the Education Act as giving rise to an absolute mandatory obligation to deliver home tuition services in accordance with such individual factors as the child's 'age, ability and any special needs'. Thus, despite the resource-led policy background against which section 298 had been enacted, resources were deemed to be irrelevant. Lord Browne Wilkinson insisted that the decision was based entirely on the interpretation of the statutory language of section 298, which he claimed to be very different from the impracticable drafting of section 2(1) CSDPA.[128]

Although the decision in *Tandy* responded in a positive way to the individual needs of a vulnerable child, the result, it should be noted, was not reached by a fundamental rights approach of the kind advocated by Laws J in *Re B*.[129] Instead, the unpredictable conclusion that on this occasion a mandatory duty should be imposed on the authority had been reached through the formal rules of statutory construction and close textual analysis of the relevant statutory provisions in accordance with the presumed intention of Parliament. Moreover, it is also notable that, by contrast with *Gloucester*, the financial impact of the House of Lord decision in *Tandy* was likely to be negligible, since only two other children had been similarly affected by the local authority policy. That did not, however, prevent the reasoning in *Tandy* from being precisely followed by lower courts, even in contexts that potentially had much greater financial implications for local authorities.[130]

Thus, following *Tandy*, the Court of Appeal in *R v Borough of Kensington and Chelsea, ex parte Kujtim*[131] interpreted section 21 of the National Assistance Act 1948 so as to conclude that the authority had a continuing duty, as opposed to a discretion, to provide shelter for an asylum seeker who was

---

[127] *Tandy* (*ibid*) 777 D–E (Lord Browne Wilkinson).

[128] *Ibid*, 776 A–H.

[129] Lord Browne Wilkinson expressly approved the decision in *Re B*.

[130] See for example *R v Birmingham City Council, ex parte Mohammed* [1998] 4 All ER 101, in which the Divisional Court interpreted s 23 Housing Grants and Construction Regeneration Act (HGCRA) 1996 in accordance with a mandatory duty to provide housing adaptations in accordance with the assessed needs of a disabled applicant, irrespective of resources available to the authority for that purpose. It was held by Dyson J that, by contrast with s 2(1) CSDPA 1970, there was no room for a subjective assessment to be made by an authority in deciding whether to approve a grant to the disabled for the purpose of adaptations 'necessary' and 'appropriate' for their needs. An authority must decide 'objectively' whether the purpose of the grant fell within the list of adaptations contained in s 23, having regard to the 'nature of the applicant's needs'.

[131] (1999) WL 478029, [1999] 4 All ER 161. The applicant, a Kosovan asylum seeker who was suffering from a depressive illness induced by stress, was evicted twice from temporary bed-and-breakfast accommodation as a consequence of extremely antisocial behaviour.

assessed as being 'in urgent need of care and attention'.[132] The recognition in *Kujtim* that such an absolute mandatory duty allowed the aggrieved claimant to 'seek or obtain by judicial review, an order requiring the local authority to perform its duty or a declaration to that effect' was followed in other post-*Tandy* decisions. For example, in *R v Wigan MBC, ex parte Tammadge*[133] the Divisional Court concluded that when an authority was in breach of statutory duty by refusing to provide larger accommodation for a very vulnerable family in accordance with their assessed needs, the court could issue mandatory orders not only to identify suitable housing within three months of the order, but also to make it available within a further three months. Furthermore, in *R (on the Application of Mukoko Batantu) v London Borough of Islington* (hereafter *Batantu*),[134] the Court (in light of *Kujtim*) held that once the local authority had concluded under section 21 National Assistance Act (NAA) 1948 that the applicant had specific needs that were not met by 'the accommodation otherwise available to him', the local authority was under a duty to provide accommodation so as to meet his lawfully assessed needs.

In light of these successes, it is not surprising that strategic campaigning lawyers have continued after the HRA to seek access to local authority welfare services or a reduction or the waiving of financial contributions from claimants, through the statutory-based paradigm of judicial review. However, an examination of local authority resource allocation disputes in which courts have been called upon to interpret the scope of local authority discretionary duties demonstrates the extent to which courts continue to steer an uncertain course between willingness to challenge the failures of government and local authorities on one hand and concerns to minimise the funding predicaments of local authorities on the other. A range of extraneous factors have influenced their conclusions: context sensitivity, reprehensible conduct on the part of authorities, the possibility of making a rugged cost benefit analysis of the impact of a decision, or the likelihood of flood gates being opened.[135] Moreover, a review of challenges founded on breach of local authority statutory duties since the HRA shows the continuing reluctance of courts to exercise their novel powers of review under section 3 HRA in accordance with fundamental rights in the ECHR, with the purpose of reminding government of their domestic and international commitments to the meeting of elementary welfare needs.

---

[132] S 21 CA requires local authorities to make arrangements to provide residential accommodation for 'persons aged 18 or over who by reason of age, illness, disability or any other circumstances are in need of care and attention which is not otherwise available to them . . .'

[133] [1998] 1 CCLR 581.

[134] [2000] WL 1741. The applicant had severe mental health problems. Assessments of his community care needs and those of his wife and four children had concluded that Batantu required larger, ground floor accommodation. However, waiting lists were such that three months later, suitable accommodation had still not been provided. In response to the applicant's argument that Islington had failed to comply with its duty under s 21 NAA 1948, Islington argued that they were entitled to take into account lack of resources when deciding how to meet his accommodation needs.

[135] See generally E Palmer, 'Resource Allocation, Welfare Rights: Mapping the Boundaries of Judicial Restraint in Public Administrative Law' (2000) 20 *Oxford Journal of Legal Studies* 63.

IV. INTERPRETING LOCAL AUTHORITY STATUTORY DUTIES POST-HRA

A. Section 17 Children Act 1989: Accommodating Children and their Families

In a series of challenges mounted after the HRA,[136] which culminated with the House of Lords decision in *G*,[137] applicants questioned whether the assessment process that lies at the heart of the Children Act 1989 can provide a trigger for the creation of mandatory duties to provide services for children 'in need' under section 17 CA.[138] Although the primary purpose of these challenges was to test the scope of local authority duties to provide accommodation for children and their parents under section 17 CA,[139] Article 8 ECHR issues were also clearly implicated in the cases. The series of cases therefore provides a focus, not only to consider the limitations of the ultra vires approach to the interpretation of local authority statutory duties, but also for debate about the use of section 3 HRA to interpret section 17 CA compatibly with the right to respect for private and family life in Article 8 ECHR.

As discussed in section II-A above, at the heart of housing legislation lies a system of prioritisation that reflects a stark reality: demand for social housing far outstrips supply, and even for the most pressing cases in the queue, there may be little prospect of success.[140] Moreover, some persons are excluded altogether from the housing queue. Intentionally homeless people and illegal immigrants who are not asylum seekers therefore have no claims under housing legislation.[141]

Notwithstanding, social services departments with obligations under Part III CA to provide welfare for children in their areas have in extreme cases adopted

---

[136] *A v Lambeth LBC* (2002) 4 CCLR 487; *W v Lambeth LBC* [2002] 2 ALL ER 901; *R (on the Application of G) v Barnet LBC* (2001) 4 CCLR 33; *R (on the Application of J (Ghanaian Citizen)) v Enfield LBC* (hereafter *Enfield*) [2002] EWHC 432, [2002] All ER (D) 209 Mar.

[137] Note 4 above.

[138] S 17(1) CA states it shall be the general duty of every local authority '(a) to safeguard and promote the welfare of children in their area who are in need; and (b) so far as is consistent with that duty, to promote the upbringing of such children by their families by providing a range of services suitable to those children's needs'.

[139] See note 5 above.

[140] See Part VI of HA 1996, precursor to the Homelessness Act 2002, the cross-heading of which is 'Allocation of Housing Accommodation'. S 167(1) provided that every local housing authority shall have a scheme ('allocation scheme') for determining priorities.

[141] S 161(1) Part VI Housing Act 1996 Part VI, the heading of which is 'Allocation of Housing Accomodation', states that every local housing authority shall have a scheme ('allocation scheme') for determining priorities. S 161(1) provided that local housing authorities shall allocate housing accommodation only to persons who are qualified to be allocated housing by that authority ('qualifying persons'). The Homelessness Act 2002, which amends rather than replaces the 1996 Act, also requires local authorities to allocate housing to 'eligible' persons and to have in place an allocation scheme. See Section II-A above. For a critique of changes to the system of housing allocation introduced by the Homelessness Act 2002, see E Laurie, 'The Homelessness Act 2002 and Housing Allocation: All Change or Business as Usual? (2004) 67 *Modern Law Review* 48.

a practice of funding or providing accommodation for vulnerable families who have been accorded low priority or have no legitimate place in the housing queue. Families who are intentionally homeless and those who have stayed beyond the dates on their visas have fallen into that category. However, the numbers of such families are growing, and disadvantaged authorities claim that they are unable to find the resources to meet spiralling demands.[142] When local authorities have had delays in meeting the assessed needs of children for transfers to suitable housing, or have refused to provide accommodation for families alongside their children, applicants have sought to enforce local authority obligations in judicial review proceedings.

A v Lambeth[143] demonstrated the acuteness of the housing crisis in Lambeth. Despite the fact that Ms A was a single parent living in 'appalling conditions' with three children under the age of 8, two of whom were autistic and severely disruptive, she was no higher than Category D (the 'mainstream category') on Lambeth's housing list.[144] Therefore, following an assessment by social services, which recorded the acuteness of the family's need to be transferred to a flat with garden space, the applicant sought to enforce the local authority duty to transfer her to accommodation suitable to her children's needs.[145]

On appeal from the decision of Scott Baker J at first instance,[146] the Court of Appeal in *A v Lambeth*[147] denied that section 17(1) CA imposes an absolute mandatory duty on local authorities to meet the specific needs of individual children following assessments, emphasising, however, that action or inaction of social services departments could be susceptible to judicial review on normal principles. The Court expressed serious concerns that if applicants like the present one should seek to jump the housing queue by the proposed route, the housing prioritisation scheme would turn into chaos. Exercised by that concern, the majority of the Court of Appeal in *A v Lambeth* (Laws LJ dissenting) decided that contrary to general belief, local authorities do not have any power under section 17 CA to assist families with their housing needs. It was held that the only accommodation duties in the Children Act 1989 are those owed to

---

[142] See the Report in *W v Lambeth* (note 155 below) 933, para 124 ('Appendix 3: Lambeth, Its Financial Difficulties and Competing Pressures'). The Appendix, which is based on evidence contained in witness statements by a former manager in the Lambeth housing department, was included by the Court of Appeal to highlight contemporary pressures on the families and children division of its social services department.

[143] Note 136 above.

[144] The Lambeth allocation scheme had seven categories. Category A related to tenants under the 'right to return' scheme; Category B covered emergencies referred by the council's housing panel; Category C related to transfers with 'some urgency', including the need for major repairs; Category D, in which the applicant had been placed, was the 'mainstream tenant category'; Category E related to homeless applications; Category related F to referrals, including social services and environmental health referrals; and Category G related to incoming nominations.

[145] Part III CA 1989 deals with services to children 'in need' and their families.

[146] Note 136 above.

[147] [2001] EWCA Civ 1624.

children separately from their parents under section 20 CA.[148] Along these lines, Chadwick LJ stated:

> In my view it would be an extraordinary result and one which in the absence of clear words I cannot hold to reflect the intention of Parliament—if the carefully structured provisions of the housing legislation, which are plainly intended to provide a fair allocation of resources among those with housing needs, were to be overridden, in specific cases, by section 17(1) of the CA.[149]

The Court of Appeal in the earlier case of *R (on the Application of G) v Barnet LBC*[150] had merely doubted whether it could ever be *practicable* for local authorities to accommodate parents with their children under section 17. In that case, a Dutch mother with a young child and no means of support refused the local authority's offer to meet her needs by funding her return to Holland, where she would have access to benefits. The council said that if she refused this offer then accommodation would be provided for the child alone under s 20 CA.[151] However, following the Court of Appeal decision in *A v Lambeth*, local authorities seemed to have no choice but to accommodate the children of visa over-stayers and intentionally homeless persons separately from their families. Therefore, since it was clear from ECHR jurisprudence that splitting families could amount to breach of Article 8 ECHR, collateral challenges followed. *R (on the Application of J (Ghanaian Citizen)) v Enfield LBC* (hereafter *Enfield*)[152] was a case in point.

In *Enfield* the applicant, the mother of a two-year-old daughter, had come from Ghana in 1995 and stayed beyond the period for which she was allowed to remain on her visa. Although HIV positive and about to be made homeless, she was, as an over-stayer, entitled neither to be placed on the housing queue nor to be accommodated under the Immigration and Asylum Act 1999. She therefore sought financial assistance towards accommodation from the social services department, which refused to help.

In the Divisional Court, Elias J concluded that in light of the earlier Court of Appeal decision in *A v Lambeth*,[153] the council had no power to fund or to provide accommodation for the applicant and her daughter under section 17 CA. However, it was acknowledged by all the parties, consistent with ECHR

---

[148] S 20 imposes a duty on the local authority to provide accommodation to children when there is no one else to care for them. S 20(1) stipulates that 'every local authority shall provide accommodation for any child in need within their area who appears to require accommodation as a result of . . . (c) the person who has been caring for him being prevented . . . from providing him with suitable accommodation and care'.

[149] *A v Lambeth* (note 147 above) 510A.

[150] [2001] EWCA Civ 540.

[151] S 20 CA 1989 provides: 'Every local authority shall provide accommodation for any child in need within their area who appears to them to require accommodation as a result of—(a) there being no person who has parental responsibility for him; (b) his being lost or having been abandoned; or (c) the person who has been caring for him being prevented (whether or not permanently, and for whatever reason) from providing him with suitable accommodation or care.'

[152] Note 136 above.

[153] Note 147 above.

jurisprudence, that the separation of mother and child would constitute a breach of Article 8 ECHR. The judge therefore decided that in light of the greater expense involved in accommodating a child without her mother, the local authority decision could not be justified in accordance with Article 8(2) ECHR. He therefore concluded that he had power under section 3 HRA to read and give effect to section 17 CA compatibly with Article 8 ECHR.

Notwithstanding this acknowledged power, Elias J preferred a different approach. Instead, he accepted the idiosyncratic argument of the Department of Health that section 2 of the Local Government Act (LGA) 2000 affords an overriding discretion to local authorities to provide financial assistance towards accommodation for families, thereby allowing them to bypass housing legislation.[154] By this evasion, there would be no need to read and give effect to section 17 CA compatibly with the Convention or invite senior courts to make what he regarded as an inevitable declaration of incompatibility under section 4 HRA.

In *W v Lambeth LBC, ex parte W*[155] the Court of Appeal had the opportunity to revisit both *Enfield* and the Court of Appeal Decision in *A v Lambeth*. The challenge concerned an intentionally homeless mother of two children, aged 4 and 15, who was living with them in cramped accommodation with her extended family. The local authority's refusal to provide funding for accommodation was endorsed by the trial judge. However, in light of *Enfield*, leave was given for the Court of Appeal in *W v Lambeth* to review the earlier Court of Appeal decision in *A v Lambeth*.

The Court of Appeal in *W v Lambeth* was in no doubt as to the correctness of the denial in *A v Lambeth* that section 17 CA gives rise to a legally enforceable duty to meet the assessed needs of claimants. Nevertheless, the Court overruled that part of the *A v Lambeth* decision that denied that the local authority had *any* power to fund or provide accommodation under section 17 CA, concluding that the earlier decision had been per incuriam.[156] Moreover, although it was accepted that Article 8 ECHR was engaged, Brooke LJ, who gave the single judgement of the Court, concluded that 'Article 8(1) rights of the applicant and her children did not affect the position'.[157]

Thus, without recourse to either section 2 LGA or section 3 HRA, the social services safety net was restored by the decision in *W v Lambeth*, in the limited form of a 'target duty', as identified by Lord Woolf in *Ali and Murshid*.[158] This would clearly relieve local authorities of the duty to meet the assessed needs of

---

[154] S 2(1) LGA 2000 is a widely framed provision concerning local authority financial powers to 'promote or improve' economic, social and environmental well-being in their localities.

[155] [2002] EWCA Civ 613, [2002] 2 All ER 901.

[156] The statutory provisions that the court in *A v Lambeth* had not had presented to it were s 122 Immigration and Asylum Act (IAA) 1999, s 17A Children Act 1989 (inserted by the Carers and Disabled Persons Act 2000) and, to a lesser extent, s 22 Housing Act 1985. Although the Court did not reject the idiosyncratic interpretation of s 2 Local Government Act (LGA) that was favoured by Elias J in *Enfield*, given their re-interpretation of s 17, there was no need to consider s 2 LGA.

[157] *W v Lambeth* (note 155 above) 85.

[158] Note 118 above.

claimants if resources did not permit. Nevertheless, the Court went on to examine the manner in which the local authority had exercised its power, concluding that Lambeth LBC had given adequate reasons for its refusal. Subsequently, observing that there were no exceptional circumstances in Ms W's case, the Court stated that if the local authority provided accommodation for that family, they would be obliged to provide accommodation for all intentionally homeless families, thereby diverting resources from others.[159]

It is clear that the prevailing concern of the Court of Appeal throughout these disputes was that the provision of accommodation for children and their families under Part III CA should not be allowed to undermine established housing schemes and that local authority discretion should be appropriately structured by reference to existing housing legislation. The Court also showed concern that local authorities should not be in breach of their HRA obligations. However, a more questionable concern, which recurred throughout the cases, was that the courts should not overstretch the resources of the local authorities involved. Thus, Ward LJ stated in the Court of Appeal decision of *R (on the Application of G) v Barnet LBC*:[160]

> [L]ocal authorities are seriously concerned as to how they can afford to meet this kind of demand as well as the multitude of other calls upon their Social Services Departments. Whatever the rights and wrongs of their predicament, experience in the Family Division and in this court supports the view that they never have enough money to do what they want to do and frequently say that they do not have enough money even to do what they have to do. The appellant, the London Borough of Barnet, is reconciled to meeting its lawful obligations, but it invites the Court to limit them.[161]

The request for courts to sympathise with the funding predicaments of local authorities in interpreting the scope of their statutory duties demonstrates the uncertainty surrounding the role of courts in these types of disputes in the United Kingdom. There has furthermore been a lack of transparency in the range of considerations that may have influenced their rulings—for example, in *Tandy*,[162] where the House of Lords considered the education needs of a very sick child. Authorities therefore have no way of knowing whether, in sensitive contexts such as that of the disabled children in *A v Lambeth*, courts might be prepared to accept that unlimited discretion of the kind implicit in *Ali and Murshid* should give way to a more potent form of two step structured obligation of the kind found in *Tammadge*[163] and *Batantu*.[164] However, since it is well

---

[159] Since the Court of Appeal decision in *W v Lambeth*, s 17 CA has been amended in the Adoption and Children Act 2003 so as to include the provision of accommodation (hitherto provided under s 20 CA) to children 'in need'.

[160] Note 150 above.

[161] *R (on the Application of G) v Barnet LBC* (note 150 above) para 1.

[162] Note 126 above.

[163] Note 133 above.

[164] Note 134 above. Notably, in *Tandy* (note 126 above), very few children were affected by the ruling, and the local authority had behaved in a confrontational manner by introducing a blanket policy by which it withdrew home tuition services on grounds of resources.

known that local authorities, rather than the central government, are likely to bear the financial brunt of these decisions, there is growing confidence among defendants, as demonstrated by this series of welfare needs cases, that courts will primarily respond to the funding predicaments of local authorities in determining the scope of local authority statutory duties.

B. Orthodoxy Reasserted: The Retreat from Kujtim?

Relying on the general duty in section 17 CA, applicants before three differently constituted Courts of Appeal (in *A v Lambeth*;[165] *W v Lambeth*;[166] and *G v Barnet*[167]) had argued unsuccessfully that section 17 CA gave rise to a mandatory duty to meet their accommodation needs.[168] However, only in *A v Lambeth* was it specifically argued that (following *Kujtim*,[169] which was in relation to adult services) the assessment process that lies at the heart of the Children Act 1989 could provide a trigger for the creation of mandatory duties to provide services for children 'in need' under section 17. The argument ran as follows. Although the duty in section 17(1) CA has been explicitly described as a general duty to provide a range of services to 'children in need', once an assessment has taken place, the duty 'crystallises' into a duty to meet their specific individual needs, enforceable by way of judicial review. Thus, the mother in *A v Lambeth* claimed that if section 17(1) were interpreted like section 21 NAA 1948 (in relation to adults suffering from disability), once the *general* duty to assess her children's needs had taken place, the local authority had a *specific* duty to provide for the residential services identified by those assessments. In other words, the applicant claimed that section 17 CA gives rise to a duty that was parallel to that found in s 21 NAA, which had been interpreted by Potter LJ in *Kujtim* as a mandatory duty to meet the assessed needs of adult claimants who are in need of 'care and attention not otherwise available to them'.[170]

However, Laws LJ regarded section 17 CA as no more than a target duty of the kind identified by Lord Woolf in *Ali and Murshid*.[171] Although he agreed that there are structured provisions allowing for a two-stage process of the kind for which the applicant contended, he refused to accept that section 17 CA gave rise to a two-step duty, or to accept the practicability of what he regarded as an

[165] Note 147 above.
[166] Note 155 above.
[167] Note 150 above.
[168] For the general duty in section 17 CA, see note 138 above.
[169] Note 131 above.
[170] See s 21(1)(a) NAA. The Court of Appeal was reminded that such an approach had led to the issue of mandatory orders in *Tammadge* (note 133 above) and *Batantu* (note 134 above), requiring social services departments to identify suitable housing within three months and to make the accommodation available within a further three months for adult disabled claimants assessed as being in urgent need of accommodation under s 21 National Assistance Act (NAA) 1948.
[171] Note 118 above.

entirely inflexible interpretation of section 17 CA—which would not only impose unmanageable burdens on authorities but also cause havoc in the established housing scheme.

It is true that there are irrefutable distinctions between the language and the structures of section 17 CA and section 21 NAA. For example, the very purpose of assessment for section 21 NAA services is to identify certain classes of vulnerable persons who are in urgent need. Also, in section 21 NAA emphasis was placed on the duty to provide adult services in accordance with Directions of the Secretary of the State. By contrast, in the drafting of section 17 CA, no specific link was drawn between the urgent character of specific services and the mandatory force of the duty to provide.

However, there is a convincing argument that the principle of assessment as a gateway to provision is the same for adult and children's services. Section 47(1) of the National Health Service and Community Care Act (NHSCCA) 1990 establishes a trigger for the enforcement of local authority duties to deliver a wide range of community care services, including section 21 NAA services, so far as is practicable and within the limits of available resources. Likewise, the assessment process in the CA provides a trigger for the enforcement of a range of general and specific welfare services for children in need. To assist local authorities in this regard, a very detailed assessment and care plan regime was produced as guidance by the Department of Health, entitled 'Framework for Assessment of Children and their Families'.[172]

Nevertheless, Laws LJ, who gave the leading judgment on this point, concluded that Parliament had taken a different view of assessments in respect of different local authority functions. There could therefore be no uniform answer regarding the extent to which assessments can trigger mandatory duties to meet the individual needs of claimants in respect of different statutory provisions. The applicants therefore appealed to the House of Lords, where *A v Lambeth* became one of three conjoined appeals in *G* concerning the scope of 17 CA.[173]

In *G* the House of Lords accepted that Article 8 ECHR was implicated in the cases. However, in relation to the arguments in *A v Lambeth*, the House of Lords reverted to the pre-*Tandy* approach to the interpretation of local authority statutory duties, holding by a majority (Lords Nicholls and Steyn dissenting) that section 17(1) CA sets out duties of a general nature, which were not

---

[172] The 'Framework for the Assessment of Children and their Families' was published by the Department of Health in 2000. It purports to provide 'a systematic way of analysing, understanding and recording what is happening to children and young people within their families and the wider context of the community in which they live'. It takes account of relevant legislation at the time of publication but is particularly informed by the requirements of the Children Act 1989, which provides a comprehensive framework for the care and protection of children. Although there is no statutory scheme to establish priorities under s 17 CA 1989 (cf s 2(1) CSDPA), as a matter of good practice, local authorities establish eligibility criteria, including risk factors such as physical danger and deteriorating health of disabled children, which allow them to provide for needs recorded as urgent by assessments.

[173] Note 4 above.

intended to be enforceable at the suit of individual claimants. Thus, as in *Ali and Murshid*,[174] it was concluded in *G* that the duty in section 17 CA was no more than a target duty, directed at all children in need within the area of the local social services authority, and not to each child 'in need'.

In reaching this conclusion, the majority in *G* were unmoved by the argument that affording such a flexible interpretation to the public authority duty would be tantamount to denying that there was any duty at all. Instead, like the Court of Appeal in *W v Lambeth*,[175] the majority in the House of Lords was more concerned about both the possible financial burdens of providing accommodation for all the children in need of accommodation in the Borough and the disruption of the statutory housing prioritisation scheme that would inevitably follow. Thus, despite the apparent inhumanity of a ruling that appeared to condone indefinite delay in meeting the needs of disabled children (and their mother), judicial determination not to interfere with the housing prioritisation scheme prevailed.

However, whereas in *A v Lambeth* the mother had been seeking a *transfer* to suitable accommodation in accordance with section 17 CA, in *W v Lambeth* and *G v Barnet*, the mothers were homeless and seeking to be housed along with their children in accordance with section 17 CA. Thus, it was clear that the issues in the latter two cases more clearly engaged Article 8 ECHR. Particularly in *G v Barnet*, where the child was fourteen months old, there were questions about whether the possibility of accommodating the baby apart from her mother (or even a threat to accommodate the mother and child separately), although satisfying the duty in section 20 CA, constituted a breach of Article 8.[176] However, the House of Lords paid scant attention to the relevance of Article 8 in either *G v Barnet* or *W v Lambeth*. Instead, the majority in *G* concluded that to arrange accommodation for the children alone would satisfy the local authority duty under section 20 CA, without having recourse to section 17 CA or to Article 8 ECHR. However, Lord Nicholls (dissenting), with whom Lord Steyn agreed, considered that in relation to section 20 CA, each case must be decided on its own facts and that a balanced view must be taken.

> Matters stand differently where the child is not old enough to understand what is going on, or if he is, he would be likely to be significantly upset at being separated from his parent. Providing accommodation for the child alone may satisfy the authority's duty under s 20 of the 1989 Act. But in this type of case the child's immediate need is for accommodation with his parent. This is a basic need. It is difficult to see how the local authority can be said to fulfil its duty under s 17(1) of the 1989 Act by accom-

[174] Note 118 above. The House of Lords refused to accept comparisons with s 298 Education Act 1993 (interpreted in *Tandy* as giving rise to a mandatory duty); or to countenance the argument that the target duty in s 17 CA crystallised into a mandatory duty once the assessment had taken place, as in *Kujtim* (note 131 above).

[175] Note 155 above.

[176] In *W v Lambeth* the children were aged 4 and 15, and the local authority proposed to arrange temporary accommodation for them with their extended family until their intentionally homeless mother could find alternative accommodation.

modating the child alone in such circumstances. It cannot be reasonable in this type of case to give greater weight to the wider financial repercussions than to the adverse consequences to the individual child in the particular case.[177]

Notably, in relation to the 'appalling' circumstances of the family in *A v Lambeth*, no attempt was made to argue that the Council was in breach of a positive duty to provide for the accommodation needs of vulnerable individuals suffering from disabilities under Article 8 ECHR.[178] Indeed, in the Court of Appeal, Laws LJ had pronounced:

> However vigorous the judicial review jurisdiction, we have to bear in mind that from first to last this case is about the construction of a statute, conditioned, certainly, by the Human Rights Act 1998 if a *true* Convention point arises, but yet no more nor less than the construction of the Act.[179]

However, shortly before the Court of Appeal decision in *A v Lambeth*, in a closely reasoned judgment in *Bernard and Another v Enfield LBC* (hereafter *Bernard*)[180] (which was later endorsed by Lord Woolf in the leading test case of *Anufrijeva*[181]), Sullivan J, after careful scrutiny of the public authority conduct, concluded that abject failure to provide for the needs of a severely disabled adult within a reasonable period of her assessments constituted a breach of Article 8 ECHR: the authority had a duty to provide assistance so that she could maintain her physical and psychological integrity.[182]

C. Positive Obligations to Protect the Vulnerable: The Approach in *Bernard*

In *Bernard*,[183] the second applicant, an adult who was severely disabled following a stroke, suffered from a range of infirmities that left her confined to a wheelchair and wholly dependent on others for her personal care, hygiene and feeding. She was cared for by her husband, the first claimant, who also looked after their six children, who ranged in age from 3 to 20. Unable to meet

---

[177] G (note 4 above) para 55.
[178] The argument that there was a breach of Arts 8 and 14 taken together was raised and peremptorily dismissed by Laws LJ in the Court of Appeal in *A v Lambeth* (note 147 above).
[179] *Ibid*, para 22 (emphasis added).
[180] [2002] EWHC 2282, [2003] HRLR 4. In chapter 3 it was noted that the case first received publicity because it was the first in which damages were awarded for breach of a public law duty under the HRA.
[181] [2004] 1 All ER 833.
[182] It is not at all clear why, in light of the opinions of the Court in *Botta v Italy* [1998] 26 EHRR 241 and *Marzari v Italy* (1999) 28 EHRR CD 175, the question as to whether a true Convention point had arisen in *A v Lambeth* was so lightly dismissed; or why no effort was made by counsel to argue that a Convention-compatible way should be found to read a statutory provision that, on its conventional reading, otherwise condoned indefinite delay or outright failure to meet the assessed needs of two extremely vulnerable children and their mother within a reasonable period of time, when serious dangers to their physical and psychological well-being had been recorded by their assessments.
[183] Note 180 above.

the mortgage payments on their owner-occupied home in Enfield, which had been adapted to suit her specific disabilities at considerable expense by Social Services, the family sold their home and moved to un-adapted rented accommodation in the London Borough of Haringey. Following a protracted dispute thereafter as to whether Haringey or Enfield had responsibility for their housing needs, the family was temporarily accommodated by Enfield Housing Department, pending inquiries, which culminated in a decision that they were intentionally homeless. However, following a protest by their solicitor against their impending eviction, Haringey Social Services Department capitulated to the extent of undertaking a number of assessments of the claimants' needs while at their temporary home.

The Haringey assessments catalogued the severely debilitating nature of the second applicant's infirmities and the resulting indignities suffered by her. They also emphasised the unsuitability and hazardous nature of the temporary housing, where she had been confined to a single living space without access to the front door, toilet or other living areas shared by her family. The Social Services Department therefore recommended an urgent request to the Housing Department for a report on the availability of a suitably adapted property, with assistance for the family to be removed to accommodation in which the applicant would be able to resume a level of independence and her care needs would be safely met.

However, despite repeated legal representations highlighting the urgency of the applicant's predicament, not only did it remain unclear whether Haringey Council had accepted responsibility for her needs, more than two years after their assessments, the claimants were still living in the same sorry circumstances, without even their most basic community care needs being met. Therefore, during a protracted legal dispute in which the Haringey Council finally admitted that they were under a statutory duty to house the claimants, leave was given for judicial review.

Following the reasoning in *Kujtim*[184] and *Batantu*,[185] Sullivan J accepted that the local authority had been in breach of its duty under section 21(1)(a) of the National Assistance Act 1948 and issued a mandatory order to make provision of suitably adapted accommodation for the claimant within a reasonable period of time; he also allowed damages for breach of statutory duty under section 8(1) HRA.[186]

The applicants had argued that the defendant's conduct constituted breaches of Articles 3 and 8 ECHR. However, when considering whether there had been a breach of Article 3, although accepting that the conditions in which the

---

[184] Note 131 above.

[185] Note 134 above.

[186] As in *Tammadge* (note 133 above), not only was the authority bound to identify an appropriate property; three months thereafter it must be adapted to meet the second claimant's needs. Moreover, if those timescales could not be met for any reason, Sullivan J required the defendant to agree to an extended period with the claimants or apply to the court for an extension.

claimants had been forced to live for 20 months could be described as degrading, particularly in view of the consequences of the second claimant's incontinence, Sullivan J was not persuaded that the 'minimum level of the severity threshold' in Article 3 had been crossed. Furthermore, although he accepted that inaction as opposed to action could in principle constitute a breach of Article 3, he thought it significant that the claimants' suffering had not been intended by the defendants[187] and that cases such as *Price v UK*[188] concerning prisoners' rights, upon which the claimants placed great reliance, 'should be treated with great caution outside the prison gates'.[189]

Thus, while accepting that protection afforded by Article 3 ECHR should be rigorously applied in the prison context even without the intention to humiliate, Sullivan J considered that a distinction could be drawn when the claimant was living 'in (admittedly deplorable conditions) in her own home, surrounded by her family in living conditions which were not deliberately inflicted upon her by the defendant'.[190] Therefore, although he was satisfied that the claimants had been obliged to remain in manifestly unsuitable accommodation for 20 months longer than would have been the case if the defendant had discharged its statutory duty towards them reasonably promptly, Sullivan J regarded the case under Article 3 to be finely balanced.

The case under Article 8 ECHR was different however. Although agreeing that the main thrust of Article 8 is to prevent arbitrary interference by public authorities with individuals' private and family life, Sullivan J in *Bernard* was not prepared to overlook the relevance of developments in ECHR jurisprudence, in which respect for private life has long been judged by the ECtHR to impose positive obligations, and in which, particularly in the wake of *Botta v Italy*,[191] respect for individuals' physical and psychological integrity has been recognised as giving rise to positive obligations of the kind at issue in *Bernard*.[192]

Thus, closely following the reasoning in *Botta*, where the claimant had likewise complained of state inaction rather than action, Sullivan J in *Bernard* recalled the ECtHR's conclusion, namely that in order to determine the scope of the indeterminate obligation of respect in a given case, 'regard must be had to

---

[187] The judge said that the claimants' case had fallen into an administrative void between the defendant's Social Services and Housing Departments. Thus, the claimants' suffering was due to the defendant's corporate neglect and not to a positive decision by the defendant that they should be subjected to such conditions.

[188] Judgment of 10 July 2001, (2002) 34 EHRR 1285. For discussion of *Price v UK*, see chapter 2, section III-C above.

[189] *Bernard* (note 180 above) paras 29–30.

[190] *Ibid*, para 29.

[191] Note 182 above. For discussion of *Botta v Italy*, see chapter 2, section III-D above.

[192] See *Markcx v Belgium* [1979] 2 EHRR 330, para 31; and *Botta v Italy* (note 182 above), where it was stated: 'Private life, in the Court's view, includes a person's physical and psychological integrity; the guarantee afforded by Article 8 of the Convention is primarily intended to ensure the development, without outside interference, of the personality of each individual in his relations with other human beings' (para 32).

the fair balance that has to be struck between the general interest and the interests of the individual, while the State has, in any event, a margin of appreciation'.[193] Further, recalling that a state has obligations of this type when it finds a direct and immediate link between the measures sought by an applicant and the latter's private and/or family life, Sullivan J considered that for present purposes it would be unnecessary to attempt to define 'family life', since it was not in dispute that 'the fundamental element of family life is the right to live together so that family relations can develop naturally and that members of a family can enjoy one another's company'.[194]

Sullivan J in *Bernard* repeated the now familiar refrain that respect for private and family life does not require the state to provide every one of its citizens with a house. He was also clear that not every breach of duty under section 21 NAA would result in a breach of Article 8 ECHR. However, since those entitled to care under section 21 are a particularly vulnerable group, as under Article 8, positive measures must be taken (by way of community care facilities) to enable them to enjoy, so far as possible, normal private and family life. Thus agreeing with the approach of Jackson J in the earlier case of *Morris v LB Newham*[195] (a dispute concerning an unlawful failure to provide accommodation under Part VII of the Housing Act 1996), he considered that whether a breach of statutory duty has resulted in an infringement of the claimants' Article 8 ECHR rights would depend upon all the circumstances of the case.[196]

Therefore, in deciding whether there had been a breach of Article 8 with regard to the Bernard family, Sullivan J concluded that following the assessments in September 2000, the defendant was under an obligation not merely to refrain from unwarranted interference in the claimants' family life, but also to take positive steps, including providing suitably adapted accommodation, to enable the claimants and their children to lead as normal a family life as possible, bearing in mind the second claimant's severe disabilities. Had those steps been taken by the authority, he argued, they would have facilitated the normal incidents of family life: the second claimant would have been able to move around her home to some extent and would have been able to play some part, together with the first claimant, in looking after their children:

> [I]t would also have secured her 'physical and psychological integrity'. She would no longer have been housebound, confined to a shower chair for most of the day, lacking privacy in the most undignified of circumstances. Instead she would have been able to operate again as part of her family and as a person in her own right, rather than being a burden, wholly dependent upon the rest of her family. In short, it would have restored her dignity as a human being.[197]

---

[193] *Bernard* (note 180 above) para 33 (Sullivan J).
[194] *Ibid*, para 34.
[195] [2002] EWHC 1262 Admin, para 59 (Jackson J).
[196] *Bernard* (note 180 above) para 32.
[197] *Ibid*, para 33.

In summary, Sullivan J concluded in *Bernard* that the Haringey Council's failure to act on the September 2000 assessments showed a singular lack of respect for the private and family life of the claimants, who were consequently condemned to living conditions that made it virtually impossible for them to have any meaningful private or family life for the purposes of Article 8 ECHR. Accordingly, the defendant was not merely in breach of its statutory duty under the NAA; its failure to act on the September 2000 assessments over a period of 20 months was also incompatible with the claimants' continuing rights under Article 8 of the European Convention.

D. A Human Rights Approach to Statutory Interpretation: Comparing *Bernard* and G

The appalling and dangerous circumstances of the two disabled children and their family and the delay that they suffered in *A v Lambeth*[198] (which ended up before the House of Lords in G)[199] are not on all fours with the circumstances of the complainants in *Bernard*.[200] However, the two cases clearly merit comparison.

Almost eighteen months before the application for judicial review of the lawfulness of the local authority conduct in *A v Lambeth*, social service assessments had recorded:

> The flat is overcrowded and damp, and the children's bedroom windows and kitchen units were broken. The family is living in appalling conditions . . . in a location very dangerous to the children, as the flat is very close to the road . . . D (one of the autistic children) has a fixation with climbing out of the window and running out of the front door . . . [T]he poor condition of the flat poses a health risk to D and his siblings. There is a risk of Mrs A breaking down without a support package to give her a break from caring for two children with autism and behavioural difficulties.[201]

Following these assessments, and by contrast with *Bernard*, some positive steps were taken before the court hearing: a few repairs were made to the property, and some respite care and placements on a holiday play scheme were arranged for the children. Therefore, although the children and their mother remained in conditions that posed serious risks to their psychological and physical health, their circumstances did not condemn them to the trapped living conditions that for Sullivan J in *Bernard* made it 'impossible to have any meaningful family life for purposes of article 8'. Nevertheless, and despite the assumption of Laws LJ that a true Convention point had not arisen, the failure of the local authority in *A v Lambeth* to provide for the accommodation needs of the children and their

---

[198] Notes 136 (first instance) and 147 (Court of Appeal) above.
[199] Note 4 above.
[200] Note 180 above.
[201] *A v Lambeth* (note 136 above) para 3.

mother arguably constituted a putative breach of the right to private and family life in Article 8 ECHR—and in light of *Bernard*, the question could reasonably have been raised.

However, a review of the case law following the decision of Elias J in *J v Enfield*[202] suggests tacit acceptance by advocates that use of the remedial provision in section 3 HRA is not appropriate in welfare needs disputes of this kind. Moreover, the intellectual gymnastics deployed in the recent Court of Appeal decision in *R (on the Application of Spink) v Wandsworth LBC* (hereafter *Spink*)[203]—far removed from the principled debate that characterised *Gloucester*[204]—suggests that in disputes requiring interpretation of the tangled web of financial powers and duties embodied in the welfare system, judicial policy has been to support the shift towards a market ethos.

Thus, despite the intention of Parliament to remove children's services from the adult welfare regime highlighted in *G*,[205] and the cogency of the applicant's arguments to that effect in *Spink*,[206] the Court of Appeal preferred the resource-led argument—that children with disabilities had been effectively drawn back into the ambit of the CSDPA. Accordingly, the Court of Appeal relied on a strict construction of a labyrinthine range of statutory powers and duties underpinned by section 29 NAA and selective extracts from the House of Lords decision in *Gloucester*, concluding in *Spink* that, as in the case of adult claimants, the costs of home adaptations for children in accordance with section 2(1) CSDPA could be legitimately recouped by the local authority. Thus, insofar as the financing of home adaptations might be an issue, consistency in the treatment of adults and children with disabilities could be achieved.

Returning then to the House of Lords decision in *G* and the interpretation therein of section 17 CA as a target duty that brooks indefinite delay in meeting the accommodation needs of even the most vulnerable children and their families, we are reminded of the limitations of the traditional ultra vires approach to the interpretation of local authority statutory duties. As we have seen, in the case of adults suffering from disabilities, the urgency of their assessed needs,

---

[202] Note 136 above.

[203] Note 7 above. In *Spink* the local authority sought to recoup expenses of £58,000 for adaptations carried out on behalf of a family with two severely disabled children. The central question was whether the local authority was entitled to recoup charges for the home adaptations in accordance with obligations to meet the needs of disabled children under s 28 A CSDPA. Although the claimants reasonably argued that the House of Lords decision in *G* (note 4 above) was authority for the proposition that in creating a wholly distinct regime for children, the Children Act 1989 had removed children from the ambit of the CDSPA, on this occasion the Court of Appeal thereby allowing the possibility of charging for those services.

[204] Note 121 above.

[205] Note 4 above.

[206] Note 7 above. In light of the emphasis in G (note 4 above) on the distinctiveness of the regime created in the Children Act 1989 and the well-documented intention of Parliament to remove those services from the umbrella of s 29 NAA 1948—and by implication from the ambit of s 2(1) CSDPA—the applicants argued that, by contrast with adults, local authorities were not entitled to charge for home adaptations for disabled children that were caught by s 17 CA.

including the need for accommodation, is a key factor to be taken into account in determining the scope of the local authority duty to provide. By contrast, however, in G the House of Lords concluded that the urgency of the needs of disabled children living in even the most appalling circumstances has no part to play in determining whether authorities are in breach of duty to provide children's services under section 17 CA.

Therefore, in pursuing the orthodox approach to the interpretation of local authority duties, which has achieved sporadic success since *Tandy*, advocates have failed to consider the potential use of section 3 HRA in cases such as *A v Lambeth* to promote a more open-textured human rights approach to the interpretation of local authority duties. As Sullivan J made clear in *Bernard*, and as we shall see further in the next chapter, not every case of prolonged failure to provide for the needs of even the most vulnerable families in accordance with their assessments constitutes a breach of Article 8 ECHR.

The decision in *Bernard* can clearly be contrasted with the apparent lack of humanity in the ruling in G. In G, as recognised by Lord Nicholls, there was no opportunity for refinement of the local authority target duty, however appalling or dangerous the children's circumstances. Thus, in cases in which breach of Article 8 ECHR is established, section 3 HRA could appropriately be invoked to remind the government as well as local authorities: in failing to provide resources to meet the accommodation needs of vulnerable disabled children and their families within a reasonable period of time, when such serious risks to their physical and psychological integrity have been recorded by assessments, they are in breach of positive obligations in the ECHR rights.

V. CONCLUSION

This chapter has shown that despite widespread perception that *Re B* marked the end of judicial intervention in contested NHS allocation decisions, UK courts have continued to contribute to the resolution of prioritisation disputes, through the development of established principles and procedures of public administrative law. Moreover, the chapter has also highlighted the extent to which established boundaries in disputes over the equitable distribution of NHS resources have been placed under strain by developments in EU law. Thus, in *Watts*, traditional blanket justifications for delay or refusal in the NHS have been found wanting by the Grand Chamber of the ECJ. Moreover, the ECJ has also emphasised the need for greater transparency and attention to the immediate clinical needs of patients in NHS prioritisation decisions, so as to render the quality of decision-making more amenable to scrutiny in domestic courts. It is notable, however, that despite exaggerated concerns before the implementation of the HRA, that Article 2 ECHR might be relied on in contested prioritisation decisions, in light of the slender stream of authority in ECHR jurisprudence, this has not transpired.

One of the central issues of the chapter has been the extent to which 'choice' has been used as a policy tool to mark an ideological shift from the traditional model of legitimate welfare dependency to contemporary neo-liberal models of social provision, which incorporate ideas of autonomy and personal responsibility for welfare. In choice-based models of the kind proposed in the Green Paper on housing,[207] the state prefers to cast itself as facilitator rather than provider. However, this chapter suggests that the shift in emphasis to quasi-consumer models of public service delivery can be used not only to mask the level of unmet need in areas of acute shortage such as housing, but also to undermine the very basis of the relationship between need and public sector provision on which the welfare state has been constructed. Thus, our review of contemporary case law has highlighted those areas of local authority welfare in which the statutory assessment process continues to imply a direct relationship between government and the meeting of individual human needs—giving rise to duties that in some cases coincide with positive protective obligations in the ECHR rights. Therefore, it has been argued that even in the post-welfare landscape, in statutory challenges involving delay or refusal of public services to some of the most vulnerable individuals caught up in the social care system, section 3 HRA provides a principled remedial tool for reminding the government of their fundamental responsibilities to meet the assessed needs of vulnerable individuals who live in abject circumstances that are inconsistent with fundamental human rights standards.

---

[207] Note 25 above.

6

Articles 3 and 8 ECHR: Failure to Provide and Positive Obligations in the Socio-economic Sphere

I. INTRODUCTION

FROM THE TIME of the enactment of the Human Rights Act (HRA) 1998, strategic human rights lawyers in the United Kingdom have been poised to test the extent to which the Act can be used to impose positive obligations on public authorities in diverse areas of social responsibility. Thus, as we have seen in chapter 4, from the time of the challenge in *Donoghue v Poplar Housing and Regeneration Community Association* (hereafter *Donoghue*)[1] until the House of Lords decisions in *R (on the Application of Qazi) v Harrow London Borough Council* (hereafter *Qazi*)[2] and *R (on the Application of Kay and Others) v London Borough of Lambeth* (hereafter *Kay*),[3] UK county courts were embroiled in litigation, the purpose of which was to test whether the negative injunction in Article 8 of the European Convention on Human Rights (ECHR) 1950—which obliges states to refrain from interfering with individuals' enjoyment of their homes—is compatible with common law and statutory rules relating to the lawful termination of different types of landlord and tenant agreements. Moreover, in chapter five we have seen that shortly after the HRA came into force, sporadic attempts were made in the local authority social care sector to test the scope of Articles 3 and 8 ECHR to prevent interference with family life—for example, by barring the separation of children from their parents, or holding public authorities to account for failing to meet the assessed needs of vulnerable children and their families to have suitable accommodation.[4]

Progress in these politically controversial claims has been slow and placed considerable strains on administrative court resources. Furthermore, divided opinions in lower courts about the potential of Articles 3 and 8 ECHR to give

---

[1] [2001] 4 All ER 604. For discussion of the case in relation to s 6 HRA, see chapter 3, section II-A above; in relation to Art 8 ECHR disputes, see chapter 4, section III-D above, especially text accompanying notes 151–6.

[2] [2003] UKHL 43, [2003] 4 ALL ER 461.

[3] [2006] UKHL 10. For discussion of *Qazi* and *Kay*, see also chapter 4, section III-D above.

[4] See generally the final section of chapter 3 above.

rise to positive obligations in welfare needs contexts, particularly in cases involving state inaction rather than direct interference with ECHR rights, has increased the scale of litigation. Over time, however, senior UK courts have had opportunity not only to revisit questions about the relevance of the negative–positive dichotomy as a basis for determining the scope of public authority obligations to give effect to rights in the ECHR, but also to consider the limits of government responsibility in complaints of administrative *failure to act*, rather than in complaints of direct interference with ECHR rights. Moreover, in *R v Secretary of State for the Home Department, ex parte Limbuela* (hereafter *Limbuela*),[5] where the executive branch of government was under direct scrutiny, the House of Lords for the first time addressed fundamental questions about state obligations to prevent poverty and destitution in a regime that has placed constraints on the potential of individuals to meet basic needs for food and shelter.

The first part of this chapter focuses on the scope of Article 8 ECHR. Its primary concern involves questions of liability for public authority inaction as opposed to direct interference by state agents with enjoyment of the ECHR rights. The focus is therefore on the Court of Appeal decision in *Anufrijeva v Southwark London Borough Council* (hereafter *Anufrijeva*),[6] a conjoined appeal of three cases that arose prior to the House of Lords decision in *Limbuela*. In *Anufrijeva*, in addition to considering crucial questions about damages,[7] the Court of Appeal considered both the scope of Article 8 to impose positive obligations in cases of undisputed failures to meet statutory obligations; and also the circumstances in which liability for breach of public authority statutory duties might coincide with liability for breach of section 6 HRA.

The second part of the chapter primarily focuses on the potential of Article 3 ECHR to impose positive obligations in welfare needs contexts. It is therefore concerned with a series of politically sensitive challenges that culminated in the House of Lords decision in *Limbuela*, against the refusal of basic welfare support to destitute asylum seekers who failed to claim asylum as soon as 'reasonably practicable' after arriving in the United Kingdom. We will also examine the important House of Lords decision in *N v Secretary of State for the Home Department* (hereafter *N*),[8] which prior to *Limbuela* had questioned whether the government was obliged to provide life-prolonging treatment to an illegal immigrant suffering from AIDS (rather than deport her to her country of origin in accordance with immigration law) in order to avoid an infringement of Article 3 ECHR.

---

[5] [2005] UKHL 66, [2006] 1 AC 396.

[6] [2003] EWCA Civ 1406.

[7] *Anufrijeva* also provided an opportunity for the Court of Appeal to examine the scope of the power to award damages under section 8 HRA, since Sullivan J had first considered the issue in *Bernard and Another v Enfield LBC* (hereafter *Bernard*) [2002] EWHC 2282, [2003] HRLR 4, [2003] LGR 423. See chapter 3 above.

[8] [2005] UKHL 31, [2005] AC 296 HL.

II. *ANUFRIJEVA*, ARTICLE 8 ECHR AND MALADMINISTRATION IN THE PROVISION OF WELFARE

The following discussion is primarily concerned with positive duties engendered by Article 8 ECHR in cases of administrative failure to act compatibly with the Convention. It therefore focuses on the Court of Appeal decision in *Anufrijeva*,[9] in which three separate applicants alleged that *failure* by public authorities to comply with statutory duties, under which they claimed to be entitled to receive welfare benefits or other qualitative improvements in their personal or family life, constituted breaches of Article 8 ECHR. In each case at first instance, it had been argued that alleged failures by public authorities to comply with statutory duties had been attributable to maladministration, which in itself (or in its effects) constitutes a breach of Article 8 ECHR—as a result of which, it was argued, claimants were entitled to damages under section 8 HRA. Each challenge therefore involved 'an allegation that the defendant was at fault in failing to take positive action, which would have averted the adverse consequences of which the complaint had been made'.[10]

Regarded as a crucial test case by Lord Woolf CJ, who gave the single judgment of the Court of Appeal, each of the conjoined cases in *Anufrijeva* involved claimants who had come to the United Kingdom to seek asylum. However, by contrast with the Article 3 disputes discussed in the second part of this chapter, the asylum status of the claimants had no material bearing on the issues of legal principle raised by the cases—although particularly in the case of the Anufrijeva family, their immigration status became the focus of a great deal of adverse media attention.

In the first case of the conjoined appeal (hereafter referred to as 'Anufrijeva's case', members of the Anufrijeva family argued that Southwark Borough Council had infringed their Article 8 ECHR right to respect for private and family life by failing to meet the special accommodation needs of Ala Anufrijeva, under section 21 of the National Assistance Act (NAA) 1948. The second case in the *Anufrijeva* appeal (hereafter referred to as 'N's case') concerned N, an asylum seeker from Libya who had been granted refugee status approximately two years after arriving in the United Kingdom. In an action for judicial review and damages against the Secretary of State, he contended that due to the maladministration of his claim for refugee status, he had received inadequate financial support over a period of almost two years and suffered psychiatric injury. Further, he argued that taken together, these circumstances constituted an infringement of his Convention rights. Finally, in the third case in the conjoined appeal (hereafter referred to as 'M's case'), an asylum seeker from Angola claimed that the three-year delay between his attainment of refugee status and

---

[9] Note 6 above.
[10] *Anufrijeva* (note 6 above) para 13 (Lord Woolf).

the granting of permission for his family to be reunited with him, infringed his right to respect for family life under Article 8 ECHR.

In Anufrijeva's case, Newman J at first instance[11] had dismissed the claim for judicial review and damages under section 8 of the HRA. He found as a fact that the local authority had been assiduous in seeking to accommodate the special needs of the disabled family member under section 21 NAA, rendering the dispute an unfortunate choice for a test case. In N's case, the first instance judge, Silber J,[12] had found that the claimant's Article 8 ECHR rights were indeed breached in the circumstances of the complaint, although Article 3 had not been breached. In M's case, the judge at first instance, Richards J,[13] had dismissed the applicant's claim against the Home Office, holding that there had been no violation of Article 8 ECHR. Accordingly, appeals were made to the Court of Appeal by the claimants in Anufrijeva's and N's cases and by the Secretary of State in M's case.

In summary the Court of Appeal held that there was no basis for impugning the factual findings of the trial judge courts in Anufrijeva's case. Similarly, in N's case it was concluded that there had been no fault in the reasoning of the judge at first instance and that the appeal should also be dismissed. Finally, in M's case, reversing the decision of the trial judge, the Court of Appeal allowed the Secretary of State's appeal, on grounds that maladministration did not infringe Article 8 ECHR because although it had caused a particularly susceptible individual like the claimant to suffer psychiatric harm, that result was not reasonably to be anticipated. However, before reaching his conclusions on these facts, Lord Woolf saw *Anufrijeva* as an opportunity to address questions as yet untested by the Court of Appeal about (a) the circumstances in which maladministration by public authorities might constitute a breach of Article 8 ECHR; and (b) the counterintuitive conclusion accepted by Sullivan J in *Bernard and Another v Enfield LBC* (hereafter *Bernard*)[14] that treatment that does not reach the severity of Article 3 degradation may nonetheless constitute positive breaches of the private life aspects of Article 8 when adverse effects on an individual's physical and moral integrity are sufficiently grave.[15]

A. The Acceptance of the Inadequacy of the Positive–Negative Dichotomy

Lord Woolf in *Anufrijeva* conceded that whether allegations are framed in terms of negative or positive breach of duty, it is possible for a range of positive

---

[11] *Anufrijeva v Southwark LBC* [2002] All ER (D) 37 Dec.

[12] *R (on the Application of N) v Secretary of State for the Home Department* [2003] EWHC 207 Admin.

[13] *R (on the Application of M) v Secretary of State for the Home Department* [2002] EWHC 3163, [2003] EWHC 319 Admin.

[14] Note 7 above.

[15] See *Anufrijeva* (note 6 above) paras 10, 33 and 39–40 (Lord Woolf).

obligations to be engendered by Article 8 ECHR—some of which might incidentally require financial expenditure on the part of the state.[16] Thus, accepting the complex nature of the right to respect in Article 8,[17] Lord Woolf first drew attention to the case of *Bensaid v United Kingdom*,[18] in which the European Court of Human Rights (ECtHR) had recently reiterated that 'not every act or measure which adversely affects moral or physical integrity will interfere with the right to respect to private life guaranteed by article 8'.[19] However, Lord Woolf also acknowledged the breadth of the ECtHR conclusion in *Pretty v United Kingdom*,[20] which affirmed that the right to respect for private life covers the physical and psychological integrity of a person and can sometimes embrace an individual's physical and social identity[21] as well as his or her right to develop relationships with other human beings and the outside world.[22] Moreover, in *Anufrijeva*, Lord Woolf recognised that the aspect of Article 8 that relates to personal development—though most clearly established in relation to private life—also has a connection with family life, so that 'if members of a family are prevented from sharing family life together, article 8(1) is likely to be infringed'.[23]

---

[16] See generally the first section of chapter 2 above. For example, the possibility of an obligation to admit relatives of settled immigrants in order to develop family life was recognised in *Gul v Switzerland* (1996) 22 EHRR 93. See also more recently *Sen v The Netherlands* (2001) 36 EHRR 81. It should be recalled that there is a well-established distinction between substantive and procedural obligations engendered by Art 8. See *Glaser v United Kingdom* (2000) 3 FCR 193. The ECtHR stated: '. . . positive obligations inherent in an effective respect for family life . . . may involve the adoption of measures designed to secure respect for family life . . . including both the provision of a regulatory framework of adjudicatory and enforcement machinery protecting individuals' rights and the implementation where appropriate of specific steps . . .' (208–9, para 63). The ECtHR has also differentiated between the introduction of a legislative or administrative scheme to ensure that Art 8 rights are respected and the competent operation of such a scheme. In relation to the latter, Lord Woolf in *Anufrijeva* considered that maladministration might give rise to a breach of Art 8.

[17] See generally chapter 2 above.

[18] (2001) 33 EHRR 205. In *Bensaid*, in addition to alleging a potential breach of Art 3, the claimant contended that his Art 8 rights would be infringed if he were expelled from the United Kingdom because of the likely effect this would have on his mental health.

[19] *Ibid*, 219, para 46.

[20] (2002) 35 EHRR 1. In *Pretty* the ECtHR, commenting on Art 8, stated '. . . the concept of "private life" is a broad term not susceptible to exhaustive definition. It covers the physical and psychological integrity of a person. It can sometimes embrace aspects of an individual's physical and social identity . . . Article 8 also protects a right to personal development, and the right to establish and develop relationships with other human beings and the outside world. Though no previous case has established as such any right to self-determination as being contained in article 8 of the Convention, the court considers that the notion of personal autonomy is an important principle underlying the interpretation of its guarantees' (35–6, para 61).

[21] 'Elements such as, for example, gender identification, name and sexual orientation and sexual life fall within the personal sphere protected by article 8' (*ibid*). See also *Bellinger v Bellinger* [2003] UKHL 21, [2003] 2 WLR 1174.

[22] See *Botta v Italy* (1998) 4 BHRC 81.

[23] *Anufrijeva* (note 6 above) para 10 (Lord Woolf). In M's case, the claim was for delay in granting necessary permission to facilitate the sharing of family life; in Anufrijeva's case, it was for failure to provide facilities that would allow the claimants to experience a satisfactory quality of family life.

Thereafter, reviewing a range of situations in which Strasbourg has recognised that states are under a 'positive obligation to introduce systems to preserve respect for family life',[24] Lord Woolf considered the limits of the proposition in the socio-economic sphere, for example when the state is asked 'to provide a home or indeed any other kind of financial support'.[25] Lord Woolf found scant authority in the jurisprudence for the proposition that a failure to provide financial support might give rise to a breach of Article 8.[26] Indeed, the most direct comment to be found was in *Andersson and Kullman v Sweden*,[27] in which two decades earlier the European Commission of Human Rights had held such an application inadmissible. However, in relation to positive obligations to provide non-economic types of statutory welfare support of the kind at issue in *Anufrijeva*, Lord Woolf recognised that there was some support in the authorities for that contention.

B. When Does Breach of Public Authority Statutory Duties Constitute Breach of Section 6 HRA?

On the central question of when a breach of statutory welfare duty might be sufficiently serious to engage Article 8 ECHR, counsel for claimants in *Anufrijeva* (Anufrijeva's case and N's case) appeared to suggest that statutory welfare schemes that provide support to refugees and asylum seekers reflect the manner in which the United Kingdom has chosen to discharge its positive obligations under the European Convention.[28] However, seeking to avoid the unacceptable conclusion that breach of Article 8 can be equated with all breaches of statutory welfare duties, it was also conceded by counsel, by reference to the decision of Sullivan J in *Bernard*,[29] that the *consequences* of breach had to be serious before the Convention would be infringed.

---

[24] *Anufrijeva* (note 6 above), paras 17–19 (Lord Woolf). See for example the recent decision in *Sen v the Netherlands* (note 16 above), where the ECtHR recognised the possibility that a state might be under an obligation to admit relatives of settled immigrants in order for them to develop family life.

[25] *Ibid*, para 20. Lord Woolf drew a distinction between *Marcic v Thames Water Utilities Ltd* [2002] EWCA Civ 64 (which demonstrated that a deterioration in the quality of life can result in infringement of Art 8, particularly when the claimant's home is affected) and cases such as *Chapman v UK* (2001) 33 EHRR 399 (where emphasis was placed by the majority on the absence of a right to a home).

[26] See R Clayton and H Tomlinson, *The Law of Human Rights*, vol 1 (Oxford, Oxford University Press, 2000) para 13.120 for comment that the positive obligations on the state to respect family life will rarely go so far as to require financial or other practical support. No mention was made of *Connors v UK* [2004] ECHR 223, Judgment of 27 May 2004 or of the dissenting judgment in *Chapman (ibid)*.

[27] (1986) 46 DR 251. In this case it was alleged that Sweden had infringed Art 8 by failing to provide a mother with financial assistance that would have allowed her to stay at home to look after her children, rather than placing them in daycare and going out to work. The European Commission of Human Rights observed: 'the Convention does not as such guarantee the right to public assistance either in the form of financial support to maintain a certain standard of living or in the form of supplying day home care places. Nor does the right under article 8 of the Convention to respect for family life extend so far as to impose on states a general obligation to provide for financial assistance to individuals in order to enable one of two parents to stay at home to take care of children' (253).

[28] See *Anufrijeva* (note 6 above) para 22.

[29] Note 7 above.

By contrast, without denying that there may be circumstances in other jurisdictions in which breach of duty in administering a statutory scheme of social security might potentially infringe Article 8,[30] counsel for the defendant in M's case (the third claimant in the conjoined case of *Anufrijeva*) argued that the current welfare system provides benefits that go far beyond any positive action required by the Convention.

However, as Lord Woolf saw it, the argument that there are positive obligations in Article 8 to make *some* provision for a minimum standard of private and family life below which states should not fall, gives rise to the problematic inference that the Convention requires all states to adhere to a single uniform core standard when giving effect to Article 8 obligations—a proposition for which he found little support.[31] Indeed, Lord Woolf considered the case of *Botta v Italy*,[32] which had been relied on by both parties, as no more than authority for an indeterminate proposition that there are *some* circumstances in which a public authority will be required to devote resources to make it possible for individuals to enjoy the rights that are entitled to respect under Article 8.[33] Moreover, he observed that although leading academic authorities suggested as long ago as 1982 that 'minimum welfare provision may now constitute a positive obligation inherent in the effective respect for private and family life by the states',[34] the ECtHR had merely accepted such a *possibility* in *Marzari v Italy*[35] and *O'Rourke v UK*.[36]

[30] Relying on the earlier Court of Appeal decision in *Carson v Secretary of State for Work and Pensions* [2003] EWCA Civ 797, [2003] 3 All ER 577.

[31] *Anufrijeva* (note 6 above) para 24. Lord Woolf considered *Botta v Italy* (note 22 above) and the more recent decision of *Zehnalova and Zehnal v Czech Republic*, App No 38621/97 (14 May 2002) unreported, to be of peripheral importance. The applicants of the latter case, who were husband and wife, complained that their Art 8 rights were infringed because, in breach of Czech law, the authorities had failed to install facilities that would enable the physically disabled wife to gain access to public buildings. However, in light of *Botta*, the ECtHR observed that Art 8 'cannot apply as a general rule . . . but only in exceptional cases where a lack of access to public buildings and those open to the public would prevent the female applicant from leading her life, so that her right to personal development and her right to make and maintain relations with other human beings and the outside world are in question . . .' (15). The female applicant had not managed to demonstrate 'the special link between the inaccessibility of the institutions mentioned and the particular needs concerned with her private life'.

[32] Note 22 above.

[33] *Anufrijeva* (note 6 above) para 28.

[34] P Duffy, 'The Protection of Privacy, Family Life and Other Rights under Article 8 of the European Convention on Human Rights' (1982) 2 *Yearbook of European Law* 191, 199.

[35] (1999) 28 EHRR CD 175. For a discussion of *Marzari* in this context, see chapter 2 above. Lord Woolf also noted the importance of the margin of appreciation in this context: 'the court went on to hold that it was not for it to review the decisions taken by the local authorities as to the adequacy of the accommodation offered to the applicant, observing, at p 180, that they had offered to carry out further works to make the accommodation suitable. In these circumstances the court held that the local authorities could be considered to have discharged their positive obligations in respect of the applicant's right to respect for his private life' (*Anufrijeva* (note 6 above) para 31 (Lord Woolf)).

[36] Application No 39022/97 (unreported) 26 June 2001. The applicant, who was in poor health, complained of infringement of his Arts 3 and 8 rights in that he was not provided with suitable accommodation after his discharge from prison. The court referred to *Marzari* (*ibid*) and observed that any positive obligation to house the homeless must be limited. Insofar as there was any obligation to house the applicant, the court considered that this was discharged by advice given to the applicant to attend a night shelter and efforts that were made to find suitable temporary or permanent occupation.

Although the ECtHR had made clear that Article 8 may oblige a state to provide positive welfare support such as housing in special circumstances, it was equally plain to Lord Woolf that 'neither article 3 nor article 8 imposes such a requirement as a matter of course: it is not possible to deduce from the Strasbourg jurisprudence any specific criteria for the imposition of such a positive duty'.[37] Nevertheless, Lord Woolf conceded in *Anufrijeva* that the work of the Parliamentary Joint Committee on Human Rights (JCHR), domestic legislation and 'our own jurisprudence since the HRA' have provided 'some assistance' in the shape of section 55 of the Nationality, Immigration and Asylum Act (NIAA) 2002, which, as he observed, envisages 'the possibility that the Secretary of State will be required to exercise his power to provide support in order to comply with the Convention'.[38]

Moreover, Lord Woolf agreed with the Attorney General's concession in *R (on the Application of Q) v Secretary of State for the Home Department* (hereafter *Q*),[39] which was later confirmed by the House of Lords in *Limbuela*,[40] that failure to provide support could constitute 'treatment' in extreme circumstances,[41] so that Article 3 ECHR could impose a positive obligation on the state to provide support for an asylum seeker. Lord Woolf therefore accepted in *Anufrijeva* that in relation to Article 3, the question of liability was not to be decided in accordance with whether there had been action or inaction on the part of authorities, and that 'if support is necessary to prevent a person in this country reaching the point of article 3 degradation, then that support should be provided.'[42]

Similarly, in the context of Article 8 ECHR, Lord Woolf also accepted that whether a case involves negative breach or positive breach, the question to be asked is: 'when might it be necessary to provide the crucial support needed to enjoy article 8 rights?'[43] Thus, although he assumed (like the Court of Appeal in *Q*) that it may be easier to identify a degree of degradation that demands welfare support than to identify 'some other basic standard of private and family life which article 8 requires the state to maintain by the provision of support', he was bound to accept in principle that

> if such a basic standard exists, . . . it must require intervention by the state, whether the claimant is an asylum seeker who has not sought asylum promptly on entering the country or a citizen entitled to all the benefits of our system of social security.[44]

---

[37] *Anufrijeva* (note 6 above) para 33.
[38] *Ibid*, para 34 (Lord Woolf). For a full discussion of these issues and the scope of section 55 NIAA, see section III below.
[39] [2003] EWCA Civ 364, [2003] 2 All ER 905.
[40] Note 5 above.
[41] The Attorney General had provided by way of example the predicament of a heavily pregnant woman.
[42] *Anufrijeva* (note 6 above) para 35.
[43] *Ibid*, para 36 (Lord Woolf).
[44] *Ibid*, para 37 (Lord Woolf).

Prior to this conclusion in *Anufrijeva* there had been few cases in which courts had offered statements of principle on the extent to which breach of specific public authority duties could give rise to a positive breach of Article 8 ECHR. In *R (Morris) v Newham London Borough Council*[45] Jackson J held that although the defendant's breach of duty had compelled the claimant and her family to live in 'grossly overcrowded and unsatisfactory accommodation' for a period of 29 weeks, this did not infringe Article 8:

> Absent special circumstances which interfere with private or family life, a homeless person cannot rely upon article 8 of the Convention in conjunction with Part 7 of the Housing Act 1996 in order to found a damages claim for failure to provide accommodation.[46]

What then were the special circumstances leading to such a finding in *Bernard*?[47]

Lord Woolf in *Anufrijeva* was mindful that a range of factors relating to the scope of the local authority's statutory duty, the culpability of the authority and the applicants' circumstances had all been pertinent to the conclusion in *Bernard* that there had been a violation of Article 8 ECHR.[48] He therefore recited a passage from *Bernard* in which Sullivan J considered the vulnerability of the group that is singled out in section 21 NAA to be crucial: 'positive measures have to be taken (by way of community care facilities) to enable them to enjoy, so far as possible, a normal private and family life'.[49] In his analysis of *Bernard*, Lord Woolf in *Anufrijjeva* furthermore recalled how in the same passage, Sullivan J had regarded as highly relevant the council's failure to act on their own assessments, thereby 'condemning claimants to living conditions which made it virtually impossible for them to have any meaningful private or family life for the purposes of article 8'.[50] Indeed, for Sullivan J these exacerbating factors made it possible to conclude that 'the defendant was not merely in breach of its statutory duty under the 1948 Act. Its failure to act . . . over a period of 20 months was also incompatible with the claimants' rights under article 8 of the Convention'.[51]

However, in light of the paucity of authority in the United Kingdom regarding the extent to which breach of local authority statutory duty might give rise

---

[45] [2002] EWHC 1262 Admin.

[46] *Ibid*, para 59.

[47] Note 7 above. For detailed discussion of the facts of this case, see chapter 5 above.

[48] In determining that there had been a breach of Art 8, Sullivan J in *Bernard* (note 7 above) stated: 'Suitably adapted accommodation would not merely have facilitated the normal incidents of family life, for example the second claimant would have been able to move around her home to some extent and would have been able to play some part, together with the first claimant, in looking after their children. It would also have secured her "physical and psychological integrity". She would no longer have been housebound, confined to a shower chair for most of the day, lacking privacy in the most undignified of circumstances, but would have been able to operate again as part of her family and as a person in her own right, rather than being a burden, wholly dependent upon the rest of her family. In short, it would have restored her dignity as a human being' (para 33).

[49] *Anufrijeva* (note 6 above) para 39.

[50] *Bernard* (note 7 above) para 33.

[51] *Ibid*, para 34.

to a concomitant breach of Article 8 ECHR, Lord Woolf also reviewed attempts made by the administrative courts in the *Anufrijeva* appeals to identify a range of principles in Strasbourg and domestic jurisprudence on the issue. Newman J in Anufrijeva's case[52] had asserted that the common feature of *Chapman*[53] and *Marzari*[54] is that in both cases the court identified a particular group of people as qualifying for the protection to be afforded by the extended reach of Article 8.[55] His assessment of Strasbourg jurisprudence therefore led him to conclude:

> [I]t will be rare for an error of judgment, inefficiency or maladministration occurring in the purported performance of a statutory duty, having application to the class or category of concept 'private and family life . . . home', to give rise to an infringement of article 8 . . . [Furthermore,] it is likely that the act or acts of the public authority will have so far departed from the performance of the public authority's statutory duty as to amount to a denial or contradiction of the duty to act.[56]

Newman J therefore maintained that it is likely that 'the circumstances of infringement will be confined to flagrant and deliberate failures to act in the face of obvious and gross circumstances affecting the Article 8 rights of individuals'.[57] Thus, he decided that extreme caution should be exercised in administrative courts when considering the extended reach of Article 8 ECHR. However, this was in contrast to the view of Silber J, who at first instance in N's case believed this test to be too narrow, preferring what he considered to be the broader approach of Sullivan J in *Bernard*.

Lord Woolf, after extensively reviewing the domestic authorities and without further discussion of the relevance of Article 8(2) ECHR, decided in *Anufrijeva* that on balance, Sullivan J had been correct in *Bernard* to accept that Article 8 is capable of imposing a positive obligation on states to provide support, even though Lord Woolf found it hard to conceive of 'a situation in which the predicament of an individual will be such that article 8 requires him to be provided with welfare support, where his predicament is not sufficiently severe to engage article 3'.[58] Furthermore, Lord Woolf acknowledged the extent to which traditional emphasis on preserving the family unit has influenced Strasbourg jurisprudence in this area, observing that 'article 8 may more readily be engaged where a family unit is involved' and that 'where the welfare of children is at

---

[52] Note 11 above.

[53] Note 25 above.

[54] Note 35 above.

[55] In *Marzari*, 'a refusal of the authorities to provide assistance in this respect to an individual suffering from a severe disease' (*Marzari*, 179); and in *Chapman* (note 25 above), 'the vulnerable position of gypsies as a minority means that some special consideration should be given to their needs. . . . To this extent there is thus a positive obligation imposed on the contracting states by virtue of article 8 to facilitate the gypsy way of life' (*Chapman*, 427, para 96). Cf arguments before the House of Lords in *Kay* (note 3 above) in relation to the ECtHR decision in *Connors v UK* (note 26 above).

[56] *Anufrijeva* (note 6 above) para 41 (Lord Woolf, citing Newman J at first instance in Anufrijeva's case (note 11 above) para 105).

[57] Anufrijeva's case (note 11 above) para 105.

[58] *Anufrijeva* (note 6 above) para 43 (Lord Woolf).

stake, article 8 may require the provision of welfare support in a manner which enables family life to continue'.[59]

Lord Woolf accordingly drew attention to the case of *R (on the Application of J) v Enfield London Borough Council*,[60] in which the claimant was homeless and faced separation from her child: 'it was common ground that, if this occurred, article 8(1) would be infringed'.[61] For Lord Woolf, therein also lay the strength of *Bernard*: 'family life was seriously inhibited by the hideous conditions prevailing in the claimants' home'.[62]

C. Maintaining the Family Unit: Levels of Culpability and the Failure to Provide

In seeking general principles to determine whether 'failure in breach of duty to provide the claimant with some benefit or advantage' can constitute a breach of Article 8 ECHR, Lord Woolf in *Anufrijeva* argued that before procedural inaction can amount to a lack of respect for private and family life, there 'must be some ground for criticising the failure to act', in other words, there must be 'an element of culpability'.[63] Furthermore, by analogy with the reasoning of the ECtHR in *Osman v UK*[64] in relation to the positive obligation under Article 2 ECHR, and the reasoning of Silber J in N's case,[65] Lord Woolf argued that there must be 'at very least some specific knowledge that the claimant's private and family life was at risk'.[66] Importantly, however, and by contrast with Newman J in Anufrijeva's case, he accepted that when the domestic law of a state imposes positive obligations in relation to the provision of welfare support, breach of these positive obligations might, without more—as in the case of *Bernard*, provide the necessary element of culpability to establish a breach of Article 8, 'provided that the impact on family life was sufficiently serious and had been foreseeable'.[67]

In sum, therefore, Lord Woolf before the Court of Appeal in *Anufrijeva* argued that a review of Strasbourg jurisprudence suggested that in complaints of 'culpable delay in administrative processes necessary to determine and give effect to article 8 rights', the approach was 'not to find an infringement unless substantial prejudice had been caused to the applicant'.[68] The example given was of early cases involving custody of children in which procedural delay was

---

[59] *Ibid.*
[60] [2002] EWHC 735 Admin. Elias J declined to use section 3 HRA; see discussion in chapter 5 above.
[61] *Anufrijeva* (note 6 above) para 43 (Lord Woolf).
[62] *Ibid.*
[63] *Ibid*, para 45.
[64] (1998) 5 BHRC 293. See generally chapter 2 above.
[65] Note 12 above (the second of the three conjoined cases in *Anufrijeva*), paras 126–48.
[66] *Anufrijeva* (note 6 above) para 45.
[67] *Ibid.*
[68] *Ibid*, para 46.

held to amount to a breach of Article 8 ECHR because of the prejudice such delay can have on the ultimate decision. For example, in *H v United Kingdom*,[69] the ECtHR held that Article 8 was infringed by delay in the conduct of access and adoption proceedings because the proceedings 'lay within an area in which procedural delay may lead to a de facto determination of the matter at issue'[70] (which, as Lord Woolf noted, was precisely what did occur). Subsequently in deciding that a complaint founded on substantial delay in granting permission for the family of a refugee to join him in the United Kingdom was inadmissible in *Askar v United Kingdom*,[71] the Commission closely followed the reasoning in *H*, observing as follows:

> In *H v United Kingdom* the court found a violation of article 8 in respect of proceedings concerning the applicant mother's access to her child which lasted two years and seven months. However, in reaching that conclusion the ECtHR decided the proceedings concerned a fundamental element of family life (whether the mother would be able to see her child again) and that they had a quality of irreversibility, lying within an area in which delay might lead to a de facto determination of the matter; whereas an effective respect for the mother's family life required that the question be determined solely in the light of all relevant considerations and not by mere effluxion of time . . .[72]

However, Lord Woolf characteristically highlighted the emphasis placed by Strasbourg on the need to have regard to resources when considering the obligations imposed on states by Article 8, 'particularly in cases where what is in issue is the grant of some form of welfare support':[73] demands on resources would be significantly increased if states were faced with claims for breaches of Article 8 simply on the ground of administrative delays. However, returning to Newman J's suggestion in Anufrijeva's case that it is likely that a public authority will have to have so far departed from the performance of its duty as to amount to a denial or contradiction of that duty before Article 8 will be infringed,[74] Lord Woolf finally considered that 'this puts the position somewhat too high', since 'in considering whether the threshold of article 8 has been reached it is necessary to have regard both to the extent of the culpability of the failure to act *and* to the severity of the consequence'.[75]

[69]   (1987) 10 EHRR 95.
[70]   *H v UK* (*ibid*) 112, para 89.
[71]   Application No 26373/95 (16 October 1995) unreported.
[72]   *Askar* (*ibid*). The Commission found that the impact of the substantial delay in Askar's case was not comparable to that in *H v UK*. It was true that in Askar's case, the subject matter of the proceedings concerned the granting of permission to enter the United Kingdom for members of the applicant's family, whom the applicant had not seen for at least six years. However, the nature of his ties to some members of the family had not been specified beyond the fact that, pursuant to Somali tradition, the applicant had on the death of his father become head of the extended family group. It was therefore not apparent that 'the delay in the proceedings had had any prejudicial effect on their eventual determination or that the effect of the passage of time is such as to prevent the proper and fair examination of the merits of the case'.
[73]   *Anufrijeva* (note 6 above) para 47 (Lord Woolf).
[74]   See note 55 and accompanying text above.
[75]   *Anufrijeva* (note 6 above) para 48.

Thus, following his painstaking review of Strasbourg authorities, Lord Woolf grudgingly accepted developments in Convention jurisprudence that had established potential liability for breach of positive obligations under Article 8 ECHR. Consequently, he was bound to accept the possibility of claiming damages under the HRA in administrative law courts. However, while conceding that maladministration by public authorities might constitute a breach of Article 8, Lord Woolf concluded before the Court of Appeal in *Anufrijeva*:

> Clearly, where one is considering whether there has been a lack of respect for article 8 rights, the more glaring the deficiency in the behaviour of the public authority, the easier it will be to establish the necessary want of respect. Isolated acts of even significant carelessness are unlikely to suffice.[76]

Although conceding the correctness of Sullivan J's approach in *Bernard*,[77] Lord Woolf in *Anufrijeva* largely ignored Article 8(2) ECHR in determining the scope of Article 8 and its potential to impose positive obligations on public authorities in welfare needs contexts. In the final analysis, much like in *Donoghue*,[78] and without reference to Article 8(2), Lord Woolf in *Anufrijeva* sought to discourage as far as possible the use of Article 8 to impose positive obligations on public authorities as a result of administrative failures such as those that arose in *Bernard*. Thus, he expressed grave concerns not only about the impact of Article 8 claims for compensatory damages on public authority finances[79] 'simply on grounds of administrative delays', but also about the impact of such claims on the efficient administration of justice. Observing the enormous costs incurred in Anufrijeva's case[80] in particular, where there appeared to have been no culpability on the part of authorities, Lord Woolf warned practitioners that incidents of maladministration of the type considered could only constitute violations of Article 8 when the consequences were sufficiently serious.

---

[76] *Ibid*, para 47.
[77] Note 7 above.
[78] Note 1 above.
[79] Lord Woolf in *Anufriyeva* (note 6 above) referred as follows to the Law Commission and the Scottish Law Commission report 'Damages under the Human Rights Act 1998' (Law Com No 266 Cm 4853, October 2000): '[It] suggests that the obvious analogy to a claim for damages under the HRA is a claim against a public authority in tort' (paras 4.14 and 4.15). The Commissions added that in the majority of situations, it is 'possible and appropriate to apply the rules by which damages in tort are usually assessed to claims under the HRA' and that it may be 'appropriate to treat those rules as the prima facie measure to be applied' unless they are in conflict with the Strasbourg approach (Law Com No 266, para 4.26). However, Lord Woolf was at pains to stress that 'the report also contained the following timely warnings as to the dangers of drawing the analogy too strictly' (*Anufriyeva*, para 49): 'the exercise is difficult and the comparisons must be treated with care' (Law Com No 266, paras 4.12 and 4.13). He regarded this as particularly important in cases such as *Anufrijeva* because there is a basic distinction between a claim under the HRA for compensation in respect of the consequences of maladministration and a claim by a member of the public against a public officer for damages for breach of a duty owed in tort. In the former case, the claimant is seeking a remedy that would not be available for misfeasance prior to the HRA.
[80] Note 11 above.

Notwithstanding, in his managerial role, Lord Woolf's concern at every stage of the judgment in *Anufrejiva* was, to limit the use of the administrative law courts to claim HRA damages in adversarial disputes with public authorities. For Lord Woolf, nothing is to be gained by using the administrative law courts to gain compensation under the HRA, since damages can already be claimed, albeit very rarely, as an adjunct to an ordinary claim for breach of statutory duty in judicial review; or more appropriately by way of complaint to a relevant ombudsman or any available internal complaints procedure. Thus, in the same way as Lord Woolf has concluded that in the overwhelming majority of welfare needs disputes, under Article 8 ECHR failure by local authorities to meet statutory obligations can be excused on grounds of lack of resources, he has also concluded in *Anufrejiva* that the proper management of court resources is a legitimate consideration to be taken into account in determining the scope of the right to public law damages under section 8 HRA.

III. ARTICLE 3 ECHR: RESPECT FOR DIGNITY

A. No Welfare for the Destitute: The Asylum Seekers' Story

The extent to which Article 3 ECHR requires states to provide a minimum level of welfare to the destitute has in the United Kingdom been the subject of a complex and controversial series of cases concerning the scope of section 55(5) of the Nationality, Immigration and Asylum Act (NIAA) 2002. In this series of cases, which culminated in the House of Lords decision in *Limbuela*,[81] administrative courts considered the circumstances in which the state's obligations (primarily under Article 3 ECHR) should extend to providing accommodation and basic necessities for large numbers of asylum seekers who, in the judgment of the Secretary of State, fail to seek asylum as soon as reasonably practicable following entry into the United Kingdom. However, from the time of the enactment of the NIAA, a schism developed in lower UK courts over the scope of section 55(5), which, as an exception to the general prohibition on providing support, authorises the Secretary of State to exercise all necessary power to avoid breaches of an individual's ECHR rights as defined by the HRA.

As Lord Phillips MR explained before the Court of Appeal in *Q*,[82] at the heart of section 55 NIAA lies a conundrum: on one hand, section 55(1) prohibits the Secretary of State from providing support to persons who are destitute; but on the other hand, section 55(5) permits him to provide support insofar as is necessary to prevent a breach of an applicant's Convention rights. Thus, mindful that Article 3 ECHR provides that no one shall be subjected to inhuman or degrading treatment, and that section 6 HRA forbids the Secretary of State to act

---

[81] Note 5 above.
[82] Note 39 above, 909, para 5.

incompatibly with Convention rights, UK courts have been required to determine (a) whether the Secretary of State can refuse support to destitute asylum seekers who have no day-to-day certainty of food or shelter—without thereby subjecting them to inhuman and degrading treatment; and (b) if there are such circumstances, how they are to be defined and 'what procedures must be used to ensure that he does not stray outside them'.[83]

The full significance of the conundrum of section 55 NIAA can be properly understood only against the background of a complex web of legislative provisions that have come about since the middle of the 1990s and that are directed at denying welfare support to asylum seekers who are awaiting the hearing of their claims.

B. Withdrawing Asylum Support: The Policy Background

In 1986 the Social Security Act introduced a comprehensive regime under which income support could be claimed by persons with no or minimal income. This included support for asylum seekers awaiting the determination of their claims. Separate provision was subsequently also made in the Asylum and Immigration Appeals Act 1993, which purported to protect asylum seekers against destitution pending the determination of their claims. However, Regulations were enacted in 1996 that restricted provision to those who made their claims immediately on entry.[84] These Regulations were primarily intended to discourage the increasingly large number of individuals who were arriving in the United Kingdom and then later claiming asylum.

At the beginning of a protracted battle in the UK courts over the legality of executive measures of this kind, the Court of Appeal in *R v Secretary of State for Social Security, ex parte Joint Council for the Welfare of Immigrants (JCWI)* (hereafter *JCWI*)[85] held by a majority that the 1996 Regulations, which had deprived 'in country' asylum seekers of benefits to which they were otherwise entitled under the Immigration and Asylum Act 1993, were ultra vires. The Court's main reason was that Parliament could not have intended to permit such a denial of fundamental entitlements in the absence of an express power. Thus, famously Simon Brown LJ observed that, although asylum seekers had been granted fuller rights than they had ever previously enjoyed, including a right of appeal, for some genuine asylum seekers, the 1996 Regulations must be regarded as having rendered their rights as nugatory:

> ... Either that, or the 1996 regulations contemplate for some a life so destitute that to my mind no civilised nation can tolerate it. So basic are the Human rights here at issue that it cannot be necessary to resort to the Convention ... to take note of their violation.[86]

---

[83] *Ibid*, para 3.
[84] Social Security (Persons from Abroad) Miscellaneous Amendments Regulations (1996/30).
[85] [1997] 1 WLR 275, [1996] 4 All ER 385. For further discussion, see chapter 4 above.
[86] *Ibid*, 481.

Furthermore, Simon Brown LJ recalled Lord Ellenborough's opinion nearly 200 years earlier that the law of humanity, which is 'anterior to all positive law', imposes obligations for 'maintaining poor foreigners' so as to 'afford them relief to save them from starving'.[87] Accordingly, although no obligation for the state arises under Article 24 of the Convention Relating to the Status of Refugees 1951 until asylum seekers are recognised as refugees, 'that is not to say that up to this point their fundamental needs can properly be ignored'.[88]

Section 11 of the Asylum and Immigration Act 1996 subsequently circumvented the ruling in *JCWI* by conferring an express power on the Secretary of State to make regulations that exclude asylum seekers from entitlement to income support. Nevertheless, this did not prevent the Court of Appeal in *R v Westminster City Council, ex parte M*[89] from concluding that asylum seekers thus deprived of the right to benefits were entitled to relief from local authorities under section 21(1)(a) NAA 1948.[90] That source of relief was, however, also cut off when, in their first term of office, New Labour enacted the Immigration and Asylum Act 1999,[91] under which the Secretary of State undertook responsibility for the provision of support to asylum seekers and set up the National Asylum Support Service (NASS) to administer the scheme.

In the first instance, section 95 of the 1999 Act authorises the Secretary of State to provide or arrange for the provision of support for asylum seekers and their dependents who appear to him either to be destitute, as defined in section 95(3),[92] or likely to become so within a prescribed period of time. In turn, however, the authorisation of the Secretary of State is contingent on section 55(1) of the Immigration and Asylum Act 2002, which provides that he may not provide asylum support unless satisfied that a claim was made 'as soon as reasonably practicable after the person's arrival in the United Kingdom'.[93] However, since there is no right of appeal from that decision[94] and no discretion on the part of

---

[87]   *R v Eastbourne (Inhabitants)* (1803) 4 East 103, 107.

[88]   *JCWI* (note 85 above) 401 (Simon Brown LJ).

[89]   (1997) 1 CCLR 85.

[90]   Lord Woolf MR held: 'the destitute conditions to which asylum seekers can be reduced as a result of the 1996 Act, coupled with the period of time which despite the Secretary of State's best efforts elapses before their applications are disposed of, means inevitably that they can fall within a class who local authorities can properly regard as being persons for whose needs they have a responsibility to meet by the provision of accommodation under section 21(1)(a)' (94). Notably, Lord Woolf added: 'The longer the asylum seeker remains in the condition, the more compelling their case becomes to receive assistance under the subsection' (*R v Westminster City Council, ex parte M (ibid)* 94).

[91]   S 116 of the Immigration and Asylum Act 1999 has amended s 21 of the 1948 Act.

[92]   S 95(3) provides that an individual is destitute 'if he does not have adequate accommodation or any means of obtaining it whether or not his other living conditions are met' or 'if he has adequate accommodation or the means of obtaining it but cannot meet his other essential living needs'.

[93]   The primary object of s 55 of the 2002 Act can be viewed 'as preventing those who are not genuine asylum seekers and those who are not in fact in need of state support from seeking assistance' (*Q* (note 39 above) para 26 (Lord Phillips MR)).

[94]   A right of appeal from the Secretary of State's decision to an asylum adjudicator is expressly excluded by s 55(10). An application for judicial review may therefore be the only remedy available.

Asylum Support Adjudicators who administer it, following the enactment of the HRA it was deemed necessary to include exceptions to the lawful applicability of section 55 of the 2002 Act.

In their second report on the Immigration and Asylum Bill 2002,[95] the JCHR expressed the view that there was a 'significant risk that section 55 could lead to a violation of Article 11(1) of the ICESCR, even in cases where the circumstances of asylum seekers denied support did not amount to a violation of one of the Convention Rights as defined in the HRA 1998'.[96] The Committee furthermore expressed its opinion that it would be difficult to envisage a case in which a person could be destitute within the terms of section 95(3) of the 1999 Act without there being a threat of a violation of Articles 3 and 8 ECHR. Moreover, the attention of Parliament was drawn to the fact that the Secretary of State had a duty under section 6 HRA to avoid such a risk.[97]

In this Report, the JCHR also expressed concerns that its recommendations in an earlier Report had not been addressed in the passage of the Bill through Parliament. Thus, section 55(5)(a) of the National Immigration and Asylum Act 2002 was inserted by government amendment in the House of Lords, after the Bill had initially passed through the Commons and despite continuing JCHR reservations about its formulation. Accordingly, section 55(5) of the 2002 Act provides that it shall not prevent 'the exercise of a power by the Secretary of State to the extent that this is necessary for the purpose of avoiding a breach of a person's Convention rights (within the meaning of the Human Rights Act 1998)'.

C. A Crisis in the Administrative Courts

Shortly after section 55 of the 2002 Act came into force, large numbers of asylum seekers, although destitute within the terms of section 95(3) of the 1999 Act, were denied support by the Secretary of State, on grounds that they had not made their asylum claims as soon as reasonably practicable. Barred from employment, they claimed to be living 'rough on the streets' with no certain prospect of food or shelter other than that which might be obtained from charitable sources, from friends or by begging or stealing.[98] As a result, the administrative courts were overwhelmed by large numbers of claims in which destitute asylum seekers not only challenged the assertion by the Secretary of State that their 'claims had not been made as soon as reasonably practicable', but also sought to argue that their abject circumstances following his refusal constituted

---

[95] JCHR, '23rd Report: Nationality Immigration and Asylum Bill: Further Report' (2002–03) HL 176 HC 1255 (23 October 2002).

[96] *Ibid*, para 15. See the final section of chapter 1 above for the content of Article 11 ICESCR.

[97] *Ibid*.

[98] Evidence to this effect was provided by charities such as Shelter, the Refugee Council and National Asylum and Support Service (NASS).

degrading and inhuman treatment under Article 3 ECHR, and consequently a breach of section 6 HRA by the Secretary of State.

The problems of case-managing large numbers of claims that require intensive scrutiny of the minutiae of individual circumstances to decide if they constitute degrading and inhuman treatment within the meaning of Article 3, were compounded by lack of guidance in the Strasbourg jurisprudence as to the potential of Article 3 to engender positive obligations to protect individuals' rights in such contexts. UK courts therefore took refuge in the decision of the ECtHR in *Pretty*,[99] which recognised that 'suffering which flows from naturally occurring illness, physical or mental may be covered by article 3, where it is, or risks being exacerbated by treatment whether flowing from conditions of detention, expulsion or other measures for which the authorities can be held responsible'.[100]

However, doubts remained in some UK courts as to whether a regime that legitimated *inaction* on the part of authorities, of the kind imposed on asylum seekers by section 55(1) of the 2002 Act constituted 'treatment' within the meaning of Article 3 ECHR. Moreover, there were uncertainties about the level (beyond the description of destitution in section 95(3) of the 1999 Act) to which the circumstances of an individual must actually fall, before reaching what has come to be described in the administrative courts as the '*Pretty* threshold':

> Where treatment humiliates or debases an individual showing a lack of respect for or diminishing his or her human dignity or arouses feelings of fear anguish or inferiority capable of breaking an individual's moral or physical resistance it may be characterised as degrading and also fall within the prohibition of article 3 . . .[101]

Furthermore, following humane Divisional Court decisions by Collins J in *R (on the Application of Q) v Secretary of State for the Home Department* (hereafter Q)[102] and Maurice Kay J (as he then was) in *R (on the Application of T) v Secretary of State for the Home Department* (hereafter T),[103] there was further confusion in the administrative courts. Questions were raised as to whether it is enough for an individual's circumstances to *verge* on *Pretty*-style suffering, so that by analogy with the concept of 'real risk' in 'intended removal' cases such as *Chahal v UK*,[104] a continuing refusal of support by the Secretary of State

---

[99]   Note 20 above.

[100]   *Pretty* (note 20 above) para 52.

[101]   *Ibid.*

[102]   [2003] EWHC 195 Admin.

[103]   [2003] EWHC 1941 Admin.

[104]   (1997) 23 EHRR 413. The applicant challenged the decision to refuse him refugee status and subsequently to deport him. The UK government argued that there was an inherent limitation on the right not to be tortured in expulsion cases, so that even when there was a 'real risk' of ill-treatment on removal, the complainant could nevertheless be deported on national security grounds. The ECtHR rejected the Government's contention, a unanimous Grand Chamber holding that in relation to alleged breaches of Art 3, 'it was not enough to have a national remedy which is "as effective as can be" in respect of a complaint that a person's deportation will expose him or her to a "real risk" of treatment in breach of Article 3 irrespective of national security issues' (para 150). The 'real risk' test has been applied by the ECtHR since *Chahal* in cases of removal to another country in which the removing state will no longer be in a position to influence events relating to the applicant's security.

would be unlawful and require a rehearing of the claim in order to avoid breach of Article 3 ECHR. Although differently constituted Courts of Appeal in Q[105] and T[106] did comprehensively address these questions, as noted by Laws LJ in the later Court of Appeal decision in R v Secretary of State for the Home Department, ex parte Adam, Limbuela and Tesema (hereafter Limbuela),[107] it was clear that many of the issues surrounding the interpretation of section 55(5) of the 2002 Act had not been satisfactorily resolved.

Insight into the extent of the divisions in the administrative courts can be found in the three conjoined appeals that came before the Court of Appeal in *Limbuela* and in the first instance decision of R *(on the Application of Zardasht) v Secretary of State for the Home Department* (hereafter *Zardasht*),[108] which followed the Court of Appeal decision in *T*.[109] Thus, as Laws LJ before the Court of Appeal noted in *Limbuela*, some courts had been persuaded to adopt an approach known as the 'real risk' test, which would accord the benefit of section 55 as soon as it could be demonstrated that the claimant would otherwise go on the streets, while other courts were continuing to insist that the usual and necessary incidents of hardship experienced by destitute asylum seekers thus denied support, would not be enough to engage Article 3 ECHR. On the second view, until evidence could be adduced that an individual's circumstances had crossed the *Pretty* threshold,[110] there would be no obligation on the Secretary of State to provide support.

Thus, for example, at first instance in *Zardasht* Newman J opined that burdens imposed on asylum seekers who have been denied support are likely to be greater than those experienced by other asylum seekers arriving in this country: 'having no home or income, being a stranger to the language and the people, experiencing loneliness, anxiety, vulnerability'.[111] Nonetheless, 'setting aside such special circumstances as ill-health that might exacerbate these conditions', he considered it to be 'essential for practitioners to realise, that simply to state what could be regarded as the obvious, namely that the applicant is homeless, sleeping rough, has no money, and is known to be vulnerable, will not be likely

---

[105] Note 39 above, 909, para 5.

[106] [2003] EWCA Civ 1285.

[107] [2004] EWCA Civ 540, [2005] 3 All ER 29. See also the later House of Lords decision (note 5 above), discussed in sections I and II above.

[108] [2004] EWCH 91. The claimant was a 20-year-old Iraqi. Support that he initially received was withdrawn following a decision that he had not claimed asylum as soon as reasonably practicable under s 55(1) of the 2002 Act. He had no specific health problems and spent 14 days sleeping rough. Newman J dismissed his application for judicial review, holding that it was not clear that 'the high threshold laid down by *Pretty* . . . had been achieved in this case' (para 39).

[109] Note 106 above. At first instance in *T* (note 103 above) Maurice Kay J, having accepted T's account of the facts (he was living rough at Heathrow Airport), decided that his condition verged on the degree of severity described in *Pretty* (note 20 above). However, the Court of Appeal (note 106 above) decided that T had only been living rough for nine days, had some shelter (albeit of 'the most precarious kind') and some sanitary facilities in the form of public lavatories and 'though unwell was not in need of immediate treatment' (para 19).

[110] For the test in *Pretty* (note 20 above), see note 101 above and accompanying text.

[111] *Zardasht* (note 108 above) para 5.

to be regarded, in the normal run of things as sufficient'.[112] Instead, he argued that if someone like the applicant in *Zardasht* (a fit and healthy man of 20 years old), 'despite being homeless . . . could obtain food from charities during the day, or other sources, and some access to washing and sanitary facilities in the course of the day', it would be possible for him to live for an extended period under such conditions 'without severe adverse consequences reducing his condition to the *Pretty* level . . .'[113]

In short therefore, the trial judge in *Zardasht* considered that even though the claimant was unable to fend for himself in the sense of obtaining gainful employment, within the concept of 'fending for himself' should be included 'assistance and support which he might be able to obtain from friends, whether new or old, and family'.[114] Thus, Newman J thought that implicit in section 55(5) of the 2002 Act was an assumption that 'from such efforts, a palliative measure may ensue, so as to prevent the seriousness of his condition sinking to the *Pretty* level', and furthermore that the burden must fall on applicants to provide evidence of present circumstances that would qualify them for section 55(5) support.[115]

In a similar vein, the first instance judge in *R (on the Application of Adam) v Secretary of State for the Home Department* (hereafter *Ex parte Adam*)[116] specifically approved the approach of Newman J,[117] arguing that any other approach would be contrary to the decision of the Court of Appeal in *Q*,[118] which had expressly rejected the 'real risk' test.[119]

By contrast, Collins J, the first instance judge in Limbuela's case,[120] continued to express the opposite view:

---

[112] *Zardasht* (note 108 above), para 7.

[113] *Ibid*, para 12.

[114] *Ibid*, para 13.

[115] *Ibid*.

[116] [2004] EWHC 354 Admin.

[117] Adam, a Sudanese national, had arrived in the United Kingdom on 15 October 2003. Although he applied for asylum the following day, he had not done so as soon as 'reasonably practicable', and support was denied. From 16 October to 10 November, when interim relief was granted, he spent his days at the Refugee Council but had to leave in the evenings; nights were spent in a sleeping bag in a car park outside the Refugee Council. His mental and physical health suffered, and he was said to have felt 'totally humiliated at having to live in a car park'. Charles J granted his claim for judicial review but concluded that four months after arrival, he had not reached the *Pretty* threshold. Approving the reasoning of Newman J in *Zardasht*, he therefore refused relief.

[118] Note 39 above.

[119] In *Q* the Court of Appeal (note 39 above) decided that the fact that there was a real risk that an individual asylum seeker might be brought so low that he or she would be driven to crime or prostitution in order to survive would not of itself engage Art 3 ECHR. The same conclusion was reached by the Court of Appeal in *T* (note 106 above): 'it is not unlawful for the Secretary of State to decline to provide support until the individual is incapable of fending for himself' (para 63).

[120] *R (on the Application of Limbuela) v Secretary of State for the Home Department* [2004] EWHC 219 Admin. Limbuela was an Angolan national, age 25, who sought asylum at the Home Office on 6 May 2003, claiming to have arrived in the United Kingdom on the same day at an unknown airport. Although initially provided with emergency accommodation by NASS, the Secretary of State subsequently decided he had not claimed asylum as soon as reasonably practicable, and support was withdrawn in accordance with s 55(1). Evicted from his accommodation,

Treatment . . . which causes someone to sleep rough, in particular in winter, to have to beg or hope for the possibility that he might find someone prepared to provide him with food, to be required to live in the same clothes for days on end, which clothes may or may not be adequate to protect him from the English climate, will, as it seems to me, in most cases be sufficient to cross the relevant threshold . . . and . . . in the case of an asylum seeker who shows that he has taken reasonable steps and that no assistance is available except by begging and hoping, then the fact that he will have to sleep rough, he has no money, he is no proper access to food or other facilities, will be likely to suffice to establish his case.[121]

Thus, although he agreed that a claimant should be obliged to put before the court evidence about 'what steps he has taken to try and get support, and what effect it has had on him if he had to sleep rough or beg or whatever', like Kay J at first instance in *T*,[122] Collins J found it 'distasteful to require that "a wait and see" policy is adopted[:] . . . let us see whether his health does deteriorate, and then if it does, he can make an application'.[123] Agreeing also with the trial judge in Tesema's case (one of the three conjoined appeals in *Limbuela*),[124] Collins LJ in Limbuela's case concluded that once an asylum seeker who is denied NASS support under section 55 has shown that he has tried but failed to find accommodation and other support, so that he will have to sleep on the streets, he will have established an imminent breach of Article 3 ECHR and corresponding entitlement to be supported under section 55.[125]

However, seeking to extricate the debate from these evidentiary issues, in his dissent before the Court of Appeal in *Limbuela*, Laws LJ argued that reliance on dicta of the Strasbourg court in *Pretty* had 'encouraged the factual abitrament on a case-by-case basis' of 'who is or is not a proper candidate for section 55(5)

Limbuela slept rough outside a police station for two days before finding a bed at a homeless shelter. Asked to leave on 28 July, he applied for judicial review of the Secretary of State's decision. He suffered from a number of medical conditions, including abdominal pain, and said he had been detained and beaten by the police in Angola. In judicial review granted by Collins J on 4 February 2004, it was accepted that, but for a grant of interim relief, Limbuela would have had to sleep rough again.

[121] *Ibid*, para 27 (Collins J).

[122] In *T* (note 103 above), Kay J had reasoned that 'when a person without such access to private or charitable funds or support is refused asylum support and must wait for a protracted but indefinite period of time for the determination of his asylum application, it will often happen that, denied access to employment and other benefits, he will soon be reduced to a state of destitution (not in the section 95 sense) . . . In those circumstances and with uncertainty as to the duration of their predicament, the humiliation and diminution of their human dignity with the consequences referred to in *Pretty* will often follow within a short period of time' (para 33).

[123] Limbuela's case at first instance (note 120 above) para 32.

[124] *R (on the Application of Tesema) v Secretary of State for the Home Department* [2004] EWHC 295 Admin. Tesema, an Ethiopian national, arrived in the United Kingdom on 13 August 2003, claiming asylum the day after. Although initially provided, it was withdrawn after a decision by the SSHD that he had not sought asylum 'as soon as reasonably practicable'. Since he immediately applied for judicial review, the applicant had not yet had to sleep rough but would have had to do so, but for a grant of interim relief. He suffered pain and loss of hearing, which he attributed to being beaten up in Ethiopia, and had psychological difficulties. Gibbs J granted his claim for judicial review on 16 February 2004.

[125] See Limbuela's case at first instance (note 120 above) paras 37–41 (Collins J).

support'—in a manner that he considered to be entirely inconsistent with 'the proper role [of courts] in judicial review: to hold public decision makers to account for errors of law'.[126] Thus, he argued:

> We are left with a state of affairs in which our public courts are driven to make decisions whose dependence on legal principle is at best fragile, leaving uncomfortable scope for the social and moral preconceptions of the individual judge.[127]

D. *Limbuela*: The Court of Appeal

By the time of the conjoined appeals in *Limbuela*[128] there were over 650 asylum benefit cases in UK administrative courts awaiting its conclusion. In each case, the respondent had failed to claim asylum at the material time; had been brought to the country by an agent who had made all the travel arrangements; and was destitute as defined by section 95 of the 1999 Act. That provision considers an individual destitute if he 'does not have adequate accommodation or any means of obtaining it (whether or not his other essential living needs are met)', or if he 'has adequate accommodation or the means of obtaining it, but cannot meet his other essential living needs'.

In each of the conjoined cases in *Limbuela*, a judge had granted the application and the Secretary of State appealed the decision. Specifically, the Secretary of State requested guidance on the legal implications of the earlier Court of Appeal decision in *Q*,[129] which was regarded as authority for the proposition that: (i) the regime imposed on asylum seekers who are denied support by reason of section 55(1) of the 2002 Act constitutes 'treatment' within the meaning of Article 3 ECHR; and (ii) 'the imposition by the legislature of a regime which prohibits asylum seekers from working and further prohibits the grant to them of support amounts to positive action directed against asylum seekers and not to mere inaction'.[130]

The majority of the Court of Appeal in *Limbuela* (Carnwath and Jacob LLJ) concluded that the appeals by the Secretary of State should be dismissed.[131] First they rejected the 'wait and see' approach, which requires an asylum seeker to show the actual onset of severe illness or acute suffering before refusal of support will constitute breach of Article 3 ECHR. Instead, they were satisfied with general evidence that support was not going to be forthcoming and that there

---

[126] See Limbuela's case at first instance (note 120 above) paras 37–41 (Collins J), para 58.
[127] *Ibid.*
[128] Note 5 above.
[129] Note 39 above.
[130] *Ibid*, para 57 (Lord Philips MR).
[131] The Court of Appeal also rejected the view of the Court of Appeal in *T* (note 106 above), namely that since Art 3 ECHR raises issues of fact and law, it is possible to overrule the trial judge on issues of fact. Instead, in *Limbuela* it was decided that the Court of Appeal could only interfere with the decision of a court below if the trial judge was plainly wrong in law.

was a 'real risk' of ensuing indignity: the 'verging on' test was 'abhorrent, illogical and very expensive'.[132] Carnwath LJ therefore stated:

> If the evidence establishes clearly that charitable support is not in practice available, and [the applicant] has no other means of 'fending for himself', then the presumption will be that severe suffering will imminently follow.[133]

Furthermore, on the issue of the government's compliance with Article 3 ECHR, the Court of Appeal thought it inappropriate that the question should be judged by the possibility of so many variable circumstances, particularly the willingness of charities to commit their funds to providing a safety net. Carnwath LJ therefore argued that once it is accepted that Article 3 is potentially in play, if the system is unable to cope, then responsibility must fall on the state to take positive protective steps to remedy it. Significantly, he viewed the obligation 'to take measures' as implying 'more than simply acting as a long-stop in individual cases as they arise', arguing: 'that may be sufficient if the alternative system of charitable support is able to cope with the generality of cases, so that article 3 suffering is truly the exception'.[134] Thus, he considered that fairness and consistency could only be achieved if the Secretary of State has in place policies that define clear criteria to be applied by the decision makers.[135]

Jacob LJ was also satisfied that evidence from various charities had shown that if a number in the order of 500 or more people were put on the streets without money and no entitlement to earn any, there was a near certainty that a substantial proportion would fall below the Article 3 ECHR threshold.[136] Thus, he too argued that even if it could not be said of any particular individual that there is more than a very real risk that denial of food or shelter will take that individual across the threshold, 'one could say that collectively the current policy of the Secretary of State will have that effect in the case of a substantial number of people'.[137] It therefore seemed to Jacob LJ that 'the current policy (which includes having no policy at all, save in the case of heavily pregnant women) is unlawful as violating article 3'.[138]

By contrast, Laws LJ, who dissented, was critical of not only such overt judicial intervention into the political arena, but also the lack of legal analysis of the difference between positive and negative obligations in the context of Article 3

---

[132] *Limbuela* (note 5 above) para 142 (Jacob LJ).

[133] *Ibid*, para 95.

[134] *Ibid*, paras 120–1.

[135] See generally *ibid*, paras 121–30. Carnwath LJ noted that although there were 10 pages of guidance on the issue of 'reasonably practicable', the question of breach of Art 3 had been dealt with very briefly (para 121). Guidance notes stated: 'it is lawful for the Secretary of State to refuse to provide support unless and until it is clear that charitable support has not been provided and the individual is incapable of fending for himself such that his condition verges on the degree of severity described in *Pretty*' (para 122).

[136] For discussion of the indeterminate Art 3 threshold (the '*Pretty* threshold'), see note 101 above and accompanying text.

[137] *Limbuela* (note 5 above) para 149.

[138] *Ibid*.

ECHR. He therefore undertook what has since become known as a 'spectrum analysis' of Article 3 ECHR: he posited the need for a difference of approach in disputes founded on allegations of direct infliction of harm by the state or its agents on the one hand, and those founded on allegations of state failure to protect in non-violence cases on the other hand. Each type of dispute lay at opposite ends of a scale of state liability for violations of Article 3, with unauthorised acts of violence, criminal acts or omissions by state agents lying somewhere in between.[139]

Thus, Laws LJ argued in *Limbuela*, whereas state violence (other than in the limited and specific cases allowed by the law such as lawful arrest or self-defence) is always unjustified, acts or omissions of the state that expose persons to suffering other than violence (whether by state agents or third parties)—'even suffering which may in some instances be as grave from the victim's point of view as acts of violence which would breach article 3'[140]—are not categorically unjustifiable, and may indeed be capable of justification if they arise in the administration or execution of lawful government policy. In such cases, he argued, 'the decision is lawful unless the degree of suffering which it inflicts (albeit indirectly) reaches so high a degree of severity, that the court is bound to limit the state's right to implement the policy on article 3 grounds.'[141]

Therefore, on the scope of executive judgment limited by Article 3 ECHR, Laws LJ claimed:

> [W]e ought to . . . acknowledge a distance between the case where a person is exposed to hardship through circumstances because the state declines, in pursuit of *proper policy*, to give him food and shelter, and the case of state violence and kindred cases of state violence: it is surely the second category which, primarily at least the drafters of the Convention must have intended to outlaw.[142]

Accordingly, he continued:

> [W]e should also recognise and respect the claim of the democratic arm of government to exercise and fulfil its powers and duties which lie within its particular responsibility, [which] . . . plainly . . . include the management of immigration control and so of asylum claims.[143]

Laws LJ furthermore cited his own judgment before the Court of Appeal in *N v Secretary of State for the Home Department*:[144]

---

[139] *Ibid*, paras 59–70 (Laws LJ). The spectrum analysis was subsequently followed by the Court of Appeal in *R (on the Application of Gezer) v Secretary of State for the Home Department* [2004] EWCA Civ 1730.

[140] *Limbuela* (note 5 above) para 68.

[141] *Ibid*, para 70.

[142] *Ibid*, para 72 (emphasis added).

[143] *Ibid*. Laws LJ expressed particular difficulties with the case of *D v UK* (1997) 24 EHRR 423: 'A claim to be protected from the harsh effect of a want of resources albeit made harsher by its contrast with the facilities available in the host country is to my mind something else altogether' (*Limbuela* (note 5 above) para 73).

[144] [2003] EWCA Civ 1369.

The idea of the 'living instrument', which is a well accepted characterisation of the Convention and some other international texts dealing with rights, no doubt gives the Convention a necessary elastic quality, so that its application is never too distant from the spirit of the time. I have difficulty in seeing that it should stretch so far as to impose on the signatory states forms of obligation wholly different in kind from anything contemplated in the scope of their agreement.[145]

Laws LJ's analysis of the scope of Article 3 ECHR marked a radical departure from earlier Court of Appeal decisions in Q[146] and T.[147] The House of Lords in fact later noted that it is difficult to identify any basis for such an analysis in Convention jurisprudence. However, Carnwath and Jacob LLJ in *Limbuela* expressed support for the spectrum analysis as a useful tool, and it was later employed in *R (on the Application of Gezer) v Secretary of State for the Home Department*.[148] It therefore provoked further discussion on appeal by the Secretary of State to the House of Lords.

E. *Limbuela*: The House of Lords Abhors the Subtraction of ECHR Rights

In the landmark House of Lords decision of *Limbuela*,[149] it was unanimously decided that section 55 NIAA 2002 had placed an unqualified duty on the Secretary of State to take positive measures to ensure that the elementary needs of asylum seekers with no other means of support are met, since a decision to withdraw support under section 55(1) NIAA was an intentionally inflicted act for which the Secretary of State was directly responsible—thereby engaging Article 3 ECHR. Thus, as Lord Bingham put it:

Where (and to the extent) that exercise of the power [under section 95 of the 1999 Act] is necessary, the Secretary of State is subject to a duty, and has no choice, since it is unlawful for him under section 6 of the [HRA] to act incompatibly with a Convention right. Where (and to the extent) that exercise of the power is not necessary, the Secretary of State is subject to a statutory prohibition, and again has no choice. Thus, the Secretary of State (in practice, of course, officials acting on his behalf) must make a judgment on the situation of the individual applicant matched against what the Convention requires or proscribes, but he has in the strict sense, no discretion.[150]

Moreover, it was unanimously agreed by the House of Lords that the obligation under Article 3 ECHR in relation to such intentionally inflicted acts was absolute, so that in determining whether the treatment in a particular case had reached the minimum level of severity, courts should not apply a more exacting test when treatment or punishment that would otherwise be found to

---

[145] *Ibid*, para 38 (Laws LJ).
[146] Note 39 above.
[147] Note 106 above.
[148] Note 139 above.
[149] Note 5 above.
[150] *Limbuela* (note 5 above) para 5.

be degrading was the result of legitimate government policy.[151] In particular, Lord Hope, who gave the most comprehensive speech in *Limbuela*, confessed to a 'feeling of unease' about Laws LJ's spectrum analysis. He decided that it was not only impossible to find any foundation for such a spectrum in the Strasburg jurisprudence but also difficult to 'find a sound basis for it in the language of article 3'.[152] For Lord Hope, the only classification to be found in the ECtHR jurisprudence was 'the result of its recognition that article 3 may require states to provide protection against inhuman or degrading treatment or punishment for which they themselves are *not* directly responsible, including cases where such treatment is administered by private individuals'.[153]

Furthermore, observing that it is impossible to embrace all human conditions that will engage Article 3 with a single simple definition, Lord Hope accepted that 'the exercise of judgment is required in order to determine whether in any given case the treatment or punishment has attained the necessary degree of severity'.[154] While agreeing that 'it is open to the court to consider whether, taking all the facts into account, this test has been satisfied',[155] he stated:

> [I]t would be wrong to lend any encouragement to the idea that the test is more exacting where the treatment or punishment which would otherwise be found to be inhuman or degrading is the result of what Laws LJ refers to as legitimate government policy: That would be to introduce into the absolute prohibition, by the backdoor, considerations of proportionality.[156]

Lord Hope therefore concluded in *Limbuela* that, irrespective of whether inhuman or degrading treatment or punishment results from deliberate infliction of harm, 'where it results from acts or omissions for which the state *is directly responsible*, there is no escape from the negative obligation on states to refrain from such conduct, which is absolute'.[157] Thus, he was clear that the 'real issue' was 'whether the state is properly to be regarded as responsible for the harm'.[158]

Moreover, their Lordships in *Limbuela* unanimously rejected the inhumanity of the 'wait and see' approach, which had echoed to and fro in the administrative courts. Lord Hope observed, by contrast with Newman J's reasoning in *Zardasht*,[159] that the power under section 55(5)(a) NIAA 2002, which enables the Secretary of State to 'avoid' a breach of Article 3 ECHR, has a prospective purpose that is wholly at odds with the need for an applicant to show that he

---

[151] *Limbuela* (note 5 above) para 5: '[I]t would be wrong to lend encouragement to the idea that the test is more exacting where the treatment . . . is the result of what Laws LJ refers to as a legitimate government policy' (para 55 (Lord Hope)).

[152] *Ibid*, para 53 (Lord Hope).

[153] *Ibid* (emphasis added).

[154] *Ibid*, para 55.

[155] *Ibid*.

[156] *Ibid*.

[157] *Ibid* (emphasis added).

[158] See *ibid*, paras 50–4 (Lord Hope).

[159] Note 108 above.

has suffered or was suffering a breach of Convention rights before becoming eligible for support: the purpose of section 55(5) was to 'prevent a breach from taking place not to wait until there is a breach and address the consequences.'[160]

Their Lordships therefore concluded that courts should look at the particular context and facts of each case, including factors such as the age, sex, health of the claimant and the length of time spent or likely to be spent without the required means of support. Moreover, their Lordships listed the kind of factors considered relevant in lower courts for determining that the requisite degree of suffering was imminent: 'any facilities or sources of support available to the applicant, the weather and time of year and the period for which the applicant has already suffered or is likely to continue to suffer privation'.[161]

In accepting the impossibility of formulating a simple test applicable in all cases, Lord Bingham was clear:

> [I]f there were persuasive evidence that a late applicant was obliged to sleep in the street, save perhaps for a short and foreseeably finite period, or was seriously hungry or unable to satisfy the most basic requirements of hygiene, the threshold would, in the ordinary way, be crossed . . . [so that] . . . in such circumstances, the Secretary of State's power to provide support under section 95 would be transformed into a duty. . . . It is not necessary that treatment, to engage article 3, should merit the description used, in an immigration context, by Shakespeare and others in Sir Thomas More when they referred to 'your mountainish inhumanity'.[162]

Furthermore, Lord Bingham did not think, as suggested by Laws LJ in the Court of Appeal, that *O'Rourke v UK*[163] was authority for the contrary proposition. Indeed it was generally agreed among their Lordships that *O'Rourke* differed from the cases at hand because, although the claimant had lived rough on the streets for 14 months to the detriment of his health, it was the claimant himself, rather than the state, who could be regarded as author of his grave misfortunes. Notwithstanding, Lord Bingham accepted that the test was a high one in circumstances of the kind at hand, which did not involve the deliberate infliction of pain or suffering.[164]

Lord Scott pursued the issue of state responsibility further, drawing a distinction between a mere *failure* to provide a minimum level of social support in accordance with lawful policy (which would *not* engage Article 3 ECHR) and

---

[160] *Limbuela* (note 5 above) para 61 (Lord Hope). Although Lord Hope was conscious that 'the legislation assumes that destitution, as defined in section 95(3) [of the 1999 Act], is not in itself enough to engage section 55(5)(a)', he was also conscious of the JCHR comment that it was 'difficult to imagine a case where a person could be destitute as defined [in statute] without giving rise to a threat of a violation of articles 3 and/or 8 of the Convention' (23rd Report (note 95 above) para 15).

[161] *Limbuela* (note 5 above) para 59 (Lord Hope). See also para 8 (Lord Bingham) and para 78 (Baroness Hale).

[162] *Ibid*, paras 7–9.

[163] Note 36 above.

[164] 'A general public duty to house the homeless or provide for the destitute cannot be spelled out of article 3' (*Limbuela* (note 5 above) para 7 (Lord Bingham)).

the *imposition* of a statutory regime 'on an individual, or on a class to which the individual belongs, barring that individual from basic social security and other state benefits to which he or she would, were it not for that statutory regime, be entitled'.[165] Thus, since asylum seekers and their dependents as temporary residents are prohibited from working,[166] the effect of the sum of measures imposed was a result, 'not of mere failure to supply such support, but of measures deliberately taken by the state to exclude them from obtaining it'.[167] On this approach, it mattered not whether they were prevented from gaining the support by their own efforts or from the state itself.[168]

Lord Brown similarly emphasised that the real issue in all the conjoined cases of *Limbuela* was 'whether the state is properly to be regarded as responsible for the harm inflicted (or threatened) upon the victim', while bearing in mind that special duties are found where the state's duty is to intervene to prevent suffering inflicted by others.[169] In particular, he rejected attempts to analyse obligations arising under Article 3 ECHR as either negative or positive, and the state's conduct as either active or passive, arguing that 'time and again these are shown to be false dichotomies'.[170] Instead, in determining the scope of the government's obligation, the fact of the matter was that the state's responsibility emanated from its own positive decision to deny rights to asylum-seekers that they had previously and that were available to other members of the community.

In generally considering the severity of deprivation that would constitute a breach of Article 3 ECHR, the House of Lord in *Limbuela* thus confirmed that there could be 'no hard and fast rules' and declined to posit a minimum core standard, stressing instead that whether there was a breach of Article 3 must be determined in the administrative courts on a case-by-case basis. However, both Lords Scott and Brown thought it relevant to consider that the most basic benefits denied to asylum seekers were available to other members of the community:

> It seems to me one thing to say as the European Court of Human Rights did in *Chapman* that within the contracting states there are unfortunately many homeless people and whether to provide funds for them is a political and not a judicial issue: quite another for a comparatively rich (not to say northerly) country like the UK to single out a particular group to be left utterly destitute on the streets as a matter of policy.[171]

In his concluding remarks Lord Brown considered Prime Minister Tony Blair's comments in his Foreword to an earlier government paper concerning the scandal of rough sleeping by groups such as care-leavers, ex-servicemen and

---

[165] 'A general public duty to house the homeless or provide for the destitute cannot be spelled out of article 3' (*Limbuela* (note 5 above), para 69.

[166] S 8 Asylum and Immigration Act 1996; Schedule, Part 1, para 3 Immigration (Restrictions on Employment) Order 1996.

[167] *Limbuela* (note 5 above) paras 66–7 (Lord Scott).

[168] See *ibid*, paras 67–9 (Lord Scott).

[169] *Ibid*, para 92.

[170] *Ibid*.

[171] *Ibid*, para 99 (Lord Brown).

ex-offenders,[172] as intolerable 'in a modern civilised society'. This observation lent weight to Lord Brown's own humane instinct that such a situation was no less tolerable 'in the case of asylum seekers who are exercising their vital right to claim refugee status and meanwhile are entitled to be here' and those who have no entitlement whatever to other state benefits.[173]

Lord Bingham, Lord Hope and Baroness Hale also emphasised that there can be 'no hard and fast rules' for determining when Article 3 ECHR is engaged. However, coming closest to the idea of a core minimum entitlement, Baroness Hale argued that in addition to individual circumstances to be taken into account, the basic requirements of shelter and some money for food would be likely to be necessary components of the duty not to violate Article 3:

> [T]his is not a country in which it is generally possible to live off the land, in an indefinite state of rooflessness and cashlessness. It might be possible to endure rooflessness for some time without degradation if one had enough to eat and somewhere to wash oneself and one's clothing. It might be possible to endure cashlessness for some time if one had a roof and basic meals and hygiene facilities provided. But to have to endure the indefinite prospect of both, unless one is in a place where it is both possible and legal to live off the land, is in today's society both inhuman and degrading.[174]

Thus, by contrast with Lord Bingham's approach, which was to determine in every case whether 'it appears on a fair and objective assessment of all relevant facts and circumstances that an individual faces an imminent prospect of serious suffering, caused or materially aggravated by denial of shelter, food or the most basic necessities of life',[175] Baroness Hale's judgment humanely suggests that it would be hard for the Secretary of State to refuse asylum support when an individual would be left without money or shelter for anything more than a short space of time.[176]

Therefore leaving aside negative return cases such as *Chahal v UK*—in which harm is inflicted or likely to be inflicted by third parties, and the state may have responsibility to intervene to prevent it—in relation to positive state obligations under Article 3 ECHR, the House of Lords indicated in *Limbuela* that attempts at elaborate legal classification of circumstances in which positive duties will arise must be subordinated to more open-textured questions about whether the state is responsible for harm. Moreover, although Article 14 ECHR was notably

---

[172] Department of Employment, Training and Rehabilitation (DETR) Rough Sleepers Unit, 'Coming in from the Cold: The Government's Strategy on Rough Sleeping' (1999). See also DETR Rough Sleepers Unit, 'Coming in from the Cold: Progress Report on the Government's Strategy on Rough Sleeping' (2000).

[173] *Limbuela* (note 5 above) para 99 (Lord Brown).

[174] Here Baroness Hale was drawing an analogy with Lord Hoffman's approval of the formulation 'persecution = serious harm + the failure of state protection' in the context of the Convention Relating to the Status of Refugees 1951: *R v Immigration Appeal Tribunal, ex parte Shah* [1999] 2 AC 629, 653.

[175] *Limbuela* (note 5 above) para 8 (Lord Bingham).

[176] Lord Brown appears to have agreed (para 102), although also deferred in principle to Lord Bingham.

not invoked in *Limbuela*, as it was in *A v Secretary of State for the Home Department*,[177] the discriminatory nature of the denial of rights to a particular group was regarded as an important and relevant issue in reaching their conclusions that such degrading and humiliating treatment could not be tolerated.

In summary, the House of Lords in *Limbuela* concluded that in determining whether there has been a breach of Article 3 ECHR, the combined effect of different legislative measures—in other words, the legal structure—should be considered as a whole, both for purposes of deciding whether there has been 'treatment' on the part of the authorities or third parties, and for deciding whether that treatment falls into the category of 'degrading and inhuman'. Crucially therefore, it was held that once the government has crossed the divide, when failure to provide support has translated into active treatment, it can no longer be sufficient for the state to rely on a general principle that the provision of state benefits is a political, issue, which is not open to judicial scrutiny.

Thus, rejecting both the mechanistic approach, which focuses on the limited range of cases in which positive steps may be necessary to *prevent* individuals from suffering,[178] and also Laws LJ's extended spectrum analysis (as inviting needless comparison with other cases), Lord Brown in *Limbuela* reiterated the observation he had made earlier in *N* before the House of Lords[179] about the manifold considerations in play and the need in all but the clearest cases 'to look at the problem in the round' when determining government responsibility and breaches of Article 3 ECHR.[180]

F. Revisiting *D v UK*: *N v Secretary of State for the Home Department* and the Limits of State Responsibility to Provide Life-saving Treatment under Article 3 ECHR

Prior to their decision in *Limbuela*[181] and in light of uncertainties about the precise boundaries of the Article 3 ECHR guarantee revealed by the ECtHR case of *D v UK*[182] and subsequent cases, the House of Lords was required in *N*[183] to consider a life and death issue, namely whether the deportation of people suffering from HIV/AIDS is consistent with the state's responsibility under Article 3 ECHR. Moreover, if as contended by the claimant in *N*, *D v UK* was authority for the proposition that there is a continuing obligation to provide life-saving treatment under the NHS, an important question in *N* was the extent to which,

---

[177] [2004] UKHL 56, [2005] 2 AC 68.
[178] See chapter 2 above for Article 3 developments in the line of cases that started with *Soerig v UK* (1989) 11 EHRR 439.
[179] Note 8 above. For further discussion of *N*, see subsection F below.
[180] See *N* (note 8 above) paras 87–9 (Lord Brown).
[181] Note 5 above. See subsection E above.
[182] Note 143 above. See generally chapter 2 above.
[183] Note 8 above.

in giving effect to their obligations under section 2(1) HRA, the House of Lords should be hidebound by Strasbourg jurisprudence.[184]

In 1998 the claimant in *N* arrived on a false passport in very poor health from Uganda. She was diagnosed as suffering from an AIDS-defining illness, of which she had been wholly unaware on arrival. However, after a long period of treatment with antiretroviral medication under the NHS, her condition stabilised to the extent that with continued access to medical facilities, her prognosis was that she would likely remain well for decades. At the same time, however, there was strong evidence that if she were deported to Uganda in accordance with requirements of immigration law, she would be unlikely to afford the necessary medical treatment there, and once denied the level of medical care she was receiving in the United Kingdom, after a period of acute physical and mental suffering, early death would follow. It was therefore recognised by the House of Lords that in light of advances in the treatment of AIDS, the reality of the choice facing the authorities was either to allow the patient to be sustained by expensive medical care in the United Kingdom for the rest of her life, or by deporting her to Uganda to precipitate an immediate decline in health and shortly after that her death.

Although the Secretary of State had refused the appellant's asylum claim, in light of the ECtHR decision in *D v UK*, an immigration adjudicator found that deportation would violate N's rights under Article 3 ECHR. However, it was unanimously concluded by the House of Lords that her deportation would not constitute a violation of Article 3. Despite evidence that she had been subjected to horrendous violence at the hands of terrorist organisations and raped by rogue elements in the Ugandan authorities, those violations had not been perpetrated by the state. She was not therefore entitled to refugee status—despite cogent humanitarian reasons for allowing her to stay.

Despite this decision, in light of obligations to take account of relevant ECHR jurisprudence, it was also necessary for the House of Lords in *N* to grapple with the implications of the ostensibly far-reaching case of *D v UK*, in which the ECtHR had further extended the scope of Article 3 protection to circumstances in which the risk of harm stems from factors that do not in themselves violate Article 3 ECHR.[185] In that case, the ECtHR accepted that there was no question of the complainant being exposed to standards of treatment in St Kitts that would in themselves violate Article 3 and recognised that aliens subject to expulsion are not 'entitled to remain in a state for the sole purpose of continuing to benefit from medical social or other forms of social assistance' but nonetheless concluded that 'in the very exceptional circumstances of this case and given the compelling humanitarian considerations at stake, it must be concluded that the

---

[184] For an important illustration of the application of s 2(1) HRA in practice, see in particular the speeches of Lord Hope (paras 37–50), Baroness Hale (paras 62–71) and Lord Brown (paras 76–99) in *N* (note 8 above).

[185] See generally chapter 2 above.

implementation of the decision to remove the applicant would be a violation of article 3'.[186]

The House of Lord in *N* was critical of the uncertainty generated by the reasoning of the ECtHR in *D v UK* and in subsequent decisions where attempts had been made to distinguish it; and they regretted the lack of direction as to the 'exceptional circumstances' that might engage the protection of Article 3 ECHR.[187] Regretting that the ECtHR 'had [not] done more to identify the criterion by which such cases were to be identified',[188] Lord Hope finally concluded in *N* that the crucial factor in *D v UK* was to be found in the applicant's medical condition at the time of the complaint: 'It was the fact that he was already terminally ill while still present in the territory of the expelling state that made his case exceptional'.[189] Moreover, a review of the case law,[190] which demonstrated that despite a number of petitions, only two AIDS cases had since been found admissible by the Strasbourg Commission,[191] confirmed for Lord Hope that D's circumstances 'had been taken as the paradigm case of what is meant by this formula'.[192] Moreover, for Lord Hope, the later decision in

---

[186] *D v UK* (note 143 above) para 54.

[187] See *N* (note 8 above) para 36 (Lord Hope). In *BB v France*, Reports of Judgments and Decisions 1998-VI, the Commission confusingly focused on the conditions in the receiving country rather than on the circumstances that made the case exceptional (2595). Compare *Bensaid v UK* (2001) 33 EHRR 205, in which it was accepted that deporting a person with mental illness could engage Art 3 ECHR. In that case, and the Court carefully analysed the type, quality and availability of mental health care in Algeria before deciding that it would not be a violation of Art 3 to deport a person with acute schizophrenic symptoms.

[188] *N* (note 8 above) para 35 (Lord Hope).

[189] *Ibid*, paras 35 and 36 (Lord Hope).

[190] See *Karara v Finland*, App No 40900/98 (29 May 1998) unreported; *MM v Switzerland*, App No 43348/98 (14 September 1998) unreported; *SCC v Sweden*, App No 46553/99 (15 February 2000) unreported; *Henao v Netherlands*, App No 13669/03 (24 June 2003) unreported; *Ndangoya v Sweden*, App No 17868/03 (22 June 2004) unreported; *Amegnigan v Netherlands*, App No 25629/04 (25 November 2004) unreported; *BB v France* (note 187 above); *Tatete v Switzerland*, App No 41874/98, judgement of 18 November 1998, E Com HR.

[191] *BB v France* (note 187 above); and *Tatete v Switzerland* (*ibid*).

[192] *N* (note 8 above) para 48. See also the observations of Baroness Hale (paras 64–6):

> In *BB v France* . . . the Commission's focus . . . did appear to be more on conditions in the receiving country than on the severity of the applicant's present condition. . . . In *Tatete v Switzerland*, Application No 41874/98, 18 November 1999, the Commission held that there were complicated questions of fact and law, so that the application could not be said to be manifestly ill founded, and once again a friendly settlement was later reached. Neither case was as extreme as *D*, although the applicant in *BB* was already very ill. All the other cases have been found inadmissible. . . . In all of these the Commission or court has asked itself whether the expulsion 'would be contrary to the standards of article 3 in view of [the applicant's] present medical condition'. Their findings in *Henao v The Netherlands* . . . are typical: 'it does not appear that the applicant's illness has attained an advanced or terminal stage, or that he has no prospect of medical care or family support in his country of origin.' Also typical is the statement of principle in *Henao* [. . .]: 'According to established case law aliens who are subject to expulsion cannot in principle claim any entitlement to remain in the territory of a contracting state in order to continue to benefit from medical, social or other forms of assistance provided by the expelling state. However, in exceptional circumstances an implementation of a decision to remove an alien may, owing to compelling humanitarian considerations, result in a violation of article 3 . . .' [. . .] In the most recent of these cases, *Amegnigan v The Netherlands* (25 November 2004), the court was faced with evidence that 'as soon as the

Bensaid v UK[193] confirmed that the high threshold set by Article 3 applies especially when the case does not concern the direct responsibility of the contracting state for the infliction of the harm. Thus, Lord Hope observed that although the ECtHR in *Bensaid* recognised the difficulties of access to medical treatment in Algeria for a patient suffering from a severe long-term psychiatric illness, the fact that his circumstances would be less favourable than those enjoyed in the United Kingdom could not be decisive: some medical treatment was 'available' to him there.[194]

Thus, the House of Lords in *N* concluded that the inference to be drawn from Strasbourg jurisprudence is that it is not necessarily a violation of Article 3 ECHR to return an AIDS patient, unless the facts are on all fours either with those in *D v UK* (in other words, if the applicant's condition is advanced or at a terminal stage) *or* with those in the HIV/AIDS cases that had been found admissible (in other words, if there will be a complete absence of palliative care or family support after deportation). Accordingly, the difficult conclusion for the House of Lords was that the circumstances of the applicant in *N* were distinguishable from those of the applicant in *D v UK* and were not exceptional: her present medical condition was not critical, and she was fit to travel. Lord Brown further observed: 'There are an estimated 25 million people living with HIV in sub-Saharan Africa and many more millions AIDS sufferers the world over.'[195]

This conclusion did not mean that their Lordships were prepared to mask the real implications of their decision for the claimant—that she would be facing certain death in her own country. They recognised the humanitarian grounds for a different solution in the applicant's case and were mindful of the proviso by the ECtHR in *D v UK*; but after considering the implications of the decision in the round, Lord Nicholls nonetheless concluded: 'Article 3 cannot be interpreted as requiring contracting states to admit and treat AIDS sufferers from all over the world for the rest of their lives';[196] and Baroness Hale agreed that it would be implying far more into the UK obligation under Article 3 ECHR than demanded by Strasbourg jurisprudence.[197] Lord Hope furthermore pointed out that any other conclusion would risk drawing large numbers of people already suffering from HIV into the United Kingdom, in the hope of remaining indefinitely.[198]

> anti-HIV therapy would be stopped, the applicant would fall back to the advanced stage of the disease which, given its incurable nature, would entail a direct threat for life' . . . but that 'the HIV virus would be suppressed as long the applicant would continue taking medication, so that there was no direct threat for life.' . . . It nevertheless concluded that, unlike the situation in *D*, 'it does not appear that the applicant's illness has attained an advanced or terminal stage, or that he has no prospect of medical care or family support in Togo, where his mother and a young brother are residing. The fact that the applicant's circumstances in Togo would be less favourable than those he enjoys in the Netherlands cannot be regarded as decisive from the point of view of article 3 of the Convention.'

[193] Note 18 above.
[194] *N* (note 8 above) para 44.
[195] *Ibid*, para 72 (Lord Brown).
[196] *Ibid*, para 17 (Lord Nicholls).
[197] *Ibid*, para 71 (Baroness Hale).
[198] *Ibid*, para 53 (Lord Hope).

Nevertheless, Lord Hope also expressed dissatisfaction with the failure of the ECtHR to address openly the distinction between *D v UK* and a contemporary AIDS cases such as *N*, in which the applicant's present state of health 'on a true analysis of the facts' was attributable to 'treatment, the continuation of which is so much at risk'.[199] Moreover, Lord Brown suggested that medical advances since *D* have now made antiretroviral treatment comparable to a life support machine,[200] while Lord Nicholls argued that an attempt to determine a 'difference of degree in humanitarian appeal by analysing a claimant's *current* state of health was an unsatisfactory basis for distinguishing between D's case and other AIDS cases'.[201] Since the humanitarian life-and-death considerations underpinning *N*, which were 'of a very high order', had not yet been openly confronted by the ECtHR, Lord Nicholls agreed that *D v UK* was no more than authority for the general proposition that 'Article 3 does not require contracting states to undertake the obligation of providing aliens indefinitely with medical treatment lacking in their own country'.[202]

It was therefore finally concluded in *N* that far from promoting a positive right to continuing medical care in the receiving state, Strasbourg jurisprudence since *D v UK* has severely limited the nature of the humanitarian response called for in such cases—a response that, by focusing respectfully on the imminence of death, should ensure that the complainant receives appropriate end-of-life treatment. This was particularly clear when Baroness Hale stated that rather than giving rise to such an impracticable undertaking, the decision can best be understood as a specific affirmation of the principle of human dignity that underpins the ECHR rights:

> But if it is indeed the case that this class of cases is limited to those where the applicant is in the advanced stages of a life threatening illness, it would appear inhuman to send him home to die unless the conditions there will be such that he can do so in dignity.[203]

IV. CONCLUSION

Although focusing on very different substantive issues, the cases of *Anufrijeva* and *Limbuela* each recognised the potential for Articles 3 and 8 ECHR to give rise to positive state duties to protect vulnerable individuals in welfare needs contexts. In *Anufrijeva*, central government responsibility for failure to provide for the welfare needs of claimants was not directly in point. Instead, in *Anufrijeva* questions about the limits of public authority obligations to provide for the needs of vulnerable individuals were characteristically discussed by reference to the potential effects of positive judicial interventions on limited

---

[199] *N* (note 8 above), para 49.
[200] *Ibid*, para 92.
[201] *Ibid*, para 14 (emphasis added).
[202] *Ibid*, para 15.
[203] *Ibid*, para 68.

public authority and court resources, and more generally by reference to the impropriety of judicial intervention in policy disputes of this kind. By contrast, in *Limbuela*, as a result of the unusual formulation of section 55(5) of the NIAA 2002, Parliament had invited the courts to engage in one of the most far-reaching policy disputes about the limits of government responsibility under the HRA to provide for the elementary needs of vulnerable individuals in the United Kingdom.

Thus, without questioning the legitimacy of the government's policy but rather its implementation, it was constitutionally appropriate for Lord Brown in *Limbuela* to note the inconsistencies between the purpose of section 55 NIAA 2002, which was to deter individuals from claiming asylum at the end of their stay,[204] and the common practice of refusing support when delay had been no more than a day or a matter of hours (as in Limbuela's case):

> I do not wish to minimise the advantages which the government seek to gain from their policy towards late claimants. But nor should these be overstated. It is in reality unlikely that many claims will be made earlier as a result of it. Nor do the statistics suggest that late claimants make a disproportionate number of the unmeritorious claims. But more important to my mind is that . . . the policy's necessary consequence is that some asylum seekers *will* be reduced to street penury. This consequence must therefore be regarded either as intended, in which case it can readily be characterised as involving degrading treatment . . ., or unintended, involving hardship to a degree recognised as disproportionate to the policy's intended aims. Either way, in my opinion, street homelessness would cross the threshold into article 3 degrading treatment.[205]

Furthermore, while entirely accepting the argument of the majority of the ECtHR in *Chapman*[206] that whether to provide funds for the many homeless people in their jurisdictions is a political not a judicial issue, Lord Brown was clear that it is quite another matter 'for a comparatively rich, not to say northerly country like the UK, to single out a particular group to left utterly destitute on the streets as a matter of policy'.[207] As Baroness Hale saw it, 'the state had taken the Poor Law policy of "less eligibility" to an extreme which the Poor Law itself did not contemplate, in denying not only all forms of state relief but all forms of self sufficiency, save family and philanthropic aid, to a particular class of people'.[208]

---

[204] 'We need to allow a reasonable period before we presume that people have come into the country for another reason and have been sustaining themselves, then when they can no longer do so, have decided that the asylum system would sustain them, being more generous than the equivalent something-for-something welfare to work system . . . People who have been in this country for some time and have decided to claim asylum can continue with that claim, but there is no reason on God's earth why we should sustain them': David Blunkett MP, Hansard HC vol 392 col 199 (5 November 2002).

[205] *Limbuela* (note 5 above) para 101 (Lord Brown).

[206] Note 25 above. See also note 55 above.

[207] *Limbuela* (note 5 above) para 99 (Lord Brown).

[208] *Ibid*, para 92 (Baroness Hale).

In *Limbuela*, the human rights framework of ECHR positive duties thus played a crucial role in determining the scope of the government's duty to provide basic food and shelter for destitute asylum seekers. Moreover, the speeches from the House of Lords decision extend further than the predicaments of asylum seekers, by suggesting that it is a basic value of the unwritten UK constitution that the state will always be responsible for preventing destitution that arises as a result of a statutory regime of the kind imposed on the claimants— that is, a regime that has removed reliable and predictable forms of social support, while at the same time preventing those whom they have made destitute from working.

Furthermore, although much that was said in *Limbuela* related to the specific regime of degradation and hardship imposed on the claimants, the case may be viewed as articulating a more general and far-reaching proposition: that the state can be held responsible to meet the basic needs of everyone in the jurisdiction, wherever existing legal structures have been directly implicated in their denial.[209] The House of Lords speeches come close to suggesting a much broader principle, namely that whenever individuals are reduced to such poverty as a result of their inability to work, through old-age mental or physical infirmity, the state has responsibility to ensure that elementary needs are met through alternative appropriately tailored legal structures.

7

Article 14 ECHR and The Unequal Distribution of Public Goods and Services in the United Kingdom

The enjoyment of the rights and freedoms set forth in this Convention shall be secured without discrimination on any ground such as sex, race, colour, language, religion, political or other opinion, national or social origin, association with a national minority or property, birth or other status.

Article 14 of the European Convention on Human Rights (ECHR) 1950

In principle it does not seem at all unreasonable that in distributing public money in the form of social security benefits the state should be obliged to treat like cases alike, although . . . there may be differences of opinion as to what makes cases relevantly different. But the virtual absence of economic rights in the convention has made it difficult to relate this principle to the enjoyment of any specific right.

Lord Hoffman in R (Carson) v Secretary of State for Work and Pensions[1]

I. INTRODUCTION

This chapter is primarily concerned with Article 14 ECHR disputes in which individuals have challenged perceived inequities in the distribution of public goods. However, by contrast with the previous chapter, which focused on issues of vulnerability, this chapter examines disputes in which unfairness is claimed on substantive grounds such as age, religion and sex. The focus here is on the key House of Lords decision in R (on the Application of Carson) v Secretary of State for Work and Pensions; R (on the Application of Reynolds) v Secretary of State for Work and Pensions (conjoined cases referred to hereafter as Carson).[2] Encouraged by recent developments in ECHR jurisprudence in cases such as Koua Poirrez v France,[3] claimants in these UK cases have tested the extent to which Article 14 taken together either with Article 1 of Protocol 1 or with

[1] [2005] UKHL 37, [2005] 2 WLR 1369, [2005] 4 All ER 545.
[2] Ibid.
[3] (2005) 40 EHRR 34. See discussion of developments in Article 14 ECHR jurisprudence in chapter 2 above.

Article 8 ECHR, can be used to challenge the proportionality of legislative measures for the distribution of discretionary socio-economic entitlements.

Developments of the kind in *Koua Poirrez* had been viewed by welfare rights campaigners such as the Child Poverty Action Group as affording potential to challenge the monetary levels at which socio-economic entitlements have been set. However, closer inspection reveals not only the precarious foundations of the *Koua Poirrez* line of authority in Strasbourg, but also the need to take into account the tension between the individualistic thrust of the ECHR rights on the one hand, and the cooperative model of social justice and citizenship on which the welfare state has been founded on the other hand. Thus, in *Carson* we see how in two very disparate areas of public provision (retirement pension and jobseeker's allowance), the House of Lords has grappled with the fundamental tension between the individualistic approach to fairness in the attainment of public goods reflected in *Koua Poirrez*, and the collectivist nature of a contributory social welfare system such as that in the United Kingdom, where the distribution of welfare goods and services has historically been determined in accordance with the political balancing of society's needs, rather than by an overriding requirement that there should be equality of outcome in the distribution of individual entitlements.

In seeking to resolve this tension in Article 14 ECHR disputes, the House of Lords has drawn a functional albeit fluid line between disputes in which discrimination (for example, on grounds of sex, race or disability) involves an assault on core values enshrined in the UK constitution, and less 'suspect' cases in which the *real* subject of challenge has been the rationality of policy choices resulting in unequal treatment of a particular individual or group. Moreover, fundamental questions were also addressed in *Carson* about the utility of the formalistic, so-called *Michalak* approach to the resolution of Article 14 disputes,[4] which has been applied by UK courts since shortly after the Human Rights Act (HRA) 1998 came into force.

In addition to dealing with specific Article 14 ECHR issues, this chapter provides a platform for more general questions about the potential of the HRA to address issues of fairness in the distribution of public goods and services. Comparisons are drawn with UK 'equalities legislation', which since the middle of the 1960s has systematically outlawed discrimination on grounds of race, sex, religion and now disability. Thus, the final section of the chapter focuses on the implications of the Equality and Human Rights Act 2006 (hereafter Equality Act), which has sought to marry traditional legislative approaches to outlawing discriminatory treatment in the provision of public goods and services, with a human rights approach to resolving these issues.[5] Under the Act, in addition

---

[4] See *Wandsworth London BC v Michalak* (hereafter *Michalak*) [2002] 4 All ER 1136. See also discussion at notes 27 and 99 below and especially discussion in section V below.

[5] The general purpose of the Committee established by the Act (see below) is to work towards the elimination of prejudice against members of groups who share a common attribute in respect of any of the following matters: age; disability; gender; proposed, commenced or completed reassignment of gender; race; religion or belief; and sexual orientation. See s 10(1)–(2) of the Equality Act 2006.

to promoting awareness of rights under specific 'equality enactments',[6] a Commission for Equality and Human Rights (CEHR)[7] will 'promote awareness understanding and protection of human rights and encourage public authorities' (including courts) 'to comply with section 6 of the Human Rights Act 1998', inter alia in matters relating to the provision of public services.[8]

Before proceeding, however, we should recall the discussion in previous chapters regarding the malleable concept of equality. Beyond its formal presence in Article 14 ECHR, the notion of equality has been recognised as fundamental to the idea of democracy itself and has been used by constitutional courts, together with principles of freedom and respect for human dignity, to impose positive obligations even in areas of socio-economic responsibility. Thus, not only has the House of Lords in *R v Secretary of State for the Home Department, ex parte Limbuela* (hereafter *Limbuela*)[9] reminded us that the 'the essence of the European Convention on Human Rights is respect for human dignity and human freedom'[10]; the principle of equality has also been shown to mean that states cannot single out a group traditionally discriminated against and subject them to this kind of treatment. Furthermore, the Court of Appeal decision in *Anufrijeva v Southwark London Borough Council* (hereafter *Anufrijeva*)[11] has confirmed that exclusion of some members of society from aspects of life essential to the attainment of their human potential, offends against the fundamental principles of equality and respect for human dignity that inform the ECHR rights. Thus, in both of these judgments we have seen how collectivist conceptions of equality have been used to inform judicial understandings of what is minimally required of governments in the provision of goods and services, particularly in a wealthy democracy such as the United Kingdom.

II. SOCIO-ECONOMIC ENTITLEMENTS AND THE LIMITS OF SUBSTANTIVE FAIRNESS IN ARTICLE 14 ECHR

Chapter one examined some attempts in other jurisdictions to rely on more broadly based equality provisions (such as the Fourteenth Amendment of the American Constitution[12]) or more advanced non-discrimination provisions (such as section 15 of the Canadian Charter of Fundamental Rights and Freedoms 1982[13]) to gain access to socio-economic entitlements. Thus, we have

---

[6] See *ibid*, s 8.

[7] To be inaugurated in October 2007.

[8] S 9 Equality Act 2006.

[9] [2005] UKHL 66, [2006] 1 AC 396.

[10] *Pretty v UK* (2002) 35 EHRR 1.

[11] [2003] EWCA Civ 1406.

[12] The Fourth Amendment to the US Constitution states: 'No state shall . . . deny to any person within its jurisdiction the equal protection of the laws'.

[13] Whereas Art 14 ECHR prohibits discrimination on grounds of sex, race, colour, language, religion, political or other opinion, national or social origin, association with a national minority and birth, by contrast, the equality provision under s 15 of the Canadian Charter spells out that every

already noted that by contrast with more general provisions in many written constitutions and human rights instruments, Article 14 ECHR has been restricted in two ways. First, the substantive arena in which discrimination or prejudice is forbidden has been restricted to the 'enjoyment of the rights and freedoms set forth in [the] Convention'.[14] Secondly, the *grounds* upon which discrimination is forbidden have been restricted to 'any ground such as [the specified grounds] or other status'.[15]

Nevertheless, as we have seen in chapter 2, the Strasbourg organs have adopted an expansive approach to the interpretation of both types of restriction,[16] gradually bringing allegations of discriminatory treatment in the allocation of economic social security benefits within the ambit of Article 14 ECHR. Indeed, more than three decades ago in *Muller v Austria*,[17] the ECHR Commission had already decided that by analogy with the proprietary right of a contributor to a private pension fund, a claim to contributory benefits in the Austrian municipal system was a 'possession', thereby grounding the complaint within the ambit of Article 14 taken together with the right to enjoyment of property protected by Article 1 of Protocol 1 ECHR.

However, the nexus between private economic property interests and social security entitlements[18] that has developed since *Muller v Austria* has been particularly problematic in countries such as the United Kingdom, where, as noted by Lord Hoffman in *Carson*,[19] 'contributions to the social security fund are hardly distinguishable from general taxation'.[20] As we have seen, this deficit has been addressed in Strasbourg by the argument that a claim to a discretionary social security benefit can have the characteristics of a possessory right, thereby falling within the ambit of Article 1 of Protocol 1, without entitling the claimant to 'anything in particular'.[21] However, this artificial line of reasoning has recently taken a new twist in the case of *Koua Poirrez v France*,[22] in which the European Court of Human Rights (ECtHR) paradoxically *emphasised* disparities between contributory and non-contributory benefits, as justification for

---

individual has a right to equal benefit and protection of the law without discrimination and in particular without discrimination based on race, national or ethnic origin, colour, religion, sex, age and mental or physical disability.

[14]   Art 14 ECHR.

[15]   *Ibid*. Cf the Canadian Constitution.

[16]   See for example *Abdulaziz v UK* (1985) 7 EHRR 471: although there was no breach of the right to respect for family life guaranteed by Art 8 ECHR (wives could join husbands abroad), there was a violation of Art 14. By refusing to allow foreign men to join partners or wives in the UK, the state was found to discriminate between men and women in the respect afforded to their family lives. See also *Ghaidan v Mendoza* [2004] 2 AC 557, [2004] UKHL 30, [2004] 2 AC 557, [2004] 3 All ER, 411: although there is no state duty to provide a home or to guarantee security in the home by a private person, if security is granted, the state must do so indiscriminately.

[17]   (1975) 3 DR 25.

[18]   See *Gaygusuz v Austria* (1997) 23 EHRR.

[19]   Note 1 above.

[20]   *Carson* (note 1 above) para 12.

[21]   See *Jankovic v Croatia* (2000) 30 EHRR CD 183.

[22]   Note 3 above, 45, para 37.

further expanding the ambit of Article 14 in the socio-economic sphere.[23] Against this jurisprudential background, it is not surprising that following the HRA, both Article 1 of Protocol 1 ECHR standing alone, and Article 14 taken together with Article 1 of Protocol 1, have been relied on to challenge the substantive fairness of government policies concerning the distribution of social security payments.

In *Carson*, the House of Lords heard two conjoined discrimination cases of this kind. The first, Carson's case, concerned alleged discrimination in the amount of state retirement pension paid to some UK citizens living abroad, by contrast with those living in the United Kingdom and elsewhere. Controversially, it was argued that the government policy of refusing to allow a British pensioner (who was resident in South Africa at the time of her retirement with a full record of social security payments) the annual cost of living increase that is available to UK pensioners and expatriates in countries with relevant treaty arrangements, constituted a breach of Article 14 taken together with Article 1 of Protocol 1 ECHR.

The applicant questioned whether the payment of different rates to some pensioners could be justified as a proportionate response to the requirement that states must balance the rights of individual claimants against those of other claimants in analogous situations under Article 14 ECHR, in order to afford consistency of treatment in the distribution of public goods. Moreover, raising similar concerns, albeit in a very different welfare context, the applicant in Reynolds' case, the second in the conjoined appeal in *Carson*, questioned inter alia whether the payment of a lower rate of contributions-based jobseeker's allowance to a claimant less than 25 years old, as a result of which she suffered financial hardship, constituted a breach of Article 14 taken together with Article 1 of Protocol 1 ECHR.

In both cases, although claims for judicial review had been refused at first instance, leave was granted to appeal to the Court of Appeal.[24] However, in a conjoined hearing and following a comprehensive review of the surrounding issues and the Strasbourg jurisprudence, Laws LJ, giving the only judgment of the Court, concluded that there had been no violation of Article 1 of Protocol 1, or of Article 14 taken together with Article 1 of Protocol 1 in Carson's case; and that there had been no violation of Article 14 taken together with Article 1 of Protocol 1, or of Article 8 or Article 1 of Protocol 1 standing alone in Reynolds' case. Accordingly, both claimants appealed to the House of Lords.

Before the House of Lords in *Carson*,[25] it was common ground that the pension and benefit entitlements of the respective claimants, as concluded by the Court of Appeal, were indeed possessions within the meaning of Article 1 of

---

[23] This issue is shortly to be considered by the Grand Chamber in the case of *Hepple v UK*, Application Nos 65731/01 and 65900/01.
[24] [2003] EWCA Civ 797.
[25] Note 1 above.

Protocol 1 ECHR.[26] Furthermore, in Carson's case specifically, consistent with *Kjeldsen v Denmark*,[27] it was agreed that foreign residence was a personal characteristic that fell within the scope of the ECHR rights, so that Article 14 was engaged. Thus, the question to be addressed by the House of Lords in Carson's case was whether the Social Security Benefits Uprating Regulations 2001 (the legislation stipulating the differences in payment rates) were ultra vires insofar as they interfered with the claimant's right not to be discriminated against in the enjoyment of her possessions, in accordance with Article 14 taken together with Article 1 of Protocol 1 ECHR. In Reynolds' case, the substantive question was whether Regulation 17(1) and Schedule 2 of the Income Support (General) Regulations 1987 (the legislation stipulating the lower rate of jobseeker's allowance for persons aged 18–24) violated the claimant's rights under Articles 14 taken together with Article 1 of Protocol 1.

The House of Lords rejected both contentions,[28] the majority holding that social security benefits were part of an interlocking system of domestic social welfare, according to which a decision to pay different rates to persons living abroad was rationally justifiable, as indeed was the decision to enter into reciprocal treaties with some countries without having to pay the same rates to all expatriates. Furthermore, in Reynolds' case, it was held that payment of jobseeker's allowance according to the prescribed age was also justifiable, since it was within the bounds of rationality to conclude that persons under 25 could as a group be regarded as having lower earnings and lower living costs. Moreover, in light of the very wide interpretation given by the ECtHR to Article 14 ECHR, it was considered necessary to distinguish between those grounds of discrimination that appear to offend against notions of respect due to individuals and those grounds that merely require some rational justification.

However, before reaching their conclusions on the facts of either Carson's or Reynolds' case, the House of Lords reviewed the potential of Article 14 ECHR to serve as a substantive equality provision of the kind contended for by the claimants. In setting the limits of their legislative intervention in Article 14 claims, they relied not so much on developments in Strasburg jurisprudence as on what they deemed to be an implicit constitutional distinction between claims of discriminatory treatment on the grounds stated in Article 14 (such as sex, race or nationality) and 'other status' challenges of the kind in *Carson*, which essen-

---

[26] Since the case of *Marckx v Belgium* [1979] 2 EHRR 330, there had been arid jurisprudential controversy as to whether Article 1 Protocol 1 ECHR applied to a person's existing possessions rather than guaranteeing a right to acquire possessions.

[27] (1976) 1 EHRR 711, 732–3, in which the Strasbourg Court held that Art 14 ECHR applied only if the discrimination was on the basis of 'a personal characteristic' (para 56). That construction had recently been adopted by the House of Lords in *R (on the Application of S) v Chief Constable of Yorkshire Police; R (on the Application of Marper) v Chief Constable of Yorkshire Police* [2004] UKHL 39, 48. However, in *Michalak* (note 4 above) Brooke LJ noted that the Strasbourg jurisprudence appeared to have moved on to accepting the engagement of Art 14 in cases in which it is hard to say that the grounds of discrimination are in any meaningful sense personal characteristics.

[28] Lord Carswell dissented.

tially raise questions of general social policy.[29] The House of Lords general review of the potential of Article 14 in this regard will be the subject of the following sections.

III. CARSON'S CASE: REFUSAL OF UP-RATED PAYMENTS TO PENSIONERS ABROAD

Since the National Insurance Act 1946, British pensioners living in other countries have generally not received up-rated pensions. However, those living in the European Economic Area and in states with which the United Kingdom has reciprocal agreements do receive them.[30] Thus, as made clear by Laws LJ before the Court of Appeal in *Carson*,[31] the issue of the refusal of up-rated pensions to expatriates is not new.[32] The question of discrimination by countries without reciprocal arrangements not only has been raised in Strasbourg[33] but has long been a matter of political debate in the UK, in light of considerable implications for the public purse.[34] Evidence was therefore provided before the Court of Appeal in *Carson* on behalf of the Secretary of State:

> Successive Governments have taken the view that the level of increases in retirement pensions relates to conditions in the UK and that it would not be right to impose an additional burden on contributors and taxpayers in the UK in order to pay pension increases to people who have chosen to become resident elsewhere in the world.[35]

[29] See for example *Carson* (note 1 above) para 17 (Lord Hoffman).

[30] Between 1948 and 1992 the United Kingdom entered into reciprocal social security agreements with a number of foreign states. However, up-rating has never been applied to pensioners living in South Africa, Australia, Canada or New Zealand. However, EEC Regulation No 1408/71 on Social Security for Migrant Workers contains detailed rules that coordinate rights granted under the different national legislations (eg, by requiring one state to take into account contributions paid in another), while EEC Regulation No 574/72 contains detailed rules for implementing Regulation No 1408/71. In practice, however, the UK's entry into the EC had little effect, because there were pre-existing reciprocal agreements providing for payment of up-rate with all member states except Denmark.

[31] Note 24 above, para 50.

[32] Laws LJ noted that 'a number of attempts in Parliament to require the government to pay the uprate to those in Ms Carson's position had foundered in both Houses of Parliament: a DSS Memorandum of 1996 submitted to the Social Security Committee of the House of Commons referred in particular to amendments tabled in both Houses in June and July 1995 during the passage of the Pensions Bill, calling for uprating to be paid. All were defeated by large majorities' (*Carson* (note 24 above) para 53).

[33] *JW and EW v UK*, Application no 9776/82 was the first case in which the Commission considered a complaint that the UK government's failure to pay an up-rated pension infringed the Convention rights of an applicant who was on the point of emigrating to Australia, where there was no reciprocal agreement. The Commission held the complaint to be inadmissible under Art 1 Protocol 1 ECHR and also rejected the complaint that there had been a violation of Art 14 ECHR read with Art 1 Protocol 1.

[34] 'According to the Secretary of State, as at January 2002, of some 900,000 pensioners and widow beneficiaries who live abroad less than half (some 420,000) receive the annual uprate. The cost of extending uprating to all pensions from the time when each was awarded would cost an additional £3bn' (*Carson* (note 24 above) para 52 (Laws LJ)).

[35] *Ibid.*

Notwithstanding this attempted justification by the Secretary of State, it was acknowledged by Laws LJ in *Carson* that 'the overall position as it stands today, is an illogical and haphazard consequence of events, including not least the conclusion of the various bilateral agreements, happening over time'.[36] Moreover, it was also acknowledged that governments generally expect that entering into reciprocal agreements affords a desirable measure of social protection for workers who move from one country to another during their working lives. Not only do such agreements generally prevent the need to contribute to both countries' social security schemes at the same time; they also ensure that benefit cover is maintained whether an individual is living in one country or another. Thus, on reaching pensionable age, workers who have been insured by the schemes of two or more countries can receive a pension from each, reflecting the amount of insurance paid in each.

However, the issue of whether to enter into reciprocal social security agreements with particular countries has continued in the United Kindgom to depend on overriding policy considerations, such as: the numbers of people moving to that country; the benefits available under the other country's scheme; how far reciprocity is possible; and the extent to which the advantages to be gained by an agreement outweigh the additional expenditure likely to be incurred by the UK government in negotiating and implementing it.

A. 'Suspect Categories', Respect for Persons and 'Weighty Reasons' for Review

Against this policy background, the House of Lords in *Carson*[37] accepted that someone in the applicant's position might be aggrieved that her treatment was inconsistent with that of a pensioner with the same contribution record who was living either in the United Kingdom or in a country with a reciprocal arrangement. However, since discrimination means failure to treat like cases alike, it was regarded as axiomatic that whether this difference in treatment constituted a violation of Article 14 ECHR must depend on whether the claimant was in an 'analogous situation' to those claimants with whom she compared herself.[38] In other words, 'discrimination can only be found under article 14 if the cases are not sufficiently different to justify an alleged difference in treatment'.[39] Thus, arguing that this question is 'partly a matter of values and partly a question of rationality', Lord Hoffman observed:

---

[36] 'According to the Secretary of State, as at January 2002, of some 900,000 pensioners and widow beneficiaries who live abroad less than half (some 420,000) receive the annual uprate. The cost of extending uprating to all pensions from the time when each was awarded would cost an additional £3bn' (*Carson* (note 24 above), para 54 (Laws LJ).

[37] Note 1 above.

[38] *Van der Mussele v Belgium* (1983) 6 EHRR 183.

[39] *Carson* (note 1 above) para 14 (Lord Hoffman).

Article 14 expresses the Enlightenment value that every human being is entitled to equal respect and to be treated as an end and not a means. Characteristics such as race, caste, noble birth, membership of a political party and (here a change in values since the Enlightenment) gender, are seldom, if ever, acceptable grounds for differences in treatment. In some constitutions, the prohibition on discrimination is confined to grounds of this kind and I rather suspect that article 14 was also intended to be so limited.[40]

However, observing also that the Strasbourg court had gradually given Article 14 ECHR a wide interpretation that approaches that of the American Fourteenth Amendment,[41] Lord Hoffman argued for the need, as in the United States, to distinguish between those grounds of discrimination that prima facie appear to offend our notions of the respect due to the individual and those that merely require some rational justification.[42] A typical example of this type of distinction can be found in the American case of *Massachusetts Board of Retirement v Murgia*,[43] in which uniformed state police officers challenged a mandatory retirement age of 50, and the Supreme Court held:

> [I]n the circumstances the appropriate test for equal protection of the laws was not strict scrutiny. The only issue was whether the mandatory retirement age had a rational basis . . . [which in this case was] . . . maintenance of a police force fit enough to carry out arduous and demanding duties.[44]

Although recognising the extension of possible grounds for discrimination in Strasbourg jurisprudence,[45] the majority of the House of Lords in *Carson* considered it permissible to draw a line of justiciability between the sensitive grounds of discrimination spelt out in Article 14 ECHR itself, and allegations of discrimination on broader grounds, which was regarded as subject to considerations of public interest and to a lesser degree of scrutiny by courts. Accordingly, as Lord Hoffman put it:

> The first category cannot be justified merely on utilitarian grounds, eg that it is rational to prefer to employ men rather than women because more women than men give up employment to look after children. That offends the notion that everyone is entitled to be treated as an individual and not a statistical unit. On the other hand, differences in treatment in the second category (eg on grounds of ability, education,

---

[40] *Ibid*, para 15.
[41] See note 12 above.
[42] *Ibid*, para 15.
[43] (1976) 427 US 307.
[44] *Massachusetts B of R v Murgia* (*ibid*) 314. The majority of the Supreme Court described the appropriate standard as a 'relatively relaxed standard reflecting the court's awareness that the drawing of lines which create distinctions is peculiarly a legislative task and an unavoidable one. Perfection in making the necessary classifications is neither possible nor necessary' (314).
[45] Lord Walker acknowledged that the wide personal characteristic test developed in *Kjeldsen v Denmark* (note 27 above) had recently been applied by the Fourth Section of the ECtHR in two admissibility decisions: *Budak v Turkey*, Application No 57345/00, 7 September 2004, unreported; and *Beale v UK*, Application No 16743/03, 12 October 2004, unreported. The questionable personal characteristic in *Beale* had been the different investigatory procedures appropriate for the police on one hand and trading standards officers on the other.

wealth, occupation) usually depend upon considerations of the general public interest. Secondly, while the courts, as guardians of the right of the individual to equal respect, will carefully examine the reasons offered for any discrimination in the first category, decisions about the general public interest which underpin differences in treatment in the second category are very much a matter for the democratically elected branches of government.[46]

Moreover, in a similar vein, Lord Walker argued:

[T]he proposition that not all possible grounds of discrimination are equally potent is not very clearly spelled out in the jurisprudence of the Strasbourg court. It appears much more clearly in the jurisprudence of the United States Supreme Court, which in applying the equal protection clause of the Fourteenth Amendment has developed a doctrine of 'suspect' grounds of discrimination which the court will subject to particularly severe scrutiny.[47]

Thus, Lord Walker noted that in *San Antonio School District v Rodriguez*[48] the US Supreme Court powerfully described the concept of a 'suspect class' as one 'saddled with such disabilities, or subjected to such a history of purposeful unequal treatment, or relegated to such a position of political powerlessness, as to command extraordinary protection from the majoritarian political process'.[49]

Developing this theme further, Lord Walker stated that although not so clearly spelt out, such a two-tier approach can also be found in Strasbourg, where the ECtHR refers for example to 'very weighty reasons' being required to justify discrimination on particularly sensitive grounds.[50] Indeed, as Lord Walker observed, this principle has for some time been identified by leading academic commentators in the Strasbourg context[51] and was recently affirmed by Lord Nicholls in *Ghaidan v Mendosa*[52] in the context of discrimination in landlord and tenant law on grounds of sexual orientation.[53] Thus, on the

---

[46] *Carson* (note 1 above) para 15.

[47] *Ibid*, para 55.

[48] (1973) 411 US 1, 28.

[49] *San Antonio School District v Rodriguez* (*ibid*) para 56.

[50] See for example *Abdulaziz v UK* (1985) 7 EHRR 501, para 78; and *Van Raalte v the Netherlands* (1997) 24 EHRR 518–19, para 39 (discrimination on grounds of sex). On the idea of a 'suspect class' of cases, see also *Carson* (note 1 above) para 45 (Lord Rodger).

[51] *Carson* (note 1 above) para 57. Lord Walker, citing *Hoffman v Austria* (1993) 17 ECHRR 293, 316, para 36; *Gaygusuz v Austria* (note 18 above) 381, para 42; and *Salgueiro da Silva Mouta v Portugal* (1999) 31 EHRR 1055, 1071, para 36, noted that the Strasbourg 'suspect' categories hitherto identified in D Harris, M O'Boyle and C Warbrick, *Law of the European Convention on Human Rights* (London, Butterworth, 1995) as 'discrimination on the grounds of race, gender or illegitimacy' had more recently been extended in C Ovey and R White (eds), *Jacobs and White: The European Convention on Human Rights*, 3rd ed (Oxford, OUP, 2002) 355–6 to include 'religion, nationality and sexual orientation'.

[52] Note 16 above.

[53] 'Where the alleged violation comprises differential treatment based on grounds such as race or sex or sexual orientation the court will scrutinise with intensity any reasons said to constitute justification. The reasons must be cogent if such differential treatment is to be justified' (*Ghaidan* (note 16 above) para 19).

assumption that where an individual lives is in principle 'a matter of choice' that, although potentially 'regarded as a personal characteristic', is 'not immutable', and that there is 'nothing intrinsically demeaning about an individual's place of residence', Lord Walker considered that a less intrusive form of scrutiny would be appropriate in such cases.[54] Interestingly, however, he also cautioned that 'social or business practices which amount to what is sometimes called a "postcode lottery" might, if devoid of any rational basis, constitute discrimination'.[55]

Notably, despite his narrow view of the constitutional boundaries of suspect categories in the ECHR rights, Lord Hoffman in *Carson* was willing to concede that there may be borderline cases in which 'it is not easy to allocate the ground of discrimination to one category or the other, since there are clearly shifts in the values of society on these matters'[56] (a point to which we shall return). Indeed, for Lord Hoffman, *Ghaidan* afforded a prime example of judicial awareness of a shift in values that has placed discrimination on grounds of sexual orientation now firmly in the first category. By contrast, he considered discrimination on grounds of old age to be 'a contemporary example of a borderline case'.[57] However, in Lord Hoffman's view, 'there is usually no difficulty about deciding whether one is dealing with a case in which the right to respect for the individuality of a human being is at stake, or merely a question of general social policy'.[58] It was into the second category that he placed Carson's case, concluding:

The denial of a social security benefit to Ms Carson on the ground that she lives abroad cannot possibly be equated with discrimination on grounds of race or sex. It is not a denial of respect for her as an individual. She was under no obligation to move to South Africa. She did so voluntarily and no doubt for good reasons. But in doing so, she put herself outside the primary scope and purpose of the UK social security system.[59]

B. Consistency of Treatment or Substantive Outcome: The Malleable Concept of Equality

Before the House of Lords, the applicant in Carson's case accepted that she would have had no legitimate complaint if the UK government had rigorously and consistently applied a constant principle that UK social security is for UK residents, with the result that pensions were refused to all expatriates. Moreover, as noted by Lord Hoffman, she made no complaint about her disentitlement to other social

---

[54] *Carson* (note 1 above) para 58.
[55] *Ibid*, para 58.
[56] *Ibid*, para 17 (Lord Hoffman).
[57] *Ibid*. Note that the Employment Equality (Age) Regulations 2006 (SI 2006/1031) came into force on 1 October 2006. For the first time in the UK, discrimination on grounds of age is prohibited in employment.
[58] *Carson* (note 1 above) para 17.
[59] *Ibid*, para 18.

security benefits, such as jobseeker's allowance and income support. Instead, the gist of her argument was that it was irrational to acknowledge her entitlement to a pension by virtue of her contributions to the National Insurance Fund on one hand, and then to refuse her the same pension as paid to UK residents who had made equal contributions on the other.

Lord Carswell expressed general agreement with the conclusion in respect of the applicant in Reynolds' case, but reached a very different conclusion from the majority in Carson's appeal. As he saw it, once it had been decided that Carson's case fell within the ambit of Article 1 of Protocol 1 ECHR for the purpose of triggering Article 14—and it was acknowledged that her residence abroad could constitute 'status' within the meaning of Article 14—logic dictated that:

> the comparison . . . should be a simple one, between the appellant . . . and other contributing pensioners who reside in the United Kingdom or in countries where their pensions are uprated by our government. She and other pensioners who reside in countries in which their pensions are not uprated are unquestionably treated differently, to their disadvantage, by reason of their residence in those countries. . . . The common factor for purposes of comparison is that all of the pensioners, in whichever country they may reside, have duly paid the contributions required to qualify for their pensions. If some of them are not paid pensions at the same rate as others, that in my opinion constitutes discrimination for the purposes of article 14.[60]

Furthermore:

> [M]any discrimination cases resolve themselves into a dispute, which can often seem more than a little arid, about comparisons and identifying comparators, where a broader approach might more readily yield a serviceable answer which corresponds with one's instincts for justice.[61]

The elaborate comparisons complained of by Lord Carswell in Carson's case, which were also criticised as something of a red herring by Lord Hoffman,[62] had appeared in argument for the Secretary of State, who had placed importance on matters such as the variation in exchange rates and the cost of living in various countries, which made it inappropriate to apply the same increase to pensioners resident abroad.[63] For Lord Carswell, such comparisons were unnecessary, since inconsistency of treatment in respect of pensioners who had paid the same contribution appeared to be tantamount to discrimination:

> It is not a matter of comparing the economic state of third countries, as the European Commission on Human Rights stated in *Corner v United Kingdom* (Application No

---

[60]   *Carson* (note 1 above), para 98.

[61]   *Ibid*, para 97 (Lord Carswell).

[62]   See *ibid*, para 26.

[63]   As explained by Lord Carswell, the Secretary of State had also argued that the Social Charter and Code of Social Security adopted by the Council of Europe, the body which produced the Convention, envisaged that payment of benefits may be suspended when the recipient is resident abroad, so that the Council cannot have considered that Art 14 was an obstacle to suspension of payment, whether or not it had in mind contributory pensions as distinct from welfare benefits payable on the basis of need (*Carson* (note 1 above) para 102).

11271/84) (unreported) 17 May 1985, which is set out in para 74 of Laws LJ's judgment [2003] 3 All ER 577, 609. It is a matter of simple justice between groups of people who have paid the same contributions. . . . That makes as little sense as arguing that pensioners in the United Kingdom could not be compared with each other because some are better off through possession of other income or because some live frugally and others spend their money in a different way.[64]

However, for Lord Hoffman, with whom the majority agreed, concentration on this single feature of the applicant's payments to the social security fund was to miscalculate the true nature of an individual's relationship with and appropriate expectations of the fund,[65] described by the ECtHR in *Van der Mussele v Belgium*[66] as 'characterised by a corpus of rights and obligations of which it would be artificial to isolate one specific aspect'.[67] Thus, Lord Hoffman argued:

Social security benefits are part of an intricate and interlocking system of social welfare which exists to ensure certain minimum standards of living for the people of this country, and an expression of what has been called social solidarity or fraternité—the duty of any community to help those of its members who are in need.[68]

Therefore, despite the treatment of such benefits by Strasbourg as possessory socio-economic entitlements in Article 14 ECHR disputes, Lord Hoffman in Carson's case considered the duty to provide social security benefits widely to have been recognised as 'national in character', by contrast with obligations recognised in treaties such as the ILO Social Security (Minimum Standards) Convention 1952 (Article 69) and the European Code of Social Security 1964.[69]

Problematically, the claimant's argument in Carson's case that she had been discriminated against in comparison with other UK pensioners failed to take account of the broad interlocking nature of the UK social security system. Instead, her argument rested on the sole premise that 'because contributions are a necessary condition for the retirement pension paid to UK residents, they ought to be a sufficient condition',[70] which implied a direct nexus between national insurance contributions and state retirement pensions, comparable with that applicable to a private pension scheme. However, as Lord Hoffman explained, national insurance contributions provide only 'part of the revenue which pays for all social security benefits and the National Health Service (the rest comes from ordinary taxation)'.[71] 'If payment of contributions were a sufficient condition of entitlement to an up-rated pension, Ms Carson should be entitled to all contributory benefits, like maternity benefit and jobseeker's allowance', but this had been no part of her argument.[72]

[64] *Ibid*, para 98.
[65] *Ibid*, para 20.
[66] (1984) 6 EHRR 163.
[67] *Van der Mussele v Belgium* (*ibid*) 180, para 46.
[68] *Carson* (note 1 above) para 18.
[69] *Ibid*.
[70] *Ibid*, para 21 (Lord Hoffman).
[71] *Ibid*.
[72] *Ibid*.

Lord Hoffman also emphasised that, although not means-tested for policy reasons, by contrast with private pension schemes, the underlying rationale of the state pension system, which is an integral part of the social security system, is needs-based. Thus, there is capacity for recouping 'part of the pension from people who have enough income to pay tax and thereby reduce the net cost of the pension'.[73] Those people who are entirely destitute would be otherwise entitled to income support, a non-contributory benefit, so that the net cost of paying a retirement pension 'to such people takes into account the fact that the pension will be set off against the claim they would otherwise have for income support'.[74] Crucially, however, none of these interlocking features were applicable to non-residents such as Ms Carson, whether at the high or low end of the means continuum. On the contrary, Lord Hoffman argued, 'her pension would go to reduce the social security benefits (if any) to which she is entitled in her new country'.[75]

Thus, while agreeing that the words 'insurance' and 'contributions' deceptively conjure up notions of a private pension scheme, Lord Hoffman made clear in *Carson* that 'from the point of view of the citizens who contribute, national insurance contributions are little different from general taxation which disappears into the communal pot of the consolidated fund'.[76] Therefore, he argued that there is no particular reason why the payment of retirement pension should be linked to the level of contributions. Indeed, as he observed, '(mainly because the present system severely disadvantages women who have spent time in the unremunerated work of caring for a family rather than earning a salary) there are proposals for change', so that over time, 'contributory pensions may be replaced with a non-contributory "citizen's pension" payable to all inhabitants of this country of pensionable age', without any corresponding change to the manner in which national insurance is collected.[77] It therefore followed:

> Once the retirement pension was no longer based on national insurance contributions, the foundation of [the claimant's] argument that she had 'earned' the right to equal treatment in respect of her pension would disappear, although she would have paid exactly the same national insurance contributions while she was working here . . .[78]

Lord Hoffman therefore considered that not only was the position of a non-resident materially and relevantly different from that of a UK resident, but the reasons for the government policy were also 'practical and fair'—even assuming, as objected by Lord Carswell, 'the reasons for the policy lie wholly in the

---

[73] *Carson* (note 1 above), para 22.
[74] *Ibid.*
[75] *Ibid*, para 23.
[76] *Ibid*, para 24.
[77] *Ibid* (Lord Hoffman).
[78] *Ibid*, para 28 (Lord Hoffman).

cost of uprating',[79] and the 'inclusion of individual pensioners in this class depended on the adventitious matter of whether this country had in the past entered into a reciprocal agreement with the particular states in which they resided'.[80] Moreover, like Lords Walker and Nicholls, Lord Hoffman concluded that once it had been accepted that the position of the applicant in Carson's case was relevantly different from that of a UK resident, and that she could not therefore claim equality of treatment, the 'amount if any which she receives must be a matter for Parliament'.[81]

IV. REYNOLDS' CASE: THE INTENSITY OF SCRUTINY IN OTHER 'STATUS DISPUTES'

In Reynolds' case, the second of the conjoined test cases facing the House of Lords in *Carson*,[82] the applicant, while she was under 25 years of age and before the birth of her son, had received jobseeker's allowance and income support at the weekly rate of £41.35, in accordance with Regulation 17(1) and Schedule 2 of the Income Support (General) Regulations 1987; section 4 of the Jobseekers Act 1995; and Regulation 79 of the Jobseeker's Allowance Regulations 1996. Had she been aged 25 or older, however, she would have received £52.20 per week. Accordingly, she claimed (although the Secretary of State did not accept all the facts in their entirety) that during a period of about eight months, despite receiving other benefits such as housing and council tax benefit and also maternity benefit during the last three months of her pregnancy, she suffered severe hardship, partly because of high expenditure on gas and electricity for the flat, and partly because she had to spend £10 a week in repaying a loan, which she had obtained to furnish the flat.

Before the House of Lords, it was argued on behalf of the applicant that there had been a breach of Article 1 of Protocol 1 in conjunction with Article 14 ECHR, in relation to both jobseeker's allowance and income support; alternatively, in relation to both benefits (but especially in relation to income support) there had been a breach of Article 8 in conjunction with Article 14 ECHR. However, in contrast to the type of jobseeker's allowance (JSA(C)) to which

---

[79] *Ibid*, para 99 (Lord Carswell). The Department of Social Security memorandum on the uprating of state retirement pensions payable to people resident abroad (Social Security Committee, 'Uprating of State Retirement Pensions Payable to People Abroad' HC (1996–97) 143 (29 January 1997)) stated: 'Agreeing to additional expenditure on pensions paid overseas would be incompatible with the Government's policy of containing the long-term cost of the social security system to ensure that it remains affordable' (para 11).

[80] *Carson* (note 1 above) para 99 (Lord Carswell). Although Lord Carswell recognised that courts should normally be slow to intervene in policy decisions of this kind, he argued somewhat abstrusely that if the government had put forward sufficient reasons of economic or state policy to justify the difference in treatment, 'I should have been properly ready to yield to its decision-power in those fields' (para 99).

[81] *Ibid*, para 25.

[82] Note 1 above.

Ms Reynolds was entitled, income support is a non-contributory, means-tested benefit. Thus, although it was conceded by the Secretary of State that job-seeker's allowance falls within the ambit of Article 1 of Protocol 1, the issue of whether entitlement to income support (a non-contributory benefit) is included in a person's 'possessions' for the purpose of Article 1 of Protocol 1 was clearly open to dispute.

However, as indicated above in the discussion of Carson's case, Strasbourg jurisprudence on the status of non-contributory social security benefits is at present 'in the melting-pot'. Moreover, since it was conceded by the Home Secretary that jobseeker's allowance is a contributory benefit that constitutes a 'possession' within the meaning of Article 1 of Protocol 1, the House of Lords decided that since the applicant in Reynolds' case was entitled to either, it should be assumed for purpose of the appeal that both income support and job-seeker's allowance fell within the ambit of Article 1 of Protocol 1 ECHR. Moreover, since the case under Article 8 in conjunction with Article 14 ECHR did not appear to add anything to her case under Article 1 of Protocol 1 in conjunction with Article 14, this part of her argument was not discussed before the House of Lords.

Since the argument in Reynolds' case was that she had been the victim of a difference in treatment on ground of her age, it was regarded as unnecessary to cover issues of principle relating to discrimination on 'other grounds' in Article 14 or to discuss the limits of judicial intervention in social policy disputes in 'non-suspect' categories, which had been fully aired in relation to Carson's case. Instead, viewing her case, like that of Carson's case, as one in which it was a matter for Parliament 'to choose' (in this case, whether different levels of benefit should be obtained according to age, and where that age differential should be set), and accepting that claimants on either side of the age divide were in 'analogous' situations, it was regarded as enough for the House of Lords to ensure that there was an objective justification for a difference in the treatment of claimants in the under-25 age group. Further, it was considered necessary for the House of Lords to consider whether the appropriate intensity of scrutiny had been applied in the Court of Appeal when considering the Secretary of State's justifications for enactment of the disputed provisions.

In seeking to explain the policy choice that had been taken, an official in the Department of Work and Pensions enumerated some of the considerations taken into account in the decision-making process, including: i) the fact that those in the 18–24 age group in general earn less than persons age 25 or over and may therefore legitimately be regarded as having lower earnings expectations; ii) the fact that the majority of those in the 18–24 age group do not live independently and may legitimately be regarded as having lower living costs than the group of claimants aged 25 or over; iii) the expectation that lower rates of job-seeker's allowance and income support for those between 18 and 24 years of age may discourage them from living independently and instead encourage them to live together with others, notably parents or other family members, which may be seen to have wider social benefits; iv) the fact that there are other aspects of the social security system that serve to prevent hardship to the minority of persons in the 18–24 age group who, like the claimant in Reynolds' case, live independently; and v) the importance, from the point of view of good administration, of basing the social security system upon clear, easily applicable rules, rather than attempting to cater to the individual situation of each claimant.

In addition, counsel for the Secretary of State elaborated on the fifth justification, by explaining that structural reforms of social security benefits in the late 1980s had drawn a distinction between 'householders' and 'non-householders', with a view to recognising that some persons entitled to income support have responsibilities for housing costs (such as rent and rates) that do not fall on other claimants. However, as subsequently pointed out in the White Paper 'Reform of Social Security',[83] 'the increase of shared housing arrangements had made the existing rules (with their connotation of a clearly identifiable head of the household) increasingly difficult to administer', which ultimately led to 'disputes which reached the social security appeal system and, in some cases, the courts'.[84] Accordingly, it was argued by the Secretary of State that however arbitrary or disadvantageous the policy may appear,

> there were sound reasons, in the interests of good administration, for providing for housing costs by other, more selective benefits (principally housing benefit and council tax benefit), both of which Ms Reynolds received.[85]

Lord Walker not only gave the most extensive review of the policy background and facts in Reynolds's case but also attended closely to the appropriate degree of scrutiny in Article 14 ECHR disputes of this kind. Thus, he recalled the observations of the trial judge Wilson J,[86] who relied on passages from *James v United Kingdom* [87] and *R v Director of Public Prosecutions, ex parte Kebeline*[88] when he stated:

> I regard it as unnecessary, indeed inappropriate, for me to address the arguments presented by [the Secretary of State] by way of justification for the demarcation with a degree of detail into which, drawing upon a statement of an eminent statistician as well as a host of other material, [counsel for Reynolds] would have me descend.

---

[83] Department of Health and Social Security (DHSS), 'Reform of Social Security: Programme for Action' (White Paper) Cmnd 9691, 1985.

[84] *Ibid*, para 2.34.

[85] *Carson* (note 1 above) para 86.

[86] *R (on the Application of Reynolds) v Secretary of State for Work and Pensions* [2002] EWHC Admin.

[87] (1986) 8 EHRR 142, which involved a challenge brought by the Duke of Westminster against certain aspects of the leasehold enfranchisement legislation. The Court rejected the challenge: '. . . the decision to enact laws expropriating property will commonly involve consideration of political, economic and social issues on which opinions within a democratic society may reasonably differ widely. The Court, finding it natural that the margin of appreciation available to the legislature in implementing social and economic policies should be a wide one, will respect the legislature's judgment as to what is "in the public interest" unless that judgment be manifestly without reasonable foundation' (para 46).

[88] [2000] 2 AC 261, 381.

Indeed, as his enthusiastic argument proceeded, I increasingly sensed the incongruity that such a debate was proceeding in court instead of in Parliament.[89]

In a similar vein before the Court of Appeal, Laws LJ had invoked the assistance of the 'rational and fair-minded person' in the *Michalak* formula[90] and accepted the need for positive justification of the less favourable treatment of a claimant under age 25 in accordance with Article 14 ECHR. Nevertheless, as noted by Lord Walker, Laws LJ had insisted that '[h]owever the depth of the justification required, the reach of the court's scrutiny of what is advanced by way of justification, is quite another matter'.[91] Thus, like Wilson J at first instance, Laws LJ had declined to be drawn into any sort of detailed debate on the appropriate demarcation age. Such a debate would be appropriate in Parliament but not in the court.[92]

It was therefore concluded by Lord Walker, distinguishing *Asmundsson v Iceland*[93] as a 'very unusual case',[94] that the courts below in Reynolds' case were entirely correct in their approach to the intensity of scrutiny: 'Demarcation lines of this kind have to be reasonably bright lines and the task of drawing them is . . . a peculiarly legislative task and an unavoidable one.'[95]

V. EQUALITY AND HUMAN RIGHTS

A. Beyond the *Michalak* Formula: The Search for a 'Material and Relevant Difference' in Article 14 ECHR Disputes

It was unanimously agreed in the House of Lords that the conjoined appeal in *Carson* provided an opportunity to revisit fundamental questions about the proper methodological approach for Article 14 ECHR disputes in the absence of

[89] Reynolds' case at first instance (note 86 above) para 28 (Wilson J) emphasis added, cited by Lord Walker in *Carson* (note 1 above) para 86. This passage from Wilson J's judgment had also been cited with approval by Laws LJ before the Court of Appeal in *Carson* (note 24 above) paras 81–2.

[90] Note 4 above. See also note 27 above and discussion in section V below.

[91] *Carson* (note 24 above) para 75 (Laws LJ), cited by Lord Walker in *Carson* (note 1 above) para 88.

[92] See *Carson* (note 24 above) paras 75–6 (Laws LJ).

[93] [2004] ECHR 60669/00. A seaman aged 30 had a serious accident at work, as a result of which he had to stop working as a seaman. His disability was assessed at 100%, making him eligible for a disability pension from a statutory contributory social security fund (the Seamen's Pension Fund), although he subsequently found work in the office of a transport company and rose to a senior position. About 14 years after his accident, the Fund, which was in serious financial difficulties, developed new rules for existing and future pensioners and thereupon reassessed the claimant's disability at 25%, which was below the threshold for any pension entitlement under the new rules. The court held this to be a breach of Article 1 of Protocol 1 ECHR, because although the claimant was still classified as 25% incapacitated, he had been deprived of the entirety of his disability pension (para 44). The ECtHR made a passing reference to differential treatment of pensioners, suggesting that the impugned measure was unjustified for purposes of Article 14 ECHR, although the Court refrained from deciding any separate issue under Article 14.

[94] *Carson* (note 1 above) paras 89–90.

[95] *Ibid*, para 91 (Lord Walker).

the enumerated grounds. A few years earlier in *Michalak*,[96] Brooke LJ had borrowed four questions from a leading textbook[97] and used them to establish whether there had been a violation of Article 14 ECHR. The questions included:

(i)   Do the facts fall within the ambit of one or more of the Convention provisions?
(ii) If so, was there a difference in treatment with respect to the rights of the complainant on one hand and the other persons put forward for comparison (the chosen comparators) on the other?
(iii) Were the chosen comparators in an analogous situation to the complainant's situation?
(iv) If so, did the difference in treatment have an objective and reasonable justification?[98]

Despite the almost uniform application by courts of this so-called *Michalak* formula, the rigidity of such an approach was a matter about which senior judges had begun to express some doubts.[99] For example, Lord Nicholls, grappling with the definition of discrimination in *Shamoon v Chief Constable of the Royal Ulster Constabulary* (hereafter *Shamoon*)[100] in the context of sex discrimination,[101] stated that in employment appeal tribunals, the 'sequential analysis [of the *Michalak* questions] may give rise to needless problems', since 'it is liable to obscure the real issue in the case, which is *why* the complainant had been treated as she had been treated'.[102]

This issue, in Lord Nicholls' opinion, first required discussion of whether the complaint 'fell within the proscribed grounds' (which would call for an examination of the facts), or whether 'there had been a difference of treatment for some other reason'.[103] Lord Nicholls considered that in the former case there is usually no difficulty in deciding 'whether the treatment afforded to the claimant on the proscribed grounds was less favourable than . . . afforded to others'.[104] However, if the answer to the latter question is 'yes', the application, in Lord Nicholls' view, will fail, without any need for potentially 'arid and confusing disputes about the identification of the appropriate comparator'.[105]

The House of Lords in *Carson* further pursued the question of whether the reduction of disputes to formulaic questions about relevant comparators was helpful. In his evaluation of the *Michalak* formula, Lord Walker in *Carson*

---

[96] Note 4 above. See also note 27 above.
[97] S Grosz, J Beatson and P Duffy, *Human Rights: The 1998 Act and the European Convention* (London, Sweet & Maxwell, 2000) 326–7.
[98] See *Michalak* (note 4 above) para 20. See also note 27 above.
[99] In *Ghaidan* (note 16 above), Baroness Hale described the *Michalak* questions 'as a useful tool, although having considerable overlap between them' (para 134). In *Carson* (note 1 above) Lord Hoffman noted in particular how he had reached his conclusion without adverting to the *Michalak* questions (para 28).
[100] [2003] UKHL 11, [2003] All ER 26.
[101] See the Sex Discrimination (Northern Ireland Order) 1976 SI 1976/1042fd.
[102] *Shamoon* (note 100 above) para 8.
[103] *Ibid*, para 11.
[104] *Ibid*.
[105] *Ibid*.

considered Lord Nicholls' *Shamoon* comments in relation to statutory discrimination to be no less apt in the context of Article 14—arguing that Strasbourg jurisprudence has made little direct use of precise comparators,[106] which are often inappropriate to the open-textured analysis required by a human rights instrument such as the ECHR. Thus, rather than looking for precise identity of position, as required by UK municipal discrimination legislation, the Strasbourg approach is to ask more broadly whether the applicant and the people who are treated differently are in 'analogous' situations.

In support, Lord Walker cited a passage from a book by David Feldman[107] in which the author argued that questions about whether people are in analogous situations 'will to some extent depend on whether there is an objective and reasonable justification for the difference in treatment', which in turn overlaps with questions about 'the acceptability of the ground and the justiciability of the difference in treatment'.[108] Feldman does not deny, however, that in some cases the ECtHR 'has rejected applications under article 14, purely on the ground that the applicant has produced no evidence that the people who were treated differently had been in analogous situations, or because the comparators are not genuinely in analogous positions'.[109] Even in cases where there has been some discussion about 'the meaning of analogous situations', according to Lord Walker in *Carson*, the ECtHR has tended, 'without any elaborate analysis or discussion of comparators [to reach] an overall conclusion as to whether in the enjoyment of Convention rights there had been unfair and unjustifiable discrimination on the grounds of some personal characteristic'.[110] For Lord Walker, this constitutes a 'process of judicial evaluation which must be sensitive to the factual context'.[111]

Nonetheless, Lord Walker agreed with Lord Hoffmann's view that there may be circumstances in which justification must be considered as a separate issue, for example in cases of positive discrimination, 'in which a category of disadvantaged persons is accorded specially favourable treatment (and others are correspondingly worse treated) precisely because of some personal characteristic (such as race or gender) of the preferred group'.[112] In those cases, Lord Walker observed, since the personal characteristic 'obviously cannot be taken

---

[106] Lord Walker noted that a great deal of learning on comparators springs from the precision required when applying definitions in the Sex Discrimination Act 1975 and the Race Relations Act 1976.

[107] D Feldman, *Civil Liberties and Human Rights in England and Wales*, 2nd edn (Oxford, OUP, 2002).

[108] *Ibid*, 144.

[109] *Ibid*. See for example *Van der Mussele v Belgium* (note 38 above) 6 EHRR; and *Johnston v Ireland* (1986) 9 EHRR 203. In the former case, comparison was drawn between a pupil advocate and other professionals such as doctors, veterinary dentists and pharmacists.

[110] *Carson* (note 1 above) paras 66–9.

[111] *Ibid*.

[112] *Ibid*, para 70 (Lord Walker). Lord Hoffman opined that it might be more logical to confine the fourth *Michalak* question (whether there is an objective and reasonable justification) to cases which are *not relevantly* different, 'for example, to achieve some legitimate teleological or administrative purpose such as correcting the effect of past discrimination or the administrative convenience of having clear distinctions' (para 32).

into account as a relevant difference negativing "analogous circumstances", positive discrimination must be justified, if at all, for reasons which focus on (and as it were make a virtue of) what would otherwise be a proscribed ground.'[113]

Lord Hoffman in *Carson* also questioned the artificiality of the *Michalak* questions, on grounds that people do not think in such a compartmentalised way. In particular, he considered the third and fourth *Michalak* questions more naturally to elide into a single question: 'is there enough of a relevant difference between X and Y, to justify difference in treatment?'[114] Lord Hoffman therefore questioned the assumption in the *Michalak* steps, that evaluations about whether there are sufficient differences between comparators to justify a difference in treatment would realistically be part of the judgment of the 'rational fair minded person' (the judge). In reality, particularly in politically sensitive claims for equal treatment of the kind at issue, 'the decision would be a matter for Parliament or the discretion of the official entrusted with statutory powers'.[115]

Therefore, in agreement with the rest of his colleagues that the *Michalak* formula should be treated with circumspection, and that a lesser degree of scrutiny is appropriate in cases falling outside the specified grounds of sex, race, nationality, etc, Lord Hoffman summarised the steps that brought him to his conclusion in *Carson*:

> (1) There is no question in this case of discrimination on a ground such as race or gender which denies Ms Carson the right to equal respect; (2) in applying a scheme of social security, it is rational and internationally acceptable to distinguish between inhabitants of the UK and persons resident abroad; (3) the extent to which the claims, if any, of persons resident abroad should be recognised as a matter for parliamentary decision.[116]

B. Competing Rights and Social Values: A Human Rights Approach

In *Carson*, Lord Hoffman recognised that courts must be sensitive to shifts in the values of society[117]—shifts that have, for example, now placed discrimination on grounds of sexual orientation firmly in the 'suspect' category of discrimination. However, as we have seen, Lord Hoffman considered discrimination on grounds of 'old age' to be 'a contemporary example of a borderline case' in which 'the right to respect for the essential individuality of a human being is at stake, rather than merely a question of general social policy'.[118]

---

[113] *Ibid*, para 70 (Lord Walker). See the *Belgian Linguistic Case* (No 2) (1968) 1 EHRR 252, 284, in which the court observed that 'certain legal inequalities tend only to correct factual inequalities' (para 10).

[114] *Carson* (note 1 above) para 30 (Lord Hoffman), citing the Court of Appeal (note 24 above) para 61 (Laws LJ).

[115] *Carson* (note 1 above) para 31.

[116] *Ibid*, para 33.

[117] *Ibid*, para 17 (Lord Hoffman).

[118] *Ibid*.

Surely discrimination on grounds of disability could be likewise labeled 'borderline', since during the past decade there has been a marked societal shift towards the recognition of the right of the disabled to enjoy the fullest possible life consistent with their disabilities and without discrimination? This right, moreover, may call for special protection in the law, as has been demonstrated not only in the international normative system for the protection of fundamental human rights[119] (despite mixed messages from Strasbourg[120]) but also in UK municipal law.[121]

It has been said that disability rights finally arrived in the United Kingdom through the enactment of the Disability Discrimination Act (DDA) 1995—nearly twenty years after protection against discrimination on grounds of race and gender was enshrined in domestic law. The Disability Rights Movement envisaged that through the DDA, charity would now give way to 'social justice' and that the 'medical model' of disability, which sees physical and mental impairment as a problem to be remedied, would accede to a new 'social model' based on the recognition that 'structures that turned impairment into the unnecessary frustration of human potential and the disablement of the flourishing individual person' could be found in the 'social economic and political environment itself'.[122] The Act was to be used not only to challenge obstacles to fulfilling human potential in the employment sphere—including the performance of public functions and political office—but also to challenge discriminatory practices and procedures in the delivery and distribution of public services across the board, from education to transport.

The Disability Rights Commission (DRC), which was established in April 2000 shortly before the HRA came into force, initially was almost wholly occupied in testing the legislative scope of the provisions of the DDA.[123] Moreover, despite its potential role in relation to 'goods and services', the DRC, like the Commission for Racial Equality and the Equal Opportunities Commission before it, was at first predominantly engaged in employment tribunal litigation, 'to the relative exclusion of work in the civil courts that might touch on areas of service provision such as health and social care every bit as important to the lives of many disabled people as employment protection'.[124]

---

[119] The United Nations Convention on the Rights of Persons with Disabilities was adopted by the UN General Assembly in September 2006. See http://www.un.org/?disabilities/?convention.

[120] See N O'Brien, 'The Disability Rights Commission and Human Rights' (summer 2006) *BIHR Brief: Newsletter of the British Institute of Human Rights* 10–16, available at http://www.bihr.org/?downloads/?newsletters/?bihr_news_summer_07-06.pdf. The author is Director of Legal Services and Operations at the Disability Rights Commission (DRC).

[121] See the Disability Discrimination Act (DDA) 1995, which for the first time in the United Kingdom made discrimination against disabled people unlawful; and the Disability Rights Commission Act 1999, which belatedly established a statutory authority to enforce and promote the DDA.

[122] O'Brien (note 120 above) 10.

[123] Litigation conformed to a legal strategy that aimed to prioritise those cases that would clarify or test the law, and so extend its impact beyond the specific circumstances of the particular case. See *ibid*.

[124] *Ibid*.

However, following the HRA and in light of the ECtHR decisions in *Botta v Italy*[125] and *Price v UK*,[126] the DRC was aware that people with disabilities and cognitive impairments who are denied access to health and social care services, adequate housing and mainstream education, and who are 'routinely excluded from the civil and judicial process and from the family and social life might look to the HRA as much as to the DDA for deliverance'.[127] Therefore, despite a slow start, the HRA has increasingly been used by the Commission as an important part of their equal opportunities strategy in the field of public services, particularly since the key test case of *R (on the Application of A, B, X and Y) v East Sussex County Council (No 2)* (hereafter *A, B, X and Y*),[128] in which Munby J found the core value of 'human dignity' and the 'right of disabled people to participate fully in the life of the community'[129] to lie at the heart of the physical and psychological integrity of every human person.

A, B, X and Y, in which the DRC acted as third-party intervener, has been viewed not only at a practical level as paving the way for the formulation of a more balanced policy by the Health and Safety Executive (HSE) in the controversial area of manual handling, but also at a more fundamental level as having 'encouraged a model for translating human rights law into human rights principles and into practical policy making on the ground'.[130] By drawing on the same 'stream of positive participatory thinking and language' as the ECtHR *Botta* judgment, and by balancing the rights of the severely disabled applicants against those of their carers, Munby J in *A, B, X and Y* demonstrated the 'communitarian dimension of human rights, with particular application to situations faced by disabled people'.[131]

Since that leading test case, a two-pronged strategy has been adopted by the DRC, whereby the Commission either makes use of a principled human rights approach, as was done in *A, B, X and Y*, or tests the legislative scope of provisions of the DDA, as was done in the House of Lords decision in *Archibald v Fife Council*.[132] Efforts have thus been made to bridge the gap between the formalism of anti-discrimination law, which is often based on fine distinctions between

[125] (1998) 26 EHRR 241. For discussion of *Botta v Italy*, see chapter 2, section III-D; chapter 5, section IV-C; and chapter 6, section II-C above.

[126] Judgment of 10 July 2001, (2002) 34 EHRR 1285. For discussion of *Price v UK*, see chapter 2, section III-C; and chapter 5 above.

[127] O'Brien (note 120 above) 11. See also R Daw, 'Human Rights and Disability: The Impact of the Human Rights Act on Disabled People' Report for the Disability Rights Commission and the Royal National Institute for Deaf People (September 2000, updated December 2005), available at http://www.drc-gb.org/?the_law/?human_rights/?human_rights_publications/ ?the_?impact_?of_?the_?human_?rights.aspx.

[128] [2003] EWHC 167. For discussion of Munby J's reasoning in *A, B, X and Y*, see chapter 3, section II-F above.

[129] *Ibid*, paras 127–9.

[130] O'Brien (note 120 above) 12. The DRC supported the High Court's approval of the HSE policy statement and promoted that policy by active disseminations to local authorities throughout the country.

[131] *Ibid*, 13.

[132] [2004] UKHL 32, [2004] 4 All ER 303.

relevant comparators, and the more open-textured application of human rights principles, so as to embrace a more positive and participatory version of egalitarianism. It has therefore been suggested that since the HRA, human rights principles have expanded the work of the DRC beyond the protection of the DDA, which has served best in traditional discriminatory contexts in which disabled people have been viewed as potential employees or consumers, rather than as full participants in every aspect of social and civic life.[133]

To date, the range of human rights test cases in which the DCR has used the strategy of third-party interventions rather than merely the partisan funding of cases, have included: a claim concerning the denial of adequate ventilation to a severely disabled child with asthma on 'quality of life' grounds;[134] a claim by a female resident of a nursing home to same-gender intimate care;[135] an effort to extend the narrow definition of 'public authority' within section 6 HRA that was established in the context of the planned closure of care homes in *Leonard Cheshire*);[136] a request for clarification as to whether policy guidance issued to doctors for the withdrawal of artificial nutrition and hydration (ANH) is compatible with core public authority obligations to act compatibly with the ECHR rights;[137] and claims testing the lawfulness of eviction of tenants for antisocial behaviour when the cause of the behaviour is disability related.[138]

---

[133] O'Brien (note 120 above).

[134] *N v B*, unreported (2004). The DRC was granted permission to intervene in a judicial review of a hospital's decision not to provide a severely disabled ten-year-old girl with medical treatment and the placing of a 'Do Not Resuscitate' order on her file against her mother's wishes. It was held that the hospital had acted unlawfully in refusing to ventilate N, and that the actions of the hospital were in breach of N's rights in Articles 2, 3, 6 and 14 ECHR. The DRC also submitted that the actions were contrary to section 19 DDA.

[135] *R (on the Application of C) v Royal Devon and Exeter NHS Foundation Trust (DRC Interested Party)*, unreported (2004). The case involved a tetraplegic adult who claimed that refusal by the NHS Trust to guarantee that necessary intimate tasks would continue as for the past thirty years to be performed by female nurses, constituted breaches of: procedural and substantive common law duties; rights in Articles 3 and 8 ECHR; and rights under the EU Charter of Fundamental Rights and Freedoms, which was incorporated in the Trusts' Constitution. Prior to a judicial review hearing, an interim injunction was obtained in September 2004, after which the NHS Trust settled, providing the guarantees sought.

[136] [2002] EWCA Civ 366, [2002] 2 All ER 936. The most recent (conjoined) test case of this kind in which the DRC has acted as intervener is *Johnson v Havering LBC, the Secretary of State for Constitutional Affairs and the National Care Association; YL v Birmingham CC, Southern Cross Healthcare, OL, VL and the Secretary of State for Constitutional Affairs* [2007] EWCA CIV 26. Leave has been granted to appeal to the House of Lords. For discussion of the role of the DRC in section 6 HRA test cases on the meaning of public authority, see further chapter 3, section II-I above.

[137] *R (on the Application of Burke) v General Medical Council* [2005] EWCA Civ 1003. The claim was brought on behalf of a patient suffering from a degenerative brain condition (spino cellebrar ataxia) who was concerned that when he inevitably became wholly dependent on others for his care and survival, doctors would have too much power to decide, based on their medical opinions about the quality of his life, whether he should survive.

[138] *Manchester City Council v Romano and Samaro (DRC as Third-party Intervener)* [2004] EWCA Civ 834.

VI. CONCLUSION

In the area of discrimination law, the House of Lords decision in *Carson*, in which the Child Poverty Action Group acted as interveners for Ms Reynolds, has significantly reduced the likelihood of further challenges against perceived inequities in the distribution of social security benefits founded on Article 14 ECHR. The House of Lords has convincingly elucidated the tension between the individualistic possessory approach to fairness in the attainment of public goods reflected in recent ECtHR decisions on the one hand and the UK model of social justice in which welfare distribution is determined in accordance with the political balancing of society's needs on the other hand. The decision has also confirmed an important constitutional justification for distinguishing the degree of scrutiny in 'other status' equality disputes of the kind that arose in *Carson* from those that are based on grounds of discrimination spelt out in Article 14. Furthermore, in subjecting the *Michalak* questions to close scrutiny, the House of Lords has highlighted the very different approach required when justifying differences of treatment under Article 14 ECHR and the complex formalistic approach based on the identification of significant comparators, which over time has developed in relation to UK 'equalities' legislation.

In our analysis of *Carson*, as in earlier chapters, we have outlined the myriad difficulties that arise when public authorities and the government are legally challenged for failing to provide access to a minimum safety net of discretionary benefits. However, by contrast with the key cases of *Limbuela*[139] and *Anufrijeva*,[140] which have been discussed fully in chapter six above, neither Carson's case nor Reynolds' case concerned questions of vulnerability, state dependency or the right to equal respect for human dignity. Indeed, there is little to associate the formal discussion of Article 14 ECHR in *Carson* either with the emergence of a human rights approach of the kind espoused by the House of Lords in *Limbuela*; or with the confirmation by the Court of Appeal in *Anufrejiva* that exclusion of some members of society from aspects of life essential to the attainment of their human potential, offends against the fundamental principles of equality and respect for human dignity in the ECHR. However, even before *Limbuela*, as indicated in chapter four above, the emergence of such a collectivist human rights approach had already been hinted at, especially by Baroness Hale in the House of Lords decision in *Ghaidan*.[141] Thus, Baroness Hale stated:

> Inequality of treatment is also damaging to society as a whole. Wrongly to assume that some have talent and others do not is a huge waste of human resources. It is also a risk to social cohesion, creating not only an underclass but an underclass with a rational grievance. It is the reverse of the rational behaviour which we now expect of government

---

[139] Note 9 above. See also discussion in chapter 4, section III-F; and chapter 6, section III-F above.
[140] Note 11 above. See also discussion in chapter 6, section II-C above.
[141] Note 16 above. See also discussion in chapter 4, section III-F above.

and the state. Power must not be exercised arbitrarily. If distinctions have to be drawn, particularly on a group basis, they must be drawn on rational grounds. . . . Last but not least, it is the purpose of all human rights instruments to secure the protection of the minimum essential rights of all individuals, including members of minority groups, who are unpopular with the majority. Democracy values everyone equally even if the majority does not.[142]

Since the enactment of the HRA there has been ongoing debate about the potential for human rights standards to act as agents for change in the field of public services. In these discussions many commentators have argued that strategic focus should be on 'mainstreaming' through the 'soft' promotion of a culture of human rights, both at a governmental level and at the micro-level of public authority service delivery.[143] Others have argued that the human rights movement should not lose the 'critical edge' that it has gained through public law litigation.[144] Yet others such as the DCR and JUSTICE actively endorse both methods. Notably moreover, it has been suggested by the DCR that the Commission for Equality and Human Rights (CEHR), inaugurated in 2007, will look to the experience of the DCR in developing its future strategy.

This chapter is not the place to second-guess the extent to which the new Commission will tackle through legal challenges either the uneven distribution of essential public services in the United Kingdom (the so-called postcode lottery) or perceived inequities in the distribution of social security benefits; or whether the Commission will focus on promoting awareness of human rights on a more general level. However, on one hand, the confident departure by the House of Lords in *Carson* from the narrow *Koua Poirrez* line of authority in Strasbourg[145] and, on the other hand, the collectivist human rights approach to equality embraced by the House of Lords in *Limbuela* provide rich examples of the incremental development of an important body of jurisprudence concerning fairness in the distribution of public goods.

---

[142] *Ghaidan* (note 16 above) para 132.

[143] See for example Baroness Hale, 'What can the Human Rights Act Do for My Mental Health?' (Winter 2005) *BIHR Brief: Newsletter of the British Institute of Human Rights* 4–7, transcript available at http://www.bihr.org/?downloads/?newsletters/?bihr-news-winter_02-05.pdf. See also in the same newsletter the work of F Klug, one of the driving forces behind the HRA, who has from the outset held the view that a highly judicialised system of enforcement would be counterproductive to the goal of creating a culture of respect for human rights. Much of the work of the British Institute of Human Rights (BIHR) has been devoted to the promotion of a culture of rights in the delivery of public services. The recent BIHR report aims to show 'how people from different backgrounds are using human rights arguments to challenge shoddy treatment from public services without having to go to court'. See BIHR, 'The Human Rights Act: Changing Lives' (2007), available at http://www.bihr.org/?downloads/?bihr_hra_changing_lives.pdf.

[144] See for example the Public Law Project (PLP), a national legal charity that 'aims to improve access to public law remedies for those whose access to justice is restricted by poverty or some other form of disadvantage'. To fulfil its objectives, PLP undertakes casework and training across the range of public law remedies. Its case work strategy prioritises socio-economic rights issues, including access to justice; legal aid scope and eligibility; court fees; Article 6 ECHR issues; contracting out of public services; accountability issues such as 'susceptibility to judicial review [and] whether the Human Rights Act applies'. See further http://www.publiclawproject.org.uk/index.html.

[145] Note 3 above. See also accompanying text.

8

Article 6 ECHR: Judicial Review, Due Process and the Protection of Socio-economic Rights

In striking the appropriate due process balance, the final factor to be assessed is the public interest. This includes the administrative burden and other societal costs that would be associated with requiring as a matter of constitutional right, an evidentiary hearing upon demand in all cases prior to the determination of disability benefits.

US Supreme Court Justice Powell in *Matthews v Eldridge*,[1]
cited by Lord Hoffman in *Runa Begum v Tower Hamlets London BC*[2]

I. INTRODUCTION

A GLANCE AT RECENT texts on the progress of the Human Rights Act (HRA) 1998 will reveal that Article 6 has been more extensively litigated in the United Kingdom than any of the other rights in the European Convention on Human Rights (ECHR) 1950, particularly in the areas of private law tort and criminal law.[3] However, much of that litigation is beyond the scope of our enquiry. Here we are primarily concerned with the way in which UK domestic courts have interpreted the scope of the right to a fair hearing in Article 6 ECHR in the context of administrative law disputes, particularly in claims concerning access to discretionary entitlements to social housing, welfare benefits or asylum support. Is the interpretation of the 'due process' right in Article 6 ECHR by the European Court of Human Rights (ECtHR) consistent with a more limited form of judicial scrutiny in administrative disputes than required in other types of disputes concerning 'civil rights', where, for example, the putative terms of a contractual agreement have been broken? Can concerns about efficiency and resources, which may not be relevant in politically sensitive public law disputes deemed to be of 'high constitutional importance', be used to justify a more limited form of judicial scrutiny in 'ordinary' administrative disputes?

[1] (1976) 424 US 319, 347.
[2] [2003] UKHL 5, [2003] 1 ALL ER 689–800, para 45.
[3] See M Amos, *Human Rights Law* (Oxford, Hart, 2006), especially ch 10, 'Article 6: Right to a Fair Trial'.

These questions were fully explored in *R (on the Application of Alconbury Developments Ltd) v Secretary of State for the Environment Transport and the Regions* (hereafter *Alconbury*)[4] and *Runa Begum v Tower Hamlets London BC* (hereafter *Begum*).[5] In those leading cases, the House of Lords addressed general issues surrounding the applicability of Article 6 ECHR in public law disputes. More specifically, in *Begum* the House of Lords had opportunity to consider the constitutional propriety of a pragmatic approach to Article 6 compliance in 'ordinary' administrative law disputes that require the adjudication of issues of primary fact and law, of the kind typically raised in housing or welfare benefit challenges.

In other areas of law as well, litigants have also tested whether the notion of a civil right in Article 6 ECHR can be used to gain access to putative socio-economic entitlements of a mixed public and private nature. In *Matthews v Ministry of Defence* (hereafter *Matthews*)[6] and *R (on the Application of Kehoe) v Secretary of State for Work and Pensions* (hereafter *Kehoe*),[7] the House of Lords, highlighting the constitutional foundations of the autonomous concept of a 'civil right', demonstrated the limits of Article 6 ECHR to afford substantive protection to positive socio-economic rights where none have previously existed. Thus, as a background to our more specific enquiry about the scope of Article 6 in public administrative law disputes over socio-economic entitlements, it is useful to set the scene by examining the approach of the House of Lords in those decisions.[8]

II. WHAT IS A CIVIL RIGHT FOR THE PURPOSES OF ARTICLE 6 ECHR?

In the determination of his civil rights and obligations or of any criminal charge against him, everyone is entitled to a fair and public hearing within a reasonable time by an independent and impartial tribunal established by law . . .

Article 6 ECHR

A. The Autonomous Concept of Civil Right in Article 6 ECHR: The Substantive Procedural Dichotomy Revisited

It is well established that the purpose of procedural guarantees in Article 6 ECHR is to protect claimants' fundamental right of access to the courts.[9]

---

[4] [2001] UKHL 23, [2001] 2 All ER 929.

[5] Note 2 above.

[6] [2003] UKHL 4, [2003] 1 All ER 689, [2003] 1 AC 1163.

[7] [2005] UKHL 48, [2005] 4 ALL ER 905–1016.

[8] In *Matthews* the dispute concerned a limitation on a private law right to sue the Crown in damages; in *Kehoe* the dispute concerned the absence of a right to enforce a statutory claim for maintenance against the applicant's husband.

[9] In *Golder v UK* (1975) 1 EHRR 524 the ECtHR said that this principle ranks as one of the universally recognised fundamental principles of law and that the right of access constitutes an element

Moreover, it is also established that although Article 6 must be broadly interpreted, it cannot by itself guarantee the content of civil rights and obligations in the substantive law of any member state. Thus, it has been recognised by UK courts that, while maintaining the flexibility of the autonomous concept of 'civil rights' intended by Strasbourg, they should not lose sight of the overriding purpose of Article 6, which is to *remove* procedural barriers to the pursuit of rights already established in national law, rather than to fashion new rights in private or public law.

Thus, in seeking to clarify the nature of the autonomous concept of 'civil rights' Lord Hope in *Kehoe* recalled an instructive passage from the decision of the European Commission of Human Rights in *Pinder v UK*[10] as the paradigmatic approach to interpreting the scope of civil rights in Article 6 ECHR:

> . . . Whether a right is at all at issue in a particular case, depends primarily on the legal system of the State concerned. It is true that the concept of a 'right' is itself autonomous to some degree. Thus, it is not decisive for the purposes of article 6(1) that a given privilege or interest which exists in the domestic system is not classified or described as a 'right' by that system. However, it is clear that the Convention organs could not create by way of interpretation of article 6(1) a substantive right which has no legal basis whatsoever in the State concerned.[11]

Moreover, Lord Hope considered the above passage from *Pinder* to suggest that each of the two words in the phrase 'civil right' has a part to play in determining whether the guarantee in Article 6(1) ECHR is engaged; furthermore, the exercise should be broken down into three stages:

> First it must be demonstrated that the applicant is seeking access to a court to enforce what the European Court will accept, according to the autonomous meaning which it gives to this word, is a 'right'. It must then be demonstrated that this is a right which the European Court will classify, again according to the autonomous meaning that it gives to it, as a 'civil' right. Then there is the question whether the 'civil right', if it is subject to some degree of limitation by the national law, is restricted or reduced to such a degree or to such an extent that the very essence of the right is impaired.[12]

---

that is inherent in the right stated in Art 6(1) ECHR (535–6, paras 35–6). The right is not absolute, however. In *Ashingdane v UK* (1985) 7 EHRR 528 the court said that limitations applied by the state on the right of access must not restrict or reduce the access left to the individual in such a way or to such an extent that the very essence of the right is impaired (546–7, para 57).

[10] (1984) 7 EHRR 462.

[11] *Pinder (ibid)* 465, para 5. Lord Hope in *Kehoe* (note 7 above) recalled that the Commission had stated that 'irrespective of whether a right in domestic law is labelled "public", "private", "civil" or something else, it is ultimately for the Convention organs to decide whether it is a "civil" right within the meaning of Article 6(1). However, in the Commission's view, Article 6(1) does not impose requirements in respect of the nature and scope of the relevant national law governing the "right" in question. Nor does the Commission consider that it is, in principle, competent to determine or review the substantive content of the civil law which ought to obtain in the State Party any more than it could in respect of substantive criminal law' (*Kehoe* (note 7 above) para 37).

[12] *Kehoe* (note 7 above) para 38 (Lord Hope).

In considering whether there has been such an impairment of the right (the third stage), the Strasbourg organs have relied on a distinction between substantive and procedural limitations—which is called into play for example, in disputes concerning the right to sue public authorities for damages in tort. When a barrier is substantive rather than procedural, thereby preempting an actionable claim, Article 6 ECHR will not be engaged.[13] By contrast where the claimant can prove the existence of a cause of action, *but for* the operation of the bar, it will be held to be a procedural barrier—and will remain so, whatever its effect, and whether it operates automatically or as a matter of discretion.[14] Thus typically, in *Matthews*,[15] where the applicant sued the Ministry of Defence on grounds that he was unable to recover tortious damages as a result of statutory limitations on his purported 'civil rights',[16] arguments turned on fine distinctions between what constitute procedural and substantive rights, in order to determine whether Article 6 ECHR was engaged.[17]

Nevertheless, the House of Lords also recognised in *Matthews* that simply to focus on fine distinctions between substantive and procedural rights does not always provide an appropriate or fail-safe approach to the question of whether the claimant has a civil right in domestic law. Thus, Lord Hoffman argued that even though the substantive–procedural distinction may be relevant, courts should not lose sight of the fundamental *constitutional purpose* of Article 6 ECHR,[18] which is, as a matter of basic first principles, to prevent contracting states from imposing restrictions on the right to bring one's dispute before the judicial branch of government, in a way that threatens the rule of law and the

---

[13] See *James v United Kingdom* (1986) 8 EHRR 123; *Pinder v United Kingdom* (note 10 above); *Golder v United Kingdom* (1975) 1 EHRR 524; *Fayed v United Kingdom* (1994) 18 EHRR 393; *Dyer v United Kingdom* (1984) 39 DR 246; and *Ashingdane v United Kingdom* (1983) 6 EHRR 69.

[14] See *Stubbings v United Kingdom* (1996) 23 EHRR 213; *Pinder v United Kingdom* (note 10 above); *Dyer v United Kingdom* (*ibid*); *Waite and Kennedy v Germany* (1999) 30 EHRR 261; *Tinnelly & Sons Ltd v United Kingdom* (1998) 27 EHRR 249; and *Fogarty v United Kingdom* (2001) 34 EHRR 302.

[15] Note 6 above.

[16] The claimant, who was suffering from asbestos related injuries, issued a claim for damages for personal injuries against the Ministry of Defence, alleging negligence or breach of statutory duty as a result of exposure to asbestos during his time of service. However, since s 10 of the Crown Proceedings Act 1947 exempted the Crown from liability in tort for injuries suffered by members of the armed forces as a result of events that occurred before 1987, a statutory certificate was issued on behalf of the Secretary of State recording this immunity but also stating, in accordance with s 10(1)(b), any liability on the part of the Ministry for injuries suffered by the claimant during service would be dealt with as a matter of pension entitlement.

[17] The House of Lords dismissed the claimant's appeal, holding that the Crown's liability in tort had been consistently precluded in respect of claims concerning the armed services both at common law and by the express terms of s 10 of the 1947 Act in cases where the Secretary of State had certified that the injury was attributable to service for the purpose of a pension in accordance with subs (1)(b); further, that in substituting the certification procedure, which effectively operated as a no-fault system of compensation for a claim for damages, s 10 imposed a limitation that operated not as a procedural bar but as a matter of substantive law under which the claimant had no civil right to which Article 6 ECHR might apply.

[18] See *Matthews* (note 6 above) paras 29–38.

separation of powers.[19] He has since consistently defended this position in other Article 6 disputes.[20]

For Lord Hoffman, therefore, in *Matthews* the question of whether the appellant should have an action in tort or a no-fault entitlement under a pension scheme had 'nothing to do with human rights'.[21] Instead, the focus should be whether the pre-1987 no-fault scheme was fair, which raised legislative issues: 'it depended upon the generosity of the pension entitlement', not on questions of human rights.[22] Thus, somewhat uncharacteristically, Lord Hoffman continued:

> Human rights are not about fairness in this sense. Human rights are the rights essential to the life and dignity of the individual in a democratic society. The exact limits of such rights are debatable and, although there is not much trace of economic rights in the 50-year-old Convention, I think it is well arguable that human rights include the right to a minimum standard of living, without which many of the other rights would be a mockery. But they certainly do not include the right to a fair distribution of resources or fair treatment in economic terms—in other words, distributive justice. Of course distributive justice is a good thing. But it is not a fundamental human right.[23]

By contrast with *Matthews*, the applicant in *Kehoe* did not seek to challenge the fairness of her economic treatment by a public body, or the fair distribution of public resources or discretionary benefits of the kind to which Lord Hoffman alluded. Rather, the case concerned a putative right *to enforce* a claim for statutory maintenance payments directly against her husband (which involved private family interests), rather than relying on the cumbersome procedures of the Child Support Agency (CSA), which was established by the Child Support Act 1991. Thus, the question raised by the dispute in *Kehoe* was not about fairness in economic terms, or whether there was a substantive or procedural bar to her right of access to court, but rather whether, as observed by Lord Brown, the Child Support Act 1991 gave the mother a right of *any* kind that could be classified as a 'right' within the meaning of Article 6(1) ECHR.

B. *R (on the Application of Kehoe) v Secretary of State for Work and Pensions*

The applicant in *Kehoe* commenced judicial review proceedings, seeking a declaration of incompatibility with Article 6 ECHR under section 4 HRA and

[19] 'Article 6 . . . is concerned with standards of justice, the separation of powers and the rule of law. It would seem to have little to do with whether or not one should have an action in tort. That is a matter of national policy. Some countries, like New Zealand, do not believe in actions in tort for personal injuries. . . . The question of whether a common law action for damages is the most sensible way of providing compensation for accident victims is controversial, and Professor Atiyah's *The Damages Lottery* (1997) demonstrates that the existing system is expensive and in many respects unfair' (*ibid*, para 35 (Lord Hoffman)).

[20] For Lord Hoffman's analysis along these lines in *Alconbury* (note 4 above) and *Begum* (note 2 above), see section III-D below.

[21] *Matthews* (note 6 above) para 26.

[22] *Ibid.*

[23] *Ibid.*

damages under section 8 HRA, contending that, properly understood, the Child Support Act 1991 gave her a right to recover financial support for her four children from her husband, and that insofar as it purported to deny her a power of direct enforcement against him, the statutory provisions were inconsistent with the right of access to a court guaranteed by Article 6.[24] At first instance, the judge concluded inter alia that the claimant's inability personally to enforce arrears of maintenance engaged her rights under Article 6 ECHR. However, a successful appeal by the Secretary of State in relation to the Article 6 point followed, and the claimant then appealed to the House of Lords.

The majority in the House of Lords (Baroness Hale dissenting) agreed with the Court of Appeal. It was decided that a system that prevented the claimant from playing any part in the process of enforcing her entitlement to child support was not incompatible with Article 6(1) ECHR: in domestic law she had no substantive right to do what was capable in Convention law of engaging the guarantees afforded to 'civil rights and obligations'. Indeed, the 1991 Act had deliberately avoided conferring on the person with care of a child, the right to enforce a child maintenance assessment against the absent parent. Since the legislature had decided that enforcement was exclusively a matter for the Secretary of State, it was not open to the House of Lords when applying Article 6(1) to create a substantive right that had no legal basis in the domestic system. Further, since Article 6(1) was not engaged, the CSA could not be said to have acted unlawfully. Accordingly, the claimant had no remedy under the HRA. The appeal was dismissed.

Baroness Hale refused to confine the meaning of 'civil rights and obligations' in Article 6 ECHR within the framework of the scheme enacted by Parliament in 1991. Instead, looking at the fundamental purpose that the Act was designed to address, she argued that at its core lay a historically prior set of fundamental values, embodied in the common law and indeed reflected in natural law, that parents have an obligation to maintain their children and that children have a corresponding 'right to obtain the benefit of that obligation'.[25] Thus, although presented as a case about adults' rights, *Kehoe* was, for Baroness Hale, in reality about children's rights:

> It is difficult to think of anything more important for the present and future good of society that our children should be properly cared for and brought up. We who are nearing the end of our productive lives will depend more than most upon the health productivity and strength of the following generations. The human infant has a long period of dependency in any event. But we have added to that by our requirements that they be educated up to the age of sixteen and disabled from earning their own living up till then. Someone must therefore look after them.[26]

The majority remained impervious to arguments of this kind, insisting that when determining whether Mrs Kehoe had a civil right for Article 6 ECHR pur-

---

[24] The judge dismissed the application for a declaration of incompatibility.
[25] *Kehoe* (note ? above) para 50 (Baroness Hale).
[26] *Ibid.*

poses, it was necessary to focus on her contemporary statutory substantive right in national law: 'Although the duty existed at common law prior to the Act, it did not provide a remedy'.[27] Furthermore, although experience had shown that the operation of the system fell short of what had been expected of it, Lord Hope concluded: 'that is the system that Parliament has laid down, and we must take it as we find it . . . It is a matter of substantive law, not of procedure'.[28]

Lord Bingham was also clear that the 1991 Act could not be interpreted as conferring any right on a parent in the position of Mrs Kehoe. Although prior to the Act she was the person to whom child maintenance would have been paid, 'directly or indirectly and subject to any deduction of benefit, as the person who incurs the expense of bringing up children . . . the right, which she has enjoyed under former legislation, has been removed, so that now the right to recover maintenance has been vested in the CSA'.[29] Furthermore, while conceding, that this was not in itself fatal to the applicant's argument, since the Strasbourg authorities are not bound by the classifications of national law, Lord Bingham insisted that the function of Article 6 ECHR is to guarantee important procedural safeguards in the exercise of rights accorded by national law; it is not ordinarily to require that particular substantive rights be accorded by national law.[30] Lord Bingham concluded:

> If national law conferred on Mrs Kehoe a right to recover child maintenance from her former husband, art 6 would guarantee her access to an impartial and independent court where her claim would be fairly determined. But art 6 does not require that she have such a right.[31]

Lord Bingham could find nothing in the Strasbourg jurisprudence to dictate a different conclusion. While he accepted that in *Golder v UK*[32] the denial of access to a solicitor constituted a violation of the applicant's rights under Article 6(1) ECHR,[33] the basis of that decision was that the constitutional right of access to a court afforded by Article 6 would be valueless unless the applicant had been able to obtain legal advice; and there was no doubt about his right in principle to sue for defamation.[34] Therefore, like Lord Hoffman in *Matthews*,

---

[27] *Ibid*, para 29 (Lord Hope).

[28] *Ibid*, para 35.

[29] *Ibid*, para 7 (Lord Bingham).

[30] Lord Bingham believed that authority for this proposition could be found in *James v UK* (note 13 above) para 81; *H v Belgium* (1987) 10 EHRR 339; *Z v UK* [2001] 2 FCR 246, paras 87 and 98; and *Matthews v Ministry of Defence* (note 6 above) paras 3, 51, 142. See *Kehoe* (note 7 above) para 8 (Lord Bingham).

[31] *Kehoe* (note 7 above) para 8.

[32] Note 9 above.

[33] *Golder v UK* (note 9 above) paras 28–36.

[34] No principle could be extrapolated from that case to assist the applicant in *Kehoe*. This also applied to *Ashingdane v UK* (1985) 7 EHRR 528, in which the court found it unnecessary to decide whether the right that the applicant sought to assert was, in Convention terms, a 'civil right' in the United Kingdom (para 54). Similarly, no principle could be extrapolated from *Philis v Greece (No 1)* (1999) 13 EHRR 741, in which the right attempting to be asserted in the national court was to professional fees for which the claimant had contracted and which (he claimed) he had earned.

Lord Bingham in *Kehoe* concluded that courts should not overlook the fundamental principle in Article 6:

> [T]he deliberate decisions of representative assemblies should be respected and given effect so long as they do not infringe rights guaranteed by the Convention. As they have made clear, it is not for the Strasbourg institutions, under the guise of applying the procedural guarantees in art 6, to impose legislative models on member states. Whether the scheme established by the 1991 Act is on balance beneficial to those whom it is intended to benefit may well be open to question, but it is a question for Parliament to resolve and not for the courts, since I do not consider that any article 6 right of Mrs Kehoe is engaged.[35]

Similarly, Lord Hope considered that, irrespective of how the privilege or interest concerned is *classified* in domestic law, it is no more open to domestic courts than to the European Court, to create a substantive right that has no prior legal basis in the domestic system. He specifically cited the ECtHR in *James v UK*[36] as 'a decision, generally acclaimed to be part of "its constant case law"',[37] recalling their words:

> Article 6(1) extends only to 'contestations' (disputes) over (civil) 'rights and obligations' which can be said, at least on arguable grounds, to be recognised under domestic law: it does not in itself guarantee any particular content for (civil) 'rights and obligations' in the substantive law of the Contracting States.[38]

Further emphasising what the ECtHR had stated in *James*, Lord Hope added:

> It is not enough to bring article 6(1) into play that the non-existence of a cause of action in domestic law may be described as having the same effect as an immunity, in the sense of not enabling the applicant to sue for a given category of harm.[39]

Lord Hope expressed sympathy for the view of Latham LJ in the Court of Appeal, who had thought it unsatisfactory that the claimant, the person with care of the child, should have no say in the conduct of the process.[40] He therefore insisted that the only source from which such a right could be derived was the 1991 Act itself, 'which gave her no such right'; 'nor was it possible to envisage how it might do so, without re-writing the scheme laid down by the Act'.[41] Concurring with this view, Lord Brown moreover decided that the only right enjoyed by those in Mrs Kehoe's position was to 'look to the CSA for the proper discharge of its public law obligations under the statute, a right which is of course of itself sustainable under the court's supervisory jurisdiction'.[42]

---

[35] *Kehoe* (note 7 above) para 10 (Lord Bingham).
[36] Note 13 above.
[37] *Kehoe* (note 7 above) para 41 (Lord Hope).
[38] *James v UK* (note 13 above) 157–8, para 81.
[39] *Kehoe* (note 7 above) para 42 (Lord Hope).
[40] See *ibid*.
[41] *Ibid*, para 43 (Lord Hope).
[42] *Ibid*, para 79 (Lord Brown).

Lord Walker was the only member of the House in *Kehoe* to consider the circumstances in which an Article 6 ECHR challenge by Ms Kehoe might be invoked in judicial proceedings: 'if for example the Child Support Agency were to refuse to enforce a claim because it made some error of law (such as misunderstanding the extent of its statutory powers), the claimant would have a sufficient interest to take proceedings by way of judicial review . . .'[43] For Lord Walker, '[w]hether she would (in any such judicial review proceedings) be securing the determination of a civil right' was open to debate, although a number of signals pointed in that direction.[44] Thus, recognising that the trend of Strasbourg jurisprudence 'is towards an ever widening interpretation of "civil rights"',[45] Lord Walker observed that the 'claimant would be acting to obtain through a social welfare agency a pecuniary benefit in which she had a direct personal interest, but in the enforcement of which the agency had a measure of discretion'.[46]

In light of Lord Walker's observation about the expansive interpretation of civil rights in administrative disputes of that kind, let us now consider the extent to which UK courts have accommodated the Strasbourg trend reflected in the proliferation of public challenges against the refusal of statutory welfare benefits, which erupted shortly after the HRA came into force.

III. THE QUALITY OF ADMINISTRATIVE JUSTICE: THE SCOPE OF ARTICLE 6 ECHR

A. 'A fair hearing by an independent and impartial tribunal established by law'

We have seen in chapter 2 that the ECtHR has decided that an administrative decision that is 'a determination of civil rights and obligations' must prima facie be made by an independent and impartial tribunal.[47] However, it has also been recognised that to provide a right to a full appeal on the merits of every administrative dispute that is 'determinative of civil rights', would be inconsistent with

---

[43] *Ibid*, para 45 (Lord Walker).

[44] *Ibid*, para 46.

[45] *Ibid*. See *Runa Begum v Tower Hamlets London BC* (note 2 above) para 6 (Lord Bingham of Cornhill). See also paras 61–9 (Lord Hoffmann); and paras 84–94 (Lord Millett).

[46] *Kehoe* (note 7 above) para 46 (Lord Walker). Lord Walker recognised parallels in private law relationships in which an individual has interests generally regarded as important legal rights, although not normally enforceable by direct action—for example, a member of an occupational pension scheme, with interests in respect of assets in the pension fund. He noted that well-settled principles of company law and trust law, to which there are also well-settled exceptions, require such persons to call on the company or the trustees to enforce rights of action that are vested, not in them, but in the company or the trustees. In such cases, the absence (as a normal rule) of a direct right of action would not be a deprivation of Art 6(1) ECHR rights but a reflection of substantive principles of British company law or English trust law. Mrs Kehoe's position under the 1991 Act was essentially the same.

[47] For discussion of relevant cases, see chapter 2, section III-F above.

the legal position in the majority of member states.[48] Thus, the ECtHR has decided that where independence is manifestly lacking in the initial administrative procedure, it may be permissible to consider whether the composite procedure of administrative decision-making, together with a right of appeal to the court, is sufficient to satisfy the guarantees afforded by Article 6 ECHR to a 'full hearing' by an independent and impartial tribunal.[49]

The need for such a flexible approach to the notion of a 'full hearing' was recognised by the ECtHR in *Bryan v UK*[50] and emphasised by Mr Bratza in his concurring opinion:

> It appears to me that the requirement that a court or tribunal should have full jurisdiction cannot be mechanically applied with the result that in all circumstances and whatever the subject matter of the dispute, the court or tribunal must have full power to substitute its own findings of fact and its own inferences from those facts for that of the administrative authority concerned.[51]

Further, Mr Bratza continued:

> Whether the power of judicial review is sufficiently wide to satisfy the requirement of article 6, in my view must depend on a number of considerations including the subject matter of the dispute, the nature of the decision of the administrative authorities which is in question, the procedure if any which exists for review of the decision by a person or body acting independently of the authority concerned and the scope of that power of review.[52]

Nonetheless, doubts have inevitably arisen in national legal systems about the type of administrative dispute in which modification of the full judicial hearing is appropriate, and the extent to which, in different types of disputes, lack of independence in the original decision-making process can be cured by a subsequent judicial hearing, confined to the legality of the administrative decision impugned.

Thus, in *Alconbury*,[53] shortly before the HRA came into force, in conjoined applications for judicial review, it was argued before the Divisional Court that certain powers of the Secretary of State relating to planning matters, compulsory purchase, railways and highways were incompatible with Article 6 ECHR, since they denied a fair and public hearing by an impartial and independent tribunal. The essential argument in all cases was that when a policy decision was

---

[48] See generally the discussion of Art 6 ECHR in chapter 2 above.
[49] A search for such flexible and workmanlike solutions has been taken in a number of cases concerning the United Kingdom. See *Bryan v UK* (1996) 21 EHRR 342; *Stefan v UK* (1998) 25 EHRR CD 130, 135; *Kingsley v UK* (2001) 33 EHRR 288, 302 and 303, paras 522–54; and *X v UK* (1998) 25 EHRR CD 88, 97. See also *Zumtobel v Austria* (1993) 17 EHRR 116, 132–3, para 32; and *ISCKON v UK* (1994) 18 EHRR CD 133, E Com HR.
[50] *Ibid.*
[51] *Bryan v UK* (note 49 above) 354.
[52] *Ibid*, para 47.
[53] Note 4 above.

taken by the Secretary of State himself, rather than by an officer appointed by him, as allowed by statute, the minister had such a direct interest in the decision that he could not be regarded as an independent and impartial tribunal. Further, it was doubted whether the availability of judicial review, or a statutory right of appeal restricted to determining the lawful exercise of ministerial discretion, could be sufficient to cure the lack of independence in the powers of the Secretary of State.

At first instance, the Divisional Court upheld these complaints, deciding that the availability of judicial review was insufficient to meet requirements for a full hearing before an independent and impartial tribunal. Declarations of incompatibility with Article 6 ECHR were therefore granted under the HRA in respect of the various powers impugned. However, on appeal by the Secretary of State directly to the House of Lords, the appeal was allowed. After an extensive review of Strasbourg case law, it was decided that the ECtHR had accepted that when certain administrative decisions that affect civil rights and that are subject to review by a court, are taken by ministers who are answerable to elected bodies, regard must be paid to both stages of the process. Thus, although the Secretary of State himself was not an independent impartial tribunal when dealing with 'called in' or recovered matters, the crucial question was whether subsequently, there was sufficient judicial control to ensure determination by such a tribunal. The House of Lords was therefore satisfied that in decisions of the kind at issue, such as planning or compulsory purchase, where in any event the Secretary of State was himself incompetent to review the disputed factual evidence, it was enough that there should be sufficient review of the legality of his decisions and of the procedures that had been followed.

Moreover, the House of Lords found nothing in Strasbourg jurisprudence to suggest that judicial control requires a rehearing or application by way of appeal on the merits. Instead, strong support was to be found in the jurisprudence of the ECtHR for the proposition that 'full jurisdiction' in public administrative law means jurisdiction to deal with a case as the nature of the decision requires, in accordance with the dictates of 'democratic accountability, efficient administration and the sovereignty of Parliament',[54] and that in disputes raising sensitive matters of public interest, the primary concern must be to separate the exercise of policy judgements by ministers directly answerable to the electorate, from the adjudicative powers of courts and tribunals confined to reviewing the lawfulness of executive discretion. Thus, for the House of Lords in *Alconbury* the crucial requirement was that there should be sufficient scrutiny of the legality of ministerial decisions and available procedures.[55] Moreover, it was

---

[54] *Alconbury* (note 4 above) para 87 (Lord Hoffman). See also *Kaplan v UK* (1980) 4 EHRR 64; and *Bryan v UK* (note 49 above). For discussion of these cases, see chapter 2, section III-F above. For further discussion of *Bryan*, see also section III-D below.

[55] This was consistent with the powerful dissent in the Commission decision in *Kaplan v UK* (*ibid*).

concluded that the judicial review jurisdiction of the High Court constituted such a review.[56]

Nevertheless, following the House of Lords decision in *Alconbury* and in light of the emphasis in *Bryan* on the need for a flexible approach that is responsive to the nature or subject of specific disputes, individual complaints have proliferated in the United Kingdom in diverse areas such as planning applications,[57] access to housing[58] and community care.[59] In these complaints, applicants have tested the extent to which compliance with Article 6 ECHR might require adaptations not only to original decision-making procedures but also to the nature of subsequent statutory appeals. Thus, in a growing number of administrative contexts, questions have been raised as to whether: (a) a full hearing to an 'independent and impartial tribunal' requires that any subsequent review of the original decision should rehearse the adjudication of disputed primary facts; (b) an application for judicial review might be sufficient to cure any violations of Article 6(1) ECHR that occurred in the original administrative decision-making process.

Although in *Alconbury*, the House of Lords had, in light of Strasbourg jurisprudence, accepted that planning disputes of the kind at issue constitute 'civil rights' for purposes of Article 6 ECHR, this could not be taken for granted in other areas of challenge. Accordingly, before considering the adequacy of

---

[56] For a detailed analysis of the House of Lords decision in *Alconbury* (note 4 above), which throws into 'relief the impact of the HRA on the freedom of the legislature to choose who should be responsible for decisions in the planning sphere', see P Craig, 'The Courts, the Human Rights Act and Judicial Review' (2001) *Law Quarterly Review* 589, 603.

[57] *Vetterlein v Hampshire County Council* [2001] EWHC Admin 560; *R (on the Application of Malster) v Ipswich Borough Council* [2001] EWHC Admin 711; and *Friends Provident v Secretary of State for Transport* [2001] EWCH Admin 820 all followed *Alconbury*. But compare *R (on the Application of Kathro) v Rhonda Cybnon Taff CBC* [2001] EWCH Admin 527, in which Richards J stated obiter that the absence of any public enquiry in the decision-making process of a local planning authority meant there was a real possibility that, in certain circumstances, a decision by an authority that was not in itself an 'independent tribunal' would not be subject to sufficient control to satisfy Art 6 ECHR; and cf also *R (on the Application of Adlard) v Secretary of State for the Environment* [2002] EWCA Civ 735, in which the Court of Appeal held that the Art 6 rights of objectors had not been infringed by the refusal of a local planning authority to accord a public hearing or indeed any form of hearing. In that case the combination of the authority's initial decision-making process coupled with judicial review by the High Court was sufficient to satisfy Art 6.

[58] In *McLellan v Bracknell Forest Borough Council* [2001] EWCA Civ 1510 the Court of Appeal held that judicial review was sufficient to resolve factual disputes concerning the termination of an introductory tenancy under s 127 Housing Act 1996. But cf *R (Brewry) v Norwich City Council* [2001] EWCA, in which Moses J took the view that the Administrative Court cannot cure 'the frequently imperceptible effects of the influence of the connection between the fact-finding body and a party to the dispute, since it has no jurisdiction to reach its own conclusion on the primary fact, still less any power to weigh the evidence' (para 64). Also compare the approach of the Court of Appeal in the homelessness cases discussed below: *Adan v Newham London BC* [2001] EWCA Civ 1961, [2002] 1 All ER 931; and *R (on the Application of Begum) v Tower Hamlets* (hereafter *Begum*) [2002] EWCA Civ 239, [2002] 2 All ER 688.

[59] See *R (Beeson) v Dorset County Council* [2001], in which Richards J held that judicial review could not compensate for the lack of an independent element in a decision-making process that involved councillors sitting on a complaints panel, where the issue that fell for decision involved a finding of fact that was dependent to a significant extent on an assessment of credibility.

procedural protection, prior to the decision of the House of Lords in *Begum*, judicial energies were devoted to addressing the logically prior question as to whether the claim gave rise to a 'civil right' within the autonomous meaning that has been granted to it by the ECtHR.

In some cases, argument turned on complex technical analysis of the meaning of a 'determination' and the proximity of the relationship between a contested public law right and a private law right such as a tenancy agreement that might materialise subsequently.[60] Alternatively, applicants emphasised that a particular public right had all the characteristics of a private law right: the mandatory force of the public law duty; the lack of discretion afforded to administrators; or the fundamental importance of a disputed public law right to the integrity and dignity of the claimant.[61] Finally, in a third category of cases, it was argued that a right to public benefits, albeit in kind rather than cash, falls within the narrow application of the doctrine established by the Strasbourg Court in *Salesi v Italy*,[62] where it had simply been held that, in light of the economic interests of the claimant in the subject matter of the dispute, social security and welfare schemes may be classed as civil rights because 'they are sufficiently well-defined to be analogous to rights in private law'.[63]

A review of Strasbourg case law in the Court of Appeal decision in *Begum*, where the court was asked to consider whether a reviewing officer's decision under section 202 of the Housing Act (HA) 1996 engaged a homeless person's civil rights for Article 6 ECHR purposes, demonstrated the degree of uncertainty as to whether different types of administrative decisions are 'determinative' of civil rights.[64] However, after answering the question in the affirmative, Laws LJ in *Begum* declared that more pressing questions lay ahead as to whether procedural guarantees in Article 6 could be satisfied in a housing review of the kind at issue, either by the degree of independence of original decision-making procedures, or by subsequent appeals from those decisions.

Thus, as in the earlier Court of Appeal decision of *Adan v Newham London BC* (hereafter *Adan*),[65] in *Begum* the substantive question was whether administrative procedures in local authority housing reviews and subsequent appeals to the County Court afforded by section 204, Part VII of the HA 1996 were compatible with procedural guarantees afforded by Article 6 ECHR. In contrast with *Adan*, however, issues of disputed fact arose in *Begum*. Therefore, it was only in the latter case that the extent to which an 'appeal of law' restricted to the

---

[60] See for example *McLellan* (note 58 above).

[61] See *R (on the Application of Hussain) v Asylum Support Adjudicator* (hereafter *Hussain*) [2001] EWHC 852 Admin, in which Stanley Burnton J held that there was a civil right to asylum support.

[62] (1998) 26 EHRR 187, 199, para 19.

[63] *Salesi (ibid)* para 19. Cf the reasoning of the House of Lords in *O'Rourke v Camden London BC* [1997] 3 All ER 23.

[64] See the arguments before the Court of Appeal in *R (on the Application of Begum) v Tower Hamlets* (note 58 above).

[65] Note 58 above.

lawfulness of the administrator's decision could be compatible with Article 6 guarantees, lay at the heart of the dispute.

B. Housing Reviews: Independence and the Right to a Full Hearing

In both *Adan* and *Begum*, housing claims by homeless applicants under Part VII of the HA 1996 had been rejected by local authorities and the original refusals upheld in internal reviews under section 202 HA.[66] Therefore, in both cases the applicants had exercised their statutory rights of appeal to the County Court under section 204 HA.[67] By such an appeal, an applicant may not only complain that the council has misinterpreted the law, but also complain of any illegality, procedural impropriety or irrationality that could be relied on in judicial review proceedings.[68]

In *Adan*, the applicant was a Dutch national of Somali origin who had fled to the United Kingdom from Holland with her children shortly after witnessing the murder of her husband outside the family home. After living for six months in Newnham in temporary accommodation with her sister, during which time her children went to school, she applied to that council for accommodation for her family. Having been turned down by the local authority on grounds that she was not 'habitually resident' in the United Kingdom, the decision was then confirmed by a different officer, who conducted an internal review pursuant to section 202 HA. The applicant thereupon exercised her statutory right of appeal to the County Court under section 204 HA.

On ordinary grounds for judicial review, she claimed that in determining the issue of 'habitual residence', the officer had taken into account irrelevant factors and failed to take into account some relevant factors: that he had not properly applied the correct legal tests or conducted a balancing exercise of the relevant factors and that his decision in all the circumstances was irrational. Accordingly, the appeal was allowed on grounds of irrationality, the matter was quashed and the decision remitted to the council for a fresh review.

However, since judgement in *Adan* was given only a few days after the HRA had come into force, the judge also noted that section 6 of the HRA made it unlawful for the council as a public authority to act in a way that is incompati-

---

[66] S 202 HA 1996 deals with the applicant's right to request a review of any decision of a housing authority as to what (if any) duty is owed to him under Part VII HA. The Secretary of State has made regulations under s 203 HA. Regulations in force at the time were the Allocation of Housing and Homelessness Review Procedures Regulations 1999, of which Reg 2 stated that when the decision of an authority or a review of an original decision by an officer of the authority is also to be made by an officer, that officer shall not be someone who was involved in the original decision and shall be senior to the officer who made the original decision.

[67] S 204 HA 1996 provides that an applicant who is dissatisfied with the decision of a reviewing officer may appeal to the County Court on a point of law arising from the review, whereupon the Court may make an order confirming, quashing or varying the decision.

[68] See *Nipa Begum v Tower Hamlets London BC* [2000] 1 WLR 306.

ble with a Convention right. He expressed concern that when conducting the fresh review, the council should not infringe the applicant's right under Article 6 ECHR to have her civil rights determined by 'an independent and impartial tribunal established by law'. He therefore directed that the review should be conducted by a different reviewing officer, who, in respect of impartiality and independence, complied with Article 6. However, on appeal by the local authority from that decision, the Court of Appeal in *Adan* set aside the judge's direction, holding that the County Court had no jurisdiction to make an order of mandamus, which was precisely what the judge had done.

Although the appeal had been allowed on grounds of the misdirection of the judge, the Court of Appeal nevertheless continued in an extended obiter dictum to consider whether the complaint procedures in Part VII HA 1996 were Article 6-compliant. Since counsel on both sides was prepared to assume that a reviewing officer employed by the council was not an independent and impartial tribunal and that the decision was a 'determination of civil rights', energies were directed to the question of whether, notwithstanding the lack of independence of the reviewing officer, the typical composite procedure of administrative decision and judicial hearing to an independent County Court was sufficient to satisfy Article 6 ECHR.

It was unanimously accepted by the Court of Appeal in *Adan* that in most cases the composite procedure would be sufficient to satisfy Article 6. However, it was also concluded that although not relevant to the present case, it would not be adequate in cases where housing officers had to resolve disputes of fact that were material to decisions.[69] In the absence of such contested facts, the County Court would have jurisdiction to correct any errors of law in the manner in which the facts had been applied to the legal issues. When, however, decisions turned on matters of disputed factual evidence, the lack of independence in the officer employed by the council to undertake a section 202 HA review could not be cured by the appeal of law afforded by section 204 HA. Thus, it was unanimously agreed by the Court that in such cases there was a danger that the procedure would not be compliant with Article 6 ECHR.

Nevertheless, the Court of Appeal in *Adan* was divided as to how, if at all, the lack of independence in the section 202 HA review could be cured by changes to the administrative procedures alone. The majority[70] considered that if a section 202 review turned on a material dispute of the primary facts, it would be open to the authority to contract out its reviewing functions, pursuant to its powers under the Local Authorities (Contracting Out of Allocation of Housing and Homelessness Functions) Order 1996.[71] In this way an independent and impartial tribunal could be appointed to conduct the review, leaving the County

---

[69] *Adan* (note 58 above) para 17 (Brooke LJ).
[70] Brooke LJ and David Steel J (Hale LJ dissenting).
[71] Order 1996 SI 1996/3205. Art 3 provides in general terms that any function of an authority under Part VII 'may be exercised by . . . such a person . . . as may be authorised in that behalf by the authority'.

Court free to review issues of law in accordance with their statutory powers under section 204 HA.

However, in her dissenting opinion, Hale LJ rejected the contracting out solution as expensive, impractical and inappropriate to the needs of vulnerable claimants and proposed that the County Court, in accordance with its obligations to act compatibly with the ECHR, could itself read the words 'appeal on a point of law' so as, if necessary, 'to include an appeal of fact', thereby rendering the composite procedure Article 6-compatible. However, the suggestion that the Court could fill in the gaps in section 202 HA so as to make the composite procedure compliant with Article 6, did not recommend itself to the majority.

Shortly after *Adan*, the County Court was presented in *Begum* with precisely the type of dispute that had been considered in theory by the Court of Appeal in *Adan* to necessitate the contracting out of section 202 HA powers, in order to cure the lack of independence in the local authority review. This was because in *Begum* the reviewing officer doubted the reasons given by the applicant for rejecting the offer made to her, namely that the flat was in a drug-ridden area; that she had been attacked there when she went to view the house; and that her husband was still living there. Thus, in light of *Adan*, in exercising her right of appeal to the County Court, the applicant claimed that the council had acted in breach of Article 6 ECHR in failing to contract out the review of her case, which centred on contested issues of fact. Albeit reluctantly, the judge at first instance was prepared to quash the local authority decision; thereafter the local council appealed.[72]

Laws LJ, who gave the single judgement of the Court of Appeal in *Begum*, agreed that when looked at in isolation, there were insufficient objective guarantees to clothe the reviewing officer's role with the qualities of independence and impartiality required by Article 6 ECHR.[73] However, contrary to the majority in *Adan*, his approach was that the compatibility of any welfare scheme with Article 6 must depend on the extent to which the scheme as a whole was likely to throw up a preponderance of factual or policy issues. If the scheme was more likely to require the exercise of judgment or policy affecting the interests of others, rather than to throw up issues of primary or secondary fact, 'a form of first instance enquiry in which the decision maker was more of an expert than a judge' would generally be compatible with Article 6 requirements for a full hearing before an independent tribunal.[74]

Moreover, Laws LJ considered that, despite the relevance of fact in a particular case, in schemes such as the present, where 'the decision maker is more of an expert than a judge',[75] an appeal limited to the ordinary grounds for judicial

---

[72] The original grounds of appeal included the normal judicial review grounds that the council had acted irrationally, had failed to make proper enquiries, did not have regard to material factors and so on.

[73] *Begum* (note 58 above) para 30 (Laws LJ).

[74] *Ibid*, para 40.

[75] *Ibid*.

review would be sufficient.[76] On the other hand, if as a whole the scheme tended systematically to throw up issues of fact, he accepted that it would be necessary for local authorities to adopt a stricter form of hearing by using conventional mechanisms for the adjudication of disputed facts, such as rights of cross examination of witnesses, access to documents and a strictly independent decision-maker.[77]

Nevertheless, Laws LJ decided that, despite the potential in some cases for contested issues of primary fact of the kind that had arisen in *Begum* in relation to section 202 HA 1996, it was not a general characteristic of the housing scheme as a whole that the exercise of local authority discretion in the distribution of a very limited stock of public housing would turn on issues of primary or secondary fact. Moreover, while he agreed with the Court of Appeal in *Adan* that want of independence in the original process could be cured by an appeal of law, even in cases where disputes of fact were at issue, he did not think that it was necessary, as suggested by Hale LJ, for the County Court to read the words 'appeal of fact' into 'appeal of law' in appropriate cases as they arose. Instead, more robustly, he considered that in any event, mirroring developments in judicial review, courts now have powers to apply a more intensive scrutiny of the facts than at first sight encapsulated in the words 'appeal of law'.[78] Accordingly, allowing the local authority appeal, Laws LJ concluded in *Begum* that there had been no breach of Article 6 ECHR and that housing allocation procedures for the homeless were compatible with Article 6.

Thus, on appeal from that decision by the claimant, the House of Lords was required to determine inter alia (i) whether the reviewing officer constituted an independent and impartial tribunal for purposes of Article 6(1) ECHR; and if not, (ii) whether the County Court on appeal under section 204 HA 1996 possessed full jurisdiction so as to guarantee compliance with Article 6(1), given that section 204 gave the County Court jurisdiction to examine only questions of law. Moreover, since the parties were in agreement that the issue of whether the applicant enjoyed anything that could properly be recognised as a civil right under Article 6 for purposes of domestic law was closely intertwined with these issues, that question was now fully addressed by the House of Lords.

---

[76] Although in *Begum* Laws LJ thought that the test for whether it is necessary to have an independent fact finder was dependent on the extent to which the administrative scheme was likely to involve findings on questions of fact nine months later, prior to the decision of the House of Lords in *Begum*, in the case of *R (on the Application of the Personal Representatives of Beeson) v Dorset CC* [2002] ALL ER Digest, he came to the conclusion that such a solution would be too uncertain: 'there is some danger we think of undermining the imperative of legal certainty by excessive debates about how many angels can stand on the head of the article 6 pin' (*Beeson*, para 15).

[77] *Begum* (note 58 above) para 40. When the scheme fell between these two, Laws LJ thought that in determining Art 6 compatibility, it would be necessary to defer to the will of Parliament as the scheme's author.

[78] *Ibid*, para 44.

C. Civil Rights and Welfare Needs: The House of Lords in Begum

Before the Court of Appeal in *Begum*,[79] Laws LJ concluded that a determination under section 202 HA 1996 engaged a homeless person's civil rights for Article 6 ECHR purposes, on grounds that '[s]uch a determination leads to the grant or withholding of a tenancy'.[80] Mindful of the less technical approach advocated by Standley Burnton J in *R (on the Application of Hussain) v Asylum Support Adjudicator* (hereafter *Hussain*),[81] Laws LJ moreover stated:

> [T]he subject matter of the scheme, dealing with the urgent provision of living accommodation for persons who will often be gravely disadvantaged (or the refusal to provide it) so touches their well-being that as a matter of our domestic law we should lean towards the application of the ECHR article 6(1) discipline.[82]

However, before the House of Lords, on the issue of whether Runa Begum had a civil right on which to found her claim, it was argued on behalf of the government now joined in the appeal, that the House of Lords decision in *O'Rourke*[83] was authority for the proposition that it is 'a necessary incident of a "civil right" that the law allows damages to make good the breach'.[84] Furthermore, it was argued that the broad discretionary area of judgement entrusted to the council as to how it would perform its duty under section 202 was inconsistent with claimant's enjoyment of a civil right for Article 6 ECHR protection. However, the House of Lords rejected this argument. Emphasising the distinction between the autonomous meaning of 'civil rights' and private law rights in national jurisdictions, and adopting the flexible approach suggested by Standley Burnton in *Hussain* and followed by Laws LJ in the Court of Appeal, the House of Lords concluded that section 193(2) HA constituted a civil right within the extended meaning of the ECHR jurisprudence:

> This was a duty owed to and enforceable by Runa Begum. It related to a matter of acute concern for her. The authority's duty gave rise to a correlative right in Runa Begum even though it was not a private law right enforceable by injunction and damages.[85]

---

[79] Note 58 above.

[80] *Begum* (note 58 above) para 25.

[81] Note 61 above.

[82] *Begum* (note 58 above) para 25. That view was consistent with the decision of the Court of Appeal in *McLellan* (note 58 above), in which it was held (in the context of the introductory tenancy scheme under Part V Housing Act 1996) that the function of the review panel under s 129 engages Art 6 ECHR civil rights and obligations.

[83] Note 55 above.

[84] *Begum* (note 2 above) para 68. In *O'Rourke* (note 63 above), the plaintiff brought an action for damages against the council following his eviction from temporary accommodation, under the precursor to s 188(1) HA 1996. Reversing the decision of the Court of Appeal, the House of Lords concluded that there was no right to private law damages in a scheme of social welfare that was intended 'to confer benefits in the general public interest' and 'where the duty to provide accommodation depended on a good deal of judgement on the part of the authority' (26).

[85] *Begum* (note 2 above) para 4 (Lord Bingham). This analysis was supported by Lord Hoffman, who stated that it is one thing to say that Parliament did not intend a breach of the council of its statutory duty under Part VII HA 1996 to be actionable in damages and quite another to say that actions of the local authority should be immune from judicial review (para 68).

This did not mean that the House of Lords thought that Strasbourg would have reached such a generous conclusion on the issue; and whether the dispute in *Begum* fell within the doctrine established before the ECtHR in *Feldbrugge v Netherlands*[86] was even more doubtful. Nevertheless, the central pragmatic concern of the House of Lords in *Begum*, was, as Lord Bingham put it, that if 'emasculation by over judicialisation of the benefits system were to be avoided', the court should embrace the principle recognised by the ECtHR in *Bryan*, namely that 'the more elastic the interpretation given to civil rights', 'the more flexible must be the approach to the requirement of independent and impartial review'.[87] Seeking support for such a flexible approach to the question of Runa Begum's civil rights, Lord Hoffman cited a passage from the joint dissenting opinion in *Feldbrugge*:

> The judicialisation of dispute procedures as guaranteed by Article 6(1) is eminently appropriate in the realm of relations between individuals but not necessarily so in the administrative sphere where organisational, social and economic considerations may legitimately warrant dispute procedures of a less judicial and formal kind. The present case is concerned with the operation of a collective statutory scheme, for the allocation of public welfare. As examples of the special characteristics of such schemes, material to the issue of procedural safeguards, one might cite the large numbers of decisions to be taken, the medical aspects, the lack of resources of the person affected, the need to balance the public interest against the need for efficient administration against the private interest . . .[88]

However, in the absence of clear authority for this contention in the ECtHR, Lord Hoffman also cited with approval the opinion of Justice Powell in the US

---

[86] (1986) 8 EHRR 425. This case, along with *Deumeland v Germany* (1996) 21 EHRR 342 (with judgments delivered by the ECtHR on the same day and are for practical purposes identical), is regarded as the starting point of Art 6 ECHR jurisprudence on social security and social welfare schemes. Mrs Feldbrugge was claiming sickness allowance on grounds that she had been unfit for work. She argued that she had not received a fair hearing from the administrative tribunal that heard her claim. On one hand, the 'right to social security' was created by public legislation that laid down qualifying conditions and rates of payment. On the other hand, there were affinities with private insurance insofar as employees paid contributions. Despite a powerful dissent from seven members of the ECtHR who argued that such an erosion of private and public law rights would lead to great uncertainty, the majority decided that the features of private law were cumulatively predominant and that the applicant's right was therefore a civil right within the meaning of Art 6. The majority of the ECtHR held:

> Mrs Feldbrugge was not affected in her relations with the public authorities as such, acting in the exercise of discretionary powers, but in her personal capacity as a private individual. She suffered an interference with her means of subsistence and was claiming a right flowing from specific rules of the legislation in force . . . [S]uch a right is often of crucial importance . . . especially . . . in the case of health insurance benefits when the employee who is unable to work by reason of illness enjoys no other source of income. In short, the right in question was a personal, economic and individual right, a factor that brought it close to the civil sphere.

See *Feldbrugge*, 434, para 37. For additional discussion, see also chapter 2, section III-F above, particularly notes 193 and 194.

[87] *Begum* (note 2 above) para 5 (Lord Bingham).

[88] *Feldbrugge* (note 86 above) 443, para 15 (cited by Lord Bingham in *Begum* (note 2 above)).

Supreme Court case of *Matthews v Eldridge*.[89] In that case, commenting on the requirements of 'due process' in the administration of a disability benefits scheme, Justice Powell had emphasised that if as a matter of right, an evidentiary hearing were provided on demand in all cases prior to the termination of disability benefits, 'the most visible burden would be the incremental cost resulting from the increased number of hearings and the expense of providing benefits to ineligible recipients pending decisions'.[90]

Therefore, having taken such a flexible approach to the question of whether Runa Begum had a civil right, the more pressing question for the House of Lords was now the extent to which in disputes over discretionary public benefits of the kind at issue, the composite procedure of administrative decision-making together with a subsequent judicial hearing confined to the legality of the decision-making process, could satisfy the requirements of Article 6 ECHR for a fair and public hearing by an independent and impartial tribunal. However, in light of emphasis placed on the absence of factual issues to justify such an affirmative conclusion in *Alconbury*,[91] a different rationalisation was required to reach the same restrictive conclusion in challenges to administrative decisions taken by local authority housing administrators about the reasonableness of an individual's wish to reject an offer of a particular accommodation, which clearly raises mixed questions of both law and fact.

D. Law, Fact and Homelessness Disputes

Emphasis placed on the policy nature of decisions by the Secretary of State in *Alconbury* had given rise to a belief in lower UK courts that more stringent safeguards would always be required in cases in which questions of primary fact are at issue. Accordingly, it was necessary in *Begum* to qualify the emphatic distinction between decisions of policy, where adjudication of the legality of administrative decisions would suffice, and those turning on issues of fact, in which case the claimant in *Begum* argued that it would *always* be necessary for an appellate court to have 'full jurisdiction to review the facts or for the primary decision making process to be attended with sufficient safeguards to make it virtually judicial'.[92]

---

[89] Note 1 above.

[90] *Matthews v Eldridge* (note 1 above) 347. (See epigraph at the beginning of this chapter.) The Supreme Court recognised that resolution of issues involving the constitutional sufficiency of administrative procedures prior to the initial termination of benefits pending review required consideration of three factors: (1) the private interest that will be affected by the official action, (2) the risk of an erroneous deprivation of such interest through the procedures used, and probable value if any of additional safeguards, and (3) the Government's interest including the fiscal and administrative burdens that the additional or substitute procedures would entail (para 44).

[91] Note 4 above.

[92] *Begum* (House of Lords decision) (note 2 above) para 37.

Lord Hoffman in *Begum* was bound to accept that in *Alconbury* he had endorsed the opinion of the Strasbourg Court in *Bryan*[93] that in the assessment of contested facts, the role of the planning officer must be attended by sufficient safeguards. Nor had he suggested that in such cases the possibility of an appeal of law would be sufficient to compensate for lack of independence on the part of administrators.[94] In *Begum*, he therefore conceded that he had incautiously created the impression in *Alconbury* that the adaptation of a review procedure for compliance with Article 6 ECHR should largely depend on the degree of factual judgement involved in the original decision-making process. Marking a retreat from this position, Lord Hoffman in *Begum* insisted that, irrespective of the degree of fact, there was compelling support in the landmark case of *Bryan* for the proposition that the relevance of factual evidence in determining questions of Article 6 compliance varies in accordance with the type of administrative dispute.[95] Thus, now he took the view:

> The great principle which *Bryan* enunciated was that in assessing the sufficiency of review it is necessary to have regard to matters such as the subject matter of the decision appealed against, the manner in which the decision was arrived at and the content of the dispute, including the desired and actual grounds of appeal.[96]

Because of the nature of *Bryan* (a planning appeal against *enforcement* proceedings), there was a possibility that the decisions of the planning inspector in that and similar cases might ultimately become subject of criminal trial, in which case disputed factual evidence would be key.[97] Lord Hoffman therefore drew attention to the importance difference between the quasi-criminal nature of the dispute in *Bryan*, which concerned breach of a planning restriction, and the housing dispute in *Begum*. Thus, as Lord Hoffman saw it, the ECtHR in *Bryan* had appropriately regarded the following safeguards in the procedure as necessary: 'the duty incumbent on each inspector to exercise independent judgement; the requirement that inspectors must not be subject to any improper influences; and the stated mission of the Inspectorate to uphold the principles of openness fairness and impartiality'.[98] By contrast, Lord Hoffman considered that those safeguards were neither necessary nor appropriate to

> the findings of fact which have to be made by central or local government officials in the course of carrying out regulatory functions (such as licensing or granting planning permission) or administering schemes of social welfare such as Part VII [of the 1996

---

[93] Note 49 above.
[94] See *Begum* (note 2 above) paras 37–42 (Lord Hoffman).
[95] *Ibid*, para 51.
[96] *Ibid*.
[97] *Bryan* involved an appeal against an enforcement notice, in which the inspector's decision that Bryan had acted in breach of planning control was binding in any criminal proceedings for failing to comply with the notice. In the UK, prior to *Bryan*, failure to comply with planning control of the kind exercised in *Bryan* was dealt with by magistrates and could therefore be regarded as analogous to a criminal matter. See *R v Wicks* [1997] 2 All ER 801.
[98] *Bryan* (note 49 above) 342, cited in *Begum* (note 2 above) paras 38–41 (Lord Hoffman).

Act]. The rule of law rightly requires that certain decisions, of which the paradigm examples are findings of breaches of the criminal law and adjudications as to private rights, should be entrusted to the judicial branch of government.[99]

Arguing that 'utilitarian considerations have their place when it comes to setting up, for example, schemes of regulation or social welfare' and that private consumer disputes are very different from disputes over a limited public housing (such as *Begum*), Lord Hoffman cited Hale LJ, who had stated in *Adan*:

> The policy decisions were taken by Parliament when it enacted the 1996 Act. Individual eligibility decisions are taken in the first instance by local housing authorities, but policy questions about the availability of resources or equity between the homeless and those on the waiting list for social housing are irrelevant to individual eligibility.[100]

Lord Hoffman was clear that *Begum* fell into the category of administrative disputes in which limited review of the facts is sufficient—disputes that were described by the Strasbourg court in *Kingsley v United Kingdom*[101] as 'typical exercise[s] of administrative discretion' and in *Bryan* as 'specialised areas of the law'.[102] In such cases, the most important factor to be considered was the 'public interest' in the costs that would necessarily arise from a more intensive adjudication of the facts. Thus, Lord Hoffman argued that in the administration of public welfare, where it would often be cheaper and more efficient to have cases decided by administrators, a less rigorous form of scrutiny satisfies the requirements of Article 6 ECHR for a full hearing. Accordingly, he took the view that, in considering the compatibility of the housing scheme as a whole with Article 6, the question must be whether, 'consistent with the rule of law and constitutional propriety', it is appropriate to entrust it to administrators. If so, it does not matter that there are many or few occasions on which they need to make findings of fact. It was therefore concluded that it would be unnecessary and inappropriate in a housing scheme already under severe economic strain, to formalise further the section 202 HA 1996 review procedure by contracting out, as proposed by the majority in *Adan*.[103]

Therefore, it was unanimously concluded in *Begum* that for utilitarian reasons of expediency and the good administration of justice, whenever an appeal against a 'typical administrative' welfare dispute lies to an adjudicative hearing,

---

[99] *Begum* (note 2 above) para 42 (Lord Hoffman).

[100] *Adan* (note 58 above) para 57 (Hale LJ), cited in *Begum* (note 2 above) para 43 (Lord Hoffman).

[101] Note 49 above.

[102] *Begum* (note 2 above) para 56 (Lord Hoffman, relying on *Kingsley* (note 49 above) and *Bryan* (note 49 above).

[103] *Begum* (note 2 above) para 43 (Lord Hoffman). In *Adan's* case, counsel for Newham detailed the number of applications received yearly and the urgency of the appeals regarding homelessness in comparison with planning appeals. It was claimed that this militated against removing appeals to a body other than the authority entrusted with the administration of the scheme. Four reasons were given for not contracting out, some of which had already been given by Hale LJ.

such as provided by the county court in the present case, the lack of a full fact-finding jurisdiction does not disqualify the tribunal for purposes of Article 6 compliance, and that ordinary principles of judicial review are invariably enough to satisfy the requirements of Article 6, whether or not, as in the present case, there are contested issues of primary fact.[104] Thus, the House of Lords agreed that the composite procedure afforded by sections 202 and 204 HA were Article 6-compatible, and the appeal was dismissed.

This was not to suggest, however, that in public law disputes in which civil rights are at issue, Article 6 ECHR precludes the investment of statutory schemes devised by Parliament with the kind of safeguards necessary to allow them to operate fairly. Thus, on one hand it was accepted in *Begum* that as a matter of due process, there must be safeguards of expertise and quality of personnel at the primary decision-making level. On the other hand, Lord Bingham was clear that in a statutory appeal of law from such an administrative process, the exercise by a court such as the County Court of the ordinary principles of judicial review is enough to satisfy the requirements of Article 6: the County Court judge can quash the authority's decision under section 204(3) HA on grounds that there had been a legal misdirection, procedural impropriety, unfairness or bias, irrationality or bad faith.[105] Moreover, that could also occur in cases in which there is a lack of evidence to support factual findings; in which factual findings are plainly untenable; or in which it can be shown that the decision-maker misunderstood or was ignorant of an established and relevant fact.[106]

Following *Alconbury*, UK courts had accepted that in disputes that raise issues of primary fact, in one way or another, it was necessary for reviewing courts to engage more fully in the merits of administrative decisions than at first sight permissible in the notion of an appeal of law. Thus, one of the most important aspects of the House of Lords decision in *Begum* was that it required reappraisal of the extent to which judicial powers of scrutiny in English administrative law—even before the HRA—had inched towards a fuller hearing of the merits of administrative decisions than is traditionally assumed by the *Wednesbury* standard of review.

E. The Standard of Judicial Review in Welfare Needs Disputes

Before the Court of Appeal in *Begum*,[107] Laws LJ had accepted that, following the HRA, the door was open to a public law jurisdiction that allows 'anxious

---

[104] The housing officer would be bound by a written report from the independent fact-finder. Lord Hoffman considered it unlikely that the Strasbourg Court would find an independent fact-finder of that kind to be more independent than an established officer of the council.

[105] *Begum* (note 2 above) para 7 (Lord Bingham).

[106] *Ibid.* See *Secretary of State for Education and Science v Metropolitan Borough of Tameside* [1976] 3 All ER 665, 675.

[107] Note 58 above.

scrutiny' of administrative decisions in appropriate cases. He thus disagreed with Hale LJ's suggestion in *Adan*[108] that 'the county court should "fill the gap" by assuming a fact finding role as necessary'.[109] Indeed, as he saw it, 'there is no gap to fill.'[110] He therefore argued:

> Given that . . . the section 202 [HA 1996] process does not of itself fulfil article 6, the judge is perfectly entitled, within the jurisdiction given him by section 204 [HA 1996], to subject the earlier decision to a close and anxious scrutiny.[111]

However, the majority in the House of Lords thought it unnecessary to consider this question in cases such as *Adan* and *Begum*, in which there were no allegations of breaches of other Convention rights such as Articles 3 or 8 in conjunction with Article 6.

It had been argued in *Begum* on behalf of the Secretary of State, that when determining whether the jurisdiction of the county court was adequate, courts should take into account the expanding scope of judicial review.[112] It was claimed that in a suitable case, this may allow a court to quash a decision on the grounds of misunderstanding of or ignorance of an established and relevant fact (as suggested by Lord Slynn in *R v Criminal Injuries Board, ex parte A*[113])—or at least the possibility of doing so when convention rights are engaged, on grounds of proportionality (as suggested by the House of Lords in *R (on the Application of Daly) v Secretary of State for the Home Department*[114]).

Lord Hoffman thought it unnecessary in *Begum* to consider the implications of either of these developments. Although he accepted that it would be open to a court exercising the review jurisdiction under section 204 HA 1996 to adopt a more intensive scrutiny of the rationality of the officer's conclusion of facts in *appropriate* cases, he nonetheless argued:

> [W]hen one is dealing with a welfare scheme, which in this particular case does not engage human rights (does not for example require consideration of article 8), then the intensity of review must be what one considers to be most consistent with the statutory scheme.[115]

Accordingly, Lord Hoffman noted how in *Pulhofer v Hillingdon*[116] seventeen years earlier, the House of Lords had famously 'contemplated a fairly low level of judicial interventionism' in such cases,[117] on grounds that

> Parliament intended the local authority to be the judge of fact. The Act abounds with the formula, when or if the housing authority are satisfied as to this or that, or have

---

108 Note 58 above.
109 *Begum* (note 58 above) paras 44–5 (Laws LJ).
110 *Ibid*, para 45 (Laws LJ).
111 *Ibid*, para 44 (Laws LJ).
112 See the House of Lords in *Begum* (note 2 above) para 48.
113 [1999] 2 AC 330, 344–5. See also *Alconbury* (note 4 above) para 53.
114 [2001] UKHL 26, [2001] 2 All ER.
115 *Begum* (note 2 above) para 48.
116 [1986] 1 ALL ER 467, 474.
117 *Begum* (note 2 above) para 48 (Lord Hoffman).

reason to believe this or that. Although action or inaction of a local authority is clearly susceptible to judicial review where they have misconstrued the Act or abused the powers or otherwise acted perversely . . . great restraint should be exercised in giving leave to proceed by judicial review.[118]

On this approach, Lord Hoffman concluded that in cases such as *Adan* and *Begum*, Article 6 ECHR compliance required no more than for courts to exercise the type of scrutiny 'most consistent with the statutory scheme in question'.[119] Nonetheless, he left open the question as to whether a fuller standard of review might be necessary in Article 6 cases in which other Convention rights are engaged.

As discussed in chapter 6, against a background of acute political controversy over delays in dealing with the claims of an increasing number of asylum seekers arriving in the United Kingdom, the introduction of the Nationality Immigration and Asylum Act 2002 resulted in increased efforts to stem the flow of resources to potentially destitute claimants. One of the primary purposes of that legislation was to grant the Secretary of State, through the operation of Asylum Support Adjudicators, responsibility for the provision of support to asylum seekers who appeared 'to be destitute or likely to become destitute' within a prescribed period.[120] Thus, section 55(5)(b) of the 2002 Act provides that the Secretary of State 'may not provide or arrange for the provision of support, if . . . [he] is not satisfied that claim was made as soon as reasonably practicable after the person's arrival in the UK'. Furthermore, a right of appeal from the Secretary of State's decision is precluded by section 55(10) of the Act.[121]

Following the 2002 Act, in *R (on the Application of Q, D, B, M, J and F) v Secretary of State for the Home Department*[122] six asylum seekers who had failed to satisfy the Secretary of State that their claims had been advanced 'as soon as was reasonably practicable' sought to challenge the refusal of their claims inter alia on that ground. In applications for judicial review, Collins J concluded that procedures for the refusal of support to asylum seekers were flawed, either when there was a failure to investigate the circumstances under which entry had been achieved,[123] or when any reconsideration of the case was

---

[118] *Pulhofer v Hillingdon* (note 116 above) 474 (Lord Brightman).

[119] *Begum* (note 2 above) para 49 (Lord Hoffman).

[120] For the purposes of s 95 of the 2002 Act, a person is destitute if (a) he does not have adequate accommodation or any means of obtaining it (whether or not his other living needs are met); or (b) he has adequate accommodation or the means of obtaining it but cannot meet his other essential living needs.

[121] S 55(10) provides that 'a decision of the Secretary of State that this section prevents him from providing or arranging for the provision of support to a person is not a decision that the person does not qualify for support for the purpose of section 103 of the Immigration and Asylum Act 1999 (appeals)'. The effect of the section is therefore to preclude the right of appeal against the Secretary of State's decision to an asylum support adjudicator.

[122] [2003] EWHC 195 Admin.

[123] 'It is an unfortunate element of the system . . . that the person at [National Asylum Support Services] who decides whether to refuse or provide support under section 55 relies on questions recorded on the form. He does not see nor does he question the claimant' (*Q (ibid)* 19 (Collins J)).

coloured by an assumption that failure to claim asylum at the port of entry was itself a justification for the refusal. Collins J therefore quashed the decisions by the Asylum Adjudicators primarily on grounds that in each case the procedures had not been fair. The Secretary of State appealed.

In the Court of Appeal case *R (on the Application of Q and Others) v Secretary of State for the Home Department* (hereafter Q),[124] in addition to the substantive issues discussed in chapter 6 above, the Court explored the fairness of the statutory regime imposed on asylum in accordance with orthodox principles and procedures of administrative law. In light of the absence of a right of appeal from the Asylum Adjudicator's decision, the Court of Appeal also considered whether procedures afforded to destitute asylum seekers in disputes in which Articles 3 and 8 ECHR are engaged were compatible with Article 6 ECHR.[125]

As we have seen, section 55 procedures require applicants to satisfy the Secretary of State that their claims have been timely. If they are unable to do so, it is then necessary for the Secretary of State to consider whether, despite the failure to qualify under section 55(1), it is necessary to provide them with support in order to avoid breaches of Articles 3 and 8 ECHR. Thus, the first issue of statutory interpretation raised by the appeal was the precise meaning to be attached to the phrase 'as soon as reasonably practicable' in section 55 of the 2002 Act.

It was submitted on behalf of the applicants that when determining what was 'reasonably practicable', it was necessary to have regard to advice given by fraudulent agents, who were anxious to get their 'charges' through immigration without detection.[126] In turn, the government argued that to take account of such mitigating factors would undermine the overriding purpose of section 55.[127] For the Court of Appeal, however, this was far from likely, given the efforts recently made by the Home Office to warn of the need to claim asylum upon arrival at the airports. As a result of these warnings, only a small number of asylum seekers could now credibly maintain that they had misunderstood the need to make an immediate claim by relying on the advice of fraudulent agents. Thus, it was concluded by Lord Phillips that 'on the premise that the purpose of coming to this country was to claim asylum and having regard both to the practical opportunity for claiming asylum and to the asylum seeker's personal circumstances',[128] the fair test of reasonable practicability should be: 'could the asylum seeker have been expected to claim asylum earlier than he or she did?'[129]

---

[124] [2003] EWCA Civ 364, 905.

[125] The Court of Appeal gave permission for the Joint Council for the Welfare of Immigrants and Liberty to make a joint intervention by way of short oral and written submissions.

[126] See Q (note 124 above) paras 18–20.

[127] Lord Phillips considered the primary object of s 55 as preventing those who are not genuine asylum seekers and those who are not in fact in need of state support from seeking assistance (*ibid*, para 26).

[128] *Ibid*, para 37.

[129] *Ibid*.

Furthermore, he concluded that 'when deciding the issue in relation to a disorientated asylum seeker in the hands of an agent, it is right to have regard to the effect of anything that the asylum seeker may have been told by his or her facilitator'.[130]

When considering the fairness of the procedures, it was accepted by both parties that the burden of proof was on the applicant to satisfy the Secretary of State in relation to the circumstances that gave rise to the need for support; nevertheless, the Secretary of State must 'set up a fair system and operate it fairly in accordance with what fairness required in that particular context'.[131] Moreover, the Court of Appeal in *Q* considered that the obligation to ensure fairness for both the applicants and the public interest was particularly high. Not only was the effect of section 55(1), which was subject to the qualification in section 55(5), to prevent the Secretary of State from providing benefits to applicants who were destitute in accordance with section 95; the questions raised by section 55(1) revolved around issues of fact in circumstances in which there could be no appeal and in which refusal would constitute a breach of the applicant's rights in Articles 3 and 8 ECHR, 'or at any rate a possibility that they may be engaged'.[132]

Thus, after a detailed examination of the general operation of the system, the Court of Appeal agreed with Collins J that since decisions were finally made by National Asylum Support Services officers (who neither saw nor questioned applicants themselves) on the basis of answers to questions on a form, it was crucial that all the necessary information was acquired and recorded on the form at the time of the initial interview.[133] Moreover, the Court was highly critical of the fact that no guidance had been given to officers on how human rights issues should be investigated and that no account was taken of the state of mind of applicants on their arrival in the United Kingdom: 'fairness required the interviewer to try to attain the precise reason that the applicant did not claim asylum on arrival, which called for interviewing skills and a more flexible approach than simply completing a standard form questionnaire'.[134] Accordingly, the

---

[130] *Ibid*, para 41.

[131] *Ibid*, paras 69–71 (Lord Phillips). See also *Gaima v Secretary of State for the Home Department* [1989] Imm AR 205, (applying *Re K (H) an Infant* [1967] 1 All ER 226, 231); and Lord Mustill's welll-known statement of 'principles of fairness' in *Doody v Secretary of State for the Home Department* [1993] 3 All ER 92, 106 (both cited by Lord Phillips in *Q* (note 124 above) para 70).

[132] See *Q* (note 124 above) paras 71–3.

[133] Asylum seekers were interviewed by administrative officers, who used standard screening forms in deciding what questions to ask. The preamble in the form initially read to applicants before interview contained no clear reference to the fact that the question to be decided was whether the applicant could show that he had applied for asylum as soon as reasonably practicable after arrival. A subsequent amendment to the original preamble contained the unhelpful statements: 'It is VITAL that all relevant information you possess in connection with when, how and where you arrived in the UK and how you travelled here today is given to us today even if you are not directly asked a question about it. Otherwise you may be refused support on the basis that you have given inadequate information to satisfy the Secretary of State that you made your asylum claim as soon as practicable after arrival in the United Kingdom. Do you understand?'

[134] *Q* (note 124 above) para 119 (Lord Phillips).

Court of Appeal decided that in each of the cases considered, Collins J had been correct to conclude that the system was not fair.

F. The Compatibility of Section 55(10) of the Nationality Immigration and Asylum Act 2002 with Article 6 ECHR

It was argued in *Q* that in not providing an appeal mechanism for asylum support, Parliament had acted incompatibly with Article 6 ECHR. However, while the government agreed that officials who take the material decisions are not independent, the decision of the House of Lords in *Begum* was relied on to contend (irrespective of the fact that Articles 3 and 8 ECHR were likely to be engaged) that the availability of judicial review, which had not been modified in any way by statute, afforded Convention-compliant access to an independent and impartial tribunal.

In considering this question, the Court of Appeal in *Q* accepted the Attorney General's assertion that the common law of judicial review has not stood still in recent years. Therefore, it was agreed that while the courts continue to refrain from merits review that require a rehearing of administrative decisions as to the facts, in 'appropriate classes of issue sensitive cases', they will today look very closely at the *process* by which facts have been ascertained and the logic of the inferences drawn from them. Moreover, it was also accepted not only that the courts have been competent since *Anisminic*[135] 'to correct any error of law, whether or not it goes to the jurisdiction', but also that 'since the coming into force of the HRA, errors of law include any failure by the state to act compatibly with the Convention'.[136] Furthermore, in light of the ECtHR decision in *Bryan*,[137] the Court of Appeal in *Q* accepted that in any event, merits review is not a necessary element of the full jurisdiction required to be vested in an independent tribunal by Article 6 ECHR, but, as recognised by Lord Hoffman in *Alconbury*,[138] full jurisdiction means 'jurisdiction to deal with the case as the nature of the decision requires'.[139]

Thus Lord Phillips in *Q* highlighted the passage in *Begum* in which Lord Hoffman had argued that 'the gap between judicial review and a full right of appeal is seldom in practice very wide . . . [and] the intensity of review must depend on what one considers to be most consistent with the statutory scheme . . .'.[140] In other words, a more intensive form of scrutiny may be necessary when

---

[135] *Anisminic Ltd v Foreign Compensation Commission* [1969] 1 ALL ER 208, [1969] 2 AC 147.
[136] *Q* (note 124 above) para 112.
[137] Note 49 above.
[138] Note 4 above.
[139] *Q* (note 124 above) paras 112–13.
[140] *Begum* (note 2 above) paras 35–7 (Lord Hoffman), cited by Phillips LJ in *Q* (note 124 above) para 114. Lord Hoffman stated further: 'even with a full right of appeal it is not easy for an appellate tribunal which has not itself seen the witnesses to differ from the decision-maker on questions of primary fact' (*Begum*, para 47).

human rights are engaged by a scheme. '[G]iven this, and given the range of other powers instanced in the *Runa Begum* case', the Court of Appeal in *Q* was satisfied that 'judicial review today is capable today of affording to an asylum seeker who is denied support under section 55, recourse to an independent and impartial tribunal which has in the Strasbourg sense, full jurisdiction to determine whether the refusal is lawful'.[141]

Nonetheless, Lord Phillips was also clear that 'were it not for the amplitude of modern judicial review and the opportunity for a more intense form of scrutiny where ECHR rights are engaged, [the Court] would have had some difficulty in holding that recourse to it was sufficient to satisfy article 6, because of the gravity discussed above of several of its human rights aspects'.[142] Thus, while accepting that an initial decision as to civil rights need not be taken by an independent and impartial tribunal to satisfy Article 6 ECHR, Lord Phillips concluded that 'at the end of the day . . . the process as a whole must be capable of fairly determining the civil rights that are in play' and that 'the inadequacies of the procedure made it impossible for the officials of the Secretary of State to make an informed determination of matters central to the asylum seekers' civil rights'.[143] As a result, the court conducting the judicial review was equally unable to do so and had no other option but to quash the decisions. However, it was concluded that if the Secretary of State were to take appropriate steps to mend the procedures, it would be possible for the 'combination of his decision-making process and judicial review of the decision reached by that process' to satisfy the requirements of Article 6.[144] Accordingly, the Court of Appeal agreed with Collins J that the provisions of section 55(10) of the 2002 Act were not incompatible with the Convention.

IV. CONCLUSION

In *Begum* the House of Lords concluded that in reviewing the legality of decisions concerning the refusal of discretionary welfare benefits, Article 6 ECHR confers no greater protection than was given all along by judicial review in the United Kingdom, unless violations of other Convention rights are at issue. Moreover, the House of Lords specifically reasserted its opinion that on grounds of public policy, maximum restraint should be exercised in giving leave to appeal in homelessness disputes, whether or not Article 6 ECHR issues are raised by the cases. Thus, in *Begum* the House of Lords has reaffirmed the controversial conclusion that it reached twenty years earlier in the notorious case of *Pulhofer*[145]—namely that given the acute housing shortages that lie at the heart

---

[141] *Q* (note 124 above) para 115.
[142] *Ibid*.
[143] *Ibid*, para 116.
[144] *Ibid*, para 117.
[145] Note 116 above.

of such disputes, nothing is to be gained by expanding established procedures or by affording more intensive scrutiny of administrative decisions than afforded by the orthodox standard of *Wednesbury* unreasonableness.

As we have seen in this chapter, there is little direct authority in *Bryan v UK*[146] on which to base the pragmatic conclusion that a distinction should be drawn between quasi-consumer administrative welfare disputes involving issues of fact and law (such as *Begum*) and quasi-criminal constitutional disputes to which the fullest protection of Article 6 ECHR is owed (such as *Bryan*). Lord Hoffman in *Begum* therefore drew inspiration instead from *Matthews v Eldridge*,[147] in which the majority of the US Supreme Court concluded that an evidentiary hearing was not required prior to the termination of social security disability payments under the Social Security Act, on grounds that 'due process is flexible and calls for such procedural protection as the particular situation demands'.[148]

By contrast, in *Goldberg v Kelly*[149] the Supreme Court had held much earlier that the Fourteenth Amendment right to due process of law required that 'welfare recipients' be afforded evidentiary hearings to determine their eligibility before their benefits were terminated by welfare authorities.[150] However, in *Matthews v Eldridge*, the majority of the Supreme Court noted with respect to claimants of disability benefits (in contrast to the welfare claimant in *Goldberg v Kelly*), 'the private interest that will be adversely affected by the erroneous termination of benefits is likely to be less in the case of a disabled worker' whose 'eligibility for financial payments is not based on financial need'.[151] Moreover, in *Matthews v Eldridge* the Supreme Court also noted that 'although hardship may be imposed, [the disabled worker's] need is likely less than the welfare recipient', since 'other forms of government assistance are likely to be available to the terminated disability recipient.'[152] Furthermore, it was also agreed by the majority in that case that medical assessment of the worker's condition 'implicates a more sharply focused and easily documented decision'.[153]

However, in the United Kingdom, by adopting a more generous interpretation of civil rights than likely to be afforded in Strasbourg, the House of Lords has refused to be drawn into comparisons between different types of public services consumers. Instead, the House of Lords conclusion in *Begum* was based on more general observations about the discretionary nature of the public welfare safety-net, which, having been long associated with shortages of supply, was said to render such arguments futile. Thus, in spite of the generous inter-

---

[146] Note 49 above.
[147] Note 1 above.
[148] *Matthews v Eldridge* (note 1 above) 339.
[149] 397 US 245 (1970).
[150] *Ibid*, 269. For a discussion of *Goldberg v Kelly*, which took place at the high-water mark of the 'due process movement' in the United States, see chapter 1, section II-B above. For discussion of due process in the United States during the 1970s and 1980s, see also chapter 1, section II-A above.
[151] *Ibid*, 332–5.
[152] *Ibid*, 343–5.
[153] *Ibid*.

pretation of 'civil rights' in Article 6 'due process' disputes that proliferated after the HRA, it has become clear since the House of Lords decision in *Begum* that Article 6 ECHR can seldom provide an answer to the frustration and disappointments of untold numbers of claimants seeking access to a limited supply of discretionary public benefits.[154]

---

[154] But now see the important case of *Tfayso v UK*, Application No 60860/00 November 2006, referred to in the preface to the paperback edition.

Afterword

M Y PROJECT ON the Human Rights Act (HRA) 1998 started in 2002 with a paper entitled 'Can the Human Rights Act 1998 Address Inadequacies and Inequalities in Public Services?'[1] By then, UK administrative law courts had begun to struggle with many of the issues that are explored in this book: the relationship between Article 6 of the European Convention on Human Rights (ECHR) 1950 and the role of courts in 'ordinary' administrative law disputes regarding discretionary housing and welfare benefits; the dynamic interpretation of Article 8 ECHR by the European Court of Human Rights (ECtHR) so as to impose positive obligations in welfare needs contexts; the interpretative limits of section 3 HRA in socio-political disputes; and the meaning of 'public function' in section 6 HRA. Happily, since then, the House of Lords has addressed many of the issues posed in my conference paper.

Moreover, there has been increasing confidence among the UK judiciary regarding what it means to *take account of* Strasbourg jurisprudence without necessarily *following* it. Thus, for example, in *Limbuela*,[2] the House of Lords placed emphatic reliance on what was identified as a strong line of Article 3 jurisprudence in order to affirm their own dynamic interpretation of the scope of Article 3 ECHR. By contrast, however, in cases such as *Begum*,[3] *Carson*[4] and *Kay*[5] the House of Lords would claim to have struck a delicate balance between adhering to the dynamic interpretations of Articles 6, 8 and 14 ECHR given by the ECtHR, and their own constitutional mandate to interpret and develop the ECHR rights in a morally defensible and culturally appropriate manner. Thus, during the past six years, among senior members of the judiciary, a sophisticated argument has arisen: that the responsibility of courts under the HRA is to develop a 'domestic code of human rights jurisprudence' that should not only be 'in tune with Strasbourg jurisprudence' but also 'fully reflect where it is appropriate to do so, our own cultural traditions and perhaps unique historic perspective of the importance of individual freedom in society'.[6]

---

[1] Presented at the Fourth Annual JUSTICE/Sweet & Maxwell conference *Making Human Rights Work* (London, October 2002).

[2] *R v Secretary of State for the Home Department, ex parte Limbuela* [2005] UKHL 66, [2006] 1 AC 396.

[3] *Runa Begum v Tower Hamlets London BC* [2003] UKHL 5, [2003] 1 ALL ER 689.

[4] *R (on the Application of Carson) v Secretary of State for Work and Pensions* [2005] UKHL 37, [2005] 2 WLR 1369, [2005] 4 All ER 545.

[5] *R (on the Application of Kay and Others) v London Borough of Lambeth* [2006] UKHL 10.

[6] The Rt Hon Lord Woolf of Barnes, 'Foreword' in L Lester and D Pannick (eds), *Human Rights Law and Practice*, 2nd edn (London, Butterworths, 2004) vi.

Notwithstanding these developments, the political landscape of the United Kingdom has undergone significant changes since the enactment of the HRA 1998. As Lord Lester and David Pannick observed in 2004, 'it had become clear six years after the election of the Blair government that it would not now have enacted the HRA 1998 if it were considering whether to do so afresh'.[7] Noting New Labour's disenchantment with the role of courts under the HRA 1998, the authors pointed out that in a television interview on 5 February 2003, Prime Minister Tony Blair stated that the position regarding asylum and illegal immigration was 'unacceptable', and that if necessary, the ministers would 'fundamentally' re-examine Britain's obligations under the Convention.[8] Furthermore, drawing attention to criticism by the Parliamentary Joint Committee of Human Rights of proposals for 'fundamental changes to the asylum and review system'[9]—which David Blunkett, then Home Secretary, astonishingly deemed to be 'compatible with the Convention rights'—Lester and Pannick sternly concluded:

> Unless the present and future administrations recognise the HRA 1998 as no ordinary law, but a constitutional measure that except in highly exceptional circumstances takes precedence over ordinary legislation the case will become overwhelming to entrench human rights by means of a new constitutional settlement and written constitution.[10]

However, approximately two years before the end of New Labour's third term of office, the call for a new constitutional settlement has come from rather different quarters. David Cameron, leader of the Conservative opposition, has said that if elected to government, he will introduce a new, 'distinctively British' bill of rights for the United Kingdom;[11] and Gordon Brown, very shortly to replace Tony Blair as New Labour Prime Minister, has also expressed his commitment to a 'new constitutional settlement'.[12] In light of emphasis on a bill of rights for the United Kingdom (as opposed to the broader regional focus of the

---

[7] Lester and Pannick (eds) (*ibid*) 20, 1.64.

[8] *Ibid*.

[9] See Clause 11 of the Asylum and Immigration (Treatment of Claimants etc) Bill 2003, Fifth Report (2003–04) HL 35, HC 304 (10 February 2004). The purpose of Clause 11 was to replace the existing immigration and asylum appeal and review systems with a single level of appeal from decisions of immigration officers in most cases. It also sought to 'oust' judicial review in cases in which it was claimed that Immigration Appeal Tribunals decisions were null by reason of lack of jurisdiction, irregularity or error of law, breach of natural justice or any other matter.

[10] Lester and Pannick (note 6 above) 1.67.

[11] Rt Hon David Cameron MP, 'Balancing Freedom and Security: A Modern British Bill of Rights' (paper presented at a conference held by the Centre for Policy Studies, 26 June 2006), available at http://www.cps.org.uk.

[12] See Brown's speech in which he launched his campaign to be leader of the Labour Party and next Prime Minister, 11 May 2007, available at http://news.bbc.co.uk/?1/?hi/?uk_politics/?6646349.stm. Brown argued: ?Government must be more open and more accountable to Parliament, for example in decisions about peace and war, in public appointments and in a new ministerial code of conduct.' He also suggested that Britain could get its first written constitution, saying: 'We need a constitution that is clear about the rights and responsibilities of being a citizen in Britain today.'

ECHR), the possible repeal of the HRA 1998 has become more than an idle threat.

Recognising the urgent need for an informed debate, JUSTICE has established its own 'Constitution Project' to examine issues surrounding a new domestic bill of rights.[13] The Project Committee, which is composed of leading academic lawyers, practitioners and constitutional scholars who have very different views on the implications of such a bill of rights,[14] has published its first discussion paper.[15] Important issues to be considered by the Committee include: the contents of such a bill of rights; amendability; enforcement; the process by which agreement might be reached; its relationship with a written constitution; and crucially, its relationship with the ECHR and with the HRA.[16]

As observed in chapter 3 above,[17] there is indeed much to be said for informed participative debate (of a kind that did not precede the HRA 1998) about a bill of rights for the United Kingdom. For example, would a bill of rights in which citizens 'have a say' include civil and political rights *and* socio-economic rights, including, for example, rights to housing or of access to health? If so, what would be the role of courts in protecting those rights? For example, would the inclusion of an express right to health prevent the closure of local hospitals (a matter of widespread public concern over which courts currently have little control)? Would courts be expected to have a greater role than they have cautiously assumed under section 3 HRA 1998 in reviewing legislation for the provision of health or welfare services to vulnerable individual caught up in the care system? In short, would such a bill of rights allow courts to hold the government to account for failures to meet the basic health and welfare needs of citizens?

On one hand, we have seen in chapter one the extent to which the historic rejection of the divisive past of South Africa provided concerted political will for the meaningful protection of socio-economic and civil and political rights in the

---

[13] See http://www.justice.org.uk/parliamentpress/index.html. The Parliamentary Joint Committee on Human Rights has also decided to inquire into whether and why a British bill of rights might be needed; what rights should be contained in such a bill of rights; what the relationship should be between a British bill of rights, the Human Rights Act and the United Kingdom's other international human rights obligations; and the impact of such a bill of rights on the relationship between the executive, Parliament and the courts. The Committee is not at this stage inquiring into other details about how a British bill of rights would work in practice, but submissions of written evidence for consideration by the Committee are being taken until 31 August 2007, after which the Committee intends to hold oral evidence sessions. See JCHR Press Notice No 38, May 28 2007; and http://www.parliament.uk/?parliamentary_committees/?joint_committee_on_human_rights/?jchrpn38_220507.cfm.

[14] Committee members include: Francesca Klug and Lord Lester, who played leading roles in the promulgation of the HRA 1998; Professors Carole Harlow and Maurice Cranston; and the political scientist Professor Vernon Bognador.

[15] 'A British Bill of Rights for the United Kingdom?' (23 March 2007). See the JUSTICE website (note 12 above). In this paper, the Committee invited JUSTICE members to partake in a public meeting on grounds that 'Gordon Brown talks of a "new constitutional settlement", and the Labour Party originally saw the Human Rights Act as the first step to establishing a deeper human rights culture. David Cameron wants a new bill of rights.'

[16] *Ibid.*

[17] See especially section II-A.

transformative South African constitution. On the other hand, we have seen the continuing resistance in the United Kingdom of the New Labour government during the past seven years to what has proved in a small number of cases to be the measured and enlightened constitutional review by senior courts, of government's interference with fundamental human rights, whether designated as civil and political rights or as socio-economic rights.[18] This is not the place to second-guess the outcome of the JUSTICE project, or indeed the likely contents of a new constitutional settlement for the United Kingdom—whether of David Cameron's or Gordon Brown's design. However, in conclusion, it seems doubtful that any future Conservative or indeed New Labour government will willingly grant a greater role to the courts in the scrutiny of health and welfare legislation in accordance with human rights standards than currently afforded by the collaborative safeguards under the HRA 1998.

---

[18] See the *Guardian Unlimited*, 23 May 2007, available at http://www.guardian.co.uk/ ?international/?story/?0,,2086261,00.html, reporting the historic decision of the Court of Appeal to allow families expelled from the Chagos Islands in order to make way for the Diego Garcia US airbase 30 years ago, to return home: 'Explaining the court?s decision, Lord Justice Sedley said that "while a natural or man-made disaster could warrant the temporary, perhaps even indefinite, removal of a population for its own safety and so rank as an act of governance, the permanent exclusion of an entire population from its homeland for reasons unconnected with their collective well-being cannot have that character and accordingly cannot be lawfully accomplished by use of the prerogative power of governance". After the ruling, a Foreign Office spokesman said ministers were "disappointed" that judges had not granted the department leave to appeal the decision. "We now have one month to lodge an appeal with the House of Lords," he added.'

Index

Administrative decision-making
constitutional limits of judicial intervention,
in 165–72
role of courts, in
law and policy, 175–7
resource allocation decisions, 162–5
Administrative law
constitutional foundations, of
ultra vires or rights, 152–6
proportionality, 157–62
Smith, 158–62
Wednesbury review, 151–165
Administrative justice
see also **Due process**
right to a fair hearing, 311–6
article 6 ECHR, 82–6,
Begum House of Lords, 320–2
civil rights, meaning of 311–22
homelessness, 322–5
housing reviews, 316–9
law and fact, 324–6
independent and impartial tribunal, 311–6
immigration and asylum, 330–1
standard of judicial scrutiny in housing/
welfare disputes, 325–30
Pulhofer, 327–31
Age discrimination
welfare claimants, 291–4
Assessment of needs
see also **Choice**
role of in public services provision, 205–6
Assisted suicide
right to dignity, 70
Asylum seekers
right to dignity
administrative court crisis, 257–62
Court of Appeal decision in *Limbuela,*
262–5
House of Lords intervention, 265–70
lack of welfare support, 254–5
withdrawal of asylum support, 255–7
right to fair trial, 330–1

Bill of Rights
background to HRA 1998, 105–6
contents of, 107–9
British Bill of Rights, 336–7
Breach of statutory duties
local authorities, generally 220–225

HRA
article 8 ECHR, breach of
Anufrejiva, 246–51
Bernard, 233- 7
section 6 HRA, 246–51
damages for, 111, 243–4

Canada
public law, developments in,
Baker 191–2
socio-economic rights protection,
through civil and political rights,
21–2
equality
Eldridge, 36
Gosselin, 38
right to life
Chaoulli, 37–38
Children
see also **right to family life**
accommodation of, generally 29–43
special needs, with 41–43
children's commissioners, 114
disability, and 134–5, 299
families and separation of, 227–8, 251
resource allocation disputes, and
225–33
Choice
EU law,
choice and entitlements, 94–6
Watts, 95–102, 218–220
housing allocation and role of, 202- 5
NHS rationing, 217–20
Rogers 214–8
role of, in public services, 200–6
mimicking private markets, 205
Citizenship
political theories of, 14–15
Civil rights
see also **Administrative justice**
article 6, in 303–7
autonomous concept, 304–7
substantive procedural limits, 306–7
Matthews, 306
pre-existing rights
Kehoe, 307–11
Civil and political rights
indivisibility of,
and socio- economic rights, 15–9

Civil and political rights (*cont.*):
  and socio- economic rights (*cont.*):
    International Covenant on Civil and
      Political Rights (ICCPR), 14
    ECHR, in, 49–86
    use of for protection of socio economic
      rights, generally, 34- 9
Clinical priority
  public services prioritisation disputes, 206–7
  EC /EU law
  targets and waiting lists 94 –5
  Watts 95–103
Collaborative Dialogue
  cooperative models of adjudication 33–4,
  JCHR and, generally, 1120 4
Constitutional review
  American political theory,
    Dworkin R, 29–33
    originalists, 30 –31
  due process, and
    Ely J, 30–1
  generally, 29–34
  UK, and, 115–117
  US constitution, nature of
    De Shaney, 18
Convention rights
  compatibility of UK legislation
    generally, 117–8
    interpretative limits, 120–30
    judicial interpretation, 118–20
    White Paper "Rights Brought Home", 118
  Strasbourg jurisprudence, taking account of,
    130–3
    criticism in
    socio-economic disputes, 133–6
    stare decisis, 136–8
Courts, role of
  see also Constitutional review
  HRA, under
    generally, 117- 120
    constitutional limits, 120–130
    Strasbourg jurisprudence, taking account
      of 130–3
      limits of s. 2 HRA 133- 136
      stare decisis 136–8
  protection of socio economic rights
    civil and political rights, through, 34–9
    constitutional review, 29–34
    institutional competencies, of 26–8
  public authority decisions, scrutiny of,
    under s.6, HRA, 140–1
    hybrid public authorities, 141–2
    identification of, 147
    parliamentary sovereignty, preservation
      of 138–40
    private power, regulation of, 143- 150
  public functions
    criticism of judicial interpretation, 142–3

meaning, 145–9,
  public/private social provision, 149
    vulnerable groups, impact 143–5
  protection of socio- economic rights,
    through
    civil and political rights, 34–9
    constitutional review, 29–34
    institutional competencies, 26–8
    South African model, 39–42
Deference
  HRA and, 115–117, 120–130,
  HRA, law and policy, and, 175–7
    landlord and tenant repossession cases,
      178–87
  human rights reasoning, and 189–95
    justification, prerequisite of, 172–4
    transparency, 174
  international public law discourse, and,
    195–196
  judicial deference in public law generally,
    151–152
  legislation, interpretation of, and
  nature of rights at issue, and 187–9
  resources, limits of judicial intervention,
    and 162–5,
  s.6 HRA, parliamentary sovereignty and,
    165–168
Degrading or inhuman treatment
  right to dignity, 69–74
Democracy
  see also **Consitutional Review, Liberty**
  human rights and
  judicial participation, in 193–4
  twenty-first century,
    conceptions of, 15–7
Deportation
  human rights and, 191–2, 270–4
Detention without trial
  terror suspects and, 193–4
Dignity
  see also **Right to dignity**
  equal respect for, 194–5
Disability
  disability rights, protection of, 298 –300
Discrimination
  age discrimination, 291–4
  conclusions, 301–2
  equal distribution of public goods, 79–81
  equality and human rights
    competing rights and social values,
      297–300
    material and relevant differences,
      294–7
  introduction, 277–9
  protection of socio-economic rights, 79–81
  socio-economic entitlements, 279–83
  up-rated pension

refusal of payments to pensioners abroad, 283–91
Due process
ECHR, and, 82–6
fourteenth amendment, and, 37
generally, 36–9
protection of welfare rights,
section 7 Canadian Charter, 38–9
US Supreme Court, 37–8

EC law
protection of socio-economic rights
Charter of Fundamental Rights 2000, 90–4
European Court of Justice, 94–102
fundamental rights, development of, 86–90
Economic Liberalism
see also **Courts, role of,**
the control of private power, HRA and, 142–150
Enforcement of socio-economic rights
South African Constitutional Court, 42–7
Equal distribution of public goods
ECHR, and, 79–81
Equality
concept, development of,
judicial, 193–5
Commission for Equality and Human Rights, 302
discrimination,
competing rights and social values, 297–300
material and relevant differences, 294–7
equal respect for dignity, 194–5
fundamental value, ECHR, 129–130
European Convention on Human Rights (ECHR)
dynamic approach, to, 50
grafting jurisprudence of positive obligations, 59–62
incremental development of positive obligations, 53–8
living instrument, 64
negative-positive dichotomy, 49–52
protection of socio-economic rights
core values, development of, 65–7
due process in public law challenges, 82–6
equal distribution of public goods, 79–81
protecting physical and psychological integrity, 74–9
respect for human dignity, 69–74
right to health treatment, 67–8
reconciling positive obligations with negative thrust, 62–3
theoretical justification for positive obligations, 64–5
EU Charter of Fundamental Rights
protection of socio-economic rights,

generally, 90–3
contents, 92–3
general principles, 93
scepticism, 93
European Court of Justice
protection of socio-economic rights
generally, 94–6
health treatment, right to, 100–2
undue delay, 96–100
Extradition
right to dignity, 73–4,

Fair trial
see **Right to fair trial**
Families
see also **Right to private and family life**
maintaining the family unit, 251–4
provision of accommodation
resource allocation disputes, 225–33
Free movement of services
NHS rationing, 217–20
Freedom
two concepts of liberty, 15–9
fear *and* want, freedom from, 13–4
social democracy, contemporary concept of, 16–7
Fundamental rights in EC/EU Law
protection of socio-economic rights
EU Charter of Fundamental Rights, 90–4
development of, 86–90

Health treatment, right to
ECHR, 67–8
European Court of Justice, and, 100–2
Homelessness
right to fair trial, 322–5
Housing
accommodating children and families, 225–33
repossession
judicial deference in public law, 178–87
right to fair trial, and, 316–9
Human dignity, respect for
core public law values, 193–4
protection of socio-economic rights
ECHR, and, 69–74
Human rights
role of UK courts
introduction, 105
socio-economic rights, as, 11–5
Human Rights Act 1998
background to
Bill of Rights, 105–6
incorporation of fundamental rights, 106–7
socio-economic rights, and, 107–9

Human Rights Act 1998 (*cont.*):
  compatibility with Convention rights
    generally, 117–8
    interpretative limits, 120–30
    judicial interpretation, 118–20
    White Paper "Rights Brought Home", 118
  conclusions, 150
  constitutional interpretation, 115–7
  horizontal effects of s.6, 140–1
  hybrid public authorities, 141–2
    identification of, 147
    legislation, interpretation of, and
      parliamentary sovereignty, 120- 130
    socio- political disputes, interpretative
      limits, 128–130
  private power, regulation of, 143–150
  public authorities
    horizontal effects of s.6, 140–1
    hybrid public authorities, 141–2
    identification of, 147
    parliamentary sovereignty, 138–40
  public functions
    criticism of interpretation, 142–3
    meaning, 145–9
    public/private social provision, 149
    vulnerable groups, impact, 143–5
  scrutiny of public authority decisions
    generally,
    s.6, HRA, 165 –172
  purpose of
    bringing rights home, 109–12
    declarations of incompatibility, 112–3
    JCHR, role of, 112–4
    structure of, 114–5
  Strasbourg jurisprudence, taking account of,
    130–3
    limits of s. 2 HRA
    socio-economic disputes, 133–6
    stare decisis, 136–8
Human Rights Adjudication
  structuring arguments
    in UK courts, 134–6
Human Rights Judges
  characteristics of, 196
Human Rights Values
  development in public law, 189–192
  international law, embodied in,
  Universal Declaration of Human Rights
    (UDHR), 16
Hybrid public authorities
  meaning of, 141–2

Immigration
  right to fair trial, 330–1
Impartiality
  right to fair trial, 311–6
Independence
  right to fair trial, 311–6

India
  socio- economic rights, protection of
    directive principles, 35
    role of courts, 38–9
Irrational allocation policies
  NHS rationing, 214–7

Joint Committee on Human Rights
  HRA, constitutional safeguards, and 112–4
  meaning of public functions, role in, 144–9
Judicial interpretation
  compatibly with Convention rights,
    generally, 117–20
  courts as public authorities, and
    horizontal effects of s.6, 140–1
  hybrid public authorities, 141–2
    identification of, 147
  legislative scrutiny, deference and
    parliamentary sovereignty, 120–130
    limits of, in socio- political disputes
      128–130
  public functions
    interpretation, criticisms of, 142–3
    meaning, 145–9
  Strasbourg jurisprudence, taking account of,
    130–3
    limits of s. 2 HRA, 133–6
    stare decisis, 136–8
  traditional approach to, 161 –4
Judicial review
  conclusions, 195–6
  constitutional foundations
    administrative law, 157–61
    pre-Human Rights Act, 156–7
    resource allocation, 162–5
    ultra vires or rights, 152–6
  introduction, 151–2
  judicial deference in public law 172–174
    democracy, 189–95
    division between law and policy, 175–7
    landlord and tenant repossession cases,
      178–87
    limits of judicial intervention, 165–72
    justification, 172–4
    nature of rights at issue, 187–9
    transparency, 174
    unified approach, 189–95
  standard in welfare disputes
    right to fair trial, 325–30
Justiciability
  amenability to review of socio- economic
    rights,
    international law, 19- 24
  domestic courts, 26–8
  issues of,
    constitutional interpretation,
    institutional competencies, 26- 27,
    legitimacy of judicial intervention, 29–34

normative content of rights, and 24–6
public interest and,
resources, 20–22,
Justification
administrative decision-making, in
giving of reasons 190–4
judicial deference in public law, 172–4
transparency 174–6,

Landlord and tenant repossession
judicial deference in public law, 178–87
Legitimate expectation
NHS rationing, 211–4
Liberty
two faces of, 15–19
fear and want, freedom from, 12–4
neo- Conservative political theorists, 17
social democracy, 16
Life-saving treatment, NHS
right to dignity, 270–4
ante- retroviral treatment 204–6
right to life, 208–10
withdrawing life support, 197
Local authorities
resource allocation disputes
accommodating children and families,
225–33
generally, 220–4
human rights approach, to 237–9
protection of vulnerable persons, 233–7

Maladministration
right to private and family life, 243–4
Anufrejiva 251–4
Margin of Appreciation
Strasbourg, 65
UK courts, and
margin of discretion 168–72
Market efficiency
see also **NHS rationing**
public services, and, 201–3
housing allocation policy, 203–4
choice, and 203–206

NHS rationing
choice and socio-economic entitlements,
217–20
legitimate interventions
generally, 210–1
irrational allocation policies, 214–7
legitimate expectation, 211–4
limits of judicial intervention, 208–10
right to life, 67–8
Normative content
socio-economic rights, 24–6

Other status disputes
Discrimination, 291–4

Parliamentary sovereignty
Human Rights Act 1998, and, 115
judicial interpretation of Convention rights,
138–40
Pensions
discrimination
pensioners abroad, 283–91
Physical integrity
protection of socio-economic rights
ECHR, and, 74–9
Positive-negative dichotomy
ECHR, 49–52
right to private and family life, 244–6
socio-economic rights, 19–22
Positive obligations
ECHR, and
incremental development, 53–8
methodological difficulties, 59–62
reconciliation with negative thrust of,
62–3
theoretical justification for, 64–5
right to dignity
asylum seekers, 254–70
conclusions, 274–6
introduction, 241–2
life-saving treatment, 270–4
right to private and family life
breach of statutory duties, 246–51
conclusions, 274–6
culpability for failure to provide, 251–4
introduction, 241–2
maintenance of family unit, 251–4
maladministration, 243–4
positive-negative dichotomy, inadequacy
of, 244–6
Prioritisation in public services
see also **NHS rationing, Resource allocation
disputes**
judicial intervention
assessment of needs, 205–6
clinical priority, 206–7
inadequacy of public resources, 200–1
individual choice, 202–5
market efficiency, 201–2
Prisons
right to dignity, 70–3
Privacy
see **Right to private and family life**
Protection of socio-economic rights
domestic courts
civil and political rights, 34–9
constitutional review, 29–34
institutional competencies, 26–8
South African model, 39–42
ECHR
developing core values, 65–7
due process in public law challenges,
82–86

Protection of socio-economic rights (*cont.*):
　ECHR (*cont.*):
　　equal distribution of public goods, 79–81
　　protecting physical and psychological
　　　integrity, 74–9
　　respect for human dignity, 69–74
　　right to health treatment, 67–8
　European protection
　　conclusion, 102–3
　　EC law, 86–102
　　introduction, 49
Psychological integrity
　protection of socio-economic rights
　　ECHR, and, 74–9
Public authorities
　horizontal effects of s.6, 140–1
　hybrid public authorities, 141–2
　identification of, 147
　scrutiny of executive action, 138–40
Public functions
　criticism of interpretation, 142–3
　meaning, 145–9
　public/private social provision, 149
　vulnerable groups, 143–5
Public goods, equal distribution of
　protection of socio-economic rights, 79–81
Public law
　common public law, emergence of, 191–192
　constitutional foundations of, generally, 152
　　–7
　democracy, 189–95
　division between policy and law 175–7
　human rights approach, 191
　human rights judges, and hallmarks of,
　　191–2
　judicial deference, role of,
　　justification, 172–4
　　landlord and tenant repossession cases,
　　　178–87
　　positivist, conception of, 167
　　transparency, 174
　　unified approach, 189–95
Public sector housing
　repossession
　　judicial deference in public law, 178–87
Public services
　conclusions, 239–40
　introduction, 197–200
　judicial intervention in prioritisation
　　disputes
　　assessment of needs, 205–6
　　clinical priority, 206–7
　　inadequacy of public resources, 200–1
　　individual choice, 202–5
　　market efficiency, 201–2
　local authority resource allocation disputes
　　accommodating children and families,
　　　225–33

　generally, 220–4
　human rights approach, 237–9
　protection of vulnerable persons, 233–7
　NHS rationing
　　choice and socio-economic entitlements,
　　　217–20
　　legitimate judicial interventions, 210–7
　　limits of judicial intervention, 208–10

Repossession
　judicial deference in public law, 178–87
Resource allocation disputes
　judicial review, 162–5
　local authorities
　　accommodating children and families,
　　　225–33
　　generally, 220–4
　　human rights approach, 237–9
　　protection of vulnerable persons, 233–7
　NHS
　　choice and socio-economic entitlements,
　　　217–20
　　legitimate judicial interventions, 210–7
　　limits of judicial intervention, 208–10
Right to dignity
　assisted suicide, 70
　asylum seekers
　　administrative court crisis, 257–62
　　Court of Appeal decision in *Limbuela*,
　　　262–5
　　House of Lords intervention, 265–70
　　lack of welfare support, 254–5
　　withdrawal of asylum support, 255–7
　conclusions, 274–6
　degrading or inhuman treatment, 69–74
　detention of vulnerable individuals, 73–4
　extradition, 73–4
　introduction, 241–2
　life-saving treatment, 270–4
　prisons, 70–3
　protection of socio-economic rights, 69–74
Right to fair trial
　administrative justice
　　civil rights, 320–2
　　homelessness, 322–5
　　housing reviews, 316–9
　　immigration and asylum, 330–1
　　independent and impartial tribunal, 311–6
　　judicial review standards in welfare
　　　disputes, 325–30
　　welfare needs, 320–2
　civil rights
　　administrative justice, 320–2
　　autonomous concept, 304–7
　　Kehoe, 307–11
　　meaning, 304
　conclusions, 331–3
　introduction, 303–4

protection of socio-economic rights, 82–6
public law challenges, 82–6
Right to life
access health treatment, 67–8
NHS rationing and, 208–10
medical ethics and,
withdrawing life support, 197
Right to private and family life
breach of statutory duties, 246–51
conclusions, 274–6
culpability for failure to provide, 251–4
interpreting local authority statutory duties,
237–9
introduction, 241–2
maintenance of family unit, 251–4
maladministration, 243–4
physical and psychological integrity, 74–9
positive-negative dichotomy, inadequacy of,
244–6
protection of socio-economic rights, 74–9

Socio-economic disputes
interpretation of Convention rights, 133–6
Socio-economic rights
composite phrase use of, 9
discretionary welfare benefits, as 9
economic rights, ascendancy of, 8- 9
fusion of social and economic rights,
reasons for 8–9
International Covenant on Economic Social
and Cultural Rights (ICESCR)
ambiguous drafting of rights, in, 8
protection in domestic courts, through
civil and political rights 34–9
relationship between, 15–9
conclusion, 47–8
discrimination, 279–83
enforcement, of
South African Constitutional Court, 42–7
human rights, understanding as, 11–5
Human Rights Act 1998, and, 107–9
negative-positive dichotomy, 19–22
NHS rationing,
discretionary welfare benefits 217–20
normative content, 24–6
protection in domestic courts, through
civil and political rights, 34–9
constitutional review, 29–34
institutional competencies, 26–8
South African model, 39–42
protection in Europe
see also **EC law, European Convention on
Human Rights**
conclusion, 102–3
EC law, 86–102
European Convention on Human Rights,
49–86

introduction, 49
unified approach to human rights, 22–4
South Africa
dedicated protection of
socio-economic rights, 39–42
enforcement of socio-economic rights,
42–7
transformative constitution, 39–40
Chalkaston P, 189–90
protecting the marginalized and excluded,
Special educational needs
local authority resource allocation disputes,
222–3
Stare decisis
interpretation of Convention rights, 136–8
Strasbourg jurisprudence
interpretation of Convention rights, 130–3

Transparency
administrative decision-making, generally
housing allocation, 202 –208
judicial deference in public law, 172–4
NHS rationing, 208- 219
Tripartite theory of obligations
explanatory and functional,
protect, respect promote rights, to
22- 24
Shue, H 23
revisiting, ECHR, 64

Ultra Vires
judicial review, constitutional foundations of
152–6
Undue delay
European Court of Justice, and, 96–100

Vulnerable groups
legislative protection, needs of,
Children Act, 1989, 225
Chronically Sick and Disabled Persons
Act (CDSPA) 1970, 221
Disability Discrimination Act 1995,
298
Education Act 1993, 232
Equality and Human Rights Act 2006, 278
National Assistance Act (NAA) 1948, 223
National Health and Community Care
Act (NHSCCA) 1990, 231
judicial interpretation of public functions,
and impact on, 143–5

Welfare needs disputes
right to fair trial
generally, 320–2
standards of review, in 325–30
White Paper "Rights Brought Home"
compatibility with Convention rights, 118